Cities, Cultures, Conversations

Cities, Cultures, Conversations

Readings for Writers

Richard Marback
Patrick Bruch
Jill Eicher
Wayne State University

Allyn and Bacon
Boston   London   Toronto   Sydney   Tokyo   Singapore

Vice President, Humanities: Joseph Opiela
Executive Marketing Manager: Lisa Kimball
Editorial-Production Administrator: Deborah Brown
Editorial-Production Service: Saxon House Productions
Text Designer and Page Layout: Glenna Collett
Composition Buyer: Linda Cox
Manufacturing Buyer: Megan Cochran
Cover Administrator: Suzanne Harbison

Copyright © 1998 by Allyn & Bacon
A Viacom Company
160 Gould Street
Needham Heights, MA 02194

Internet: www.abacon.com
America Online: keyword: College Online

Library of Congress Cataloging-in-Publication Data

Marback, Richard.
    Cities, cultures, conversations / Richard Marback, Patrick Bruch, Jill Eicher.
        p.   cm.
    ISBN 0-205-18456-1 (paperbound)
    1. Readers—City and town life.   2. City and town life—United
States—Problems, exercises, etc.   3. Sociology, Urban—United
States—Problems, exercises, etc.   4. English language—Rhetoric.
5. Readers—Sociology, Urban.   6. College readers.   I. Bruch,
Patrick.   II. Eicher, Jill.   III. Title.
PE1127.C53M37   1998
808'.0427—DC21   97-16287
                                                                       CIP

Printed in the United States of America
10 9 8 7 6 5 4 3 2 1   01 00 99 98 97

Contents

PART 7   Urban Styles   402

Preface

WHY CITIES?

Why read and write about cities? What can you learn about language from reading and writing about cities? Whether you live in a rural area, the suburbs, or a city, you have knowledge of cities and urban culture in the United States today. When you think about it, your knowledge of cities comes from a variety of sources. You may have firsthand experience with urban environments, or you may have friends or family who talk with you about their urban experiences. But you certainly have a sense of cities and urban life from books, magazines, movies, music, newspapers, school, and television. Because you are surrounded by talk about cities, you have opportunities to think and talk about city life and urban issues. So wherever you live, you have some sense, some idea, of what cities are like, who lives in cities, and how cities figure in the current culture.

This book asks you to bring the knowledge and experience of cities that you already have to the task of improving your writing. What you know of urban culture and the ways you have of making sense of what you hear about cities from your family and friends and from the mass media can be valuable resources for learning more about how to read critically and how to write effectively. As the title of this book, *Cities, Cultures, Conversations,* suggests, our view is that what we think and how we act are both shaped by the ways we use language. What we think about cities—whether we enjoy them or are afraid of them—as well as how we act in response to urban environments—whether we avoid them or seek them out—depend on the ways we talk with others about the perils and promises of city life.

Throughout *Cities, Cultures, Conversations,* we use terms such as *city life, urban environment,* and *urban experience* to describe both the direct experience of city life and common knowledge about cities and city life available through the mass media. More often than not, mass media images are more persuasive than direct experience. Even if they have never been there before, many people already have ideas about cities like Miami drawn from the news, from television shows, or from the movies. *Cities, Cultures, Conversations* provides an opportunity to evaluate critically   such images of urban life. *Cities, Cultures, Conversations* also asks you to consider what makes the urban landscape such an important site for communicating our fears and hopes for our world. Critically discussing experiences and perceptions of the meaning of urban life, you will learn reading, thinking, and writing strategies and skills that will be useful in your other courses and in your life as a citizen.

The chapters in this book bring together readings on specific features of urban life: the idea of cities, communities and neighborhoods; crime; urban art; style; suburban sprawl; and politics. The readings have been chosen for what they say and for how they say it. Questions, discussions, and writing prompts in each part direct you to think critically about the topics and to produce various kinds of writing that respond to and build on both your own experiences and the articles you have read.

Cities, Cultures, Conversations includes several features intended to facilitate your ability to bring your knowledge and experience to the task of improving your writing. These features are as follows:

1. To get you started, Part 1 takes you step-by-step through several essays, examining the writing and reading processes, and allowing you to begin to think about cities and urban life through freewriting exercises. As you work your way through this first part, keep in mind that what you already know about cities and that how you already talk about urban life are important. Use what you know and how you talk to take part in the conversation that asks, "Why cities?"
2. Beginning with Part 2, the readings are divided into separate thematic parts.
3. Each part begins with two or more quotes and a brief introduction that explains the issues addressed by the essays in the particular part.
4. Beginning with Part 2, the introductory essay is followed by some prereading exercises. These exercises are intended to get you to reflect on what you already know about the topic so that you can read the essays in each part with your own thoughts in mind.
5. Each essay is preceded by a short introduction that lets you know something about the author and invites you to think about the topic.
6. Every essay is followed by questions for discussion that ask you to reflect on what was said in the essay, to consider the effectiveness of the writing, and to relate the essay to your own experience. In discussions and in your writing, you are encouraged to draw on what you already know, to use your knowledge and experience to make sense of what an author writes, and even to disagree with an author.
7. In Parts 2 through 7, there are several more discussion questions at the end of each part that ask you to relate the essays to one another. These questions also ask you to think more generally about the topic itself and to make some judgments of your own.
8. The longer writing assignments at the end of each part often ask you to go out into your community and talk to people there or to gather information. Just as

we encourage you to bring prior knowledge of and experience with cities to the classroom, we encourage you, through these assignments, to bring what you have learned in the classroom to the people around you and to the places where you live.

Acknowledgments

We would like to thank the following reviewers whose comments and advice helped us make this a better and more useful anthology: Grant Boswell, Brigham Young University; Douglas Bucholz, Community College of Philadelphia; Linda Daigle, Houston Community College; Nancy Downs, University of Illinois at Chicago; Faun Bernbach Evans, Chicago State University; Reg Gerlicka, Henry Ford Community College; Sherrie Gradin, Portland State University; Michael G. Moran, University of Georgia; Ruth Y. Reed, Macomb Community College; Carol Stein, Community College of Philadelphia; Stuart Stelly, University of New Orleans; and Mary Trachsel, University of Iowa. We have been fortunate to receive and have the opportunity to implement their many useful suggestions.

Reading, Writing, and Talking about Cities

THE ABILITY TO READ, write, and speak in accordance with the code sanctioned by a culture's ruling class is the main work of education, and this is true whether we are discussing ancient Athens or modern Detroit. These rules are of course inscribed in a rhetoric, a systematic designation of who can speak, when and where they can speak, and how they can and must speak. Educational institutions inculcate these rules, determining who is fit to learn them and who has finally done so—in other words, who is authorized to be heard. A rhetoric codifies these rules for the members of a society. It is therefore never simply a set of disembodied principles that discuss the way language is used for purposes of persuasion or communication. It is a set of strictures regarding the way language is used in the service of power. It designates who may have access to power and who may not, doing so in a way even more effective than legal sanctions with all of their punitive devices. To use Althusser's term a rhetoric serves as an important ideological state apparatus. It affirms economic, social, political, and cultural arrangements, doing so in the name of passing on to the young the "natural" rules that govern discursive and, more important, non-discursive practices. A society rarely, if ever, of course sees its rules regarding discourse as a social construction designed to serve a particular set of power arrangements, offering these rules instead as normal, "in the nature of things."

—*James Berlin*

1

IN LOOKING AT HISTORY with a subtle historical sense, I also have in mind the fundamental question: What do we have in common? By history, I mean the human responses to a variety of different processes over time and space—various social structures that all human beings must respond to. In responding to these circumstances, the problem has been that most of us function by a kind of self-referential altruism, in which we're altruistic to those nearest to us, and those more distant, we tend to view as pictures rather than human beings. Yet, as historical beings, as fallen and fallible historical beings, we do have a common humanity. We must not forget our long historical backdrop. The present is history—that continues to inform and shape and mold our perceptions and orientations.

The political challenge is to articulate universality in a way that is not a mere smokescreen for someone else's particularity. We must preserve the possibility of universal connection. That's the fundamental challenge. Let's dig deep enough within our heritage to make that connection to others.

We're not naive; we know that argument and critical exchange are not the major means by which social change takes place in the world. But we recognize it has to have a role, has to have a function. Therefore, we will trash older notions of objectivity, and not act as if one group or community or one nation has a god's-eye view of the world. Instead we will utilize forms of intersubjectivity that facilitate critical exchange even as we recognize that none of us are free of presuppositions and prejudgments. We will put our arguments on the table and allow them to be.

—*Cornel West*

THE CITY HAS ALWAYS BEEN man's single most impressive and visible achievement. It is a human artifact which has become an object in the world of nature. Cities are a plural phenomenon: There are many of them, but though each has its individual history, they all seem to exemplify similar patterns. The most basic of these is the interpenetration of past and present. On the one hand there is the visible city of streets and buildings, frozen forms of energy fixed at different times in the past and around which the busy kinetic energy of the present swirls. On the other hand there are the subconscious currents arising in the minds of the city's living inhabitants from this combination of past and present. These currents include the city's ties with the realm of the dead through its temples, cemeteries, and ceremonies as well as its old buildings, and also its functions as the seat of secular power, embodied in kings, governments, and banks.

—*Burton Pike*

INTRODUCTION

Cities

Why cities? When we think of cities we think of places that we can point to on a map, places like Baltimore, Kansas City, Newark, Portland, and San Antonio. But cities are more than just places we can find on maps, where a lot of people live and many things have happened. Cities are also places that have meaning, significance, and value for us because of what they represent in the wider culture. In this part we will ask you to explore the question, Why cities? by asking you to talk and think and read and write about what cities are, what we know about them, how we know about them through our culture, and how we represent them in our conversations. Doing this will introduce you to the themes of this book: cities, cultures, and conversations. Trying to answer the question, Why cities? will also lead you to appreciate how representations of urban culture are linked to issues of learning writing.

Anyone who has experience with contemporary culture through magazines, newspapers, television, radio, music, or the movies has ideas about the meaning, significance, and value of cities. As a consumer of mass media images and as a participant in contemporary culture, you not only have a lot of knowledge about cities, you also use that knowledge when you communicate with others. When you hear or read about a particular city, almost automatically you draw upon what you previously heard or read about that city to judge what you are hearing or reading now. Using the widely available cultural knowledge of cities and urban life in this way, you take part in challenging and even perpetuating the meanings, significance, and values cities and urban spaces have in contemporary American culture. To begin to demonstrate this to yourself, complete the following freewriting exercise.

1 Freewriting Exercise   Take a few moments now to write down on a separate sheet of paper all the things each of the following cities evokes for you: Anchorage, Alaska; Birmingham, Alabama; Cleveland, Ohio; and Denver, Colorado.

Looking at your list, you should discover that even if you have never been to any of these cities, you have ideas and opinions about them. Compare your list to the lists of other members in your class. How do they compare? Do people who have been to, or even lived in, Anchorage, Birmingham, Cleveland, or Denver have different lists than people who have never been to any of these cities? Talk about the lists in class. How would you account for the differences? When you compare lists among people who have never been to any of these cities, how similar are they? Where might these similarities come from? What do these similarities tell you about how people form impressions of cities?

Our ability to communicate with others is often helped or hindered by the similarities and differences in our perceptions. What we think about certain cities, and even how we respond initially to people from those cities, therefore greatly influences our abilities to communicate by providing us opportunities to identify shared assumptions, meanings, points of view, and values. The ways in which we talk and write about cities are, therefore, also functions of the way we have learned to perceive those places and the people who live there. Whatever individual perceptions we have, we generate these perceptions through our responses to others. Because we create our individual perceptions out of widely available information, we can say that the assumptions, meanings, points of view, and values we collectively create and negotiate through our talk about cities come to us from a variety of widely available sources.

Consider the example of Philadelphia. Philadelphia is commonly referred to as the "city of brotherly love." In addition, most people who do not live in Philadelphia, or who have never been there, think of it as the location of the *Rocky* movies or as the home of the Liberty Bell or even as the place where racial tensions led police to firebomb the homes of African American separatists. If we only know of Philadelphia through the movies, or through history books, or through news accounts, we only have a partial picture of the city. Philadelphia is all of these things; it is a location for popular films, a historic site, and an urban landscape torn by racial tensions. But Philadelphia is also more than just the sum of these things. As a city in which we can locate our dreams of heroic struggle, as in the *Rocky* movies, or our nightmares of racial violence, as in the firebombing of the MOVE home, Philadelphia communicates our hopes, dreams, anxieties, and fears about living in the United States today.

As the example of Philadelphia suggests, even though not everyone lives in a large city, or even in a major metropolitan area, everyone has experience with representations of cities. Whether you live in a rural area, the suburbs, or a city, you have knowledge of cities and urban culture in the United States today. When you think about it, your knowledge of cities comes from a variety of sources. You may have firsthand experience with urban environments, or you may have friends or family who talk with you about their experiences. But you certainly have a sense of cities and urban life from books, magazines, movies, music, newspapers, school, and television.

Pause for a moment and consider what you know about a city such as New York. We know a lot about New York City from the television shows *NYPD Blue*, *Seinfeld*, and *David Letterman*. What do you know about New York City from newspapers and magazines such as the *New York Times*, *The New Yorker*, or the *Village Voice*? Through music we have images of New York as the "city that never sleeps." What perceptions of New York City do you have from movies such as *Clockers* or *Taxidriver*? And while it may seem trivial, representations of New York City are available in commercials as well, as when a character rejects a picante sauce because it is "made in New York City!"

To make explicit some of the specific sources for your images and representations of cities other than New York, complete the following freewriting exercise.

2 Freewriting Exercise   Identify as many different sources as you can for representations of specific cities. Describe those representations of specific cities. So, for example, whether or not you like their music, you could describe what you know about Los Angeles from Coolio, Ice-T, or NWA. Draw from as many different kinds of media as you can, including books, magazines, school, and television, and talk with friends and relatives.

Compare your lists and descriptions with the lists and descriptions of others. Discuss among yourselves the similarities and differences of your lists. What cities and sources have you included that they have not? What cities and sources have they included that you have not? How do you account for these differences? What do the differences say about you? In what ways might these differences influence your relationships with others?

The point of identifying all that you already know about cities is not simply to demonstrate to yourself the wealth of images you have about places you may never have been before. That we can have so much information available to us about places we have never experienced suggests that those places serve as important sites for our exchange of attitudes, beliefs, and values with others. What matters most then is that you act and think and communicate in certain ways through your use of those images. Because you are surrounded by talk about cities, you are influenced to think of cities in certain ways at the same time that you are influenced to act in certain ways toward city life and to talk in certain ways about urban issues. So wherever you live, you have some sense, some idea, about what cities are like, who lives in cities, and how cities figure in the current culture. Through your use of representations of cities, you choose what you will say and do and what you won't say and do, where you will go and where you won't go, who you will talk to and who you won't talk to.

Before proceeding to the next section, discuss these points with the other members of your class. To begin the discussion, consider the following questions: What do the representations of cities so far discovered and discussed ask you to do? Do they invite you into cities? Do they scare you away? Just how do you respond to these representations? Do you seek out city life or avoid it? Why do you respond one way as opposed to another? Further consider the way representations of cities influence your talk. How do you talk about cities? Do you talk positively or negatively? In what ways does your talk about cities match talk available through the mass media? In what ways does your talk differ from talk in the mass media? How would you explain these similarities and differences? And finally, what does your talk about cities say about your attitudes, beliefs, and values?

Cultures

By using this book to read and write about cities, about our experiences of them, about our attitudes toward them, and about our ways of representing them, you are investigating the many ways in which we make sense of our world and find our place in it. You are investigating the ways we use language to orient our-

selves in the world; by reading and thinking and writing about cities you therefore have an opportunity to develop new ways of using written language to orient yourself and your actions in contemporary culture.

In the previous section, you read and wrote about the fact that, whether we
realize it or not, most of us read and write and talk about cities and urban experiences every day. From newspapers and magazines to TV news, political
speeches, and movies, we are all surrounded with language about what it is like
to live in an urban setting. Through this language, we gain images of places
many of us have never been to. The bustling business world of Wall Street, the
gleaming skyscrapers of Dallas, the crime-ridden inner-city streets of
Washington, D.C., the glitter of Las Vegas, the mosaic of separate ethnic areas in
Los Angeles, and the aging, abandoned factories of northern industrial cities like
Detroit are all images that any of us can picture. Each of these images—a fast-
paced financial center, towering glass buildings, crime-ridden inner cities, and
abandoned factories—represents the city as a certain kind of place. By representing specific cities as certain kinds of places, we are in a way determining our
potential actions in those places. We would, for example, expect to have completely different experiences in Las Vegas and Detroit. So when we go to those
places, we go expecting to do some things and not others.

3 Freewriting Exercise   Take a few minutes to consider how our representations of places influence our actions in those places. Discuss the
following questions with the other members of your class: Just what
influence might representations of Las Vegas and Detroit have on our
actions? How accurate or effective are they in telling us what these cities
are like? And in telling us what these cities are like, how accurate or
effective are they in telling us what contemporary American culture is
like? And in telling us something meaningful about cities and contemporary culture, how forcefully do these representations influence our
actions?

Like any language, the language about cities used by the media, by politicians, and by us and our friends encourages us to think about cities in certain
ways—and not to think about them in other ways. This language also encourages
some types of action and discourages others. For example, an advertisement for
perfume may picture the city as sophisticated and cultured, whereas an advertisement for an automobile may picture the city as noisy and congested with traffic. At the same time, a political candidate's speech may depict the city as criminal and dangerous. Each of these images tries to shape our ideas about cities and
influence our actions within them, encouraging us to desire a particular fra-
grance or a new car, or to "get tough on crime" by building more prisons and hiring more police officers. As these examples show, the ways we represent cities
in pictures and in print have everything to do with how we are asked to feel
about cities—whether we consider them glamorous or decayed, inviting or dangerous. They also have everything to do with what we do in response to our per-

ceptions. Images and discussions of cities are thus also about what we want to do in cities: Do we want to shop there for things like perfume? Do we see ourselves participating in urban life from within a car? Or do we want to hire more police and build more prisons in order to make cities more safe?

Shopping, driving, and even "getting tough on crime" are all features of contemporary urban culture. Culture can be defined as the vast range of activities people engage in day after day. Of course, culture is not simply the sum of everyone's everyday activities; culture can also be defined as what we value most in our social lives. What people do with their lives on a daily basis expresses what they value most. For example, the daily activities of fighting crime and of spreading information about crime demonstrate how much of an issue people believe crime is and what they consider important to do in response to crime. Crime prevention is thus an activity that communicates shared as well as competing values and perceptions. As such an activity, crime prevention is part of our culture. By thus investigating daily activities such as crime prevention, we are investigating cultural activities. By thinking about crime prevention in terms of how people represent their activities and the value of those activities, we are investigating culture itself.

Take a few minutes now to clarify for yourself just what you think culture is by freewriting in response to the following prompt.

4 Freewriting Exercise   Illustrate urban culture by describing all the day-to-day activities and practices that constitute it. Include not only descriptions of all the things people do as participants in an urban culture but also explanations of what those activities mean. Why do those activities matter? Also, what makes those activities distinctly urban?

Exchange your descriptions and explanations of urban activities with the other members of your class. There are probably some explanations that you all seem to agree on and others that you do not agree on. Talk for a few minutes about your agreements and disagreements. Use the following to get the conversation going: As a class, define urban culture. What daily activities does your definition of urban culture include? What mass media representations of cities support this definition? What representations contradict it? Now generate a list of activities that might be considered urban but are excluded by your definition of urban culture. Are these activities promoted or not in the mass media? Through the general culture? Why?

For the most part, what people believe about cities today is communicated through their culture, and by what they do in and with cities. Thus, perfume and car ads, political speeches, and urban images in rap music influence what we think about Los Angeles, Chicago, Miami, or Memphis. By reading ads and listening to speeches or songs, we are participating in contemporary culture. When we agree with, challenge, disagree with, or reflect on the representations of cities made available through ads, speeches, and songs, we are negotiating the representations of cities available through contemporary culture. In negotiating representations of cities, we are interacting with others, just as we take in and respond to the images, meanings, and values expressed by others in their representations of urban culture.

You are therefore more than just a consumer of mass media images of cities; you are a producer of urban images as well. When you think about cities and discuss urban issues such as crime and unemployment, you too represent cities. You have considered earlier in this part whether you repeat what your family and friends say about your city and other cities. You have also considered the extent to which the mass media is a source for your talk about cities. Growing up in the United States, we learn about our world, and about our cities, both directly at home and in school, and indirectly by repeating and believing what we hear and see every day on the radio, on television, in magazines, and from other people. In this section of Part I, we are asking you to consider the ways you contribute to urban culture and representations of cities.

Buying a product, going into an urban area, or voting for one candidate as opposed to another are all things that everyone does. Often, the choices we make when we buy something, go somewhere, or vote for someone are choices we talk about with others. Most of us have had the experience of having to defend or explain what we do to family and friends. By defending or explaining our actions, we are fashioning representations of what we believe to be appropriate, desirable, just, or simply possible actions. We are asking others to accept representations of the world that make a specific kind of sense out of our actions. When it comes to defending or explaining our actions in and our attitudes toward cities and urban culture, we are attempting to persuade others to accept our visions of what city life and urban culture are and ought to be. To develop this point for yourself, take several minutes to complete the following freewriting exercise.

5 Freewriting Exercise   What do we need in order to lead quality lives in cities? Generate a list of about five or six criteria for evaluating the quality of daily life in cities. Briefly explain why each category matters. Then use your criteria to create a ranked list of the ten best cities to live in in the United States.

Share your criteria and your list of cities with the other members of your class. You might even want to develop collaboratively a set of criteria for ranking cities and then as a group create a list of the ten best cities based on these new criteria. Discuss among yourselves the interactions of representations of cities available throughout our culture and the things you do in and toward cities. To facilitate your discussion, consider the following questions: What kind of life do you value most through these criteria? What kinds of activities do your criteria make most desirable? Why do these criteria and not others provide you a quality life? Following your criteria, what kind of life do you value least? According to your criteria, what kinds of activities are least desirable? In what ways do your criteria attempt to persuade others that some ways of living are less desirable than others? What might the appeal of your criteria be? In what ways does your list of cities also attempt to persuade others to desire some activities and so some places over other places?

The criteria you used to rank cities indicate what it is you think cities should be like and what people should be able to do in cities. Ideas about what makes a city a place where we would want to live or not want to live are widely circulated throughout the mass media. Some of the criteria you have developed for yourself about the quality of life in cities are probably criteria that you share with others because you all share the same broad cultural networks.

To come to a better understanding of the relationships among urban culture and representations and actions, consider the criteria used each year by *Money* magazine to determine and rank the best cities to live in in the United States. In the July 1996 issue of *Money* magazine, the "nine broad categories" used to rank American cities were as follows: economy, health, crime, housing, education, weather, transit, leisure, and arts. These categories are not otherwise defined for readers of *Money* magazine. Stop and consider for a moment what these categories might mean. What are we being asked to value when *Money* magazine evaluates cities in terms of "economy"? Or "education"? Or "leisure"? Consider why these categories are and/or should be significant. Observe as well whether any of these categories match your list of categories. Why do you think you use categories other than those used by *Money*? What do the differences in categories have to do with the differences in the people generating the lists? What do the differences in categories tell us about the people generating the lists? About the people those lists are meant to persuade?

Through their categories, the editors at *Money* magazine generated a list of three hundred cities. According to the criteria used by *Money* magazine, the best city to live in in the United States is Madison, Wisconsin; the 2nd most desirable city is Punta Gorda, Florida; 3rd is Rochester, Minnesota; 4th is Fort Lauderdale, Florida; and 5th is Ann Arbor, Michigan. Of major cities, San Francisco is 13th; Phoenix and Houston are 34th and 35th respectively; Portland, Oregon is 48th; Nashville ranks 101st; Atlanta ranks 115th; New York City is 231st; and Cincinnati is 257th. The 300th city on the list is Rockford, Illinois.

The editors of *Money* magazine think that cities should be specific kinds of places where people can do certain things and they have used their categories to persuade us of their views. Discuss your reactions to the *Money* magazine list of the best cities with the other members of your class. Consider some of the following questions: Do you agree with their choices of the top five cities? Why or why not? What reasons might you give to explain your agreements or disagreements with the editors of *Money* magazine? Given their choices of the best cities in the United States, just what seems to be their view of cities? There seems to be more to the list than simply an attempt to get everyone to recognize that Madison is the best city to live in. What else do you think *Money* magazine's list of the best cities in the United States does? What do you think they are trying to persuade us to feel and think and do? And finally, what do you think might be the possible consequences of a ranked list of cities?

Conversations

Now that we have considered the kinds of places cities are, as well as the ways we make use of them as a part of our culture, we will in this section explore more thoroughly the connections among cities and cultures and conversations, as well as the possibilities for learning writing that are inherent in conversations about cities.

So far, we have examined how our ideas about cities are more often than not incomplete, inconsistent, and sometimes even inaccurate because our knowledge of United States cities comes to us from so many different places and in so many different ways. For example, popular images of cities, such as those available through *Money* magazine, political speeches, horrifying crime stories, and glamorous movies and advertisements, simplify cities and city life. Since we base our ideas about particular cities largely on popular images, our images of those cities will also necessarily be incomplete and stereotypical. So, for instance, we might think Nashville is simply the home of the Grand Ole Opry, or that San Francisco is only Alcatraz, Chinatown, and Fisherman's Wharf.

When you think about it, the representations of cities that we see and hear are partial in two senses of the term. First, they are incomplete—any city is always more than any one image we might have of it, more than a desperate ghetto or a bustling business. Second, these images take a political viewpoint or slant that encourages *you* to take a side on a subject such as graffiti or the Los Angeles riot or welfare, often by making a partial image relate to an obvious or commonsense conclusion. Together, the incompleteness and partial viewpoint of any mass media image or news story or essay create a picture of a city that, if not balanced with countering images and texts, results in oversimplified ways of understanding and expressing our experiences.

Additionally, the partiality of images makes it easier for certain groups to give authority to their ways of seeing, interpreting, and communicating about our lives together. For example, in the fairly recent past, the power to represent urban ghetto life on television was used to make being poor and isolated seem fun. Thus, shows like *Sanford and Son* or *Good Times* represented ghetto life in Watts (the scene of an urban rebellion in 1965) and Chicago public housing (which now serves as a national image of urban collapse) as a life of family unity, loving relationships, and relaxed joviality. Of course, these representations of ghetto life are *partially* true. People who live in Watts or Cabrini-Green can and do have families and can and do experience loving relationships. But exclusively emphasizing these aspects of anyone's life ultimately misrepresents their existence by excluding everything else they experience. But this is exactly the point: The truth that is highlighted is one that makes sense of the world and our relationships in order to support existing relationships of authority and power. Thus, representations of poverty as happy and fun-loving ask us to ignore the economic, social, and political isolation of the urban poor by asking us to believe that poor people like to be poor, or at least that they choose to remain poor. And representations such as *Sanford and Son* and *Good Times* ask us to believe this whole-heartedly, not as *partially* true (in both senses of the term). In order to explore these ideas, complete the following freewriting exercise.

6 Freewriting Exercise Brainstorm a list of several specific mass media texts that you are familiar with and that represent cities. First think about the central message of each text. If each of the texts says one thing about cities and city life, what is it? After listing these central messages, compare your lists with those of your classmates. Discuss the similarities and differences in your lists and discuss the ways that the messages you've listed are incomplete. What do the texts leave out, and what do the absences reveal about the partiality of the texts?

We know from experience that no single image can do justice to the actual diversity of cities. Cities are extremely complicated; they are multifaceted places that mean many different things to different people. As we have seen, in order to fight for what they want out of cities, different people fight over how cities are depicted to the rest of us—to city residents, to suburban residents, to voters, to consumers, to the middle class, to the poor, and to people of different races and ethnic backgrounds. It is important to recognize that these different people struggle from different positions in social- and cultural-power relationships. An unemployed homeless resident of a particular neighborhood clearly has less influence over how her neighborhood will be represented to others than a wealthy real estate developer who owns property in the neighborhood. And since, as this example can suggest, the ways in which cities are represented have real impact on real people, then how we think, view, and talk about cities is of extreme importance because those things determine what actions will seem permissible to us, what actions will seem good, and what actions will seem heartless or destructive. In the instance of the homeless person and the real estate developer, the real estate developer can convince others that gentrifying the neighborhood is a good thing to do despite the fact that the homeless will remain homeless and will be forced to find shelter elsewhere. Thinking, viewing, and talking about cities, about homelessness and gentrification, about public housing and the quality of urban life are important to all of us as citizens and not just to city dwellers, for cities are central to American business, politics, and culture; thus urban spaces are central to all of our lives and to what it means to be an American today.

Cities assume this central place in our culture and our consciousness because they provide us with ways of communicating about things that really matter to or bother us in the current world. For example, through images of cities and city life, we can communicate with each other about such fundamental issues as welfare, unemployment, crime, education, personal freedom, racism, family values, technology, business and economics, the environment, and

women's rights, among other things. In order to make the United States a working democracy, we must learn to participate through our language as thoughtful,
knowledgeable citizens. Such thoughtfulness demands that we take the time and
make the effort to learn to read about our cities and our nation in a thorough and
critical way. In addition, we must take the time to talk and write about cities in
ways that conscientiously try to express the values that we believe in. If we
believe in democracy and the importance of everyone having his or her say and
participating in making knowledge about the world, then we must resist the
temptation to use writing to both ignore the partiality of our views and silence
different points of view.

7 Freewriting Exercise   Take several minutes to consider the idea that different ways of using language and writing are ways of acting out different forms of citizenship. For several minutes, brainstorm a list of roles
that a citizen might play or a list of differing definitions of citizenship like
worker, political agitator, community worker, union leader, parent,
planning supervisor, block club member, or religious leader. After
exhausting your ideas individually, share your list with a group and discuss together how different public roles or forms of citizenship demand
different ways of using literacy.

By thinking of cities and writing as conversations, we can reflect upon the
purposes, perhaps even the social or cultural purposes, of learning writing. If we
conceive of cities as forms of writing, as conglomerations of communication
between people through architecture and neighborhoods, through art and clothing and music, through daily activities and forms of entertainment, as well as
through the mass media, then writing takes on new meaning and the purposes
for learning writing also take on new meanings. Perhaps, more than anything
else, the image of a conversation taking place within a system of relationships—
where some parts of the conversation support authority while some parts of the
conversation resist it and most parts of the conversation both support *and* resist
it at the same time—suggests that by learning to write we learn to be a part of a
democratic society struggling over questions of who has the authority to contribute to the public discussion of issues. Learning writing we also learn other
ways of making sense of the contributions that others make to any conversation.

Consider this idea more fully by taking a few minutes to think and talk about
the ways that you have learned literacy in school. What are the practices, the
activities, the rituals, of learning writing? Like any part of the culture, these practices communicate underlying values and assumptions. What cultural values and
beliefs underlie the literacy experiences you and your classmates have had?
What are the values that you think would ideally underlie writing instruction and
literacy practices? What would it mean to teach literacy and writing according to
those values? What would be the hoped for outcomes?

The topic of the city lends itself to an image of writing as a conversation, a
communicative encounter in which the object is not to win a debate or to be

"right," but to try and make connections and appreciate the complexities of issues and perspectives. When we do take positions through writing, we should do so in a way that pays attention to where those positions come from and what they do to others when they represent a phenomenon as complex as a city. In particular, this means being conscious of how some ways of writing assume cultural authority because they replicate prevailing distributions of authority and power. Responsible use of cities to represent issues and to enact beliefs depends on actively discussing how we use cities and what we use them for.

This suggests that the idea of a conversation should not be romanticized. The conversation always taking place in, about, and through cities—on the evening news, in political speeches, on *Sanford and Son* or *COPS*—is not an ideal democratic, open discussion of positions. Instead, the conversation takes place in a system of power relations and through images that create the possible positions at the same time that they struggle to establish dominance for a particular perspective. Thus, part of using the city as a physical and imaginary point of discussion involves working to appreciate the ways that positions within the conversation, as well as ways of contributing perspectives, are given meanings by the ways that they reinforce or challenge how power is currently arranged.

Now that you have read and written and thought and talked about cities, cultures, and conversations, we ask that you turn what you have discovered to the task of reading about cities in order to learn about writing.

THINKING, READING, AND WRITING MORE CRITICALLY ABOUT CITIES

The essays collected in *Cities, Culture, Conversations* are all focused on cities and urban issues. The issues that define cities are quite complex, as demonstrated by the diversity of the positions on cities taken by people in this book. Together, images taken from movies, television, magazines, newspapers, and other media shape our conversations about cities and America and cause us to believe certain things about our cities, our culture, and ourselves. These images thus also work to cause us to act in certain ways toward our cities, cultures, and each other. Building on these ideas, we would like to offer some strategies for successfully using the essays and exercises collected in the remaining parts of this book to learn writing as a way of participating in public conversations about life in the United States today.

In the preceding sections, we have asked you to think about cities as places that are significant in our culture, a significance we negotiate through our representations of cities and urban spaces in a range of conversations. Thinking about cities as collections of competing images can help us as we learn writing because it offers us a way to step back from everyday life and look at the texts and conversations through which we all make sense of our cities, our culture, our expe-

riences, and our place as American citizens. By looking at your own urban experiences and the essays, advertisements, and movies that try to make sense of
those experiences, you can use this book to help you become an active participant in discussions about contemporary American issues, such as crime, education, and race. The readings we have collected here and the questions we offer
encourage thinking, reading, and writing about cities as ways of thinking, reading, and writing about citizenship.

In order to think and write about cities and their issues, you will need to ana-
lyze both popular images of cities—in the news, TV, and movies—as well as the
more politicized and academic discussions. Popular, politicized, and academic
images and texts all contribute to discussions of urban experience. Once you
begin to understand the complexity of the many different perspectives on cities,
you will be able to take part in the discussions on cities by thinking and writing
about urban issues in a manner that responds to the issues themselves as well
as to what has already been said. This book has been developed with exactly
these goals in mind.

This first part serves as an introduction to thinking, reading, and writing
about cities by providing a guided tour of how to use the other parts in this book.
It looks at the issue of how we represent cities to ourselves and others and at
what the consequences of those representations of cities might be. Using "A Nice
Place to Visit, but . . ." as an example essay, we will explain and demonstrate the
ways in which this book can facilitate your becoming an informed reader,
thinker, and writer who partakes in discussions about cities, contemporary urban
culture, and citizenship. Specifically, this part explores the relationships between
how cities are represented in written and visual texts and how people feel toward
cities. At the same time, we discuss reading and writing strategies that you may
have encountered previously in your school careers. A brief demonstration of
their uses and purposes may help to provide a context for your work with this
book. We provide this context by taking you step-by-step through the same kinds
of exercises you will find in all of the other parts. Each of the other parts in this
book focuses on a different urban issue: graffiti and music, crime and violence,
neighborhoods and communities, style, suburbanization, and civil unrest.

Getting Started: Think about What You Already Know

Each part begins with an introduction that discusses that part's topic in a general way, then asks you to contemplate and write about what you already think and
believe about that topic—largely based upon your own experiences and the
beliefs you've absorbed from the media, from your reading, and from your family and friends. At the beginning of this part, we briefly discussed how our images
of cities are formed through newspapers, magazines, political speeches, movies,
and our conversations with family and friends. Take a few minutes now to recall
the freewriting and brainstorming you have thus far done. Discuss with the members of your class your general impressions of cities and urban spaces. Have you

decided just what cities contribute to American culture? Discuss as well what cities and urban spaces mean in your life. How do you represent cities in your conversations? How are cities represented in the media? In school? In your home? How do or don't these conversations interact? Why?

Although it often seems that schools and school writing are completely separate from the rest of our lives, your classroom discussions about cities and your understanding of how to write and when to write will, throughout this book, be connected to the broader conversations of cultural life in this country. So, your experiences outside of school are essential to your ability to respond to urban issues in school.

8 Freewriting Exercise   Try writing for ten minutes without stopping about the parts of the conversation about city life that are most important to you. For example, are you interested or actively involved in a particularly "urban" music? Are you involved in neighborhood politics? Or are you interested in city government? Do you watch the news or go see movies? Whatever part of the conversation you focus on, write in as much detail as possible about the assumptions of this part of the conversation. What does it assume about cities? After you are done, compare what you have with other members of your class. Where do you agree? Where do you disagree? Why? How does what you already believe about cities show the extent to which you and your classmates already participate in similar and different conversations about urban experiences and the quality of urban life?

Reading Critically

Keeping in mind the ideas you came up with from writing about the ways in which you already participate in discussions about cities, next you will turn to the readings. Here and in each part that follows, several readings are presented on a particular topic. Every reading is preceded by an introduction and followed by questions and writing assignments. Finally, each part ends with questions and writing assignments that offer ways to tie the various essays in the part together.

Here we will start with the sample essay, "A Nice Place to Visit, but . . ." written by Judith Martin.

The Essay's Introduction.   Before each essay, an introduction tells you about the author and where the essay was published, and gives you some information and questions about the essay itself. Here is the introduction to Martin's essay:

Judith A. Martin is director of the Urban Studies Program at the University of Minnesota–Twin Cities. "A Nice Place to Visit, but . . . ," originally published in The Utne Reader *in 1994, describes the ambivalence Americans have toward their cities. Through examples, Judith Martin draws her readers' attention to the ways people embrace their cities and the ways they reject their cities. She makes her readers aware of how seemingly positive terms can often be perceived to have negative connotations. As you read "A Nice Place to Visit, but . . . ," keep in mind the words you have learned to evaluate cities. Are you someone who embraces cities and an urban lifestyle? Or are you someone who rejects cities?*

After reading the introduction to an essay, think for a moment on what you got out of it. Having read the introduction to "A Nice Place to Visit, but . . . ," what did you learn about Martin? About where the essay was originally published? What information can you gather about the essay even before having read it? How else does the introduction help you read the following essay? The questions at the end of the introduction are intended to push you to keep thinking about your own previous ideas and attitudes about cities while reading Martin's essay. Our hope is that you will use your prior knowledge about cities to question what any of the authors has to say. We also hope that you will use what the authors have to say to reflect on and add to your prior knowledge.

Reading the Essay.   Now read through Martin's essay, keeping in mind the discussions you've already had about cities.

A Nice Place to Visit, but . . .

Judith A. Martin

AMERICANS ARE LOCKED into a long-term love/hate relationship with their cities. As a nation we are now approximately 45 percent suburban and 25 percent rural. Most of us judge cities on hearsay more than on our own experience of urban communities. Our perceptions of urban life are now derived largely from the bad news we see nightly on television or read in the newspaper over breakfast. On the plus side, many Americans partake of the cultural life cities offer—theater, museums, concerts, professional sports, ethnic restaurants. Cities are still seen as the source of sophistication and glamour. Yet on balance, most of us seem to think of cities as places with a lot of problems and only a few redeeming characteristics.

Judith A. Martin. "A Nice Place to Visit, but . . ." From *Utne Reader* 65 (Sept./Oct. 1994): 121–124. Reprinted by permission of Judith A. Martin, Director, Urban Studies Program, University of Minnesota–Twin Cities.

But where did our tainted view of cities originate? They did not spring full blown from the drug/crime/violence litany of recent years. These ideas are nearly as old as our country. As the future of the young United States was being forged in the late 18th century, our current inner conflict about cities was clearly foreshadowed.

Thomas Jefferson promoted the idea of an agrarian society in which yeoman farmers with strong connections to the land would safeguard the new democratic state. Alexander Hamilton had an opposite view. Promoting manufacturing as the most desirable economic path for the new country, he envisioned eventual urbanization. Through the 1960s, Hamilton seemed to have won this debate. Railroads and canals (and eventually highways and airports) created a national economy focused on cities. But now, as communications technology leaps forward and cocooning instincts take hold, many people have abandoned the face-to-face relationships that characterize urban life. Jefferson seems ascendant.

Through the late 19th and early 20th centuries, the conflict between urban and agrarian coalesced into a view of American cities as risky but exciting, dark and colorful at the same time. Cities were industrial power-houses (Carl Sandburg lauded Chicago, calling it "hog butcher to the world"). They were ethnic melting pots where immigrants became Americans. They were cultural centers filled with vaudeville houses, theaters, movie palaces, and department stores. They had busy big downtowns where all of the city could, and sometimes did, come together.

Two faces of American cities coexisted for a century. There was the debilitating, dangerous, and polluted environment captured forever in photographs of the Lower East Side and Ellis Island by Jacob Riis and Lewis Hine. Alternatively, there was the alluring, glamorous place where Fred Astaire and Ginger Rogers danced in evening clothes atop skyscrapers during the Depression. The reality of city living, for most people, fell between these extremes, and was neither so glamorous nor so depressing.

Since the 1950s and the advent of television, our perceptions of American cities have clearly owed more to popular culture than to lived experience. In the late 1950s and early 1960s, bus driver Ralph Kramden and sewer worker Ed Norton lived with their wives in a New York tenement; Ricky Ricardo, a Cuban bandleader, lived in a building where neighbors invade your private space at every opportunity. Both of these were high-density/high-intensity situations where laughter was a necessary antidote to inherent stress. Then there's the Ozzie Nelson family and the Anderson family whose father knew best, both properly ensconced in small city or suburban habitats. Lucy and Ricky, Alice and Ralph are funnier, but would you move into their apartments or choose them to be your neighbors?

Fast-forward to the 1970s when, among the urban images saturating the airwaves, we had the hilarity of life in high-rise public housing on *Good Times* counterbalanced by the amusingly reactionary Queens neighborhood of Archie Bunker. More recently, the darker urban verisimilitude of Stephen Bochco's "Blues" (*Hill Street* and *NYPD*) extended a cultural viewpoint already imprinted by decades of private eye/detective series. Such entertainments confirmed most Americans' notions that cities are threatening places filled with folks who are out to do you harm.

Neither Jefferson nor Hamilton could have imagined the complex cultural mix of the 1990s American city. For that matter, neither could most folks who grew up in cities—even big cities—as late as the 1950s.

Much about the character and structure of American urban life has shifted radically in recent decades. The people of the world are on the move, and America is once again becoming a nation of immigrants, from Asia, Africa, and Latin America now instead of from Europe. New forms of international business obliterate familiar urban factory scenes as well as traditional local retailers. Buyouts and "restructuring" eliminate jobs in the cities and inner suburbs, while we build new office towers, industrial parks, and subdivisions further out on the metropolitan fringe.

What kinds of images and perceptions do we want for the new American urban condition? We should hope for something better than the stereotyped jokes and terrors that have heretofore obscured rather than revealed the revolution in our lifestyles. As we once did with the old industrial immigrant cities, we need new eyes and new voices to present the many faces of our fast-changing metropolitan scene. We now need only to find them and listen.

Annotating

As you read the essay, you may want to employ some methods to help you gain the most from your reading. Many scholars use what are termed *annotations* to facilitate their reading. Annotating is the process of making notes and marks right on the pages of the essay as you read it, in order both to help you make sense of it as you read and to help you remember the main points of the essay and your reactions to it when you look at it later. Annotating therefore involves both making sense of the text as you read and making comments upon it for later use. Your notes and comments may prove helpful when you review the essay, compare it to other essays, or refer to it as you write your own essay. Annotating often involves:

- Underlining main points or summarizing them in the margin
- Commenting next to points that you find particularly helpful, offensive, or interesting

- Defining key words that you had to look up in the dictionary
- Underlining or circling especially good quotes from the text
- Making a note of a connection you see between what you're reading and something else
- Noting what writing strategies an author is using to be persuasive.

Here is a sample annotated version of Martin's text:

A Nice Place to Visit, but . . .

Judith A. Martin

AMERICANS ARE LOCKED into a long-term love/hate relationship with their cities. As a nation we are now approximately 45 percent suburban and 25 percent rural. Most of us judge cities on hearsay more than on our own experience of urban communities. Our perceptions of urban life are now derived largely from the bad news we see nightly on television or read in the newspaper over breakfast. On the plus side, many Americans partake of the cultural life cities offer—theater, museums, concerts, professional sports, ethnic restaurants. Cities are still seen as the source of sophistication and glamour. Yet on balance, most of us seem to think of cities as places with a lot of problems and only a few redeeming characteristics.

But where did our tainted view of cities originate? They did not spring full blown from the drug/crime/violence litany of recent years. These ideas are nearly as old as our country. As the future of the young United States was being forged in the late 18th century, our current inner conflict about cities was clearly foreshadowed.

Thomas Jefferson promoted the idea of an agrarian society in which yeoman farmers with strong connections to the land would safe-

Margin annotations:

70% Americans live outside cities

Our beliefs about cities: from media

Main Point: 2 views of cities—
1. glamourous
2. dangerous

But this is from lived experience, not just the media, right?

def: contaminated

def: repetitive verbal responses

goes into history of tainted views

def: small-time farmers who owned own farms

T. Jefferson: agrarian society

A. Hamilton: urbanization & manufacturing

guard the new democratic state. Alexander Hamilton had an opposite view. Promoting manufacturing as the most desirable economic path for the new country, he envisioned eventual urbanization. Through the 1960s, Hamilton seemed to have won this debate. Railroads and canals (and eventually highways and airports) created a national economy focused on cities. But now, as communications technology leaps forward and cocooning instincts take hold, many people have abandoned the face-to-face relationships that characterize urban life. Jefferson seems ascendant.

Through 1960s, urbanization winning; since — U.S. retreating from cities

def: united

Through the late 19th and early 20th centuries, the conflict between urban and agrarian coalesced into a view of American cities as risky but exciting, dark and colorful at the same time. Cities were industrial powerhouses (Carl Sandburg lauded Chicago, calling it "hog butcher to the world"). They were ethnic melting pots where immigrants became Americans. They were cultural centers filled with vaudeville houses, theaters, movie palaces, and department stores. They had busy big downtowns where all of the city could, and sometimes did, come together.

Late 19th–early 20th cent.: glamourous & dangerous views united

Aren't these mostly real lived urban experiences?

Here — images in photos & movies

Two faces of American cities coexisted for a century. There was the debilitating, dangerous, and polluted environment captured forever in photographs of the Lower East Side and Ellis Island by Jacob Riis and Lewis Hine. Alternatively, there was the alluring, glamorous place where Fred Astaire and Ginger Rogers danced in evening clothes atop skyscrapers during the Depression. The reality of city living, for most people, fell between these extremes, and was neither so glamorous nor so depressing.

Aren't photos of poor immigrants more real than musicals?

Reality in between glamourous & dangerous (for most)

Since 1950s TV — has produced most of our images of cities

Since the 1950s and the advent of television, our perceptions of American cities have clearly owed more to popular culture than to lived experience. In the late 1950s and early 1960s, bus driver Ralph Kramden and sewer worker Ed Norton lived with their wives in a

New York tenement; Ricky Ricardo, a Cuban bandleader, lived in a building where neighbors invade your private space at every opportunity. Both of these were high-density/high-intensity situations where laughter was a necessary antidote to inherent stress. Then there's the Ozzie Nelson family and the Anderson family whose father knew best, both properly ensconced in small city or suburban habitats. Lucy and Ricky, Alice and Ralph are funnier, but would you move into their apartments or choose them to be your neighbors?

> *1950s–Early 1960s TV shows in cities:*
> *The Honey-mooners,*
> *I Love Lucy,*
> *Ozzie & Harriet,*
> *Father Knows Best*

> *Doesn't really discuss race*

Fast-forward to the 1970s when, among the urban images saturating the airwaves, we had the hilarity of life in high-rise public housing on *Good Times* counterbalanced by the amusingly reactionary Queens neighborhood of Archie Bunker. More recently, the darker urban verisimilitude of Stephen Bochco's "Blues" (Hill Street and NYPD) extended a cultural viewpoint already imprinted by decades of private eye/detective series. Such entertainments confirmed most Americans' notions that cities are threatening places filled with folks who are out to do you harm.

> *1970s TV shows—*
> *Good Times,*
> *All in the Family*

> */*
> *shows w/ racial theme*

> *def: having the appearance of truth*

> *TV shows recently:*
> *NYPD Blue,*
> *Hill Street Blues*
> **
> *cop shows*

Neither Jefferson nor Hamilton could have imagined the complex cultural mix of the 1990s American city. For that matter, neither could most folks who grew up in cities—even big cities—as late as the 1950s.

Much about the character and structure of American urban life has shifted radically in recent decades. The people of the world are on the move, and America is once again becoming a nation of immigrants, from Asia, Africa, and Latin America now instead of from Europe. New forms of international business obliterate familiar urban factory scenes as well as traditional local retailers. Buyouts and "restructuring" eliminate jobs in the cities and inner suburbs, while we build new office towers, industrial parks, and subdivisions further out on the metropolitan fringe.

> *Current changes in cities:*
> *Now—new wave of immi-grants—Asia, Africa, Latin America*

> *Changes in jobs—abandoning of cities for suburbs*

> *Again—how is this about images? Is this supposed to be the truth about cities now?*

What kinds of images and perceptions do we want for the new American urban condition? We should hope for something better than the stereotyped jokes and terrors that have heretofore obscured rather than revealed the revolution in our lifestyles. As we once did with the old industrial immigrant cities, we need new eyes and new voices to present the many faces of our fast-changing metropolitan scene. We now need only to find them and listen.

We need new images to represent the 1990s city

Does this mean that images are accurate?

Summarizing

It is also a good idea to summarize any essay you read. Summarizing a text gives you the chance to clarify for yourself what you think of the essay and the author's position. A summary is simply a much shorter version of a text, put into your own words. We are all familiar with the principles of summarizing, for every day we summarize movie plots, newspaper articles, and even events that happen in our lives when we tell them to someone else. You begin the process of summarizing written texts when you make marginal notations on the essay's main points. When writing a summary, start by looking over the main points you annotated. Then see if you left anything out—or put in too much—by thinking about the following: What are the main points of the essay? What is the author's viewpoint or opinion in this essay? What is the essay's purpose? How is the essay organized? (Is it divided into parts? Is it comparing two or more things? Does it incorporate history? Does it include personal stories?) When summarizing, it is important to remember that some things must be left out; you want to focus in on what seems most important to you.

Here's a sample summary of Martin's essay:

About 70 percent of Americans live outside cities. Most of us base our ideas about cities on images derived from the media. We have two main images of cities: the glamorous center of culture and night life, and the crime-infested ghetto. These two images have a long history, dating from debates in the late 1700s between Thomas Jefferson and Alexander Hamilton about how to envision America. In the late nineteenth to early twentieth centuries the two images were united, as the city was both risky and exciting. From the 1950s to the present, these two images of the city have been produced for us mostly by TV sitcoms and crime drama shows. However, there have been recent major changes in cities: Our population is changing as we experience a huge wave of immigrants from Latin America, Africa, and Asia. Also, new modes of international business are making urban factories obsolete, with many businesses now relocating to the suburbs. These changes have made the glamorous and dangerous images of the city outdated, and we need new images to represent more accurately United States cities as they are now.

This summary of Martin's essay both paraphrases her main idea—"Most of us base our ideas about cities on images derived from the media"—and identifies how she supports her claims—"The two images have a long history. . . ." Summarizing offers opportunities for reviewing an essay, comparing it to other essays, and writing your own informed essays. But summarizing also demands that you spend some time clarifying an author's main points and acknowledging the author's style. Summary thus prepares you for more thoughtful, informed consideration of a text and the issues it raises. By summarizing an essay, you develop a clear understanding and a definite perspective from which to engage a text and an issue.

Answering the Discussion Questions

To further explore an issue, each of the readings in this book is followed by a set of questions. The first three questions direct you to the content of the reading; that is, they attempt to help you understand what the essay is about, what its perspective is, and how it compares to your own ideas. The next three questions are form questions. They ask you to focus more on how the essay is written, what kind of language it uses, what kinds of facts or emotions it brings in, how it is organized, and how these things influence your perception of the author's ideas. These form questions are intended to help you better understand how writers use different methods to achieve different goals by eliciting different reactions from different audiences. Now read, think about, and write answers to the following questions on Martin's essay:

Content
1. According to Martin, what are the two most common images of cities operating today? Do you agree with her? How do you think these two kinds of images are given authority? That is, how is each kind of image made to seem real?

2. At the end of her essay, Martin suggests that, because our cities are currently undergoing so much change, we need to change the images we have of cities. Remembering that images are always partial, what do you think these new images should be like? Who should produce them? Why? How would they be more useful than the images currently being used and who would they be useful to?

3. Martin says that since the introduction of television, "our perceptions of American cities have clearly owed more to popular culture than to lived experience." What do cities owe to popular culture? As you think of cities, which of your images of them grow out of your own and your family's experiences, and which do you take from TV shows, movies, and advertisements?

Form

   1. Martin gives a short historical overview of American attitudes toward cities. How does this history contribute to the way that you understand cities as conversations? In what ways does the conversation seem static? In what ways does it seem to be always changing?

   2. Martin says that since the 1950s, our images of cities have come mostly from popular culture, such as TV. What are her pre-1950s examples of the American city? What impact do her examples have on your reading of her essay and your understanding of pre-1950s images of cities?

   3. How would you describe Martin's tone? How does her tone help us to appreciate her opinion about images of cities? In what ways does she seem to think our images of cities are good? In what ways does she seem to think our images are bad?

Using Your Own Experiences for the Writing Prompts

Two brief writing assignments follow these questions. These assignments ask you to write using ideas gained from the essay and your own ideas and experiences with urban environments and media images of cities. The writing assignments may also ask you to do some additional research of some kind—talking to others, reading other essays, or researching your city's history. When we write, we always write in response to something else; whether it's something someone else said or something we saw, read, or experienced, our writing is best thought of as a response to someone or something. When you write in response to an essay on cities, write in response not only to the essay but also to how the essay makes you feel and how well it seems to match your experience with cities. Draw on what you already know. After you have read an essay, ask yourself how it compares with your experiences. What would you say differently as a result of your experiences? Why would you say it differently? Use your experiences to challenge and question what the writer says. At the same time, use what the writer says to help you rethink the meanings of your experiences from different viewpoints. Your experiences can be used as evidence in an argument; but you can also use someone else's experiences to rethink your own understanding, impressions, values, and perceptions. We encourage you to make notes on your own experiences and how they do or do not support any writer's point. Throughout your written responses, find ways to explain the similarities and differences. Reflect in writing on what it might take to get you to agree with a particular writer, or what it might take to get him or her to agree with you.

   Here are the writing prompts for Martin's essay. Write out your responses and share them with others in your class.

   1. Watch an episode of a television show that takes place in an American city. Write a response both to Martin and to the show that discusses the validity of her perception of two kinds of images of cities.

   2. Describe your city as fully as you can based upon your own experiences and thoughts. Then interview one of your parents or someone else who is a generation older than you and who has lived in your city for many years. Ask that person to describe your city during her or his childhood and to describe it now. Then write out how, according to this person, your city's image has changed over the years. Also write out what the city's image is now, according to the two of you. In what ways do you agree on the city's image? In what ways do you differ? If you differ, why do you think that is?

CONTINUING THE CONVERSATION

After you have answered questions about an essay, such as Martin's, you will have compared it with your own experiences and ideas. Now you will read other essays on the same topic. After reading several of these essays, you will probably begin to understand the various positions on that topic and get a sense of your own position. You should begin to see that, taken together, you and the other writers are having a written conversation about the issues. A written conversation is much like a spoken conversation, except that each person's contributions to the discussion take place separately in various magazines and newspapers. Each contribution to a written conversation is thus a response to what others have said on the topic—just as in an ordinary conversation—but written conversations generally involve more participants, and each person's contributions tend to be more thoughtful and more thoroughly worked out than they would be if the people were conversing in the same room. As Martin's essay suggests, individual cultural conversations also try to make sense of other conversations. Her essay comments, for example, on the ways in which TV shows talk about cities; the conversation between TV shows thus becomes an example in a written conversation about images of cities. Further, many important topics in American culture, such as issues of race, family, religion, and crime, are never resolved once and for all; discussions of these topics have been ongoing for centuries. And because they are important conversations, they will continue.

Here are excerpts from two more essays about images of cities that will help you see a conversation emerging about how cities are represented. As you read each excerpt, annotate it, looking for both the main points and the author's viewpoint, and thinking about your own comments. Also, look over the introduction to each essay to help you better understand the author and her or his essay's perspective on cities. Then summarize each essay briefly in your own words, using your annotations and the questions listed above (under "Summarizing") to help you. When you're through with summarizing, look over the questions after each essay and try to answer them. These questions should help you to understand the essay and relate it to other essays.

The following excerpt is taken from "Disneyfication of the Metropolis," first published in the Journal of Urban Affairs. *The author, Stacy Warren, is a professor in the Department of Geography and Anthropology at Eastern Washington University. As a teacher and researcher of urban affairs, Warren attempts to make known to her students and her readers how urban planning achieves positive or negative results. In "Disneyfication of the Metropolis," she chronicles Seattle's experiences with the urban planners of the Walt Disney Company. Increasingly aware of how decayed their cities have become, city officials have turned to comparing their cities to clean, efficient, "urban-like" places such as Disney World. City officials have thus turned as well to the designers of Disney World for possible solutions to their problems with decay and inefficiency. Describing Seattle's attempted "Disneyfication," Warren suggests ways for people in other cities to think about their own urban renewal projects. Her article sets up a distinction between the Disney experts and the people of Seattle. Through this distinction she raises questions about who might know what's best when it comes to city planning. As you read this essay, think about whether you think private experts or public citizens should have more authority in urban planning, and why.*

Disneyfication of the Metropolis: Popular Resistance in Seattle

Stacy Warren
Eastern Washington University

CONSIDER A LIST of the most formidable design influences on the North American city: Ebenezer Howard, Daniel Burnham, Frederick Law Olmstead, Le Corbusier, Robert Moses, Jane Jacobs, Mickey Mouse. Mickey Mouse? Strange though it may seem, this Walt Disney Company spokesrodent has become the somewhat frivolous symbol of an entirely serious new urban style: the city built in the Disney image. Millions of dollars have been spent

Stacy Warren. "Disneyfication of the Metropolis: Popular Resistance in Seattle." From *Journal of Urban Affairs* 16, 2(1994): 89–107. Reprinted by permission of JAI Press Inc.

by planners, architects, and others who consciously look toward Disney as an expert on the creation of livable public space. Suburban shopping malls, inner city festival markets, small town main streets, residential neighbor-hoods and, in a few cases, whole cities have been shaped according to the lessons of Disney theme parks. Even the Walt Disney Company itself, through its recently created Disney Development arm, has become a significant play-er in the Disneyfication of the metropolis. As architect Frank Gehry, a some-times collaborator with Disney, has commented, it is indeed precarious to not be co-opted by the mouse: the Disney influence has become firmly entrenched in the North American city.

We now have over 20 years of Disneyfication to evaluate. Has Mickey Mouse become, as architectural critic Peter Blake hoped at the onset, the "savior of our cities"? Is he, as Landau more gloomily predicted, the great rodent "dictator"? These questions raise vital theoretical and empirical issues, because Disneyfication represents not merely a new architectural style but also a whole approach to urban planning. The Disney city, as it expands across space, has sparked vigorous debate concerning the politics of urban planning. Who participates in the creation and evolution of the Disney city? Who are its citizens and what powers and rights are they granted? What advantages does the Disney city offer and what problems does it introduce? What happens when an urban form honed behind the protective confines of theme park walls is translated into the real world? Do real city residents have the agency to resist and transform the Disney version of urban utopia through political processes in their community? . . .

When Walt Disney opened his first theme park in Anaheim, California, in 1955, he not only popularized a new form of outdoor entertainment but also planted the seeds of a new urban vision. With Disneyland, Disney purported to offer the antidote to the traditional amusement park, whose rickety roller coasters, soggy hot dogs, and obnoxious barkers he considered seedy, bor-ing, and unsuitable for children. Disney's carefully designed and landscaped park would be magical entertainment for the whole family, its five "lands" offering in Walt Disney's own words "a metropolis of the future . . . above all a place for people to find happiness and knowledge."

Observers rapidly concluded that Disney's creation transcended mere amusement. The developer James Rouse, for instance, declared before a Harvard University audience in 1963 that Disneyland was "the greatest piece of urban design in the United States today." Blake, upon the 1971 opening of Florida's Walt Disney World, called the second park "the most interesting new town in the United States", leading him to speculate that "in this turbulent century, urban man might, just possibly, be saved by a mouse." Where Detroit, Newark, or Los Angeles failed, where places such as Pruitt Igoe came crashing down in the disgrace of their own dust, Disney succeeded. The Disney parks, as architect Robert Venturi lamented, were "nearer to what people really want than anything architects have ever given them."

Fans of the Disney city attributed its success to three crucial urban components: The Disney city looked good, it "worked" as advertised, and people felt comfortable in it. Walt Disney, borrowing from the Hollywood stage set and his own somewhat romanticized childhood memories, created landscapes of exquisite charm, architecturally and aesthetically unified down to the last detail, trimmed with lush greenery, and spotlessly clean. The Imagineers, Disney's stable of set designers, animators, architects, and engineers who were responsible for theme park design, spoke of achieving a synergy of elements where theme, design, scale, and landscaping came together as one harmonious package. Veteran Disney designer John Hench explained how Disney's vision was aimed directly at curing the ills of contemporary urban space:

> Visual elements [in Disneyland] would be designed to complement one another (nonthreatening) rather than compete (threatening) as they often do in the outside world. Most urban environments are basically chaotic places, as architecture and graphics scream at the citizen for attention . . . A journey down almost any street will quickly place the visitor into visual overload as all the competing messages merge into a kind of information gridlock.

Of paramount importance was that the space be people-friendly. Buildings were scaled for the pedestrian through the clever use of a forced perspective technique where nearly full-scale ground floors tapered to increasingly smaller scales with each subsequent level. Buildings on Walt Disney World's Main Street U.S.A., for instance, are seven-eighths scale on the first floor, one-half full height on the second, and less than one-third full size on the third. Consequently, what are actually two story buildings appear three floors high, meant to create a streetscape that seems vibrant and bustling yet still nonthreatening. Buildings in the original Disneyland were built to an even smaller and more intimate scale, leading some Disney observers to criticize the newer Walt Disney World for being "overbearing . . . almost oppressive."

The rest of the surroundings were designed with the pedestrian in mind. The pathways, spokes, and corridors of the overall layout were designed with computer analysis to control where people paused, where they kept moving, and where they turned off, thus smoothing out potential traffic snarls. Attractively shaded park benches were liberally scattered throughout and even the sidewalks were constructed of a special resilient asphalt that, Disney advertised, never tired your feet. Buildings were repainted as often as needed, streets steam-cleaned each morning, and plantings tended to almost constantly.

It was urban space that ran smoothly. Architectural historian Renyer Banham commented with some amazement that at Disneyland "one can step off the pavement and mingle with buses and trains on Main Street in a manner that would lead to sudden death or prosecution outside." The myriad forms of transportation, which included monorails, steam trains, submarines, horse-drawn carriages (virtually everything, in fact, except the private automobile) always ran on time and never broke down. Transportation was transformed from grueling necessity into pleasant adventure. Technology in general could be counted on to enhance, not undermine, the urban experience. There were never any power blackouts or brownouts to rain on Disney's nightly electrical parade. Inside Disneyland, as Charles Moore, Dean of Berkeley's School of Architecture, commented, "everything works, the way it doesn't seem to anymore in the world outside."

People loved it. Surrounded by cheerful landscapes and smiling employees, theme park guests and academics alike responded favorably to the environment....

In fact, the whole Disney city promised to live up to Walt's own description of it as "the happiest place on earth", crime-free, drug-free, corruption-free, poverty-free, racial-conflict-free, free, in short, of the plethora of urban problems that faced every other urban space across North America.

What started as amusement space in the realm of unmitigated nonsense was mass marketed into a credible urban model. Disney was recast as a bona fide urban planner....

Numerous architects, developers, and planners incorporated Disney techniques into their designs for suburban shopping malls, inner city festival marketplaces, revitalized small town main streets, new satellite residential neighborhoods, and, in a few cases, entire cities such as Seaside, Florida. Significantly, the Walt Disney Company itself has played an increasingly active role in the Disneyfication of North America....

It was no coincidence that by the early 1960s, people acknowledged in Disney's creations a powerful and comprehensive urban vision. Disney himself, dismayed by what he perceived to be uncontrolled sprawl surrounding Los Angeles in the years before his death, displayed a growing interest in urban design. Walt Disney World's EPCOT Center, as originally conceived by Disney, was to be truly an Experimental Prototypical Community of Tomorrow, a working city of 20,000 permanent residents, radial in design, complete with a 50-acre glass domed downtown, suburbs, manufacturing areas, and cultural districts linked by state-of-the-art transportation systems. It would be built "from scratch on virgin land", according to Disney, because "the need is not just for curing old ills of old cities." In EPCOT, the latest technologies would be showcased to instruct the city's paying visitors how properly planned technology could ensure a smooth running city. Disney's carefully orchestrated social contract, which would outlaw such urban ills as unemployment, public drunkenness, unmarried cohabitation, and pet ownership, completed the urban landscape."In EPCOT there will be no slum areas because we won't let them develop", Disney explained. The overall effect was to be truly utopian: a site that proposed imaginative solutions to urban problems that, Disney hoped, would "influence the future of city living for generations to come."

Disney died before EPCOT could be built as planned, but the Walt Disney Company has carried on his legacy. The company began its experiments within the Walt Disney World property in Florida on 28,000 acres that were meant to provide the theme park with a buffer zone, a ring of land that the company, free from competition, could shape into whatever it deemed best. The State of Florida granted the right to set building codes, construct roads, levy taxes, and even build a nuclear power plant (an option that Disney, so far, has declined to pursue). In the same agreement, the company was also exempt from paying local impact fees for development projects.

By the mid-1980s, encouraged by new CEO Michael Eisner, Disney officially stepped beyond theme park walls and into the real world. Theme park development had slowed: EPCOT, now much transformed from Walt Disney's original vision, was completed in 1982 and the Disney Company was not yet fully involved in plans for the Euro Disney project in France. Eisner took advantage of this relative lull to explore new business opportunities. The Imagineers were given a bold new agenda: Diversify, they were told, and apply Disney's world famous expertise in design, crowd management, transportation, and efficient entertainment to urban spaces. Disney, Eisner hoped, could corner the market on the planning and development of mixed use, public/private retail-entertainment facilities.

The story of Disney's experience as urban planning consultant for the City of Seattle highlights the enormous appeal that the Disney city holds and the richly problematic nature of its implementation in the real world. Disney came to town to fix Seattle Center, an aging civic center area originally constructed for the 1962 World's Fair and since transformed into heterogeneous public space where visitors can frequent the science museum or the opera, watch a hockey game, wander through flower gardens, hear an outdoor concert, listen to a political rally, or ride the roller coaster. Patron composition is as diverse as that of the activities: elderly women in furs, gang members in colors, suburban families with young children, the homeless, tourists from other countries. All frequent Seattle Center. . . .

Disney's involvement with the area dates back to the late 1950s when Disney staff helped design the original fairgrounds. During the same period he also worked on other projects. He had considerable input into the 1964 World's Fair in New York and Disney himself (unsuccessfully) offered his talents to the City of Las Vegas in 1960 with the idea of installing a monorail down the center of town to alleviate traffic congestion. The focus of the current case study begins in the early 1980s, when Seattle Center was over two decades old and beginning to seem no longer quaint but, in the words of a local newspaper, "a bedraggled relic." The sorry state of the civic center was virtually a citywide scandal. City Hall and Seattle Center management decided that it was time to fundamentally rethink the best use for this space and they decided the best people to help would be the Disney Company.

The Seattle Center project was Disney's first, and to date most extensive, foray into urban planning on non-Disney property. The complete 74-acre site, incorporating a variety of urban functions, intrigued the Imagineers. They made it clear from the start that they were not simply interested in fine tuning the amusement zones, but in developing and possibly also financing and operating the entire site. They proposed assistance in architecture, design, site layout, landscaping, crowd and traffic management, and security. Vice President of Imagineering Patrick Scanlon, in what would become a recurring theme, assured Seattle that Disney had no plans to foist a Disneyland North or EPCOT West upon the city: They envisioned creating something truly unique for the area.

Negotiations with Disney began in 1986 in order to hammer out a contract that would include the creation of blueprints for three alternative renovation schemes and the provision of all related financial and socioeconomic data. Initially, the prognosis for this joint effort looked good. Seattle Mayor Charles Royer praised what he perceived to be Disney's special talents at helping cities create "excellent people places", adding that Disney was "probably the best in the world" at urban entertainment planning. City representatives were confident that Disney could successfully reshape the center, organize the chaos, and harmonize the currently inefficient use of space. Disney would clean up the grounds, both literally and figuratively, eliminating all those unwanted elements that ranged from litter to undesirable visitors. In the words of City Councilmember George Benson, Disney "is the answer."

As involvement with Disney proceeded, however, trouble began to brew. Over the next three years, the situation would deteriorate to the point that Disney ultimately would be dismissed. Friction centered on two general issues: (1) Disney's seeming inability to create designs for Seattle Center that meshed with the needs and desires of Seattle residents and (2) apparent unwillingness to remedy the situation by seeking advice, or even taking advice when offered, from local quarters. The implications were disturbing: In spite of Disney's success within theme park walls, the company perhaps had neither the talent nor the political inclination to excel in actual urban space. . . .

The final blow came when Disney released its financial projections: The total bill for Seattle Center's renovation, which Disney had first estimated at $60 million, now stood at $335 million. This revelation left council stunned.

The Disney plan, if implemented, would force the city into a position where an admission fee would be virtually inevitable and symbolized the true private and exclusionary nature of Disney's so-called public planning venture. Council, upon the encouragement of the official advisory group, informal coalitions, and many vocal citizens, decided it was time to send Disney packing. A local architectural firm was engaged to develop a new round of three alternative plans for Seattle Center. The topic had so galvanized the city, in fact, that several additional firms submitted plans, unsolicited and at their own expense. When the Environmental Impact Statement was undertaken in 1989, council chose five plans from the many it had received. The Disney plan, however, was not among them. Seattle's involvement with Disney officially had come to an end.

Seattle's experience with Disney ranged from initial euphoric hopes that Disney could recreate in Seattle Center the same kind of magic that had so skillfully been designed in their theme parks to local residents' realization that the Disney plan introduced more urban problems than it solved. The dynamic hegemonic processes that underscored this experience revealed, to Seattle residents, a fundamental contradiction in Disneyfied space. Its charming surface and smooth running infrastructure would only be achieved through planning practices that are unacceptably authoritarian in the real world. Disney's demands for special political concessions, insistence that, as privileged holders of Disney knowledge, the company knew better than locals what Seattle needed, and the company's refusal to acknowledge any dissenting opinions left many Seattleites feeling patronized and insulted. To make matters worse, the urban space that Disney offered failed to capture local culture or adequately incorporate the ethnic and age diversity of Seattle Center patrons or even look good on paper....

It is important to acknowledge that, throughout the whole process, there were elements of the Disney city that held and continued to hold great appeal. People responded quite favorably to a vision of urban space that is clean and safe, where the buildings and landscaping have been carefully designed and tended, where traffic proceeds smoothly and the trains run on time, where all are welcome, and where traditional urban ills, such as poverty, unemployment, and racial and class tensions, have been dealt with, in effect, an urban space where each person is empowered and true community can grow. Significantly, Seattle residents in the end were able to appropriate what they liked from the Disney city and discard what they did not like through political channels.... Almost as soon as the Imagineers' bags were packed, the City of Seattle began holding citizen participation panels to hammer out a more compatible version of the civic center's future.

The newly renovated Seattle Center, when completed, will represent the efforts of many local architects, planners, designers, and other citizens who specifically rejected an autocratic, outside force in order to retain control over their space. Their interest in maintaining the character of the center, as a sometimes chaotic mingling of uses that offers meaningful landscapes to groups ranging from the homeless to wealthy operagoers without reducing options for a middle class norm, stems from their concern to speak for those who are not directly involved in the planning process. In the words of a local homeless man who filled out a questionnaire during the planning process, "thank you for having me and other individuals to be part of the [Seattle] Center—warmth etc. as a homeless person." That a homeless person, as perhaps the strongest symbol of disenfranchisement in the city, should form a constituent part of the planning for the new Seattle Center speaks to the powers of true citizenship embedded in hegemonic processes.

Discussion Questions

Content
1. What reasons does Warren give for the Walt Disney Company's getting involved in urban planning? Why do city planners, such as those in Seattle, want Disney to help them plan their cities? What potential benefits can you imagine that Disney might gain by helping cities to plan revitalization projects?

2. According to the essay, in what ways was Disney successful and in what ways were they unsuccessful in planning for a real urban environment, i.e., the Seattle Center? Why do you think that is?

3. What might a utopian city be like? Disneyland claims to be a utopian place, "the happiest place on earth," because it's "crime-free, drug-free, corruption-free, poverty-free, racial-conflict-free." Would the utopian city you imagine have the same characteristics as Disneyland for the same reasons Disneyland has them? How and why would your utopia differ from the Disneyland model?

Form
1. Warren's essay moves through three sections in which she discusses Disney. What is the topic of each and what positive effects do you think Warren accomplishes by dividing the essay as she does?

2. What does Warren mean by the term *Disneyfication*? What tone or attitude does the word communicate to you? What does this tone reveal about Warren's perspective of Disney, of the city, of the meaning of the word *revitalization*?

3. In her essay, Warren concludes that Disney's involvement in the planning of the Seattle Center was a failure. Could she have drawn a different moral from the story of Disney's involvement? What leads her to her conclusions? Point to specific parts of her essay to discuss how Warren's conclusions seem valid to you or not.

Writing Prompts

1. Consider a place in your area that you think should be redeveloped. Who do you think should decide how it is to be redeveloped? Disney? City planners? Someone else? Write an essay in which you describe the advantages and disadvantages of each as the developer.

2. Using the concept and word *Disneyfication*, describe a recent development in your area. How do the streets, the buildings, the development's purpose, and the people who use the development make the development seem "Disneyfied" or not?

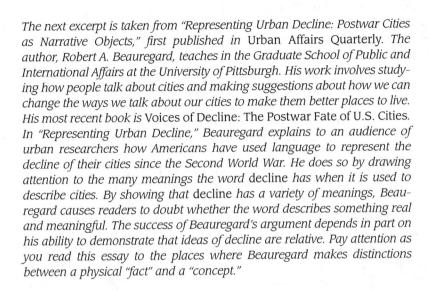

The next excerpt is taken from "Representing Urban Decline: Postwar Cities as Narrative Objects," first published in Urban Affairs Quarterly. *The author, Robert A. Beauregard, teaches in the Graduate School of Public and International Affairs at the University of Pittsburgh. His work involves studying how people talk about cities and making suggestions about how we can change the ways we talk about our cities to make them better places to live. His most recent book is* Voices of Decline: The Postwar Fate of U.S. Cities. *In "Representing Urban Decline," Beauregard explains to an audience of urban researchers how Americans have used language to represent the decline of their cities since the Second World War. He does so by drawing attention to the many meanings the word* decline *has when it is used to describe cities. By showing that* decline *has a variety of meanings, Beauregard causes readers to doubt whether the word describes something real and meaningful. The success of Beauregard's argument depends in part on his ability to demonstrate that ideas of decline are relative. Pay attention as you read this essay to the places where Beauregard makes distinctions between a physical "fact" and a "concept."*

Representing Urban Decline: Postwar Cities as Narrative Objects

University of Pittsburgh

THE DECLINE OF CITIES IN THE UNITED STATES after World War II shocked most urban commentators. Although many of them realized that the Depression and the war had siphoned capital away from investment, thus weakening the physical fabric of cities, and that the decentralization of the 1920s might well continue, few anticipated the rapid deterioration of older industrial cities. Such a reversal of fortunes cried out for explanation, and commentators searched for those conditions and events that gave causal impetus to the ostensible fall of once-mighty U.S. cities.

Robert A. Beauregard. "Representing Urban Decline: Postwar Cities as Narrative Objects." From *Urban Affairs Quarterly* 29 (Dec. 1993): 187–202. Copyright © 1993 by Sage Publications, Inc. Reprinted by permission of Sage Publications, Inc.

Almost without exception, the inherent instability of the concept of urban decline has been ignored in the resultant explanations, an avoidance linked directly to the difficulties one faces in fixing the meaning of cities. Although one can count the movement of people from central cities to suburbs, the fall in the dollar value of urban real estate, the metropolitan shifts of employment from core to periphery, or the expansion in the numbers of abandoned buildings, the *meaning* of these phenomena *as urban decline* is not so easily grasped. Just as the concept of cities resists rigid classification, the notion of urban decline stands as one of its elusive attributes....

To what does urban decline refer? Is it the loss of population and employment from the city (a common interpretation), or is it the shrinking of the middle class, the expansion of minotity and low-income populations, and the increasing incidence of fiscal difficulties? What about physical deterioration? Is it increasing crime, AIDS, and homelessness? ...

At the root of this indeterminacy is the ongoing difficulties of making clear what is being talked about when one mentions decline. One of the culprits is the instability of the meaning of *urban* across the history of urban theory. From Tönnies to Castells, notions of *the city* and *the urban* have been continuously challenged and redefined. Tönnies and other early sociologists understood the city to be the opposite of community—that is, of places where social relations are characterized by face-to-face interactions, psychological ties, fully realized personalities, and fully expressed roles. The city thus had no identity independent of a more desirable type of human settlement; the city was community's antithesis.

Weber, for example, boldly confronted the city's ephemerality and emerged with an ideal type that limited it to medieval settlements. Any human settlement that had a marketplace and political and legal autonomy was a city. However, this approach effectively emptied the category of cities except for specific settlements in the Middle Ages. By fixing the meaning of the city in this way, Weber removed it as an object of study.

Robert Park devised his meaning of city by drawing on the natural sciences, particularly biology. He wrote of the ecological dynamics of human settlements, linking notions of community to environment and space and thereby giving cities a geographical dimension. For Park, ecological competition and its subsequent equilibrium pivoted on growth in the city's central business district. The city thus became, at least implicitly, any human settlement with such a natural area. Despite being a student of Park, Louis Wirth rejected this approach, preferring instead to focus on urbanism as a way of life. Yet, he simultaneously anchored his notion of urbanism in an ecological triumvirate of size, density, and heterogeneity. Moreover, Wirth's claim that urbanism could not be confined to a specific type of human settlement weakened his claim to a stable definition of the city.

Early theorists of the city subsequently abandoned any attempt to specify its meaning, preferring instead to focus on the social relations that occur within places assumed to be cities. The notion of cities was so close to exploding into fragments—thus unsettling urban sociology—that theorists and researchers steered clear. The complexity of meanings swept into its vortex made the city a dangerous site for theorizing.

The instability of urban is not solely responsible for the inconstant nature of urban decline. The term *decline* is also a culprit. Just as the meaning of urban is elusive, the meaning of decline is equally problematic but in a different way. One illustration of this appears when narratives of civilization and national decline intersect with those of urban decline. The common ground is decline as a reference to loss and loss as a sign of weakness and disgrace. . . .

Many urban commentators have argued that without cities and the agricultural surpluses that enabled people to wrest themselves from subsistence activities, civilization was simply not possible. Cities mark the turning point between agricultural societies lacking in elaborate cultural and political developments and urban societies in which the Aristotelian attributes of a civil society emerge. Within cities, people are free to pursue intellectual and artistic endeavors, explore innovative economic activities, and participate in self-governance.

The blooming of capitalism in the mid-nineteenth century set the stage for the coming of modern society in which cities solidified their function as pinnacles of civilization. The fine arts flourished in the modern city, democracy was strengthened, and affluence released a burgeoning middle class from its minority status. Moreover, within the modern city, governments begin to control the spaces of the city, bringing to them a cohesive image of what constitutes a place of progress and opportunity.

From this perspective, to speak of the decline of cities is to refer to the demise of a particular notion of civilization widely held by middle- and upper-class elites. Urban decline brings not just the threat of crime, falling property values, and higher taxes, but, more important, and symbolically embedded in any announcement of urban decline, decline threatens to undermine the identity of those whose lives have transcended subsistence and whose social contributions appear in intellectual, artistic, political, and even economic realms. To the extent that modern civilization is built on capitalism, any threat to civilization is a threat to those who live off capitalism's great powers to generate affluence, even while it also creates deep poverty. For these reasons, the decline of cities taps fundamental insecurities about highly valued ways of life. Though suburban growth might fill the void left by urban decline and despite its function as a vehicle for postwar affluence, suburbs are rarely considered to be among the fruits of civilization.

To the degree that *civilization* is simultaneously a reference to specific leisure pursuits and to the political economy that produces those opportunities and to the extent that the growth of cities is associated with the rise of civilization, both as an "engine" of civilization and as a place where one lives an urbane existence, any decline in cities threatens the civilized way of life. Thus urban commentators cannot refer to urban decline without setting in motion subtle harmonics that cause many listeners and readers to reflect on the precariousness of their way of life. . . .

Consider decline as representing a loss of power and status, and consider this loss as only assessable in relation to memory of what was and expectation of what might be. To this extent, individuals experience loss because of what they remember about how they were, either as a nation or as city dwellers, and they fear the loss because they had expected a much different and more desirable national and urban future. As this loss unfolds, the collective understanding of the past is revised. Memory (and history) is rewritten to lessen the current loss or to deepen alarm over an impending future. When national and urban prowess have been ostensibly diminished, for example, many commentators inflate the past so that decline is more ominous and deflate the future so that the tasks before the nation are not as daunting.

From this perspective, national decline and urban decline are not simply a result of the dynamics of development but, rather, a violent affront to the American character. Allowing oneself, the cities, or the nation to fall short of an understood potential is unacceptable and a sign of weakness. Weak and uncompetitive, susceptible to more powerful and prosperous nations, no longer "the best," facing a future that one can neither control nor anticipate with great expectations, and deprived of the lifestyle to which one has become accustomed are the meanings of urban decline that surface as one explores its intersection with other popular and scholarly debates.

A popular belief is that Americans are antiurban. Commentators, from magazine writers to academics, enjoy pointing out how households fled the cities when transportation and housing technology made suburban living possible. For many of these commentators, the decentralization and deconcentration of cities that began in the late nineteenth century are natural phenomena previously constrained only by the concentration of employment, the costs of commuting, and the expense of suburban housing. Even the more critical commentators seldom question the purported Jeffersonian desire of Americans to live in the country. In fact, one frequently reads the ironic comment that despite the avowed preference of many people to live outside of the cities, most people live within them. The observation signals the constraints on an antiurban prejudice.

The claim that Americans dislike cities pivots on romantic notions of an agrarian life that existed prior to the onset of the industrial age and on a political belief in the greater democratic tendencies of gentleman and yeoman farmers. Instead of representing the pinnacle of civilization, industrialization brought grimy, oppressive, and dangerous cities populated by propertyless classes with anarchistic tendencies and a bent for mob behavior. Elements of that argument traveled to the postwar period. There, the agrarian and yeoman ideals became reinterpreted as the suburban lifestyle, concerns about the industrial city were refocused on ghettos, race was introduced as an additional reason for avoiding cities, and mob rule became crime (whether organized or random), illegal drugs, and riots. From this perspective, Americans have had every reason to reject their cities.

Yet, one would be overstating the case by accusing Americans of being antiurban. Evidence to the contrary is equally accessible, if not equally publicized. Large numbers of people live in urban places, and one frequently hears stories of vibrant urban neighborhoods with residents who find it inconceivable that they might relocate to the suburbs. The national news media daily extol events within cities: professional sports, symphonic recitals, personal tragedies, corporate successes and failures, engineering feats, ethnic celebrations, architectural achievements, political scandals, and scientific breakthroughs. Most rural and suburban lives fall within the domain of economic, cultural, and social forces flowing from the cities, and, throughout history, numerous public commentators have marveled at cities and equated them with the modern world.

One can better describe Americans as ambivalent toward cities. One does not have the choice of cities or no cities. Escape from the city, no matter how deep within prairie or forest, is no escape from the city's influence and is no solution, except on the most individualistic of terms. Americans have not as much rejected the city as they have struggled with how to incorporate its presence into the mythology and reality of life in the United States. The struggle has been one of reconciling an agrarian heritage with an industrial present, mediating between individualism and the necessities of collective action, and balancing freedom against government protection from the vagaries of capitalism. These oppositional tendencies speak to the American character, and their fleeting resolutions define that character as ambivalent.

Thus the onset of postwar urban decline did not bring widespread rejoicing. If antiurbanism had been deeply entrenched in the collective psyche, one would have expected celebration and then been surprised by its absence. Instead, urban decline engendered two responses: One response was further flight from the older industrial cities (yet also flight into newer cities of the Southwest, South, and West), and another response was alarm and concern. The decline of the cities that had built American prosperity was not a welcomed event. In the postwar period, suburban living made sense in part because of an urban presence. The city provides the jobs, finance, culture, and professional sports. It houses the poor and minorities, and its govern-ment carries burdens that make suburban affluence possible. One can hardly applaud the decline of cities if it undermines the bases of suburban prosperity.

Therefore, Americans have treated urban decline ambivalently. On the one hand, decline threatens the American way of life and points to weak-nesses in the national fabric; on the other hand, it represents the "just rewards" due profligate, immoral, and cancerous cities. Urban decline can be interpreted as something that city dwellers brought onto themselves because they failed to make the investments, to institute the social controls, and to commit themselves seriously to the continuous renewal of their envi-ronments. If the cities were to disappear, then, those living outside of them would be better off because they would no longer be threatened.

Of course, cities cannot disappear. Physical places can, but their resi-dents still have to go someplace. On reflection, urban decline is and has always been a serious threat to suburban living, not its affirmation. To elimi-nate the cities is to relocate the nation's urban problems. The most likely response to such complicated relationships and consequences is ambiva-lence.

Consequently, urban decline, either as a symbol or objective measure of cities, does not resolve the confusion that anchors the American urban sen-sibility. On the contrary, it intensifies and builds on ambivalence to produce not a simple benign neglect of cities in decline or an aggressive and massive counterstrategy but a mixture of rejection and sympathy, flight and rein-vestment, and helplessness and hope. Whether a theorist or a popular com-mentator, one cannot present urban decline as an attribute of cities in the absence of deep-rooted insecurities within the American psyche. Whether or not one opts to explore how that ambivalence shapes attitudes toward and the meanings attached to urban decline, its resonances cannot be com-pletely suppressed.

Urban decline is more than a multidimensional empirical indicator and more than its surface manifestations; it is multirepresentational and replete with symbolic resonances. Quite diverse meanings are forged into this single attribute frequently attached to postwar cities. Using this concept, urban commentators attempt to make sense of postwar cities and find themselves only more entangled in the briar patch of interpretation.

Just as the many narratives of urban decline often use dismal assess-ments as a springboard to optimistic commitment, critical and reflective the-orists should probe this analysis of urban decline for positive guidance. Four prescriptions can be derived from the previous discussion. First of all, it is important that scholars of the city recognize the cultural and symbolic reso-nances of what seem to be objective, stable, and immediately comprehensi-ble interpretations. Any time scholars use a phrase like urban decline, they bring to the foreground the rhetorical dimension of their work. In this article, I have attempted to show this for urban decline, but similar conditions hold any time scholars attempt to explain the city.

Second, simultaneous to recognizing the rhetoric surrounding cities, urban commentators need to grasp the significance of the issue of representation. No single best or valid way of understanding the city exists, only different ways. Given uneven development, why do we focus on decline in the absence of growth? Or why ignore capital investment in the built environment and characterize developmental trends in terms of employment and population shifts? Moreover, representational choices are not just tied to the objects that are the focus of attention. The issue of representation also extends to choices between analysis and narrative, objectivism and relativism, and expert opinion and personal impressions. Each way of representing the city provides different interpretations and insights and different meanings. The city cannot be understood in just one way.

Third, the discussion implicitly points out the disconnectedness of analysis and action in the realm of urban policy and collective mobilization. Anxiety-provoking diagnoses, such as that of urban decline, cannot lay claim to aggressive remedy, rapid flight, or calm indifference. What is done about urban problems, if anything, often has little relation to the actual depth of those problems. Most important, though, interpretation must also be seen as a realm of action, one in which meanings are socially negotiated and rhetorically constructed.

Finally, because urban commentators are part of a society that generates the injustices of urban decline, they cannot escape responsibility for them. Although the degree of their responsibility and the extent of their obligations to act vary, they cannot place themselves outside the web of inequalities that link the problems of the cities to the settings in which they live.

The obligations of urban theorists are to demystify urban decline by "unpacking" its many meanings, to point to the complex array of narratives that create these meanings, and to expose the material construction of the ideology of decline. To ignore what urban decline means and how those meanings are created is to succumb to an uncritical theoretical stance highly vulnerable to representational repression.

Discussion Questions

Content

1. What point is Beauregard making about urban decline? What is he saying about people who theorize and write about urban decline?

2. Beauregard says that the terms *urban* and *decline* have been defined in several ways. What are some of the different definitions for *urban* and *decline*? Why does it matter that these terms have multiple definitions?

3. Beauregard says, "No single best or valid way of understanding the city exists, only different ways." What does he mean by this? Do you agree with him?

Form

1. At the beginning of his essay, Beauregard asks, "To what does urban decline refer?" In what ways does he answer this question? In what ways does he fail to answer this question?

2. What key words besides *urban* and *decline* does the author use to discuss urban decline? How do these words help us make sense of the idea of decline?

3. Beauregard draws four conclusions from his discussion of how people have represented urban decline. Do these conclusions seem to you to follow from what he has presented? Are there other conclusions implied in his essay?

Writing Prompts

1. In another of his essays, Beauregard asks the question, "What do our cities tell us?" Write an exploratory essay in which you answer the question, "What does my city tell me?"

2. Write a description of the major city in your area, trying to use the key words and phrases that the city's residents typically use to describe it. Discuss whether the most commonly used words and phrases evoke decline or renewal. Then discuss in some detail what image of your city these words and phrases evoke.

REEXAMINING YOUR EXPERIENCES AND YOUR ENVIRONMENT

Now, think again about your experiences in light of the conversation that you are joining. How do the various authors' ideas relate to your experiences of the topic and your ideas about the topic? In this case, how do Martin's, Beauregard's, and Warren's ideas about images of cities relate to your experiences of those images and your ideas about the meanings of those images? At this point, it is often helpful to make a list of things you think you can bring to the existing conversation. In order to begin such a list, simply write out what you think could be added to the conversation. When you look at the ways these "experts" talk about cities, what is left out?

Next, think about the city you live in or a city that you have experience with or knowledge of. How is the conversation about contemporary urban culture taking place in your environment? In other words, what kinds of images are circulating in and about your city? What are those images trying to accomplish? What can those images reveal about your city, its residents, or its culture? Just as Warren examines a revitalization project in Seattle to say something about how people think about cities and their purposes, you can focus on a local example to say something that applies to more cities than your own. In most cases, it will not be difficult to relate something from your environment to the conversation you are trying to join: simply be on the lookout for a usable case or example.

For instance, consider a typical evening news program. The lead story asserts that the old baseball stadium downtown has become outdated, dilapidated, and inconvenient to current fans. Some fans argue that the old stadium is unattractive and that a new one would attract more support for the team. City officials suggest that a new stadium would bring money downtown, attracting more suburbanites and tourists to games, urban restaurants, and other businesses. The team owner adds that, given the high salaries of athletes, stadiums must produce even more revenue in order to support the team. So the owner proposes a new stadium at a new location that would feature restaurants, retail outlets, and luxury suites, while at the same time revitalizing a depressed and decayed area of the inner city. Fans imagine easier parking and freedom from homeless beggars and crime in the new, well-planned stadium development area. City officials, the team owner, and fans contribute to the conversation about a new stadium by using images of decline (the old stadium is outdated) and renewal (a new stadium will revitalize the city and the team).

But then the news report reveals that not everyone talking about the stadium issue, or the future of the city, uses images of decline and renewal in the same ways. The "old stadium fan club" wants to preserve the old stadium as a functional historical monument. Local parking lot, restaurant, souvenir shop, and bar owners want to keep the stadium where it is so that they can stay in business. Residents of the neighborhood surrounding the old stadium argue that it has given a special meaning to their neighborhood for as long as they can remember; and residents of the proposed new stadium site do not want their neighborhood bulldozed to provide space for the parking lots and new businesses that will surround the new stadium. These participants in the conversation represent the existing city quite differently from the way their opponents do.

Making new sense of the issue means offering a new way to think about something. In this case, you might use some ideas from your readings to make new sense of the stadium controversy. Alternatively, you could use the stadium or other discussion in your city to make some new sense out of how images function to create cities and shape people's actions. In either case, you're trying to look around yourself, look at your own world, and interpret that world in a way that contributes to the conversation of culture. Each of the essays we've read so far in this part seeks to participate in the conversation going on in culture to say something about a specific place or set of examples. Martin speaks of how TV represents cities; Warren discusses how various groups in Seattle represented revitalization; Beauregard speaks about the language of urban studies and how that language represents cities.

Next, we offer an essay in which the author, Jerry Herron, uses a sign in a pizza shop window to launch a discussion of the ways in which people have pictured and used his city throughout its history. As you read "Niki's Window: Detroit and the Humiliation of History," think about the different ways in which your city has been represented throughout its history and how those changing images of your city still remain within its current face. As usual, Herron's essay is preceded by an introduction and followed by discussion questions.

Jerry Herron lives in Detroit, where he teaches in the English Department and directs the American Studies Program at Wayne State University. He is the author of two books, Universities and the Myth of Cultural Decline *and* AfterCulture: Detroit and the Humiliation of History. *He writes regular columns and restaurant and movie reviews for local newspapers in Detroit. In "Niki's Window," first published in* Georgia Review, *Jerry Herron describes the window of what is now a restaurant in a section of Detroit known as Greektown. By exploring the history of that window, and of the building, and of the people who have owned the building, Herron reveals how the history of places can be transformed and forgotten. He describes something unique about contemporary American cities and our memories of their histories. The effect of this essay derives from the way Herron repeatedly returns the reader's attention to Niki's window as a point where recollecting and forgetting come together. As you read, reflect on the effect Herron's repeated return to Niki's window has on your attitude toward his argument.*

Niki's Window:
Detroit and the Humiliation
of History

Jerry Herron

We as a nation seem to be self-destructing—environmentally, economically and culturally. Detroit is just doing it more quickly and more willfully.

—Marvin Krueger in a letter to *The New York Times*

I

WHO COULD HAVE ANTICIPATED finding the sign in Niki's window? Nobody, I expect, and that's both the wonder of it and the shame. Niki's sign tells the truth—the whole truth. It faithfully represents what it stands for,

Jerry Herron. "Niki's Window: Detroit and the Humiliation of History." From *The Georgia Review* 47.2 (Summer 1993): 362–375. Reprinted by permission of the author.

which is what has happened to history in Detroit: the most historically representative city in America, the one place that everybody can agree they no longer want any part of. Think about what has gone on, and gone wrong, in Detroit: riots and white flight, plant closings and industrial collapse, murders and carjackings, assaults, arson, and drug wars—all the kinds of trouble that people who've moved away were hoping to leave behind. And unlike in Los Angeles, say, or Washington, DC, the troubles here are not relieved by the operatic distractions of a Hollywood or a national government.

Eloquence notwithstanding, Niki's sign goes largely unnoticed. Maybe that's because no one, individually, is responsible for creating this remarkable historical text; there's no author to claim credit for its prodigal intelligence. Or maybe the sign gets ignored because it is so clearly a reminder of unwanted things. Or maybe its moment has not yet come. Niki's sign records a city that nobody has figured out how to need or even tolerate: the city that appears after the culture of middle-class expectations, which had once sustained America, gives way and falls apart.

II

There's nothing mysterious about the sign on its surface: red and white letters painted on a pane of plate glass in the window of Niki's Taverna, an inexpensive restaurant in a part of the old business district referred to locally as "Greektown." The sign names the place as belonging to Niki: NIKI'S. But that's where the simplicity ends. First, there is no Niki. *Niki* is the name invented by a Greek dishwasher and school dropout named Dennis Kefallinos, who immigrated to America at age fourteen, worked hard, saved his money, and now— some twenty years later—has come to own three restaurants, several parcels of real estate, and a food distribution company.

Thanks to Niki's success, Kefallinos no longer has to wash dishes. He wears suits, and the dishwashers work for him. His photograph accompanies an article in the *Detroit News*: "Horatio Algers Without Diplomas." A handsome, smiling man, "Niki" lounges pridefully against the front of his restaurant, right next to the sign. "To make it happen in this country is easier now than thirty years ago," he told the interviewer. "Making it happen"—that's what Niki is good at, which is how he got his picture in the paper and how he qualifies as one of Detroit's Horatio Algers. The reporter has confused Alger—a philanthropic Harvard graduate—with his self-made characters, but no matter. In a way, conflation is precisely the point and the reason to congratulate the immigrant Kefallinos on his becoming Niki, who mocks our natives' disbelief in Horatio Alger clichés with the visible fact of his improvised success. As he points out, "There's no such thing as, 'I can't make it happen.' I don't buy that." And why should he?

Niki's story of opportune self-creation is no less true of Greektown itself. Like the stylized waiter's portrait he uses as a logo—a kind of ethnic happy face—this historic "town" is largely make-believe. Greektown is actually just one block of Monroe Street and a block or two of a cross street, Beaubien, where Niki set up his business. This part of the city was first settled in the eighteenth century by French farmers (among them Antoine Beaubien, whose property line became the street in front of Niki's). The French were followed a hundred years later by German immigrants, who arrived in great numbers after the failed revolution of 1848, but the Germans seem not to have wanted to memorialize their arrival by inventing a Germantown to live in. The buildings they put up are architecturally undistinguished and utilitarian.

Civic pride demanded something grander, something perpetually more up-to-date, to serve as the center of the city, so for much of the twentieth century, this part of Detroit was essentially forgotten. That's why there's enough of it still standing to be converted now by entrepreneurs who want to help their neighbors rediscover the romance of the urban past. It would take quite a few years, however, to arrive at the point at which the past would feel like something to capitalize on rather than conceal. And by then the depopulation of Detroit would have so altered its demographic character (with more than seventy percent of the population having become black and nearly a third of the residents living in poverty) that certain realities could best be dealt with through proxies, like the invented Niki, whose simulacral Greek waiter offers a blandly acceptable stand-in for otherwise threatening differences of race and class that history has left painfully unresolved.

Goings-on are unabashedly touristic in Niki's home town, where practically nobody, including Greeks, still lives. What's left of the old neighborhood, like the few remaining tables in the Macedonia Cafe, has been pushed aside by conversion. Video arcade games, Street Fighter II and Super Street Fighter II, have taken over the space where Greek men used to sit playing cards, smoking cigarettes, and drinking sweet coffee out of tiny cups. Now visitors—generally white, suburban, and middle-class—come to this inner city as if looking for something valuable their parents or grandparents forgot in the rush to get up and out and on to a better life.

Greektown is not so much a place, then, as it is a way of reinventing one of the oldest, and now most profitably "restored," parts of Detroit. No city is immune to this kind of entrepreneurial ersatz, even ones where residents pride themselves on being *genuinely* historical: Boston, New York, San Francisco, Baltimore, Philadelphia. They've all got neighborhoods like Greektown, where tourists "return" to an urban theme park to buy souvenirs of a time and place—usually ethnic, crowded, and working-class—that the people formerly caught in couldn't wait to escape.

III

Greektown is where many residents take out-of-town visitors, or where they go themselves, especially on summer evenings if the weather is nice. Here, for the space of one block, Detroit puts on a recognizable, urban scene. Monroe Street is narrow, barely two lanes wide; pedestrians jaywalk leisurely among the slow-moving cars. Buildings, made of weathered red brick, are as old as any in the city and low—two or three stories—with no space between them. All the storefronts are filled, most with Greek restaurants and bakeries and markets, one after the other: Simeon Bakery, the Athens Bar, the Golden Fleece, the Athens Bakery, the Laikon Cafe, the Olympia, the Grecian Gardens, Pegasus Restaurant, the Hellas (which claims to be the original Greek restaurant on Monroe Street), the New Parthenon, Astoria Pastry, Aegean Ice Cream, and so on. At the end of the block are the Romanesque towers of St. Mary's Catholic Church—the single unconverted site on the street, and consequently the only one that requires the explanation of an historic marker.

By dinnertime, there are lines of people on the sidewalks, waiting to get into restaurants, especially at the Laikon and the Hellas with its wraparound windows. Rollerbladers cruise by on Monroe; vendors sell roses "for the lady." There's even a sketch artist who will do your portrait, and a guy in improvised Elizabethan costume who will produce a sonnet to suit the occasion. Couples stroll along eating ice cream cones, holding hands. Conventioneers with plastic badges—"Hi! I'm Bob"—travel in packs, talking loudly after having had too much to drink. They're the ones most likely to stop and stare through the window at Lindos to watch the belly dancer perform on stage. But generally the crowd is well-behaved and, except for the teenagers, largely white. The average visitor to Greektown, according to a recent consumer survey, is thirty-four years old, has an income of more than $40,000 and resides eight miles north in suburban Oakland County, one part of which contains the highest concentration of millionnaires per square foot in America.

IV

The centerpiece of Niki's neighborhood, an enclosed minimall comprised of several nineteenth-century brick structures, is a gaudy piece of fakery called "Trapper's Alley" that opened in 1985. There is no alley, but there are—or once were—trappers; they came here to sell their pelts and hides to Traugott Schmidt, who immigrated from Germany in 1852. That historic recollection provides the organizing theme of this "festival market," as it is subtitled, but the history is purely generic and might apply equally well to almost any American city—a point the developers, Cordish Embry & Associates, have been quick to capitalize on elsewhere. Trapper's Alley, with its exposed red brick and brass reproduction fittings, merely stands for *pastness* as such. Nothing locates it in *this* city; nothing connects it to events specifically and uniquely defining Detroit, any more than do the products sold in the shops.

Aside from the usual fast-food outlets—Popeye's Fried Chicken, Sbarro's Pizza—there's the Purple Store with its stock of cheap items, all of which are colored purple; and there's the little novelty boutique, Lefties Corner, specializing in T-shirts and mugs that sloganeer on behalf of left-handedness. Across the way is Get Sauced, where the inventory consists of improbable and high-priced condiments: tiny bottles of Nervous Nellie Hot Pepper Jelly for $6.95 and Blueberry Chutney for $7.95. There are also obscene greeting cards, scented oils or sticks of incense, tiny crystals on simulated gold chains, and "readings" available from Corry the Psychic. These are not the kinds of retailers that typically show up in suburban malls, where shopping is more directly tied to necessity. In contrast, most products here are meant as jokes—which puts an odd spin on the notion of renewal. The city once stood for an urbane, commercial superiority; now it is represented by little, imported souvenirs that memorialize the inconsequence of time spent in urban space. Only a single T-shirt vendor has kept the faith. Fit To A Tee is still committed to history, after a fashion; there you can buy a shirt imprinted to mimic a dictionary definition: "Detroit *n* /di troit' / Fr *détroit*, strait: 1. Industrial city in SE Michigan where the weak are killed and eaten."

The creation of Trapper's Alley has generally called for the erasure of such powerful, if ridiculous, impressions. While the space appears to be historical, it happily imposes none of the burdens that a still untranscended past might entail. This is precisely what is meant by its designation as "festival marketplace," and what makes it the unofficial city hall of Greektown. Here the past gets interpreted as a perpetual carnival, which is quite the opposite of the historical realities of the place. Within this space, the nostalgia for history can be shared, just as city life once was, but the experience is purely recreational: a holiday interruption, a freak. This is nowhere more obvious than at The Fudgery, where a staff of black teenagers nightly puts on an a cappella doo-wop show while they prepare the fudge, slapping great blobs of the gooey stuff down onto marble slabs for shaping. These are the same menacing kids of urban crime statistics, and suburban paranoia, now fully domesticated. They—or the parties responsible for this popular performance—turn racial difference into a smiling entertainment option, rather than something real and troubling.

The rootlessness that such projects pander to and profit from is what marks the real difference between Niki and his suburban visitors. He *chose* to become an alien, urged on by innocent (if canny) dreams, and in that he simply followed the example of countless others before him who went off looking to found their own particular "City Upon a Hill." This seems, more or less, to have been what Antoine Laument had in mind when he entered the service of Louis XIV and ended up inventing both himself and Detroit, which he first called *Fort Pontchartrain du Détroit*, in commemoration of his patron, Count Pontchartrain, and to signal the fort's location. Once Laument arrived here, out of reach of his superiors, the hardscrabble traveler translated himself into the gentility of Antoine de la Mothe, Sieur de Cadillac. "Cadillac" made it happen, just as Niki would later, only a few blocks from the spot where the founder planted his flag. Each man turned homelessness to social credit, and found among strangers a fortune to be made. But this matter of choosing to become an alien separates Niki and Cadillac from native residents who discover they have no hometown to return to, except in the contrived spaces of entrepreneurs. It's not opportunity these people sense, but something else.

V

Nobody could have anticipated Niki's sign because it wasn't really made, in any usual sense; it was arrived at. The sign is a complex assemblage that becomes visible right out in front of the taverna, where large glass windows come into opposition, meeting at an angle of about a hundred degrees with doors at the point of intersection. The panes are old, with slight undulations in their surfaces. On the left, red and white letters spell out Niki's name. Business got so good on Niki's side of the building that he bought out the bakery next door, knocked down the interior walls, and doubled the size of his operation. The deal probably didn't cost much because the Acropolis, as the bakery had been called, had never become a success; the Greeks who owned it didn't speak much English and seemed only interested in doing business with other Greeks. So Niki came easily by his extra space—and also the rest of his sign, which didn't emerge until after he had scraped the competition's impermanent signature off the neighboring glass. Then, a wonderful thing happened. The history Niki had been so busily (and successfully) obliterating signed itself—surreptitiously—right on the window of his restaurant. Once the sign of the Acropolis was removed, another and much older sign became visible. Faint impressions left on the glass surface—in the right light—can be seen to spell out "Dodge Brothers."

The brothers referred to are John and Horace Dodge, founders of the automobile company that still bears their name. The Boydell Building, as Niki's place on Beaubien Street was then called, housed their machine shop from 1901 until 1903, when they put up a bigger plant a couple of blocks east on Monroe at Hastings. It was here on Beaubien, though, that they had their first great success, building engines and transmissions for Ransom Olds's "Merry Oldsmobiles" after his own factory burned down. More important, this is likely the place where the brothers met Henry Ford, for whom they contracted to produce the running gear of the Model A, the car that would make all three of them rich men. Ford had only an idea at the time. He lacked both a factory and capital, and he had failed in two previous ventures, so backing of any sort was hard to arrange. His success depended on John and Horace—men who had come to town to invent things and who brought with them a gambler's nerve. The result of their gamble is well known; it is no less surely, if ambiguously, inscribed on the face of this city than it is inscribed on Niki's window.

Like those barely visible impressions, which are an inadvertent memorial to the famous brothers' tenancy, the city itself has been rendered transparent as it has been deprived of genuine historical presence—the cultural paint between the lines. Abandonment now becomes the justification for the precise acts of stripping—actual as well as metaphoric—that fulfill the prophecy already scripted for Detroit: America's first urban domino to fall. The popular representations of the city are nothing, then, except expediency: a general need to imagine the worst but to imagine it as both titillatingly close and exotically distant.

VI

Figure and ground, and the power of names: The celebrated Model A wasn't really a Ford at all; it was a Dodge engine and chassis, underneath a Wilson carriage body, assembled piecemeal by workers paid with other men's money. Henry had the sense to name it and to stamp the radiator with his figure, though that famous Ford ellipse was another man's doing as well. No matter: even after he has been seen through, Henry is no less real. The same cannot be said, however, for the "Renaissance City" that middle-class evacuation has enabled us to *literally* see through. The city is neither one thing nor the other, neither the empty dark places nor the shiny restored ones; it is both at once, back and forth: a kind of monumental gestalt puzzle. Clearly it would be difficult to write a history based on a figure such as that, because narratives, even postmodern ones, still operate only one line at a time, left to right, just as they always have. Perhaps the history that comes *after* middle-class culture can be gotten at only by other means, such as the sign in Niki's window, which is there both to signify and to be seen through.

This is the point Niki has made so clear in his appropriation of the Dodge Brothers' old machine shop. His historic restoration, like most others, didn't restore anything at all; on the contrary, it mocks the precise failure of narrative production that makes Detroit so ambiguous a symbol of humiliated American pride. Niki renovated the abandoned space on Beaubien, where nobody wants to make cars any more, by translating the visible signs of dereliction into valorizing props. The exposed brick walls, the old shop floors, and the outmoded industrial fittings all testify to the authenticity of his anachronistic enterprise; they vouch for the quality of his improbable—if famous—"square Greek pizzas" offered up in this museum of abandonment. Patrons pay happily for the privilege of condescending to a past made to seem comfortingly contrived and therefore no longer implicated in their lives and fates.

And out front is the sign, where those panes of plate glass angle in toward each other to form a self-regarding V, the all-but-invisible Dodge Brothers reflecting on the pizza man's prideful self-inscription. Yet despite all the seeing through that goes on, it would be wrong to assume that this place, or the supposedly postmodern visitors in it, exists beyond or outside of history—regardless of what the visitors buy or say or do. No matter how far people move away, in other words, they are still moving—back and forth—on behalf of the city and what we have made of it. But the history that is revelant and determining now and the forms that—without excuses—it comes in, are not ones easily reduced to text. Instead, it is at places like Niki's, where the past is simultaneously restored and effaced, honored and degraded, that things—however briefly—become clear. That is why Detroit, the most humiliated of cities, is also the most representative: because it has endured, more than any other, what we have made of history; because it has been the most seen through. For the same reason, however, it is also the city that becomes finally, the hardest to know.

Discussion Questions

Content

1. What do you take as the main idea of Herron's essay? Does he announce it at the beginning? Just when does the main idea become apparent?

2. What distinction is Herron making between real history and what he calls both "pastness" and "nostalgia"? What are the consequences of this distinction; that is, why do you think it matters that we recognize the difference between history and pastness?

3. What do you understand Herron to mean when he says that Detroit's history has been humiliated? How do you understand his descriptions of Niki's patrons as people who "pay happily for the privilege of condescending to a past made to seem comfortingly contrived and therefore no longer implicated in their lives and fates"?

Form

1. What does the sign in Niki's window represent, according to Herron? How does the sign function stylistically in the essay?

2. Herron's essay seems to begin again in every section. How does this repetition affect the way you read the essay? How do you read this form differently from the way you would read a more typically organized essay?

3. Is Herron's essay convincing? In what ways does he persuade you to look differently at cities or at representations of cities?

Writing Prompts

1. Think about a well-known site in your city. Write an essay describing the many ways in which the site both is used and symbolizes the city. Speculate on how people's attitudes toward the site shape their use of it. Speculate about what the site may have meant for past generations and what that reveals about how the city has changed.

2. Write an essay about your city that has multiple beginnings, as Herron's essay does. Use the same thought-provoking sentence to begin each section. In each section, however, try to discuss the city from a different aspect or in a different way.

MAKING NEW SENSE OF THE CONVERSATION

Having read and considered several points of view on a topic, you are now ready to return to your own experiences, your own environment, and take a position within the conversation. Often, your entry into the conversation will take the form of an essay. It is important that this essay do more than simply rehash existing positions and arguments. Instead, use your experience to help readers familiar with the conversation think differently about the issues. Use your experience to ask others to consider an issue from your point of view. At the same time, use your entry into the conversation to make new sense of your own experiences and see new connections between your experiences and the broader culture.

Herron's essay serves as our last example because it brings together the multiple layers of conversation that are always taking place in our culture. On the one hand, Herron is reading the conversation taking place in Detroit between people from all around the Detroit area who visit Niki's and come to Greektown and either worry about or have hope for the city's future. On the other hand, Herron's essay is also contributing to the discussion begun by Martin, Beauregard, and Warren about what our cities mean to our culture and why they mean what they do. In talking and writing about cities, you too will be taking part in these kinds of conversations; you will be participating in a dialogue with people you live with that will shape the places you live, and at the same time, you will be contributing to a conversation about urban experience in United States culture. So, now it's your turn; use the following prompts to begin your contribution.

PART 1 DISCUSSION QUESTIONS

1. The authors in this part provide terms for talking about our cities and explaining what they mean to us. When taken together, how accurately do these terms express all that we think and feel about our cities? What other terms would you use to talk and write about cities? What additional ideas and perspectives do these terms represent concerning our sense of American cities?

2. How do people you know talk about major cities like Chicago, Detroit, Los Angeles, and Miami? Which words or phrases do they all use to characterize cities? Comparing their talk to the essays in this part, discuss how their ideas, perceptions, and values are part of larger "conversations" about cities, their purposes, and their possibilities.

3. Which do you think has more influence over the ways we perceive our cities: our firsthand experiences of cities or the ways we talk about cities? How do our experiences of cities and our talk about cities influence each other? As you consider these questions, think about the ways we can have opinions about cities we have never visited because we have seen or heard about these cities through the mass media.

PART 1 WRITING ASSIGNMENTS

1. Talk to people you know about your city or about their perceptions of another major city, such as Dallas or New Orleans. Ask them to tell you what they think of the city; find out whether they think the city is in decline or on the rise. Once you have three or four different perspectives, write a dialogue in which you have characters representing each of the different views debating the question: What should we do about our city? Have each of the characters speak at least three times. Make sure that when each character speaks, she or he has at least four lines of dialogue. At the end of the debate, no one side should appear to have won.

2. According to Stacy Warren, Seattle officials turned to the Disney Company for help in renovation because they believed that Disneyland is a living example of a smoothly running city. Write a creative piece in which you describe what Seattle, or any other city, might be like if the Disney Company rebuilt it. Would that city be the "happiest place on earth"?

3. Write an essay that describes your city and has the title, "A Nice Place to Visit, but . . ." Explain the many reasons why your city is a nice place to visit. Then, after describing each of the positive aspects of your city, qualify your description with a passage that begins, "But . . ."

4. Over the course of several days, pay attention to the ways in which American cities are represented in the mass media. Observe how cities are talked about or visually portrayed in advertising, newspapers, magazines, televised news, television shows, popular music, and popular movies. Write an essay in which you bring the variety of words and pictures together to explain what you consider the major popular image of American cities today.

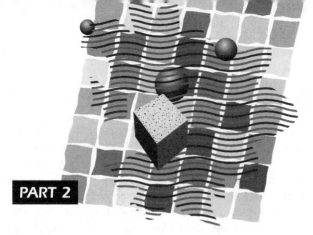

Neighborhoods and a Sense of Community

OFF THE MAIN ROAD, white asphalt boulevards with avenues of palm trees give onto streets that curve pleasingly around golf courses and small lakes. White ranch-style houses sit back from the streets on small, impeccably manicured lawns. A glossy four-color map of the town put out by a real-estate company shows cartoon figures of golfers on the fairways and boats on the lakes, along with drawings of churches, clubhouses, and curly green trees. The map is a necessity for the visitor, since the streets curve around in maze fashion, ending in culs-de-sac or doubling back on themselves. There is no way in or out of Sun City Center except by the main road bisecting the town. The map, which looks like a child's board game (Snakes and Ladders or Uncle Wiggily), shows a vague area—a kind of no-man's-land—surrounding the town. As the map suggests, there is nothing natural about Sun City Center. The lakes are artificial, and there is hardly a tree or a shrub or a blade of grass that has any correspondence in the world just beyond it. At the edges of the development, there are houses under construction, with the seams still showing in the transplanted lawns. From there, you can look out at a flat brown plain that used to be a cattle ranch. The developer simply scraped the surface off the land and started over again.... Sun City Center has age restrictions, of course. For a family to be eligible to live in Sun City, at least one member must be fifty, and neither there nor in Kings Point can residents have children under eighteen. But with one exception no Sun Citian I talked to said he or she had chosen the town because of the age restrictions. When I asked Mrs. Krauch why she and her husband had chosen an age-segregated community she looked startled. "Oh, I didn't feel I would just be with a lot of older people," she said. "And Sun City Center isn't like that!" Sun Citians would certainly be horrified to know that some retirees in St. Petersburg and Tampa look upon their town as an old-age ghetto. When Sun Citians speak of a "retirement community," what they usually mean is a life-care center or a nursing home. They came to Sun City Center for all the amenities spelled out in the advertising brochures and for a homogeneity that had little to do with age. In a country where class is rarely discussed, they had found their own niche like homing pigeons. And once they were home they were happy. "Lots of fine people," one resident told the community newspaper. "This is a cross section of the better people in the nation."

—Frances Fitzgerald

THERE IS A HOUSING PROJECT standing now where the house in which we grew up once stood, and one of those stunted city trees is snarling where our doorway used to be. This is on the rehabilitated side of the avenue. The other side of the avenue—for progress takes time—has not been rehabilitated yet and it looks exactly as it looked in the days when we sat with our noses pressed against the windowpane, longing to be allowed to go "across the street." The grocery store which gave us credit is still there, and there can be no doubt that it is still giving credit. The people in the project certainly need it—far more, indeed, than they ever needed the project. The last time I passed by, the Jewish proprietor was still standing among his shelves, looking sadder and heavier but scarcely any older. Farther down the block stands the shoe-repair store in which our shoes were repaired until reparation became impossible and in which, then, we bought all our "new" ones. The Negro proprietor is still in the window, head down, working at the leather.

These two, I imagine, could tell a long tale if they would (perhaps they would be glad to if they could), having watched so many, for so long, struggling in the fishhooks, the barbed wire, of this avenue.

The avenue is elsewhere the renowned and elegant Fifth. The area I am describing, which, in today's gang parlance, would be called "the turf," is bounded by Lenox Avenue on the west, the Harlem River on the east, 135th Street on the north, and 130th Street on the south. We never lived beyond these boundaries; this is where we grew up. Walking along 145th Street, for example, familiar as it is, and similar, does not have the same impact because I do not know any of the people on the block. But when I turn east on 131st

Street and Lenox Avenue, there is first a soda-pop joint, then a shoeshine "parlor," then a grocery store, then a dry cleaners', then the houses. All along the street there are people who watched me grow up, people who grew up with me, people I watched grow up along with my brothers and sisters; and, sometimes in my arms, sometimes underfoot, sometimes at my shoulder—or on it—their children, a riot, a forest of children, who include my nieces and nephews.

When we reach the end of this long block, we find ourselves on wide, filthy, hostile Fifth Avenue, facing that project which hangs over the avenue like a monument to the folly, and the cowardice, of good intentions. All along the block, for anyone who knows it, are immense human gaps, like craters.

—*James Baldwin*

PHOTOGRAPHS OF THE OLD DOWNTOWN in its 1940s prime show crowds of Anglo, black, and Mexican shoppers of all ages and classes. The contemporary Downtown "renaissance" renders such heterogeneity virtually impossible. It is intended not just to "kill the street" as Kaplan feared, but to "kill the crowd," to eliminate that democratic mixture that Olmsted believed was America's antidote to European class polarization. The new Downtown is designed to ensure a seamless continuum of middle-class work, consumption, and recreation, insulated from the city's "unsavory" streets. Ramparts and battlements, reflective glass and elevated pedways, are tropes in an architectural language warning off the underclass Other. Although architectural critics are usually blind to this militarized syntax, urban pariah groups—whether young black men, poor Latino immigrants, or elderly homeless white females—read the signs immediately.

This strategic armoring of the city against the poor is especially obvious at street level. In his famous study of the "social life of small urban spaces," William Whyte points out that the quality of any urban environment can be measured, first of all, by whether there are convenient, comfortable places for pedestrians to sit. This maxim has been warmly taken to heart by designers of the high corporate precincts of Bunker Hill and its adjacent "urban villages." As part of the city's policy of subsidizing the white-collar residential colonization of Downtown, tens of millions of dollars of tax revenue have been invested in the creation of attractive, "soft" environments in favored areas. Planners envision a succession of opulent piazzas, fountains, public art, exotic shrubbery, and comfortable street furniture along a ten-block pedestrian corridor from Bunker Hill to South Park....

In stark contrast, a few blocks away, the city is engaged in a relentless struggle to make the streets as unlivable as possible for the homeless and the poor. The persistence of thousands of street people on the fringes of Bunker Hill and the Civic Center tarnishes the image of designer living Downtown and betrays the laboriously constructed illusion of an urban "renaissance." City Hall has retaliated with its own version of low-intensity warfare.

—*Mike Davis*

INTRODUCTION

What can your neighborhood teach you about city life? Are the people in your neighborhood the people you identify with? Many times our neighborhoods are such a fundamental part of our lives that we don't think about the lessons that they teach us: Every day they teach us about who we are, what holds us together, and what tears us apart.

In urban areas in the United States, neighborhoods define themselves in a number of ways. Many older cities, such as San Francisco, Houston, Miami, and New York, have distinct ethnic neighborhoods in which people have lived for generations. People who live in San Francisco's Chinatown district, for example, either are from mainland China or Taiwan or are descended from immigrants from those countries. Miami has a sizable community of Cuban Americans, and Detroit's Middle Eastern community is among the largest in the United States. Urban communities can also be defined in economic terms, with people of the same socioeconomic class living in neighborhoods distinct from those in which richer or poorer persons live. Persons living in the same area may share a common ethnic heritage or socioeconomic status because these things force them together or because they feel more comfortable living around people they have things in common with, things like heritage, religion, or language.

Just what neighborhoods and communities are depends, then, on a combination of cultural, economic, geographic, and social factors. Yet whatever the factors are that define your neighborhood, your experiences of living with these factors can be quite telling. You have probably had the experience of traveling through an unfamiliar part of your city and feeling uncomfortable. Or maybe you have, or someone you know has, preconceived notions about people because they are from communities other than yours—and thus they have different ethnic, racial, or economic identities.

By thinking about the combination of factors that define neighborhoods and communities and how people respond to those factors, we come to understand something important about the experience of living in an urban setting. As you read the essays in this part, you will be asked to consider the things that contribute to the promises and the problems of urban communities. In large urban areas, where people of different ethnic heritages, racial identities, and economic statuses interact every day, communities become a source of comfort and stability. However, while the ethnic, racial, or economic identities that largely define urban communities can provide safety and security for the communities' residents, they can also inspire mistrust and suspicion of people who have different ethnic, racial, or economic identities.

The readings in this part explore questions about living in cities, considering what it means to form neighborhoods and communities within larger urban settings. Addressed in this part are the questions of what a home is and why a home matters. Through a comparison and contrast of people living in a camp of makeshift shelters with people coming and going in a nearby hotel, Jim Burklo's essay, "Houselessness and Homelessness," challenges us to rethink what it means to be homeless. In "Homeplace: A Site of Resistance," bell hooks describes the anxiety she felt as a child when she left the security of her neighborhood to visit her grandmother. She recalls the attachment she felt to her grandmother's house—what it meant to her and why she considered it a "homeplace." She uses these reflections to develop an expanded sense of *homeplace,* a term that expresses for her the importance of feelings of belonging and attachment in a world of anger, discrimination, and frustration.

Jerome Charyn considers the isolation and misunderstanding that result from rigid boundaries in his essay "The Rough Adventure of the Street. . . ." Charyn proposes that the vitality and meaningfulness of city life are experienced only by venturing into the streets to experience the "disorder" of urban living. Camilo José Vergara describes the negative consequences of the creation of boundaries in his essay "Our Fortified Ghettos." He explains the tragic consequences that result when people shape their communities in response to fears and anxieties about crime. In her essay "A Beautiful Day in the Neighborhood," Mary Kay Blakely collects her experiences, thoughts, and feelings occasioned by moving to Manhattan. She reflects on her fears and anxieties as she encounters street people in her new neighborhood.

Questions of boundaries, of who is an insider and who an outsider, and of labeling and categorizing people are explicitly discussed by Gary Okihiro in "Is Yellow Black or White?" Through examples of recent racial tensions between African Americans and Asian Americans, Okihiro raises questions about how people come to define their community membership in racial terms. He suggests that defining racial identity and community membership in terms of black and white oversimplifies race by excluding Asian Americans, defining them as sometimes black and sometimes white.

Several of the essays address the topic of urban living through personal reflection. In "Silent Dancing," Judith Ortiz Cofer tells about her conflicted experiences growing up in New Jersey. By combining personal recollection with descriptions of family home movies, she describes how her father, a man of Puerto Rican descent, was ashamed of living among other Puerto Ricans. Mike Rose reflects on the persons and places he knew growing up in East Los Angeles in "I Just Wanna Be Average." He explains the many ways in which he felt like a member of his community and yet longed to belong to a different community, to just "be average."

The writers of these pieces all have different views about what counts as a community and about what constitutes community membership. They address the complex issues of identity and urban living, of deciding who we are, of how we can get along with others, and of how we create boundaries between communities and how we can cross them. These issues are important to persons living in cities in close proximity to one another; the authors collected in this part all suggest ways of addressing these issues without agreeing on any final solutions.

As you read the essays in this part and write about urban neighborhoods and communities, you will be asked to think about how your sense of community shapes your feelings of familiarity and unfamiliarity, comfort and discomfort, identity and difference. You will be asked to consider how your idea of community shapes your perceptions of yourself and influences your interactions with others. Some questions worth considering include: How do people define their neighborhood or community within a larger urban space? In terms of race? culture? class? geographic or attitudinal boundaries? With your classmates, you will also provide perspectives on the following questions: When do the barriers we erect between ourselves and others work to benefit everyone? When do they work against everyone's best interests? And perhaps most importantly, how can we develop senses of ourselves and our communities that respond most positively to others? You will probably discover that our sense of neighborhood and community identity is largely a matter of language: of how we have learned to speak and write about where we come from and how we recognize and talk about where we feel that we belong.

PREREADING ASSIGNMENTS

1. Take a few minutes to freewrite your impressions of your community. Describe important people, places, and events. Explain how you feel about these people, places, and events.

2. Spend ten minutes writing down everything that words associated with the idea of community mean to you. Consider including words such as *neighborhood, family, home,* and *neighbors.*

3. Brainstorm for fifteen minutes about the problems facing urban neighborhoods in this country today. What might these problems be? Draw from your own experiences, from what other people have told you, and from what you learn through the news. Discuss possible causes of these problems, and suggest a number of alternative solutions.

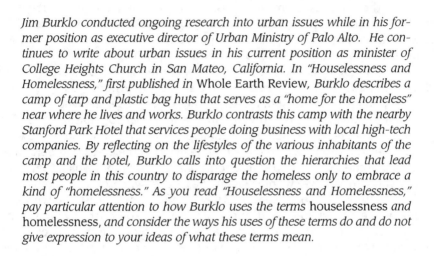

Jim Burklo conducted ongoing research into urban issues while in his for-mer position as executive director of Urban Ministry of Palo Alto. He con-tinues to write about urban issues in his current position as minister of College Heights Church in San Mateo, California. In "Houselessness and Homelessness," first published in Whole Earth Review, *Burklo describes a camp of tarp and plastic bag huts that serves as a "home for the homeless" near where he lives and works. Burklo contrasts this camp with the nearby Stanford Park Hotel that services people doing business with local high-tech companies. By reflecting on the lifestyles of the various inhabitants of the camp and the hotel, Burklo calls into question the hierarchies that lead most people in this country to disparage the homeless only to embrace a kind of "homelessness." As you read "Houselessness and Homelessness," pay particular attention to how Burklo uses the terms* houselessness *and* homelessness, *and consider the ways his uses of these terms do and do not give expression to your ideas of what these terms mean.*

Houselessness and Homelessness

Jim Burklo

A CLUSTER OF HUTS, all blue tarps and black plastic bags, straggles along the creek that demarcates Palo Alto and Menlo Park, California. This camp has been functioning since I came to town in 1979. It functioned as a home for the homeless during the seven years that I served as director of the Urban Ministry of Palo Alto, which offers hospitality and other services to people on the streets. I now live about a quarter of a mile from this camp, and pass it every day on my way home from my job as the minister of a church. I check in with the residents of this camp whenever I check out books at the Menlo Park Library, which offers hot and cold running water in its bathrooms and is not far down the railroad tracks from the creek.

Looming on the top of the creek bank above the camp is the Stanford Park Hotel, an expensive place for a different kind of homeless people to stay. It is a place for people to sleep and eat and use hot and cold running water while they do business with high-tech industrial corporations. The

Jim Burklo. "Houselessness and Homelessness." From *Whole Earth Review* (Summer 1995): 66–69.

people who stay at the Stanford Park Hotel have the money and skills needed to live most anywhere, and as a result, a lot of them live nowhere. So much of their lives is spent in hotels, airport shuttles, and jet aircraft that they suffer from homelessness. They have houses somewhere, but often they lack homes anywhere. The people sleeping under the tarps and plastic bags in the creek bed below them have homes, but lack houses.

There is little romance in the houseless homeless life, as I learned in my work with people on the streets. But in a striking way, homeless people are more at home than the rest of us. According to the jet-setters who are members of my church, there isn't much romance in global nomadism, either. The people in the creek are indigenous, unlike the inter-urban wanderers who stay in the Stanford Park Hotel. The people living in the creek bed belong to a certain "home slice" of a specific geographic radius within which they have found ways to survive, within which they have synchronized themselves with the natural and social seasons. They know whom to trust and whom to avoid, where to get free food and clothes, which dumpsters contain the items they most need. People often asked me why the folks we served at Urban Ministry didn't move to Fresno or Modesto or other places where the cost of living is lower. I'd answer that homeless people, ironically, tend to be homebound. Most folks who live in houses are part of a mass culture, a world culture, that enables us to be unbolted from Palo Alto or Menlo Park, California, and twisted into place in Boston or Singapore or Atlanta or London. Our skills and our lifestyles are useful and acceptable just about anywhere, making us interchangeable parts in the world economic machine. We communicate with money, a language that most people everywhere understand well.

A few homeless people aren't indigenous—they are on the streets temporarily, as a result of a personal disaster of a transitory nature. Often, these folks adamantly refuse to be called homeless, even though they live in the bushes like the rest. They are still interchangeable nuts belonging to the world economic engine; they just happened to spin off their bolts and land in the gutter for a while, and in the meantime, they cling tenaciously to their passports as world citizens. If they stay in the gutter too long, they might become indigenous, a fate which frightens them. These people tend to be more isolated and emotionally upset than the long-term houseless people around them. They are acutely homeless, in every sense of the word, and often this suffering motivates them to rapidly return to jobs and houses again.

But few homeless people are interchangeable, portable economic units of the New World Order. Moving out of the hometown is a frightening prospect for someone so dependent on such a locally idiosyncratic web of delicate social and natural ecology. Most homeless people can't speak the global language of money. Their survival depends on intimate knowledge of a set of locally specific individuals—other homeless people, cops, storekeepers, library employees, and social service workers.

Some of the most "homeful" people I know are technically homeless. At Urban Ministry, we served a 93-year-old woman who, for a period of months, slept on a park bench at night. She'd been kicked out of the residential hotels in town because she was a pack rat and never cleaned her rooms. We had no trouble finding board and care placements for her, but she refused them, because they were in Mountain View, the next town to the south. "I live in Palo Alto," she bluntly informed us, and returned to her park bench until we persuaded the managers of the subsidized senior housing in her hometown to let her name jump the waiting list and get her a place indoors again. Practically every merchant in town knew her well, since, at her plaintive request, many of them were storing her moldy boxes in their storerooms so that neither she nor her possessions would be separated from her place of residence, which was the whole of downtown Palo Alto. Until she died, she was a town character who made a major contribution to the character of the town. Palo Alto really isn't the same without her smiling ancient face greeting people on the sidewalks.

"Indigenous" need not connote "indigence." It is not a term that necessarily indicates poverty or houselessness. It is a mistake to presume that only seniors or disabled or houseless or unemployable people are homebound. Whether poor or rich, indigenous people have characteristic relationships to specific geographic places. They belong where they are, and where they are belongs to them—or ought to belong to them. If they go elsewhere, by force or by choice, they tend to suffer physically, psychologically, and spiritually. But being indigenous doesn't have to be a crippling or marginalizing condition on home turf.

Each local place has its characters, upon whom the character of the place depends. Each place has people who have developed roles or businesses that are site-specific. Their skills and their habits are not geographically transferable. They might be able to move elsewhere and have the money to live for a while, or even for a long time. But, emotionally, they would dry up inside. Many older people with money retire and move, only to discover too late that they are indigenous to their home town. Outside of that geographic radius, life makes no sense.

In today's world economy it is not considered safe to be indigenous. Our places in the system are temporary assignments, subject to the whims of global forces. To become indigenous is to risk losing a place anywhere, including one's dwelling "unit." We're accustomed to the global economic system. We are attached to its material abundance, even as our souls groan at the loss of any real home on the planet. But to embrace the indigenous life is a bold move that has deep pleasures and rewards for self and others. There is a wonderful intimacy that results from the face-to-face, year-in and year-out relationships that can only come by acting as if you are indigenous to a local place. The great attraction, and the great revulsion, that people have toward rural life is the prospect of becoming dependent on a local culture, to the exclusion of being able to fit into the world economy ever again.

I became a minister in order to create and sustain indigenous societies, groups of people who belong to each other in a local urban area over a long period of time. A lot of the volunteers who came to help us at Urban Ministry were spiritually homeless people with jobs and homes, yearning to taste the fruits of indigenous living. They were attracted to the sense of belonging to a place that exists among people who live on the streets. In fact, I noticed that volunteering with us was an excellent way for newcomers to Palo Alto to get to join the town and its people. It's ultimately impossible to know the streets without knowing the street people.

I went to work as the minister of a local church in order to serve home-less people who live in houses as well as in creek beds. I'm in a church because it is not a support group or a therapy group, made up of people who are looking for something specific from each other, for a specific peri-od of time, before moving on to the next group. A church or temple is a place where people go for good, for keeps, for birth and life and death. I'm interested in organized religion only insofar as it creates and maintains deep and intimate relationships in a community of people who have come together to live indigenously, for good. Understandably, lots of people—particularly those who want to fit in anywhere on earth, in any nation or cul-ture—fear the sectarian nature of most religious congregations, the propri-etary language and habits that go with people who have strong links to tra-dition and to a local church or synagogue community. People are afraid to give up their homelessness, much as they suffer from it. People will hang tribal masks on the walls of their condos, but they are afraid of wearing the masks and doing the indigenous rituals in which they were used. And peo-ple are afraid of having a home that is so precious to them that they would have a hard time leaving it when they receive New World Orders to move elsewhere.

I'm haunted by the words of a man who attends the church I serve. He's a Ph.D. with a job in a high-tech Silicon Valley firm. He said that if he had to go to another office party where people did nothing but exchange small-talk, another gathering of people who had no intimacy and no real connec-tion with each other, he would scream. I heard his soul crying out for a place to call home, a specific local circle of people worth taking the risk of depend-ing upon for his spiritual survival. A place and a people that, if he left them, would render him heartsick.

One of the marks of indigenous people is the persistent presence of annoying people among them. A church is not an indigenous community unless there are a few people in it who are permanent thorns in the sides of the rest of its members. One of the marks of non-indigenous societies is that they throw out obnoxious participants, or the societies fall apart because the rest of the participants leave and join or create other groups. At the Urban Ministry, we had our share of annoying homeless people who drank coffee at our drop-in center every day. They reminded me that I belonged to a truly local community of indigenous human beings. Go to a city council meeting anywhere, and listen to the people who speak during the part of the meeting devoted to "oral communication" from citizens. Listen to the ones who go up to the mike week after week, causing consternation or irritation among the council members. Those oral communicators are indigenous people. If they weren't there at the city council meeting, you would know that your town was a stone-cold-dead suburb, a place belonging everywhere, and, thus, to nobody.

A place cannot hope to be home to anyone unless there are people in that place who are indigenous to it. People who are gears in the global clockwork yearn deeply for the sentiments that come from indigenous living, but fear that they would have to give up too much in order to live that way themselves. Avoiding eye contact, they will pass by local houseless indigenous people, and they will proceed on their way to shop for conversation pieces at the ethnic art store. As they commute from faceless condos to faceless tilt-up industrial headquarters buildings, they will listen to Garrison Keillor on the car radio as he describes the latest doings among the indigenous citizens of mythical Lake Wobegon. To create a homey atmosphere, spiritually homeless people will buy antiques from quaint locations. They will travel to charming spots for vacations and "leave their hearts" with the indigenous residents, who have the good sense to keep their own hearts where they keep their bodies—at home.

In my travels, I have observed that the greater the number of indigenous people in a place, the fewer houseless people there are in that place, relative to the population. In a culture of people who can live anywhere, and, thus, live nowhere in particular, you will find a subset of people who are reduced to living on the streets. In a culture of people who really live where they are, who are living in a permanent manner and are dependent on the local people around them, there is a social web that prevents all but a very few folks from having to live outdoors. The houseless homeless are our canaries. When they fall into the creek bed, the rest of us need to pay attention to what has become of our communities, and take the risks and rewards that come from making the choice to live indigenously in them.

Discussion Questions

Content

1. What meanings does Burklo give for the terms *houselessness* and *homelessness*? Consider not only the definitions he provides but also the implications he suggests. In what sense are homeless people homeless? In what sense are homeless people not homeless?

2. If a person had to choose, which would be preferable, homelessness or houselessness? Or perhaps something else? When considering these questions, take into account Burklo's uses of the terms *homelessness* and *houselessness*. What do people give up when they become houseless? What do they give up when they become homeless? Why do they give these things up? Do the people in the camps and in the hotel give up the same things? If so, what are they? If not, why are they so different?

3. One of Burklo's suggestions is that the plight of the houseless and the attitudes and practices of the affluent homeless are intertwined. Just what does Burklo see as the relationship between the affluent homeless and the indigent houseless? Consider the ways in which the affluent and the indigent might view each other. How do you think attitudes of houselessness among financially successful people influence their attitudes toward homelessness and their perceptions of the homeless? How might different attitudes of houselessness among the poor influence their attitudes toward homelessness and their perceptions of the wealthy homeless?

Form

1. Burklo's article progresses by developing a comparison and contrast between the "homeless" and the "houseless." What comparisons does Burklo make between the homeless and the houseless? What contrasts? How do these comparisons and contrasts build as the article progresses in order to make readers think differently about themselves and the homeless? About homelessness and houselessness? Is Burklo's strategy effective? For what kind of readers? For people who are homeless or for people who are houseless? How would you rewrite the article for readers who are either homeless or houseless?

2. Do Burklo's comparisons and contrasts seem fair to you? In what ways is he fair or even unfair? Through his comparison and contrast of the two groups does he give too much or too little respect to either the homeless or the houseless? Indicate specific passages where you consider Burklo fair and/or unfair in his discussion of the homeless and the houseless. How might your representations of these two groups differ from Burklo's? Why would your comparison and contrast of the houseless and the homeless represent the houseless and the homeless one way as opposed to another? And how would your representations of these groups influence your narrative?

3. One of Burklo's controlling themes is the sense of place. Through his discussion of the homeless and the houseless, Burklo draws out specific ideas about what a sense of place is, why a sense of place is important to have, and how a sense of place has gotten lost in the age of high-speed travel. Identify passages from the article in which Burklo explains his ideas of place. Do his ideas seem to you more old-fashioned or more forward thinking? Why? What are your ideas about place? How does your perception of his attitude about place influence your reception of his conclusions about homelessness and houselessness?

Writing Prompts

1. Describe your attitudes, feelings, ideas, and perceptions about where you live. Do you feel you live in a home? Or is it just a house? Explain through your discussion what it takes to make some place a home. Also try to explain why where you live is or is not a home.

2. Compare and contrast what appear to you to be the differences between the homeless and the houseless people in your area. Do the indigent homeless people in your area seem to you more rooted in one place and more dependent on each other? Do the affluent homeless people in your area seem less connected to the people and places around them?

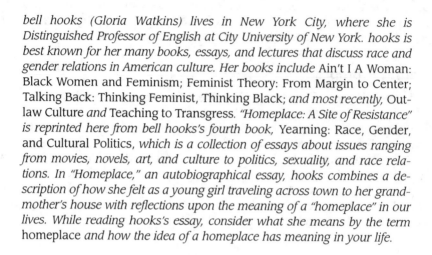

bell hooks (Gloria Watkins) lives in New York City, where she is Distinguished Professor of English at City University of New York. hooks is best known for her many books, essays, and lectures that discuss race and gender relations in American culture. Her books include Ain't I A Woman: Black Women and Feminism; Feminist Theory: From Margin to Center; Talking Back: Thinking Feminist, Thinking Black; *and most recently,* Outlaw Culture *and* Teaching to Transgress. *"Homeplace: A Site of Resistance" is reprinted here from bell hooks's fourth book,* Yearning: Race, Gender, and Cultural Politics, *which is a collection of essays about issues ranging from movies, novels, art, and culture to politics, sexuality, and race relations. In "Homeplace," an autobiographical essay, hooks combines a description of how she felt as a young girl traveling across town to her grandmother's house with reflections upon the meaning of a "homeplace" in our lives. While reading hooks's essay, consider what she means by the term* homeplace *and how the idea of a homeplace has meaning in your life.*

Homeplace:
A Site of Resistance

bell hooks

WHEN I WAS A YOUNG GIRL the journey across town to my grandmother's house was one of the most intriguing experiences. Mama did not like to stay there long. She did not care for all that loud talk, the talk that was usually about the old days, the way life happened then—who married whom, how and when somebody died, but also how we lived and survived as black people, how the white folks treated us. I remember this journey not just because of the stories I would hear. It was a movement away from the segregated blackness of our community into a poor white neighborhood. I remember the fear, being scared to walk to Baba's (our grandmother's house) because we would have to pass that terrifying whiteness—those white faces on the porches staring us down with hate. Even when empty or vacant, those porches seemed to say "danger," "you do not belong here," "you are not safe."

bell hooks. "Homeplace: A Site of Resistance." *Yearning: Race, Gender, and Cultural Politics*, pp. 41–49. Reprinted by permission of South End Press.

Oh! that feeling of safety, of arrival, of homecoming when we finally reached the edges of her yard, when we could see the soot black face of our grandfather, Daddy Gus, sitting in his chair on the porch, smell his cigar, and rest on his lap. Such a contrast, that feeling of arrival, of homecoming, this sweetness and the bitterness of that journey, that constant reminder of white power and control.

I speak of this journey as leading to my grandmother's house, even though our grandfather lived there too. In our young minds houses belonged to women, were their special domain, not as property, but as places where all that truly mattered in life took place—the warmth and comfort of shelter, the feeding of our bodies, the nurturing of our souls. There we learned dignity, integrity of being; there we learned to have faith. The folks who made this life possible, who were our primary guides and teachers, were black women.

Their lives were not easy. Their lives were hard. They were black women who for the most part worked outside the home serving white folks, cleaning their houses, washing their clothes, tending their children—black women who worked in the fields or in the streets, whatever they could do to make ends meet, whatever was necessary. Then they returned to their homes to make life happen there. This tension between service outside one's home, family, and kin network, service provided to white folks which took time and energy, and the effort of black women to conserve enough of themselves to provide service (care and nurturance) within their own families and communities is one of the many factors that has historically distinguished the lot of black women in patriarchal white supremacist society from that of black men. Contemporary black struggle must honor this history of service just as it must critique the sexist definition of service as women's "natural" role.

Since sexism delegates to females the task of creating and sustaining a home environment, it has been primarily the responsibility of black women to construct domestic households as spaces of care and nurturance in the face of the brutal harsh reality of racist oppression, of sexist domination. Historically, African-American people believed that the construction of a homeplace, however fragile and tenuous (the slave hut, the wooden shack), had a radical political dimension. Despite the brutal reality of racial apartheid, of domination, one's homeplace was the one site where one could freely confront the issue of humanization, where one could resist. Black women resisted by making homes where all black people could strive to be subjects, not objects, where we could be affirmed in our minds and hearts despite poverty, hardship, and deprivation, where we could restore to ourselves the dignity denied us on the outside in the public world.

This task of making homeplace was not simply a matter of black women providing service; it was about the construction of a safe place where black people could affirm one another and by so doing heal many of the wounds

inflicted by racist domination. We could not learn to love or respect ourselves in the culture of white supremacy, on the outside; it was there on the
inside, in that "homeplace," most often created and kept by black women,
that we had the opportunity to grow and develop, to nurture our spirits. This
task of making a homeplace, of making home a community of resistance, has
been shared by black women globally, especially black women in white
supremacist societies.

I shall never forget the sense of shared history, of common anguish, I felt
when first reading about the plight of black women domestic servants in
South Africa, black women laboring in white homes. Their stories evoked
vivid memories of our African-American past. I remember that one of the
black women giving testimony complained that after traveling in the wee
hours of the morning to the white folks' house, after working there all day,
giving her time and energy, she had "none left for her own." I knew this story.
I had read it in the slave narratives of African-American women who, like
Sojourner Truth, could say, "When I cried out with a mother's grief none but
Jesus heard." I knew this story. I had grown to womanhood hearing about
black women who nurtured and cared for white families when they longed
to have time and energy to give to their own.

I want to remember these black women today. The act of remembrance
is a conscious gesture honoring their struggle, their effort to keep something for their own. I want us to respect and understand that this effort has
been and continues to be a radically subversive political gesture. For those
who dominate and oppress us benefit most when we have nothing to give
our own, when they have so taken from us our dignity, our humanness that
we have nothing left, no "homeplace" where we can recover ourselves. I want
us to remember these black women today, both past and present. Even as I
speak there are black women in the midst of racial apartheid in South Africa,
struggling to provide something for their own. "We . . . know how our sisters
suffer" (Quoted in the petition for the repeal of the pass laws, August 9,
1956). I want us to honor them, not because they suffer but because they
continue to struggle in the midst of suffering, because they continue to
resist. I want to speak about the importance of homeplace in the midst of
oppression and domination, of homeplace as a site of resistance and liberation struggle. Writing about "resistance," particularly resistance to the
Vietnam war, Vietnamese Buddhist monk Thich Nhat Hahn says:

> . . . resistance, at root, must mean more than resistance against war. It is a resis-
> tance against all kinds of things that are like war . . . So perhaps, resistance
> means opposition to being invaded, occupied, assaulted and destroyed by the
> system. The purpose of resistance, here, is to seek the healing of yourself in
> order to be able to see clearly . . . I think that communities of resistance should
> be places where people can return to themselves more easily, where the con-
> ditions are such that they can heal themselves and recover their wholeness.

Historically, black women have resisted white supremacist domination by working to establish homeplace. It does not matter that sexism assigned them this role. It is more important that they took this conventional role and expanded it to include caring for one another, for children, for black men, in ways that elevated our spirits, that kept us from despair, that taught some of us to be revolutionaries able to struggle for freedom. In his famous 1845 slave narrative, Frederick Douglass tells the story of his birth, of his enslaved black mother who was hired out a considerable distance from his place of residence. Describing their relationship, he writes:

> I never saw my mother, to know her as such more than four or five times in my life; and each of these times was very short in duration, and at night. She was hired by Mr. Stewart, who lived about twelve miles from my house. She made her journeys to see me in the night, traveling the whole distance on foot, after the performance of her day's work. She was a field hand, and a whipping is the penalty of not being in the field at sunrise . . . I do not recollect of ever seeing my mother by the light of day. She was with me in the night. She would lie down with me and get me to sleep, but long before I waked she was gone.

After sharing this information, Douglass later says that he never enjoyed a mother's "soothing presence, her tender and watchful care" so that he received the "tidings of her death with much the same emotions I should have probably felt at the death of a stranger." Douglass surely intended to impress upon the consciousness of white readers the cruelty of that system of racial domination which separated black families, black mothers from their children. Yet he does so by devaluing black womanhood, by not even registering the quality of care that made his black mother travel those twelve miles to hold him in her arms. In the midst of a brutal racist system, which did not value black life, she valued the life of her child enough to resist that system, to come to him in the night, just to hold him.

Now I cannot agree with Douglass that he never knew a mother's care. I want to suggest that this mother, who dared to hold him in the night, gave him at birth a sense of value that provided a groundwork, however fragile, for the person he later became. If anyone doubts the power and significance of this maternal gesture, they would do well to read psychoanalyst Alice Miller's book, *The Untouched Key: Tracing Childhood Trauma in Creativity and Destructiveness*. Holding him in her arms, Douglass' mother provided, if only for a short time, a space where this black child was not the subject of dehumanizing scorn and devaluation but was the recipient of a quality of care that should have enabled the adult Douglass to look back and reflect on the political choices of this black mother who resisted slave codes, risking her life, to care for her son. I want to suggest that devaluation of the role his mother played in his life is a dangerous oversight. Though Douglass is only one example, we are currently in danger of forgetting the powerful role black women have played in constructing for us homeplaces that are the site for resistance. This forgetfulness undermines our solidarity and the future of black liberation struggle.

Douglass's work is important, for he is historically identified as sympathetic to the struggle for women's rights. All too often his critique of male domination, such as it was, did not include recognition of the particular circumstances of black women in relation to black men and families. To me one of the most important chapters in my first book, *Ain't I A Woman: Black Women and Feminism,* is one that calls attention to "Continued Devaluation of Black Womanhood." Overall devaluation of the role black women have played in constructing for us homeplaces that are the site for resistance undermines our efforts to resist racism and the colonizing mentality which promotes internalized self-hatred. Sexist thinking about the nature of domesticity has determined the way black women's experience in the home is perceived. In African-American culture there is a long tradition of "mother worship." Black autobiographies, fiction, and poetry praise the virtues of the self-sacrificing black mother. Unfortunately, though positively motivated, black mother worship extols the virtues of self-sacrifice while simultaneously implying that such a gesture is not reflective of choice and will, rather the perfect embodiment of a woman's "natural" role. The assumption then is that the black woman who works hard to be a responsible caretaker is only doing what she should be doing. Failure to recognize the realm of choice, and the remarkable re-visioning of both woman's role and the idea of "home" that black women consciously exercised in practice, obscures the political commitment to racial uplift, to eradicating racism, which was the philosophical core of dedication to community and home.

Though black women did not self-consciously articulate in written discourse the theoretical principles of decolonization, this does not detract from the importance of their actions. They understood intellectually and intuitively the meaning of homeplace in the midst of an oppressive and dominating social reality, of homeplace as site of resistance and liberation struggle. I know of what I speak. I would not be writing this essay if my mother, Rosa Bell, daughter to Sarah Oldham, granddaughter to Bell Hooks, had not created homeplace in just this liberatory way, despite the contradictions of poverty and sexism.

In our family, I remember the immense anxiety we felt as children when mama would leave our house, our segregated community, to work as a maid in the homes of white folks. I believe that she sensed our fear, our concern that she might not return to us safe, that we could not find her (even though she always left phone numbers, they did not ease our worry). When she returned home after working long hours, she did not complain. She made an effort to rejoice with us that her work was done, that she was home, making it seem as though there was nothing about the experience of working as a maid in a white household, in that space of Otherness, which stripped her of dignity and personal power.

Looking back as an adult woman, I think of the effort it must have taken for her to transcend her own tiredness (and who knows what assaults or wounds to her spirit had to be put aside so that she could give something to her own). Given the contemporary notions of "good parenting" this may seem like a small gesture, yet in many postslavery black families, it was a gesture parents were often too weary, too beaten down to make. Those of us who were fortunate enough to receive such care understood its value. Politically, our young mother, Rosa Bell, did not allow the white supremacist culture of domination to completely shape and control her psyche and her familial relationships. Working to create a homeplace that affirmed our beings, our blackness, our love for one another was necessary resistance. We learned degrees of critical consciousness from her. Our lives were not without contradictions, so it is not my intent to create a romanticized portrait. Yet any attempts to critically assess the role of black women in liberation struggle must examine the way political concern about the impact of racism shaped black women's thinking, their sense of home, and their modes of parenting.

An effective means of white subjugation of black people globally has been the perpetual construction of economic and social structures that deprive many folks of the means to make homeplace. Remembering this should enable us to understand the political value of black women's resistance in the home. It should provide a framework where we can discuss the development of black female political consciousness, acknowledging the political importance of resistance effort that took place in homes. It is no accident that the South African apartheid regime systematically attacks and destroys black efforts to construct homeplace, however tenuous, that small private reality where black women and men can renew their spirits and recover themselves. It is no accident that this homeplace, as fragile and as transitional as it may be, a makeshift shed, a small bit of earth where one rests, is always subject to violation and destruction. For when a people no longer have the space to construct homeplace, we cannot build a meaningful community of resistance.

Throughout our history, African-Americans have recognized the subversive value of homeplace, of having access to private space where we do not directly encounter white racist aggression. Whatever the shape and direction of black liberation struggle (civil rights reform or black power movement), domestic space has been a crucial site for organizing, for forming political solidarity. Homeplace has been a site of resistance. Its structure was defined less by whether or not black women and men were conforming to sexist behavior norms and more by our struggle to uplift ourselves as a people, our struggle to resist racist domination and oppression.

That liberatory struggle has been seriously undermined by contemporary efforts to change that subversive homeplace into a site of patriarchal domination of black women by black men, where we abuse one another for not conforming to sexist norms. This shift in perspective, where homeplace is not viewed as a political site, has had negative impact on the construction of black female identity and political consciousness. Masses of black women, many of whom were not formally educated, had in the past been able to play a vital role in black liberation struggle. In the contemporary situation, as the paradigms for domesticity in black life mirrored white bourgeois norms (where home is conceptualized as politically neutral space), black people began to overlook and devalue the importance of black female labor in teaching critical consciousness in domestic space. Many black women, irrespective of class status, have responded to this crisis of meaning by imitating leisure-class sexist notions of women's role, focusing their lives on meaningless compulsive consumerism.

Identifying this syndrome as "the crisis of black womanhood" in her essay, "Considering Feminism as a Model for Social Change," Sheila Radford-Hill points to the mid-sixties as that historical moment when the primacy of black woman's role in liberation struggle began to be questioned as a threat to black manhood and was deemed unimportant. Radford-Hill asserts:

> Without the power to influence the purpose and the direction of our collective experience, without the power to influence our culture from within, we are increasingly immobilized, unable to integrate self and role identities, unable to resist the cultural imperialism of the dominant culture which assures our continued oppression by destroying us from within. Thus, the crisis manifests itself as social dysfunction in the black community—as genocide, fratricide, homicide, and suicide. It is also manifested by the abdication of personal responsibility by black women for themselves and for each other ... The crisis of black womanhood is a form of cultural aggression: a form of exploitation so vicious, so insidious that it is currently destroying an entire generation of black women and their families.

This contemporary crisis of black womanhood might have been avoided had black women collectively sustained attempts to develop the latent feminism expressed by their willingness to work equally alongside black men in black liberation struggle. Contemporary equation of black liberation struggle with the subordination of black women has damaged collective black solidarity. It has served the interests of white supremacy to promote the assumption that the wounds of racist domination would be less severe were black women conforming to sexist role patterns.

We are daily witnessing the disintegration of African-American family life that is grounded in a recognition of the political value of constructing homeplace as a site of resistance; black people daily perpetuate sexist norms that threaten our survival as a people. We can no longer act as though sexism in black communities does not threaten our solidarity; any force which estranges and alienates us from one another serves the interests of racist domination.

Black women and men must create a revolutionary vision of black liberation that has a feminist dimension, one which is formed in consideration of our specific needs and concerns. Drawing on past legacies, contemporary black women can begin to reconceptualize ideas of homeplace, once again considering the primacy of domesticity as a site for subversion and resistance. When we renew our concern with homeplace, we can address political issues that most affect our daily lives. Calling attention to the skills and resources of black women who may have begun to feel that they have no meaningful contribution to make, women who may or may not be formally educated but who have essential wisdom to share, who have practical experience that is the breeding ground for all useful theory, we may begin to bond with one another in ways that renew our solidarity.

When black women renew our political commitment to homeplace, we can address the needs and concerns of young black women who are groping for structures of meaning that will further their growth, young women who are struggling for self-definition. Together, black women can renew our commitment to black liberation struggle, sharing insights and awareness, sharing feminist thinking and feminist vision, building solidarity.

With this foundation, we can regain lost perspective, give life new meaning. We can make homeplace that space where we return for renewal and self-recovery, where we can heal our wounds and become whole.

Discussion Questions

Content

1. hooks explains that a "homeplace" is where she learned "dignity, integrity of being," where she learned "to have faith." What values does she oppose to these? What places does she associate with these other values? How do you respond to these divisions? Do they seem accurate or fair to you? Why, or why not?

2. What is a "homeplace"? Who is responsible for making it a "homeplace"? How does it differ from a public, "non-homeplace"? Can you think of any home-

places that you have experienced? Just how important do you think it is for people to have a homeplace?

3. In what ways does hooks challenge and contribute to debates about family values? What new ideas or points of view does she introduce into the debate
over family values? In what ways does she seem to you just to repeat what has
already been said?

Form

1. How does hooks use the opening personal recollection to introduce larger social issues? Do you find her opening effective? Why or why not?

2. hooks's essay combines family memories with scholarly discussion. Does
this combination of personal and scholarly styles give voice to an otherwise
silenced perspective? Just what might that silenced perspective be? Do you think
it is a voice and a perspective we should listen to? Why or why not?

3. Do you find hooks's writing powerful and convincing? What is it about
the style or structure of her essay that does or does not make it powerful? Would
you rewrite her essay to make it more powerful or more convincing? In answer-
ing this question, refer either to specific passages you think you would like to see
written differently or refer to specific passages you think are good just the way
they are. Explain why you think they do or do not need revision.

Writing Prompts

1. Using hooks's essay as a model, reflect on an experience or person in
your past. Use your recollection of that experience or person to give expression
to your understanding of a larger social issue.

2. Write an essay comparing and contrasting two places in your city that
demonstrate what you take to be the distinction between a homeplace and a
nonhomeplace.

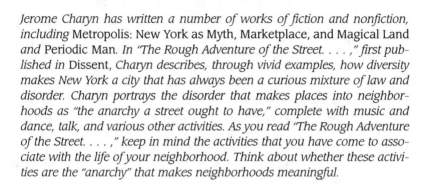

Jerome Charyn has written a number of works of fiction and nonfiction, including Metropolis: New York as Myth, Marketplace, and Magical Land *and* Periodic Man. *In "The Rough Adventure of the Street. . . ," first published in* Dissent, *Charyn describes, through vivid examples, how diversity makes New York a city that has always been a curious mixture of law and disorder. Charyn portrays the disorder that makes places into neighborhoods as "the anarchy a street ought to have," complete with music and dance, talk, and various other activities. As you read "The Rough Adventure of the Street. . . ," keep in mind the activities that you have come to associate with the life of your neighborhood. Think about whether these activities are the "anarchy" that makes neighborhoods meaningful.*

"The Rough Adventure of the Street. . . ."

Jerome Charyn

"**C**ITIES, LIKE DREAMS," Calvino tells us, "are made of desires and fears, even if the thread of their discourse is secret, their rules are absurd, their perspective deceitful, and everything conceals something else" (*Invisible Cities*).

Calvino is right, of course. New York is the ultimate dream city: monstrous, rude, gentle, brilliant, and dumb. It has all the arrogance and snobbery of a small village, and the pure delight of an empire sitting by the sea. It can never be adequately defined or circumscribed, because it's a city that didn't grow out of an idea that made practical sense. The Dutch arrived like phantoms, thinking they were traders, and did not realize that they'd been seduced by a very strange island. They never conquered Manhattan. They built a tiny settlement at the edge of the island, called it New Amsterdam, and forgot they'd ever left home. It was a magic harbor. The British took it from them, renamed the island, but they couldn't really turn it into an English town. New York had its own peculiar babble, its own peculiar tongue.

It was a mythical landscape: Europe's dream and desire of a fabulous kingdom, a kingdom of unlimited wealth. But this *new world* of New Amsterdam and New York wasn't so readily decipherable. It had convicts, rabbis, merchants, witches, soldiers, slaves. It was a village that grew into a gigantic Monopoly board. Somehow it always stank of wealth.

And it didn't matter who were its kings. The English, the Dutch, or even the French, who could have crept down from Canada (New France) to steal the whole pie. The island always withstood authority and centers of power, even if it was King George's own capital of British America during the Revolutionary War. The Tories danced on this island throughout most of the revolution, while American soldiers died on prison ships in the harbor. Tory landlords discovered the miracle of real estate. They charged fortunes for tiny houses and tents. But there was an anarchy in King George's village that went much deeper than any idea of the Crown.

NEW YORK HAS ALWAYS BEEN a curious mixture of law *and* disorder. It's no accident that the worst gangs the world has ever seen came out of an old slophouse called the Brewery over a hundred and fifty years ago. It was a "housing project" in lower Manhattan for poor blacks, the immigrant Irish, dwarfs, beggars, the lame, and the blind. There were at least two murders a night inside the Brewery. There were mad, raving songs. There was highway robbery in the halls. There was child prostitution. There was arson. There was rape. And yet somehow the Brewery learned to police itself. Its tenants managed to survive . . . except for those two murders a night.

The Irish moved out of the Brewery, entered politics, and soon controlled the town. For a while it seemed as if the Irish had established their own state on the island of Manhattan. They managed politics, the police, and crime. Irish spinster ladies taught in the schools. Irish priests invented their own little Vatican. Irish gangs destroyed their Republican rivals and transformed the Democrats into a party of immigrants and thieves. The thieves were often compassionate. They would steal your money and give your daughter a jar of milk.

The Irish didn't have palaces on Fifth Avenue. They never entered Wall Street. They weren't land speculators or millionaires. But the Irish ran New York. They fashioned its day-to-day existence. They built its underground railroads and its bridges. They'd fled the Old World during potato famines, until there were more Irish in New York than in all of Dublin. And then . . .

The Italians and the Russian Jews arrived. They lived in their own little Breweries. They scratched, they starved, they finagled, they married, they stole, they died, they danced with the Irish, and then pushed the Irish out of the way. And suddenly New York was a Jewish-Italian town. With Arnold Rothstein. Fannie Brice. Fiorello LaGuardia (who was Italian and Jewish). Lucky Luciano. Arthur Miller. Lauren Bacall. Danny Kaye. Diane Arbus. Norman Mailer. Martin Scorsese. Robert De Niro. Barbara Streisand. John Gotti. Ed Koch . . .

But the honeymoon is over. At the very point of their "apotheosis," the Jews in New York have become a dying breed. And the Italians are sinking into the suburbs. Now we have the Chinese, the Koreans, Cambodians, West Indian blacks . . . and God knows what complexion New York will have in fifty years. But it doesn't matter.

A Chinese mayor in 2035 will have to live with the same anarchy that tugs at the city's heart. Because underlying the city's fabric is a kind of dream song that doesn't pay much attention to spectacular rises and falls. It's a type of murderous energy that has little to do with race or religion, City Hall, or the New York Stock Exchange.

Now, in 1987, New York wears an odd metaphysical mask: blacks have grown invisible. Harlem is like a burnt-out Vietnamese village with bits of decoration at its borders. Black children ride on the trains, beating out songs on their seats, "rapping" about those moonscapes they live in. No one really listens. A few of the children become graffiti artists, breakdancers, or comedians, like Eddie Murphy, but the rest are stranded on their moonscapes: concrete bunkers we call housing developments.

Y ET THOSE ARE THE LUCKY ONES, in a way. At least they have an address. In New York, an "address" is harder and harder to find, particularly for Latinos and blacks. Who wants to build low-income housing when realtors can make fortunes building towers for the rich? It's part of the same metaphysics. As the poor multiply, so do the rich. The middle class have become their own small underprivileged country. Shoemakers disappear. Corner groceries are a relic of a different past. Every block in Manhattan needs an ice-cream parlor. The realtors and the young rich want to sculpt the city into a fairyland of fashion shops. And so we have a fake seaport, a convention center that looks like an isolated tomb of glass, a vertical shopping mall at Herald Square that has its own imbecilic theme song: whole floors dedicated to different city neighborhoods. It looks and feels like a home for androids. Who goes there?

A black man I discovered selling tiny bottles of perfume outside on the corner seemed to have much more expertise and enthusiasm than any of the human mannequins behind those glass walls.

And so, it would seem, this endless construction, the desire to build vertical and horizontal towers, and entomb ourselves in glass, has a chance of turning Manhattan into a moonscape for the rich. But not even all that glass, that constant duplication of boxes shooting into the sky, can destroy the anarchy that exists inside Manhattan's grid.

Under the streets there's an entire system of abandoned subway stations, abandoned tunnels, abandoned tracks, a Plutonian world that mocks all the massive building above ground. Pluto prefers his own republic. A few yards from the Yale Club is a door that leads to an "outland" of tunnels under Grand Central Station. Various drifters have their own "streets" within these tunnels. There's even a Burma Road.

IF YOU WANT TO "DISCOVER" NEW YORK, go into the dunes: visit those caves in the South Bronx where breakdancing began as ritualized warfare between rival gangs. Or stroll down Ninth Avenue, which hasn't been gentrified, and one can still feel an electric charm, a *sense* of neighborhood with some of the anarchy a street ought to have. The old and the young mixing, mingling, with all kinds of quarrels and courtship rites.

Or go to Brighton Beach, where the Russian Jews have descended, drinking borscht and wearing 1950s' American clothes. Visit Mafia country in Bath Beach, where the young bloods stand in front of restaurants wearing their silkiest shirts. Travel to the Lower East Side, where the Chinese, the Latinos, and elderly Jews occupy the parks and the streets as if they'd all come out of a single crib.

Go up to the Grand Concourse and discover Art Deco buildings that some merchant prince built for his favorite daughter fifty years ago. THE CAROLINE or THE BEVERLY will be chiseled in stone above the front door ...

Museums and opera houses cannot get you into the blood of a town. They are splendid attempts at order in a disordered world. But we have to be Marco Polo in Manhattan, and risk that rough adventure of the street.

Discussion Questions

Content

1. Charyn describes New York City as a place of both "law" and "disorder." List the aspects of New York City life that Charyn associates with law. List the aspects of city life he associates with disorder. From the items on the lists, define *law* and *disorder*. What do these terms mean? Can you think of any items that could be added to either list? Relate these lists to each other. What sense do you make of their relationship to each other? Just how is it that these lists describe a neighborhood?

2. What do you think Charyn means by the "rough adventure of the street"? If the adventure of the street is "rough," can it also be desirable or worthwhile? If

so, how? If not, why not? Ask yourself if the adventure of the street needs to be rough. Couldn't it be something else? If so, what else might it be? If not, why can't it be any other way?

3. Charyn writes that the best way to experience city life in New York City is in the streets of its neighborhoods, taking the chance to interact with people different from yourself. Just how would someone go about experiencing city life in New York City? Or in any city for that matter? What would he or she do? Where would he or she go? Who would he or she talk to? Do you even think the experience of different people, places, and things is worthwhile? Specifically, would it be more worthwhile than a visit to the city's museums? Why? Or, why not?

Form

1. Charyn opens his essay with a quote from the author Italiano Calvino. What does the quote do for you as a reader to introduce Charyn's essay? What does it ask you to think about? How does Charyn develop, or fail to develop, the thoughts you have in response to the quote? How might you use the quote to begin an essay?

2. Charyn concludes that "we have to be Marco Polo in Manhattan" if we want to "discover" New York. Identify phrases and descriptions in the essay that use the language of discovery. In what ways does this language support Charyn's main point about how to experience Manhattan? What does the language of discovery prevent us from thinking about? Think of another set of phrases and descriptions that could be used to encourage people to go out and experience the streets of your city.

3. What place does Charyn's chronology of New York immigration have in the essay? How do you think the chronology strengthens or weakens his main points? Were these people somehow adventurers and discoverers? If so, in what ways? In what ways weren't they adventurers or discoverers? And how do you think our activities of adventure and discovery differ from theirs?

Writing Prompts

1. Write a creative piece describing the "rough adventure of the street" that someone might have in your city. Include details not only of disorder but also of law. What might someone encounter that he or she wouldn't otherwise expect? How is that encounter rough? Dangerous? Exciting?

2. Write to persuade someone from outside your area that a visit to your city would be better spent exploring the streets than visiting a museum. Try to convince him or her, for example, that the streets are more fun, dangerous, interesting, and full of history and life than the museum.

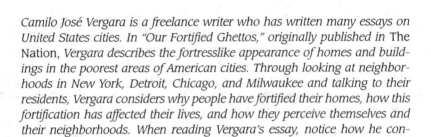

Camilo José Vergara is a freelance writer who has written many essays on United States cities. In "Our Fortified Ghettos," originally published in The Nation, *Vergara describes the fortresslike appearance of homes and buildings in the poorest areas of American cities. Through looking at neighborhoods in New York, Detroit, Chicago, and Milwaukee and talking to their residents, Vergara considers why people have fortified their homes, how this fortification has affected their lives, and how they perceive themselves and their neighborhoods. When reading Vergara's essay, notice how he contrasts words that evoke the military with words that evoke the home and family. Think about the reasons why he chose such opposite kinds of language and what kind of impact this choice has upon you as a reader.*

Our Fortified Ghettos

Camilo José Vergara

PLACES WE ASSOCIATE with awful events tend to become fixed in our minds with a peculiar intensity. At 2258 Mack Avenue on Detroit's East Side there stands a 120 year-old gray wooden cottage, a former farmhouse. The roof has black holes left from a fire that raged on the afternoon of February 17, 1993. Glass windowpanes are gone, but the metal bars are still visible. "A sad day," says Ms. Jones, a neighbor. "All I could see was the smoke. The bars stopped them, the smoke killed them. It made me sick. I had to go to bed."

Outside, around the cottage, are mementos placed there by people trying to come to terms with the tragedy: a red ribbon tied to the doorknob; stuffed animals arranged on the front steps; a bright yellow tricycle parked in the weeds; a table with a large clock, its hands stuck at 2 o'clock, the time of the fire, and next to it a neat line of children's shoes. A crude billboard depicts the faces of three angelic children; four ovals, each framing a cross, represent the others.

LaWanda Williams, 9; Nikia Williams, 7; Dakwan Williams, 6; La Quinten Lyons, 4; Venus Lyons, 2; Anthony Lyons, 7 months; Mark Brayboy, 2—all died when left alone in their "prison house." In the preceding five months another six people in Detroit, most of them children, had also died trapped by fires in barred and barricaded houses.

Fortification epitomizes the ghetto in America today, just as back alleys, crowded tenements and lack of play areas defined the slum of the late nineteenth century. Buildings grow claws and spikes, their entrances acquire metal plates, their roofs get fenced in, and any additional openings are sealed, cutting down on light and ventilation. Glass windowpanes in first-floor windows are rare. Instead, window openings are bricked in or fitted with glass bricks. In schools and in buses, plexiglass, frosty with scratches, blurs the view outside.

Even in areas where statistics show a decrease in major crime, fortification continues to escalate, and as it does, ghettos lose their coherence. Neighborhoods are replaced by a random assortment of isolated bunkers, structures that increasingly resemble jails or power stations, their interiors effectively separated from the outside. Throughout the nation's cities we are witnessing the physical hardening of a new order, streetscapes so menacing, so alien, that they would not be tolerated if they were found anywhere besides poor, minority communities. In brick and cinderblock and sharpened metal, inequality takes material form.

THE UNITED STATES POST OFFICE is the main symbol of the federal government in the ghetto. But where one might expect reassuring classical buildings decorated with eagles and images of the old Pony Express, there are instead squatty concrete blocks with iron grating. The only unifying national symbols are the American flag on the outside and, on the inside, the F.B.I. most-wanted poster.

In a truly democratic society there would be no great differences in the quality of buildings the government constructs for the same purposes in different communities. Yet in the ghetto, form does not follow function so much as it does fear. A building's adaptations for survival announce the existence of a state of urban war, a fact that even Washington cannot ignore.

"Post offices should look friendly, identifiable, efficient and stylistically typical of local buildings—not like factories," concluded a study published in 1989 in *Progressive Architecture*. Certainly, the fortresslike ghetto post office is "stylistically typical." The same can be said of the most modest representation of the postal system: apartment-building mailboxes, which are often covered by a locked iron grid. In dangerous buildings in New York City, the boxes are kept in a separate locked room.

Commercial establishments are just as heavily defended. Already in 1975, businessman Phillip Cyprian of Gary, Indiana, figured that even if his clothing store were housed in an all-steel building with no windows or doors, burglars would still find a way to enter and clean him out. "They'd take cutting torches and do it and never get caught," he reasoned. So Cyprian decided to move out. Entrepreneurs who stayed behind have applied measures only a little less drastic than those in his bleak architectural vision.

"We try to block up anything at all that can give people the idea this place is an easy target," explains the owner of a warehouse in Camden, New Jersey. In Detroit, a fenced roof, blocked windows and a jail door help to make Singleton Cleaners a difficult target, while its bright colors announce to drivers that the establishment is indeed in business. At a Newark Kentucky Fried Chicken franchise, a large plastic menu is protected with plexiglass and an iron grating, obscuring much of the writing.

Churches also turn into fortresses. In Brownsville, Brooklyn, St. Luke's Community Church, formerly a Jewish catering hall, had the misfortune of being located across the street from a rubble-filled vacant lot. After school, neighborhood children used to throw bricks at the church, breaking windows, so the congregation simply blocked them. The Lighthouse Gospel M.B. Church in Chicago gets a little daylight through a cross made of glass bricks.

Most of these structures are accented by razor-ribbon wire. It was not until the late 1970s that this wire, formerly common only in prisons and military installations, came into large-scale civilian use. First strung atop fences around warehouses and factories, more recently it has become a favorite device for domestic defense, separating roofs of adjacent apartment buildings, securing the space between structures and protecting the perimeter. Yet despite awesome fortifications, buildings are still broken into and burned, and the streets, now invisible to those inside, are even more threatening.

Choice public spaces are open for only a few hours during the day, while others are allowed to fall into disrepair, to harbor drug dealers and to function as open dumps. In "people's parks"—places accessible only with a key—those enjoying the green grass, trees and flowers seem to be themselves part of an exhibit for passers-by. Fences dwarf the tiny spaces.

Within such environments, police are perceived as distant, taking a long time to answer calls and often refusing to come at night. Dogs and security guards protect the few who can afford them. And if one is to believe residents, just about everybody keeps a gun. Thus, people defend their homes. Those living in townhouses and private dwellings surround the borders of their property with fences enclosing the house and family car. In addition, they bar their first floor windows and often install clearly visible burglar alarms, red lights blinking. The most effective defense is not physical, however, but social, as people watch after one another's dwellings, question strangers and call the police.

In South Central Los Angeles a basic fortress is a bungalow with a small green lawn. The dwelling's first line of defense is an iron door, usually painted black. Metal bars on the windows add further protection, changing the once-friendly character of the wood and stucco houses. Less visible are the iron spikes to ward off trespassers.

In urban sections where apartment buildings are the characteristic abode, outsiders are discouraged from loitering in lobbies, harassing residents, selling drugs and stealing mail by locked extensions made of iron fencing that jut out, removing sections of sidewalk from public use. Where there are courtyard entrances, these are closed off with heavy gates topped with razor-ribbon wire.

Inside buildings, a guard dog chained to the stairway railing calls attention to suspicious movements. In dangerous projects, metal doors to apartments have as many as four locks, including one at the center that releases two cross-shaped bars. Between the dogs and the door locks, however, are often-dark hallways, and little can be done to defend those.

Besides the profusion of physical barriers against crime, in violent neighborhoods in New York City, Newark and Chicago, social arrangements have evolved that befit a state of war. Groups of disabled and elderly residents going from their secure buildings to check-cashing outlets and the supermarket require police or security guards for escorts. At the entrance of shelters and welfare offices, guards face photographs and composite drawings of people wanted for crimes.

Milagros Jimenez, a small middle-aged woman, the president of her building's tenant association and a South Bronx resident, tells of her courageous struggle to save her building: "I would go with Gladys to the roof at two or three in the morning, to watch so that people would not go there to do drugs and to kick out those who were doing drugs. Since we were with God and I was with another brave person, I was not afraid."

People also resort to religion and magic. As protection against evil, Elizabeth Valentin, also a resident of the South Bronx, keeps saints and voodoo statues by her bed. She credits these images with having saved her during at least five muggings.

Signs are widely used as warnings. A piece of cardboard on an apartment window of a Chicago Housing Authority project, Altgeld Gardens in South Riverdale, reads: "No Trespassing. Due to an epidemic of AIDS do not enter my apartment when I am absent. Game is over dude." Other prominently displayed notices alert intruders that they will be attacked by dogs or even shot. A warning sign in front of a house on Hillman Avenue in Youngstown, Ohio, reads:

Yo' Homes, rock starz, body sellarz, bad boyz
Do *NOT*
1. "CHILL" Here
2. "CLOCK" Here
3. "HANG TUFF"

4. SELL rockz HERE
5. READ Too LONG
   In other words
   STROLL!
   Yes, this means you2

Yet even these kinds of signs, as well as letters and numbers bearing the names, addresses and purposes of edifices, are often stripped by thieves and vandals. Interiors have also been modified. In businesses and public offices, bullet-proof plexiglass separates attendants and clients; people are buzzed in only after being screened by a receptionist.

CONCERN FOR SECURITY has led to a new brutalism. Fortification creates a conflict between the desire to make people feel welcome and the grim need for defense. Those who live or work in such buildings say that the outside appearance has little to do with the quality of what is offered inside.

The manager of a forbidding day shelter in Chicago declares himself proud of offering the best meals of any shelter in the city. A recreation worker at the Hillside Community Center, which looms like an arsenal on Milwaukee's north side, boasts that great basketball games are played inside. And a South Bronx resident comments that despite the menacing claws on the roof and metal shutters on the windows, her neighborhood public library is always busy.

Those involved in the erection of fortresses deny that their buildings are in any way extraordinary. A Salvation Army official who took part in designing a bunkerlike building in Chicago explained: "There are windows there, a clerestory window in the chapel above, and small windows along the side. We don't spend enormous amounts on large windows, but to call this building a fortress seems to be a little overkill. It is not like a Strategic Air Command blockhouse, where I served when I was in the service, where you work in the basement and you have to go upstairs to see if the sun ever came up that day."

But a South Bronx resident was so surprised by what she heard about the High Bridge Branch of The New York Public Library that she "had to come here and check it out and take some books out." Another, commenting on the metal spikes that ring the roof's perimeter, said, "It is sad, isn't it? I guess they don't want people on the roof." A guard at the Office of Family Services in the South Bronx laughed at the comparison between his workplace and a prison, saying: "Too small for a jail—it does not cover enough ground. In New York you never find a jail this small." Yet most people interviewed perceived that the defenses were there to protect them, and nobody expressed a wish that they be removed. Instead, people strive to soften the unfriendliness of their environments, decorating homes and businesses with lively paintings, ornate wrought-iron designs and plantings. But underneath the surface, the fortress remains.

Plans that a quarter-century ago gave rise to polemics against the "school of brutalism" that was so prominent in the 1960s have become widely accepted in ghetto neighborhoods. "It is strange that those designs that were made to provoke an outrageous response should become every-day normality—what you have to have to get through the day," remarks Marshall Berman, professor of political science at City College in New York.

WHAT DOES IT MEAN to live in a windowless world lined with sharp things that protect by threatening to cut, puncture and impale? A world characterized by animals that bark and bite, crude warning signs, bars that keep some out but may also prevent escape? A world defined by security guards and razor-ribbon wire, by streets, hallways and nights that don't belong to you? People in these neighborhoods express their dislike of forti-fication but accept it as inevitable.

Fortification has profound consequences. Where defenses are aggres-sively displayed they create bizarre, shunned streetscapes of distorted sur-vivors and ruined losers. The time spent opening and closing so many locks and gates, connecting and disconnecting alarms, nervously looking over one's shoulder, feeding guard dogs and explaining one's business to security personnel can become exhausting and detracts from other activities. Blocking the openings in buildings forces people to consume more electrici-ty for artificial lighting and cooling, while increasing their isolation and sense of imprisonment. Scarce resources that should be devoted to basic needs and services are used instead for security and fortification. And residents feel powerless in their cages because they believe that crime is out of control.

Detroit's 2258 Mack Avenue has an aura. Terrible images pass through one's mind upon seeing the broken, old-fashioned cottage surrounded by tokens of sorrow. A few blocks east along Mack Avenue, on the corner of Meldrum, the writing on the wall of an abandoned building says: "We remember that when people lose their lives as a consequence of injustice their spirit wanders, unable to pass over—seeking resolution." The message is repeated clearly and neatly several times to make sure someone notices.

Discussion Questions

Content

1. Vergara argues that "in brick and cinderblock and sharpened metal, inequality takes material form." What are the kinds of inequality Vergara is refer-ring to? What do you think it means for inequality to take material form? Refer to specific evidence he provides to support your answers. Does he seem to you to be right when he describes inequality in physical terms? Why or why not?

2. In addition to physical architectural barriers, what other forms of barriers against crime does Vergara discuss? Why are they important to this essay? What do the descriptions of the various barriers tell us about our ideas of space and security? What conclusions can you draw from Vergara's descriptions about the quality of life in urban neighborhoods?

3. What does Vergara see as the consequences of the fortification of our neighborhoods? Do fortifications build a sense of community? Do they contribute to feelings of despair? Do you agree with his conclusions? Explain your reasons for either agreeing or disagreeing with Vergara.

Form

1. How does Vergara begin his essay? Why do you think Vergara begins the essay as he does? What does the opening discussion do for you to prepare you to react to the main body of the essay? Just what did you think the essay was going to be about after you read the opening? Did you think you would like it? Did you think you would agree with what it has to say? Just what was it about the opening that made you think this way? How might you have begun the essay?

2. Vergara draws examples from a number of cities. Why does he use so many examples from so many different places? What does the variety of examples show? What would have been demonstrated if Vergara had only used examples from one city? For you, how much do the examples contribute to the persuasiveness of the essay? Would he need more examples to persuade you? Or could he have done it with fewer examples? Why do you think you are either more or less easily persuaded through examples about urban fortification?

3. What words or phrases does Vergara use to influence the way we understand his examples? Pick a place in the essay where Vergara seems to you to be explicitly using words or phrases to influence our reading of his examples. What point of view do these words and phrases reveal? How do these words or phrases attempt to influence you? What do they appeal to? Your reason? Your emotion? Your experience? Just how effective is Vergara's influence? You can judge his effectiveness by explaining the sense you make of his examples. Is this the sense he seems to want?

Writing Prompts

1. Write a response to Vergara's essay that uses your own examples to agree or disagree with his portrayal of urban life.

2. Describe how one building you frequently use is "fortified." Include obvious and not so obvious fortifications. That is, describe not only the various locks and latches, barricades and barriers, but also things such as highly visible open spaces in and around the building, security cameras, warning signs, and information desks. Reflect on how these "fortifications" influence the way you behave in this space; describe what you do differently as a result of these barriers. Reflect as well on your perceptions of this space: Does it *feel* fortified?

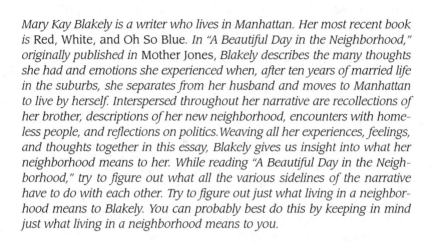

Mary Kay Blakely is a writer who lives in Manhattan. Her most recent book is Red, White, and Oh So Blue. *In "A Beautiful Day in the Neighborhood," originally published in* Mother Jones, *Blakely describes the many thoughts she had and emotions she experienced when, after ten years of married life in the suburbs, she separates from her husband and moves to Manhattan to live by herself. Interspersed throughout her narrative are recollections of her brother, descriptions of her new neighborhood, encounters with homeless people, and reflections on politics. Weaving all her experiences, feelings, and thoughts together in this essay, Blakely gives us insight into what her neighborhood means to her. While reading "A Beautiful Day in the Neighborhood," try to figure out what all the various sidelines of the narrative have to do with each other. Try to figure out just what living in a neighborhood means to Blakely. You can probably best do this by keeping in mind just what living in a neighborhood means to you.*

A Beautiful Day in the Neighborhood

Mary Kay Blakely

WELL PAST MIDNIGHT on a steamy summer night last year, I clutched the handle next to the passenger's seat in a large U-Haul truck as it bounced through construction barricades on the Cross Bronx Expressway, listening to my cargo crash against the walls as Howard, knuckles white with tension, swung the loose steering wheel to keep us on course. Sheer guts had put him in the driver's seat. This man, from whom I've now been divorced a little longer than the decade we were married, inspired groans from our teenage sons with his contentment in the 55 mph lane on interstate highways. Ryan and Darren, the main glue between us for nearly 20 years, were following in the car behind, all of us exhausted and a little slaphappy after lifting and toting since dawn.

I was acutely aware that this was "the first day of the rest of your life"— certainly, it was destined to be the last day of life as I'd known it. A recently

Mary Kay Blakely. "A Beautiful Day in the Neighborhood." From *Mother Jones* (Nov./Dec. 1995): 46–51+. Mary Kay Blakely is the author of *Red, White, and Oh So Blue,* published by Scribner, and *American Mom,* published by Algonquin Books of Chapel Hill and Washington Square Press.

paroled mother/writer/suburbanite, I was about to begin a solo life in New York City; the first time in 47 years I would not have to filter every decision through the needs and expectations of other people. The irony of having my once-husband and two former dependents launch me into independence made this surreal journey somehow more provocative.

The close relationships in our postnuclear family continually baffled friends, but I wasn't surprised when Howard called from Ann Arbor and volunteered his two-week vacation to help me pack my emptying nest in Connecticut. The sturdy friendship we retrieved from our divorce was rebuilt slowly from the powerful alloy of regret and apology, an interactive chemistry that eventually produces genuine change. We'd never imagined, when we naively recited those vows to love and honor each other for life back in 1970, we would mainly be providing each other unlimited opportunities for mercy.

Mercy is the antidote for the crushing pain that invariably follows the loss of innocence, and only the numb don't need it. Most recently, Howard had to forgive the hard time I gave him with a memoir I'd just finished on 20 years of motherhood. Long familiar by now with the public compromises of an exwife who writes, he said reading the manuscript made him feel "like a jerk or a fool." When I asked him to identify the offending passages, it took three weeks before he called back. "It wasn't what you wrote that made me feel like a fool," he said quietly, utterly undefended. "It's my *life* I wish I could revise." Only in hindsight was it clear how he'd taken this fork instead of that, how decisions made in Michigan affected people he loved in Connecticut. Growing instead of shrinking from the truth, he understood we had no control, of course, over what other people would do with it.

The first review had arrived by fax that morning, shortly before I unplugged and packed the machine. I asked if the noxious label that would be appearing next to his name again and again had hurt. "Yeah," he admitted, it got to me." He smiled ruefully, said he'd had a sudden image of us appearing together on a "Geraldo" show: "Deadbeat Dads and the Women Who Love Them." We laughed. Then we kept moving.

THESE ARE PERILOUS TIMES for anyone living outside "the traditional family," since the reigning politicians are determined to bring back the social dictatorship of the '50s. Certainly, the contemptuous labels we've had to live under—broken home, latchkey children, absentee mother, deadbeat dad—make it difficult for outsiders to recognize all the thinking and striving most postnuclear families do.

It's more than a little frightening to see how swiftly the White Guys' Movement has revived the old formula for ridding a country of its conscience during hard economic times: First, you label whole segments of the population as the Other. Then, when the suffering comes, it's possible to believe they deserve it. If any of your own relatives turn out to be among the despised populations—a gay son, maybe, a divorced sister—well, mercy is notably absent from the current roster of family values.

Since the neighborhood I was moving into was teeming with Others— accented immigrants, hyphenated Americans, single moms, low-income families—I knew that casualties from the "Contract on America" would be falling within my direct line of vision. It was already impossible to walk through the Upper West Side without encountering lifeless bodies laid out on every block, the parched bottom layer of the trickle-down economy. This reality apparently doesn't look so bad if you take it in through numbers and indexes in *The Wall Street Journal,* where investors declare a "good economy" if profits are up. There is scant coverage on the business pages and rarely any photos, of people going down. Mothers and children are so invisible in the national news, investors might not even know we are out here, laboring in the same economy. Business columnists uniformly regard the collapse of communism as "the triumph of capitalism." *Triumph?* From the passenger window, capitalism without compassion looks a lot like Calcutta.

As HOWARD TOOK THE EXIT on the Upper West Side and aimed the truck down Broadway, I looked out the window at the street people I'd driven past hundreds of times, but never as a neighbor. What did being a "good neighbor" mean in this community, where the utterly destitute and the fantastically wealthy live within blocks of each other? How would I stay in touch with reality, when the daily reality is so unreal? Do I put on an armband, own my affinity with the Others—or do I wear mental blinders, try not to know what I know? I've never been able to establish any distance from street people—I keep thinking they're my relatives. I still scan their faces for signs of my brother Frank, even though I know it's irrational since I delivered the eulogy at his funeral more than a decade ago.

I'm more or less resigned to my role as an easy mark for panhandlers—a readily identifiable "Sucker Man," as my son Darren would say in sticky situations, remembering a childhood toy with suction cups that glowed in the dark. I feel especially sucked in by street people with obvious symptoms of mental illness. Frank's madness used to terrify me, as it did him, and I spent years looking into his wild eyes on psychiatric wards, trying to make contact, trying to stare fear down by knowing it. If you make eye contact with panhandlers, know their stories, the buck in your pocket is already in their hands. I think of these tiny contributions as payments against my huge debt to all the strangers who were kind to Frank.

We lost him periodically, between hospitals and jail cells and mental institutions and home—those scary times when this frail, brilliant, desperately ill young man was "out there" somewhere, totally dependent on the compassion of others. Walking through Manhattan, I still make sidewalk diagnoses of manic depression, autism, schizophrenia, paranoia … all being treated on the streets since political reformers in the late '60s stopped "warehousing" the mentally ill. Few voters back then understood the loathsome "warehouses" were the last stop for the most helpless, or that the alternative to inept and underfunded hospitals would be no care at all. A theater of the absurd, America's sidewalks reflect the insanity of a national health care policy that now jails the mentally ill before treating them.

HOWARD HAD ACQUIRED A NEW NICKNAME that week after he'd dropped a 27-inch television a customer had brought in for repairs. "Hey, Crash!" the wise guys he worked with now greeted him, "How's it goin'?" With all my material possessions in the U-Haul, I had nothing to lose with Crash at the wheel since my alternate driver was Anthony, the Connecticut neighhor who'd shorn the roof off a delivery van when he plowed into a sign that read, "Clearance—8'." ("Sure I saw it," he later told the hospital staff. "I forgot I was in the stupid truck.") I already missed Anthony and the rest of the gang who regularly camped out around our kitchen table.

I loved that raucous household, blooming with growth and optimism. The quiet solitude after Ryan and Darren left for college felt abrupt. In truth, our quality time together was sometimes down to five minutes a day by then, and the main noise was running water. My landlady had been shocked by our water bills and asked if she should send a plumber to check for leaks. "No," I confessed, "I'm growing male adolescents here. They need a lot of showers." I offered to pay the difference, since watering teenagers was more economical and effective than therapy, and ultimately easier on the environment. The boys would emerge in elevated moods, skin flushed and wrapped in terry cloth. Every time I would come across those alarming headlines about young male violence and try to imagine what might save us, I'd think: Showers. If every kid in America had enough private time in the bathroom to get a grip, to feel just great for a moment … wouldn't it have to improve civilization?

I was lucky to find a "prewar" apartment. Manhattan shorthand for big rooms that haven't been subdivided into six studios with pantry kitchens and broom-closet bathrooms. Space is so precious in New York, custody suits over rent-controlled apartments are common when couples split up. After postwar prosperity devolved into today's social Darwinism, whole working-class families now read, watch television, eat, make love, fight, cry, laugh, yell, and sleep all in the same room.

Driving through Harlem a few years ago, I got lost in an urban canyon between tall, crumbling buildings. The narrow street was solidly double-parked, and I noticed every car was occupied: One man was reading by flash-light, another was having a cigarette, a pair of teenagers was car-dancing to a radio, another pair was sinking slowly into the seat. Here, on the streets, people were in the only private room at home. It's no wonder tempers flare and violence erupts during steamy summers in the city. Who can take a shower in a car?

My neighborhood is "in transition," as we say, between an elegant past and present cruelties, a microcosm of the growing class divisions in America. One block west of my building uniformed doormen with epaulets safeguard well-to-do residents who are likely to be liberal, generous contributors to the soup kitchen in the nearby cathedral. One block east, crack vials litter the sidewalks where street people and drug addicts spend the night. The haves and havenots live cheek by jowl here—with remarkable civility I think, given the givens. The thief who would eventually steal my car radio did not break any car windows, and left a screwdriver behind on the seat. When the car was broken into again a week later nothing was taken. Somebody evidently just needed a room.

My suburban habit of getting close to neighbors is trickier here because they come and go—sometimes within the same day. It's hard to learn all their names without mailboxes. And the names sometimes change. The woman with the wild gray hair and bedroom slippers who growls at pedes-trians on the west side of Broadway calls herself "Bad Bertha," but when she's sitting quietly on the east side, her hair tucked neatly into a bun and feet prettily aligned in ballet shoes, her name is "Irena." The exuberantly manic guy who works the street outside the Hungarian Pastry Shop calls himself "the Lord's Apostle" and sings a gospel rap that sounds like a kind of Gregorian Dixie. One rhyme made me laugh, and a laugh in Manhattan is worth a buck to me: "I love Christ, Jesus Christ/The only Man who's been here twice...."

But there was a dramatic shift in my street relationships when Howard, the boys, and I were finishing renovations on the apartment. That whole week, nobody hit on us for money. Instead, panhandlers grinned and nodded when we passed them during errands and lunch breaks, as though we were old comrades. Maybe they only solicit suburban commuters, I thought, and now recognize us as neighbors. Then I realized how we were dressed: paint-splattered T-shirts, sweaty kerchiefs, shoes covered with sawdust and Spackle. Crash's work outfit was truly special—Howard had grabbed a pair of old sweats from the Goodwill pile in Connecticut and didn't discover the cord was missing until he put them on in New York. We searched the vacant apartment for a piece of string or elastic, but all we came up with from work supplies was a roll of duct tape. Even the craziest panhandlers weren't tempted to solicit change from a guy wearing a cummerbund of silver duct tape.

If our degrees of separation could melt with a change of attire perhaps the current experiment with "casual days," when corporations relax formal dress codes on Fridays, should go even further. Maybe Mondays should be down-in-the-socks day. Princely executives could become paupers once a week and get to know the folks who are so invisible to *Wall Street Journal* readers. In their starched collars and knotted ties and pressed twill, so many of the Suits who bustle down Broadway dodging strollers and shopping carts look either uncomfortable or angry, as if everybody wants their stuff. Most everybody probably does.

But suppose they relieved themselves of this burden once a week, surrendered their gaberdine armor and leather belts for a Goodwill outfit and roll of duct tape. Would they be less angry if nobody was hitting on them? If they got grins and nods on the streets, if they made eye contact and learned the names of the Others, would they be tempted to open up membership in the tight little group of "we Americans"? It's almost too poignant to imagine, but could the in-it-together camaraderie on the streets even move the white guys to share their drugs? The comprehensive health coverage for Congress and the military is costing taxpayers a bundle, but that entitlement program never appears on the Republicans' list of "financial burdens."

Party strategist William Kristol chastised GOP colleagues for compromising their economic goals after Democrats launched an aggressive campaign with the "politics of compassion" during the last presidential election. Addressing a conference on C-Span, he warned his fellow Republicans not to be sidetracked by worries about poor people next time. If the rich could become richer still, objections to ruthlessness become moot: "The politics of growth trump the politics of compassion," he declared over and over. Greed trumps mercy every time. It was late at night when I heard this game plan in my hotel room almost two years ago. I couldn't think of anyone to call, anything to do. Now Kristol is publisher of a new, right-wing magazine financed by Rupert Murdoch, and Kristol's colleagues have taken Capitol Hill. Should I have called 911?

AFTER UNLOADING AND RETURNING the truck, my tired crew crashed on mattresses flush with the floors and didn't get up until noon. The next day, muscles sore but freshly showered, we were in elevated moods after lunch in a local Chinese-Cuban restaurant. "Chinese-Cuban-Americans," I said, wondering how I would keep track of the hyphens here. Imagine fleeing the Gang of Four and landing in Castro country."

"Yeah," Howard said, "then risking your life in an open boat and washing up here just in time for the Gingrich Gang." Ryan and Darren gave each other a worried look, familiar by now with their progenitors' habit of getting worked up over politics. They hated hearing about suffering they couldn't do anything about. If we were going to saddle them with family values of mercy and justice in these mean times, they wanted to know how to fend off despair. Though we are not regular churchgoers—the religion in our post-nuclear family is an interfaith amalgam of Catholic beatitudes and Lutheran heresies and Zen koans—I suggested a visit to St. John the Divine.

The largest Episcopal cathedral in North America, its towering spire of magnificent masonry now sits sullenly under rusted iron scaffolding, renovations stalled once more while fundraising efforts are applied to more immediate emergencies. Dean James Morton has the formidable task of convincing wealthy parishioners deeply committed to art and historic preservation that their first obligation, as Episcopalians, is to serve the community—in their case, ceaseless waves of troubled kids, addicted veterans, dying homosexuals, and homeless immigrants. In the turf wars between the Suits and the Others in this West Side Story, the cathedral is the parking lot where miracles happen.

Still beautiful despite its present humility, the stately edifice is buzzing with civilian activity. Before New York adopted a recycling program, parishioners brought their garbage to church, where the homeless turned aluminum cans into cash. Two biologists now work out of the church to restore the urban watershed in Upper Manhattan, and hold community workshops on environmental issues. The doors are open to anyone who wants in—on the Feast of St. Francis, when members bring pets to the procession honoring all God's creatures, even elephants come to St. John the Divine.

In the park next to the interfaith elementary school at the church, we stopped before an installation by sculptor Frederick Franck. A row of six steel panels are aligned on the lawn perpendicular to the path, each with a silhouette of the same human figure cut from the center, the first one slightly larger than life, the last a miniature version of the shrinking figure itself. The inscription quotes the Great Law of the Haudenosaunee, the Six Nations Iroquois Confederacy: "In all our deliberations we must be mindful of the impact of our decisions on the seven generations to follow ours." Franck titled the sculpture *Seven Generations,* but there are only six figures. The viewer, standing squarely at the mouth of the tunnel, must become the seventh. We each took turns looking through the five ghostly silhouettes, connecting with the tiny figure at the end. Step aside from your place in the human chain, it disappears.

How did the Iroquois chiefs come to their remarkably long view of personal responsibility? How did they make the connection between their business decisions in Michigan and domestic life in Connecticut? Were they all in difficult relationships? Did they speak the hard truth, argue and apologize, let mercy change them? Seemingly larger than life in their war paint and headdresses, did the chiefs declare a casual day at the Haudenosaunee Council, light the pipe and pass it around? Did they inhale?

The architects of the Republican Party's future can't be worried about the next seven generations—William Kristol said it's not even practical to care about most of *this* one. "You cannot in practice have a federal guarantee that people won't starve," he told *Harper's* during a candid forum with five other white guys, explaining how Republicans envision the future. Some people will have to suffer, but "that's just political reality," said author David Frum. Obviously unaware of Dean Morton's work with New York Episcopalians, Frum apparently doesn't think "the sort of people who make $100,000 contributions to the Republican Party" can get behind poor people. "Republicans are much more afraid of angry symphonygoers than they are of people starving to death," he said.

The main problem with running a merciless government is that in a democracy, millions of voters have to agree to starvation. This requires a certain "finesse," said media adviser Frank Luntz. "I'll explain it in one sentence: I don't want to deliver bad news from a golf course in Kennebunkport." Republicans are depending on Rush Limbaugh, the undisputed master of political spin, to keep people dizzy and laughing about starvation plans. Labeling people like me "compassion fascists" for trying to get people like him interested in mercy, Limbaugh is so popular even *The New York Times* compromised its editors when marketing executives hired him to advertise the newspaper. In the new morality of bottom-liners, it's OK to have a propagandist represent the "newspaper of record," if it increases sales. Vice must be spun into virtue before we can get to the Republican future, but everybody's doing their part.

Several years ago, Ivan Boesky spoke to students at the University of California while on tour to promote a new book. "Greed is healthy," he inspired them. "You can be greedy and still feel good about yourself." Boesky's invocation of avarice didn't stir any action from Republican crusaders fighting "a cultural war . . . for the soul of America," in which Pat Buchanan sees the enemies as "radical feminists and homosexuals." Talk about a dazzling public relations coup: The party championing morality in America has declared that charity is impractical, greed is healthy, compassion is fascist, and mercy is the responsibility of other people. If future schoolchildren have to recite a prayer written by these folks, whatever will it say? "Dear God, please give me more of everything than I'll ever need and I promise not to care about anyone else."

THOUGH I'M NOT AN EPISCOPALIAN, visiting St. John's always makes me wish I could pray. I envy the solace my family and friends have talking to God. My own spiritual meditations are generally addressed to my brother Frank, the euphoric madman who left abruptly at age 36, delirious with love and forgiveness as he answered God's call. I still want him to tell me: *Is* heaven better than the transient hotel where the Chicago police found his body? Sitting in the garden at St. John's, I remembered our last conversation on the lawn at Elgin State Hospital. He asked me why I loved him and I said, "Because you are a fool, and I love fools."

"But Jesus said, 'There are no fools,'" he replied, quoting a scriptural fragment from his seminarian days.

"I know," I replied. "But I think what Jesus really meant is that we are all fools," I said, paraphrasing J.D. Salinger. I told him I thought he was the king of fools. He laughed, said I must be the queen.

I don't blame God for the scrambled thinking that led to Frank's suicide. I can't even be sure there is a God. I believe my divinely crazy brother heard God say what he wanted to hear. Many mentally ill people think they are in direct touch with the Almighty. The Lord's apostle outside the pastry shop, the toothless guy at D'Agostino, even Bertha on her bad days will offer the panhandler's benediction: "God bless you," they say, whether the quarter comes or not. Republican Christians today are getting some frenzied directives as the political scene becomes ever crazier, and they too hear exactly what they want to hear: God wants everybody to get married, wants women to stay home, doesn't want gays in the military, doesn't want national health insurance. I can't share their faith that a supreme benevolence is behind all these messages, but if the polls are correct and most Americans do think somebody's God should be directing all our lives, let's please not pick the one who's inspiring pro-lifers to get automatic weapons. Until we have a firmer grip on our common reality, maybe we could all follow the harmless god who's telling the autistic disciple on 34th Street, over and over: "Go to Macy's nine-to-five, Go to Macy's nine-to-five." We could leave the credit cards home, stay out of trouble. Just look.

IT WAS A BEAUTIFUL SUMMER NIGHT on Broadway as we walked home from our last dinner together, grateful there were no more boxes to move. When a U-Haul truck rattled down the street, Crash laughed and asked, "Do you think they'd have less business if the company was named, 'U-Bust-Your-Ass'?" Our laughing foursome attracted looks from our neighbors, but few grinned or nodded, as if we'd become strangers again. Darren noticed too.

"This is too weird," he said. "People are staring at us because we look so *normal*. Like Mom and Pop and the two boys from Iowa." He was struck by the irony of having been labeled the weirdos in almost every neighborhood we've lived in, then arriving here—where weirdos abound—and being mistaken for regular guys.

"We should wear a sign," he said. "We're Not What You Think."

Maybe everyone should wear that sign through the next election, since there's so much confusion about the Other. As bad decisions in Washington crush good people in Harlem, even "liberal" politicians are telling us to pre-pare for further compromises—live a little leaner, do more charity work, tighten our belts. What can they be thinking? My neighhors are already liv-ing in cars, doing-it-yourself, holding pants up with duct tape. There is plen-ty of self-help and personal responsibility out here, where people watch each other's kids and take mostly working vacations, if we take them at all.

How did the white guys ever get the impression they are doing all the work? Because they are earning all the big bucks? Why are the Republicans so mad—why so furious with mothers? Do they need more Prozac? Since all the female labor sustaining them at home and at work is so invisible, so seemingly profitless, they can't seem to hold the picture that somebody's valuable work is responsible for the fact their children are alive, their Contracts are typed. The arrogance and ignorance of the current political leadership is so stupefying, you don't even want to argue with these boys—you "just want to *slap* them," as a high-ranking official recently told Molly Ivins. Maybe that's why the white guys loathe mothers so much—we remind them they have to share, take turns, grow up.

THE NEXT MORNING we loaded the roof of Howard's car so high with the boys' sports equipment, easels, and trunks, we had to make one last trip to the hardware store for longer bungee cords. It was a hectic departure as the Clampetts hit the road, and I waved from the curb as they mouthed their final goodbyes through the window. Still smiling, I stayed on the curb for a long time, sorry the party was over. Letting go rarely comes naturally to me, and I felt my worry reflexes kick in as the car turned the corner.

Almost every family value Howard and I tried to give our sons will give them nothing but trouble, if they choose to live them. As two young, edu-cated white guys who could qualify as insiders if they got behind the Contract on the rest of us, there are bound to be days they'll feel like Sucker Man, stuck with mercy when greed is called trump. I know it's a peculiar wish for a mother, but I hope they never quite fit in with their crowd. Certainly their affinity with their dad, a truly original odd man out, was a heartening sign. I could see them all laughing for the next 750 miles. Folding my arms, I looked up at the cathedral. I wished I could pray. I remembered my religious instructor's belief that we were all fools, walking from one hallowed ground to the next. Dear God, I thought, please let us be merciful fools.

Discussion Questions

Content

1. Why do you think Blakely entitled her essay "A Beautiful Day in the Neighborhood"? What is it that's beautiful in her descriptions, for example, of the street people in Manhattan? In what sense can the scenes she describes be considered beautiful?

2. Through reflecting on her new Manhattan neighborhood, Blakely introduces discussions of such things as capitalism and the failure of the mental healthcare system. Are you persuaded by her movement from her specific encounters to national problems? Why or why not? In what ways do you think local problems are related, if at all, to national policies and problems?

3. Does Blakely's description of her neighborhood seem familiar to you? Are the problems and possibilities she finds in Manhattan the same problems and possibilities you have experienced elsewhere? If so, what are those problems and possibilities? And why do you think they are so familiar? Are they an inescapable part of urban life? If the problems and possibilities she describes are unfamiliar to you, then why should you care about what she has to say?

Form

1. The pretext of Blakely's essay is her experience moving into an apartment in Manhattan, but the essay includes much more than a description of her activities. What are all the other elements of the essay? How do the other stories, descriptions, and reminiscences relate to the main narrative of moving into a new apartment? Do you think the additional materials add to or take away from the story of moving? What do they add or take away? Why do you read Blakely's essay this way?

2. From the start of her essay, Blakely makes it clear that she is moving into the city after living most of her adult life in the suburbs. How do you think Blakely's perspective influences her reactions to her new neighborhood in Manhattan? Are her encounters with street people naive? Does her essay seem to you to express a "suburban" perspective on the city? With reference to the essay itself, explain just what you think Blakely's perspective is. Imagine, as well, how different her essay might be if she were moving from Manhattan to the suburbs, or from Manhattan to another urban neighborhood. Would her essay have the same impact?

3. After reading Blakely's essay, do you feel hope or despair? Comfort or discomfort? Refer to the passages in her essay that you think had the most influence over how you responded to the essay as a whole. What is it about these particular passages that had such an impact on you?

Writing Prompts

1. Write a narrative reflecting on the thoughts and feelings you had on an occasion when you were moving. Try as much as you can to follow Blakely in letting the moving experience lead to discussions of other people or larger issues. If you have never had the experience of moving, write a fictional narrative in which you imagine what someone might think and feel as he or she prepared for life in a new home. Again, lead the narrative into discussions of other people and larger issues.

    2. Rewrite Blakely's essay with the title "An Ugly Day in the Neighborhood."

Gary Okihiro lives in the Pacific Northwest. He has written several books on Asian Americans and Asian American issues, including Cane Fires: The Anti-Japanese Movement in Hawaii, 1865–1945 *and* Reflections on Shattered Windows: Promises and Prospects for Asian American Studies. *"Is Yellow Black or White?" is excerpted from Okihiro's book of essays* Margins & Mainstreams: Asians in American History and Culture. *In this essay, Okihiro discusses the recent violent clashes between Korean storeowners and their African American clientele in several American cities. Reflecting upon these clashes, Okihiro asks, "Is Yellow Black or White?"—in other words, he explores how Asian Americans are perceived as being either black or white, when in fact they are neither. Notice how Okihiro keeps repeating the question, "Is yellow black or white?" and how his answer to the question keeps changing. Think about why he keeps changing his answer.*

Is Yellow Black or White?

Gary Okihiro

> Everytime I wanna go get a fucking Brew
> I gotta go down to the store with a tool
> Oriental ones (can you count) mother-fuckers
> They make a nigger mad enough to cause a ruckus
> Thinking every brother in the world's on the take
> So they watch every damn move that I make
> They hope I don't pull out a gat and try to rob
> their funky little store, but bitch, I gotta job.
> So don't follow me up and down your market
> Or your little chop-suey ass will be a target
> Of the nationwide boycott
> Choose with the people
> That's what the boy got
> So pay respect to the Black fist
> Or we'll burn down your store, right down to a crisp
> And then we'll see you
> 'Cause you can't turn the ghetto into Black Korea.

Gary Okihiro. "Is Yellow Black or White?" In *Margins and Mainstreams: Asians in American History and Culture* (Seattle: University of Washington Press, 1994), pp. 31–63. Reprinted with the permission of University of Washington Press.

BETWEEN 1985 AND 1990 in New York City, there were three major protests against Korean storeowners in African communities, while in Los Angeles, as one boycott ended in the summer of 1991, another began, and within a six-month period, five Korean grocery stores were firebombed. In a Los Angeles courtroom, the television monitors showed fifteen-year-old Latasha Harlins punch Soon Ja Du and turn to leave the store, when Du lifts a gun and fires pointblank at Harlins's head, killing her. On December 15, 1991, Yong Tae Park died of bullet wounds received during a robbery of his liquor store the previous day; Park was the seventh Korean storeowner killed in Los Angeles by African male suspects that year. "Black Power. No Justice, No Peace! Boycott Korean Stores! The Battle for Brooklyn," the poster read. "Crack, the 'housing crisis,' and Korean merchants is a conspiracy to destabilize our community.... The Korean merchants are agents of the U.S. government in their conspiracy to destabilize the economy of our community. They are rewarded by the government and financed by big business." In south central Los Angeles in April and May 1992, following the acquittal of police officers in the beating of African American Rodney G. King, Koreatown was besieged, eighteen-year-old Edward Song Lee died in a hail of bullets, nearly fifty Korean merchants were injured, and damage to about 2,000 Korean stores topped $400 million. Parts of Japantown were also hit, and losses to Japanese businesses exceeded $3 million. Is yellow black or white?

In laying the intellectual foundation for what we now call the model minority stereotype, social scientists William Caudill and George De Vos stated their hypothesis: "there seems to be a significant compatibility (but by no means identity) between the value systems found in the culture of Japan and the value systems found in American middle class culture." That compatibility, they cautioned, did not mean similarity but rather a sharing of certain values and adaptive mechanisms, such that "when they [Japanese and white middle-class Americans] meet under conditions favorable for acculturation ... Japanese Americans, acting in terms of their Japanese values and personality, will behave in ways that are favorably evaluated by middle class Americans." Although Caudill and De Vos tried to distinguish between identity and compatibility, similarity and sharing, subsequent variations on the theme depicted Asians as "just like whites." And so, is yellow black or white?

The question is multilayered. Is yellow black or white? is a question of Asian American identity. Is yellow black or white? is a question of Third World identity, or the relationships among people of color. Is yellow black or white? is a question of American identity, or the nature of America's racial formation. Implicit within the question is a construct of American society that defines race relations as bipolar—between black and white—and that locates Asians (and American Indians and Latinos) somewhere along the divide between black and white. Asians, thus, are "near-whites" or "just like blacks." The construct is historicized, within the progressive tradition of American history, to show the evolution of Asians from minority to majority status, or "from hardship and discrimination to become a model of self-respect and achievement in today's America." "Scratch a Japanese-American," social scientist Harry Kitano was quoted as saying, "and you find a Wasp," and Asians have been bestowed the highest accolade of having "outwhited the Whites." The construct, importantly, is not mere ideology but is a social practice that assigns to Asian Americans, and indeed to all minorities, places within the social formation. Further, the designations, the roles, and the relationships function to institute and perpetuate a repression that begets and maintains privilege. Asian Americans have served the master class, whether as "near-blacks" in the past or as "near-whites" in the present or as "marginal men" in both the past and the present. Yellow is emphatically neither white nor black; but insofar as Asians and Africans share a subordinate position to the master class, yellow is a shade of black, and black, a shade of yellow.

We are a kindred people, African and Asian Americans. We share a history of migration, interaction and cultural sharing, and commerce and trade. We share a history of European colonization, decolonization, and independence under neocolonization and dependency. We share a history of oppression in the United States, successively serving as slave and cheap labor, as peoples excluded and absorbed, as victims of mob rule and Jim Crow. We share a history of struggle for freedom and the democratization of America, of demands for equality and human dignity, of insistence on making real the promise that all men and women are created equal. We are a kindred people, forged in the fire of white supremacy and struggle, but how can we recall that kinship when our memories have been massaged by white hands, and how can we remember the past when our storytellers have been whispering amid the din of Western civilization and Anglo-conformity? . . .

We are a kindred people, African and Asian Americans. We share a history of migration, cultural interaction, and trade. We share a history of colonization, oppression and exploitation, and parallel and mutual struggles for freedom. We are a kindred people, forged in the fire of white supremacy and tempered in the water of resistance. Yet that kinship has been obscured from our range of vision, and that common cause, turned into a competition for access and resources. We have not yet realized the full meaning of Du Bois's poetic insight: "The stars of dark Andromeda belong up there in the great heaven that hangs above this tortured world. Despite the crude and cruel motives behind her shame and exposure, her degradation and enchaining, the fire and freedom of black Africa, with the uncurbed might of her consort Asia, are indispensable to the fertilizing of the universal soil of mankind, which Europe alone never would nor could give this aching world."

Is yellow black or white? In 1914, Takao Ozawa, a Japanese national, filed for naturalization on the basis of his over twenty-eight-year residence in the United States and the degree of his "Americanization." Further, Ozawa contended, Asians were not specifically excluded under the naturalization laws, and thus he should be considered a "free white person." The U.S. Supreme Court rendered its decision on November 13, 1922, rejecting Ozawa's application and claim. Only whites and Africans were accorded the privilege of naturalization, wrote Associate Justice George Sutherland, and although the founding fathers might not have contemplated Asians within the meaning of either black or white, it was evident that they were not included within the category of "free white persons." Ruled Sutherland: "the appellant is clearly of a race which is not Caucasian, and therefore belongs entirely outside the zone on the negative side." The marginalization of Asians—"entirely outside the zone"—was accompanied by their negation as "nonwhites"—"on the negative side"—in this institutionalization of the racial state. Yellow is not white.

But yellow is not black either, and the question posed is, in a real sense, a false and mystifying proposition. The question is only valid within the meanings given to and played out in the American racial formation, relations that have been posited as a black and white dyad. There are other options. Whites considered Asians "as blacks" or, at the very least, as replacements for blacks in the post–Civil War South, but whites imported Chinese precisely because they were not blacks and were thus perpetual aliens, who could never vote. Similarly, whites upheld Asians as "near-whites" or "whiter than whites" in the model minority stereotype, and yet Asians experienced and continue to face white racism "like blacks" in educational and occupational barriers and ceilings and in anti-Asian abuse and physical violence. Further, in both instances, Asians were used to "discipline" African Americans (and other minorities according to the model minority stereotype). That marginalization of Asians, in fact, within a black and white racial formation, "disciplines" both Africans and Asians and constitutes the essential site of Asian American oppression. By seeing only black and white, the presence and absence of all color, whites render Asians, American Indians, and Latinos invisible, ignoring the gradations and complexities of the full spectrum between the racial poles. At the same time, Asians share with Africans the status and repression of nonwhites—as the Other—and therein lies the debilitating aspect of Asian–African antipathy and the liberating nature of African–Asian unity.

On November 27, 1991, about 1,200 people gathered outside Los Angeles City Hall to participate in a prayer vigil sponsored by the African–Korean American Christian Alliance, a group formed the previous month. A newspaper reporter described the "almost surreal" scene:

Elderly Korean American women twirling and dancing with homeless men in front of the podium. Koreans and street people in a human chain, holding hands but not looking at each other. Shoes and clothing ruined by cow manure, which had been freshly spread over the rally grounds in an unfortunate oversight. Alliance co-chair Rev. Hee Min Park startled rally-goers when he began quoting from Martin Luther King's famous "I have a Dream" speech. Black homeless people listened in stunned silence at first, as the pastor's voice with a heavy immigrant accent filled the slain black minister's familiar words. Then a few began chanting "Amen" in response to Park's litany.

Park's articulation of King's dream reminds me of Maxine Hong Kingston's version of the story of Ts'ai Yen, a Han poetess kidnapped by "barbarians," in her book *The Woman Warrior*. Although she had lived among them for twelve years, Ts'ai Yen still considered the people primitive, until one evening, while inside her tent, she heard "music tremble and rise like desert wind." Night after night the barbarians blew on their flutes, and try as she might, Ts'ai Yen could not block out the sound. "Then, out of Ts'ai Yen's tent, which was apart from the others, the barbarians heard a woman's voice singing, as if to her babies, a song so high and clear, it matched the flutes." After she was ransomed, Ts'ai Yen brought her songs back to her people, who sang them to their own instruments. Concluded Kingston, "They translated well."

Discussion Questions

Content

1. Okihiro makes an argument for African Americans and Asian Americans being "a kindred people." Summarize the argument. Do you find it persuasive? Why or why not? If Okihiro's argument is persuasive, how does it transform your ideas about interracial relations? If it is not persuasive, do you think there are any kinds of arguments to be made for improving interracial relations?

2. Does Okihiro seem hopeful or skeptical about African American and Asian American relations? At what points in the essay is he hopeful? At what points is he skeptical? Are you hopeful or skeptical? What makes you hopeful? What makes you skeptical?

3. In your experience, are Asian Americans treated more like African Americans or like European Americans? How do Native Americans and Latin Americans get treated? Do you think that the treatments of the various groups reflect a larger social pattern? Just what do you think that pattern is?

Form

1. Throughout the essay, Okihiro repeats the question, "Is yellow black or white?" What are the various answers he gives? What do you think repeating the question contributes to the development of the essay?

2. Okihiro begins his essay with lyrics from Ice Cube's "Black Korea." What effect does opening the essay in this way have on you as a reader? Do you find that his use of the song makes you angry and incapable of listening to his essay? Or does the song make you even more open to what he has to say? Explain your response.

3. Okihiro ends his essay by quoting Maxine Hong Kingston, "They translated well." What does this mean in the context of Okihiro's essay? Who is doing the translating? What is he or she translating? How do we know when he or she has translated well? And what are the consequences of translating well? After having reflected on the quote, what overall effect does this ending to the essay have on you as a reader?

Writing Prompts

1. Write about your personal experience with someone of a different racial background. How did this experience change your perceptions of that person's racial group? How did the experience reinforce what you already believed?

2. Interview two people from different racial or ethnic groups, asking them about their experiences living in your city. Specifically, ask each person how his or her race or ethnicity influences his or her experiences of urban life. In your report of the interviews, explain how the two people's answers differ. Explain these differences. Also explain how their answers are similar. Do the similarities suggest to you any common bonds? Describe what these common bonds might be.

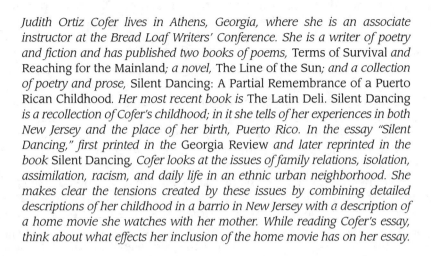

Judith Ortiz Cofer lives in Athens, Georgia, where she is an associate instructor at the Bread Loaf Writers' Conference. She is a writer of poetry and fiction and has published two books of poems, Terms of Survival *and* Reaching for the Mainland; *a novel,* The Line of the Sun; *and a collection of poetry and prose,* Silent Dancing: A Partial Remembrance of a Puerto Rican Childhood. *Her most recent book is* The Latin Deli. *Silent Dancing is a recollection of Cofer's childhood; in it she tells of her experiences in both New Jersey and the place of her birth, Puerto Rico. In the essay "Silent Dancing," first printed in the* Georgia Review *and later reprinted in the book* Silent Dancing, *Cofer looks at the issues of family relations, isolation, assimilation, racism, and daily life in an ethnic urban neighborhood. She makes clear the tensions created by these issues by combining detailed descriptions of her childhood in a barrio in New Jersey with a description of a home movie she watches with her mother. While reading Cofer's essay, think about what effects her inclusion of the home movie has on her essay.*

Silent Dancing

Judith Ortiz Cofer

WE HAVE A HOME MOVIE *of this party. Several times my mother and I have watched it together, and I have asked questions about the silent revelers coming in and out of focus. It is grainy and of short duration, but it's a great visual aid to my memory of life at that time. And it is in color—the only complete scene in color I can recall from those years.*

We lived in Puerto Rico until my brother was born in 1954. Soon after, because of economic pressures on our growing family, my father joined the United States Navy. He was assigned to duty on a ship in Brooklyn Yard—a place of cement and steel that was to be his home base in the States until his retirement more than twenty years later. He left the Island first, alone, going to New York City and tracking down his uncle who lived with his family

Judith Ortiz Cofer. "Silent Dancing." Reprinted with permission from the publisher of *Silent Dancing: A Partial Remembrance of a Puerto Rican Childhood* (Houston: Arte Publico Press—University of Houston, 1990).

across the Hudson River in Paterson, New Jersey. There my father found a tiny apartment in a huge tenement that had once housed Jewish families but was just being taken over and transformed by Puerto Ricans, overflowing from New York City. In 1955 he sent for us. My mother was only twenty years old, I was not quite three, and my brother was a toddler when we arrived at *El Building*, as the place had been christened by its newest residents.

My memories of life in Paterson during those first few years are all in shades of gray. Maybe I was too young to absorb vivid colors and details, or to discriminate between the slate blue of the winter sky and the darker hues of the snow-bearing clouds, but that single color washes over the whole period. The building we lived in was gray, as were the streets, filled with slush the first few months of my life there. The coat my father had bought for me was similar in color and too big; it sat heavily on my thin frame.

I do remember the way the heater pipes banged and rattled, startling all of us out of sleep until we got so used to the sound that we automatically shut it out or raised our voices above the racket. The hiss from the valve punctuated my sleep (which has always been fitful) like a nonhuman presence in the room—a dragon sleeping at the entrance of my childhood. But the pipes were also a connection to all the other lives being lived around us. Having come from a house designed for a single family back in Puerto Rico—my mother's extended-family home—it was curious to know that strangers lived under our floor and above our heads, and that the heater pipe went through everyone's apartments. (My first spanking in Paterson came as a result of playing tunes on the pipes in my room to see if there would be an answer.) My mother was as new to this concept of beehive life as I was, but she had been given strict orders by my father to keep the doors locked, the noise down, ourselves to ourselves.

It seems that Father had learned some painful lessons about prejudice while searching for an apartment in Paterson. Not until years later did I hear how much resistance he had encountered with landlords who were panicking at the influx of Latinos into a neighborhood that had been Jewish for a couple of generations. It made no difference that it was the American phenomenon of ethnic turnover which was changing the urban core of Paterson, and that the human flood could not be held back with an accusing finger.

"You Cuban?" one man had asked my father, pointing at his name tag on the Navy uniform—even though my father had the fair skin and light-brown hair of his northern Spanish background, and the name Ortiz is as common in Puerto Rico as Johnson is in the U.S.

"No," my father had answered, looking past the finger into his adversary's angry eyes. "I'm Puerto Rican."

"Same shit." And the door closed.

My father could have passed as European, but we couldn't. My brother and I both have our mother's black hair and olive skin, and so we lived in El

Building and visited our great-uncle and his fair children on the next block. It was their private joke that they were the German branch of the family. Not many years later that area too would be mainly Puerto Rican. It was as if the heart of the city map were being gradually colored brown—*café con leche* brown. Our color.

The movie opens with a sweep of the living room. It is "typical" immigrant Puerto Rican decor for the time: the sofa and chairs are square and hard-looking, uphol-stered in bright colors (blue and yellow in this instance), and covered with the transparent plastic that furniture salesmen then were so adept at convincing women to buy. The linoleum on the floor is light blue; if it had been subjected to spike heels (as it was in most places), there were dime-sized indentations all over it that cannot be seen in this movie. The room is full of people dressed up: dark suits for the men, red dresses for the women. When I have asked my mother why most of the women are in red that night, she has shrugged, "I don't remember. Just a coincidence." She doesn't have my obsession for assigning symbolism to everything.

The three women in red sitting on the couch are my mother, my eighteen-year-old cousin, and her brother's girlfriend. The novia *is just up from the Island, which is apparent in her body language. She sits up formally, her dress pulled over her knees. She is a pretty girl, but her posture makes her look insecure, lost in her full-skirted dress, which she has carefully tucked around her to make room for my gorgeous cousin, her future sister-in-law. My cousin has grown up in Paterson and is in her last year of high school. She doesn't have a trace of what Puerto Ricans call* la mancha *(literally, the stain: the mark of the new immi-grant—something about the posture, the voice, or the humble demeanor that makes it obvious to everyone the person has just arrived on the mainland). My cousin is wearing a tight, sequined, cocktail dress. Her brown hair has been light-ened with peroxide around the bangs, and she is holding a cigarette expertly between her fingers, bringing it up to her mouth in a sensuous arc of her arm as she talks animatedly. My mother, who has come up to sit between the two women, both only a few years younger than herself, is somewhere between the poles they represent in our culture.*

It became my father's obsession to get out of the barrio, and thus we were never permitted to form bonds with the place or with the people who lived there. Yet El Building was a comfort to my mother, who never got over yearn-ing for *la isla*. She felt surrounded by her language: the walls were thin, and voices speaking and arguing in Spanish could be heard all day. *Salsas* blasted out of radios, turned on early in the morning and left on for compa-ny. Women seemed to cook rice and beans perpetually—the strong aroma of boiling red kidney beans permeated the hallways.

Though Father preferred that we do our grocery shopping at the supermarket when he came home on weekend leaves, my mother insisted that she could cook only with products whose labels she could read. Consequently, during the week I accompanied her and my little brother to *La Bodega*—a hole-in-the-wall grocery store across the street from El Building. There we squeezed down three narrow aisles jammed with various products. Goya's and Libby's—those were the trademarks that were trusted by *her mamá*, so my mother bought many cans of Goya beans, soups, and condiments, as well as little cans of Libby's fruit juices for us. And she also bought Colgate toothpaste and Palmolive soap. (The final *e* is pronounced in both these products in Spanish, so for many years I believed that they were manufactured on the Island. I remember my surprise at first hearing a commercial on television in which Colgate rhymed with "ate.") We always lingered at La Bodega, for it was there that Mother breathed best, taking in the familiar aromas of the foods she knew from Mamá's kitchen. It was also there that she got to speak to the other women of El Building without violating outright Father's dictates against fraternizing with our neighbors.

Yet Father did his best to make our "assimilation" painless. I can still see him carrying a real Christmas tree up several flights of stairs to our apartment, leaving a trail of aromatic pine. He carried it formally, as if it were a flag in a parade. We were the only ones in El Building that I knew of who got presents on both Christmas day AND *día de Reyes*, the day when the Three Kings brought gifts to Christ and to Hispanic children.

Our supreme luxury in El Building was having our own television set. It must have been a result of Father's guilt feelings over the isolation he had imposed on us, but we were among the first in the barrio to have one. My brother quickly became an avid watcher of Captain Kangaroo and Jungle Jim, while I loved all the series showing families. By the time I started first grade, I could have drawn a map of Middle America as exemplified by the lives of characters in *Father Knows Best, The Donna Reed Show, Leave It to Beaver, My Three Sons*, and (my favorite) *Bachelor Father*, where John Forsythe treated his adopted teenage daughter like a princess because he was rich and had a Chinese houseboy to do everything for him. In truth, compared to our neighbors in El Building, *we* were rich. My father's Navy check provided us with financial security and a standard of life that the factory workers envied. The only thing his money could not buy us was a place to live away from the barrio—his greatest wish, Mother's greatest fear.

In the home movie the men are shown next, sitting around a card table set up in one corner of the living room, playing dominoes. The clack of the ivory pieces was a familiar sound. I heard it in many houses on the Island and in many apartments in Paterson. In Leave It to Beaver, *the Cleavers played bridge in every other episode; in my childhood, the men started every social occasion with a hotly debated round of dominoes. The women would sit around and watch, but they never participated in the games.*

Here and there you can see a small child. Children were always brought to parties and, whenever they got sleepy, were put to bed in the host's bedroom. Babysitting was a concept unrecognized by the Puerto Rican women I knew: a responsible mother did not leave her children with any stranger. And in a culture where children are not considered intrusive, there was no need to leave the children at home. We went where our mother went.

Of my preschool years I have only impressions: the sharp bite of the wind in December as we walked with our parents towards the brightly lit stores downtown; how I felt like a stuffed doll in my heavy coat, boots, and mittens; how good it was to walk into the five-and-dime and sit at the counter drinking hot chocolate. On Saturdays our whole family would walk downtown to shop at the big department stores on Broadway. Mother bought all our clothes at Penney's and Sears, and she liked to buy her dresses at the women's specialty shops like Lerner's and Diana's. At some point we'd go into Woolworth's and sit at the soda fountain to eat.

We never ran into other Latinos at these stores or when eating out, and it became clear to me only years later that the women from El Building shopped mainly in other places—stores owned by other Puerto Ricans or by Jewish merchants who had philosophically accepted our presence in the city and decided to make us their good customers, if not real neighbors and friends. These establishments were located not downtown but in the blocks around our street, and they were referred to generically as *La Tienda, El Bazar, La Bodega, La Botánica*. Everyone knew what was meant. These were the stores where your face did not turn a clerk to stone, where your money was as green as anyone else's.

One New Year's Eve we were dressed up like child models in the Sears catalogue: my brother in a miniature man's suit and bow tie, and I in black patent-leather shoes and a frilly dress with several layers of crinoline underneath. My mother wore a bright-red dress that night, I remember, and spike heels; her long black hair hung to her waist. Father, who usually wore his Navy uniform during his short visits home, had put on a dark civilian suit for the occasion: we had been invited to his uncle's house for a big celebration. Everyone was excited because my mother's brother Hernan—a bachelor who could indulge himself with luxuries—had bought a home movie camera, which he would be trying out that night.

Even the home movie cannot fill in the sensory details such a gathering left imprinted in a child's brain. The thick sweetness of women's perfumes mixing with the ever-present smells of food cooking in the kitchen: meat and plantain *pasteles*, as well as the ubiquitous rice dish made special with pigeon peas—*gandules*—and seasoned with precious *sofrito* sent up from the Island by somebody's mother or smuggled in by a recent traveler. *Sofrito* was one of the items that women hoarded, since it was hardly ever in stock at La Bodega. It was the flavor of Puerto Rico.

The men drank Palo Viejo rum, and some of the younger ones got weepy. The first time I saw a grown man cry was at a New Year's Eve party: he had been reminded of his mother by the smells in the kitchen. But what I remember most were the boiled *pasteles*—plantain or yucca rectangles stuffed with corned beef or other meats, olives, and many other savory ingredients, all wrapped in banana leaves. Everybody had to fish one out with a fork. There was always a "trick" pastel—one without stuffing—and whoever got that one was the "New Year's Fool."

There was also the music. Long-playing albums were treated like precious china in these homes. Mexican recordings were popular, but the songs that brought tears to my mother's eyes were sung by the melancholy Daniel Santos, whose life as a drug addict was the stuff of legend. Felipe Rodríguez was a particular favorite of couples, since he sang about faithless women and brokenhearted men. There is a snatch of one lyric that has stuck in my mind like a needle on a worn groove: *De piedra ha de ser mi cama, de piedra la cabezera . . . la mujer que a mi me quiera . . . ha de quererme de veras. Ay, Ay, Ay, corazón, porque no amas. . . .* I must have heard it a thousand times since the idea of a bed made of stone, and its connection to love, first troubled me with its disturbing images.

The five-minute home movie ends with people dancing in a circle—the creative filmmaker must have set it up, so that all of them could file past him. It is both comical and sad to watch silent dancing. Since there is no justification for the absurd movements that music provides for some of us, people appear frantic, their faces embarrassingly intense. It's as if you were watching sex. Yet for years, I've had dreams in the form of this home movie. In a recurring scene, familiar faces push themselves forward into my mind's eye, plastering their features into distorted close-ups. And I'm asking them: "Who is *she*? Who is the old woman I don't recognize? Is she an aunt? Somebody's wife? Tell me who she is."

"See the beauty mark on her cheek as big as a hill on the lunar landscape of her face—well, that runs in the family. The women on your father's side of the family wrinkle early; it's the price they pay for that fair skin. The young girl with the green stain on her wedding dress is *La Novia*—just up from the Island. See, she lowers her eyes when she approaches the camera, as she's supposed to. Decent girls never look at you directly in the face. *Humilde*, humble, a girl should express humility in all her actions. She will make a good wife for your cousin. He should consider himself lucky to have met her only weeks after she arrived here. If he marries her quickly, she will make him a good Puerto Rican-style wife; but if he waits too long, she will be corrupted by the city—just like your cousin there."

"She means me. I do what I want. This is not some primitive island I live on. Do they expect me to wear a black mantilla on my head and go to mass every day? Not me. I'm an American woman, and I will do as I please. I can type faster than anyone in my senior class at Central High, and I'm going to be a secretary to a lawyer when I graduate. I can pass for an American girl anywhere—I've tried it. At least for Italian, anyway—I never speak Spanish in public. I hate these parties, but I wanted the dress. I look better than any of these *humildes* here. *My* life is going to be different. I have an American boyfriend. He is older and has a car. My parents don't know it, but I sneak out of the house late at night sometimes to be with him. If I marry him, even my name will be American. I hate rice and beans—that's what makes these women fat."

"Your *prima* is pregnant by that man she's been sneaking around with. Would I lie to you? I'm your *Tiá Política*, your great-uncle's common-law wife—the one he abandoned on the Island to go marry your cousin's mother. *I* was not invited to this party, of course, but I came anyway. I came to tell you that story about your cousin that you've always wanted to hear. Do you remember the comment your mother made to a neighbor that has always haunted you. The only thing you heard was your cousin's name, and then you saw your mother pick up your doll from the couch and say: 'It was as big as this doll when they flushed it down the toilet.' This image has bothered you for years, hasn't it? You had nightmares about babies being flushed down the toilet, and you wondered why anyone would do such a horrible thing. You didn't dare ask your mother about it. She would only tell you that you had not heard her right, and yell at you for listening to adult conversations. But later, when you were old enough to know about abortions, you suspected.

"I am here to tell you that you were right. Your cousin was growing an *Americanito* in her belly when this movie was made. Soon after she put something long and pointy into her pretty self, thinking maybe she could get rid of the problem before breakfast and still make it to her first class at the high school. Well, *Niña*, her screams could be heard downtown. Your aunt, her mamá, who had been a midwife on the Island, managed to pull the little thing out. Yes, they probably flushed it down the toilet. What else could they do with it—give it a Christian burial in a little white casket with blue bows and ribbons? Nobody wanted that baby—least of all the father, a teacher at her school with a house in West Paterson that he was filling with real children, and a wife who was a natural blond.

"Girl, the scandal sent your uncle back to the bottle. And guess where your cousin ended up? Irony of ironies. She was sent to a village in Puerto Rico to live with a relative on her mother's side: a place so far away from civilization that you have to ride a mule to reach it. A real change in scenery. She found a man there—women like that cannot live without male company—

but believe me, the men in Puerto Rico know how to put a saddle on a woman like her. *La Gringa*, they call her. Ha, ha, ha. *La Gringa* is what she always wanted to be...."

The old woman's mouth becomes a cavernous black hole I fall into. And as I fall, I can feel the reverberations of her laughter. I hear the echoes of her last mocking words: *La Gringa, La Gringa!* And the conga line keeps moving silently past me. There is no music in my dream for the dancers.

When Odysseus visits Hades to see the spirit of his mother, he makes an offering of sacrificial blood, but since all the souls crave an audience with the living, he has to listen to many of them before he can ask questions. I, too, have to hear the dead and the forgotten speak in my dream. Those who are still part of my life remain silent, going around and around in their dance. The others keep pressing their faces forward to say things about the past.

My father's uncle is last in line. He is dying of alcoholism, shrunken and shriveled like a monkey, his face a mass of wrinkles and broken arteries. As he comes closer I realize that in his features I can see my whole family. If you were to stretch that rubbery flesh, you could find my father's face, and deep within *that* face—my own. I don't want to look into those eyes ringed in purple. In a few years he will retreat into silence, and take a long, long time to die. *Move back, Tío*, I tell him. *I don't want to hear what you have to say. Give the dancers room to move. Soon it will be midnight. Who is the New Year's Fool this time?*

Discussion Questions

Content

1. What do you consider to be the main points that Cofer is making about growing up a Latina in an urban neighborhood? Support your answer with references to her essay.

2. Cofer says that a place to live outside of the barrio was her father's "greatest wish" and her mother's "greatest fear." Why did her father wish to live outside the barrio? Why did her mother not want to leave? What do their feelings say about their respective attitudes about neighborhood and community? How do you think Cofer herself felt about this issue? Who seems to you to have the best sense of neighborhood? Why?

3. Cofer suggests that her father wanted his family to isolate themselves from their Latino neighbors and that he had encountered racism in his experience with the dominant culture. How can he hold these two positions simultaneously? Why would he want to isolate himself from his neighbors instead of joining with them? In what ways do you think his desire for isolation is a response to racism? How widespread do views such as her father's seem to you?

Form

1. How are the alternating sections of the text organized? Is one form of text primary and the other secondary? If so, which are the primary sections? What is it about certain sections that you consider them primary? In considering these questions, think about how the title "Silent Dancing" relates to the nonitalicized text.

2. Identify the form of Cofer's essay. Is it personal reflection? Objective description? Or does it combine several forms? If so, which ones? Just how effective is Cofer's style? What does the form of the essay do for you as a reader? Explain your response with references to the essay itself.

3. What does Cofer's decision to use italicized and nonitalicized text demonstrate to you about her purpose in writing the essay? How might you use both italicized and nonitalicized text in an essay about growing up?

Writing Prompts

1. Choose a handful of family photographs or home movies. Describe the images in the pictures and explain how you feel about them now. Also try to reflect on how your perceptions of these images have, or have not, changed over the years. Did you look at them differently four or five years ago?

2. Describe a home depicted in a television show. Provide details about the setting of the home, the people in it, and the action that takes place there. Compare the way the show portrays life in that home with what you think it would really be like to live in that type of home.

Mike Rose grew up and currently lives and works in Los Angeles. He is a professor of education at UCLA. Mike Rose is well known for his criticisms of traditional education and has written a number of articles on this subject for journals in English studies and education. He has also written two books on this issue: When a Writer Can't Write *and* Writer's Block. *"I Just Wanna Be Average" is excerpted from Rose's educational autobiography,* Lives on the Boundary: The Struggles and Achievements of America's Underprepared. *In* Lives on the Boundary, *Rose describes the ways in which he, like many other Americans, experienced discrimination and exclusion from educational opportunities and the advancement they promise. In "I Just Wanna Be Average," Mike Rose recalls moving to and growing up in South Los Angeles. He remembers both his family's home and the people and places that characterized his neighborhood. Through these recollections, Rose reflects upon how his urban neighborhood experiences caused him to long for the mainstream, middle-class existence depicted in television and movies. While reading "I Just Wanna Be Average," consider what forces cause Rose and many of us to believe that our lives could somehow be better if only we were more "average."*

I Just Wanna Be Average

Mike Rose

BETWEEN 1880 AND 1920, well over four million Southern Italian peasants immigrated to America. Their poverty was extreme and hopeless—twelve hours of farm labor would get you one lira, about twenty cents—so increasing numbers of desperate people booked passage for the United States, the country where, the steamship companies claimed, prosperity was a way of life. My father left Naples before the turn of the century; my mother came with her mother from Calabria in 1921. They met in Altoona, Pennsylvania, at the lunch counter of Tom and Joe's, a steamy diner with twangy-voiced waitresses and graveyard stew.

For my mother, life in America was not what the promoters had told her father it would be. She grew up very poor. She slept with her parents and brothers and sisters in one room. She had to quit school in the seventh grade to care for her sickly younger brothers. When her father lost his leg in a railroad accident, she began working in a garment factory where women sat crowded at their stations, solitary as penitents in a cloister. She stayed there until her marriage. My father had found a freer route. He was closemouthed about his past, but I know that he had been a salesman, a tailor, and a gambler; he knew people in the mob and had, my uncles whisper, done time in Chicago. He went through a year or two of Italian elementary school and could write a few words—those necessary to scribble measurements for a suit—and over the years developed a quiet urbanity, a persistence, and a slowly debilitating arteriosclerosis.

When my father proposed to my mother, he decided to open a spaghetti house, a venture that lasted through the war and my early years. The restaurant collapsed in bankruptcy in 1951 when Altoona's major industry, the Pennsylvania Railroad, had to shut down its shops. My parents managed to salvage seven hundred dollars and, on the advice of the family doctor, headed to California, where the winters would be mild and where I, their seven-year-old son, would have the possibility of a brighter future.

At first we lived in a seedy hotel on Spring Street in downtown Los Angeles, but my mother soon found an ad in the *Times* for cheap property on the south side of town. My parents contacted a woman named Mrs. Jolly, used my mother's engagement ring as a down payment, and moved to 9116 South Vermont Avenue, a house about one and one-half miles northwest of Watts. The neighborhood was poor, and it was in transition. Some old white folks had lived there for decades and were retired. Younger black families were moving up from Watts and settling by working-class white families newly arrived from the South and the Midwest. Immigrant Mexican families were coming in from Baja. Any such demographic mix is potentially volatile, and as the fifties wore on, the neighborhood would be marked by outbursts of violence.

I have many particular memories of this time, but in general these early years seem a peculiar mix of physical warmth and barrenness: a gnarled lemon tree, thin rugs, a dirt alley, concrete in the sun. My uncles visited a few times, and we went to the beach or to orange groves. The return home, however, left the waves and spray, the thick leaves and split pulp far in the distance. I was aware of my parents watching their money and got the sense from their conversations that things could quickly take a turn for the worse. I started taping pennies to the bottom of a shelf in the kitchen.

My father's health was bad, and he had few readily marketable skills. Poker and pinochle brought in a little money, and he tried out an idea that had worked in Altoona during the war: He started a "suit club." The few customers he could scare up would pay two dollars a week on a tailor-made suit. He would take the measurements and send them to a shop back East and hope for the best. My mother took a job at a café in downtown Los Angeles, a split shift 9:00 to 12:00 and 5:00 to 9:00, but her tips were totaling sixty cents a day, so she quit for a night shift at Coffee Dan's. This got her to the bus stop at one in the morning, waiting on the same street where drunks were urinating and hookers were catching the last of the bar crowd. She made friends with a Filipino cook who would scare off the advances of old men aflame with the closeness of taxi dancers. In a couple of years, Coffee Dan's would award her a day job at the counter. Once every few weeks my father and I would take a bus downtown and visit with her, sitting at stools by the window, watching the animated but silent mix of faces beyond the glass.

My father had moved to California with faint hopes about health and a belief in his child's future, drawn by that far edge of America where the sun descends into green water. What he found was a city that was warm, verdant, vast, and indifferent as a starlet in a sports car. Altoona receded quickly, and my parents must have felt isolated and deceived. They had fallen into the abyss of paradise—two more poor settlers trying to make a go of it in the City of the Angels.

LET ME TELL YOU ABOUT OUR HOUSE. If you entered the front door and turned right you'd see a small living room with a couch along the east wall and one along the west wall—one couch was purple, the other tan, both bought used and both well worn. A television set was placed at the end of the purple couch, right at arm level. An old Philco radio sat next to the TV, its speaker covered with gold lamé. There was a small coffee table in the center of the room on which sat a murky fishbowl occupied by two listless guppies. If, on entering, you turned left you would see a green Formica dinner table with four chairs, a cedar chest given as a wedding present to my mother by her mother, a painted statue of the Blessed Virgin Mary, and a black trunk. I also had a plastic chaise longue between the door and the table. I would lie on this and watch television.

A short hallway leading to the bathroom opened on one side to the kitchen and, on the other, to the bedroom. The bedroom had two beds, one for me and one for my parents, a bureau with a mirror, and a chest of drawers on which we piled old shirt boxes and stacks of folded clothes. The kitchen held a refrigerator and a stove, small older models that we got when our earlier (and newer) models were repossessed by two silent men. There was one white wooden chair in the corner beneath wall cabinets. You could walk in and through a tiny pantry to the backyard and to four one-room rentals. My father got most of our furniture from a secondhand store on the next block; he would tend the store two or three hours a day as payment on our account.

As I remember it, the house was pretty dark. My mother kept the blinds in the bedroom drawn—there were no curtains there—and the venetian blinds in the living room were, often as not, left closed. The walls were bare except for a faded picture of Jesus and a calendar from the *Altoona Mirror*. Some paper carnations bent out of a white vase on the television. There was a window on the north side of the kitchen that had no blinds or curtains, so the sink got good light. My father would methodically roll up his sleeves and show me how to prepare a sweet potato or avocado seed so it would sprout. We kept a row of them on the sill above the sink, their shoots and vines rising and curling in the morning sun.

The house was on a piece of land that rose about four feet up from heavily trafficked Vermont Avenue. The yard sloped down to the street, and three steps and a short walkway led up the middle of the grass to our front door. There was a similar house immediately to the south of us. Next to it was Carmen's Barber Shop. Carmen was a short, quiet Italian who, rumor had it, had committed his first wife to the crazy house to get her money. In the afternoons, Carmen could be found in the lot behind his shop playing solitary catch, flinging a tennis ball high into the air and running under it. One day the police arrested Carmen on charges of child molesting. He was released but became furtive and suspicious. I never saw him in the lot again. Next to Carmen's was a junk store where, one summer, I made a little money polishing brass and rewiring old lamps. Then came a dilapidated real estate office, a Mexican restaurant, an empty lot, and an appliance store owned by the father of Keith Grateful, the streetwise, chubby boy who would become my best friend.

Right to the north of us was a record shop, a barber shop presided over by old Mr. Graff, Walt's Malts, a shoe repair shop with a big Cat's Paw decal in the window, a third barber shop, and a brake shop. It's as I write this that I realize for the first time that three gray men could have had a go at your hair before you left our street.

Behind our house was an unpaved alley that passed, just to the north, a power plant the length of a city block. Massive coils atop the building hissed and cracked through the day, but the doors never opened. I used to think it was abandoned—feeding itself on its own wild arcs—until one sweltering afternoon a man was electrocuted on the roof. The air was thick and still as two firemen—the only men present—brought down a charred and limp body without saying a word.

The north and south traffic on Vermont was separated by tracks for the old yellow trolley cars, long since defunct. Across the street was a huge garage, a tiny hot dog stand run by a myopic and reclusive man named Freddie, and my dreamland, the Vermont Bowl. Distant and distorted behind thick lenses, Freddie's eyes never met yours; he would look down when he took your order and give you your change with a mumble. Freddie slept on a cot in the back of his grill and died there one night, leaving tens of thousands of dollars stuffed in the mattress.

My father would buy me a chili dog at Freddie's, and then we would walk over to the bowling alley where Dad would sit at the lunch counter and drink coffee while I had a great time with pinball machines, electric shooting galleries, and an ill-kept dispenser of cheese corn. There was a small, dark bar abutting the lanes, and it called to me. I would devise reasons to walk through it: "'Scuse me, is the bathroom in here?" or "Anyone see my dad?" though I can never remember my father having a drink. It was dark and people were drinking and I figured all sorts of mysterious things were being whispered. Next to the Vermont Bowl was a large vacant lot overgrown with foxtails and dotted with car parts, bottles, and rotting cardboard. One day Keith heard that the police had found a human head in the brush. After that we explored the lot periodically, coming home with stickers all the way up to our waists. But we didn't find a thing. Not even a kneecap.

When I wasn't with Keith or in school, I would spend most of my day with my father or with the men who were renting the one-room apartments behind our house. Dad and I whiled away the hours in the bowling alley, watching TV, or planting a vegetable garden that never seemed to take. When he was still mobile, he would walk the four blocks down to St. Regina's Grammar School to take me home to my favorite lunch of boiled wieners and chocolate milk. There I'd sit, dunking my hot dog in a jar of mayonnaise and drinking my milk while Sheriff John tuned up the calliope music on his "Lunch Brigade." Though he never complained to me, I could sense that my father's health was failing, and I began devising child's ways to make him better. We had a box of rolled cotton in the bathroom, and I would go in and peel off a long strip and tape it around my jaw. Then I'd rummage through the closet, find a sweater of my father's, put on one of his hats—and sneak around to the back door. I'd knock loudly and wait. It would take him a while to get there. Finally, he'd open the door, look down, and quietly say, "Yes, Michael?" I was disappointed. Every time. Somehow I thought I could fool him. And, I guess, if he had been fooled, I would have succeeded in redefining things: I would have been the old one, he much younger, more agile, with strength in his legs.

The men who lived in the back were either retired or didn't work that much, so one of them was usually around. They proved to be, over the years, an unusual set of companions for a young boy. Ed Gionotti was the youngest of the lot, a handsome man whose wife has run off and who spoke softly and never smiled. Bud Hall and Lee McGuire were two out-of-work plumbers who lived in adjacent units and who weekly drank themselves silly, proclaiming in front of God and everyone their undying friendship or their unequivocal hatred. Old Cheech was a lame Italian who used to hobble along grabbing his testicles and rolling his eyes while he talked about the women he claimed to have on a string. There was Lester, the toothless cabbie, who several times made overtures to me and who, when he moved, left behind a drawer full of syringes and burnt spoons. Mr. Smith was a rambunctious retiree who lost his nose to an untended skin cancer. And there was Mr. Berryman, a sweet and gentle man who eventually left for a retirement hotel only to be burned alive in an electrical fire.

Except for Keith, there were no children on my block and only one or two on the immediate side streets. Most of the people I saw day to day were over fifty. People in their twenties and thirties working in the shoe shop or the garages didn't say a lot; their work and much of what they were working for drained their spirits. There were gang members who sauntered up from Hoover Avenue, three blocks to the east, and occasionally I would get shoved around, but they had little interest in me either as member or victim. I was a skinny, bespectacled kid and had neither the coloring nor the style of dress or carriage that marked me as a rival. On the whole, the days were quiet, lazy, lonely. The heat shimmering over the asphalt had no snap to it; time drifted by. I would lie on the couch at night and listen to the music from the record store or from Walt's Malts. It was new and quick paced, exciting, a little dangerous (the church had condemned Buddy Knox's "Party Doll"), and I heard in it a deep rhythmic need to be made whole with love, or marked as special, or released in some rebellious way. Even the songs about lost love—and there were plenty of them—lifted me right out of my socks with their melodious longing:

> Came the dawn,
> and my heart and her love and the night
> were gone.
> But I know I'll never forget
> her kiss in the moonlight Oooo . . .
> such a kiss Oooo Oooo such a night . . .

In the midst of the heat and slow time the music brought the promise of its origins, a promise of deliverance, a promise that, if only for a moment, life could be stirring and dreamy.

But the anger and frustration of South Vermont could prove too strong for music's illusion; then it was violence that provided deliverance of a different order. One night I watched as a guy sprinted from Walt's to toss something on our lawn. The police were right behind, and a cop tackled him, smashing his face into the sidewalk. I ducked out to find the packet: a dozen glassine bags of heroin. Another night, one August midnight, an argument outside the record store ended with a man being shot to death. And the occasional gang forays brought with them some fated kid who would fumble his moves and catch a knife.

It's popular these days to claim you grew up on the streets. Men tell violent tales and romanticize the lessons violence brings. But, though it was occasionally violent, it wasn't the violence in South L.A. that marked me, for sometimes you can shake that ugliness off. What finally affected me was subtler, but more pervasive: I cannot recall a young person who was crazy in love or lost in work or one old person who was passionate about a cause or an idea. I'm not talking about an absence of energy—the street toughs and, for that fact, old Cheech had energy. And I'm not talking about an absence of decency, for my father was a thoughtful man. The people I grew up with were retired from jobs that rub away the heart or were working hard at jobs to keep their lives from caving in or were anchorless and in between jobs and spouses or were diving headlong into a barren tomorrow: junkies, alcoholics, and mean kids walking along Vermont looking to throw a punch. I developed a picture of human existence that rendered it short and brutish or sad and aimless or long and quiet with rewards like afternoon naps, the evening newspaper, walks around the block, occasional letters from children in other states. When, years later, I was introduced to humanistic psychologists like Abraham Maslow and Carl Rogers, with their visions of self-actualization, or even Freud with his sober dictum about love and work, it all sounded like a glorious fairy tale, a magical account of a world full of possibility, full of hope and empowerment. Sindbad and Cinderella couldn't have been more fanciful.

Discussion Questions

Content

1. What does the essay title, "I Just Wanna Be Average," suggest about the contents of the essay? What does it mean to be average? Does Rose seem to think he was average? Or is he recalling the ways in which he wasn't average? What is it about his neighborhood that seems to you average or not? In the neighborhood he describes, why do you think anyone would just want to be average?

2. Near the end of this essay, Rose briefly describes the violence of his neighborhood as providing "deliverance." He also writes that it wasn't the violence of South Los Angeles that "marked" him. What sense do you make of these views? How can urban violence provide deliverance? At the same time, in what ways does urban violence "mark" people?

3. Through his discussion of his mother and father and the people of Vermont Avenue, Rose explains what it meant to him to belong to this community. Is his attitude reminiscent of yours? When you think about it, do you have similar feelings about the people in your community? Who are those people? What do they do and why do you feel as you do about them? And how do these feelings demonstrate what you value about your community?

Form

1. Many people would describe Rose's essay as realistic and straightforward. Would you agree or not? What words, phrases, or sentences can you point to in support of your position?

2. Rose's essay contains both descriptions of places and storytelling narratives. Can you find a passage of each? Why do you think Rose combines both elements in his essay? What might the essay be like if it consisted simply either of description or of storytelling? Do you think it would be a better or a worse essay? Why?

3. How does Rose's style influence your impressions of what city life was like in South Central Los Angeles? How do these impressions of city life compare to those produced by Cofer's style in her essay? Just how important is a writer's style when he or she wants to create impressions of city life? Why? Explain what styles you think might be inappropriate for creating impressions of urban communities.

Writing Prompts

1. Using a very realistic style like Rose's, write an essay describing a recent day in your neighborhood. Try and concentrate on providing detailed descriptions of places and people and events.

2. Write a description of your life that shows readers why and how you "just wanna be average."

PART 2 DISCUSSION QUESTIONS

1. bell hooks values a "homeplace" because a homeplace provides protection. Camilo José Vergara exposes most vividly the negative aspects of a need for protection and security. How do they and the other authors create visions of home as secure and safe? As dangerous? As isolating and stifling? In what ways do you think the idea of a home in cities is all these things at the same time? Or don't you think this? Would you want a home to be anything else?

2. One of the defining features of community discussed in these essays is race. Refer to specific essays to generate several other defining features of community. Once you have a list of features of community, rank the items. Which are more important than the others? Why are some more important than others? Are there some that should be more important but are not? Are there other features you would include that aren't available from the essays?

3. To the authors of these essays, our identity is created by our homes and neighborhoods. How are cities places where people are made to feel at home? How are cities places where people are not made to feel at home? In what ways do you think cities contribute to or take away from people's sense of home?

4. Are any of the issues of community that are discussed in the readings issues in your city? Which ones? In what ways are issues of community issues that your city shares with all other cities? In what ways are these issues played out uniquely in your city? How do you think your city's residents can best deal with these issues?

5. What ideas about the urban neighborhood experience do you think all the essays share? Do you even think there is an urban neighborhood experience that can be shared from city to city and person to person? If so, just what might the specifics of that uniquely urban neighborhood experience be? If not, then what is it about the neighborhoods in different cities that makes them each unique unto themselves?

PART 2 WRITING ASSIGNMENTS

1. Write a personal essay exploring what it means to be a member of your community. Include details about the people and places that have the most value for you. Try to give your readers a strong sense of your community as a place. Give you readers a sense of what it means to you to belong, or to want not to belong, to that community.

2. Write an essay in which you discuss the kinds of physical, mental, and emotional barriers that identify your neighborhood. Who and what do these barriers keep in? Who and what do they keep out? How do these agreed-upon barriers shape the ways urban people think and act toward themselves, toward each other, and toward their surroundings?

3. Consider what it is about cities that makes neighborhoods so necessary. Think about what characteristics of neighborhoods both unify and divide cities. Then, write about an incident that happened in your city in which neighborhood identity created both a sense of unity and at the same time caused a feeling of antagonism among people.

4. Write a description of the culture of your neighborhood for someone totally unfamiliar with it. Consider the following: What do its residents share that brings them together? How is this sharing beneficial? Do some people have trouble associating themselves with your neighborhood? How and why do they have trouble? What is your neighborhood's relationship to the rest of the city? How does that relationship reflect your neighborhood's culture?

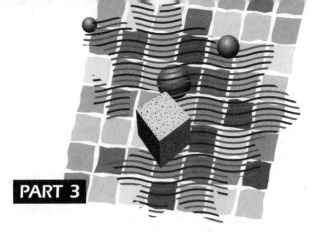

Crime in Our Cities

MANY INDIVIDUAL EVENTS on the current cultural landscape conspire to make me obsessed with contemporary debates over "multiculturalism" in both the art world and the culture at large, but my concern is grounded first and foremost in my observation of the impact of present material conditions of an increasing sector of the population. These material conditions, which include widespread homelessness, joblessness, illiteracy, crime, disease (including AIDS), hunger, poverty, drug addiction, alcoholism, as well as the various habits of ill health, and the destruction of the environment are (let's face it) the myriad social effects of late multinational capitalism.

In New York City where I live the population most affected by these conditions consists largely of people of African, Latino, or Asian descent, some of whom are gay—blacks either from, or one or two generations removed from, the South, the Caribbean, or Africa, or Latinos of mixed race from the Caribbean or Central or South America, or Asians from Korea, the Philippines, or China. In other parts of the country, the ethnic composition of the population that is most economically and politically disenfranchised may vary to include more poor whites, women, and children of all races and ethnicities, gays, Native Americans, and Chicanos. In New York City this population, which accounts for more than half the population of the city, is menaced in very specific ways by inadequate and formidably expensive housing and medical care, by extremely shoddy and bureaucracy-ridden systems of social services and public education, by an inefficient, militaristic police force, and by increasing street violence and crime promoted by drug trafficking and high rates of drug addiction.

One of the immediate consequences of this system is that most people who are not rich, white, and male (and therefore virtually never leave the Upper Eastside) live in fear in New York City. And contrary to the impression that one might get based on the overreporting of those incidents that involve black-on-white crime, it is women, children, and old people, and especially young men of color, who live under the greatest and most constant threat.

—*Michelle Wallace*

THE POLICE DEPARTMENT and the armed forces are the two arms of the power structure, the muscles of control and enforcement. They have deadly weapons with which to inflict pain on the human body. They know how to bring about horrible deaths. They have clubs with which to beat the body and the head. They have bullets and guns with which to tear holes in the flesh, to smash bones, to disable and kill. They use force, to make you do what the deciders have decided you must do....

Which laws get enforced depends on who is in power. If the capitalists are in power, they enforce laws designed to protect their system, their way of life. They have a particular abhorrence for crimes against property, but are prepared to be liberal and show a modicum of compassion for crimes against the person—unless, of course, an instance of the latter is combined with an instance of the former. In such cases, nothing can stop them from throwing the whole book at the offender. For instance, armed robbery with violence, to a capitalist, is the very epitome of evil. Ask any banker what he thinks of it.

If Communists are in power, they enforce laws designed to protect their system, their way of life. To them, the horror of horrors is the speculator, that man of magic who has mastered the art of getting something with nothing and who in America would be a member in good standing of his local Chamber of Commerce.

"The people," however, are nowhere consulted, although everywhere everything is done always in their name and ostensibly for their betterment, while their real-life problems go unsolved. "The people" are a rubber stamp for the crafty and sly. And no problem can be solved without taking the police department and the armed forces into account. Both kings and bookies understand this, as do first ladies and common prostitutes.

—*Eldridge Cleaver*

ACCORDING TO RICHARD ERICSON and Clifford Shearing, there are two distinct faces of the law, one symbolic, the other operational. Legal discourse must appeal to values and principles to provide specific laws and, simultaneously, their merits. It must also move along the terrain of coercion, control, and force. Resistance to and transgressions of the law are a given. Someone has to do the dirty work. "There is the discourse of the public culture: its normative sentiments about the rule of law provide a legitimizing symbolic canopy for the work of police and other legal agents. There is also the discourse of the operational reality of social control on behalf of the state: the law allows police and other legal agents to take the actions they deem necessary, and yet be able to construe them and account for them in terms which make them publicly acceptable."

The law exists as a codified, if evolving, set of constitutional provisions and amendments, legislative statutes, executive orders, judicial opinions, and criminal codes. Yet there is no easy one-to-one correspondence between the occurrence of an action, the determination that that action constitutes the specific breaking of a law, and the decision to arrest the actor for that transgression. Layers upon layers of intervening discretion, knowledge, compromises, and interpretations break apart the theoretical correspondence. These intervening considerations often come as a surprise to a trusting or naïve citizenry.

—*Robin Wagner-Pacifici*

INTRODUCTION

Every day, newspaper headlines and televised news reports tell of violent crimes in our nation's cities. Often these reports emphasize the most senseless, violent, and extreme crimes. They give the impression that lawless and violent persons are everywhere: Families who take a wrong turn while driving in the city are gunned down by drug-dealing gang members; babies sleeping in their cribs are killed by stray bullets. In these images of violence, the mass media make assumptions about peace and tranquillity—that they are only to be hoped for and found outside of cities. The mass media also use language that plays on people's fear, frustration, and despair, making crime prevention and personal safety important concerns for all Americans. The language of fear in the mass media has spawned a market for self-protection and crime-prevention products. Just think of the many ads for antitheft devices, burglar alarms, and self-defense courses that appear on television and the radio, in newspapers and magazines. The fear of crime provoked by our talk about crime has also created a "get tough on crime" political climate. Politicians create election campaigns that manipulate people's beliefs, fears, and perceptions of just how widespread violence is in our cities. Think about the campaign rhetoric of people running for public office; they typically promise "tougher laws," "stricter sentencing," and "more police and prisons"—all of which are designed to "get criminals off the street."

However, crime is also a reality. You may know someone who has been the victim of a crime; you may even have been the victim of a crime yourself. We live every day with the realities of crime, as well as with ideas about the extent and nature of crime generated by advertising, news, politics, TV, movies, and music.

Like everyone else in the United States, you have to deal with actual crime and its prevention, mass-media-produced images of crime, and your attitudes about crime—which are generated by both real-world crime and the mass media. Whether you believe criminal behavior is the fault of deviant persons or the fault of those individuals' environments depends upon and determines how you respond to crime.

How should we respond to violent crime? How can we best make sense of violent crime? Are violent crimes the acts of deviant persons who should be locked up? Or are violent crimes somehow expressions of a violent society? Or should we understand violent crimes as something in between? The ways in which you respond to these questions and how you talk about them have important implications not only for how you view and act on crime, but also for how you live your life and act in your community.

The essays in this part explore some of the ways in which the real effects of urban violence and crime are represented and manipulated for purposes of law enforcement, social organization, politics, and entertainment. Using statistics gathered from his own police department, Daryl Gates, in "Guns Aren't the Only Issue," describes what he considers the root cause of violence in American cities and explains what he thinks will curb the spread of violence. As Gates explains, he does not believe it is guns that make people criminal.

In "Live from Death Row," Mumia Abu-Jamal describes what it is like to be accused of a crime and to be sentenced to death row. Abu-Jamal, a former radio reporter, was convicted of the 1982 death of a Philadelphia police officer. He has consistently maintained his innocence and has argued that police vengeance and racial intolerance of his views resulted in an unfair trial and an unjust conviction. Overall, Abu-Jamal gives us insight into the lives and perceptions of people classified as criminals.

Bruce Shapiro explores the ways in which the realities of crime can be quite different from news images of crime. In "One Violent Crime," Shapiro explains how his experience as a victim of a violent crime got used in a news story about a crime bill. He describes not only how he felt seeing himself on television, but also how his experience was unrelated to the bill it was used to illustrate. He concludes that "getting tough on crime" isn't the answer, for his attacker would not have been stopped by tougher crime legislation.

Mike Davis and Sue Ruddick discuss the different perceptions people have of crime and criminals. In "War in the Streets," they describe some of the ways in which law enforcement officials and politicians talk about crime, violence, and gangs; the authors explain the consequences that follow from our describing crime as a "war." Cheryl Russell also discusses perceptions in her essay "True Crime," weighing the crime statistics gathered by law enforcement agencies against the perceptions of crime among most Americans. She concludes that attitudes toward crime are shaped more powerfully by images than by the realities of crime. These attitudes, she suggests, will shape our behaviors in the coming years.

In "Saving Youth from Violence," Frank Hechinger assembles evidence from a variety of sources to demonstrate that problems of violence in our cities are answerable only when we take into account the cultural, economic, political, psychological, and social realities of contemporary urban life. For Hechinger, saving youth from violence is clearly more than a matter of limiting access to guns. Luis Rodriguez also argues that there is more to addressing crime than controlling guns. In "Turning Youth Gangs Around," Rodriguez writes about his experiences with young gang members in Chicago. He explains that they are not criminals and that they are not inherently violent; instead, he argues, members of gangs are in need of direction, responsibility, and encouragement.

Taken together, these articles offer a range of responses to the issue of violent crime in American cities. The articles raise some of the most important questions Americans face as we search for ways to respond adequately to the images and realities of violence in our society. Should the government "get tough on crime"? What does it mean to "get tough"? How does talk about crime using terms such as "get tough" and "war" ask us to think about people and their actions? Whose perceptions, expectations, and interests does the talk act on? Whose does it ignore? Do we want to live with each other in "us against them" ways? When reading and writing about these and related questions, you will have an opportunity to see how people use talk about urban violence for the purposes of either instilling fear, despair, and blame or fostering hope, promise, and community.

PREREADING ASSIGNMENTS

1. Freewrite for ten minutes about a violent or nonviolent crime that recently happened to you or to someone you know—or that you or someone you know recently committed. Consider different kinds of crime—everything from rape and murder to cheating on taxes and buying beer underage. What was the experience like? Did it change your perceptions about crime? About cities? How did it change your perceptions about crime, cities, and fear of crime? How did it not change your perceptions about crime?

2. List all the terms that you frequently hear the media use to discuss crime. Then try to explain what the list tells us about media perceptions of crime. What types of terms and images are used most often? Why do you think such language and images are used? Is it to scare people? Or is it to make them feel secure? Or vengeful? Or something else? How might crime as depicted in the mass media be different from crime in real life? If you see a difference between crime in real life and crime as depicted in the media, how do you account for that difference?

3. Try to describe your own attitudes toward crime. What do you think causes crime? Is a crime simply the act of a "criminal" individual who chooses to do wrong? If so, then what makes someone a criminal? Or is crime caused by social factors such as poverty, lack of opportunity, racism, a violent society? Or is it some of both? Explain your answers.

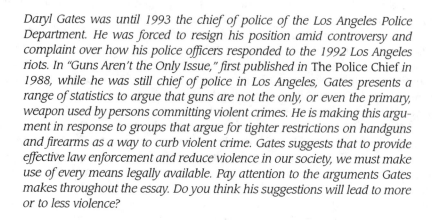

Daryl Gates was until 1993 the chief of police of the Los Angeles Police Department. He was forced to resign his position amid controversy and complaint over how his police officers responded to the 1992 Los Angeles riots. In "Guns Aren't the Only Issue," first published in The Police Chief *in 1988, while he was still chief of police in Los Angeles, Gates presents a range of statistics to argue that guns are not the only, or even the primary, weapon used by persons committing violent crimes. He is making this argument in response to groups that argue for tighter restrictions on handguns and firearms as a way to curb violent crime. Gates suggests that to provide effective law enforcement and reduce violence in our society, we must make use of every means legally available. Pay attention to the arguments Gates makes throughout the essay. Do you think his suggestions will lead to more or to less violence?*

Guns Aren't the Only Issue

Daryl F. Gates

Chief of Police,
Los Angeles Police Department, California

GUNS, KNIVES, CHAINSAWS, syringes, rope and blunt objects serve many diverse legitimate purposes. Unfortunately, they are all part of a long list of items used for a common purpose. They are tools of violence in our violence-prone population. In Los Angeles, each of those instruments has been used to commit the ultimate violence—murder. It is no surprise that the murder weapon of choice, however, is a gun.

In 1986, of 831 homicide victims in Los Angeles, 520 were murdered by suspects using a gun. Of these, 374 murderers used a handgun, 35 used a rifle, 56 used a shotgun and 55 used an unknown type of firearm. Of 2,411 forcible rapes, 277 rapists used a gun; of 30,105 robberies, 9,862 robbers used a gun; and of 33,560 aggravated assaults, 7,911 suspects used firearms.

Daryl F. Gates. "Guns Aren't the Only Issue." Reprinted from *The Police Chief* (March 1988): 55. Copyright held by the International Association of Chiefs of Police, Inc., 515 N. Washington Street, Alexandria, VA 22314. Further reproduction without the express permission from IACP is strictly prohibited.

Of those 66,907 violent crimes, 28 percent were committed by criminals armed with guns.

Viewed in that light, perhaps it is understandable that in the desire to reduce violence in our society, we have focused on reducing access to the favored instrument of death more strongly than we have on the wielders of those instruments. In my view, we should not limit our primary attention to only those who are canny enough to select the best tool for their violence. Rather, we should give equal attention to the other 72 percent of violent crimes where some instrument other than a gun was unlawfully used.

Through education, prevention, swift prosecution and commensurately severe punishment, we should focus on the core of the problem—violent people. In keeping with that concept, and in concert with other criminal justice agencies and community organizations, the LAPD is developing wide-ranging programs that are designed to break the cycle of criminal violence.

By way of example, I shall describe one program that has been designed to attack the criminal connection between narcotics, violence and weapons. The bonding agents of this destructive linkage include the following facts:

- The average age of first use of marijuana is 10 years.
- Marijuana is usually the *introductory* drug of abuse that leads to abuse of hard narcotics.
- Narcotics abuse is an epidemic, fueled by a multi-billion dollar narcotics industry that severely threatens the survival of our society.
- Criminals at all levels, including street gangs and organized crime, are heavily involved in narcotic trafficking.
- Major narcotic seizures are often accompanied by seizures of sophisticated firearms and other weapons that are possessed in violation of existing laws.
- Sixty-one percent of the homicides committed in Los Angeles are related to narcotics.

All of the instruments cited earlier have been used as murder weapons in narcotic-related homicides.

The department's attempt to dismantle this nexus includes vigorous enforcement of the many gun laws, but our primary focus is on the common denominator—the people who comprise or supply the illicit drug market. Our strategy is to remove the profits of the narcotic industry by arresting traffickers and abusers at all levels, interdicting their product, seizing assets of suppliers and buyers, vigorously prosecuting offenders, and curbing our society's enormous appetite for illicit drugs through prevention and education programs.

In 1986, the LAPD compiled some impressive statistics in pursuing its strategy. More than 6½ tons of cocaine, 66 pounds of heroin and over 800,000 units of PCP were seized, as were substantial quantities of most other narcotics and illicit drugs. The total street value of all narcotic seizures was $2.8 billion. In addition, over $29.7 million in cash and 2,194 guns were seized. The department made over 46,000 narcotic arrests. Despite those numbers, no claim is made that the narcotic industry has been crippled in Los Angeles. To the contrary, it is still the city's number one crime problem. However, LAPD is making its presence felt and will continue to do so until the anticipated results of these long-range educational programs are achieved.

The centerpiece of our educational programs is DARE (Drug Abuse Resistance Education), the purpose of which is to produce future generations of drug-free Americans. The program was started in 1983 as a joint effort of the LAPD and the Los Angeles Unified School District, which developed the curriculum. It is taught by uniformed police officers in every elementary and junior high school in the district. DARE gives children the skills to recognize and resist both the subtle and the overt pressures that cause them to experiment with drugs and alcohol. The program has spread to 398 communities in 31 states, to Department of Defense overseas schools and to New Zealand.

So far, the effects of the program on students, teachers, parents and the community have exceeded our expectations. Obviously, it is a long-range program. The extent of DARE's ultimate success will be measured by the decline in the demand for drugs. Without a demand, there is no profit, no market competition and no drug-related violence. Therefore, there is no application of the tools of violence, including guns. When those things happen, the nexus will have been broken.

Skeptics might say that such programs take too long, that the results are too uncertain, that commitments are too tenuous and that quick-fix solutions are better. Many of their violence reduction quick-fix solutions focus almost exclusively on guns. But I think they err through omission. Certainly, the many gun laws we now have must be strictly enforced and vigorously prosecuted. But to suggest that the violence now committed by using guns would be eliminated if guns were not lawfully available is a gross exaggeration of their causal connection with the total problem of criminal violence.

I think a far more effective approach is to increase our intolerance for any form of criminal violence, regardless of the weapon used. We must strive to eliminate our tendency to resolve social conflicts through violence. Until then, we must use to the fullest extent those tools of deterrence that are now constitutionally available. This includes capital punishment when appropriate—and it is appropriate far more frequently than it is used.

Discussion Questions

Content

1. What does Gates consider the main cause of violence in America today? What are some of his suggestions for addressing this?

2. What assumptions about crime and law and order does Gates have? Pick out of the article words, phrases, or sentences that express these assumptions. Why would someone make these assumptions and not others? In what ways do these assumptions seem fair, and in what ways do they seem unfair? Do they lay blame for crime in the appropriate place? Or do they draw our attention away from the "real" causes of crime? What might some other assumptions about crime and law and order be? How would Gates's article be different if he wrote it from those assumptions?

3. Gates suggests that, at least for now, we should fight to end violence through constitutionally available "tools of deterrence." How do you evaluate his argument? Is it logical to "fight" violence? What else can we do?

Form

1. What terms does Gates use to characterize the violence of criminals? What words does he use to characterize the force used by police officers? What attitudes does Gates have about the police and about criminals? In what ways do these attitudes determine his conclusions about violence?

2. Gates supplies a wealth of statistics to support his claims that the LAPD programs are effective in combating crime. How well do his statistics support his case? How can the statistics be read as supporting the argument that the LAPD programs are not successful?

3. Whom do you imagine Gates is arguing against in this essay? Indicate specific passages that suggest whom he is opposing. Do you think these are the same people who would be reading *The Police Chief*, the magazine in which this essay originally appeared? If not, why do you think he published the piece there?

Writing Prompts

1. Write a response to "Guns Aren't the Only Issue" in which you explain to Gates how you feel about his many attitudes and responses to crime.

2. Write an essay describing what you think are the real issues behind "the crime issue." How are these issues different from those typically referred to in discussions of crime? Why do you think crime discussions usually refer to certain issues and not others?

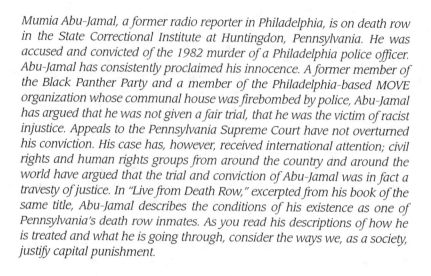

Mumia Abu-Jamal, a former radio reporter in Philadelphia, is on death row in the State Correctional Institute at Huntingdon, Pennsylvania. He was accused and convicted of the 1982 murder of a Philadelphia police officer. Abu-Jamal has consistently proclaimed his innocence. A former member of the Black Panther Party and a member of the Philadelphia-based MOVE organization whose communal house was firebombed by police, Abu-Jamal has argued that he was not given a fair trial, that he was the victim of racist injustice. Appeals to the Pennsylvania Supreme Court have not overturned his conviction. His case has, however, received international attention; civil rights and human rights groups from around the country and around the world have argued that the trial and conviction of Abu-Jamal was in fact a travesty of justice. In "Live from Death Row," excerpted from his book of the same title, Abu-Jamal describes the conditions of his existence as one of Pennsylvania's death row inmates. As you read his descriptions of how he is treated and what he is going through, consider the ways we, as a society, justify capital punishment.

Live from Death Row

Mumia Abu-Jamal

DON'T TELL ME about the valley of the shadow of death. I live there. In south-central Pennsylvania's Huntingdon County, a 100-year-old prison stands, its Gothic towers projecting an air of foreboding, evoking a gloomy mood of the Dark Ages. I and some forty-five other men spend about twenty-two hours a day in a six-by-ten-foot cell. The additional two hours may be spent outdoors, in a chain-link fenced box, ringed by concertina razor wire, under the gaze of gun turrets.

Welcome to Pennsylvania's death row.

I'm a bit stunned. Several days ago the Pennsylvania Supreme Court affirmed my conviction and sentence of death, by a vote of four justices (three did not participate). As a black journalist who was a Black Panther way back in my yon teens, I've often studied America's long history of legal lynchings of Africans. I remember a front page of the *Black Panther* newspaper, bearing the quote: "A black man has no rights that a white man is bound to respect," attributed to U.S. Supreme Court Chief Justice Roger Taney, of the infamous *Dred Scott* case, where America's highest court held that neither Africans nor their "free" descendants are entitled to the rights of the Constitution. Deep, huh? It's true.

Perhaps I'm naive, maybe I'm just stupid—but I thought the law would be followed in my case, and the conviction reversed. Really.

Even in the face of the brutal Philadelphia MOVE massacre of May 13, 1985, that led to Ramona Africa's frame-up, Eleanor Bumpurs, Michael Stewart, Clement Lloyd, Allan Blanchard, and countless other police slaughters of blacks from New York to Miami, with impunity, my faith remained. Even in the face of this relentless wave of antiblack state terror, *I thought my appeals would be successful.* I still harbored a belief in U S. law.

The realization that my appeal had been denied was a shocker. I could understand intellectually that American courts are reservoirs of racist sentiment and have historically been hostile to black defendants, but a lifetime of propaganda about American "justice" is hard to shrug off.

I need but look across the nation, where, as of October 1986, blacks constituted some 40 percent of men on death row, or across Pennsylvania, where, as of August 1988, sixty-one of 113 men—over 50 percent—are black, to see the truth, a truth hidden under black robes and promises of equal rights. Blacks constitute just over 9 percent of Pennsylvania's population and just under 11 percent of America's.

As I said, it's hard to shrug off, but maybe we can do it together. How? Try out this quote I saw in a 1982 law book, by a prominent Philadelphia lawyer named David Kairys: "Law is simply politics by other means." Such a line goes far to explain how courts really function, whether today, or 138 years ago in the *Scott* case. It ain't about "law," it's about "politics" by "other means." Now, ain't that the truth?

I continue to fight against this unjust sentence and conviction. Perhaps we can shrug off and shred some of the dangerous myths laid on our minds like a second skin—such as the "right" to a fair and impartial jury of our peers; the "right" to represent oneself; the "right" to a fair trial, even. They're *not* rights—they're privileges of the powerful and rich. For the powerless and the poor, they are chimeras that vanish once one reaches out to claim them as something real or substantial.

Don't expect the media networks to tell you, for they can't, because of incestuousness between the media and the government, and big business, which they both serve. I can.

Even if I must do so from the valley of the shadow of death, I will....

I have lived in this barren domain of death since the summer of 1983.

For several years now I have been assigned disciplinary-custody status for daring to abide by my faith, the teachings of John Africa, and, in particular, for refusing to cut my hair. For this I have been denied family phone calls, and on occasion I have been shackled for refusing to violate my beliefs.

Life here oscillates between the banal and the bizarre.

Unlike other prisoners, death-row inmates are not "doing time." Freedom does not shine at the end of the tunnel. Rather, the end of the tunnel brings extinction. Thus, for many here, there is no hope.

As in any massive, quasi-military organization, reality on the row is regimented by rule and regulation. As against any regime imposed on human personality, there is resistance, but far less than one might expect. For the most part, death-row prisoners are the best behaved and least disruptive of all inmates.

It also is true, however, that we have little opportunity to be otherwise, given that many death units operate on the "22 + 2" system: twenty-two hours of locked in cell, followed by two hours of recreation out of cell.

All death rows share a central goal: "human storage" in an "austere world in which condemned prisoners are treated as bodies kept alive to be killed," as one study put it.

Pennsylvania's death-row regime is among America's most restrictive, rivaling the infamous San Quentin death unit for the intensity and duration of restriction. A few states allow four, six, or even eight hours out of cell, prison employment, or even access to educational programs. Not so in the Keystone State.

Here one has little or no psychological life. Here many escape death's omnipresent specter only by way of common diversions—television, radio, or sports. Televisions are allowed, but not typewriters: one's energies may be expended freely on entertainment, but a tool essential for one's liberation through judicial process is deemed a security risk.

One inmate, more interested in his life than his entertainment, argued forcefully with prison administrators for permission to buy a nonimpact, nonmetallic, battery-operated typewriter. Predictably, permission was denied for security reasons. "Well, what do y'all consider a thirteen-inch piece of glass?" the prisoner asked. "Ain't that a security risk?"

"Where do you think you'll get that from?" the prison official demanded.

"From my television!"

Request for typewriter denied.

Television is more than a powerful diversion from a terrible fate. It is a psychic club used to threaten those who dare resist the dehumanizing isolation of life on the row. To be found guilty of an institutional infraction means that one must relinquish television.

After months or years of noncontact visits, few phone calls, and ever-decreasing communication with one's family and others, many inmates use television as an umbilical cord, a psychological connection to the world they have lost. They depend on it, in the way that lonely people turn to television for the illusion of companionship, and they dread separation from it. For many, loss of television is too high a price to pay for any show of resistance.

HARRY WASHINGTON SHRIEKS out of an internal orgy of psychic pain: "Niggers! Keep my family's name outcha mouf! Ya freaks! Ya filth! Ya racist garbage! All my family believe in God! Keep your twisted Satanic filth to y'all-self! Keep my family's name outch'all nasty mouf!"

I have stopped the reflexive glance down in front of Harry's cell. For now, as in all the times in the past, I know no one is out near his ground-level cell—I know Harry is in a mouth-foaming rage because of the ceaseless noises echoing within the chambers of his tortured mind. For Harry and I are among the growing numbers of Pennsylvanians on death row, and Harry, because of mind-snapping isolation, a bitterly racist environment, and the ironies, the auguries of fate, has begun the slide from depression, through deterioration, to dementia.

While we both share the deadening effects of isolation, and an environment straight out of the redneck boondocks, Harry, like so many others, has slipped. Many of his tormenters here (both real and imagined) have named him "Nut" and describe him as "on tilt." Perhaps the cruel twists of fate popped his cork—who can say? A young black man, once a correctional officer, now a death-row convict. Once he wore the keys, now he hears the keys, in an agonizing wait for death. The conditions of most of America's death rows create Harry Washingtons by the score.

Mix in solitary confinement, around-the-clock lock-ins, no-contact visits, no prison jobs, no educational programs by which to grow, psychiatric "treatment" facilities designed only to drug you into a coma; ladle in hostile, overtly racist prison guards and staff; add the weight of the falling away of family ties, and you have all the fixings for a stressful psychic stew designed to deteriorate, to erode, one's humanity—designed, that is, by the state, with full knowledge of its effects.

Nearly a century ago, a Colorado man was sentenced to death for killing his wife. On his arrival at Colorado State Penitentiary, James Medley was placed in solitary. Medley promptly brought an original writ of habeas corpus in the U.S. Supreme Court, which in 1890 consisted of six Republicans and three Democrats. In the case, *In re Medley*, 134 US 160 (1890), the Court reached back to old English law, to the early 1700s of King George II, to conclude that solitary confinement was "an additional punishment of the most important and painful character" and, as applied to Medley, unconstitutional.

Fast-forward nearly a century, to 1986, to the infamous federal court decision of *Peterkin v. Jeffes,* where Pennsylvania death-row inmates sought to have solitary confinement declared unconstitutional, and one hears a judge deny relief, saying, in the immortal words of now-Chief Justice Rehnquist, "Nobody promised them a rose garden"—that is, solitary is OK.

The notion that human progress is marked by "an evolving standard of decency," from the less civilized to the more civilized, from the more restrictive to the less restrictive, from tyranny to expanding freedom, dies a quick death on the rocks of today's Rehnquistian courts. Indeed, what other court could make the Republican-controlled, Southern-Harlan-Fuller Court of the 1890s seem positively radical by comparison?

Harry continues his howlings and mindless mutterings of rage at no one in particular.

THERE IS A QUICKENING on the nation's death rows of late—a picking up of the pace of the march toward death. The political prod is sparking movement, and judges in death cases are beginning to find themselves under increasing pressure to make the final judgment.

As murder rates rise in American cities, so too does the tide of fear. Both politicians and judges continue to ride that tide that washes toward the execution-chamber's door. No matter that of the ten states with the highest murder rate, eight lead the country in executions that supposedly deter; no matter that of the ten states with the lowest murder rate, only one (Utah) has executed anyone since 1976. No matter that the effectiveness of the death penalty is not really debated; no matter that the contention that the death penalty makes citizens safer is no longer seriously argued.

States that have not slain in a generation now ready their machinery: generators whine, poison liquids are mixed, gases are measured and readied, silent chambers await the order to smother life. Increasingly, America's northern states now join the rushing pack, anxious to relink themselves with their pre-*Furman* heritage.

Deterrence? The March 1988 execution of Willie Darden in Florida, exceedingly well publicized here and abroad, should have had enormous deterrent effect, according to capital theories. But less than eleven hours after two thousand volts coursed through Darden's manacled flesh, a Florida corrections officer, well positioned to absorb and understand the lessons of the state ritual, erupted in a jealous rage and murdered a man in the maternity wing of a hospital.

Seems like a lesson well learned to me.

Long-termers on the row, those here since 1984, recall a small but seemingly significant event that took place back then. Maintenance and construction staff, forced by a state court order and state statute to provide men with a minimum of two hours daily outside exercise, rather than the customary fifteen minutes every other day, erected a number of steel, cyclone-fenced boxes, which strikingly resemble dog runs or pet pens. Although staff assured inmates that the pens would be used only for disciplinary cases, the construction ended and the assurances were put to the test.

The first day after completion of the cages, death cases, all free of any disciplinary infractions, were marched out to the pens for daily exercise outdoors. Only when the cages were full did full recognition dawn that all the caged men were African.

Where were the white cons of death row?

A few moments of silent observation proved the obvious. The death-row block offered direct access to two yards: one composed of cages, the other "free" space, water fountains, full-court basketball spaces and hoops, and an area for running. The cages were for the blacks on death row. The blacks, due to racist insensitivity and sheer hatred, were condemned to awaiting death in indignity. The event provided an excellent view, in microcosm, of the mentality of the criminal system of injustice, suffused by the toxin of racism.

VISITS ARE AN EXERCISE IN HUMILIATION. In Pennsylvania, as in many other death states, noncontact visits are the rule. It is not just a security rule; it is a policy and structure that attempts to sever emotional connection by denying physical connection between the visitor and the inmate. Visits are conducted in a closed room, roughly eighty square feet in size. The prisoner is handcuffed and separated by a partition of shatterproof glass, steel trim, and wire mesh.

What visitors do not see, prior to the visit, is a horrifying spectacle—the body-cavity strip search. Once the prisoner is naked, the visiting-room guard spits out a familiar cadence:

"Open yer mouth.
Stick out your tongue.
You wear any dentures?
Lemme see both sides of your hands.
Pull your foreskin back.
Lift your sac.
Turn around.
Bend over.
Spread your cheeks.
Bottom of yer feet.
Get dressed."

Several prisoners have protested to the administration that such searches are unreasonable, arguing that body-cavity strip searches before and after noncontact visits cannot be justified. Either allow contact visits, they argue, or halt the body-cavity strip searches. But prison officials have responded to this proposal as they have to repeated calls by the condemned for allowance of typewriters: refusal, due to security risk.

For the visitor, too, such visits are deeply disturbing. In *Rhem v. Malcolm*, the often-cited case on prison conditions in New York, Judge Lasker quoted expert testimony from Karl Menninger, the late psychiatrist, who described noncontact visiting as "the most unpleasant and most disturbing detail in the whole prison," and a practice that constitutes "a violation of ordinary principles of humanity." Dr. Menninger stated: "[I]t's such a painful sight that I don't stay but a minute or two as a rule. It's a painful thing. . . . I feel so sorry for them, so ashamed of myself that I get out of the room."

The ultimate effect of noncontact visits is to weaken, and finally to sever, family ties. Through this policy and practice the state skillfully and intentionally denies those it condemns a fundamental element and expression of humanity—that of touch and physical contact—and thereby slowly erodes family ties already made tenuous by the distance between home and prison. Thus prisoners are as isolated physiologically as they are temporally and spatially. By state action, they become "dead" to those who know and love them, and therefore dead to themselves. For who are people, but for their relations and relationships?

Hurled by judicial decree into this netherworld of despair, forcefully separated from relationships, overcome by the dual shame of their station and the circumstances of the crime that led them to death's door, a few succumb to the shady release of suicide. Some fight Sisyphean battles, struggling to prove their innocence and reverse unjust convictions. Others live as they are treated—as "shadows of [their] former selves, in a pantomime of life, human husks."

To such men and women, the actual executions are a fait accompli, a formality already accomplished in spirit, where the state concludes its premeditated drama by putting the "dead" to death a second time.

IN THE MIDST OF DARKNESS, this little one was a light ray. Tiny, with a Minnie Mouse voice, this daughter of my spirit had finally made the long trek westward, into the bowels of this man-made hell, situated in the south-central Pennsylvania boondocks. She, like my other children, was just a baby when I was cast into hell, and because of her youth and sensitivity, she hadn't been brought along on family visits until now.

She burst into the tiny visiting room, her brown eyes aglitter with happiness, stopped—stunned—staring at the glassy barrier between us and burst into tears at this arrogant attempt at state separation. In milliseconds, sadness and shock shifted into fury as her petite fingers curled into tight fists, which banged and pummeled the plexiglass barrier, which shuddered and shimmied but didn't shatter.

"Break it! Break it!" she screamed. Her mother, recovering from her shock, bundled up Hamida in her arms, as sobs rocked them both. My eyes filled to the brim. My nose clogged.

Her unspoken words echoed in my consciousness: "Why *can't* I hug him? Why *can't* we kiss? Why *can't* I sit in his lap? *Why can't we touch?* Why not?" I turned away to recover.

I put on a silly face, turned back, called her to me, and talked silly to her. "Girl, how can you breathe with all them boogies in your nose?" Amid the rolling trail of tears, a twinkle started like dawn, and before long the shy beginnings of a smile meandered across her face as we talked silly talk.

I reminded her of how she used to hug our cat until she almost strangled the poor animal, and Hamida's denials were developing into laughter. The three of us talked silly talk, liberally mixed with serious talk, and before long our visit came to an end. Her smile restored, she uttered a parting poem that we used to say over the phone: "I love you, I miss you, and when I see you, I'm gonna kiss you!" The three of us laughed and they left.

Over five years have passed since that visit, but I remember it like it was an hour ago: the slams of her tiny fists against that ugly barrier, her instinctual rage against it—the state-made blockade raised under the rubric of security, her hot tears.

They haunt me.

Discussion Questions

Content

1. What are some of the conditions Abu-Jamal describes? What is "life" on death row like?

2. What is Abu-Jamal's claim about the relationship between the death sentence and crime in our cities? What larger claims about crime, criminality, social order, and deterrence can you draw from this piece?

3. Abu-Jamal describes the dehumanization of life on death row. What kind of attitudes toward death row inmates do you think the prison officials and corrections officers have to have in order to enforce these conditions? What public attitudes about crime and criminals influence how we view and interact with people convicted of crimes? In what ways are these attitudes just or injust?

Form

1. The title of Abu-Jamal's book is *Live from Death Row*. In the selection from the book reprinted here, Abu-Jamal emphasizes isolation and death. What might he be saying with his title, and to whom? To us? To himself?

2. Abu-Jamal uses language in certain ways to suggest that the death penalty is used largely against African Americans and people of color. Highlight specific passages in which he makes these claims. What facts does he use? Where does he get his information? At what points do you find his claim compelling? At what points is it not persuasive? Explain your answers.

3. The selection reprinted here ends with Abu-Jamal describing a visit with his daughter. How do you respond to this passage? What is it about the way Abu-Jamal sets up the visit that makes you respond in this way? What do you think your response to the essay might be if the selection began rather than ended with the visit?

Writing Prompts

1. Write an essay describing what you might experience and feel if you were convicted of a crime and cut off from all contact with other persons.

2. Ask several different people their views on the death penalty. Also, listen to the news and read the newspaper for information on the death penalty debate in states other than your own. Once you have a variety of opinions, write a dialogue that explores the many things people have to say about the death penalty. Avoid making any judgments about who's right and who's wrong. Just present what they have to say and have them state some of the reasons they have for their views.

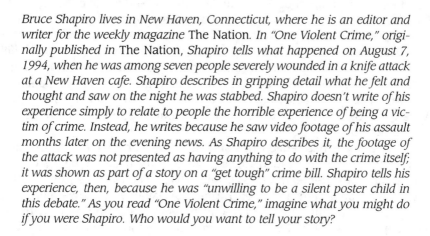

Bruce Shapiro lives in New Haven, Connecticut, where he is an editor and writer for the weekly magazine The Nation. *In "One Violent Crime," originally published in* The Nation, *Shapiro tells what happened on August 7, 1994, when he was among seven people severely wounded in a knife attack at a New Haven cafe. Shapiro describes in gripping detail what he felt and thought and saw on the night he was stabbed. Shapiro doesn't write of his experience simply to relate to people the horrible experience of being a victim of crime. Instead, he writes because he saw video footage of his assault months later on the evening news. As Shapiro describes it, the footage of the attack was not presented as having anything to do with the crime itself; it was shown as part of a story on a "get tough" crime bill. Shapiro tells his experience, then, because he was "unwilling to be a silent poster child in this debate." As you read "One Violent Crime," imagine what you might do if you were Shapiro. Who would you want to tell your story?*

One Violent Crime

Bruce Shapiro

ALONE IN MY HOME I am staring at the television screen and shouting. On the local evening news I have unexpectedly encountered video footage, several months old, of myself writhing on an ambulance gurney—skin pale, shirt open and drenched with blood, trying desperately to find relief from pain.

On the evening of August 7, 1994, I was among seven people stabbed and seriously wounded in a cafe a few blocks from my house. Any televised recollection of this incident would be upsetting. But tonight's anger is quite specific, and political, in origin: My picture is being shown on the news to illustrate why my state's legislature plans to lock up more criminals for a longer time. A picture of my body, contorted and bleeding, has become a propaganda image in the crime war. I had not planned to write about this assault. But for months now the politics of the nation have in large part been the politics of crime, from last year's federal crime bill to the "Taking Back Our Streets" clause of the Contract with America. With a welter of reactions to my

Bruce Shapiro. "One Violent Crime." From *The Nation* (April 1995): 437, 445–452. Reprinted with permission from *The Nation* magazine © The Nation Company, L.P.

own recent experience, one feeling is clear: I am unwilling to be a silent poster child in this debate.

Here is what happened: At about 9:45 P.M. I arrived at the coffeehouse on Audubon Street with two neighborhood friends, Martin and Anna. We sat at a small table near the front; about fifteen people were scattered around the room. Just before ten, as Martin went over to the counter for a final refill, chaos erupted. I heard him call Anna's name. I looked up and saw his arm raised and a flash of metal and people leaping away from a thin, bearded man with a ponytail. Tables and chairs toppled. Without thinking I shouted to Anna, "Get down!" Clinging to each other, we pulled ourselves along the wall toward the door.

What actually happened I was only tentatively able to reconstruct later. Apparently, as Martin headed toward the counter the thin, bearded man, whose name we later learned was Daniel Silva, asked the time from another patron, who answered and then turned to leave. Without warning, Silva pulled out a hunting knife and began moving about the room with de-monic speed, stabbing six people in a matter of seconds. Among these were Martin, stabbed in the thigh and the arm, the woman behind the counter, stabbed in the chest and abdomen while phoning the police, and Anna, stabbed in the side as we pulled each other toward the door.

I had gone no more than a few steps down the sidewalk when I felt a hard punch in my back followed instantly by the unforgettable sensation of skin and muscle tissue parting. Silva had stabbed me about six inches above my waist, just beneath my rib cage. Without thinking, I clapped my hand over the wound before the knife was out, and the exiting blade sliced my palm and two fingers.

"Why are you doing this?" I cried out. I fell, and he leaned over my face, the knife's glittering blade immense. He put the point into my chest. I remember his brown beard, his clear blue-gray eyes looking directly into mine, and the round globe of a streetlamp like a halo above his head.

"You killed my mother," Silva answered. At my own desperate response—"Please don't"—he pulled the knifepoint out of my chest and dis-appeared. A moment later I saw him flying down the street on a battered bicycle.

I lay on the sidewalk, screaming in pain. Every muscle in my back felt locked and contorted; breathing was excruciating. A woman in a white-and-gray plaid dress was sitting on the curb in a stupor, covered with blood. Up the street I saw a police car's flashing lights, then another's, then an officer with a concerned face and a crackling radio was crouching beside me. I stayed conscious as the medics arrived and I was loaded into an ambulance.

Until August 7 Daniel Silva was a self-employed junk dealer and a home-owner. He lived with his mother and several dogs. He had no arrest record. A police detective who was hospitalized across the hall from me recalled Silva as a socially marginal neighborhood character. He was not, apparently, a drug user. He had told neighbors about much violence in his family—showing one a scar on his thigh he said was from a stab wound.

A week earlier, Silva's seventy-nine-year-old mother had been hospitalized for diabetes. After a few days the hospital moved her to a new room; when Silva saw his mother's empty bed he panicked, but nurses swiftly took him to her new location. Still, something seemed to have snapped. On the day of the stabbings, police say, Silva released his dogs, set fire to his house, and rode away on his bicycle as his home burned. He arrived on Audubon Street evidently convinced that his mother was dead.

WHILE I LAY IN THE HOSPITAL, the big story on CNN was the federal crime bill then being debated in Congress. Even fogged by morphine I was aware of the irony. I was flat on my back, with tubes in veins, chest, penis, and abdomen, the result of a particularly violent assault, while Congress was busy passing the anticrime package that I had criticized in print just a few weeks earlier. Night after night, unable to sleep, I watched Republicans and Democrats fall over one another to prove who could be the toughest on crime.

A few days after I returned home, the bill passed. What I found when I finally read its 412-page text was this: Not a single one of those pages would have protected me or Anna or Martin or any of the others from our assailant. Not the extended prison terms, not the forty-four new death-penalty offenses, not the three-strikes-and-you're-out requirements; not the summary deportations of criminal aliens. The even stiffer provisions of the Contract with America, including the proposed abolition of the Fourth Amendment's search and-seizure protections, still would have offered me no practical protection.

On the other hand, the mental-health and social-welfare safety net shredded during the 1980s might have made a difference in the life of someone like my assailant—and thus in the life of someone like me. Silva's growing distress in the days before August 7 was obvious to his neighbors. He had muttered darkly about relatives planning to burn down his house. A better-funded, more comprehensive social-service infrastructure might have saved me and six others from untold pain and trouble.

In fact, it was in no small measure the institutions of an urban community that saved my life that night. The police officer who found me was joined in a moment by a phalanx of emergency medics, and his backups arrived quickly enough to chase down my assailant three blocks away. In minutes I was taken to nearby Yale–New Haven hospital—built in part with the kind of public funding so hated by the right—where several dozen doctors and nurses descended to handle all the wounded. If my stabbing had taken place in the suburbs, I would have bled to death.

One thing I could not properly appreciate in the hospital was how deeply other people were shaken by the stabbings. The reaction of most was a combination of decent horrified empathy and a clear sense that their own presumption of safety had been undermined. But some who didn't bother to acquaint themselves with the facts used the stabbings as a sort of Rorschach test on which they projected their own preconceptions. Some present and former Yale students, for instance, were desperate to see in my stabbing evidence of the great dangers of New Haven's inner city. One student newspaper wrote about "New Haven's image as a dangerous town fraught with violence." A student reporter from another Yale paper asked if I didn't think the attack proved that New Haven needs better police protection. Given the random nature of this assault, it's tempting to dismiss such sentiments. But city-hating is central to today's political culture. Newt Gingrich excoriates cities as hopelessly pestilent, crime-ridden, and corrupt. Fear of urban crime is the right's basic fuel, and defunding cities is a central agenda item for the new congressional majority.

"WHY DIDN'T ANYONE try to stop him?" That question was even more common than the reflexive city-bashing. I can't begin to guess the number of times I had to answer it. Each time, I repeated that Silva moved too fast, that it was simply too confusing. And each time, I found the question not just foolish but offensive.

"Why didn't anyone stop him?" To understand that question is to understand, in some measure, why crime is such a potent political issue. To begin with, the question carries not empathy but an implicit burden of blame; it really asks, "Why didn't *you* stop him?" It is asked because no one likes to imagine oneself a victim. It's far easier to imagine assuming the aggressive power of the attacker, to embrace the delusion of oneself as Arnold Schwarzenegger: *If I am tough enough and strong enough, I can take out the bad guys.*

The country is at present suffering from a huge version of this same delusion, a myth nurtured by historical tales of frontier violence and vigilantism and by the action-hero fantasies of film and television. Bolstered by the social Darwinists of the right, who see society as an unfettered marketplace in which the strongest individuals flourish, this delusion frames the crime debate.

To ask, "Why didn't anybody stop him?" is to imply only two choices: Rambo-like heroism or abject victimhood, fight or flight. And people don't want to think of themselves choosing flight. In last year's debate over the crime bill, conservatives successfully portrayed themselves as those who would stand and fight; liberal were portrayed as ineffectual cowards.

But on the receiving end of a violent attack, the fight-or-flight dichoto-my didn't apply. Nor did that radically individualized notion of survival. At the coffeehouse that night there were no Schwarzeneggers, no stand-alone heroes. But neither were there abject victims. The woman behind the counter helped one of the wounded out the back window; Anna, Martin, and I clung to one another as we escaped; and two patrons who had never met sought a hiding place together around the corner. In the confusion and panic of life-threatening attack, people reached out to one another. This sounds simple, yet it suggests that there is an instinct for mutual aid that poses a profound challenge to the atomized individualism of the right.

I do understand the rage and frustration behind the crime-victim move-ment, and see how the right has harnessed it. Anyone trying to deal with the reality of crime, as opposed to the fantasies peddled to win elections, needs to understand the complex suffering of those who are survivors of such trau-mas, and the suffering and turmoil of their families. I have impressive physi-cal scars, but to me the disruption of my psyche is more significant. For weeks after the attack, I awoke nightly, agitated, drenched with sweat. Any moment of mental repose was instantly flooded with images from that night. Sometimes my mind simply would not tune in at all. My reactions are still out of balance and disproportionate. I shut a door on my finger, not too hard, and my body is suddenly flooded with adrenaline, nearly faint. Walking on the arm of my partner, Margaret, one evening I abruptly shove her to the side of the road because I have seen a tall, lean shadow a block away. An hour after an argument, I find myself quaking with rage, completely unable to restore my sense of calm.

What psychologists call post-traumatic stress disorder is, among other things, a profoundly political state, in which the world has gone wrong, in which you feel isolated from the broader community by the inarticulable extremity of experience. I have spent a lot of time in the past few months thinking about what the world must look like to those who have survived repeated violent attacks—to children battered in their homes and prisoners beaten or tortured behind bars—and to those, like rape victims, whose assaults are rarely granted the public ratification that mine was.

If the use of my picture on television unexpectedly brought me face-to-face with the memory of August 7, some part of the attack is relived for me daily as I watch the gruesome, voyeuristically reported details of the deaths of Nicole Brown Simpson and Ronald Goldman. And throughout the Colin Ferguson trial, as he spoke of falling asleep and having someone else fire his gun, I heard Daniel Silva's calm, secure voice telling me I had killed his moth-er. When I hear testimony by the survivors of that massacre—on a train as comfortable and familiar to them as my neighborhood coffee bar is to me—I feel a great and incommunicable fellowship.

But the public obsession with these trials, I am convinced, has no more to do with the real experience of crime victims than do the posturings of politicians. I do not know what made my assailant act as he did. Nor do I think crime and violence can be reduced to simple political categories. I do know that the answers will not be found in social Darwinism and individualism, in racism, in dismantling cities and increasing the destitution of the poor. To the contrary: every fragment of my experience suggests that the best protection from crime and the best aid to victims are the very social institutions most derided by the right. As a crime victim and a citizen, what I want is the reality of a safe community—not a politician's fantasyland of restitution and revenge. That is my testimony.

Discussion Questions

Content

1. Why does Shapiro say that he is "unwilling to be a silent poster child" in the debate over crime?

2. According to Shapiro, certain politicians have effectively manipulated our opinions of crime in order to gain support for certain public policies. What does this mean? Does Shapiro suggest that these policies are actually working to eliminate crime or not? What relationships between opinion, public policy, and real crime does Shapiro see? Do you believe him? What support do you find for your position in his essay?

3. What do you make of Shapiro's attitude toward violence and anticrime legislation? In what ways does his attitude make sense to you? What experiences with crime cause your attitudes toward crime to be similar to or different from Shapiro's?

Form

1. How does Shapiro use his experience as a crime victim to relate media coverage of crime, the politics of crime, and the situation of his attacker? What do you find effective about the connections he draws? What about them do you find ineffective? Are you more or less prone to believe what he has to say because he claims in the article to be a victim of a crime? Why or why not?

2. What effect does Shapiro's description of his attack have on you as a reader? Do you empathize with him? In what ways is it fair of him to use his attack in this way? In what ways is it unfair?

3. Shapiro describes his feelings of helplessness during his attack and explains his desire to do something to stop his attacker. What popular images of heroes and crime fighters does his description invoke? How do such popular images influence the ways in which Shapiro has presented his story? How do these images influence the manner in which we read his story?

Writing Prompts

1. Recall something that happened to you that you then heard someone else describing. Write a personal essay explaining how it made you feel to overhear the other person's retelling of your story. Consider the following: Did the person get the story right? Why was the person retelling your experience? Was it appropriate for that person to be using and telling your story in the way and for the purposes that he or she did?

2. Write an essay explaining what you think happens to specific events when they are presented in the news or in political debates. Use an event you are familiar with. Consider the choices people make. What information do they emphasize? What do they downplay?

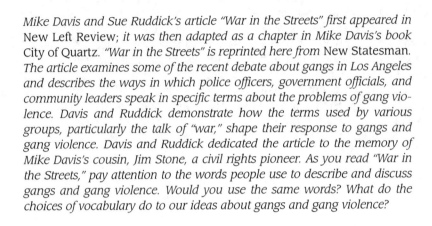

Mike Davis and Sue Ruddick's article "War in the Streets" first appeared in New Left Review; *it was then adapted as a chapter in Mike Davis's book* City of Quartz. *"War in the Streets" is reprinted here from* New Statesman. *The article examines some of the recent debate about gangs in Los Angeles and describes the ways in which police officers, government officials, and community leaders speak in specific terms about the problems of gang violence. Davis and Ruddick demonstrate how the terms used by various groups, particularly the talk of "war," shape their response to gangs and gang violence. Davis and Ruddick dedicated the article to the memory of Mike Davis's cousin, Jim Stone, a civil rights pioneer. As you read "War in the Streets," pay attention to the words people use to describe and discuss gangs and gang violence. Would you use the same words? What do the choices of vocabulary do to our ideas about gangs and gang violence?*

War in the Streets

Mike Davis with Sue Ruddick

ON A WEEKEND IN EARLY APRIL Los Angeles police and sheriff's units arrested more black youth than at any time since the Watts Riots of 1965. A thousand extra-duty patrolmen, backed by elite tactical squads and a special anti-gang task force, imposed Chief Daryl Gate's "Operation Hammer" on ten square miles of black Los Angeles. Like a Vietnam-era search-and-destroy mission—of which many LA police are in fact veterans—the Los Angeles Police Department (LAPD) saturated the streets with its "Blue Machine", "jacking up" thousands of local teenagers at random like surprised peasants. Kids were humiliatingly forced to "kiss the sidewalk" or spreadeagle against police cruisers while officers checked their names against computerised files of gang members. 1,453 were arrested and processed in mobile booking offices, mostly for petty offences like delinquent traffic tickets or curfew violations. Hundreds more, uncharged, had their names entered on the force's gang roster for future surveillance.

Mike Davis with Sue Ruddick. "War in the Streets." From *New Statesman* (Nov. 1988): 27–30. Reprinted with permission from New Statesman & Society.

Chief Gates, who earlier in the year had urged the "invasion" of Colombia, derided civil libertarian protests. "This is war ... we're exceedingly angry .... We want to get the message out to the cowards out there, and that's what they are, rotten little cowards—we want the message to go out that we're going to come and get them." To reinforce the military analogy, the chief of the district attorney's Hardcore Drug Unit added: "This is Vietnam here."

The "them"—the analogical Vietcong—are the members of local *black* gangs, segmented into several hundred fighting "sets" and loosely aligned into two hostile super-gangs, the "Crips" and the "Bloods"—universally distinguished, as everyone who sees Dennis Hopper's *Colors* will know, by their colour-coding of shoelaces, T-shirts and bandannas (red for Bloods, blue for Crips). In the official gang version, reheated and sensationalised by Hollywood, these gangs comprise veritable urban guerrilla armies organised for the sake of rock-cocaine ("crack") and outgunning the police with their huge arsenals of Uzi and Mac-10 automatics. Although the gang cohorts are hardly more than high-school sophomores, local politicians frequently compare them to the "murderous militias of Beirut".

This very real epidemic of youth violence has been inflated by law enforcement agencies and the media into something quite phantasmagoric. The city attorney's office has steadily increased its estimates of hard-core gang membership from 10,000 to 50,000. Local newspapers and television have amplified this figure to 70,000–80,000, while Sheriff's "gang experts" have invoked a spectre of 100,000 "rotten little cowards" overrunning Los Angeles County. Meanwhile an Andromeda strain of Crips and Bloods is reported to have infiltrated the entire west, with accounts of local spores from Seattle to Denver, even mutant white variants in Tucson (such, at least, is the fantasy of hysterical parents).

As long as the actual violence was more or less confined to the ghetto, the gang wars were a fantasy projection and a voyeuristic titillation for white yuppie Westsiders. Then last December frisson became fear as gang hit-men, in a mistaken moment, gunned down a young woman outside a theatre in the posh Westwood Village entertainment district. Westwood's influential merchants, who had recently induced the police to use curfew ordinances to repel non-white youth from the Village, clamoured for extra police protection, while Westwood councillor Zev Yaroslavsky, the Koch-like mayoral candidate, posted a huge reward for apprehension of the "urban terrorists".

The dramatically differential press coverage of, and preferential police response to the Westwood shooting ignited the simmering resentment of black community leaders. They blasted Yaroslavsky, the police and Mayor Bradley for their failure to respond comparably to mayhem in their South-central neighbourhoods. For several weeks the council chambers resounded to an arcane debate over relative police response times in different divisions and the comparative allocations of personnel. This ideologically circumscribed and loaded debate, focusing on the demand for a more "equal" and vigorous prosecution of the war against gangs, provided a long-sought-after signal for the ambitious chief of police who had been broadly distrusted, if not openly reviled, by the black community for his consistent cover-up of the Los Angeles police's racism and brutality.

After the Westwood shooting, black demands for police reinforcements gave Gates an unexpected opportunity to make the pro-police coalition hegemonic in all parts of the divided and socially polarised metropolis. By appearing to respond to the outcry from black neighbourhoods, Gates was able to capture the born-again support of black politicians. To guarantee maximum media coverage, dramatising the department's need for more personnel and resources, Gates launched the first of his anti-gang sweeps. This so-called Gang Related Active Trafficker Suppression program (GRATS) targetted "drug neighbourhoods" for raids by 200–300 police under orders to "stop and interrogate anyone who they suspect is a gang member, basing their assumptions on their dress or their use of gang hand signals". Thus, on the flimsy "probable cause" of red shoelaces or high-five handshakes, the taskforces in February and March mounted nine sweeps, impounded 500 cars and made nearly 1,500 arrests. By Good Friday Chief Gates was gloating over the success of GRATS in drastically curtailing street violence. A few hours after his speech, however, gang members mowed down a crowd on a South-central street corner, killing a 19-year-old woman.

Hysteria again took command in the Civic Center. Yaroslavsky claimed that the city was "fighting a war on gang violence ... that's worse than Beirut". Gates, frantic to retain the limelight, announced the escalation of GRATS into the HAMMER, with deployment of his force's full manpower resources. The first of the thousand-cop *blitzkriegs* hit the streets of South-central LA. Although black politicians rallied almost unanimously to the Hammer, police spokespersons complained of less than enthusiastic support at the embattled grassroots. Civil rights organisations reported an unprecedented number of complaints, in the hundreds, about illegal police harassment.

Given an open warrant to terrorise gang members and crack dealers, the police predictably exceeded the call of duty. On 5 April they shot down an unarmed teenager cowering behind a small palm tree on Adams Boulevard. He was alleged to be reaching suspiciously into his pants; more importantly, he was a "suspected gang member". A few weeks later, Hammer forces, storming a supposed "rock house", poured double-ought buckshot into an 81-year-old retired construction worker. No drugs were actually found, there was strong suspicion that the police had an incorrect address, and the victim's niece—a witness—testified that he had been killed with his hands up. The police department simply replied that gangs were paying off elderly people to use their homes as sales points.

In a season when every gang murder was a headline atrocity, these two police homicides caused barely a blip. One of the few groups willing to criticise the Hammer was the Southern California chapter of the American Civil Liberties Union. Attorney Joan Howarth, who defends youth civil liberties for the ACLU, was vigorous in denouncing the catch-as-catch-can sweeps as "publicity stunts", designed to glorify Gates and to shift scarce tax resources to the greedy LAPD. Howarth pointed out that the Hammer involved the massive infringement of youth civil rights—not to mention police shootings—with little practical effect except to enrage gangs while increasing their outlaw prestige. She emphasised the relative ineffectiveness of repression—short of police death-squads or mass internment—in countering the economic or psychological inducements to gang membership. Despite nearly a thousand Crips and Bloods segregated in their own special wing of LA's county jail, and the several thousand more incarcerated at all levels of the penal system, from youth camp to death row, gang recruitment has remained strongly on the upswing.

James Hahn, LA's aggressive young city attorney, has also questioned the efficacy of mere shows of force like the Hammer. But if Gates' persona is that of a General Westmoreland, then Hahn's approach is reminiscent of an ambitious bureaucrat in an authoritarian state like South Africa or Chile. From his standpoint the underlying problem is the law itself, with its "excessive" guarantees of due process to criminal individuals. Like the prosecutors of Communists earlier this century, he proposed to criminalise an entire class, in this case gang members, and to suspend their protections under the Bill of Rights.

As the legislature continues to debate gang criminalisation under the shadow of California's newly conservatised Supreme Court (which would almost certainly sustain the constitutionality of such legislation), progressive opposition is desultory. Joan Howarth of the ACLU complains, more in sadness than bitterness, that "progressives have virtually deserted us on this issue ... the left has been largely shut out of the policy debate which is now totally framed by the Reaganite right and its Democratic shadow. There is no progressive agenda on crime, and, consequently, no challenging of the socioeconomic forces that have produced the burgeoning counter-culture of gang membership."

In justifying this aggressive strategy, the gangbusters themselves look no further than to recapitulation of traditional white prejudice—ie, "family failure" in the ghetto, abetted by indulgent welfarism and the decline of paternal role models, has created a feral population of grave social menace. Thus mayoral challenger Yaroslavsky, once the McGovern organiser at UCLA, now snarls when asked about the "economic roots of the gang problem". As head of the city council's finance committee, Yaroslavsky has been responsible for issuing Chief Gates' blank cheques. In a city where emergency care for the poor has virtually collapsed, where 50,000 nightly go homeless, and where non-white infant mortality levels are inching upwards towards third world levels—Yaroslavsky has put firepower above all.

In past years this pitiless approach to juvenile crime might simply have been dismissed as the venom of white backlash. But this time there is an angry "blacklash" as well. The qualitatively new, and disturbing, element is the swelling support of black leadership for the "war on gangs". Thus the National Association for the Advancement of Colored People controversially endorsed Hahn's attempt to impose martial law on a gang called the Playboy Gangsters operating on the edge of rich white neighbourhoods, while the South Central Organising Committee has led the fight for greater police deployment against street youth.

The trend is probably national. Although Jesse Jackson continues to campaign for a programme of rescuing ghetto youth, including gang members, others argue that vigilantism has become the order of the day. In an essay written from Oakland, "Ground Zero", the novelist Ishmael Reed predicts that the time is fast approaching when the black working class—"people who've put in time at stupid dull jobs all their lives and suffered all manner of degradation so that their children might become achievers"—will have to take the offensive against "black terrorists … the brutal crack fascists". Comparing daily existence in East Oakland to the oppression in Haiti under the Tontons Macoutes, Reed pours scorn on the white liberals from the Berkeley and Oakland hills "who have 'Out of Nicaragua' bumper stickers on their Volvos but are perfectly willing to tolerate drug fascists who prey upon the decent citizens of Oakland." In order to save black America, Reed canvasses the idea of a curfew for 18-to-24-year-olds and a much sterner community invigilation of youth.

Black revulsion against youth criminality—indeed the perception that dealers and gangs threaten the very integrity of black culture—is thus the catalyst for a realignment of the usual politics of law and order, laying the basis for a potential tidal-wave majority for repression. The traditional antipathy between inner-city black communities and the police is now overlaid by a more urgent, transposed fear of gang culture. Once fiery nationalist intellectuals like Reed openly float the idea that a "sacrifice" of the criminalised stratum of the young may be the only alternative to the dissolution of a community fabric heroically built up over generations of resistance to racist white America. How is it, in days of such apparent rainbow hopes, that relations between old and young in the black community have grown so grimly foreboding?

Over the last 10 years white-collar and professional blacks have abandoned the plains of South-central LA for upscale homes in the city. Working-class blacks in the flatlands have faced relentless economic decline. City resources have been absorbed in financing the corporate renaissance of downtown, but black small businesses have withered and jobs programmes have virtually disappeared. Most devastatingly, the old Eastside manufacturing belt of auto, steel, rubber and electrical plants, upon which working-class black LA always looked for high-wage jobs and occupational mobility, has been entirely restructured. Gross manufacturing employment still managed to expand, but "reindustrialisation" has overwhelmingly centred on minimum-wage sweatshops.

Blacks in California, especially young men, have been excluded from the latest suburban job booms. It is a stunning fact—emblematic of institutional racism on a far more rampant scale than usually admitted these days—that most of California's job and residential growth areas have black populations of one per cent or less. Apart from losing mobility in relocated industrial or transport jobs, young blacks have been locked out of the more attractive service-sector entry-level positions. Young black males, for example, are most apparent by their absence in the sales force of regional shopping malls—jobs coveted by white teenagers. On the other hand, young blacks willing to accept menial service jobs find themselves in a losing competition with new immigrants, not least because of clear employer opinions about labour "docility". As a result, unemployment among black youth in LA County, despite unbroken regional growth and a new explosion of conspicuous consumption, remains at a staggering 45 per cent.

This bias in labour-market trends affecting young black men is so specific and extreme that it is no wonder that black scholars increasingly invoke the "endangered black male", the "new black morbidity", or white society's de facto "declaration of war". What is happening to black males in the labour market is only one dimension, albeit crucial, of the socio-economic crisis, the poverty, especially among the young, the dismantling of youth employment schedules, segregation in the schools, cutbacks in youth policies which has incubated the counter-economy of youth crime and drug dealing.

Revisiting Watts nearly a generation after a famous pioneering study of its problems, UCLA industrial relations economist Paul Bullock discovered that conditions had grown far worse since 1965. At the core of community despair was endemic youth unemployment. The only rational option open to youth—at least in the neoclassical sense of individual economic choice—was to sell drugs. Indeed as power resources in the community have declined, ghetto youth, refusing simply to become "expendable" have regrouped around the one social organisation that seems to give them clout: the street gang.

Since the militarisation of federal drug enforcement in south Florida in 1982, Los Angeles, according to US attorney Robert Bonner, has displaced Miami as "the principal distribution centre for the nation's cocaine supply". At the street level, retailing is franchised to the gangs who run the so-called "rock houses", fortified apartments or bungalows that act as drug convenience stores. In South-central LA rock or crack houses are now more common than liquor stores; the police estimate that there are 150, maybe 200, houses, each turning over more than $5,000 per day ($25,000 on welfare and social security cheque days). The rock houses—employing usually four youth: a leader, a setter, a guard and a look-out—transform the powder into the crystalline rock form suitable for smoking and sell it on.

Cocaine was until recently a glamour drug. Then, in 1983–84, $25 rock hit the streets of LA and a few other cities. It is important to remember that crack is not simply cheap cocaine, but a quite lethal form. Indeed it is the most addictive substance known to science—an absolute commodity that permanently enslaves its consumers. As the street supply has burgeoned, gang rivalries have exploded into violent battles over sales territories and profits.

The appearance of crack has given gang culture a terrible, almost irresistible momentum. Economic pathology, not surprisingly, is a more powerful causal factor than putative syndromes of "family breakdown" or "ghetto culture". Which is not simply to reduce the gang phenomenon to mere economic determinism. Gang bonding has always offered a terrible and total love, a solidarity which closes out other empathies and transmutes self-hate into a festival of rage. But the Crips and Bloods—decked out in Gucci T-shirts and expensive Nike airshoes, ogling rock dealers driving by in BMWs—are also authentic creatures of the age of Reagan. Their world view, above all, is formed of an acute awareness of what is happening down on the Westside, where gilded youth, at moral degrees "less than zero", practise the insolent indifference and hungry avarice that are probably also forms of street violence.

The shattering effects of gang violence and crack addiction upon lower-income communities pose urgent, and immensely difficult, problems for advocates of grassroots politics and rainbow coalition. How to steer between support for the police on the one hand and ignoring the cries of desperation from terrorised working-class families on the other?

The tactical responses from the left have so far not been brilliant. Thus, Mark Naison, a distinguished historian of black history, proposes "dramatic measures to break the stranglehold of criminal elements in poor neighbourhoods". His programme includes placing "drug-related offenders in work camps in rural areas, physically removing them from the neighbourhoods, while new youth programmes are put in place"; "more vigilant law enforcement at the local level, something which community residents in every low income neighbourhood have been demanding for years"; and "a national service requirement should be instituted immediately sending *millions* of middle-class youngsters into poor neighbourhoods to staff day-care centres and clinics, work in schools and community centres and set up programmes in theatre, music, and sports". The half-baked character of these proposals betrays the superficiality of analysis and the scant concern for juvenile civil liberties. And realistically, what strategy does he propose to generate the social resources to reconstruct the political economy of the inner city?

Practically all the ideas put forward, like gun control, are almost irrelevant to the scale of the problem at hand. The first and greatest nightmare is rampant youth poverty and inequality—the reduction of our children to social refuse. For socialists this is the "deep structure" of the problem of juvenile crime that must take precedence in every discussion, whether of etiology or of treatment. Legalising cocaine will not alter the structure of minority youth employment or turn the gangs into pacifists. By the same token, to seek palliatives at the level of a "left law and order programme" in the name of the "working class" may be a worse delusion.

Meanwhile more repression only sows dragon's teeth. If, as Gates, Hahn and Bradley all maintain, the gangs really are an "urban guerrilla army" and this is really "war", then only extermination will ultimately conquer. The strictly punitive strategy, now embraced by all sides of the political establishment, including many blacks and liberals, will assuredly make the nightmare worse. The logic of civil libertarians has never been more compelling: the rights taken away from gang members will be rights denied all minority youth; the walls put around gangs will imprison whole communities; the police state once expanded will not easily be contracted.

The social polarisation across Los Angeles, and late imperial America as a whole, has been internalised as a firestorm of self-violence within oppressed communities; it is not an uprising of the poor against the rich. The gangs are solidly rooted in old-fashioned economic survivalism, the "getting your own piece" ethos that Americans worship. As the novelist Claude Brown reminds us: "The nation's young crack dealers are merely pursuing the American dream along what they see as the only channel open to them— drug-dealing entrepreneurial ventures. True, it's a high-risk endeavour, but so is life in America for minority youth. As they see it, what alternatives do they have."

Yet we should never concede that this is a "lost generation". As LA inner-city organisers constantly point out, the gangs flourish in part because more humane and radical role models were literally shot down by the police in the 1960s. Nothing is more important than an alternative model of youth culture and self-organisation, a different channel for passion and group-bonding that points towards the resumption of the struggle for liberation. It is disappointing that the immense excitement of the Rainbow Coalition has not been translated into the creation of a "Rainbow youth movement" in the inner cities, drawing from the examples of SNCC, the Panthers, the "Comrades" of Soweto, and so forth. Like so much else, this remains both a dream deferred and a last hope.

Discussion Questions

Content

1. According to the article, what circumstances led to the "war" in Los Angeles and what conclusions could residents, activists, police, and politicians draw from the events?

2. What do you think are the main points of the article? How do your perceptions of the main points of the article differ from the perceptions of other students in your class? In what ways do they differ? Why do you think they differ?

3. The authors argue that neither tougher law enforcement nor widespread social programs alone can address the issue of crime. What possible solutions are left? Is a combination of solutions the answer? How so?

Form

1. What consequences follow from the way in which LAPD, the city government, and even the article's authors describe the inner city as "Vietnam"? What consequences follow from their speaking about police work in terms of "war" and "terrorism"? What does such talk allow us to say? What does it prevent us from saying? Are these the things we want to be saying? Why or why not?

2. How would you characterize the tone of the article? How does the tone encourage you to respond to the article? Does it make you agree with the article? Does it anger you? Or does it sadden you? Explain why.

3. Davis and Ruddick demonstrate that images of war and violence are widespread in talk about crime. They even describe how these images are important to movies like *Colors*. What images from movies, songs, and television do Davis and Ruddick use in talking about crime? What is the relationship between the language of the article and the language of violence in popular culture? What do these languages have to do with real crime?

Writing Prompts

1. Think of a word other than *war* to describe urban violence. Use the images associated with that word to discuss crime in American cities.

2. Imagine and write a conversation between community residents, a community activist, a police officer, and a politician in which each of the participants gives his or her perspectives on what to do about crime. Allow each participant to speak at least three times. When each participant speaks, have him or her speak for at least three lines. In the end, do not let any participant win the discussion.

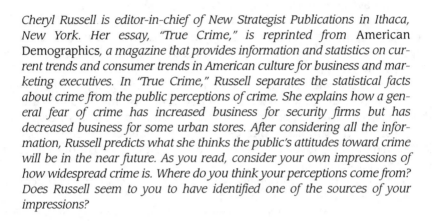

Cheryl Russell is editor-in-chief of New Strategist Publications in Ithaca, New York. Her essay, "True Crime," is reprinted from American Demographics, *a magazine that provides information and statistics on current trends and consumer trends in American culture for business and marketing executives. In "True Crime," Russell separates the statistical facts about crime from the public perceptions of crime. She explains how a general fear of crime has increased business for security firms but has decreased business for some urban stores. After considering all the information, Russell predicts what she thinks the public's attitudes toward crime will be in the near future. As you read, consider your own impressions of how widespread crime is. Where do you think your perceptions come from? Does Russell seem to you to have identified one of the sources of your impressions?*

True Crime

Cheryl Russell

THE HOUR IS LATE. The city street lies dark and empty. Solitary footsteps echo on the pavement. Ahead, an ominous shape lurks in a storefront. Suddenly you're face to face with a gun-wielding, homicidal maniac. You panic. Is it time to run, or time to turn off the TV?

Crime in America has come home. Ask anyone; they can tick off the names, dates, and grisly details from the Oklahoma bombing, the O.J. Simpson double-murder trial, the kidnapping and murder of Polly Klaas, the drowning of Susan Smith's children, the roadside slaying of Michael Jordan's father, the Long Island Railroad massacre, the never-ending string of post office shootings, and on and on. Crime was the number-one issue of concern to the public in 1994, according to the Conference Board. Ninety percent of Americans say that crime is a "serious" problem.

No one escapes the repercussions of Americans' obsession with crime. Some segments of the economy even profit from it. Forty-three percent of Americans have had special locks installed on their doors, and 18 percent have burglar alarms, according to a 1993 Gallup Poll. Half of American house-holds own guns, and sales of personal-security devices such as mace and pep-per spray have been brisk in recent years.

More businesses are hurt than helped by the fear of crime. Downtown areas lose shoppers to suburban shopping malls, while tourists and home-buyers shy away from areas where the media have publicized particularly heinous offenses.

Not only do Americans think crime is a terrible problem; they believe it's getting worse. Nearly nine in ten say there was more crime in 1993 in the U.S. than there was a year before, according to a Gallup poll. This perspective accounts for the popularity of a get-tough attitude toward criminals, from stiffer penalties for juvenile offenders to three-strikes-you're-out life terms for repeat felony criminals.

Support for the death penalty has grown from just under 50 percent in the early 1960s to 80 percent in 1994.

But is crime really overwhelming America? The public says yes, but crime statistics are contradictory—and so are the experts. Separating the myths from the facts is the best way to understand the current mood of the public. And when you take a close look, one thing becomes clear. Every organization should position itself for a future in which fear of crime is likely to play a major role.

Fuel for Fear

Crime has become a hot issue for a number of reasons, beginning with the media. The public's concern with crime rises and falls in lockstep with media reporting about the issue. High-profile crimes create sensational news cov-erage. And the greater the news coverage, the larger the proportion of Americans who cite crime as the most important problem facing the coun-try, according to a 1994 analysis in *The Public Perspective* by Jeffrey D. Alderman, director of polling for ABC News. Public concern with crime fol-lows news coverage of crimes with an exactness that proves the importance of the media in shaping public opinion.

In 1994, a *Los Angeles Times* poll asked Americans whether their feelings about crime were based on what they read or saw in the media, or on what they had personally experienced. While 65 percent named the media, only 21 percent named personal experience, and 13 percent said both.

Another reason for the public's heightened concern about crime is the expansion of the middle-aged population. People in the huge baby-boom generation, now aged 31 to 49, are more concerned than young adults about crime. Baby boomers are also more active in protecting themselves from crime. People aged 30 to 49 are more likely than those younger or older to have installed special locks, to have a dog for protection, to have bought a gun, to carry a weapon, or to have a burglar alarm.

In 1995, 38 percent of all American adults are in the 35-to-54 age group, a larger proportion than at any time since the 1950s. The share in this age group will rise to 40 percent by 2000. The middle-aged population is struggling to protect its homes, careers, financial assets, and especially its children. No wonder crime is one of its top concerns.

There is some evidence that the public's fear of crime is driven by a burgeoning population of parents and the crime-crazy media, but not by the facts. Overall crime rates are lower today than they were in the early 1980s. At that time, baby boomers were crime-prone young adults who drove the rates up. And while most Americans believe the crime problem is severe, they think it is much worse elsewhere than it is in their community. Seventy-nine percent of Americans think crime is one of the nation's biggest problems, but only 14 percent name crime as one of the biggest problems in their neighborhood. Sixty-one percent of Americans say they feel "very safe" at home. And most Americans say they are not afraid to walk alone at night near their home.

The average American's fear of crime may be a fear for the future. Forty-three percent say that crime in their local area is increasing. While most Americans feel safe in their home and neighborhood, many do not feel secure in their community or when traveling elsewhere. These feelings will intensify in the years ahead, because those most afraid of crime are a growing segment of the population. Moreover, the worst crime does appear to be on the rise.

A Look at the Data

How bad is the crime scene? The answer isn't easy to find, because the United States keeps two sets of books on crime. One, the FBI's Uniform Crime Reports (UCR), is an annual collection of reported crime in over 16,000 communities across the country. The figures are voluntarily submitted to the FBI by police agencies in those communities. Overall, 95 percent of the population is covered by the police agencies that submit their crime data to the FBI, including 97 percent of the metropolitan population and 86 percent of non-metro residents.

The second data set on crime is the Justice Department's national survey of households, called the National Crime Victimization Survey. In this survey, interviewers ask respondents whether anyone in the household has been a crime victim in the past year. Because many crimes are never reported to police, the National Crime Victimization Survey uncovers much more crime than the police report to the FBI.* By comparing these two data sets, analysts can estimate the amount of crime reported to police.

In 1992, only 39 percent of what the Justice Department refers to as "victimizations" were reported to police. Yet the public's willingness to report crime varies by type of crime. In 1992, the public reported 53 percent of rapes, 51 percent of robberies, 49 percent of assaults, 41 percent of household theft, and 30 percent of personal theft. Motor-vehicle theft is most likely to be reported to the police—75 percent in 1992—because such thefts must be reported to make claims on auto insurance.

Over time, the gap between actual and reported crime has narrowed as Americans have become increasingly willing to complain of misdeeds. The 39 percent reporting level of 1992 was up from 32 percent in 1973. The proportion of aggravated assaults reported to the police increased from 52 percent to 62 percent during those years. The proportion of personal theft reported to police rose from 22 to 30 percent. Today's older, better-educated public is more comfortable interacting with authorities than was the public of two decades ago. This increases the likelihood of reporting crime. In addition, the introduction of 911 emergency phone services makes it easier for people to report crime.

The two databases on crime seem to contradict each other in many cases. The Uniform Crime Reports show crime rising over the past 20 years, while the National Crime Victimization Survey shows crime falling. The total crime rate rose from 4,850 offenses per 100,000 population in 1974 to 5,660 per 100,000 in 1992, a 17 percent increase, then dropped slightly to 5,483 per 100,000 in 1993, according to the UCR. In contrast, the household survey shows the percentage of households "touched" by crime falling from 32 to 23 percent from 1975 to 1992. The exclusion of murder and arson from the household survey cannot explain this contradiction, because the two datasets show crime rates moving in opposite directions even for specific types of crime. For example, the UCR statistics show the rate of aggravated assault rising from 2.16 to 4.42 assaults per 1,000 people between 1974 and 1992, a 105 percent increase. In contrast, the victimization survey shows the aggravated assault rate falling from 10.4 to 9.0 assaults per 1,000 people aged 12 or older during those years.

The trends revealed by the two datasets agree in only two areas. Both show burglary declining and motor-vehicle theft rising. But while the FBI finds that the burglary rate fell 19 percent between 1974 and 1992, the household survey says it fell 48 percent. And while the FBI reports that motor-vehicle theft is up 37 percent, the household survey says just 7 percent.

*The FBI collects statistics on murder and non-negligent manslaughter, forcible rape, robbery, aggravated assault, burglary, larceny, motor-vehicle theft, and arson. The National Crime Victimization Survey covers all but murder/non-negligent manslaughter and arson.

Which dataset is right? The public finds the FBI's rising crime rates most believable, because it is closer to the carnage they see on TV. But most experts believe that the trends revealed in the victimization survey are more accurate because of changes in Americans' propensity to report crime. As people report a larger proportion of crime to police, then the UCR statistics will show an increase even if crime rates remain the same. For example, the fact that a larger proportion of aggravated assaults was reported to police in 1993 than in 1974 could account for much of the increase in aggravated assault reported in the UCR.

The trends in the UCR statistics are questionable because of reporting problems. Yet the trends revealed by the victimization survey may not be completely accurate because they are affected by changes in household size, household location, and the age structure of the population. Single-person households are less likely to be victimized by crime than are larger households. Households in central cities are more likely to be victimized than those in suburban areas. If household size declines and an increasing share of households are located in the suburbs, as in the past 20 years, the proportion of households victimized by crime will decline while crime rates remain unchanged.

The Justice Department reports that if households in 1992 were the same size as those in 1975, the proportion "touched" by crime would have been 23.7 percent in 1992 rather than 22.6 percent. But it would still fall far below the 32 percent of 1975. Adjusting for changes in household location would raise it even further, because it turns out that most of the decline in the proportion of households touched by crime is due to the drop in property crime rather than violent crime. The victimization survey shows the burglary rate dropping by 47 percent between 1973 and 1992, household larceny falling by 22 percent, and personal theft down 35 percent. Violent crime rates, on the other hand, have barely budged.

The changing age structure of the population also affects the crime trends revealed by the victimization survey. . . . Adults are much more likely to be victimized by crime than are older people. Even if crime rates remain unchanged, the overall crime rate should have dropped over the past two decades due to the aging of the population. The fact that the victimization survey shows no significant decline despite the aging of the population suggests that the age-adjusted rate of violent crime is actually on the rise.

Both datasets show violent crime increasing as a proportion of all crime. In the UCR, violent crime grew from 10 to 14 percent of all reported crime from 1974 to 1993. The victimization survey shows the same trend, with violent crime growing from 15 to 20 percent of all crime during those years. This trend alone is enough to alarm the public, since a larger share of the crime around them is of the most-feared type—the random act of violence committed by a stranger.

The UCR shows the rate of violent crime rising fairly steadily since the mid-1970s, peaking in 1992, and standing just below that peak in 1993. The household survey shows the rate of violent crime rising through the early 1980s, falling slightly, then rising again in the early 1990s. The latest statistics from both surveys show violent crime rates today to be close to their all-time high. No wonder people are alarmed.

The trend in violent crime is especially ominous, because the young-adult population—the segment most likely to commit acts of violence—is currently at a low point, due to the small baby-bust generation. As the young-adult population expands with the children of the baby boom in the next decade or so, we can expect a significant increase in violent crime simply because of demographic change.

Small, Southern, and Dangerous

Crime may be pervasive, but each crime is local. This adds another layer of confusion to the crime story. The media's obsessive reporting of every gory detail has increased the public's fear of crime in areas where well-publicized crimes occur. Because the largest number of crimes occur in the most populous metropolitan areas, many people have an exaggerated sense of danger in these places. At the same time, they feel safe in smaller metropolitan areas that may be more dangerous than some big cities. This public confusion is documented in a 1993 Gallup poll that asked Americans to rank cities according to their danger of crime. Out of a list of 15 cities, Americans correctly ranked Miami and New York as first and second in crime danger. UCR statistics show that the metropolitan area with the highest violent crime rate is Miami, with 2,136 per 100,000 people.* Second is New York, with 1,866. The public ranked Washington, D.C., as the 4th most dangerous city, with two-thirds saying Washington, D.C. is a dangerous place to live or visit. But its violent crime rate (771 per 100,000 people) places it 88th among the 245 metro areas reporting violent crimes to the FBI in 1993. This rate is far below that of San Francisco or Dallas. Yet only 42 percent of the public think San Francisco is dangerous, and just 24 percent think Dallas is dangerous.

The metropolitan area with the third-highest rate of violent crime is one most Americans have never heard of: Alexandria, Louisiana. The fourth is no surprise—Los Angeles–Long Beach. Fifth is Tallahassee, Florida. Other lesser-known cities on the top-ten list are Baton Rouge, Louisiana; Little Rock, Arkansas; Jacksonville, Florida; and Pueblo, Colorado.

The UCR statistics show that the South is a region plagued by crime. Of

---

* The National Crime Victimization Survey is not large enough to supply data for metropolitan areas, so the Uniform Crime Reports are the only source of local data on crime.

the ten metros with the highest rates of violent crime, seven are in the South. Of the top 20, 16 are in the South. Of the top 50, 35 are in the South. Several factors account for the South's high rate of crime. One is the warm climate, which allows people to get out and into trouble year-round. The rate of violent crime peaks in July and August, when hot weather shortens tempers, according to the FBI.

Another reason for the South's high rate of violent crime may be the rapid growth of many of the region's metropolitan areas. The list of the nation's fastest-growing metros looks very similar to the list of the most dangerous. Florida alone is home to 9 of the 50 metropolitan areas with the highest rates of violent crime: Miami (1), Tallahassee (5), Jacksonville (8), Gainesville (11), Tampa (15), Ocala (22), Orlando (26), Fort Lauderdale (41), and Lakeland (45). Other fast-growing metros are also on the list, such as Charlotte-Gastonia, North Carolina (16) and Las Vegas (49). These popular metropolitan areas—many touted as wonderful retirement and recreation areas—have much higher crime rates than the cities Americans fear, such as Atlanta (54th in its rate of violent crime), Boston (85), Washington, D.C. (88), and Philadelphia (114).

The FBI's local crime rates are often criticized by civic leaders in crime-prone cities. And in fact, many variables can skew these data. If fewer robberies are reported in New York City than in Tallahassee, for example, New York's rate will look too low, while Tallahassee's will look too high. When Tallahassee launched an aggressive campaign against sex crimes in the mid-1980s, the number of reported rapes increased three times faster than the overall crime rate. Wherever police are aggressive against criminals but approachable to the public, a high proportion of total crimes will be reported.

Still, the FBI data are the only source of information on local crime rates. And the same regional patterns show up in the crime most difficult to hide: murder. New York ranks 5th and Washington, D.C. ranks 28th among the 255 metropolitan areas that supplied their 1993 murder statistics to the FBI. But the nation's highest murder rate is in New Orleans, followed by Shreveport-Bossier City, Louisiana; Jackson, Mississippi; and Jackson, Tennessee. Of the ten metropolitan areas with the highest murder rates, seven are in the South. Among the top 20, 17 are in the South. Among the top 50, 38 are in the South.

Murder is not included in the Justice Department's victimization survey. But the UCR statistics show that 24,530 Americans were murdered in 1993, or 9.5 murders per 100,000 people. This rate is up 20 percent from a low of 7.9 in 1984 and 1985. This is cause for concern, because the increase occurred despite the shrinking size of the crime-prone young-adult population.

The Next Decade of Crime

The experts agree that violent crime will increase in the years ahead, for demographic reasons alone. The number of Americans aged 15 to 24 is projected to rise 14 percent between 1995 and 2005. Those most likely to commit crime or to be victimized by crime are teenagers and young adults. What's more, crime-prone age groups are getting wilder in the 1990s. The violent crime victimization rate for 16-to-19-year-olds rose from 73.8 to 77.9 per 1,000 between 1989 and 1992, according to the Justice Department's survey. The rate for 12-to-15-year-olds rose from 62.9 to 75.7, and the rate among 20-to-24-year-olds rose from 57.8 to 70.1. Young black men are now so vulnerable to crime that homicide is the leading cause of death for black men aged 15 to 24.

Violent crime may also increase as people's sense of community dwindles. The emergence of highly individualistic generations in the U.S. and other countries has weakened community standards and eroded public trust. The percentage of Americans who think most people can be trusted fell from 55 percent in 1960 to 36 percent in 1993. The emergence of a highly individualistic population that is indifferent toward public judgment has disturbing consequences that ripple through society. One of the consequences is an increase in violence at society's margins.

As violent crime increases in the next decade, the powerful baby-boom generation will have children entering the age group most likely to be victimized by crime. These converging trends will probably increase public hysteria over crime in years to come. Specifically:

- Expect middle-aged Americans to demand more protection for their children, whether they are toddlers in day care or young adults in college. Institutions of higher education are likely to discover that the old-fashioned policy of *in loco parentis* has powerful advantages as a marketing tool. Strict on-campus discipline will appeal to fearful parents who are unwilling to grant their children independence at the vulnerable age of 18.
- The public's fear of crime will ensure an ongoing fascination with true crime stories. In this respect, the O.J. Simpson trial is just a harbinger of things to come. Expect at least one major crime story to be at the top of the news at all times from now on.
- The public will shy away from gratuitous fictional violence, because they are so afraid of the real thing. Audiences will demand happy endings from their fiction because there are so many tragedies in real life.
- The personal-security industry will offer increasingly creative high-tech ways to protect oneself, from alarms and security cards to hidden cameras. A growing number of crimes will be captured on videotape and fed to the suppliers of 24-hour news.

- The gun lobby will lose power as an older, educated public demands reasonable compromise in the gun control debate. A growing number of politicians will advocate gun control as their constituents tire of random violence.
- Retailers, restaurateurs, shopping malls, office buildings, train stations, and other public places will offer more visible security. Expect growing demand for guards, metal detectors, and escorts. Even neighborhoods will become more security-conscious. When the baby-boom generation retires, it may retreat behind the walls of a gated community.

Discussion Questions

Content

1. According to Russell, why have Americans become obsessed with crime?

2. What does crime have to do with the idea of community and our hopes for the future? In what ways do people's ideas about crime and their fear of crime lead them to think about their communities and their futures in specific ways?

3. Given the information that Russell presents—the crime statistics and the explanations of public attitudes—what sense do you make of the American fear of crime? In what ways is it justified? In what ways do you believe it is unjustified? What does our fear of crime say about Americans as a whole?

Form

1. Russell describes how Americans are assaulted with crime through their televisions. In what similar ways does she assault us to "bring crime home"? What are the effects on you as the reader when she uses these techniques?

2. Russell's article is written for businesspeople interested in the attitudes of consumers. How do you think this purpose shapes the manner in which she presents her information? What is she trying to get businesspeople to think and do? How would her article be different if her intended audience were, say, a neighborhood watch group? Or a sociology class?

3. Does Russell's essay treat facts and attitudes equally? Or does she favor one over the other? Indicate some passages that show how she treats facts and attitudes. What is the effect of these treatments on you as a reader?

Writing Prompts

1. Using the information and statistics provided by Russell, write an essay persuading tourists of how safe or unsafe American cities are.

2. Describe the ways in which your feelings about crime are both similar to and different from those of most Americans.

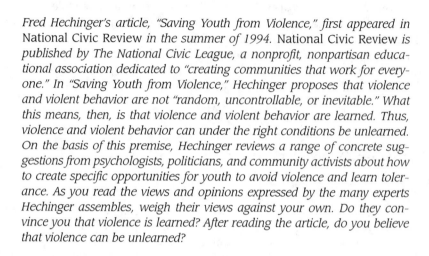

Fred Hechinger's article, "Saving Youth from Violence," first appeared in National Civic Review *in the summer of 1994.* National Civic Review *is published by* The National Civic League, *a nonprofit, nonpartisan educational association dedicated to "creating communities that work for everyone." In "Saving Youth from Violence," Hechinger proposes that violence and violent behavior are not "random, uncontrollable, or inevitable." What this means, then, is that violence and violent behavior are learned. Thus, violence and violent behavior can under the right conditions be unlearned. On the basis of this premise, Hechinger reviews a range of concrete suggestions from psychologists, politicians, and community activists about how to create specific opportunities for youth to avoid violence and learn tolerance. As you read the views and opinions expressed by the many experts Hechinger assembles, weigh their views against your own. Do they convince you that violence is learned? After reading the article, do you believe that violence can be unlearned?*

Saving Youth from Violence: Charting New Paths to Safety

Fred M. Hechinger

THERE IS A GROWING BELIEF among experts that the trend toward ever-more violent behavior in America can be reversed. The report of the American Psychological Association's commission on youth and violence concluded from psychological research that violence is not a random, uncontrollable, or inevitable occurrence: "Many factors, both individual and social, contribute to an individual's propensity to use violence, and many of these factors are within our power to change. . . . There is overwhelming evidence that we can intervene effectively in the lives of young people to reduce or prevent their involvement in violence."

Ronald G. Slaby, a psychologist at Harvard University and a member of the APA commission, concurs: "Violence is learned, and we can teach children alternatives."

Fred M. Hechinger. "Saving Youth from Violence: Charting New Paths to Safety." From *National Civic Review* 83, 2 (Spring/Summer 1994): 126–138. Reprinted with permission from *National Civic Review*.

Some Strategies Against Violence

Carnegie Corporation of New York president David A. Hamburg observes: "You have to assume that if kids grow up in reasonably good shape, and with some sense of decent opportunities, then the risk of taking to the gun will be much less, even in a television-saturated community."

Reversal of the trend of violence among the young, Hamburg says, calls for the teaching of "pro-social behavior" at home, in child care centers and pre-school programs. "By pro-social behavior, I mean constructive interaction with other human beings—sharing, taking turns, learning to cooperate, helping others. This is very fundamental. It used to be assumed that children got this outside school. This was never a sound assumption, and it is less so now than it ever was. I believe that if you don't get a foundation in the elementary pattern of sharing and cooperation before arriving in school, the odds are very much against you."

At its earliest stage, violence prevention begins with good health care for mother and child and the bonding of the child to a caring adult. It involves stimulating the development of non-confrontational skills in language and behavior from the very start of life.

As they grow up, says David Satcher, director of the Centers for Disease Control and Prevention and former president of Meharry Medical College in Nashville, "young people must have a reason to believe that they can change the future for themselves and others. Then it is much easier to deal with violence and substance abuse and teen-age pregnancy. We've found that those problems were not the problems; they were the symptoms. When young people don't have any hope for the future, they'll do anything."

Attention to violence prevention must take into account the social and cultural mores guiding children's attitudes and behavior. For example, aggressive behavior and victory at all costs are deeply imbedded in the American ethos. "The term 'aggressive' in America's entrepreneurial culture is considered very positive," Hamburg notes, adding, "It doesn't necessarily mean violence. It does mean taking the initiative, being vigorous, being determined, hanging in there, being resourceful, not giving up easily. That sense of aggression, another word for assertiveness, is very important for kids to have, but we need to distinguish it very clearly from moving to violence."

Assertiveness, taught as a social skill, helps young adults learn how to take advantage of opportunities offered by health services and job training. It teaches youngsters how to resist unwanted pressures and intimidation, resolve conflicts non-violently, and make smart decisions about schooling, drugs and weapons. Says Hamburg, "It gets youngsters to stop and think! What is it you want, and how can you get it peacefully instead of believing that violence will get it for you every time?"

Morton Deutsch, director of the International Center for Cooperation in Conflict Resolution at Teachers College Columbia University, stresses the importance of teaching skills in conflict resolution—of making students aware that violence begets violence, that there are other ways to express anger, and that nonviolent alternatives to dealing with conflict are available. He calls clear communication and effective listening to what others are saying critical to the resolution of conflict and to becoming alert to the biases, misperceptions and stereotyped thinking, in oneself and in others, that foster conflict....

For children and adolescents in impoverished communities, social support systems and life-skills training are needed in a wide variety of settings. Social supports can include school-based health clinics, home-visiting programs, adult mentoring, and church-based youth activities. "People must have a dependable infrastructure and enduring relationships with adults as well as peers," says Hamburg. "There is potential in these approaches to provide constructive alternatives to joining violent groups."

One way this goal is being pursued is through programs that build a strong and continuing connection between parents and schools in the children's early years. Established in 1968 by James P. Comer at Yale University, the School Development Program, for example, links academic and social support as a means of improving children's success in school and society. The message is that consistent attention to the development and education of infants, toddlers, children, and adolescents offers the best hope for change.

The success of the early childhood approach already has been demonstrated by the Perry Preschool Program, in Ypsilanti, Michigan, sponsored by the High/Scope Educational Research Foundation and supported in part by Carnegie Corporation of New York. The program, enrolling poor, black children at age three or four, has shown remarkably positive results in youngsters' subsequent behavior as adolescents and young adults. Those who participated in the program have engaged in significantly less unlawful and criminal behavior than those who did not have the benefits of early intervention to promote cognitive and social development.

Early intervention also should deal with the classroom bully. To dismiss violent, anti-social behavior in children as a phase of normal development is viewed by many educators as a denial of reality. Bullies usually pick on smaller, relatively defenseless classmates. Unless their behavior is stopped, class bullies may be on the way to terrorizing neighborhoods.

Dan Olweus, professor of psychological science at the University of Bergen, Norway, who has conducted extensive studies of bullying, reports: "When we follow the former school bully to age 23, we find a four-fold increase in criminal behavior."

Norway has produced training materials for teachers, an information folder for parents and video cassettes that show episodes from the everyday lives of two children who have been victims of bullying. Interventions to eliminate bullying include setting firm limits against unacceptable behavior, protecting potential victims, making all students aware of the problem, and actively involving teachers and parents in the prevention of bullying. In the Norwegian program, bullying incidents dropped by more than 50 percent in a two-year period. At the same time, anti-social behavior, such as theft, vandalism and truancy, also declined significantly. Students reported that they were happier in school.

The school remains the institution to which parents look for help in their daily struggle to do the best for their children. It is the place where the campaign against violence needs to be given educational focus and where, in practical terms, children and youth should be able to find protection from the dangerous street culture, not for a few hours but throughout the day....

Charting New Paths to Safety

Adolescent Development in 1993 published a report, *A Matter of Time: Risk and Opportunity in the Nonschool Hours.* In the foreword, David Hamburg wrote that youth organizations "can provide young adolescents with social support and guidance, life-skills training, positive and constructive alternatives to hazards such as drug and alcohol use, gang involvement, early sexual activity, and crime, and they can create opportunities for meaningful contributions to the community."

Emphasis on the early years in efforts to prevent youngsters from later joining violent gangs does not mean that the problem of existing gangs can be ignored. The Community Youth Gang Service Project in Los Angeles is an example of what might be done to make gangs less violent. This program, also part of the Education Development Center's network of violence prevention and treatment programs, works directly with gang members, encouraging them to settle disputes by non-violent means, establish "neutral territories" that are safe for everybody, and work toward agreements on periods of peace.

Mentoring. For some young people, the outreach of youth organizations is sufficient; others need more direct contact with a trustworthy adult. In his book, *The Kindness of Strangers: Adult Mentors, Urban Youth and the New Voluntarism,* Marc Freedman writes that mentors can contribute to the ability of inner-city youth to cope with very difficult circumstances. One of the rich sources of mentoring, Freedman writes, "has been the African-American community. Many organizations have initiated projects focused on linking inner-city youngsters with successful African-American men and women—individuals who, in many instances, were themselves raised in inner-city neighborhoods...."

Because mentoring can have virtually unlimited faces, it enables individuals, as Freedman puts it, "to participate in the essential but unfinished drama of reinventing community, while reaffirming that there is an important role for each of us in it." The beneficiaries of mentoring are less likely to be drawn into the nihilism of violence.

Since adolescents and even children constitute the greatest number of perpetrators and victims of violence, policies and programs aimed at the prevention of violence should concentrate on measures that affect and protect those vulnerable age groups.

For the short term, the criminal justice system must be revised to deal effectively with youthful offenders and with adults who entice minors into criminal activities, especially in the use of guns and drugs, and to protect children and youth against domestic violence.

More effective policing would help communities to defeat the violence around them, make the schools and access to them safe, and drive the drug dealers and other threats to peace out of the housing projects.

Protection of young people's records was instituted with the best of intentions at a time when children's and adolescents' misbehavior rarely included serious crimes. Under present conditions, some experts believe the approach sends the wrong message to youngsters: that they can expect leniency in the punishment of serious crimes. It encourages criminal adults too, particularly in the drug trade, to use armed youngsters as junior partners, relatively immune to serious penalty.

Educational and legislative action aimed at reducing the threat of gun violence is making some headway, in part because the nation's police forces have become an effective lobby for gun control. President Clinton has made a strong appeal for it, saying the nation never will be able to lower its health care costs if the streets continue to be a battleground for armed teenagers.

The Brady Law imposes a waiting period of five business days on purchasers of firearms in order to allow time for a background check, as well as to ensure a "cooling-off" period to prevent crimes of passion and momentary rage. But it clearly is no more than an interim measure, as even most of its supporters admit, because in the world of embattled streets, housing projects and schools, firearms are not bought through legal commercial channels; they are traded, like drugs in alleys, from vans and through a host of illegal suppliers.

The process of disarming would best begin with children and teenagers, the group that commits the most serious gun-related crimes and suffers most as victims of such crimes. Colorado Governor Roy Romer has made it a priority "to get the bullets off the streets and guns out of the hands of our kids." Colorado recently passed legislation to ban possession of handguns by persons under age 18 and to make it illegal for adults to provide handguns to juveniles, to expedite prosecution of cases involving minors and guns, and to expand detention space and programs, including "boot camps" for those who violate the law. Utah has enacted similar legislation.

There are other interim measures to protect young people that can be considered:

- Make schools, and the way to and from school, as safe as possible from guns and other weapons.
- Severely penalize adults, including parents, who either purposely or through neglect allow children to gain access to firearms.
- Treat gun violence resulting in injuries and death as serious crimes, regardless of the perpetrator's age, and make available the records of such crimes once the adolescent reaches the age of 16.

The long view. A review of rapidly emerging developments raises troublesome questions. Are the programs to prevent youth violence beginning to work? How can statistics showing the success of pilot intervention programs be reconciled with equally reliable reports of escalating violence among ever more—and younger—perpetrators and victims?

Part of the answer is that, even as anti-violence actions gain support, violence-creating conditions do not remain static. More guns, the epidemic of crack cocaine, the continuing deterioration of family life, the decline of civic virtue, the spread of poverty and unemployment, the relentless show of violence by the entertainment media—all remain winners in what still is an unequal contest.

President Clinton already has issued his impassioned appeal: "Unless we deal with the ravages of crime and drugs and violence—unless we recognize that it's due to the breakdown of the family, the community and the disappearance of jobs—and unless we say some of this cannot be done by government because we have to reach deep inside the values, the spirit, the soul, and the truth of human nature, none of the other things we seek to do will ever take us where we need to go."

Delbert Elliott puts the matter bluntly: "Once involved in a life-style that includes serious forms of violence, theft and substance abuse, those from disadvantaged families and neighborhoods find it very difficult to escape this life-style. There are fewer opportunities for conventional adult roles, and they are more embedded in and dependent upon gangs and the illicit economy that flourishes in their neighborhoods. . . . The evidence suggests that those who are successful in making the transition into conventional work and family roles give up their involvement in violence. We must target our interventions to facilitate a successful transition into conventional adult roles for all youth."

For the long term, basic answers must be found in broadly conceived education. The crisis calls for the enlistment of schools and communities in offering effective programs of conflict resolution and cooperative learning, providing teenagers with a sense of belonging, competing constructively with the allure of gangs, creating community schools that operate beyond the normal school day, and fostering responsible family planning, family-life education, healthy child development, and the recovery of humane values with a sense of responsibility toward the rights of others. It calls for a personal commitment to mentoring by credible and dedicated adults and peers. It calls for government and business to provide young people with access to community services and jobs.

In the end, vanquishing youth violence will require a public stance that violence is socially unacceptable and that the nation's economic and social policies should reflect a society that despises rather than tolerates and even glorifies violence.

Discussion Questions

Content

1. Has Hechinger made a convincing case for the view that violence is "not a random, uncontrollable, or inevitable occurrence"? If so, what evidence from the article convinces you of this opinion? If not, what evidence does not convince you? Explain why you are convinced by some evidence and not by other evidence.

2. What information about crime has Hechinger neglected? What persons other than psychologists, sociologists, and community activists would you like to hear from? Why do you believe it is important to hear from these people? What might they add to the conversation about what urban violence?

3. Do you agree with Hechinger's suggestion that we live in a society that "tolerates and even glorifies violence"? Why or why not? Do you think this tolerance or glorification is a cause of violence? Support your answer by considering such things as computer games like "Doom," sports (for example, football), and violent movies.

Form

1. Hechinger must present the suggestions of a number of experts in some kind of order; some are first, some are in the middle, and others are last. In what order does he present the suggestions? Who is first? Who is in the middle? Who is last? How does Hechinger relate one expert's views to another? What assumptions seem to you to be made in the transitions between each expert? How do these assumptions influence your reading of the experts' suggestions?

2. How would you characterize the insights of some of Hechinger's experts? Are they valuable? important? misguided? uninformed? Overall, how does each expert's character contribute to or detract from Hechinger's conclusion? In the end, are you persuaded to share the experts' views on violence or not? Explain your response with references to the experts themselves.

3. Consider the range of strategies Hechinger suggests that we need to use in order to end violence. Given his suggestions, do you believe that violence is insurmountable? Has the organization of Hechinger's essay left you with the impression that, in reality, nothing can be done to end violence? If so, why? If not, why not? How might Hechinger rewrite the article to make an end to violence seem more possible or less possible?

Writing Prompts

1. Drawing from the information collected by Hechinger, write a proposal for an anticrime program for youth in your area.

2. Write an essay that agrees or disagrees with Hechinger's view that American society—especially TV, music, and movies—glorifies violence. Use examples from current television programs, movies, and music to support your view.

*Luis Rodriguez lives in Chicago, where he is a community activist and direc-
tor of the Tía Chucha Press. His most recent book,* Always Running, *is a
memoir of gang life in Los Angeles. In "Turning Youth Gangs Around," originally published in* The Nation, *Rodriguez tells of his experiences working
with young people across the country and talking with them about gang
violence. He draws on this experience to argue for an inclusive and imaginative response to gang violence. As you read "Turning Youth Gangs
Around," consider what Rodriguez's point of view is on children who join
gangs. Does he think they are naturally violent? How does his view of gang
members shape his solutions? Think as well about your own attitudes
toward gangs. What solutions are presupposed from the point of view of
your perspective?*

Turning Youth Gangs Around

Luis J. Rodriguez

PEDRO* IS A THOUGHTFUL, articulate and charismatic young man; he listens, absorbs and responds. His movements are quick, well-developed during his years surviving in the streets of Chicago. Pedro is a 20-year-old gang
leader. For most of his life, he has lived off and on between his welfare mother and an uncle. He has been kicked out of schools and has served time in
youth detention facilities. He is also a great human being.

For four months in 1993, the courts designated me as his guardian under
a house arrest sentence. He was respectful and polite. He meticulously
answered all my messages. He was loved by my 6-year-old son. His best
friend happens to be my 19-year-old son Ramiro.

During his stay, I gave Pedro books, including political books to help him
become more cognizant of the world. One of these was *Palante,* a photo-text
about the Young Lords Party of the 1970s. Pedro, whose family is from Puerto
Rico, began to open up to an important slice of history that, until then, he'd
never known about. Pedro read *Palante* from cover to cover—as he did other
books, for the first time ever.

Luis J. Rodriguez. "Turning Youth Gangs Around." From *The Nation* (Nov. 94): 605–609. Reprinted with
permission from *The Nation* magazine. © The Nation Company, L.P.

*Some of the names in this article were changed.

When Pedro was released from house arrest, he moved out of the neighborhood with his girlfriend and her small boy. He found a job. He remained leader of the gang, but was now talking about struggle, about social change, about going somewhere.

Last November, Pedro was shot three times with a .44. He was hit in his back, leg and hand. Ramiro and I visited him at the Cook County Hospital. He lived, but he was not the same after that. One day during Pedro's hospital stay, the same gang that had shot him ambushed and killed Angel, a friend of Ramiro and Pedro. Angel, an honor student at one of the best schools in the city, was on his way to school; a news account the next day failed to mention this, reporting only that he was a suspected gang member, as if this fact justified his death.

I tried to persuade Pedro to get his boys to chill. I knew that Ramiro and the others were all sitting ducks. Pedro went through some internal turmoil, but he decided to forbid retaliation. This was hard for him, but he did it.

Unfortunately, the story doesn't end there. Earlier this year, Pedro allegedly shot and killed one of the guys believed to be behind Angel's murder and his own shooting. Pedro is now a fugitive.

I TELL YOU THIS to convey the complexity of working with youths like Pedro, youths most people would rather write off, but who are also intelligent, creative and even quite decent. The tragedy is that it is mostly young people like these who are being killed and who are doing the killing. I've seen them in youth prisons, hospitals and courts throughout the land: young people who in other circumstances might have been college graduates, officeholders or social activists. Unfortunately, many find themselves in situations they feel unable to pull out of until it's too late.

I've long recognized that most youths like Pedro aren't in gangs to be criminals, killers or prison inmates. For many, a gang embraces who they are, gives them the initiatory community they seek and the incipient authority they need to eventually control their own lives. These are things other institutions, including schools and families, often fail to provide. Yet without the proper guidance, support and means to contribute positively to society, gang involvement can be disastrous.

This August, a media storm was created when 11-year-old Robert Sandifer of Chicago, known as "Yummy" because he liked to eat cookies, allegedly shot into a crowd and killed a 14-year-old girl. A suspected member of a Southside gang, Yummy disappeared; days later he was found shot in the head. Two teenage members of Yummy's gang are being held in his death. Hours before his murder, a neighbor saw Yummy, who told her, "Say a prayer for me."

This is a tragedy, but without a clear understanding of the social, economic and psychological dynamics that would drive an 11-year-old to kill, we can only throw up our hands. Yet it isn't hard to figure out the motive forces behind much of this violence.

Sandifer, for example, was a child of the Reagan years, of substantial cuts in community programs, of the worst job loss since the Great Depression, of more police and prisons and of fewer options for recreation, education or work. Here was a boy who had been physically abused, shuttled from one foster home to another, one juvenile justice facility after another. At every stage of Robert's young life since birth, he was blocked from becoming all he could be. But there was nothing to stop him from getting a gun. From using it. And from dying from one.

No "three strikes, you're out," no trying children as adults, no increased prison spending will address what has created the Pedros and Yummys of this world. Such proposals deal only with the end results of a process that will continue to produce its own fuel, like a giant breeder reactor. This is not a solution.

Gangs are not new in America. The first gangs in the early 1800s were made up of Irish immigrant youths. They lived as second-class citizens. Their parents worked in the lowest-paid, most menial jobs. These youths organized to protect themselves within a society that had no place for them. Other immigrants followed identical patterns. Today the majority of gang members are African-American and Latino, and they face the same general predicaments those early immigrants did. But today something deeper is also happening. Within the present class relations of modern technology-driven capitalism, many youths, urban and rural, are being denied the chance to earn a "legitimate" living. An increasing number are white, mostly sons and daughters of coal miners, factory workers or farmers.

Los Angeles, which has more gang violence than any other city, experienced the greatest incidence of gang-related acts during the 1980s and early 1990s, when 300,000 manufacturing jobs were lost in California. According to the Gang Violence Bridging Project of the Edmund G. "Pat" Brown Institute of Public Affairs at California State University, Los Angeles, the areas with the greatest impoverishment and gang growth were those directly linked to industrial flight.

At the same time, the state of California suffered deep cuts in social programs—most of them coming as a result of the passage in 1978 of Proposition 13, which decreased state funding for schools after a slash in property taxes. Since 1980, while California's population has jumped by 35 percent, spending for education has steadily declined. Yet there has been a 14 percent annual increase in state prison spending during the past decade; the state legislature has allocated $21 billion over the next ten years to build twenty new prisons.

Almost all areas in the United States where manufacturing has died or moved away are now reporting ganglike activity. There are seventy-two large cities and thirty-eight smaller ones that claim to have a "gang problem," according to a 1992 survey of police departments by the National Institute of Justice. Chicago, also hard hit by industrial flight, has many large multigenerational gangs like those in L.A.

What has been the official response? In Chicago "mob action" arrests have been stepped up (when three or more young people gather in certain proscribed areas, it is considered "mob action"), as have police sweeps of housing projects and "gang infested" communities. Recently there have been calls to deploy the National Guard against gangs, which is like bringing in a larger gang with more firepower against the local ones. This, too, is not a solution.

I agree that the situation is intolerable. I believe most people—from the Chicago-based Mothers Against Gangs to teachers who are forced to be police officers in their classrooms to people in the community caught in the crossfire—are scared. They are bone-tired of the violence. They are seeking ways out. First we must recognize that our battle is with a society that fails to do all it can for young people—then lays the blame on them.

It's time the voices for viable and lasting solutions be heard. The public debate is now limited to those who demonize youth, want to put them away, and use repression to curb their natural instincts to re-create the world.

I have other proposals. First, that we realign societal resources in accordance with the following premises: that every child has value and every child can succeed. That schools teach by engaging the intelligence and creativity of all students. That institutions of public maintenance—whether police or social services—respect the basic humanity of all people. That we rapidly and thoroughly integrate young people into the future, into the new technology. And finally, that we root out the basis for the injustice and inequities that engender most of the violence we see today.

Sound farfetched? Too idealistic? Fine. But anything short on imagination will result in "pragmatic," fear-driven, expediency-oriented measures that won't solve anything but will only play with people's lives.

Actually, the structural economic foundation for such proposals as I've roughly outlined is already laid. The computer chip has brought about revolutionary shifts in the social order. The only thing that isn't in place is the non-exploitative, non-oppressive relations between people required to complete this transition.

I know what some people are thinking. What about being tough on crime? Let me be clear: I hate crime. I hate drugs. I hate children murdering children. But I know from experience that it doesn't take guts to put money into inhumane, punishment-driven institutions. In fact, such policies make our communities even less safe. It's tougher to walk these streets, to listen to young people, to respect them and help fight for their well-being. It's tougher to care.

For the past two years, I've talked to young people, parents, teachers and concerned officials in cities as far-flung as Hartford, Brooklyn, Phoenix, Seattle, Lansing, Denver, Boston, El Paso, Washington, Oakland, San Antonio and Compton. I've seen them grope with similar crises, similar pains, similar confusions.

Sometimes I feel the immensity of what we're facing—talking to Teens on Target in Los Angeles, a group made up of youths who have been shot, some in wheelchairs; or to teenage mothers in Tucson, one child caring for another; or to incarcerated young men at the maximum security Illinois Youth Center at Joliet. I felt it when a couple of young women cried in Holyoke, Massachusetts, after I read a poem about a friend who had been murdered by the police, and when I addressed a gym full of students at Jefferson High School in Fort Worth and several young people lined up to hug me, as if they had never been hugged before.

BECAUSE I HAVE TO DEAL WITH people like Yummy and Pedro every day, I decided this summer to do something more than just talk. With the help of Patricia Zamora from the Casa Aztlán Community Center in Chicago's Mexican community of Pilsen, I worked with a core of young people, gang and nongang, toward finding their own solutions, their own organizations, their own empowerment.

In the backyard of my Chicago home, some thirty people, mostly from the predominantly Puerto Rican area of Humboldt Park (my son's friends, and Pedro's homeys) and Pilsen, were present. They agreed to reach out to other youths and hold retreats, weekly meetings and a major conference. All summer they worked, without money, without resources, but with a lot of enthusiasm and energy. They hooked up with the National Organizing Committee, founded in 1993 by revolutionary fighters including gang members, welfare recipients, trade unionists, teachers and parents from throughout the United States. The N.O.C. offered them technical and educational assistance.

The young people's efforts culminated in the Youth '94 Struggling for Survival Conference, held in August at the University of Illinois, Chicago. More than a hundred young people from the city and surrounding communities attended. They held workshops on police brutality, jobs and education, and peace in the neighborhoods. A few gang members set aside deadly rivalries to attend this gathering.

Although there were a number of mishaps, including a power failure, the youths voted to keep meeting. They held their workshops in the dark, raising issues, voicing concerns, coming up with ideas. I was the only adult they let address their meeting. The others, including parents, teachers, counselors, resource people and a video crew from the Center for New Television, were there to help with what the young people had organized.

Then the building personnel told us we had to leave because it was unsafe to be in a building without power. We got Casa Aztlán to agree to let us move to several of their rooms to continue the workshops; I felt we would probably lose about half the young people in the fifteen-minute ride between sites. Not only did we hang on to most of the youths, we picked up a few more along the way. In a flooded basement with crumbling walls in Casa Aztlán we held the final plenary session. The youths set up a round-table, at which it was agreed that only proposed solutions would be entertained. A few read poetry. It was a success, but then the young people wouldn't let it be anything else.

Youth Struggling for Survival is but one example of young people tackling the issues head-on. There are hundreds more across America. In the weeks before the November 8 elections in California, thousands of junior high and high school students, mostly Latino, walked out of schools in the Los Angeles area. Their target: Proposition 187, intended to deny undocumented immigrants access to education, social services and non-emergency health care.

These young people need guidance and support; they don't need adults to tell them what to do and how to do it; to corral, crush or dissuade their efforts. We must reverse their sense of helplessness. The first step is to invest them with more authority to run their own lives, their communities, even their schools. The aim is to help them stop being instruments of their own death and to choose a revolutionary service to life.

We don't need a country in which the National Guard walks our children to school, or pizza-delivery people carry sidearms, or prisons outnumber colleges. We can be more enlightened. More inclusive. More imaginative.

And, I'm convinced, this is how we can be more safe.

Discussion Questions

Content

1. What image of gang members does Rodriguez offer for his readers? Are the gang members portrayed as criminals or victims? How do you think his portrayal of gang members enables or disables discussion about the gang problem?

2. What are Rodriguez's proposals for "turning youth gangs around"? What kinds of beliefs are his proposals based on? Are these valid beliefs? Why or why not?

3. In his solutions, Rodriguez seems to suggest that enforcing laws breeds violence and that engaging youth in self-government leads to safety. Do you agree with this? Why or why not? Is it more important to encourage youth to obey the law or to involve them in making decisions for themselves? Which activity seems to you to encourage nonviolent behavior?

Form

1. How well does the beginning anecdote work to establish Rodriguez's authority on the subject of helping gang members? Does it make Rodriguez more or less credible for you? Why?

2. Why do you think Rodriguez anticipates that people will label his proposal "farfetched" and "too idealistic"? Just how idealistic do you think his proposals are? What might be more realistic? Why? What is it about the ways we think about problems like urban violence that makes community-based activism seem "too idealistic" to cope really with violence?

3. In his essay, do you think Rodriguez is able to bring compassion and action together? Why or why not?

Writing Prompts

1. Write an essay exploring the meaning of the ideas of "compassion" and "action" for you. Narrate some of your experiences with compassion and with action. Describe the ways in which they do and do not influence each other. Was the way in which compassion and action came together ideal? How could their coming together have been better?

2. Write a letter to Rodriguez explaining what you think of his ideas and efforts. Discuss what you consider to be the causes of gang violence. Given these causes, discuss what you think he should do to address gang violence.

PART 3 DISCUSSION QUESTIONS

1. What metaphors and images do the authors in this part most often use when discussing crime? How widely does their use of these metaphors and images seem to vary? Do some use them without hesitation? Do others use them in ways that are ironic or troublesome? To what extent do you think the debate about crime in American cities is a debate about how we talk about crime?

2. Among the authors in this part, there are at least two opposing views about crime. For some, it is an act of random, lawless violence. For others, it is a predictable consequence of the way in which American society is organized. Identify each of the authors in this part as holding one or the other view. How do their views of crime as either random or predictable determine what issues they debate? To what extent do you think we can explain the debate on crime in this country as a debate about how crime is discussed?

3. Several of the authors in this part relate the facts of crime and perceptions of crime to images of crime in movies, music, and television. Other authors don't consider the role popular culture may play in perpetuating violence. Should we consider popular culture and its influence on our lives when discussing crime? Which author do you most agree with on this issue? Which author do you most disagree with? Explain why you think images of popular culture are or are not important to our considerations of crime and its prevention.

4. Many of the authors in this part make suggestions as to what needs to be done either to eliminate or to curb violent crimes in America today. At the same time, several of these authors suggest that there is no easy or guaranteed solution. What are their various proposals? How much do they resemble one another? How much do they differ? How effective do you think each of these solutions would be? Try to imagine other solutions they have not thought of. Consider why the ways they talk about crime have prevented them from proposing your solutions.

5. If all the authors in this part were brought together to have a debate on crime, what would they talk about? What issues do you think they would agree to discuss? How would they debate these issues? Where would they agree? And why? At what points do you think they would reach an impasse in their discussions? Can you imagine what it might take for them to move beyond any impasse?

PART 3 WRITING ASSIGNMENTS

1. Write a personal essay in which you explain how you feel about crime in American cities. Explain how you feel when you go out to certain places. Where do you feel secure? Unsafe? How much do you worry about your own protection? Why? In what ways does your awareness of crime influence your behavior?

2. The issues raised in this part—issues of how we talk about crime and of what that talk does—are related to issues raised elsewhere in this book. Choose one essay from this part and one essay from another part of this book, and write a paper that demonstrates how these essays when taken together say something about the larger meaning of life in American cities.

3. Identify what you consider to be the two most important issues raised by the authors in this part. Write an essay in which you explain why you chose these issues. Evaluate the positions presented on these issues, and argue whether you think the issues are best addressed as issues of fact or issues of perception.

4. Use the information presented in this part to persuade people in your area about how they should think about crime and about what they should do in response to crime.

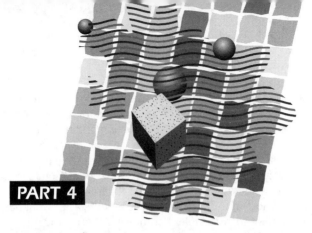

Expressions of City Life in Urban Art

IN PRACTICE what often occurs when a person walks into the sterile museum setting and tries to grapple with a difficult piece of contemporary work,
is that the viewer is left with the questions "What does this work mean?"
"Why don't I understand it?" and then, if the work generates a bit of uneasiness or anger, as it often does, the question becomes, "Is it art?" In Chicago's
Museum of Contemporary Art I have heard such queries directed at pieces
by such artists as Joseph Beuys, Rebecca Horn, Christian Boltanski. Recently,
standing in front of a Rauchenberg painting, I heard a man say, "I could make
something like that." ...

When Scott Tyler placed the U.S. flag on the gallery floor at the School of
the Art Institute of Chicago, all these issues were raised. The initial reaction
of many viewers was fury generated by the placement of the flag in such a
compromised position. And this rage was followed by a series of questions:
What is this strange thing called "installation"—a form that is neither painting, sculpture, nor photography but in Tyler's case an amalgam of all three?
Why was this piece shown within the confines of the Art Institute of
Chicago—a well-respected and prestigious venue? In reference to this last
query, the location of the exhibit was an issue that needed immediate clari-
fication. Tyler's installation, "What Is the Proper Way to Display a U.S. Flag?"
was not chosen for exhibition by the twentieth-century curator of the muse-

um but rather by a faculty committee selecting work for a student exhibition. Misinformed, thousands of Chicagoans in protest thought it was time to stop contributing their tax dollars to the Art Institute. The School of the Art Institute insisted on making the distinction between the function of a school and that of a museum, in the hope that it would change the perception of the work, but the damage was already done.

—Carol Becker

THE POWERFUL APPARATUSES of contemporary commercial electronic mass communications dominate discourse in the modern world. They supply us with endless diversion and distraction mobilized to direct our minds toward advertising messages. They colonize the most intimate and personal aspects of our lives, seizing upon every possible flaw in our bodies, minds, and psyches to increase our anxieties and augment our appetites for consumer goods. Culture itself comes to us as a commodity. The artistry and historical consciousness of a Rahsaan Roland Kirk becomes obscured by our contexts of reception. We buy records and attend concerts, watch films and television commercials as a matter of course. Rarely do we ask about the origins and intentions of the messages we encounter through the mass media; sometimes we forget that artists have origins or intentions at all, so pervasive are the stimuli around us.

Yet mass communications also embody some of our deepest hopes and engage some of our most profound sympathies. People ingeniously enter those discourses to which the have access; the saxophone or the guitar, the stage or the camera can offer precious and unique opportunities for expression. For some populations at some times, commercialized leisure is history—a repository of collective memory that places immediate experience in the context of change over time. The very same media that trivialize and distort culture, that turn art into commodities, and that obscure the origins and intentions of artists also provide meaningful connection to our own pasts and to the pasts of others. But they do so only indirectly, constrained by the nonlinear biases of the electronic media as well as by a commercial matrix hostile to the kinds of empathy, inquiry, and analysis basic to historical thinking.

—George Lipsitz

CULTURE IN AMERICA is likely to be spelled these days with a hyphen. Watch it on TV. There's *Cuban-American* singing star Gloria Estefan in a music video on MTV Latino. See it at the cinema. The film version of *The Joy Luck Club*, based on the popular novel by Chinese-American author Amy Tan, could be playing nearby. Theater? There's the modern-dance show Griot New York, directed by Jamaican-American choreographer Garth Fagan. Poetry? Buy a book of verse by St. Lucian-born, Nobel-prizewinning poet Derek Walcott, who teaches at Boston University. Painting? New York's Asia Society is holding a show that tours the country next year featuring Asian-American visual artists who emigrated from Vietnam, Thailand and elsewhere in Asia.

And that's just the beginning. "All American art is a function of the hybrid culture that resulted from centuries of immigration to this nation," says David Ross, director of the Whitney Museum of American Art. "We're just more dramatically aware of it today." American culture used to be depicted as a Eurocentric melting pot into which other cultures were stirred and absorbed. The recent waves of newcomers have changed that. Today it seems more like a street fair, with various booths, foods and peoples, all mixing on common sidewalks.

The celebration was a long time coming. To be an immigrant artist is to be a hyphen away from one's roots, and still a thousand miles away. But it is often that link to a foreign land—another way of seeing things—that allows such artists to contribute ideas to American culture that are fresh and new. That slim hyphen, that thin line that joins individual Americans to their past, is also what connects all America to its future.

—Christopher John Farley

INTRODUCTION

One of the unique roles that cities play in American culture is to provide a space in which many different kinds of people encounter one another. In many cities, art provides opportunities for these encounters. Through art, members of different groups use urban materials and urban space to communicate about urban life and experience. In your daily life, you can find ways in which music, sculpture, murals, and graffiti have been infused with senses of urban life. Also, these various forms of urban art are used by artists, residents, and others to represent what city life is like, what it means, and where it is leading.

Understanding how urban art functions to give meaning to city life involves thinking about how art draws on the urban context for its subject matter. In addition, it necessitates thinking about how art, in its artistic forms and choice of medium (paint, metal, sound, etc.), represents the city. Art represents the city in order to comment on or even to change the quality of city life. From your own experience, you can probably list several forms of urban art in your city that are deemed acceptable, and several that are seen as a problem or even a nuisance. Thus, writing and thinking about urban art involves more than merely considering what a piece of urban art means in and of itself; we must think as well about what particular forms of urban art mean in broader discussions about how urban spaces should look and how they should be used and shared.

The essays in this unit provide ways of viewing urban art simultaneously as "art" and as part of public culture. In "Art and Context: A Personal View," Daria Dorosh discusses the connections between her own art and New York City, where it is located. Stating that she has become uncomfortable with the separation between "museum" art and everyday life, Dobosh chronicles her attempts to integrate art and life and to contribute to the urban community through her work. Dorosh suggests that the city is the artist's canvas. She also offers insight into the collaborative relationships that some urban artists form as they try to make use of the materials of urban life, such as concrete and stone, in their art. In addition, she demonstrates that urban artists work together to gain the technical expertise of architects, lawyers, and others, for a commitment to public urban art involves legal, economic, and civic considerations. Her essay also helps us to see some of the ways in which what has traditionally been called "high art" is being connected to urban life.

Graffiti is the most controversial of the urban art forms that use public space as their canvases. As Leonard Kriegel indicates in his essay, "Graffiti: Tunnel Notes of a New Yorker," graffiti's status as art is a matter of considerable debate. Kriegel's discussion not only takes a position on graffiti's "illegal" use of public space as a canvas, but also considers the meaning of graffiti's artistic expressions and reflects upon the responsibilities of graffiti artists to communicate effectively. In his essay, Kriegel compares the graffiti he saw during his childhood and the graffiti he sees today in New York. Drawing a distinction between what he calls "political," communicative graffiti and those that he sees every day in New York, Kriegel wonders about the future of a city that calls graffiti "art." Writing from the perspective of a graffiti artist, Chaka Jenkins, in his essay, "As the Sun Sets We Rise," tries to show us how and why graffiti culture is important to him. Jenkins's perspective directly opposes Kriegel's feeling that graffiti is unintelligible, and so the two essays provide a glimpse into how debates over urban art do or do not help different people understand one another.

The controversy that surrounds urban art is also represented in Judith McWillie's essay, "(Inter)Cultural (Inter)Connections." Here, McWillie discusses the urban African American tradition of "found art" installations or "yard shows" in terms of the controversies they raise in cities and in terms of their connections to African folk culture. She argues that yard shows provide creative outlets for commentaries on the past and present situations of specific areas.

In "The Rap on Rap," written for The *New Republic,* David Samuels explores the ramifications of sales data indicating that rap music's "primary audience is white and lives in the suburbs." Using these figures as a critical tool with which to question rap music's self-promotion as an "authentic" artistic expression of contemporary American city life, Samuels suggests that rap's history can be read as a story of turning racist images of African Americans into a risk-free consumable product for white teenagers.

In "When Black Feminism Faces the Music, and the Music Is Rap," Michelle Wallace deals with the tensions between a commitment to the right of free expression and the feminist role of resistance to discourses of male dominance and female exploitation. Claiming that, "a large part of the appeal of pop culture is that it can offer symbolic resolutions to life's contradictions," Wallace explores the ways that rap is connected to larger social notions of male dominance, concluding that, "when it comes to gender, rap has not resolved a thing."

Finally, in her essay "The Iconography of Chicano Self-Determination: Race, Ethnicity, and Class," Shifra Goldman considers the ways in which urban Chicano art forms have responded to the racial, ethnic, and class contexts of life within the United States. Considering the urban art forms that Chicanos have used to explicitly turn the city into a canvas, such as paintings, murals, plays, and public celebrations, Goldman traces images of Chicano cultural affirmation and political solidarity.

The essays in this part ask questions about urban art forms that help us to understand the contributions that urban art can make to our understanding of our lives and our surroundings. In reading the contributions to this part, then, we might join these authors in considering questions like: To what degree does urban art attempt to communicate across different cities and between cities and their suburbs? If there is a "message" to urban artistic expressions, to whom is that message addressed? What responsibilities do critics have to the urban art forms they respond to? What responsibilities do the urban artists have to depict and decorate their cities in certain ways? How are urban art forms used by city residents and others to think about and "picture" city life?

PREREADING ASSIGNMENTS

1. Freewrite for ten minutes about how and where you learned to define art. What do you think are art's characteristics? What do you think are art's purposes? Push yourself toward details of your experiences that might explain why you define art the way you do.

2. Make a list of key words that you would expect to hear in a discussion or debate about urban art. What kinds of people use which terms, and what advantage do they gain by their uses of those terms?

3. Spend ten minutes recalling situations in which your friends or family discussed their ideas about different kinds of urban art, such as graffiti, rap music, municipal sculpture, etc. What different opinions did people express? What roles do they see for these kinds of art? What is it about art that we take seriously?

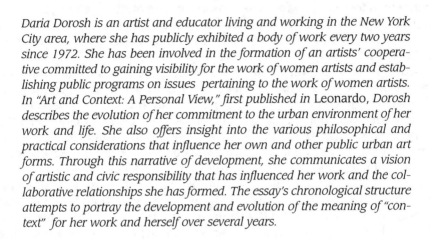

Daria Dorosh is an artist and educator living and working in the New York City area, where she has publicly exhibited a body of work every two years since 1972. She has been involved in the formation of an artists' cooperative committed to gaining visibility for the work of women artists and establishing public programs on issues pertaining to the work of women artists. In "Art and Context: A Personal View," first published in Leonardo, *Dorosh describes the evolution of her commitment to the urban environment of her work and life. She also offers insight into the various philosophical and practical considerations that influence her own and other public urban art forms. Through this narrative of development, she communicates a vision of artistic and civic responsibility that has influenced her work and the collaborative relationships she has formed. The essay's chronological structure attempts to portray the development and evolution of the meaning of "context" for her work and herself over several years.*

Art and Context: A Personal View

Daria Dorosh

I. Influence of Place

NEW YORK CITY, where I live and work as an artist, has engendered the issues I address in my work, as well as its form, scale, medium and visual vocabulary. My history and development as an artist have been shaped by the process of working and exhibiting here. This history, in turn, is the foundation for directions that are still to be expressed. For me, the most exciting changes in my work have come from engagement and response to a particular environment.

Conversely, the experience of leaving the city periodically to continue my work in a different setting generated certain conflicts that made clear to me the connection between art and place. Many summers spent in south-

Daria Dorosh. "Art and Context: A Personal View." From *Leonardo* 21, 4 (1988): 361–366. Reprinted with the permission of MIT Press Journals.

eastern Vermont helped me recognize that my paintings were rooted in a city experience. I used color for its properties of contrast and temperature rather than for its ability to evoke seasons or time of day. The imagery in my work, though abstract, had references to architectural form and electric light. I sometimes used fragments of the landscape for pattern but only after filtering nature through memory or the flatness of a photograph. To work on a 12-foot painting or drawing in my New York studio was exhilarating, but large work has specific space requirements as to where it can be made or viewed. I delighted in the intimate scale and clutter of the summer houses I rented, but I was troubled that the kind of painting I did in my city studio did not belong in them. Over the course of many Vermont summers, I began to wonder who was the audience for my work and where did my work belong once it left my studio. The engrossing process of making a painting is reason enough to make art, yet I feel a responsibility to the finished work as well. I care about its existence and place in the world, even though I know that artists traditionally have little control over the future of their work. Eventually, these questions found their way into the work itself, stirred by the dissonance of working in a rural environment rather than in the one which I had become accustomed.

I think that exhibiting in New York has a specific impact on how an artwork looks. With hundreds of galleries competing for an international art-viewing audience, it becomes paramount to produce a dynamic exhibition in order to have the work noticed. The neutral space of the gallery is made for art that can make this setting come alive. It is exciting to participate in a large-scale work that presses at the boundary of the gallery space, as does the sculpture of Richard Serra or the huge paint-encrusted canvases of Anselm Kiefer. By nature, exhibits are temporary events, performances, after which the artwork goes on to a more permanent location. With help from skilled dealers and the press, some artists' work finds its way into museum, private, or corporate collections, which can provide the kind of space this work requires. It is not meant for the modest living spaces or budgets of most people; the scale of the work has built into it a particular clientele and marketplace.

New York has many art worlds with many different audiences, yet little of the art that is produced here is intended to affect the quality of public life in the city. When I leave the context of the art circle—namely museums, galleries and art schools—there is little evidence that what I do as an artist really matters or even exists. Without the integration of art into everyday life, the public arena feels incomplete to me. Although numerous factors have made this situation what it is, I have determined to work toward the integration of art with place by incorporating my concerns in the artwork itself.

II. Early Work and Influences

I have had the opportunity to exhibit a body of work every 2 years since 1972, when I joined a group of women artists to form a nonprofit art organization and gallery. Complete freedom to follow the natural direction of my work without the pressures of the marketplace allowed my work to go through a personal evolutionary process. I first exhibited small semiabstract watercolors—abbreviations of places I had visited. The clarity and immediacy of the medium held an attraction for me. My images were always frontal and become increasingly more abstract over several years, until I realized that the edge of pigment deposited between two areas of color as they met was becoming the essence of my painting.

By 1975, I wanted to bring a physical dimension to my work. Watercolor seemed too limited for what I needed to express. This led to a body of work of slim plaster reliefs that were poured to a thickness of 1/4 inch and then carved and painted with watercolor. The theme of these works was a sense of the void as described in a creation chant of the Maori of New Zealand, which poetically evokes place on a universal scale.

In 1976, I felt the need to regain the expressiveness of color. To investigate how I perceived color I used a Polaroid camera to gather hundreds of fragments of light, color and place. The outcome of each photo could never be anticipated, and this kept me aesthetically involved. Each photo was a piece in a puzzle and needed to be integrated into a larger composition. Color photocopying was the next stage in the process and left its own signature on the Polaroid composites: it unified the collage surface, translated the color into a strange mechanical palette and left a wonderful tactile ridge, somewhat like the plaster reliefs I had been doing previously. The new color range I discovered for my next body of work was influenced by the color photocopy process. My colors now were electric and raw, sometimes deep and muddy, in the sense that many colors applied in layers of oil crayon were active in the same area. In these very physical and luminous works, my scale also changed to 5-foot-square works, and I was able to experience the new pleasure of being surrounded by the image I was making.

From 1978 to 1981, my work generally took the form of large drawings in oil crayon on muslin-backed paper. For the imagery, I used Polaroids of places, which I transformed by cutting, composing and photocopying them and then drawing from them. The compositions were frontal, relating to the edges of the picture plane; and the vertical and horizontal areas intersected, creating an illusion of depth. During this time, I became increasingly aware that I could make these works only in my New York studio because of their large size and because I needed the distance from my source, nature, in order to restructure the photographic material freely.

III. Challenging the Separation of Art and Place

In the summer of 1981, while in Vermont, I started a body of work in which I acknowledged my struggle with location. The resulting nine works were shown at A.I.R. Gallery in New York under the title "Paintings/Resistant Spaces: Paintings in Combination with Photographs and Chairs". Each work consisted of an abstract painting set into its own environment, which took the form either of a chair or of a large black-and-white photograph of a domestic interior.

In these works, furniture was used to make the work 'house scale', yet the work did not comply with what one might expect 'house art' or 'gallery art' to be. The chairs were not appropriated into the artwork as art objects, and the photographs acted not as art but as visual information around the painting. An equilibrium was maintained between the painting and the object so that neither became subordinated to the other; rather, the objects had to maintain their inherent nature in order to activate the painting in the composition. I gave each painting its own reference point, and thus the gallery was no longer the springboard for the work.

At the same time, my experience of the average domestic interior made me want to challenge the conventional manner in which art is displayed there. I envisioned making paintings for unexpected locations in houses, such as alongside windows and doorframes, rather than centered on a wall. I felt that a small work placed in counterpoint with a room could stimulate a dramatic interaction between art and place. That summer, I took photographs in our rented house to extract images of windows, walls with doors and pieces of furniture and then had large black-and-white blow-ups made. I cut out a place on the wall in the photo and, after mounting the cut photograph on Masonite, I composed and painted an image in the open space.

The result was surprising. Two modes of representing reality, painting and photography, when locked into each other, manifested their differences and did not assume their usual roles. The photograph, usually representative of reality, showed its abstract side through its flat, non-tactile surface and cropped geometric form. It enveloped the painting, acting as a frame and taking it into its own image. In contrast, the painting, although abstract, seemed more real because of its painterly surface, luminous color, spatial illusion and architectural references to the interior in the photograph. I discovered that a dynamic relationship is created when two separate visual vocabularies operate as a unit.

IN FOUR OF THE WORKS, I used the chair to achieve similar effects and to pull the space in the painting closer to the space in the room. Maintaining its function, the chair stood 6 inches in front of the painting. The painting relied on the structure of the chair as a reference for its image; yet, because of the juxtaposition, new aspects of both objects surfaced. The household chair, with its particular history and characteristics, evoked the presence of the human figure and relegated the painting to the role of background in the composition. Obstructed by the chair, the painting became less of an icon; yet, because of its ability to 'activate' the chair, it became even more powerful.

The titles of these works, such as *Interstice, Twice Around, Between* and *Margin*, were chosen to convey the essence of these interactions—namely, the transition between art and object, illusion and reality, abstraction and realism. I gave up the autonomy of the painting in these juxtapositions; yet, once I allowed art to come into being from this new vantage point, innumerable possibilities presented themselves for exploration. The dialogue that was initiated between art and an aspect of place has affected the course of my work ever since.

In 1984, I decided to initiate a series of collaborations with architects for my next exhibition at A.I.R. Gallery. The process of looking for architects willing to participate in a collaboration was instructive in itself. After several attempts, I found four architects with highly individual sensibilities who wanted to work collaboratively for an exhibition. I met with each of them initially to identify a shared point of reference for both painting and object. Subsequently, each collaborative unit developed in its own framework, giving me the opportunity to work on four different projects.

My premise was that a conscious relationship could be established between art and the built environment in which both were separate but equally necessary to each other. I wanted to know what the nature of collaboration was, what was important to preserve in a collaborative situation, and whether different points of view could coexist in one framework if the aesthetic domain were different. It was also important to me that all of us worked in a manner consistent with our individual concerns and the work we produced for the show could function independently after the exhibition.

IV. Four Collaborations

The architect Mary Pepchinski, with whom I share an interest in the city, designed a writing desk with storage spaces in the form of an urban skyline which included a 'billboard' rectangle that could hold a 9-by-16-inch painting. Harriet Balaran and I decided to do a light-hearted variation on the decorator's habit of matching a painting to a couch, except in this case the *Lounge on Four Spheres*—a black, lacquered-wood structure on bowling balls—was designed to 'match' a given painting. Elizabeth Diller and I addressed the conceptual theme of 'gravity—levity, vantage point—vanishing point' by juxtaposing her mirror assemblage and my painting. Although the two objects were next to each other, the contrasting way that mirror and painting manifest illusion held the two objects in a relationship of differences. Donna Robertson produced a brooding dark green fence that evoked both a picket fence and a frontier stockade with towers. My large dark painting created in the same outdoor mood, hung on the wall behind the fence, slightly obstructed, or protected, by the structure. Our mutual point of reference was the expression of boundary or edge.

With this exhibition, I was able to devise a context for my paintings within the gallery space. Now I was ready to go further—to let go of the protective territory of the gallery and make work intended to be an integral and permanent part of a place. To do this, I had to identify place as both subject and context before I could begin to work.

V. The City as Artist's Studio

I began to view New York City as a large open studio for site-specific work. Using the photograph again, I chose various public spaces—such as the lobby of the Museum of Modern Art, the New York Convention Center, subway stations, parts of Broadway—and made drawings within them. It was exciting to envision art on a grand scale in surroundings that had a ready-made audience. The floor surface in these places became the canvas on which I could weave an illusion of abstract forms under the feet of people traversing the space.

At the same time, I began researching and visiting public spaces built in past eras to help me define possibilities for the present. I found diverse cultural and historical models—for example, the gardens of China, which combine nature, art and spirit into one experience; urban parks such as the Buttes-Chaumont in Paris, which represents the aesthetics of nature re-created by man; and the urban public spaces of Italy, designed to encourage sociability and dramatic interaction among its residents. Looking at these and other examples, I began to define my personal criteria for public art.

First of all, I wanted to create work specifically for a site. Existing in the public realm, it would need to be incorporated into a functional surface or structure, such as the floor, wall or seating, rather than be an autonomous, contemplative art object. Its setting would render it vulnerable, thus requiring the use of appropriate durable, low-maintenance materials. It would have to be a permanent installation, showing a commitment from the community and allowing it the possibility of becoming part of an historical context. Furthermore, public art belongs to a large audience and must come about through a complex process that includes administrative assistance and financing. The artist must be willing to work with many groups and individuals who pool their skills and resources to bring the work to realization.

Finally, I wanted to put art directly within the city environment, to create a celebratory site in which art functions as place, even as it counters the sobriety of the city workplace through its nature as art.

My first drawing for a site-specific artwork for New York City was done in 1985 and titled *A Pedestrian Bridge for 57th Street between 5th and 6th Avenues*. Most people, myself included, get to the galleries and stores located on both sides of this street by running through traffic mid-block to avoid going to the far corners to cross. I felt inspired to solve this problem aesthetically. I took many photographs of the street and chose a view that provided a dramatic setting for a pedestrian bridge. Using oil pastels on an enlarged photograph of the site, I composed a bridge of titled asymmetrical forms with surfaces flooded by colored lights. Since this area is reputed to be the center of contemporary art, it seemed fitting that the bridge be designed by an artist as a functional and aesthetic marker for the street.

The enormous gap between artistic vision and implementation has relegated this proposal to the conceptual realm. However, it set in motion a dialogue with city agencies, such as the New York City Department of Transportation, which continues to this day, and I discovered the complex mechanisms for putting anything permanent in a public space.

VI. European Influences

My growing interest in public art coincided with several summers spent teaching and travelling in France and Italy. This exposure made a significant impact on the formal direction of my work. Seeing art and architecture in their historical and social setting revealed new dimensions in works I had known only through reproductions. I found the buildings in the countryside of France compelling in their dense, massive forms, where roof and wall became an continuous surface of stone in which occasional small openings for windows were unpredictably placed and often shuttered. This introspective quality seemed to belong to a particular time and location. Upon visiting Le Corbusier's Chapelle do Notre Dame du Haut, built in 1950 in Ronchamp, I could see its connection to this history of massive form, tactile surface and small windows opening to the outside world. Before seeing it in the context of French rural architecture, I had admired it as an abstract modern work alone.

This contact with France eventually turned my imagery inside out. I had been painting layers of abstract, open spaces receding from the edges of the picture plane; now my imagery began to resemble a dense self-contained object reminiscent of a diatom suspended in a colorful void. An equally important influence on my work at this time was the magnificently public-spirited architecture of Italy, with its generous entryways, dramatic use of stairs and decorative surfaces in fresco and stone. In the churches of Siena, Ravenna and Assisi, I saw the potential of marble and mosaic and the excellent opportunities that floors presented for embedded images.

VII. New Directions

In 1985, a fusion of impressions became evident in my work. I began to work on marble and granite surfaces making drawings and simulated inlaid stone and metal in the shape of floating geometric forms. I continued drawing on photographs of existing sites but also started a series of site-specific line drawings in actual locations. To continue my work while travelling in Europe, I used tape to 'draw' on architectural forms in public areas; I then photographed the image before removing the tape. One of these 'drawings' was done in Paris, on the Quai St. Bernard, along the Seine. These temporary drawings allowed me to experience the effect of my two-dimensional configurations on an environmental scale. As a painter, I was excited to see the bonding of imaginary space with an existent functional surface.

I was eager to work on a permanent installation and had been gathering information on commissions through the '% for Art' programs around the country. Public art programs have been attracting growing numbers of artists, particularly sculptors, who want to work on large-scale projects that are set up as collaborations with architects. In the early seventies, artists like Robert Smithson opened up the issue of site-specific art—earthworks—that moved out of the gallery space. I see public art today as another stage in this direction, but one that has its own characteristics. Any monumental work that strives to exist in the public arena, no matter how temporary, like the installations of Christo, requires funding and coordination on a grand scale. The artists actively working in this direction, such as Mary Miss, Elyn Zimmerman or Joyce Kozloff, work with teams of people, including program administrators, architects, engineers, contractors and lawyers, to bring a project to realization. During this process, the time frame or even the outcome is hard to predict. Robert Irwin writes about this in his book *Being and Circumstance*. One difference between 'earthworks' and public art is that the latter exists in a social or urban setting and must go through a process of evaluation and acceptance by its 'users', who also provide the funding and take responsibility for maintaining the work.

Although procedures for artists to apply for these projects have been in place for some time, I wondered if it were possible to initiate a public art project myself, as the next step necessary for the evolution of my work. I decided to bring together all my resources to find out.

VIII. Traffic Island Transformation

I was attracted to a site in lower Manhattan that seemed to have the right characteristics for a successful public art project. The site, a painted traffic island at a 'T' intersection, was in the midst of a business area with an active pedestrian flow. It was on a broad street, spacious yet protected at this intersection by office buildings on three sides. The corporations around the site could serve as potential sources of funding for the project since it would be designed for their employees. I started with inquiries at the New York Department of Transportation to find out what I needed to do to take a design proposal through the city channels. Project funding was a key issue. Drawing on my experience with grants and organizational work as well as my extensive file on architects, I wrote a proposal to do a design study for this space. The interdisciplinary design team I brought together included myself as artist and project coordinator, an architect whose special area of interest was street furniture, and a landscape architect who had a strong background in urban parks. We agreed to work collaboratively to arrive at a design concept; in addition, I would seek additional funds to exhibit our design to the business community and for possible realization of the project.

With sponsorship from a nonprofit organization, letters of support from the community and two advisors, I obtained funds to do a design study and we have been working on this project since 1986.

Working collaboratively, our design team has researched the potential of the site and developed a plan for integrating art, architecture and landscaping. Our premise is to use various paving materials and to treat the sidewalk as if it were a painted canvas on which a large-scale illusion of abstract forms is embedded. Street furniture and landscaping areas will be woven into the illusion to relate to the image or to act as counterpoint. To me, New York has always been a city of vertical views, whether looking up at the skyscrapers or downward from places like the World Trade Center, which is my favorite vantage point. The scale and illusion in my pavement 'painting' are made to be seen from the tops of buildings in the area. On the street level, it will function as an outdoor public space with seating, plantings and small-scale detailing in the materials for pedestrians to enjoy.

IX. Conclusion

The design study has led to a subsequent project titled *Urban Transformation*. It exists in a time frame more familiar to architects and city planners than to artists. As I take it through procedures with city agencies, community groups and corporate boards, the project is continually moving closer to realization. I am satisfied with the many new issues this endeavor required me to consider because my personal goals as an artist need to be realized in a social context. I am going outside the artworld boundaries to do my work because I want to contribute something I value to the built environment. For me, New York is a communal space, always in the process of being shaped by the people who live and work here. In the course of this pursuit, I have been affected and changed as well. My materials now include paving surfaces, such as cement, bricks and granite, as well as paint, and the scale of my work is flexible, from a watercolor to several city blocks. What remains constant, however, is the spirit evolving within my work as an artist; this remains the essence of what I have to contribute.

Discussion Questions

Content

1. How do you think Dorosh interprets the current relationship between art and the public? What does she seem to feel the relationship should be? What forces do you think influence the current relationship? In what ways?

2. How does Dorosh define an artwork's context? In what ways does she believe that we respond differently to a painting that is part of its urban environment and one that is traditionally presented as an art object?

3. Dorosh states that little of the art produced in New York City "is intended to affect the quality of public life in the city." How does Dorosh believe art can affect public life? In what sense do you agree with her and in what ways are art's influences on public life limited?

Form

1. In this essay, Dorosh mixes personal experiences with her thoughts about art and cities. Do her personal experiences lend authority to her interpretations? What are the effects on you as a reader of this combination of interpretations and personal experiences?

2. How would you describe Dorosh's attitude toward her pending projects that will combine her own and other peoples' art in public spaces in New York City? What words or phrases best capture her attitude? Given this attitude, why do you think she ends her essay the way she does?

3. Readers may have expectations of Dorosh's writing since she is an artist. In what ways does her essay seem "artistic" and in what ways does it fail to meet your expectations? In what kinds of environment would the style of her writing lend authority to her ideas, and in what situations would the style of her writing detract from her authority?

Writing Prompts

1. Write an essay that challenges what you understand to be commonly held beliefs about the purposes and functions of urban art installations like the ones Dorosh describes.

2. Write an essay that compares and contrasts the kind of public urban art that Dorosh describes with other forms of urban art. What values do the different kinds of sanctioned and unsanctioned urban art have in common? What are their differences?

Leonard Kriegel is an essayist and novelist who currently lives in New York city. He is the author of nonfiction: Working Through: A Teacher's Journey in the Urban University; On Men and Manhood; *and* Falling Into Life. *He has also published novels, including* Quitting Time. *In "Graffiti: Tunnel Notes of a New Yorker," originally published in* The American Scholar, *Kriegel reflects upon the changing nature of graffiti in New York City over the course of his lifetime. The essay offers a vision of New York as it was in the days of World War II and compares that vision to today's urban environment. The essay also takes up the debate over the status of graffiti as either art or an illegal pollutant of the city and city life. Kriegel argues that graffiti most eloquently captures and represents the current state of affairs in urban America.*

Graffiti:
Tunnel Notes of a New Yorker

Leonard Kriegel

WHEN I WAS EIGHT, I loved to run with my friends through the tunnel leading into Reservoir Oval in the North Central Bronx. The Oval occupied the site of a former city reservoir dredged by the WPA and then landscaped with playgrounds, wading pools, softball fields, a quarter-mile dirt track, and some of the finest tennis courts in the city—all ringed by attractive bush- and tree-lined walks that provided a natural shield for the sexual probings of early adolescence. Nothing else that bordered our neighborhood—not the wilds of Bronx Park or the chestnut trees of Van Cortlandt Park or the small camel-humped rock hill in Mosholu Parkway down which we went belly-whopping on American Flyer sleds in winter—fed us so incontrovertible a sense that America's promise now included us as did the long green and gray sweep of Reservoir Oval.

We would run through that entrance tunnel like a pack of Hollywood Indians on the warpath, our whoops echoing off the walls until we emerged from its shadows into the lush green lawns and brick walks and playing fields. Our portion of the Bronx was an ethnically mixed stew of immigrant families and their children, many of whom had fled Manhattan's crowded Lower East Side tenements for the spacious, park-rich green borough where Jonas Bronck had followed his cow across the Harlem River three hundred years earlier. The Bronx was still the city's "new" borough in 1941. Sparsely settled until after World War I, our neighborhood contained typical New York working- and lower-middle-class families on the rise in an America emerging from the Depression.

We children had already been assimilated into the wider American world. All of us—Irish and Italian Catholic as well as Eastern European Jew—believed we could ride the dream of success to a singular destiny. We were not yet of an age where we could physically journey into that wider America the books we read and the movies we saw told us was ours for the taking. The Oval was where we played together. It was also where we sometimes fought each other over myths that grew increasingly foreign and more raggedly European with each passing day. (Not that we were unaware of our parents' cultural baggage: marriage between Italian and Irish Catholics was still considered "mixed" in 1941.)

Occasionally, I would chance the Oval alone, in search of more solitary adventure. A curious metamorphosis would envelope me at such times: the entrance tunnel seemed darker and more threatening, the shadows warning me to move cautiously past walls peppered with graffiti. Alone, I let loose no war whoops to echo through that emptiness. Instead, I picked my way carefully through that dark half-moon of enclosed space, as if the graffiti scrawled on its surface held the clue to my future. There was something menacing about words scrawled on walls. Like an archaeologist probing ruins, I might turn in terror at any moment and run back to the security of my apartment three blocks south of the Oval.

Most of the graffiti was of the "John loves Mary!" kind, no different from the scribbled notes we passed one another in the P.S. 80 school yard down the hill. But it was also on that tunnel's walls that I first read the rage and fury of those who stained the world with conspiratorial fantasies. As rage exploded like bullets, words burrowed into my consciousness. "Roosevelt Jew Bastard!" "Unite Unite / Keep America White!" "Father Coughlin Speaks Truth!" "Kill All Jews!" In the raw grasp of age-old hatreds, politics was plot and plot was history and that reality seemed as impregnable as it was inescapable.

Like adults, children learn to shape anger through the words they confront. The graffiti on that tunnel wall mobilized my rage, nurturing my need for vengeance in the midst of isolation. It wasn't simply the anti-Semitism I wanted vengeance upon; it was my own solitary passage through that entrance tunnel. As I moved through it alone, the tunnel was transformed into everything my budding sense of myself as embryonic American hated. Walking through it became an act of daring, for graffiti had converted its emptiness into a threat that could only be taken the way it was offered—a threat that was distinctly personal.

In no other part of that huge complex of fields and walks was graffiti in great evidence. Other than the occasional heart-linked initials carved into the green-painted slats of wooden benches, I remember nothing else defacing the Oval. One emerged from that tunnel and the graffiti disappeared—all of it, "John loves Mary!" as well as "Kill All Jews!" It was as if an unwritten compact had been silently agreed upon, allowing the tunnel leading to the Oval to be scrawled over (despite occasional whitewashing, the tunnel was dark and poorly lit) while the rest of that huge recreation complex remained free of the presence of graffiti. Running that tunnel alone was an act of purgation, rewarded when one was safely home with the illusion (and occasionally the reality) of ethnic harmony.

Other than that tunnel, the presence of graffiti was localized to a few alleys and subway stations and public urinals in the New York I remember from the forties and fifties. Until the sixties, even chalk and paint adhered to the unwritten laws of proportion in neighborhoods like mine. Buildings had not yet been crusted over with curlicued shapes and exploding slashes, zigzagging to a visual anarchy that testified to a love of color and line overwhelmed by hatred of the idea that color and line do not dictate the needs of community. Even the anti-Semitic graffiti of that tunnel remains in my memory as less the product of hatred than an expression of the distance existing between groups struggling to claim a portion of the American past.

IN AN ESSAY PUBLISHED IN 1973, Norman Mailer labeled graffiti a "faith," a word that struck me even back then as an odd use of language when applied to what a graffiti writer does. From the perspective of that eight-year-old child moving through that tunnel entrance, graffiti was the very antithesis of faith. It embodied a poetics of rage and hatred, a syntax in which anyone could claim the right, if he possessed the will, to impose his needs on others. But rage is not faith, as even an eight-year-old knew. It is simply rage.

In today's New York—and in today's London and Paris and Amsterdam and Los Angeles—the spread of graffiti is as accurate a barometer of the decline of urban civility as anything else one can think of. Paradoxically, even as it spread, graffiti was hailed as one of the few successful attempts the voiceless in our nation's cities made to impose their presence on urban culture. If graffiti is now the most obvious form of visual pollution city landscapes are forced to endure (even more polluting than those paste-up false windows with flower pots that grow like urban ivy on the deserted apartment houses fronting the Major Deegan Parkway in the East Bronx), it has assumed for New Yorkers the shape and frame of this city's prospects. Where expectation is confused with coherence, those savage slashes on brick and sidewalk embody our idea of all that city life is and all that we can now expect it to be.

In books and photographic essays, graffiti is heralded as the art structuring the real urban landscape that the poor confront in their daily lives. "Graffiti makes a statement!" is the rallying cry of those who defend its presence. True enough—even if one believes that the statement graffiti makes chokes the very idea of what a city can be. One can argue that it is not what the statement says but the style the statement employs that lends graffiti its insistent singularity. But the evidence of the streets insists that graffiti is an urban statement whose ultimate end is nothing less than the destruction of urban life. Regardless of whether it is considered art or public nuisance, graffiti denies the possibility of an urban community by insisting that individual style is a more natural right than the communitarian demands of city life.

Defenders of graffiti may insist that its importance lies in the voice it gives to anger and that its triumph resides in the alternative it offers to rage. Perhaps so. But anyone who walks through the streets of today's New York understands that the price graffiti demands is an emotional exhaustion in which we find ourselves the victims of that same rage and anger supposedly given voice—*vented* is today's fashionable word—by these indiscriminate slashes of color plastered against brick and wall and doorway and telephone booth.

CONTEMPORARY GRAFFITI is not particularly political—at least not in New York. On those few times when one spots graffiti that does seek to embrace a message, the politics seem prepubescent sloganeering. Few openly political sayings are lettered onto these buildings and walls. Even the huge graffiti-like wall mural of a small Trotskyite press that one sees driving north on West Street in lower Manhattan speaks not of politics but of a peculiar Third World clubbiness more characteristic of the early 1970s than of our time. Malcolm X, Che Guevarra—originally offered as a pantheon of Third World liberators, the faces over the years have taken on the likeness of the comic-book superheroes in whose image one suspects they were originally conceived and drawn. The future they appeal to is curiously apolitical, as if the revolution they promise lies frozen in a nineteenth-century photograph in which reality assumes the proportions of myth. One has the impression that these are icons that have been hung on the wall for good luck, like a rabbit's foot or one of those plastic Jesuses one sees hanging from the rear-view mirrors of battered old Chevys.

The single most effective political graffito I have seen over the past few years was not in New York. Last summer, as I drove through streets filled with the spacious walled-in homes and immaculate concrete driveways of a wealthy Phoenix suburb, on my way to visit Frank Lloyd Wright's Taliesin

West, I came across "Save Our Desert" slashed in large dripping red letters across a brown sun-drenched adobe wall surrounding one of the huge sun palaces that root like cacti in the nouveau riche wilds of Goldwater County. Here was a graffito in which politics was central, a gauntlet thrown at the feet of developers for whom the Arizona desert is mere space to be acquired and used and disposed of for profit.

Perhaps because it is more traditional, political graffiti seems more understandable than these explosions of line and color and ectoplasmic scrawl now plastered like dried mucus against New York's brick and concrete. "Save Our Desert!" may be simplistic, but at least it expresses a desire to right a balance deemed unjust and unnecessary. Political graffiti intrudes on privacy by voicing a specific protest. This alone serves to distinguish it from the public stains New Yorkers now assume are as natural as blades of grass growing between the cracks in a sidewalk.

To deny this city's painful decline over the past three decades is to deny the obvious. One can measure that decline through the spread of graffiti. The process began with the insistence that these mindless blotches and savage strokes embodied a legitimate, if admittedly different, sense of fashion, that they could be viewed—indeed, they had to be viewed—as a "natural" expression of the new and daring.

Like everything else in this city, graffiti demands an emotional investment from those who defend it. One can only vindicate these slashes and blobs of color because their presence is so overwhelming. What choice do we have but to demand that the world recognize the "art" in these urban voices? Anything else forces us to examine the consequences of what we have allowed through the intimidating fear of not being in fashion. Even as acceptance is demanded, graffiti continues to pound against the city, having grown as mechanical and fixed as the sound of the boom boxes in the streets below our windows. We label graffiti "real," we label it "authentic," we label it "powerful." Like true pedants, we discuss the nuances of these different voices. We create graffiti martyrs from Keith Haring, dead of AIDS, and from Basquiat, dead of a drug overdose. In their deaths, we tell ourselves, our city lives. For their art is "urban." And urban counts. Urban must count. If not, why have we permitted what has been done to this city we claim to love?

If the graffiti plastered first on subway cars and then on billboard and doorway and brick truly constitutes an art form, then it is an art that seeks to rip out the root idea of what supposedly created it—the idea that a specifically urban culture exists. Defended as a creative act in which the city itself becomes the artist's canvas, the paradox of graffiti is the extent to which its existence connotes an implicit hatred of what a city is and what it can offer its citizens. At the core of graffiti's spread lurks the dangerously romantic notion that the city is a place of such overwhelming evil that it must be torn apart, savaged into its own death, its residents given a "voice" in the irrational hope that in this way its more urbane voices will be stilled. Graffiti slashes at the heart of New York, the heart of urbanity, by attacking the city's splendid nineteenth-century monuments of cast-iron architecture in the resurrected Soho neighborhood of lower Manhattan as indifferently as it attacks the playful 1930s art deco apartment house façades that once made the now-dingy Grand Concourse in the Bronx so singularly playful an example of urban aspiration.

New Yorkers stand like helpless mannequins before the onslaught. Graffiti does not, after all, destroy lives. It is not like the scourge of crack, or the horrendous spread of AIDS, or the rising tension in our neighborhoods between blacks and Jews and between blacks and Asians. Graffiti is no more than a background for the homeless who cage themselves in makeshift cardboard boxes or laundry baskets at night or the crazies who walk the streets engaged in heated dialogues with Jesus or Lenin or Mary Baker Eddy or George Steinbrenner or the dead yet still-celebrated Basquiat. Graffiti is innocent, or so we continue to tell ourselves even in the face of powerful evidence to the contrary. "No one ever died from graffiti!" a friend impatiently snaps, as I point out a deserted bank on the northwest corner of Fourteenth Street and Eighth Avenue, its once-attractive façade gouged and stabbed by slashes of black spray paint. "There are more important problems in this city."

Of course, there *are* more important problems in this city. Yet none speak more directly to the true state of affairs in this New York than the mush-rooming graffiti in our streets. And nothing traces the actual state of those streets better than the insistence graffiti makes that there are neither rules nor obligations for the survival of urban hope and aspiration. The prospect of a voice for the voiceless illuminates every dark alley in the New Yorker's mind, like the reflection of one of those stars already extinguished millions and millions of light years away. But is that to be all those of us who claim to love this city are finally left with, these dead light gleanings of one false revolution after another, beneath whose costly illusions—in the name of fashion—we have bent this great and wounded metropolis out of time and out of function and perhaps even out of its future?

Discussion Questions

Content

1. On what basis does Kriegel distinguish between contemporary and traditional graffiti? In what ways does the distinction seem valid to you and in what ways does it seem questionable?

2. Kriegel contends that "the spread of graffiti is as accurate a barometer of the decline of urban civility as anything else one can think of." What do you think

Kriegel means by the phrase "urban civility" and what do you think of this interpretation of graffiti? What do you think graffiti, as a communicative practice, stands for, other than a decline in civility? If graffiti is spreading, what does that show about our culture?

3. What kind of portrait of New York does Kriegel paint when he remembers his childhood, and what, other than graffiti, seems to make that city different from the current one? How do particular words or phrases work to construct the past differently from the present in this essay?

Form

1. In what ways does Kriegel engage arguments opposed to his? What positions do you think he ignores?

2. Kriegel argues in favor of political graffiti. How does the organization of his essay lead us to agree with him that some graffiti are good and some are not?

3. Kriegel connects the increase in graffiti to New York's decline. How is his essay organized to connect graffiti and decline? Does the connection seem valid to you?

Writing Prompts

1. Write an essay that either challenges or supports a distinction between political and nonpolitical graffiti. Use examples from your city or campus to support your distinction.

2. Write an essay that explains the purpose and social significance of graffiti. Explore your community to find examples of graffiti that you can use to support your interpretation of what graffiti means.

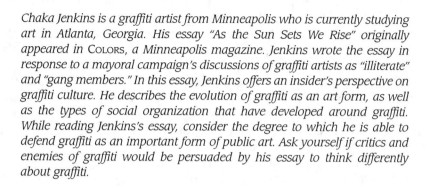

Chaka Jenkins is a graffiti artist from Minneapolis who is currently studying art in Atlanta, Georgia. His essay "As the Sun Sets We Rise" originally appeared in Colors, *a Minneapolis magazine. Jenkins wrote the essay in response to a mayoral campaign's discussions of graffiti artists as "illiterate" and "gang members." In this essay, Jenkins offers an insider's perspective on graffiti culture. He describes the evolution of graffiti as an art form, as well as the types of social organization that have developed around graffiti. While reading Jenkins's essay, consider the degree to which he is able to defend graffiti as an important form of public art. Ask yourself if critics and enemies of graffiti would be persuaded by his essay to think differently about graffiti.*

As the Sun Sets We Rise: The Life and Times of a Graffiti Artist

Chaka Jenkins

ON A GRAY-SKIED WEDNESDAY AFTERNOON within the confines of my first-floor lab, I recline my head on a soft blue cushion, relaxing, pondering life's poisons over a glass of mango Snapple. An excessive dose of underground hip-hop seeps thickly out of my makeshift boombox. As the beat hits the audio canals and liquid trickles slowly down my esophagus, I allow my eyes to wander over 200 hundred cans of Krylon, American Accent, Plasticote, and the old-time favorite, Rustoleum.

It's an indescribable pleasure to observe large quantities of paint, especially when the stash of paint is within my possession. Immaculate colors and labels stand in single-file rows—plums, real greens, mauves, silvers, reds and blues. Sacks upon sacks of adjustable spray nozzles lay scattered on the floor. From an aerial position the white nozzles form a subconscious pattern on the dark-brown carpet.

For me every day is the same. Work among the zombies who have already submitted to government corporate flux, then backtrack my way to the residence, avoiding unnecessary confrontation with divine evil, occasionally waving to comrades of both genders. When I finally reach my destination I enjoy many methods of relaxation. After my meditation, I focus my mind on subjects that negate any remnants of my work. I enter my euphoric graffiti, or (as some refer to it) aerosolic art, which in some ways destroys the negative connotations of the word graffiti. Whether it be called aerosolic or graffiti, the action of rebelliously painting is my soul and energy, my breath of life, my walk and talk, my 360 degrees of bona fide culture. I am far from alone. Our members run deep and thorough, yet I'm aware that the numbers of people who can't see or feel it in its proper context rank massive next to ours. We are a clandestine group, writing graffiti by night after the sun has set on others' daytime fortunes.

My very good friend Jeanne Lee at *Colors* thought it would be interesting for me to write an article regarding the life and ethics of a graffiti artist. Due to my lack of trust I was hesitant. Newsmen with cameras have greedily requested access to hidden meccas of pieces, asked for names and crews, history, and so on. Many uninformed people were influenced by that irresponsible ad campaign by candidate (now Mayor) Sharon Sayles Belton during last year's Minneapolis election. When I first saw her ad on television, set against a backdrop of graffiti that others were painting over as she pledged to rid the city of it, I was shocked. It was funny and detrimental all at once. It was just living fact about how foul all politicians must be in order to function in the political arena.

The Sayles Belton campaign told the public that graffiti artists are illiterate and gang members. People actually believed it. That newsman was stupid to think I would reveal precious locations for commercial fame. If you stumble upon it, that's one thing, but to lead you to it—I don't think so. It is very ironic that numerous articles have been written about us but not by us. Once again, outside entities define our culture, telling us what we dress, look, and smell like. Pure arrogance in the highest form.

Before I get in depth with this article I would like to first give love and powerful positive shouts to all brethren and sistren representing graffiti all around and especially in Minneapolis, where I used to lay my head. I hope I represent us properly, as is rarely done outside our intimate circles. I really hope toys out there learn something valuable and the means to shed their neophyte curse.

Some History

Graffiti started in the streets. It is rugged and rough and has adopted codes of existence which in the last resort may result in violence. Graffiti at its core is not violent, but has evolved to something totally removed from its original form. Graffiti is the attitude that subdues average linear letters and twists, bends, and shapes them. Letters are primary; characters (images, pictures, portraits) are secondary. Graffiti is visual slang.

Most of the graffiti styles in Minneapolis and St. Paul originated elsewhere. In 1985 or 1986 a brother from Brooklyn named Jek put brothers on the North Side down with styles. I knew most of the old school brothas but not enough history to splurge upon. I do know that graffiti in Minnesota started in North Minneapolis. I knew brothers who caught rek were Jek, Viper, EB Too Much, Payton, Stage, Oops, Smak, and Rey. Graffiti, of course, was here before Jek, due to the movies "Wildstyle," "Style Wars," and "Beat Street." From what I heard, Jek formulated styles out of his black book like no other, to produce solid students. But that graffiti died out in 1987 or 1988 due to people getting busted and the introduction of crack.

Tag-banging is based on neighborhoods taggin', scrapping, and shooting. The only thing that separates taggers from street organizations is the nicknames of the members, the crew name and the jazzy style of writing. When I first was fully in tune with the graffiti scene in Los Angeles in 1987 and 1988, groups were assembled along with gang-banging. As time progressed, the rules changed. People crossed out each other more blatantly, causin' rougher measures to enforce respect for your crew. As confrontations arose, people literally got beat down. Some kids who caught the beatings had older siblings who were involved in the gangs. Regardless of who did the beating, they had to handle the situation in gang formation. Blood is the strongest connection.

Everybody in L.A. had some siblings who bang. Some graffiti crews were in the same radius as the gangsters, sometimes sharing membership. So problems escalated. Some people do not see the separation between the two, just a lifestyle. The similarity lies in the high level of respect you must command. In the world of the streets, whatever you bring upon yourself you must handle adequately.

I was involved in some of the early tag-banging in the summer of 1988. Downtown Huntington Park in L.A. was the spot for the Tuesday $2 matinee. The theater was packed more than 300-deep with taggers.

I remember standing in line forever to enter, talking to the homies, checking out the female writers trooping in packs. After you paid your $2, you entered the clutches of stern-faced security guards who would thoroughly check for any object used for marking or carving. But being so youthful and sneaky, we always managed to get our supplies in.

After I was clear, I would enter a sloping red-velour carpet trail down the aisle to find my crew. I would look for the hats with the crew initials embroidered on the side, then slide in, give a few handshakes and proceed to observe the chaos in motion. Side doors would blast open like explosives to reveal sunlight and 20 kids rushing into the dark black forest of angry adolescents to quickly fit in as if they had been in the movie for hours. Kids would tag on the screen as the projector showed the film. Rarely would I be able to focus my attention on the movie. I mostly came for the ambiance.

When people label graffiti writers as gangs it gives a wide range of misconceptions. The first misconception is the word "gang." Who do you fit to it? The president's committee, the pope, judges, police, FBI, CIA or USDA? Nope. Dark-skinned people with the lowest form of a gang which is visible, thanks to our good friend media.

Bombin', Piecin' and Stayin' Safe

A tag is a signature used with a Pilot, mean streak or thin or fat cap connected to some Krylon. A fat cap is best so your tag is most seen. Entering a throw-up along with taggin' in my view is bombing. A throw-up can consist of initials of your name or your whole name or crew. Usually throw-ups are bubbly. Sometimes they are sprayed fat in a mist with a fat cap just to lightly cover them. When you're finished, a thick outline is applied to pull everything together. Throw-ups are very visible. Throw-ups are done in a light and dark color or done in the darkest color with no fill-in. Good combinations include true blue and white; red and white; silver and black; red and silver; gold and red; and blue and silver.

The next step is two cans of clean, stylized letters that don't connect. Then comes piecing. Piecing is a learning experience. You learn from what you didn't do before. Then you try to include all input for the next piecing. Letter formation is more critical than the colors or concepts. You should be able to manifest your wild style in two colors. Cleanliness is appreciated from everyone.

When I piece, I look for clean, smooth walls that can best serve my letter size. Visible or invisible, I mostly look for potential yards to start up new locations. I'll piece anywhere, high or low; the same with bombing. Developing styles is cool, but if you can't outdo what you wish to go over, don't do it. Take it somewhere else. If you go over someone's work with bullshit, you will be handled roughly. Plain and simple.

To prepare the wall for piecin', you can roll primer over it, go over someone else's piece who you can outdo, go over your own stuff, or paint right on the wall, depending on how good the wall is. There is no set method. Everyone does it differently. I like to fill in my dimensions first, then handle the fill of the piece. When doing this, I try to feel and become one with my environment, allowing myself to be aware of intruders. I look out a lot. I also have a watch out. It feels good to do it illegal.

To all toys: Watch and feel. Don't ever overexaggerate. You will cause attention to yourself. If you get caught, shut up and be quiet. Tell them nothing. If this is what you want to do, why snitch out a buddy who loves to do what you love also? If you are in school, stop taggin' on your backpack. Become silent with your skills, like you're some superhero by night, student by day.

Toys

A toy is what every graffiti writer is when starting off. Writers who say they were never toys are lying. I was a toy when I first started writing in the summer of '85 in Los Angeles. After watching "Wildstyle" and reading the book, I named myself Toy because of my beginning status. As I evolved, I realized naming myself Toy was a dis to myself. People who remembered me from junior high would shout, "Hey, Toy," and I would be ready to fight. The '94 toys of Minnesota refuse to listen to their elders. They are the ultimate hardheads. They lack feelings, dedication, soul, spirit, and foundation. Honestly, they're not even doing graffiti. Without these elements they move further and further away from what they say they're so interested in.

Metaphorically speaking, a beginning jazz musician can't start doing solos or delving into the depths of fusion or improvisation unless the fundamental aspects of simplicity are followed, memorized, and become as easy to do as breathing. After that process is completed, one can move on. I think the chain of evolution goes like this: toy to tagger to bomber and finally to full-fledged writer who tags, bombs, and pieces.

Toys are the biggest enemy to a small scene like the Twin Cities where they misrepresent us and outnumber us six times over. Toys are the low end of our culture, and in this town they will be our demise. I personally have nothing against some toys. They must learn somewhere. Yet I won't take a toy under my wing to school him or her, because I feel it would be in vain. In 1994 everyone's authenticity is challenged due to heavy exploitation. I question toys up and down about why they wish to be a part of the rich and talented culture. Is it a fad? Can you feel it? Most toys I interrogate don't pass. They know nothing. It hurts tremendously. I ask myself what is to come of what people have risked their lives for?

Some toys really want, feel it, live it, and love it but get bunched in with the others who outnumber us all. They follow the unseen rules and show development through time. Time converts toys or condemns them to the abyss.

Outro

The Wall of Fame used to be legal. The owners of the building said it was okay as long as good taste was kept, discriminating against no one. This year the Wall of Fame is still legal, according to the owners of the building. But you piece at your own risk from a consistent swarm of cops who apprehend on site. To be free from harassment you must get permission from the city. Most artists don't know that, and most artists won't go through the motions just to paint on the wall. So in turn the wall creates more illegal graffiti, and more negative things for politicians, cops, and other organizations to talk about. It's just another form to kill what they can't have their hand in controlling. In the eyes of the government, it's only legal when the government controls it. But then it wouldn't be graffiti anymore. Graffiti is a sign of discord and of the corruption within our communities. We get upset and take it to the streets.

Graffiti will forever stay illegal. The best a city can do is to donate abandoned walls for practice without trying to make money, or trying to control and destroy it. Make graffiti legal without government strings. It's a radical thought that everyone's too scared to try.

Discussion Questions

Content

1. What purpose does graffiti serve in Jenkins's life? What does he feel is important about graffiti, and how is this importance connected to his stated reasons for writing his article?

2. Jenkins states that graffiti "has evolved to something totally removed from its original form." In what senses does his essay develop this idea? Does Jenkins present graffiti as properly a stable art form or one that is always changing? What reasons does he give for his position and how would you respond to it?

3. Jenkins suggests that outsiders have written and passed laws about graffiti that ignore "writers." In what ways do you think that his essay does a good job of expanding the discussion about graffiti, and what are the essay's limitations?

Form

1. How does Jenkins's tone change in the different sections of the essay? In what ways can the issue of authority be used to understand these shifts in tone?

2. When and how does Jenkins use language and discuss ideas that fit your expectations of a graffiti writer? When and how do his language and ideas seem most unlike what you would expect?

3. Does Jenkins's primary audience seem different in the various sections? List his primary audience for each section. Discuss other ways in which he could have addressed these audiences without special sections.

Writing Prompts

1. Write an essay that considers the importance of insiders' perspectives on marginal cultures like graffiti culture. Why are such perspectives important, and what are their potential drawbacks?

2. After reviewing the essays by Kriegel and Jenkins in this part, write an essay that evaluates the degree to which the various sides of the graffiti debate understand and address each other's concerns. To what degree do Jenkins and Kriegel communicate with each other and to what degree do they seem to miscommunicate?

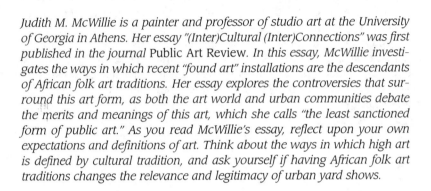

Judith M. McWillie is a painter and professor of studio art at the University of Georgia in Athens. Her essay "(Inter)Cultural (Inter)Connections" was first published in the journal Public Art Review. *In this essay, McWillie investigates the ways in which recent "found art" installations are the descendants of African folk art traditions. Her essay explores the controversies that surround this art form, as both the art world and urban communities debate the merits and meanings of this art, which she calls "the least sanctioned form of public art." As you read McWillie's essay, reflect upon your own expectations and definitions of art. Think about the ways in which high art is defined by cultural tradition, and ask yourself if having African folk art traditions changes the relevance and legitimacy of urban yard shows.*

(Inter)Cultural (Inter)Connections

Judith M. McWillie

THE INTERSECTION of the Southern Railroad and Highland Avenue in the Normaltown district of Memphis, Tenn., is a busy urban crossroads that divides the fashionable suburbs of the city's east side from the racially segregated neighborhoods of the Orange Mound district to the southwest. From the late 1960s until shortly before his death in 1990, Eddie Williamson offered himself as a bridge across these boundaries. Living as a "squatter" on a narrow grass embankment flanking the south side of the railroad tracks, Williamson created a huge yard show that local shop owners and residents described as "Parking Lot Eddie's bottle garden."

The focus of Williamson's life, as well as his contributions to the neighborhood, revolved around this 100-foot by 25-foot work. Assembled from discarded bottles, sprouting stalks and seedlings, carpet and fabric remnants, mattresses and bedsprings, oil lamps, shopping carts, chrome hubcaps and other found objects, it was a sprawling testament to the artist's strength and tenacity. Glass bottles set in troughs next to the curb marked its parameters. Other bottles were planted in rows, marking discrete zones within the site itself. While transporting found objects to the site, Williamson

Judith M. McWillie. "(Inter)Cultural (Inter)Connections." From *Public Art Review* (Summer/Fall 1992): 14–15. Reprinted with permission of the author.

often filled discarded jars and buckets with cuttings from plants that had somehow managed to break through the neighborhood's veneer of concrete and asphalt. Likewise, within a two-block radius of the central installation, he cultivated virtually every patch of exposed earth, pulling weeds from the crumbling edges of parking lots where they intersected the bases of buildings, exposing enough raw ground to plant zucchini and watermelon. These he later harvested and distributed free to patrons of the adjacent shopping center.

The yard show itself was another kind of cultivated oasis—a cosmogonic axis whose design honored the horizontal sweep of the railroad tracks and resonated with the patchwork grids of rural subsistence gardens. Williamson sometimes camped in a tent-like, pyramid-shaped shelter in the center; later he moved to a used car parked next to a meat market.

Farther afield, he collected broken pots, vases, and other ceramic vessels from dumpsters and installed them in the shallow alcoves that spontaneously develop in the façades of shopworn buildings. These wall shrines were complemented by bundles of carefully selected found objects that he mounted in alleyways and median strips. Together with his gardens and plantings, Williamson's art ritually inverted the identity of an arid commercial district.

For all their range and longevity, however, African-American yard shows such as Eddie Williamson's remain the least sanctioned form of public art, not only in the precincts of academia where they are now being investigated and documented, but sometimes in the cities that host them, as well. Their religious origins are rarely understood, while their political effects remain even more obscure. However, surveys in both urban and rural settings (by Robert Farris Thompson and Grey Gundaker of Yale University, and by this author) reveal a strikingly consistent pattern of cultural invention operating on a scale that transcends the local folklore attached to them.

Perhaps the most famous contemporary yard shows were created in the late 1980s by 37-year-old Tyree Guyton and his family in Detroit's Heidelberg Street neighborhood. Like Eddie Williamson, Guyton voraciously collected cast-off consumer objects and resurrected them in a visionary context. He used the neighborhood's condemned and abandoned houses as armatures, covering them with so many objects that the superstructures beneath were barely exposed. The disorientation of familiar items, the sheer density and mass of their cumulative effect, seemed to defy gravity. Almost immediately, the carnivalesque spectacle of Guyton's work attracted tourists and discouraged the crack cocaine dealers who had moved into the abandoned houses. Guyton reversed the neglect of his neighborhood and correspondingly focused attention on the community's needs, an achievement that made him an instant celebrity. He was featured on the NBC Nightly News and in an unusually broad spectrum of publications ranging from *The National Star* (a crown jewel of the pulp press similar to *The National Enquirer*), to *People* and *Connoisseur* magazines. In 1990, the Detroit Institute of the Arts sponsored a solo exhibition of Guyton's work in which he arrived daily and dressed the walls and floors with still more newly rescued objects. This exhibition marked the first occasion in which African-American yard dressing was consciously imported into a fine arts context.

While there are obvious precedents for the use of found objects in 20th-century Western art, both the origins and purposes of yard shows such as Guyton's and Williamson's predate modernism and continue to transmit African cultural signatures no less than in the past. Robert Farris Thompson suggests that "minkisi," sacred medicines from the Kongo region of West Africa (Angola and Zaire), the ancestral homeland of many African-Americans, establish an appropriate paradigm for understanding the symbology and social values encoded within them.

"Minkisi" are charms made from ritual configurations of objects and substances said to affect spiritual power in those who honor them. Although in West Africa "minkisi" were primarily composed of natural substances and carvings, in the New World the tradition was expanded to include all manner of commercially manufactured items from the West as well. This was a "cloaking" device employed by slaves as they encountered the suppression of African traditional religion and material culture. The use of ordinary objects for ritual purposes thus became a crucial strategy of spiritual continuity and cultural resistance. As vessels of coded communication, these objects were easily recognized by the initiated; as the ordinary props of everyday existence, uninformed slave owners simply overlooked them.

In *The Four Moments of the Sun: Kongo Art in Two Worlds*, Thompson quotes the 18th-century historian L'Abbé Proyart's reaction to the dressed houses and fields he encountered along the coast of northern Kongo. "The most determined thief would not dare cross their threshold when he sees it thus protected by these mysterious signs." While in Africa, as well as in the United States, the yard was the center of family life, Eugene Genovese points out that in the West Indies, "it was much more than a social center and a means of additional food. The slaves buried their dead there; the yard took on a religious significance . . . One did not walk into another's yard without permission." In North America, where the yard and the cemetery were most often separate, the long-standing custom of using found objects as votives on graves reinforced the connection of these two spaces. The idiom of found-object grave decoration radiated across the United States from the southeastern Atlantic coast, generating a lexicon of material signs, directly related to Kongo religion, that later became the basis of yard show iconography. The late anthropologist Robert Plant Armstrong used the term "syndedic" to describe these processes and to signify modes of development in which "linear, evolutionary growth tends less to dominate than does ardent proliferation."

Shells, clocks, tires, automobile wheel casings, wagon wheels and other signs of circular or spiral time involve the Kongo life cycle of spiritual return in which the soul travels counter-clockwise around the "four moments of the sun": i.e., birth, ascendency, death, and triumphant return as an ancestor. Diamond-shaped ideograms inscribed on graves and used as *bricolage* houses further add to the material extensions of this tradition. Circles indicating little suns occasionally appear at the nodes of the diamond in African-American vernacular painting, sculpture, and textiles.

In Kongo cosmology, the passage beyond life also includes a journey across "kalunga," a watery region where everything is upside-down and reversed as a reflection. Metal and terra cotta pipes signal this journey, both as water bearers and as "bridges between worlds" capable of transmitting messages from the beyond. Ceramic shards and broken pots, as well as inverted porcelain bowls and basins represent "the reversing power of death." Mirrors, glass, mica, tinfoil, chrome objects—all carriers of mystic flash—hold the spirit at an appropriate distance from the living while allowing those remaining to see into the next world. Lamps light the way to the deceased along their spiritual journey. The last used objects of family and loved ones seal covenants of communication between the living and the dead. Trees planted directly on graves evoke "immortality and perdurance." Bottle trees, one of the first idioms to translate the dialogic powers of the cemetery into the context of yards, summon spirits that guard the land against intruders while also capturing and containing malevolent forces.

Today, some African-American grave sites are beginning to assume the volume and complexity of yard shows. A grave in New Orleans, photographed in April 1991, serves as an example of how the use of found-object votives is continuously updated, refreshing a tradition that has always stressed authenticity over orthodoxy. Here, the idiomatic water-bearing pipe is juxtaposed with its contemporary counterpart, a child's circular plastic swimming pool. This grave, along with another in Holly Hill, S.C., is literally wired together with the personal effects of the deceased. Deep within the enclosure of the South Carolina grave is a small "headstone" where the wheel of a child's bicycle is cemented onto a wooden slab.

However, the transition from the modestly dressed graves and yards of rural Southern communities to the explosive shaping and elaboration of the idiom by those we call artists involves a quantum leap through politics as well as tradition. In spite of Tyree Guyton's national visibility and renown, for example, a court order allowed the city of Detroit to disassemble his houses in 1991 on the grounds that they violated local zones and ordinances. One of the witnesses at Guyton's court hearing was Robert Farris Thompson, who tried in vain to convince the city of the historical and spiritual significance of the artist's work.

Likewise, during the 20 years Eddie Williamson lived at the Highland and Southern crossroads in Memphis, legal machinations chronically threatened his work. The neighborhood's merchants and restaurateurs championed Williamson, but transient motorists complained of the "junk yard" adjoining the railroad tracks. Houston Brown, owner of the Southern Meat Market across the street from the site, and a close friend of Williamson's, marshalled support from a local television station and hired a lawyer to represent his friend in court battles with the city health department. Brown remains inspired by Williamson's legend, maintaining an archive on him and pointing out the peach trees he planted, now fully grown, along the tracks where he built the bottle garden.

"As long as it was at least 25 feet from the center of the tracks, the railroad allowed it," said Brown. "The city health department got onto him, but all three cases against him were dismissed. This was back in the 1970s when, unlike today, it was illegal to live on the street. At one point they tried to prove him mentally incompetent, so Channel 13 got a psychiatrist who declared him sane. Another time, when he was living in the car, they said he had to store his belongings at least 18 inches above the ground. That was when we got the shopping carts—in order to be in compliance with that law. Eddie refused Social Security and his service pension, not wanting to take any money from the government. He earned what money he had from cleaning up the alleys and parking lots. It's the way he wanted to live and he deserves credit for doing what he wanted to do. He was just different, and he was going to do what he wanted to do regardless."

Four years before his death, Williamson permitted the city to strip the site of his yard show since ill health prevented him from further maintaining it. He continued to live in the car next to Brown's meat market, however, developing his wall shrines and found-object votives until his death at the age of 68.

The assaults on Eddie Williamson and Tyree Guyton's works are local manifestations of a more persuasive cultural contrast in which the myth of the "hard-edged autonomous individualist," a myth at the core of 20th-century Western art, gives way to a more community-oriented connective impulse in the larger context of Afro-Atlantic tradition. That Eddie Williamson and Tyree Guyton would galvanize their local communities, using as their only tools the waste and refuse of consumer culture, is wholly compatible with an African spiritual system based on interconnectedness, empathy, and the sanctity of personal relationships. Their works can thus be understood as nodes of power activated by still more yard shows in hundreds of "private" spaces across the United States. Yard shows challenge our social and aesthetic presumptions in ways "yet to be fully estimated." "I suggest," says Thompson, "that the coming of the artistic traditions of West Africa to the New World provided life insurance on a hemispheric scale and that the full range of possibility embodied in this history helps us to understand some of the central issues of our time."

Discussion Questions

Content

1. What connections does the author suggest exist between urban "found art" and African folk art forms? How do these connections influence the way that you understand "found art"?

2. What similar urban issues might both Guyton and Williamson be addressing? How are their installations similar commentaries on urban life?

3. McWillie states that urban art installations like those of Williamson and Guyton "remain the least sanctioned form of public art." What evidence does she offer to support this claim, and how can you explain resistance to "found art" installations in urban environments?

Form

1. McWillie separates her discussion of Guyton and Williamson from her discussion of the African folk arts. How do you explain this separation? To what degree and in what ways does it enhance or weaken her argument?

2. McWillie ends her essay with a quotation. Do you find that this form of closing serves a particularly powerful rhetorical purpose? Where else in the essay could this quotation have appeared, and what would its rhetorical effect have been?

3. Near the end of her essay, McWillie suggests a "community-oriented connective impulse" in the art she describes. How do you understand this suggestion? In what ways do the structure and organization of her essay seem to mirror this impulse?

Writing Prompts

1. Find a "yard show" in your area that either intentionally or unintentionally assembles diverse "found" materials. Compare that exhibit, installation, or collection to either Williamson's or Guyton's, as you understand them from McWillie's essay. What commentary do you think your "yard show" provides on contemporary culture?

2. Write a "found" piece using only phrases that you overhear, read, or find in one hour. After sharing this piece with others, think and write about what this activity suggests or reveals about a key concept in your understanding of writing, such as originality, correctness, focus, or intention.

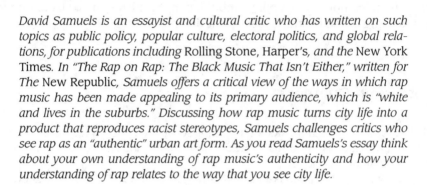

David Samuels is an essayist and cultural critic who has written on such topics as public policy, popular culture, electoral politics, and global relations, for publications including Rolling Stone, Harper's, *and the* New York Times. *In "The Rap on Rap: The Black Music That Isn't Either," written for* The *New Republic, Samuels offers a critical view of the ways in which rap music has been made appealing to its primary audience, which is "white and lives in the suburbs." Discussing how rap music turns city life into a product that reproduces racist stereotypes, Samuels challenges critics who see rap as an "authentic" urban art form. As you read Samuels's essay think about your own understanding of rap music's authenticity and how your understanding of rap relates to the way that you see city life.*

The Rap on Rap:
The Black Music That Isn't Either

David Samuels

THIS SUMMER Soundscan, a computerized scanning system, changes *Billboard* magazine's method of counting record sales in the United States. Replacing a haphazard system that relied on big-city record stores, Soundscan measured the number of records sold nationally by scanning the bar codes at chain store cash registers. Within weeks the number of computed record sales leapt, as demographics shifted from minority-focused urban centers to white, suburban, middle-class malls. So it was that America awoke on June 22, 1991, to find that its favorite record was not *Out of Time*, by aging college-boy rockers R.E.M., but *Niggaz4life*, a musical celebration of gang rape and other violence by N.W.A., or Niggers With Attitude, a rap group from the Los Angeles ghetto of Compton whose records had never before risen above No. 27 on the Billboard charts.

From *Niggaz4life* to *Boyz N the Hood*, young black men committing acts of violence were available this summer in a wide variety of entertainment formats. Of these none is more popular than rap. And none has received quite the level of critical attention and concern. Writers on the left have long viewed rap as the heartbeat of urban America, its authors, in Arthur Kempton's words, "the pre-eminent young dramaturgists in the clamorous theater of the street." On the right, this assumption has been shared, but greeted with predictable disdain.

Neither side of the debate has been prepared, however, to confront what the entertainment industry's receipts from this summer prove beyond doubt: although rap is still proportionally more popular among blacks, its primary audience is white and lives in the suburbs. And the history of rap's degeneration from insurgent black street music to mainstream pop points to another dispiriting conclusion: the more rappers were packaged as violent black criminals, the bigger their white audiences became.

If the racial makeup of rap's audience has been largely misunderstood, so have the origins of its authors. Since the early 1980s a tightly knit group of mostly young, middle-class, black New Yorkers, in close concert with white record producers, executives, and publicists, has been making rap music for an audience that industry executives concede is primarily composed of white suburban males. Building upon a form pioneered by lower-class black artists in New York between 1975 and 1983, despite an effective boycott of the music by both black and white radio that continues to this day, they created the most influential pop music of the 1980s. Rap's appeal to whites rested in its evocation of an age-old image of blackness: a foreign, sexually charged, and criminal underworld against which the norms of white society are defined, and, by extension, through which they may be defied. It was the truth of this latter proposition that rap would test in its journey into the mainstream.

"Hip-hop," the music behind the lyrics, which are "rapped," is a form of sonic bricolage with roots in "toasting," a style of making music by speaking over records. (For simplicity, I'll use the term "rap" interchangeably with "hip-hop" throughout this article.) Toasting first took hold in Jamaica in the mid-1960s, a response, legend has it, to the limited availability of expensive Western instruments and the concurrent proliferation of cheap R&B instrumental singles on Memphis-based labels such as Stax-Volt. Cool DJ Herc, a Jamaican who settled in the South Bronx, is widely credited with having brought toasting to New York City. Rap spread quickly through New York's poor black neighborhoods in the mid- and late 1970s....

ALTHOUGH MUCH IS MADE OF RAP as a kind of urban streetgeist, early rap had a more basic function: dance music. Bill Stephney, considered by many to be the smartest man in the rap business, recalls the first time he heard hip-hop: "The point wasn't rapping, it was rhythm, DJs cutting records left and right, taking the big drum break from Led Zeppelin's 'When the Levee Breaks,' mixing it together with 'Ring My Bell,' then with a Bob James Mardi

Gras jazz record and some James Brown. You'd have 2,000 kids in any community center in New York, moving back and forth, back and forth, like some kind of tribal war dance, you might say. It was the rapper's role to match this intensity rhythmically. No one knew what he was saying. He was just rocking the mike."

Rap quickly spread from New York to Philadelphia, Chicago, Boston, and other cities with substantial black populations. Its popularity was sustained by the ease with which it could be made. The music on early rap records sounded like the black music of the day: funk or, more often, disco. Performers were unsophisticated about image and presentation, tending toward gold lamé jumpsuits and Jericurls, a second-rate appropriation of the stylings of funk musicians like George Clinton and Bootsy Collins.

THE FIRST RAP RECORD to make it big was "Rapper's Delight," released in 1979 by the Sugar Hill Gang, an ad hoc all-star team drawn from three New York groups on Sylvia and Joey Robinson's Sugar Hill label. Thanks to Sylvia Robinson's soul music and background, the first thirty seconds of "Rapper's Delight" were indistinguishable from the disco records of the day: light guitars, high-hat drumming, and hand-claps over a deep funk bass line. What followed will be immediately familiar to anyone who was young in New York City that summer:

> I said, hip-hop, de-hibby, de-hibby-dibby,
> Hip-hip-hop you don't stop.
> Rock it out, Baby Bubba to the boogie de-bang-bang,
> Boogie to the boogie to be.
> Now what you hear is not a test,
> I'm rapping to the beat . . .
> I said, "By the way, baby, what's your name?"
> She said, "I go by the name Lois Lane
> And you can be my boyfriend, you surely can
> Just let me quit my boyfriend, he's called Superman."
> I said, "he's a fairy, I do suppose
> Flying through the air in pantyhose . . .
> You need a man who's got finesse
> And his whole name across his chest" . . .

Like disco music and jumpsuits, the social commentaries of early rappers like Grandmaster Flash and Mellie Mel were for the most part transparent attempts to sell records to whites by any means necessary. Songs like "White Lines" (with its anti-drug theme) and "The Message" (about ghetto life) had the desired effect, drawing fulsome praise from white rock critics, raised on the protest ballads of Bob Dylan and Phil Ochs. The reaction on the street was somewhat less favorable."The Message" is a case in point."People hated that record," recalls Russell Simmons, president of Def Jam Records. "I remember the Junebug, a famous DJ of the time, was playing it up at the Fever, and Ronnie DJ put a pistol to his head and said, 'Take that record off and break it or I'll blow your fucking head off.' The whole club stopped until he broke that record and put it in the garbage."

It was not until 1984 that rap broke through to a mass white audience. The first group to do so was Run-DMC, with the release of its debut album, *Run-DMC,* and with *King of Rock* one year later. These albums blazed the trail that rap would travel into the musical mainstream. Bill Adler, a former rock critic and rap's best-known publicist, explains:"They were the first group that came on stage as if they had just come off the street corner. But unlike the first generation of rappers, they were solidly middle class. Both of Run's parents were college-educated. DMC was a good Catholic schoolkid, a mama's boy. Neither of them was deprived and neither of them ever ran with a gang, but on stage they became the biggest, baddest, streetest guys in the world." When Run-DMC covered the Aerosmith classic "Walk This Way," the resulting video made in onto MTV, and the record went gold.

Rap's new mass audience was in large part the brainchild of Rick Rubin, a Jewish punk rocker from suburban Long Island who produced the music behind many of rap's biggest acts. Like many New Yorkers his age, Rick grew up listening to Mr. Magic's Rap Attack, a rap radio show on WHBI 1983, at the age of 19, Rubin founded Def Jam Records in his NYU dorm room. (Simmons bought part of Def Jam in 1984 and took full control of the company in 1989.) Rubin's next group, the Beastie Boys, was a white punk rock band whose transformation into a rap group pointed rap's way into the future. The Beasties' first album, *Licensed to Ill,* backed by airplay of its authentic frat-party single "You've Got to Fight for Your Right to Party," became the first rap record to sell a million copies.

The appearance of white groups in a black musical form has historically prefigured the mainstreaming of the form, the growth of the white audience, and the resulting dominance of white performers. With rap, however, this process took an unexpected turn: white demand indeed began to determine the direction of the genre, but what it wanted was music more defiantly black. The result was Public Enemy, produced and marketed by Rubin, the next group significantly to broaden rap's appeal to young whites.

Public Enemy's now familiar mélange of polemic and dance music was formed not on inner-city streets but in the suburban Long Island towns in which the group's members grew up. The children of successful black middle-class professionals, they gave voice to the feeling that, despite progress toward equality, blacks still did not quite belong in white America. They complained of unequal treatment by the police, of never quite overcoming the color of their skin:"We were suburban college kids doing what we were supposed to do, but we were always made to feel like something else," explains Stephney, the group's executive producer.

Public Enemy's abrasive and highly politicized style made it a fast favorite of the white avant-garde, much like the English punk rock band The Clash ten years before. Public Enemy's music, produced by the Shocklee brothers Hank and Keith, was faster, harder, and more abrasive than the rap of the day, music that moved behind the vocals like a full-scale band. But the root of Public Enemy's success was a highly charged theater of race in which white listeners became guilty eavesdroppers on the putative private conversation of the inner city. Chuck D denounced his enemies (the media, some radio stations), proclaimed himself "Public Enemy #1," and praised Louis Farrakhan in stentorian tones, flanked onstage by black-clad security guards from the Nation of Islam, the SIWs, led by Chuck's political mentor, Professor Griff. Flavor Flav, Chuck's homeboy sidekick, parodied street style: oversize sunglasses, baseball cap cocked to one side, a clock the size of a silver plate draped around his neck, going off on wild verbal riffs that often meant nothing at all.

The closer rap moved to the white mainstream, the more it became like rock 'n' roll, a celebration of posturing over rhythm. The back catalogs of artists like James Brown and George Clinton were relentlessly plundered for catchy hooks, then overlaid with dance beats and social commentary. Public Enemy's single "Fight the Power" was the biggest college hit of 1989:

> Elvis was a hero to most
> But he never meant shit to me, you see
> Straight-up racist that sucker was simple and plain
> Motherfuck him and John Wayne
> 'Cause I'm black and I'm proud
> I'm ready and hyped, plus I'm amped
> Most of my heroes don't appear on no stamps
> Sample a look back, you look and find
> Nothing but rednecks for 400 years if you check.

After the release of "Fight the Power," Professor Griff made a series of anti-Semitic remarks in an interview with *The Washington Times*. Griff was subsequently asked to leave the group, for what Chuck D termed errors in judgment. Although these errors were lambasted in editorials across the country, they do not seem to have affected Public Enemy's credibility with its young white fans.

PUBLIC ENEMY'S THEATRICAL BLACK NATIONALISM and sophisticated noise ushered in what is fast coming to be seen as rap's golden age, a heady mix of art, music, and politics. Between 1988 and 1989 a host of innovative acts broke into the mainstream. KRS-One, now a regular on the Ivy League lecture circuit, grew up poor, living on the streets of the South Bronx until he met a New York City social worker, Scott La Rock, later murdered in a drive-by shooting. Together they formed BDP, Boogie Down Productions, recording for the Jive label on RCA. Although songs like "My Philosophy" and "Love's Gonna Get 'Cha (Material Love)" were clever and self-critical, BDP's roots remained firmly planted in the guns-and-posturing of the mainstream rap ghetto.

The ease with which rap can create such aural cartoons, says Hank Shockee, lies at the very heart of its appeal as entertainment: "Whites have always liked black music," he explains. "That part is hardly new. The difference with rap was that the imagery of black artists, for the first time, reached the level of black music. The sheer number of words in a rap song allows for the creation of full characters impossible in R&B. Rappers become like superheroes. Captain America or the Fantastic Four."

By 1988 the conscious manipulation of racial stereotypes had become rap's leading edge, a trend best exemplified by the rise to stardom of Schoolly D, a Philadelphia rapper on the Jive label who sold more than half a million records with little mainstream notice. It was not that the media had never heard of Schoolly D: white critics and fans, for the first time, were simply at a loss for words. His voice, fierce and deeply textured, could alone frighten listeners. He used it as a rhythmic device that made no concessions to pop-song form, talking evenly about smoking crack and using women for sex, proclaiming his blackness, accusing other rappers of not being black enough. What Schoolly D meant by blackness was abundantly clear. Schoolly D was a misogynist and a thug. If listening to Public Enemy was like eavesdropping on a conversation, Schoolly D was like getting mugged. This, aficionados agreed, was what they had been waiting for: a rapper from whom you would flee in abject terror if you saw him walking toward you late at night.

IT REMAINED FOR N.W.A., a more conventional group of rappers from Los Angeles, to adapt Schoolly D's stylistic advance for the mass white market with its first album-length release, *Straight Out of Compton*, in 1989. The much-quoted rap from that album, "Fuck the Police," was the target of an FBI warning to police department across the country, and a constant presence at certain college parties, white and black:

"Fuck the Police" coming straight out the underground
A young nigger got it bad 'cause I'm brown
And not the other color. Some police think
They have the authority to kill the minority . . .
A young nigger on the warpath
And when I'm finished, it's gonna be a bloodbath
Of cops, dying in L.A.
Yo, Dre I've got something to say: Fuck the Police.

Other songs spoke of trading oral sex for crack and shooting strangers for fun. After the release of *Straight Out of Compton*, N.W.A.'s lead rapper and chief lyricist, Ice Cube, left the group. Billing himself as "the nigger you love to hate," Ice Cube released a solo album, *Amerikkka's Most Wanted*, which gleefully pushed the limits of rap's ability to give offense. One verse ran:

I'm thinking to myself, "why did I bang her?"
Now I'm in the closet, looking for the hanger.

But what made *Amerikkka's Most Wanted* so shocking to so many record buyers was the title track's violation of rap's most iron-clad taboo—black on white violence:

Word, yo, but who the fuck is heard:
It's time you take a trip to the suburbs.
Let 'em see a nigger invasion
Point blank, on a Caucasian.
Cock the hammer and crack a smile:
"Take me to your house, pal . . ."

Ice Cube took his act to the big screen this summer in *Boyz N the Hood*, drawing rave reviews for his portrayal of a young black drug dealer whose life of crime leads him to an untimely end. The crime-doesn't-pay message, an inheritance from the grade-B gangster film is the stock-in-trade of another L.A. rapper-turned-actor, Ice-T of *New Jack City* fame, a favorite of socially conscious rock critics. Taking unhappy endings onto glorifications of drug dealing and gang warfare, Ice-T offers all the thrills of the form while alleviating any guilt listeners may have felt about consuming drive-by shootings along with their popcorn.

It was in this spirit that "Yo! MTV Raps" debuted in 1989 as the first national broadcast forum for rap music. The videos were often poorly produced, but the music and visual presence of starts like KRS-One, LL Cool J, and Chuck D proved enormously compelling, rocketing "Yo!" to the top of the MTV ratings. On weekends bands were interviewed and videos introduced by Fab Five Freddie; hip young white professionals watched his shows to keep up with urban black slang and fashion. Younger viewers rushed home from school on weekdays to catch ex-Beastie Boys DJ Dr. Dre, a sweatsuit-clad mountain of a man, well over 300 pounds, and Ed Lover, who evolved a unique brand of homeboy Laurel and Hardy mixed with occasional social comment.

With "Yo! MTV Raps," rap became for the first time the music of choice in the white suburbs of middle America. From the beginning, says Doug Herzog, MTV's vice president for programming, the show's audience was primarily white, male, suburban, and between the ages of 16 and 24, a demographic profile the "Yo!"'s success helped set in stone. For its daytime audience, MTV spawned an ethnic rainbow of well-scrubbed pop rappers from

MC Hammer to Vanilla Ice to Gerardo, a Hispanic actor turned rap star. For "Yo" itself, rap became more overtly politicized as it expanded its audience. Sound bites from the speeches of Malcolm X and Martin Luther King became de rigueur introductions to formulaic assaults on white America mixed with hymns to gang violence and crude sexual caricature.

HOLDING SUCH POLYGLOT RECORDS TOGETHER is what *Village Voice* critic Nelson George has labeled "ghettocentrism" a style-driven cult of blackness defined by crude stereotypes. P.R. releases, like a recent one for Los Angeles rapper DJ Quik, take special care to mention artists' police records, often enhanced to provide extra street credibility. When Def Jam star Slick Rick was arrested for attempted homicide, Def Jam incorporated the arrest into its publicity campaign for Rick's new album, bartering exclusive rights to the story to *Vanity Fair* in exchange for the promise of a lengthy profile. Muslim groups such as Brand Nubian proclaim their hatred for white devils, especially those who plot to poison black babies. That Brand Nubian believes the things said on its records is unlikely: the group seems to get along quite well with its white Jewish publicist, Beth Jacobson of Electra Records. Anti-white, and, in this case, anti-Semitic, rhymes are a shorthand way of defining one's opposition to the mainstream. Racism is reduced to fashion, by the rappers who use it and by the white audiences to whom such images appeal. What's significant here are not so much the intentions of artist and audience as a dynamic in which anti-Semitic slurs and black criminality correspond to "authenticity," and "authenticity" sells records.

THE SELLING OF THIS KIND of authenticity to a young white audience is the stock-in-trade of *The Source,* a full-color monthly magazine devoted exclusively to rap music, founded by Jon Shecter while still an undergraduate at Harvard. Shecter is what is known in the rap business as a Young Black Teenager. He wears a Brooklyn Dodgers baseball cap, like Spike Lee, and a Source T-shirt. As editor of *The Source,* Shecter has become a necessary quote for stories about rap in *Time* and other national magazines.

An upper-middle-class white, Shecter has come in for his share of criticism, the most recent of which appeared as a diatribe by the sometime critic and tinpot racist Harry Allen in a black community newspaper, *The City Sun,* which pointed out that Shecter is Jewish. "There's no place for me to say anything," Shecter responds, "Given what I'm doing, my viewpoint has to be that whatever comes of the black community, the hip-hop community which is the black community, is the right thing. I know my place. The only way in which criticism can be raised is on a personal level, because the way that things are set up, with the white-controlled media, prevents sincere back-

and-forth discussion from taking place." The latest venture in hip-hop marketing, a magazine planned by Time Warner, will also be edited by a young white, Jonathan van Meter, a former Condé Nast editor.

In part because of young whites like Shecter and van Meter, rap's influence on the street continues to decline. "You put out a record by Big Daddy Kane," Rubin says, "and then put out the same record by a pop performer like Janet Jackson. Not only will the Janet Jackson record sell ten times more copies, it will also be the cool record to play in clubs." Stephney agrees: "Kids in my neighborhood pump dance hall reggae on their systems all night long, because that's where the rhythm is. . . . People complain about how white kids stole black culture. The truth of the matter is that no one can steal a culture." Whatever its continuing significance in the realm of racial politics, rap's hour as innovative popular music has come and gone. Rap forfeited whatever claim it may have had to particularity by acquiring a mainstream white audience whose tastes increasingly determined the nature of the form. What whites wanted was not music, but black music, which as a result stopped really being either.

White fascination with rap sprang from a particular kind of cultural tourism pioneered by the Jazz Age novelist Carl Van Vechten. Van Vechten's 1926 best seller *Nigger Heaven* imagined a masculine, criminal, yet friendly black ghetto world that functioned, for Van Vechten and for his readers, as a refuge from white middle-class boredom. In *Really the Blues,* the white jazzman Mezz Mezzrow went one step further, claiming that his own life among black people in Harlem had physically transformed him into a member of the Negro race, whose unique sensibility he had now come to share. By inverting the moral values attached to contemporary racial stereotypes, Van Vechten and Mezzrow at once appealed to and sought to undermine the prevailing racial order. Both men, it should be stressed, conducted their tours in person.

The moral inversion of racist stereotypes as entertainment has lost whatever transformative power it may arguably have had fifty years ago. MC Serch of 3rd Bass, a white rap traditionalist, with short-cropped hair and thick-rimmed Buddy Holly glasses, formed his style in the uptown hip-hop clubs like the L.Q. in the early 1980s. "Ten or eleven years ago," he remarks, "when I was wearing my permanent-press Lee's with a beige campus shirt and matching Adidas sneakers, kids I went to school with were calling me a 'wigger,' 'black wanna-be,' all kinds of racist names. Now those same kids are driving Jeeps with MCM leather interiors and pumping Public Enemy."

THE WAYS IN WHICH RAP has been consumed and popularized speak not of cross-cultural understanding, musical or otherwise, but of a voyeurism and tolerance of racism in which black and white are both complicit. "Both the rappers and their white fans affect and commodify their own visions of street culture," argues Henry Louis Gates, Jr., of Harvard University, "like buying Navajo blankets at a reservation roadstop. A lot of what you see in rap is the guilt of the black middle class about its economic success, its inability to put forth a culture of its own. Instead they do the worst possible thing, falling back on fantasies of street life. In turn, white college students with impeccable gender credentials buy nasty sex lyrics under the cover of getting at some kind of authentic black experience."

Gates goes on to make the more worrying point: "What is potentially very dangerous about this is the feeling that by buying records they have made some kind of valid social commitment." Where the assimilation of black street culture by whites once required a degree of human contact between the races, the street is now available at the flick of a cable channel—to black and white middle class alike. "People want to consume and they want to consume easy," Hank Shocklee says. "If you're a suburban white kid and you want to find out what life is like for a black city teenager, you buy a record by N.W.A. It's like going to an amusement park and getting on a roller coaster ride—records are safe, they're controlled fear, and you always have the choice of turning it off. That's why nobody ever takes a train up to 125th Street and gets out and starts walking around. Because then you're not in control anymore: it's a whole other ball game." This kind of consumption—of racist stereotypes, of brutality toward women, or even of uplifting tributes to Dr. Martin Luther King—is of a particularly corrupting kind. The values it instills find their ultimate expression in the ease with which we watch young black men killing each other: in movies, on records, and on the streets of cities and towns across the country.

Discussion Questions

Content

1. Samuels claims that "the more rappers were packaged as violent black criminals, the bigger white audiences became." What evidence does he offer to support this claim? What makes or does not make this evidence convincing to you?

2. Identify what you consider to be some of the dangers or drawbacks of Samuels's perspective that white audiences have determined the shape of rap music. Does rap have anything to do with reality? Is it, in your opinion, mostly fact, mostly exaggeration, or mostly fiction, and what makes you think so?

3. At the end of his essay, Samuels argues that, "This kind of consumption—of racist stereotypes, of brutality toward women, or even of uplifting tributes to

Dr. Martin Luther King—is of a particularly corrupting kind." What do think of this suggestion that commodity consumption corrupts experience? What are the values of commodity consumption and what kind of relations between people does consumption presuppose?

Form

1. What effect does the historical background information provided by Samuels have on you as a reader? What does this history suggest about the relationship between writing and "truth"?

2. How does Samuels's title, "The Rap on Rap," relate to the way he organizes and develops his essay. Does his essay seem like a rap to you in any way?

3. In terms of the form of his argument, the nature of his quotations, and the style of his writing, what kind of an essay would you say that Samuels has written? Does it seem academic, popular, journalistic? Identify key passages that demonstrate the essay's affiliation with one or more kinds of writing.

Writing Prompts

1. Write an essay discussing the ways in which other media (movies, television, magazines) represent cities and their African American residents in ways similar to rap music.

2. Samuels suggests that our understanding of urban culture is shaped by mass media images created for profit. Write an essay that explains your perceptions of the media's role in determining the relationships that different kinds of people have with one another. For instance, how does the media shape the relationships between men and women, or between Arab Americans and other Americans?

Michelle Wallace is a feminist scholar at the City University of New York. In "When Black Feminism Faces the Music, and the Music Is Rap," which appeared originally in the New York Times, *Wallace deals with the tensions between a commitment to the right of free expression and the feminist role of resistance to discourses of male dominance and female exploitation. Thus, she attempts to be supportive of rap music's creative and critical energy, while challenging the ethical vision that unquestioningly supports rap's negative representations of women in lyrics and videos. Claiming that "a large part of the appeal of pop culture is that it can offer symbolic resolutions to life's contradictions," Wallace explores the ways that rap is connected to larger social notions of male dominance, concluding that, "when it comes to gender, rap has not resolved a thing." As you read Wallace's essay, pay attention to how she argues in favor of rap music's right to free expression in such a way that she can still argue against rap's negative representations of women.*

When Black Feminism Faces the Music, and the Music Is Rap

Michelle Wallace

LIKE MANY BLACK FEMINISTS, I look on sexism in rap as a necessary evil. In a society plagued by poverty and illiteracy, where young black men are as likely to be in prison as in college, rap is a welcome articulation of the economic and social frustrations of black youth.

In response to disappointments faced by poor urban blacks negotiating their future, rap offers the release of creative expression and historical continuity: it draws on precedents as diverse as jazz, reggae, calypso, Afro-Cuban, African and heavy-metal, and its lyrics include rudimentary forms of political, economic and social analysis.

But with the failure of our urban public schools, rappers have taken education into their own hands; these are oral lessons (reading and writing being low priorities). And it should come as no surprise that the end result emphasizes innovations in style and rhythm over ethics and morality. Although there are exceptions, like raps advocating world peace (the W.I.S.E. Guyz's "Time for Peace") and opposing drug use (Ice-T's "I'm Your Pusher"), rap lyrics can be brutal, raw and, where women are the subject, glaringly sexist.

Given the genre's current cross-over popularity and success in the marketplace, including television commercials, rap's impact on young people is growing. A large part of the appeal of pop culture is that it can offer symbolic resolutions to life's contradictions. But when it comes to gender, rap has not resolved a thing.

Though styles vary—from that of the X-rated Ice-T to the sybaritic Kwaneé to the hyperpolitics of Public Enemy—what seems universal is how little male rappers respect sexual intimacy and how little regard they have for the humanity of the black woman. Witness the striking contrast within rap videos: for men, standard attire is baggy outsize pants; for women, spike heels and short skirts. Videos often feature the ostentatious and fetishistic display of women's bodies. In Kool Moe Dee's "How Ya Like Me Now," women gyrate in tight leather with large revealing holes. In Digital Underground's video "Doowutchyalike," set poolside at what looks like a fraternity house party, a rapper in a clown costume pretends to bite the backside of a woman in a bikini.

As Trisha Rose, a black feminist studying rap, puts it, "Rap is basically a locker room with a beat."

The recent banning of the sale of 2 Live Crew's album "As Nasty as They Wanna Be" by local governments in Florida and elsewhere has publicized rap's treatment of women as sex objects, but it also made a hit of a record that contains some of the bawdiest lyrics in rap. Though such sexual explicitness in lyrics is rare, the assumptions about women—that they manipulate men with their bodies—are typical.

In an era when the idea that women want to be raped should be obsolete, rap lyrics and videos presuppose that women always desire sex, whether they know it or not. In Bell Biv De-Voe's rap-influenced pop hit single "Poison," for instance a beautiful girl is considered poison because she does not respond affirmatively and automatically to a sexual proposition.

In "Yearning: Race, Gender, Cultural Politics" (Southend, 1990), bell hooks sees the roots of rap as a youth rebellion against all attempts to control black masculinity, both in the streets and in the home. "That rap would be anti-domesticity and in the process anti-female should come as no surprise," Ms. hooks says.

At present there is only a small platform for black women to address the problems of sexism in rap and in their community. Feminist criticism, like many other forms of social analysis, is widely considered part of hostile white culture. For a black feminist to chastise misogyny in rap publicly would be viewed as divisive and counterproductive. There is a widespread perception in the black community that public criticism of black men constitutes collaborating with a racist society.

The charge is hardly new. Such a reaction greeted Ntozake Shange's play "For Colored Girls Who Have Considered Suicide When the Rainbow Is Enuf," my own essays, "Black Macho" and "The Myth of the Superwoman," and Alice Walker's novel "The Color Purple," all of which were perceived as critical of black men. After the release of the film version of "The Color Purple," feminists were lambasted in the press for their supposed lack of support for black men; such critical analysis by black women has all but disappeared. In its place is "A Black Man's Guide to the Black Woman," a vanity-press book by Shahrazad Ali, which has sold more than 80,000 copies by insisting that black women are neurotic, insecure and competitive with black men.

Though misogynist lyrics seem to represent the opposite of Ms. Ali's world view, these are, in fact, just two extremes on the same theme: Ms. Ali's prescription for what ails the black community is that women should not question men about their sexual philandering, and should be firmly slapped across the mouth when they do. Rap lyrics suggest just about the same: women should be silent and prone.

There are those who have wrongly advocated censorship of rap's more sexually explicit lyrics, and those who have excused the misogyny because of its basis in black oral traditions.

Rap is rooted not only in the blaxploitation films of the '60s but also in an equally sexist tradition of black comedy. In the use of four-letter words and explicit sexual references, both Richard Pryor and Eddie Murphy, who themselves drew upon the earlier examples of Redd Foxx, Pigmeat Markham and Moms Mabley, are conscious reference points for the 2 Live Crew. Black comedy, in turn, draws on an oral tradition in which black men trade "toasts," stories in which dangerous bagmen and trickster figures like Stackolee and Dolomite sexually exploit women and promote violence among men. The popular rapper Ice Cube, in the album "Amerikkka's Most Wanted," is Stackolee come to life. In "The Nigga Ya Love to Hate," he projects an image of himself as a criminal as dangerous to women as to the straight white world.

Rap remains almost completely dominated by black males and this mindset. Although women have been involved in rap since at least the mid-80s, record companies have only recently begun to promote them. And as women rappers like Salt-n-Pepa, Monie Love, M. C. Lyte, L. A. Star and Queen Latifah slowly gain more visibility, rap's sexism may emerge as a subject for scrutiny. Indeed, the answer may lie with women, expressing in lyrics and videos the tensions between the sexes in the black community.

Today's women rappers range from a high ground that doesn't challenge male rap on its own level (Queen Latifah) to those who subscribe to the same sexual high jinks as male rappers (Oaktown's 3.5.7). M. C. Hammer launched Oaktown's 3.5.7, made up of his former backup dancers. These female rappers manifest the worst-case scenario: their skimpy, skintight leopard costumes in the video of "Wild and Loose (We Like It)" suggest an exotic animalistic sexuality. Their clothes fall to their ankles. They take bubble baths. Clearly, their bodies are more important than rapping. And in a field in which writing one's own rap is crucial, their lyrics are written by their former boss, M. C. Hammer.

Most women rappers constitute the middle ground: they talk of romance, narcissism and parties. On the other hand, Salt-n-Pepa on "Shake Your Thang" uses the structure of the 1969 Isley Brothers song "It's Your Thing" to insert a protofeminist rap response: "Don't try to tell me how to party. It's my dance and it's my body." M. C. Lyte, in a dialogue with Positive K on "I'm Not Havin' It," comes down hard on the notion that women can't say no and criticizes the shallowness of the male rap.

Queen Latifah introduces her video, "Ladies First," performed with the English rapper Monie Love, with photographs of black political heroines like Winnie Mandela, Sojourner Truth, Harriet Tubman and Angela Davis. With a sound that resembles scat as much as rap, Queen Latifah chants "Stereotypes they got to go" against a backdrop of newsreel footage of the apartheid struggle in South Africa. The politically sophisticated Queen Latifah seems worlds apart from the adolescent, buffoonish sex orientation of most rap. In general, women rappers seem so much more grown up.

Can they inspire a more beneficent attitude toward sex in rap?

What won't subvert rap's sexism is the actions of men; what will is women speaking in their own voice, not just in artificial female ghettos, but with and to men.

Discussion Questions

Content

1. Reread the first line of Wallace's essay. Given her argument, why do you think she feels that sexism in rap is "necessary"? Why does she think it is "evil"? Do you think sexism in rap is both necessary and evil? Why?

2. What does Wallace suggest it is that makes her position as a black feminist particularly difficult? How does her argument demonstrate an attempt to deal with these difficulties?

3. Wallace argues, at the end of her essay, that "what won't subvert rap's sexism is the actions of men; what will is women speaking in their own voice." Do you find this position convincing? What vision of gender roles does this argument support? What makes or does not make that seem like a feminist position to you?

Form

   1. Follow the development of Wallace's argument. What does she discuss first, second, and so on? How can you explain this arrangement? Would you characterize it as an optimistic, hopeful way of organizing her discussion or not? Why?

   2. As does David Samuels in the preceding essay on rap in this section, Wallace provides some historical background to support her interpretation. What effect does the placement of historical information have on you as a reader? What purposes do you think this historical information serves in furthering each side of Wallace's argument that sexism in rap is necessary and evil?

   3. As you look at Wallace's article on the page, you might notice that this essay is built of many very brief paragraphs. What does this tell you about her essay? What do you think are the strengths of this form and what do you think are its drawbacks?

Writing Prompts

   1. Find a claim in Wallace's essay that you either support or disagree with. Write an essay that seeks to understand how and why people would disagree with your position. Try to sort out the values or ethical principles that underlie each of the positions including your own.

   2. Among the essays in this part, you have encountered perspectives on rap music by two authors. Write an essay that discusses the ways in which each of these authors' perspectives are partial. Offer some analysis of how each of their perspectives supports a particular cultural group's authority to define rap. Which of the perspectives is most convincing to you? Which of the perspectives do you think would be most convincing to mainstream American culture? Why?

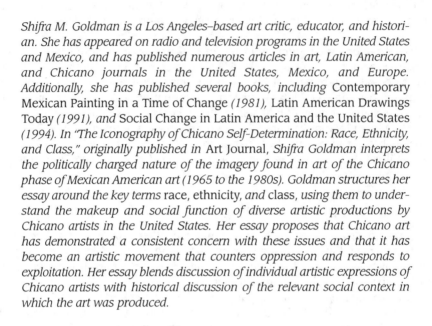

Shifra M. Goldman is a Los Angeles–based art critic, educator, and histori- an. She has appeared on radio and television programs in the United States and Mexico, and has published numerous articles in art, Latin American, and Chicano journals in the United States, Mexico, and Europe. Additionally, she has published several books, including Contemporary Mexican Painting in a Time of Change *(1981),* Latin American Drawings Today *(1991), and* Social Change in Latin America and the United States *(1994). In 'The Iconography of Chicano Self-Determination: Race, Ethnicity, and Class," originally published in* Art Journal, *Shifra Goldman interprets the politically charged nature of the imagery found in art of the Chicano phase of Mexican American art (1965 to the 1980s). Goldman structures her essay around the key terms* race, ethnicity, *and* class, *using them to under- stand the makeup and social function of diverse artistic productions by Chicano artists in the United States. Her essay proposes that Chicano art has demonstrated a consistent concern with these issues and that it has become an artistic movement that counters oppression and responds to exploitation. Her essay blends discussion of individual artistic expressions of Chicano artists with historical discussion of the relevant social context in which the art was produced.*

The Iconography of Chicano Self-Determination: Race, Ethnicity, and Class

Shifra M. Goldman

IN SEVERAL CITIES in the Southwest and Midwest with sizable enclaves of Chicanos, there are to be found considerable numbers of images that have become leitmotifs of Chicano art. In their ubiquity, these motifs demonstrate that the Chicano phase of Mexican-American art (from 1965 to the 1980s)

Shifra M. Goldman. "The Iconography of Chicano Self-Determination: Race, Ethnicity, and Class." From *Art Journal* 49, 2 (Summer 1990): 167–173. Reprinted by permission of the College Art Association, Inc. Reprinted in Shifra M. Goldman, *Dimensions of the America: Art and Social Change in Latin America and the United States,* Chicago: University of Chicago Press, 1994.

was nationally dispersed, shared certain common philosophies, and established a network that promoted a hitherto nonexistent cohesion. In other words, it was a *movement,* not just an individual assembly of Mexican-descent artists. In what follows, Chicano art is examined as statements of a conquered and oppressed people countering oppression and determining their own destiny, though not all the producers of these images necessarily saw their production in the political way they are framed below. Examples have been chosen specifically to show how, in response to exploitation, artists have taken an affirmative stance celebrating race, ethnicity, and class.

Race

Without setting forth theories of how and why racism is instituted and continues to exist, it can be said briefly that the Anglo-Saxon settlers of the North American colonies brought racism with them from Europe; found it useful in the genocidal subjugation of the Indian peoples and the expropriation of their lands; used it as a rationalizing ideology for African slavery; and practiced it in the subjugation of the mestizo (mixed-blood) Mexicans in the nineteenth century. In the 1840s, when Anglos were anxious to seize Mexican territory, racial assertions bolstered that desire. Mexican soldiers, it was said, were "hungry, drawling, lazy half-breeds." The occupation of Mexico was in order since, as documented in the *Illinois State Register,* "the process which had been gone through at the north of driving back the Indians, or annihilating them as a race, has yet to be gone through at the south." In the 1930s one American schoolteacher claimed that the "inferiority of the Mexicans is both biological and class"—a reference both to the Indian component of Mexican *mestizaje* (admixture) and to the Spanish, who were considered among the "inferior" peoples of Europe because of their Moorish inheritance. Supposed racial inferiority eventually served to create in the United States a colonized cheap labor pool, which not only worked for less at the dirtier, harder jobs but was used to threaten white workers demanding higher wages, shorter hours, and unions.

One of the first issues Chicano artists addressed in the 1960s was the question of their Indian heritage. The earliest expression was an embracing of pre-Columbian cultures in order to stress the non-European racial and cultural aspects of their background. Directly related to the question of racial identity, the 1969 Plan Espiritual de Aztlán, formulated at a national gathering in Denver, stated: "We are a Bronze People with a Bronze Culture." Actually, the earliest colonists, moving northward from New Spain or Mexico in the sixteenth century, had mingled with the Pueblo Indians of New Mexico, and that process continued throughout the centuries. However, under the pressure of Anglo racism, this fact was hidden or denied as Mexicans designated themselves "Spaniards."

In 1968, in Del Rey, California, Antonio Bernal painted two murals on the outside walls of the Teatro Campesino headquarters that exemplify the iconography prevalent in the politicized murals of the 1970s. On one panel, pre-Columbian elites line up in flat horizontal bands, headed by a woman. There is little doubt that this scene was borrowed from the Maya murals of Room I in the temple at Bonampak, Chiapas, Mexico. Like the all-male standing dignitaries at Bonampak, the Bernal figures wear headdresses with long feathers. On the second panel is a sequence of admired leaders from the period of the Mexican revolution to the present, headed by the figure of a *soldadera* (a woman soldier—perhaps the legendary La Adelita) wearing a bandolier and carrying a curved sword. She is followed by the revolutionaries Francisco "Pancho" Villa and Emiliano Zapata, the nineteenth-century outlaw-hero Joaquín Murieta, César Chávez of the United Farm Workers, Reies López Tijerina of the New Mexico land-grant struggles, a Black Panther with the features of Malcolm X, and Martin Luther King, Jr. The figures in both murals are represented in appropriate garb with significant emblems and carrying objects related to their respective roles in the social process. All are organized processionally on a single ground line and are painted with unmodeled brilliant color against a plain background. Bernal applied the Maya style to modern as well as ancient personalities in order to establish a stylistic homogeneity. In what amounts to an affirmation of racial pride, the Spanish (presumably white) lineage is deemphasized while the dark-skinned indigenous heritage is stressed. The mural is unique in two respects: (1) for the prominence given activist women, which is unusually sensitive for this male-dominated period of Chicano art, and (2) for the suggested alliance between Mexicans and the African-American civil-rights movement, which seldom again comes up so directly.

Like Indianist culture in Latin America, Chicano indigenism was often of an archaizing and romantic character, setting up the values of Indian culture and civilization as an alternative to European values. In the search for an affirmation of heritage in the extinguished past, the urge toward the creation of a heroic mythology was strong. Thus, in cultural terms, the concept of Aztlán—which defines the Southwest as the home of the original Aztecs and therefore their link to the present Chicano population—is itself a speculative bit of history not verified by archaeology.

A parallel notion, widely disseminated in visual and literary forms by Chicanos (who were 90 percent working class until the mid-twentieth century or later) is that they were the descendants of the elite rulers of the Aztec, Maya, or Toltec states. The hundreds, perhaps thousands of pyramids, warriors, and adaptations of pre-Columbian religious sculptures and paintings, as well as Aztec and Maya princes and princesses, that permeate Chicano art are a testimony to this preoccupation.

One of the most ubiquitous of the latter images derives from the purportedly Aztec legend of the lovers Popocatépetl ("the smoking mountain") and Ixtaccíhuatl ("the white woman"), the names of two snow-capped volcanoes in the rim of mountains surrounding the Valley of Mexico. In the most popular version, a princess dies and her warrior lover builds two pyramids, on one of which he places her; on the other he stands holding a torch to illuminate her sleeping body. Most versions of the story concur on the postures of the lovers: the peaked mountain represents the erect guardian, the flat-topped mountain is the sleeping woman. Almost invariably, however, Chicano images show the male figure carrying a voluptuous, often half-nude princess à la Tarzan and Jane. This melodramatic variation of the traditional iconography very probably derives from the popular chromolith calendars printed in Mexico and widely distributed with local advertising in Mexican communities of the United States. The Texas sculptor Luis Jiménez modified the calendar-derived image in a color lithograph showing the scantily clad body of the princess draped across the warrior's knees in a manner reminiscent of Michelangelo's *Pietà*. The print includes also a blooming prickly-pear cactus, an eagle, and a serpent—legendary symbols that led the nomadic Aztecs to their city of Tenochtitlán in the Valley of Mexico—as well as snow-clad volcanoes and a large maguey cactus.

Other scenes in Chicano art illustrate the fusing of pre-Columbian motifs with contemporary issues. One of the earliest such usages was the 1971 mural painted on two interior walls of a Las Vegas, New Mexico, high school by the Artes Guadalupanos de Aztlán. Their naïve representation is tempered by adaptations of the dramatic foreshortening and polyangular perspective characteristic of the Mexican muralist David Alfaro Siqueiros. On one wall, dominated by feather-adorned pre-Columbian Indians, a sacrifice scene takes place. The second wall, echoing the first, illustrates modern sacrifice: a symbol of the Vietnam War, followed by a crucified Christ beneath whose arms a mother with twin babies surmounts a flag-draped coffin with the slogan "15,000 Chicanos muertos en Vietnam. Ya basta!" (15,000 Chicanos dead in Vietnam. Enough!). Functioning in a similar vein is a 1973 poster by Xavier Viramontes of San Francisco in which the slogan "'Boycott Grapes" is flanked by red, white, and black thunderbird flags of the United Farm Workers Union. Above, a brilliantly colored feather-bonneted pre-Columbian warrior holds in his hands bunches of grapes from which blood drips over the words.

Some indigenous motifs illustrate the recognition by Chicano artists that modern North American Indians have been similarly oppressed. For example, Victor Ochoa rendered a modern Native American on the exterior wall of the Centro Cultural de la Raza of San Diego: the Apache chief Geronimo, whose consistent defiance of the government in the late nineteenth century serves as a symbol for contemporary resistance. Alliances between Chicanos and Native Americans appear also in a silkscreen poster produced in the mid-1970s by the Royal Chicano Air Force (RCAF) of Sacramento. A nineteenth-century Indian is shown with painted face and a feather in his hair; half of his face is covered by a U.S. flag from which blood drips. The slogan states "Centennial Means 500 years of Genocide! Free Russell Redner, and Kenneth Loudhawk." No images of Chicanos appear in the poster; nevertheless, a Chicano presence and an endorsement of Native American struggles that paralleled the Chicanos' own are implied by the RCAF logo that appears on the poster.

More recently, Chicano artists have reflected their empathy, brotherhood, and involvement with the Maya Indians of Central America who are resisting genocidal decimation from dictatorial governments supported by U.S. military aid and advisers. Among such artworks are Yreina Cervántez's 1983 silkscreen *Victoria Océlotl,* which is concerned with Guatemala, and Roberto Delgado's series of monotypes titled *Border Series,* in which silhouetted pre-Columbian designs and shadowy Indian figures of today are interlaced with helicopters. As in Vietnam, the U.S.-supplied helicopters of Central American warfare against civilian populations have become the visual symbols of violent repression.

Ethnicity

Ethnicity is not an individual construct but the residue of societal processes that may have taken generations to evolve. Without embarking on a discussion of the nationalism to which ethnicity is obviously related, we can define it as a set of activities, traits, customs, rituals, relationships, and other emblems of signification that are rooted in group histories and shared to differing degrees by the members of a given national/ethnic group.

Perhaps the greatest difference between nationality and ethnicity is that the former is a given that exists by virtue of birth in a certain place and time whose manifestations are transparent enough not to be open to question. More concretely, a national group is considered such when it is politically independent (like a "sovereign state"), no matter how loose or rudimentary its structure, no matter how dependent or infiltrated it may be by other states. Ethnicity, however, needs to be maintained and is often in an embattled posture vis-à-vis a dominant national culture that surrounds and threatens to overwhelm (either acculturate or totally assimilate) an ethnic identity separated by years or generations from its national source. A multicultural and multiethnic political structure such as that of the United States is extremely likely to be large and complex enough to involve social stratification and the crosscutting of ethnicity with social inequality. Both these factors exacerbate ethnic consciousness, since the experience of discrimination is related to one's identity and thus to one's ethnicity, which is an important aspect of that identity.

There is evidence to suggest that, beginning in the late 1970s, with the possibility and actualization of social mobility for a segment of educated Chicanos, ethnicity—severed from its socioeconomic aspirations for an entire group—has become an acceptable component of dominant ideology. Nevertheless, true to form, the multiethnic political structure has exerted its defining and structuring powers by conflating all "ethnics" of Latin American descent into a single group designated "Hispanic." At the same time, the practice of milder and subtler stereotyping continues to be exercised as the occasion arises. Needless to say, the "acceptable ethnics" are those who can be assimilated into the middle class and who accept the values of the "American Dream" as a realizable goal.

When Anglo-Americans first began to penetrate areas of the Southwest, then part of Mexico, many points of disagreement became apparent. The Anglos spoke English, were primarily Protestants, came from primarily southern states, and were proslavery; the Mexicans were Spanish-speaking, Catholic, tolerant of feudal peonage, but opposed to slavery. Their diets were different, their family attitudes at variance, and their racial stock diverse. As conquerors, the Anglo-Americans attacked not only the political and economic power of the former Mexican territory but the culture of its inhabitants. "Colonialism," said Frantz Fanon, "is not satisfied merely with holding a people in its grip. . . . By a kind of perverted logic, it turns to the past of oppressed people, and distorts, disfigures, and destroys it." As the dominant society and controller of power, the Anglos continued their attack on Mexican culture from the time of penetration to the present—through stereotypes, the prohibition of spoken Spanish at schools, and the scorning of cultural manifestations. Chicano artists therefore attacked stereotypes, insisted not only on the use of Spanish but also on the validity of "interlingualism," and stressed the celebration of cultural symbols that identified their ethnicity.

The stereotype, critic Craig Owens writes, is "a form of symbolic violence exercised upon the body [or the body politic] in order to assign it to a place and to keep it in its place. [It] works primarily through intimidation; it poses a threat . . . [it] is a gesture performed with the express purpose of intimidating the enemy into submission." The insidious aspects of such gestures is that they "promote passivity, receptivity, inactivity—docile bodies. . . . To become effective, stereotypes must circulate endlessly, relentlessly throughout society" so that everyone may learn their significations. It is abundantly clear that the dominant culture persistently considers cultural traits differing from its own to be *deficiencies;* the cultures being declared deficient (Black, Chicano, Puerto Rican, Filipino, and hundreds of Native American groups) are considered so with respect to Anglo culture—a reflection of the ideologies that have served to justify the relationship of inequality between European and Third World peoples.

As an image, the Virgin of Guadalupe has a long history in Mexico as the nation's patron saint. In the United States it has been carried on all farmworker demonstrations. It is a constantly repeated motif in artworks of all kinds, an affirmation of institutional and folk Catholicism. The institutional aspect of the Guadalupe began in 1531 as part of the evangelical process directed at the indigenous people by the Spanish Catholic Church. Evangelization was accomplished by means of a miraculous event: the apparition of a *morena* (dark-skinned) Indian Virgin to a humble peasant, Juan Diego, at Tepeyac, site of the shrine dedicated to the benevolent Aztec earth goddess Tonantzin—or "our mother."

A series of paintings and mixed-media works done in 1978–79 by the San Francisco artist Yolanda López takes the Virgin through a number of permutations. In one she addresses the syncretic nature of Mexican Catholicism, identifying the Guadalupe with the Aztec earth goddess Tonantzin by surrounding the latter with *guadalupana* symbols of mandorla, crown, star-covered cloak, crescent moon, angel wings, and four scenes from the Virgin's life. In others of the series, she places her grandmother, or her mother, or a modern Mexican Indian woman and child, or the artist herself as a runner, in various ensembles combined with the Virgin's symbols—a total secularization. When charged with sacrilege, López defended her images as those of "Our Mothers; the Mothers of us all." The syncretic revival of Coatlicue/Tonantzin in conjunction with the Guadalupe pays tribute not only to the racial and religious affirmations of the Chicano movement but to the particular idols of feminist artists as well.

Among ethnic affirmations that appear in Chicano artworks in response to scornful denigration from the dominant culture are the inclusion of such foods as the humble tortilla, bean, chile pepper, and nopal (prickly-pear cactus); the use of the Spanish language in texts; the rites of folk healing among rural Mexicans; the image of the *calavera* (skull or animated skeleton) as a death motif; and the celebration of the Día de los Muertos—an annual cemetery ritual in rural Mexican communities (which, ironically, is slowly disappearing with Mexican urbanization and has long been commercialized for the tourist trade). Since the early 1970s Día de los Muertos ceremonies have been celebrated increasingly in the Chicano barrios of large cities, sometimes with processions. Home altars associated with the Día de los Muertos were revived by Chicanos for gallery display, using the folk crafts and traditional format but also introducing contemporary variations. One example, by San Francisco artist René Yáñez, includes images of Diego Rivera, Frida Kahlo, and skeletons, and a hologram within a domed form of El Santo—a mysterious and legendary Mexican wrestler of the 1940s whose trademark was a silver head mask slit only at the eyes, nose, and mouth, and who maintained his anonymity like Superman's Clark Kent. On this cloth-covered altar, accompanied by two candlesticks made of twisted wire "flames," El Santo has truly become a "saint" as well as an icon of popular culture. Like López's Guadalupes, Yáñez's altar has been divested of any religious intent.

Although the Mexican presence in the United States predates the Anglo, it has constantly been increased and reinforced by Mexican immigration to provide rural and urban labor. The greatest movement of people north was during the years of the Mexican Revolution, roughly 1910 to 1920, and many of these immigrants headed to the big cities of Los Angeles and San Antonio where a particularly urban ethnic expression arose by the 1940s: the Pachuco. The most famous (or infamous) attack against the Pachucos was that known as the "Zoot Suit Riots." Fanned by the Hearst press in 1943, xenophobic U.S. servicemen invaded the barrios and downtown areas of Los Angeles to strip and beat the zoot-suiters in the name of "Americanism." (This was the same period in which Japanese in the U.S. were herded into concentration camps.)

Some Chicanos have glamorized the Pachuco into the status of a folk hero—as did Luis Valdez in 1978 in the play *Zoot Suit,* where the proud, defiant stance of the character created by Edward James Olmos epitomizes the myth. El Pachuco, in the play, becomes the alter ego of Mexican-American youth, the guardian angel who represents survival through "macho" and "cool hip" in the urban "jungle" filled with racist police, judges, and courts. In the l940s a policeman actually stated that "this Mexican element considers [fisticuffs in fighting] to be a sign of weakness . . . all he knows and feels is the desire to use a knife . . . to kill, or at least let blood." This "inborn characteristic," said the policeman, makes it hard for Anglos to understand the psychology of the Indian or the Latin. The "inborn characteristic" is a reference to pre-Columbian sacrifice, especially of the Aztecs, and the inference, of course, is that since the Aztecs were savages, so are their descendants.

The real Pachuco, drawn from family portraits of the time, is a less heroic personage in his baggy pants, long coat, and chain borrowed from Black entertainer Cab Calloway, and as he was immortalized in Mexican film by the actor Tin Tan as an expression of border culture. This is how he is presented in paintings by César A. Martínez of San Antonio, which derive from old family photograph albums of the 1940s. Martínez's style is totally contemporary in its use of fields of thickly brushed paint and in its pop consciousness, which allows the inclusion of the entire trademark, with parrot and tree limb, of La Parot Hi-Life Hair Dressing above the image of a Pachuco combing back his thick hair in the characteristic ducktail style of the 1940s.

Class

Class divisions in the southwestern United States, which was once part of New Spain and Mexico, have existed since the first conquest in 1598. Juan de Oñate, a millionaire silver-mine owner from Zacatecas, Mexico, then led an expedition into New Mexico, colonizing the area and subjugating the Indians. In the semifeudal, semimercantile, preindustrial period that followed, Indians and lower-class mestizos formed the "working class." With the Anglo conquest in 1848, some Anglos married women from wealthy Mexican landowning families to form a bilingual upper class (in southern Texas and California, particularly), but by and large Mexicans in the Southwest were stripped of their land and proletarianized. As *vaqueros* (the original cowboys, as distinguished from the elegantly dressed *charros* of the upper classes), as miners, as members of railroad section gangs, as agricultural laborers—and more recently as industrial and service workers—Mexican-Americans and Chicanos have been mostly of the working class.

Emigdio Vásquez of Orange, California, fills his murals and easel paintings with both well-known and anonymous heroes of the agricultural and industrial working class derived from historical and contemporary photographs, but without the impersonality of photorealism. His mural introduces an Aztec eagle warrior, a Chicano, and a Mexican revolutionary at the left, followed by a railroad boilermaker, a rancher, a miner, and migrant crop pickers. The procession ends with portraits of César Chávez and a representative of the Filipino workers in the fields of Delano, California, who formed an alliance with the Mexican workers to set up what, in the 1960s, became the United Farm Workers Union.

Following on the heels of the Black civil-rights struggle in the United States, which influenced all the subsequent social-protest movements of the 1960s, farm workers' activism provided an important class encounter for Chicanos. It was an economic movement, but also a cultural one, expressing itself with a flag (the black thunderbird on a red-and-white ground), the Virgin of Guadalupe banner in all processions, and the magazine *El Malcriado* with caricatures by Andy Zermeño and reproductions of Mexican graphics. During the course of a very effective grape boycott, for example, the Nixon administration in the 1960s increased its purchase of grapes for the military forces. In one issue of *El Malcriado* Zermeño shows Richard Nixon himself being fed grapes by a fat grower, who emerges from his coat pocket, while his bare feet trample out the "juice" of farm workers' bodies in a wooden vat. On the ground, in a pool of wine/blood, lies a dead body labeled "La Raza." The legend across the cartoon reads "Stop Nixon." Another cartoon addresses the dangers of pesticide crop spraying. In it a gas-masked aviator sweeps low over fleeing farm workers while clouds of poison envelop them. Rows of graves line the background.

Other aspects of labor that have found their way into Chicano art include the steel mills of Chicago, the garment-industry sweatshops of Los Angeles, and the Mexican maids (often undocumented) in Anglo households whose vocabulary is limited to the household and for whose employers little books of Spanish phrases for giving orders have been printed. In recent years, Chicano artists have become increasingly involved with the question of undocumented workers crossing into the United States to supplement their inadequate Mexican income. Although these workers are secretly recognized by U.S. employers as beneficial to the economy (and business profits), the flow is unregulated and, in times of depression or recession, the workers are scapegoated in the media to divert unemployed U.S. workers from recognizing the source of their own misery. In this ideological campaign, the border patrol of the U.S. Immigration and Naturalization Service (INS) plays a brutal role by rounding up and harassing the Mexicans. The sculptor David Avalos of San Diego has made this theme a central part of his artistic production. In a mixed-media assemblage, Avalos combines an altar format with that of a donkey cart used for tourist photographs in the commercial zone of the border town of Tijuana, Mexico. His sardonic sense of humor is expressed in the sign painted before the untenanted shafts of the cart: "Bienvenidos amigos" (Welcome friends)—usually addressed to the U.S. tourist but not, of course, to the Mexican workers. The upper part of the cart, shaped like an altar with a cross above and nopal cactus on either side below two votive candles, has been painted as a flower-filled landscape with barbed wire within which an INS officer searches an undocumented worker whose raised arms echo a crucifixion scene.

In poetically articulating the importance given the class struggle by Chicanos, the Plan Espiritual de Aztlán said the following: "Aztlán belongs to those who plant the seeds, water the fields, and gather the crops, and not to foreign Europeans." The plan called for self-defense, community organizations, tackling economic problems, and the formation of a national political party. It called on writers, poets, musicians, and artists to produce literature and art "that is appealing to our people, and relates to our revolutionary culture." The note of self-determination, however romantically phrased, is struck here, in 1969.

In conclusion, it can be said that Mexican-American and Chicano culture in the United States has been characterized by three manifestations: that of cultural resistance (which started at the time of the first contact with Anglo-American penetration of the Southwest); cultural maintenance, which includes all aspects of ethnicity; and cultural affirmation, which celebrates race, ethnicity, and class and reached its strongest and most national expression, in my opinion, during the Chicano period.

Discussion Questions

Content

1. Judging from Goldman's essay, why are race, class, and ethnicity such central concerns for Chicano artists?

2. How are Goldman's definitions of race, ethnicity, and class connected to Chicano history and the urban experience?

3. What are the ways other than through race, class, and ethnicity in which Chicano art can be understood? What is the difference between looking at art for its political content and looking at art in other ways?

Form

1. How do the sections in Goldman's essay develop a single main idea?

2. What stylistic techniques does Goldman use to make her interpretations of art appear to be factual observations?

3. How effectively do you think Goldman incorporates historical detail into her interpretations of art? What purpose does the historical detail serve?

Writing Prompts

1. Goldman uses Latino history to interpret the meanings of recurring images in recent and contemporary Latino art. Write an essay in which you use your knowledge of current history to understand how a currently popular image (Mickey Mouse, sixties hippies, etc.) is used in an art form with which you are familiar.

2. Using the ideas from other essays in this part concerning how art forms like graffiti or hip-hop are interpreted and evaluated by outsiders, write an essay that challenges or defends Goldman's interpretations of Chicano art.

PART 4 DISCUSSION QUESTIONS

1. Each of the essays in this part implicitly makes suggestions about how art can or cannot contribute to public life. What common ground do some or all of these authors share? What role do you think public art plays in the quality of life, and the way life is represented, in your city?

2. Several of the art forms described in this part have raised controversies concerning the definition and purposes of art. How do you think urban art forms have expanded the term *art* in your lifetime? How can you connect those redefinitions to the nature of urban environments?

3. Many of these essays suggest that urban art helps people to understand what city life is all about. From your experience, what are the most significant aspects or issues of urban living? Which art forms do you think most adequately represent these aspects or issues, and why?

4. The authors in this part describe the art forms most prevalent in specific environments. What forms of sanctioned and unsanctioned public expression predominate in your community? Think about the ways in which official sanctioning influences what can or cannot be expressed by public art. What is the usefulness of official sanctioning?

5. These essays make connections between artists' personal lives and their public expressions. What personal values does each of these authors think that contemporary urban art expresses? If these authors met to discuss the values of urban art, what differences would they have to work out?

PART 4 WRITING ASSIGNMENTS

1. Write a personal essay explaining the similarities and differences between your own responses to a form of urban art and those of others who are close to you. Include specific incidents that help to show the values that you and these others either share or don't share.

2. Write a persuasive essay that attempts to convince a specific audience that they should reconsider their opinion on the legitimacy or importance of a specific form of urban art. Be sure to keep in mind the values and beliefs that this audience would have.

3. Write a position statement that communicates your stand on what are appropriate forms of public art. Be sure to clearly express your reasons for holding the position you take and offer examples to help make your position clear.

4. Use a key word to compare and contrast the important issues in discussions of urban art with the important issues raised in another part of this book. For example, the term *barrier* could be the focus of a discussion of issues in urban art and neighborhoods, etc.

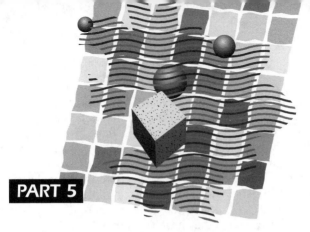

Cities and Suburbs

To THE OUTSIDE OBSERVER, Levittown appears to be a community on which the national American culture has been imprinted so totally as to leave little room for local individuality. The houses express the current national residential style: pseudo-Colonial fronts borrowed from the eighteenth century glued on a variety of single-family house styles developed between the eighteenth and twentieth centuries, and hiding twentieth century interiors. Schools are contemporary, modular, one-story buildings that look like all other new schools. The shopping center is typical too, although the interior is more tastefully designed than most. It consists mainly of branches of large national chains, whose inventory is dominated by prepackaged national brands, and the small centers are no different. The old "Mom and Pop" grocery has been replaced by the "7 to 11" chain, which, as its name indicates, opens early and closes late, but sells only prepackaged goods so that each store can be serviced by a single cashier-clerk. Even the Jewish and Italian foods sold at the "delis" are cut from the loaf of a "pan-ethnic" culture that is now nationally distributed....

The impact of the media is most apparent among children; they are easily impressed by television commercials, and mothers must often fight off their demands on shopping trips. But the adults are seldom touched deeply; media content is always secondary to more personal experience. For example, people talked about articles on child-rearing they had seen in popular magazines, but treated them as topics of conversation rather than as possible guides for their own behavior.

—*Herbert J. Gans*

BY 1950, New York City, Chicago, and Philadelphia and many smaller cities had all stopped growing. Not that the metropolitan regions surrounding these cities were not vigorous, but 1950 is probably as good a date as any to mark the end—or, more accurately, the beginning of the end—of traditional, concentrated cities.

One reason that it's not easy to clearly identify what has happened and is happening to cities is that urban terminology is very inaccurate. Terms such as "city" and "suburb" are used as if they represent two distinct polarities. In fact they are often only polemical categories: depending on your point of view, either bad (dangerous, polluted, concrete) cities and good (safe, healthy, green) suburbs, or good (diverse, dense, stimulating) cities and bad (homogeneous, sprawling, dull) suburbs. The reality is more complicated.

Like "bourgeois" or "capitalist," "suburb" is one of those words that is difficult to use in a precise discussion because it describes something that has become a stereotype. And like most stereotypes, it is composed of clichés. For example, compared with urban housing, suburban housing is held to be monotonous, although urban tenements and industrial-era rowhouses are equally standardized and repetitive. Another cliché holds that suburban areas are rich, white, and white-collar. While this was true of the first suburbs, suburban areas have grown to include a diversity of incomes, classes, and, increasingly, ethnic and racial groups. (A manifestation of this growing diversity is the appearance of ethnic restaurants and food stores in suburban malls.) Indeed, it is the cities that are more likely to be homogeneous with more than their representative share of the poor, of blacks, and of Hispanics.

Only in a legal sense is the difference between urban and suburban clear: everything inside the city limits is urban, and everything outside is suburban. On the ground, there is often little distinction between the physical appearance of urban and suburban neighborhoods or the life they contain. Of course, there is a marked contrast between crowded inner-city neighborhoods and the outer suburbs, where large houses stand on one-acre lots, but these are the two extremes. In most cities—especially those newer cities that grew in the postwar period—urbanites live in houses, mow lawns, drive cars, and shop at malls, just like their suburban neighbors. Even a city like New York, once one leaves Manhattan, is composed of many neighborhoods in which houses with front gardens and backyards line the streets.

—*Witold Rybczynski*

ON 1,200 FLAT ACRES of potato farmland near Hicksville, Long Island, an army of trucks sped over new-laid roads. Every 100 feet, the trucks stopped and dumped identical bundles of lumber, pipes, bricks, shingles, and copper tubing—all as neatly packaged as loaves from a bakery. Near the bundles, giant machines with an endless chain of buckets ate into the earth, taking just 13 minutes to dig a narrow, four-foot trench around a 25-by-32 ft. rectangle. Then came more trucks, loaded with cement, and laid a four-inch foundation for a house in the rectangle.

After the machines came the men. On nearby slabs, already dry, they worked in crews of two and three, laying bricks, raising studs, nailing lath, painting, sheathing, shingling. Each crew did its special job. . . . [A] new one was finished every 15 minutes. . . .

The Government has actually spent little cash itself. But by insuring loans up to 95% of the value of a house, the Federal Housing Administration made it easy for a builder to borrow the money with which to build low cost houses. The Government made it just as easy for the buyer by liberally insuring his mortgage. Under a new housing act signed three months ago, the purchase terms on low cost houses with Government guaranteed mortgages were so liberalized that in many cases buying a house is now as easy as renting it. . . . Thus an ex-G.I. could buy a Levitt house with no down payment and installments of only $56 a month.

—Time *Magazine, July 3, 1950*

INTRODUCTION

By the 1920s, most older cities had spawned a handful of close-lying suburbs. However, since the "baby boom" began in this country in the late 1940s, the growth of the suburbs has increased dramatically. Prior to the 1950s, little new housing had been built in the United States for almost thirty years. Veterans returning from the Second World War and their new families wanted new housing to separate them from crowded cities such as New York, Chicago, and Atlanta. Thus, suburbs as we know them today were first developed in the late 1940s and early 1950s to accommodate the increased demand for single-family homes. In addition, many people felt suburbs provided an escape from the social problems of big cities.

In the 1950s, suburbs were primarily places where people lived and cities were the places where they worked; today, suburbs are places where people live, work, shop, visit the doctor, and do all the things they once did in cities. Suburban areas have grown so large that they often seem like cities themselves. In fact, many people who live in suburbs rarely if ever go into the major city in their area.

When you read and write about cities and suburbs, you are investigating a topic that has significance today. We have all heard the term *urban sprawl*. If you live in an urban area such as Atlanta or New York or San Diego, you know that the suburbs stretch for miles in every direction, reaching into other counties, and in some cases into other states or, in the case of San Diego, into another country. As a result of this rapid growth, cities are no longer the cultural, professional, or residential centers of urban living. The increasing urbanization of suburban areas not only has introduced urban problems into the suburbs (problems such as crime, poverty, and overcrowding), but has also encouraged us to view suburbs as the new American cities. Also, as more and more people move into the suburbs, and as the suburbs move further and further out into the country, suburbs create problems for traditional urban and rural areas by encroaching on rural lands and altering rural lifestyles. Additionally, suburbs create significant problems for cities because they attract population, businesses, and tax dollars.

The writers whose essays are collected in this part examine both the history and the current state of suburbs. Discussing the impact that suburbanization has had upon Americans' lifestyles, these authors consider such ideas as sense of community and beliefs about political responsibility.

In "The Buy of the Century," Alexander O. Boulton provides a historical overview of the first post–World War II American suburb, Levittown, New York. He explains why Levittown and other suburbs were built, how people lived in them, and what they have come to mean. Nicholas Lemann also provides a historical perspective on the evolution of suburbs through his discussion of Naperville, Illinois, comparing the suburbs of the 1950s to Naperville in the 1980s. In his discussion of current-day Naperville, "Stressed Out in Suburbia," Lemann sees parallels between increased urbanization in suburbia and rising stress levels among its residents. David J. Dent provides a different historical perspective in "The New Black Suburbs." Dent describes the emergence of black suburbs in the 1980s and 1990s in terms of the continuing struggle for civil rights among middle and upper-middle-class African Americans.

Although they provide differing viewpoints on the topic, both Robert Reich and David Moberg describe the negative consequences suburbanization has had on major American cities such as Dallas, Philadelphia, and New York. In "Secession of the Successful," Reich argues that the American flight to the suburbs reflects a loss of commitment to community. He calls on Americans, no matter where they live, to renew their sense of urban togetherness and responsibility for the less fortunate. David Moberg similarly argues for a recommitment to community in "Separate and Unequal." Moberg documents how the suburban separation from cities has generated inequalities that spell economic and social loss for both cities and suburbs. He concludes that suburban reinvestment in cities is to everyone's mutual benefit.

In "America's New City: Megalopolis Unbound," Robert Fishman explains the causes and effects of our country's current suburban growth. In light of the rapid growth of urban areas in suburbs, he encourages us to rethink our ideas about what cities are. Joel Garreau also asks us to think about suburbs as new kinds of cities. Garreau uses the term *Edge City* to express what he thinks urban areas in the United States have become. Like Fishman, Garreau asks us to look at our "edge cities" as completely new kinds of urban communities. Garreau nonetheless argues that edge cities aren't really unique because they are only the latest manifestation of the basic American desire for constant change.

In "Park Slope: Notes on a Middle Class Utopia," Jan Rosenberg describes a gentrified Brooklyn neighborhood that she characterizes as a "post-urban" neighborhood. Rosenberg sees in Park Slope a neighborhood that represents an improvement on both traditional urban and suburban lifestyles. Finally, Peter Shaw, in "Let a Hundred Cities Bloom," explains why he thinks rebuilding and reinvesting in major cities is a wasted effort. Shaw proposes what he considers an obvious and more appropriate solution to the problems of inner cities.

Reading these essays, you will be asked to consider several questions about suburbanization: What forces have caused suburbanization to occur in the United States? How have the suburbs changed over the past few decades and why? What impact has the changing role of suburbs had upon how we perceive cities? Have suburbs left cities behind? Or have large metropolitan areas of cities and their surrounding suburbs become the new cities? Do suburban residents have economic and moral responsibility for what has happened to inner cities? Is the increasing suburbanization of the United States a change for the better or for the worse? Or is change just change, and not necessarily good or bad? Reflect upon these questions and your tentative answers to them as you read the essays collected in this part. Consider how your answers change as you read what the authors of these essays have to say, and as you debate the changes associated with suburbanization with your class. Overall, think about how the language used to describe suburbs and cities, especially statements like "pursuing the American dream" or "abandoning the cities," shapes what we think suburbanization means. Furthermore, consider how we use terms such as these to persuade others—and ourselves—to have certain beliefs about the changes suburbanization has caused in American cities.

PREREADING ASSIGNMENTS

1. Spend approximately ten minutes brainstorming about the meaning of the term *suburbanization*. Consider questions such as the following: What is the process of suburbanization? What is a suburb? Who lives in a suburb? What is the quality of life in suburbs? How are suburbs different from cities?

2. Take a few minutes to write down all the words you associate with suburbs and all the words you associate with cities. Compare and contrast the lists. How are they alike? How are they different? What words have you included on the cities list and not on the suburbs list? Which list has more positive terms? Which has more negative terms? What sense do you make of the similarities and differences? Compare your lists with those of your classmates. Talk about the similarities and differences in your lists.

3. Freewrite about how suburbanization has had an impact upon your life. If you have grown up in a suburban area, how has suburbanization influenced your perception of cities? If you have grown up in a major city, how has your city, and so your life, been influenced by suburbanization?

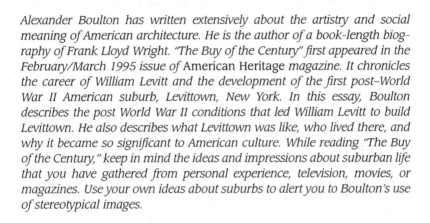

Alexander Boulton has written extensively about the artistry and social meaning of American architecture. He is the author of a book-length biography of Frank Lloyd Wright. "The Buy of the Century" first appeared in the February/March 1995 issue of American Heritage *magazine. It chronicles the career of William Levitt and the development of the first post–World War II American suburb, Levittown, New York. In this essay, Boulton describes the post World War II conditions that led William Levitt to build Levittown. He also describes what Levittown was like, who lived there, and why it became so significant to American culture. While reading "The Buy of the Century," keep in mind the ideas and impressions about suburban life that you have gathered from personal experience, television, movies, or magazines. Use your own ideas about suburbs to alert you to Boulton's use of stereotypical images.*

The Buy of the Century

Alexander O. Boulton

YEARS LATER, after the fall of his financial empire, William Levitt remembered with some satisfaction the story of a boy in Levittown, Long Island, who finished his prayers with "and God bless Mommy and Daddy and Mr. Levitt." Levitt may well have belonged in this trinity. When he sold his company in 1968, more Americans lived in suburbs than in cities, making this the first suburban nation in history, and his family was largely responsible for that.

Jim and Virginia Tolley met William Levitt in 1949 after waiting in line with three thousand other ex-GIs and their families to buy houses. Bill Levitt pointed to a plot on a map spread out on a long table and advised the Tolleys to buy the house he would build on that spot. Thanks to a large picture window with an eastern exposure, the Tolleys' home, Levitt promised, would have sunshine in the coldest months of winter, and its large overhanging eaves would keep them cool in the summer. The Tolleys, who lived in a three-room apartment in Jackson Heights, bought the unbuilt house.

Alexander O. Boulton. "The Buy of the Century." From *American Heritage* (Feb/Mar 1995): 62–69. Reprinted by permission of *American Heritage* magazine, a division of Forbes, Inc. © Forbes, Inc., 1995.

Their story was shared by the more than 3.5 million Americans who had lacked new housing in 1946, housing that had not been built during the Depression and the war. People kept marrying and having babies, but for almost two decades nobody was building new homes.

In providing affordable housing for thousands of Americans after the war, the Levitts were following a basic American success formula; they were at the right place at the right time. Abraham, the patriarch of the family, had been a real estate lawyer in Brooklyn. His two sons, William and Alfred, briefly attended New York University before they began to buy land and design and build houses on a small scale. Alfred was the architect, learning his trade by trial and error, while William was the salesman and became the more public figure. The Second World War transformed their business. Encouraged by wartime contracts for large-scale housing projects, they followed the same mass-production principles that earlier in the century had been developed to build automobiles and that in wartime made ships and airplanes, tanks and guns.

Levittown, Long Island, thirty miles east of New York City, was the first of their postwar projects. Levittown was not the earliest planned community in the country, but it was certainly the biggest, and it is still considered the largest housing project ever assembled by a single builder. Between 1947 and 1951 the Levitts built more than seventeen thousand houses, along with seven village greens and shopping centers, fourteen playgrounds, nine swimming pools, two bowling alleys, and a town hall, on land that had once been potato farms. In addition, the company sold land for schools at cost and donated sites for churches and fire stations.

Following the course of other American industries, the Levitts expanded both horizontally and vertically. They purchased timberland in California and a lumber mill, they built a nail factory, they established their own construction supply company to avoid middlemen, and they acquired a fleet of cement trucks and grading equipment. Instead of the product moving along a production line, however, the Levitt house stood stationary while men, material, and equipment moved around it. At its peak of efficiency the Levitt organization could complete a house every fifteen minutes. Although these were not prefabricated houses, all the materials, including the preassembled plumbing systems and precut lumber, were delivered to the site ready for construction. Twenty-seven steps were required to build a Levittown house, and each work crew had its specialized task. One man did nothing but move from house to house bolting washing machines to the floor. William Levitt liked to say his business was the General Motors of the housing industry. Indeed, the automobile seems to have inspired many of Levitt's practices. He even produced new house models each year, and a few Levittown families would actually buy updated versions, just as they bought Detroit's latest products.

THE FIRST STYLE, a four-and-a-half room bungalow with steeply pitched roof, offered five slight variations in the placement of doors and windows. The result, according to a 1947 *Architectural Forum*, was "completely conventional, highly standardized and aptly described as the public's favorite adjective, 'cute.'" A couple of years later the same publication moderated its tone of easy scorn to pronounce the style "a much better-than-average version of that darling of the depression decade—builder's Cape Cod."

Levittown houses were not what the popular 1960s song called "little boxes made of ticky-tacky." They were exceptionally well built, the product of some of the most innovative methods and materials in the industry. Taking a page from Frank Lloyd Wright's Usonian houses, Levittown houses stood on concrete slab foundations (they had no basements), in which copper coils provided radiant heating. The Tolleys were among the first customers for the 1949 ranch-style houses that replaced the earlier Cape Cod design. The ranches featured Thermopane glass picture windows, fireplaces opening into two rooms, and carports instead of garages. In addition, they had build-in closets and bookcases and swinging shelf units that acted as walls to open up or close the space between kitchen, living room, and entry passage. At twenty-five by thirty-two feet the new houses were two feet longer than the earlier models, and they offered as standard features built-in appliances that were only just coming into general use; many houses contained Bendix washing machines and Admiral television sets. The fixed price of $7,990 allowed the Levitts to advertise "the housing buy of the century." It was probably true. Levitt and his sons seemed to be practically giving homes away. Thousands of families bought into new Levittowns in Pennsylvania, New Jersey, Illinois, Michigan, and even Paris and Puerto Rico. The techniques that the Levitts initiated have been copied by home builders throughout the country ever since.

Despite its immediate success, from the earliest days Levittown also stood as a metaphor for all the possible failings of postwar America. The architectural critic Lewis Mumford is said to have declared the tract an "instant slum" when he first saw it, and he certainly was aiming at Levittown when he condemned the postwar American suburb for its "multitude of uniform, unidentifiable houses, lined up inflexibly, at uniform distances, on uniform roads, in a treeless communal waste, inhabited by people of the same class, the same income, the same age group, witnessing the same television performances, eating the same tasteless pre-fabricated foods, from the same freezers, conforming in every outward and inward respect to the same common mold." Some of the early rules, requiring owners to mow their lawns every week, forbidding fences, or banning the hanging out of laundry on weekends, did indeed speak of the kind of regimentation Mumford snobbishly abhorred.

Today's VISITOR to the original Long Island Levittown might be surprised by many of those early criticisms. Now almost fifty years old, most of the houses have been so extensively remodeled that it is often difficult to distinguish the basic Cape Cod or ranch inside its Tudor half-timbering or postmodern, classical eclecticism. Greenery and shade trees have enveloped the bare landscape of the 1950s and Japanese sand gardens, Renaissance topiary, and electrically generated brooks and waterfalls decorate many of Levittown's standard sixty-by-one-hundred-foot plots. The place now seems not the model of mass conformity but a monument to American individualism.

Probably Levittown never was the drab and monotonous place its critics imagined. For many early residents it allowed cultural diversity to flourish. Pre-war inner-city neighborhoods often had ethnic divisions unknown in Levittown. Louis and Marylin Cuviello, who bought a one-bathroom house in 1949 and reared eleven children there, found themselves moving in a wider world than the one they had known in the city. She was a German-American married to an Italian-American, and in their Levittown neighborhood most of the householders were Jewish. During their first years there the Cuviellos took classes in Judaism at the local synagogue, and they often celebrated both Passover and Christmas with their neighbors.

But this American idyll was not for everyone. In 1949, after Gene Burnett, like his fellow veteran Jim Tolley, saw advertisements for Levittown in several New York papers, he drove to Long Island with his fiancée. The Levittown salesman he met refused to give him an application form. "It's not me," the agent said. "The builders have not at this time decided to sell to Negroes." This pattern of racial exclusion was set in 1947, when rental contracts prohibited "the premises to be used or occupied by any person other than members of the Caucasian race." In 1992 Gene Burnett, now a retired sergeant in the Suffolk County, Long Island, Police Department, told a reporter, "I'll never forget the ride back to East Harlem."

There were other such episodes. Bill Cotter, a black auto mechanic, and his family sublet a house in Levittown in 1953. When his sublet expired, he was informed that he would not be allowed either to rent or to own a house in Levittown. Despite the protests of friendly neighbors, who launched a petition drive in their behalf, Cotter, his wife, and their five children were forced to vacate. These racial policies persisted. As late as the 1980s real estate agents in the area assured white home buyers that they did not sell to blacks, and in 1990 the census revealed that .03 percent of Levittown's population—127 out of more than 400,000—was African-American.

Levittown has been both celebrated and denounced as the fruit of American laissez-faire capitalism. In fact, it may more accurately be described as the successful result of an alliance between government and private enterprise. Levittown and the rise of American suburbia in general could not have happened without attractive loan packages for home buyers guaranteed by the FHA and the VA. Tax breaks, such as the deductibility of mortgages, encouraged suburbanites, who were also helped by a burst of federally funded highway construction. For almost half a century after World War II, the government has played a major role in helping consumers obtain the products of industry—washing machines, television sets, cars, and, especially, houses. For most of us it's been a great ride.

LEVITTOWN RESIDENTS have mixed feelings about their unique heritage. Periodically some of them have attempted to redraw the boundaries of the towns so they could have more elegant addresses. More recently, proud members of the Levittown Historical Society have worked to encourage a new appreciation for their community. They are pushing to establish historic landmark districts while they try to preserve the few houses that have remained relatively unchanged over the years. They are also casting a wide net among their neighbors and former neighbors to gather artifacts and memorabilia for a museum. Recently the Smithsonian Institution announced that it was looking for an original Levittown house to add to its American domestic-life collection. Some African-American groups continue to question the virtue of memorializing a policy of exclusion, but the history-minded residents are pressing ahead, and Eddie Bortell, the Historical Society's vice president, is optimistic. If the work of the historical society has helped bring attention to some of these painful questions, he says, then that in itself is a reward for its efforts.

Discussion Questions

Content

1. According to Boulton, why were Levittown houses "the buy of the century"?

2. In the essay, Boulton describes the major economic, political, and social factors that led to the establishment of suburbs in the late 1940s. Which of these conditions do you think is more important to the establishment of suburbs? Which conditions seem to you to be the least important? Explain why you rank the conditions as you do.

3. In what ways do suburbs represent both the realization of the American dream and "all the possible failings of postwar America"? Consider, for example, the possibility that suburbs create for homeownership; at the same time, consider just who gets to own homes and who doesn't. Think about the possibilities of homeownership as a success of mass production; at the same time, think about the cultural and social consequences of the sameness of the houses.

Form

1. After describing objections to Levittown, Boulton writes that "probably Levittown never was the drab and monotonous place its critics imagined." How does he support this claim? How important to his essay does this claim seem to you? If his support of this claim is or is not convincing to you, how does that influence your reading of the essay as a whole?

2. What effect does Boulton's juxtaposition of historical writing and descriptions of present-day Levittown have on you as a reader? For your answer, refer to specific passages in the essay. Explain, through references to these passages, why you respond as you do.

3. Near the beginning of his essay, Boulton tells the story of Jim and Virginia Tolley. What was your first reaction when you read their story? Why do you think Boulton put it so near the beginning of the essay? How does their story affect your reading of the remainder of the essay? Just how would you have responded to the essay if their story was not included? Explain your answer.

Writing Prompts

1. Describe your home—both the inside and the outside—and tell what you and your family have done to personalize it. Through the description, tell how the place you live in reflects who you are. Provide the details, for example, of how you have decorated a particular room with plants, nicknacks, memorabilia, awards, or photographs. Provide descriptions of the ornamentation, furnishings, and plantings on the inside and outside of your home.

2. Write an essay that supports your opinion as to whether or not American suburbia is, as Lewis Mumford called it, a "multitude of uniform, unidentifiable houses, lined up inflexibly, at uniform distances, on uniform roads," and inhabited by similar people.

Nicholas Lemann is a prolific essayist who has written articles for the New York Times Book Review, Gentlemen's Quarterly, *the* Atlantic, *and* Current. *His topics include party politics, social problems, and American lifestyles. In "Stressed Out in Suburbia," originally published in the* Atlantic, *he describes Naperville, Illinois, a suburb thirty miles west of Chicago. Comparing and contrasting the suburbs of the 1950s with Naperville in the 1980s, Lemann emphasizes the lifestyle changes that have taken place in suburban America in the last forty years. In particular, Lemann demonstrates that people still move to the suburbs for the same reasons as they did forty years ago; but he concludes that life in the suburbs has changed dramatically in that period of time. While reading this essay, keep the title, "Stressed Out in Suburbia," in mind, and use it to help you get to the main points of the essay. Once you do this, you can identify and evaluate the kinds of stress Lemann documents.*

Stressed Out in Suburbia

Nicholas Lemann

I RECENTLY SPENT SOME TIME in Naperville, Illinois, because I wanted to see exactly how our familiar ideas about the suburbs have gotten out of date. Naperville is thirty miles west of the Chicago Loop. It had 7,000 residents in 1950, 13,000 in 1960, 22,600 in 1970, and 42,600 in 1980, and just in this decade it has nearly doubled in population again, to 83,000 this year. Driving there from Chicago, you pass through the West Side ghetto, the site of riots in the late sixties, and then through a belt of older suburbs at the city limits. Just when the suburbs seem to be dying out, you arrive in Oak Brook, with its collection of new shopping malls and office towers. The seventeen-mile stretch from Oak Brook west through Naperville to the old railroad city of Aurora has the look of inexplicable development common to booming areas that were recently rural. Subdivisions back up onto cornfields. Mirrored-glass office parks back up onto convenience-store parking lots. Most of the trees are saplings.

THE HISTORY OF NAPERVILLE as an urban village begins in 1964, when AT&T decided to build a major facility there for its research division, Bell Labs, along the new Interstate 88. Before that, as the next-to-last stop on the Burlington & Northern line from Chicago, Naperville attracted some hardy long-distance commuters, but it was mainly an independent small town, with frame houses and streets laid out in a grid.

Bell Labs opened in 1966 and is still by far the largest employer in Naperville—7,000 people work there, developing electronic switching systems, and another 3,000 work at a software-development center in the neighboring town of Lisle. In 1969 Amoco moved its main research-and-development facility from the industrial town of Whiting, Indiana, to a site in Naperville along the interstate, near Bell Labs. Today more than 2,000 people work there. All through the seventies and eighties businesses have built low-slung, campus-style office complexes up and down I-88, which Governor James R. Thompson in 1986 officially subtitled "The Illinois Research and Development Corridor." There are now four big chain hotels on the five-mile stretch that runs through Lisle and Naperville. In Aurora, Nissan, Hyundai, and Toyota have all established distribution centers, and four insurance companies have set up regional headquarters.

In the fifties the force driving the construction of residential neighborhoods in the suburbs was that prosperity had given young married couples the means to act on their desire to raise children away from the cities. In the eighties in Naperville there is still some of this, but the real driving force is that so many jobs are there. Dozens of new residential subdivisions fan out in the area south of the office complexes and the old town center. In this part of town, whose land Naperville aggressively annexed, the school district has built three new elementary schools since 1984 and added to seven others. A new junior high school opened this fall, another one is under construction, and last spring the town's voters passed a bond issue to build another elementary school and additions to two high schools.

In *The Organization Man,* William Whyte was struck by how removed the place he studied—Park Forest, Illinois, the fifties equivalent of Naperville, brand-new and also thirty miles from the Loop—was from Chicago and from urban forms of social organization. Naperville is even more removed, mainly because downtown commuters are a small minority of the new residents. Nearly everybody in Park Forest worked in Chicago. Only five thousand people take the train from the Naperville station into Chicago every day; most people work in Naperville or in a nearby suburban town. The people I talked to in Naperville knew that they were supposed to go into Chicago for the museums, theater, music, and restaurants, so they were a little defensive about admitting to staying in Naperville in their free time, but most of them do. Though Naperville has many white ethnics (and a few blacks and Asians), it has no ethnic neighborhoods. There are ethnic restaurants, but many of them are the kind that aren't run by members of that ethnic group. Naperville is politically conservative but has no Democratic or Republican organizations active in local politics. Nobody who can afford a house lives in an apartment. There are only a few neighborhood taverns. Discussions of Chicago focus on how much crime is there, rather than on the great events of municipal life.

In distancing itself from Chicago, Naperville has continued a trend that was already well under way in Whyte's Park Forest. Otherwise, most of the ways in which Naperville is different from Whyte's Park Forest and places like it were not predicted by the suburbia experts of the time.

Naperville is much more materially prosperous, and at the same time more anxious about its standard of living, than Park Forest was. The comparison isn't exact, because Park Forest was a middle-middle-class community dominated by people in their late twenties and early thirties; Naperville is more affluent and has a somewhat fuller age range. Nonetheless, since Naperville is the fastest-growing town in the area, it can fairly be said to represent the slice of American life that is expanding most rapidly right now, as Park Forest could in the fifties. The typical house in Park Forest cost $13,000 and had one story (the most expensive house there by far, where the developer lived, cost $50,000). The average house in Naperville costs $160,000 and the figure is higher in the new subdivisions. Plenty of new houses in town cost more than $500,000. Most of the new houses in Naperville have two stories; in fact, the small section of fifties and sixties suburbia in Naperville is noticeably more modest than the new housing.

Obviously one reason for the difference is that Park Forest in the early fifties was only a very few years into the postwar boom, which left the middle class vastly better off than it had been before. Another is that the consumer culture was young and undeveloped in the fifties. Middle-class people today want to own things that their parents wouldn't have dreamed of.

T HE AFFLUENCE OF NAPERVILLE is also a byproduct of what is probably the single most important new development in middle-class life since the fifties (and one almost wholly unanticipated in the fifties), which is that women work. Park Forest was an exclusively female town on weekdays; when Whyte wrote about the difficulty of being a "superwoman," he meant combining housework with civic and social life. In Naperville I heard various statistics, but it seems safe to say that most mothers of young children work, and the younger the couple, the likelier it is that the wife works. When *Business Week* did a big story on the "mommy track" last spring, it used a picture of a woman from Naperville. What people in Naperville seem to focus on when they think about working mothers is not that feminism has triumphed in the Midwest but that two-career couples have more money and less time than one-career couples.

In the classic suburban literature almost no reference is made to punishingly long working hours. The Cheever story whose title is meant to evoke the journey home at the end of the working day is called "The Five Forty-Eight," and its hero is taking that late a train only because he stopped in at a bar for a couple of Gibsons on the way from his office to Grand Central Station. In Naperville the word "stress" came up constantly in conversations. People felt that they had to work harder than people a generation ago in order to have a good middle-class life. In much of the rest of the country the idea holds sway that the middle class is downwardly mobile and its members still never live as well as their parents did. Usually this complaint involves an inexact comparison—the complainer is at an earlier stage in his career, works in a less remunerative field, or lives in a pricier place than the parents who he thinks lived better than he does. In Naperville, where most people are in business, it's more a case of people's material expectations being higher than their parents' than of their economic station being lower. A ranch-style tract house, a Chevrolet, and meat loaf for dinner will not do any more as the symbols of a realized dream. Also, a changed perception of the future of the country has helped create the sense of pressure in Naperville. Suburbanites of the fifties were confident of a constantly rising standard of living, level of education, and gross national product in a way that most Americans haven't been since about the time of the 1973 OPEC embargo. The feeling is that anyone who becomes prosperous has beaten the odds.

It is jarring to think of placid-looking Naperville as excessively fast-paced, but people there talk as if the slack had been taken out of life. They complain that between working long hours, traveling on business, and trying to stay in shape they have no free time. The under-the-gun feeling applies to domestic life as well as to work. It's striking, in reading the old suburban literature today, to see how little people worried about their children. Through many scenes of drunkenness, adultery, and domestic discord, the kids seem usually to be playing, oblivious, in the front yard. Today there is a national hyperawareness of the lifelong consequences of childhood unhappiness (hardly an issue of *People* magazine fails to make this point); the feeling that American children can coast to a prosperous adulthood has been lost; and the entry of mothers into the work force has made child care a constant worry for parents. The idea that childhood can operate essentially on autopilot has disappeared.

The most reliable connection between subdivision residents and the community is children. Adults meet through the children's activities. I often heard that new neighborhoods coalesce around new elementary schools, which have many parent-involving activities and are also convenient places to hold meetings. The churches (mostly Protestant and Catholic, but the town has places of worship for Jews and even Muslims) have made an effort to perform some of the same functions—there is always a new church under construction, and eight congregations are operating out of rented space. The Reverend Keith Torney, who recently left the First Congregational Church in Naperville, after eighteen years, for a pulpit in Billings, Montana, told me, "We try to create a community where people can acquire roots very quickly. We divided the congregation into twelve care groups. Each has twenty to thirty families. They kind of take over for neighbors and grandma—they bring the casserole when you're sick. People come here for a sense of warmth, for a sense that people care about you."

There isn't any hard information on where new Naperville residents come from or where departing ones go. Most of the people I met had moved to Naperville from elsewhere in the Chicago area, often from the inner-ring suburbs. They came there to be closer to their jobs along I-88, because the schools are good and the crime rate is low, and because Naperville is a place where the person who just moved to town is not an outsider but the dominant figure in the community. If they leave, it's usually because of a new job, not always with the same company; the amount of company-switching, and of entrepreneurship, appears to be greater today than it was in the fifties. Several of the new office developments in the area have the word *corporate* in their names. (I stayed in a hotel on Corporetum Drive.) Since the likes of AT&T and Amoco don't call attention to themselves in this way, the use of the word is probably a sign of the presence of new businesses. People's career restlessness, and companies' desire to appear regally established right away, are further examples of the main message I got from my time in Naperville: the suburbs and, by extension, middle-class Americans have gone from glorifying group bonding to glorifying individual happiness and achievement.

THE BAD SIDE OF THIS CHANGE in ethos should be obvious right now: Americans appear to be incapable of the social cohesion and the ability to defer gratification which are prerequisites for the success of major national efforts. But a good side exists too. Representations of middle-class life in the fifties are pervaded with a sense of the perils of appearing to be "different." William Whyte wrote a series of articles for *Fortune,* and the photographs that Dan Weiner took to illustrate them (which are included in *America Worked,* a new book of Weiner's photographs) communicate this feeling even more vividly than *The Organization Man* does: the suburban kaffeeklatsch and the executive's office come across as prisons. There can't be much doubt that the country is more tolerant now than it was then.

Discussion Questions

Content

1. What are the specific features of 1950s suburbia and current-day suburbia that Lemann compares and contrasts?

2. In what ways do you think the essay elaborates on the topic suggested by the title, "Stressed Out in Suburbia"? In what ways are the issues and problems described by Lemann sources of stress for suburbanites? Just where do these stresses seem to come from? Are they products of suburbia itself? Or are they brought to the suburbs by the people who move there? Support your view through references to the essay.

3. According to Lemann, much has changed in suburbs like Naperville in thirty years. Paradoxically, the one thing that has also changed while continuing to thrive is the suburban dream. After reading Lemann's essay, would you say there is such a thing as a suburban dream anymore? Just what has that dream been? What has it become? What do you think it could (or even should) be?

Form

1. How does Lemann's comparison of 1950s suburbia to current-day suburbia help support the points he makes about suburban life? Take at least one example of his comparison from the essay; explain what point you think it helps Lemann make and how you see the comparison helping him make that point. Also, evaluate Lemann's uses of the comparison. Do you think, for example, that he would have had to make the case differently if he was writing about a different suburb?

2. What strategies does Lemann use most often to support his generalizations? Does he provide specific empirical evidence? Does he make appeals to experts? Does he use hearsay? How persuasive are these strategies for you? Why are these strategies as persuasive for you as they are? What other strategies for support might you find more or less persuasive? Explain your preferences with reference to the essay.

3. At the end of his essay, Lemann states that suburbs are now both better and worse than they were in the 1950s. How can suburbs be better *and* worse at the same time? In what sense might Lemann be using the words *better* and *worse* so that he can use them in this way? Do you find his paradoxical conclusion more or less satisfying than you would a conclusion stating that suburbs are *either* better or worse? Explain your preference in terms of your response to the essay. Would it be a better or a worse essay with a clear-cut, either/or conclusion?

Writing Prompts

1. Interview a family about their lifestyle twenty years ago. Ask about the pace of their life, how long they worked, what they did for entertainment, where they spent most of their time. Ask them to reflect as well on whether they were more stressed then or if they are more stressed now. With this information, write an essay comparing and contrasting that family's lifestyle with your own. Whose is more stressful?

2. Write an essay that explores both what is positive and what is negative about the city–suburb division in your area.

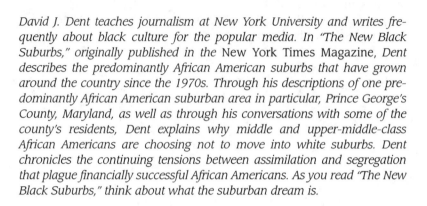

David J. Dent teaches journalism at New York University and writes fre-
quently about black culture for the popular media. In "The New Black
Suburbs," originally published in the New York Times Magazine, *Dent*
describes the predominantly African American suburbs that have grown
around the country since the 1970s. Through his descriptions of one pre-
dominantly African American suburban area in particular, Prince George's
County, Maryland, as well as through his conversations with some of the
county's residents, Dent explains why middle and upper-middle-class
African Americans are choosing not to move into white suburbs. Dent
chronicles the continuing tensions between assimilation and segregation
that plague financially successful African Americans. As you read "The New
Black Suburbs," think about what the suburban dream is.

The New Black Suburbs

David J. Dent

A GENERATION AGO, peaceful civil rights demonstrators faced violent
resistance in the fight for a racially integrated society. Years later, Barron and
Edith Harvey, who are black, would embody the hopes of that struggle. In
1978, the couple moved into a white, upper-middle-income neighborhood
in Fairfax County, Va., a suburb of Washington. During their seven years there,
no crosses were burned in their yard and no racial epithets were muttered
at them within earshot. There were a few incredulous stares, a few stops by
the police, who had mistaken Barron for a criminal, and a run-in with an elementary school principal over the absence of blacks in the curriculum at the
Harveys' daughter's school.

"You expect those kinds of things in a white neighborhood, and, all
things being equal, we would have stayed," says Barron Harvey, chairman of
the accounting department at Howard University and an international business consultant.

But the Harveys left in 1985—not because Fairfax was inhospitable, but because they wanted to become part of another Washington suburb, Prince George's County in Maryland. Prince George's—a county that George Wallace won in the 1972 Presidential primary—was fast becoming the closest thing to utopia that black middle-class families could find in America.

What some consider the essence of the American dream—suburbia—became a reality for a record number of blacks in the 1980's. In 1990, 32 percent of all black Americans in metropolitan areas lived in suburban neighborhoods, a record 6 percent increase from 1980, according to William H. Frey, a demographer at the University of Michigan Population Studies Center specializing in population and racial redistribution patterns. As an increasing number of black Americans head for the suburban dream, some are bypassing another dream—the dream of an integrated society. These black Americans are moving to *black* upper- and middle-class neighborhoods, usually pockets in counties that have a white majority.

The growing popularity of these neighborhoods over the past decade has coincided with the increasing enrollment at black colleges and booming interest in African and African-American history, art, music and literature. These trends seem to represent a retreat from the days of the early post-civil-rights era, when status in the black community was often tied to one's entree into the once-forbidden worlds of white America.

Black suburbs have sprung up across the country. In the Miami area, there is Rolling Oaks in Dade County. Around St. Louis, black suburbs exist in sections of Black Jack, Jennings, Normandy and University City in St. Louis County. In the Atlanta suburbs, black majority communities include Brook Glen, Panola Mill and Wyndham Park in DeKalb County. And in the Washington area, Prince George's County itself has a black majority.

Racial steering, though illegal, may lead some blacks in the Washington area to the predominantly black neighborhoods of Prince George's. But for most, it is a deliberate, affirmative choice.

"I don't want to come home and always have my guard up," says David S. Ball, a senior contract administrator who works on railroad projects in the Washington area. Ball and his wife, Phillis, moved from Washington to a predominantly black subdivision in Fort Washington, Md. "After I work eight hours or more a day," he says, "I don't want to come home and work another eight."

Ball says his family didn't have to live in an *all*-black neighborhood. Currently, Ball says, his block comprises seven black families and three white families.

Barron Harvey adds: "We always wanted to make sure our child had many African-American children to play with, not just one or two. We always wanted to be in a community with a large number of black professionals, and to feel part of that community. We never really felt like we were part of Fairfax."

For some Prince Georgians, like Radamase Cabrera, 39, one reason for the move was a profound sense of disillusionment.

"I think the integration of black folks in the 60's was one of the biggest cons in the world," says Cabrera, an urban planner for the city of Washington. Cabrera was one of a small number of blacks attending the University of Connecticut at Storrs in 1970. "I was called a nigger the first week there and held by the police until this white girl told them I hadn't attacked her. You want to call me a separatist, so be it. I think of myself as a pragmatist. Why should I beg some cracker to integrate me into his society when he doesn't want to? Why keep beating my head up against a wall, especially when I've been there."

While the racial balance of Prince George's population of 729,268 may indicate an integrated county—50.7 percent black, 43.1 percent white, 6.2 percent other—census data suggest a segregated county. More than half of all the census tracts in Prince George's are at least 70 percent white or 70 percent black. Some experts predict the county will be two-thirds black by the end of the century.

Some white residents prefer to see the county serve as a model for true integration.

"Here we have a place that is nearly 50-50," says Margery A. Turner, a white resident and senior research associate, specializing in housing for the Urban Institute. "We should be using this opportunity to show the country there are places where integration can work. I'm not suggesting we limit blacks. But I do think we should avoid resegregating. Separateness sustains prejudice, which sustains inequality."

Cabrera, however, disagrees. "What I reject is this notion that we are aiming toward an integrated county," he says. "African-Americans should be aiming toward an ability to control our own destiny."

THE CHANGING RACIAL COMPOSITION of Prince George's is not immediately evident when entering the county on Route 495, known throughout the Washington area as the Beltway. Many of the exits off the Beltway lead to neighborhoods with names like Enterprise Estates and Paradise Acres—subdivisions stocked exclusively with single-family houses for middle- and upper-income families. The county's transformation becomes clear when you enter those neighborhoods and see that most of the girls jumping rope on the sidewalk and most of the boys dribbling basketballs in driveways are black.

Ben Jones, a real-estate agent who lives in Prince George's County, is riding by the manicured lawns and well-kept colonial and ranch-style houses of

Paradise Acres. He identifies house sales he has made by the profession of the buyer: a vice president of the World Bank, an assistant superintendent of schools, lawyers, professors and doctors.

Jones went on his own search for a black neighborhood in 1980. While riding through a then-undeveloped Mitchellville section, he saw four elaborate full-brick, four-bedroom ranch houses, a trailer and a black man walking out of the trailer. He decided to stop and introduce himself to the man, who turned out to be a realtor. "I assumed it would become a black neighborhood because there was a black real-estate agent," Jones says. Today all but a handful of the 83 families in that subdivision, Paradise Acres, are black.

Jones, a nuclear-weapons specialist at the Department of Energy at the time, had been living in an all-white working-class neighborhood in Upper Marlboro, the county seat, for a decade. When he moved to Mitchellville, he saw a business opportunity in the large number of blacks moving into the county and eventually quit his government job to become a full-time real-estate agent. He has sold 355 homes throughout Prince George's County— all to blacks, with the exception of about four sales to whites. "I don't exclude whites," says Jones. "But most of my sales come from contacts and referrals. There are few whites who will come to a black agent."

The black presence in Prince George's County can be traced to the late 17th century, when blacks were forced into the county as slaves. "Many eventually owned land, and many of their children are still here," says Alvin Thornton, a professor of political science at Howard University who has lived in the county for 20 years.

Descendants of those original black families have lived through segregation, the county's resistance to open housing laws in the late 1960's, court-ordered busing and fears of violence. David Ball remembers that Prince George's was viewed as a rural county full of "rednecks" in which the few pockets of blacks were subjected to police brutality and a citizenry that lived by a brand of justice loaded with "good old boy" rules. Ball never thought he would cherish living in the county he once regarded as racist. Even three years ago, when he and his wife began looking seriously at suburbia, Prince George's County wasn't on the list. They first looked at houses in Montgomery County, but they couldn't find a neighborhood that combined good value for their money and a neighborhood with a significant black presence.

"I really wasn't interested in moving into an all-white neighborhood and being the only black pioneer down there," Ball says.

Harold and Patricia Alexander have grown with Prince George's County. Patricia Alexander's mother, Claudia Sims, bought a town-house condominium in Prince George's County in the early 1970's. Harold Alexander was a premed student at Howard University at the time; Patricia was supporting them both with her salary as a secretary at the university. The couple moved into the county, and the second bedroom of Claudia Sims's town house became the Alexanders' home.

THEIR MIGRATION was part of a population boom, stimulated by the rapid construction of garden apartments and condominiums in the late 1960's and early 1970's. Like the Alexanders, many of the new black residents didn't go deep into the county. Instead, many moved to communities closer to the predominantly black Southeast Washington border.

"When we first moved into the county, it was very uncomfortable," says Patricia Alexander. "We heard stories about the police and racism. So, you know, you go to work, you come home and lock the door."

The new black residents of the 1970's laid the base that eventually drew large numbers of blacks in the 1980's. "You have to look at it in two stages," says Thornton, who has studied the county's migration patterns. "The great surge in the 70's came because many blacks were doing what other people were doing. They wanted better schools, more space, a backyard and less density. But that first period was met with massive white resistance, police brutality and court-ordered busing."

The second stage was inadvertently propelled by the county's Economic Development Corporation. It tried to entice developers to create industries and build houses that would woo white-collar professionals. The selling points of the county were these: the cheaper rural land of Prince George's contrasted with the overdeveloped tracts in neighboring counties; Prince George's road-improvement plan, and the presence of the Goddard Space Flight Center, the world's largest space research facility, Andrews Air Force Base and the University of Maryland at College Park. The campaign reaped $10 billion in new investments in the county, which included the construction of homes for mid- to high-level executives.

Diana V. Jackson, director of development for the corporation, says the majority of those new homeowners were blacks—something that startled the county's white leadership, according to many political activists and black realtors.

"The county officials underestimated the money within the black middle class in Washington," says Larry Lucas, a Washington lobbyist and former minority-population specialist for the Census Bureau. "It's one of the largest concentrations of middle-class blacks in the country. A lot of the subdivisions were really built for whites, but before whites could come out and buy them, black folks were coming in and buying them and when blacks started buying them, whites wouldn't look at them."

After four years of living in the county, the Alexanders, who by now had two children, were comfortable with the idea of moving farther from the Washington border. In 1977 they moved into a middle-income neighborhood of new four-bedroom split-level homes, and found virtually all the residents on their block were like them.

"The second stage was not met with that resistance because you had some white flight and a coming of age of black identity in the county," says Thornton. "There was a critical enough mass of black people by the 80's so blacks could feel they were a part of the county. That's when you get people who move here because they want to live in a black community."

Harold Alexander has benefited from the influx of blacks. His medical practice has increased, and four months ago, the Alexanders made another move inside the county—this time into a $1 million mansion.

The increasing number of blacks in the county and pressure from the N.A.A.C.P. have led to major changes in the police department, where 37 percent of the force is now black, compared with 8 percent in 1978. For many, fear of police brutality has nearly vanished.

Hodari Abdul-Ali, who owns a chain of bookstores in the area, says, "I know that what happened to Rodney King can happen anywhere, but there's much less likelihood of it happening here."

Abdul-Ali's main store had been located near Howard University in Washington. Two years ago, after Abdul-Ali noticed an increasing number of customers were coming from Prince George's County, he opened a store there. It outsells his four other stores.

Barron Harvey visits the store at least twice a month, and the books he buys often become grist for conversations at the family's summer pool parties, when the Harveys' backyard is full of neighborhood friends. Edith Harvey, who lived in predominantly white towns all her life, says that in Prince George's, neighbors have comprised the core of her social life for the first time. The Harveys seldom entertained when they lived in Fairfax, but today they have people over at least twice a month.

"When I'm socializing with people who are not African-American, I have to do a lot of explaining," says Edith Harvey, an education specialist for the Department of Education. "It's stressful because you know it's your responsibility to educate whites who have a sincere interest in understanding an issue. But it's more like work when you should just be socializing. If it's a black social setting, it's more like sharing ideas than educating."

The social networks that provide a forum to share ideas in Prince George's have grown over the past decade. Churches and traditional black middle-class social and professional organizations—like the Links, Jack and Jill and graduate chapters of black fraternities and sororities—have increased their membership in the county, some by as much as fourfold.

The Ebenezer African Methodist Episcopal Church has revitalized itself by moving its congregation to Prince George's. Membership at the 136-year-old church had dwindled to fewer than 100 members. Since the relocation from Washington in 1983, membership has grown to nearly 7,000, and donations have provided $10 million for the construction of a new church building.

Ebenezer holds forums every month, during which many Prince Georgians hear about the latest news and battles in the county's school system. The school system is now 66 percent black, compared with 22 percent in 1971–72. There is widespread agreement among black and white parents to move away from busing as a means of achieving racial balance, which doesn't occur naturally, because of residential separation in Prince George's. Many parents want the school system to continue to build its nationally lauded magnet programs, which feature specialized classes meant to attract a diverse student population.

But there is dissension over the new multicultural curriculum: many white parents object to it, while some black parents are pushing for an Afrocentric approach.

"I believe it's the next step in the battle," says the Rev. Dr. Granger Browning, pastor of Ebenezer and an advocate for an Afrocentric curriculum in the public schools. "It's a fight for our children, and we will win."

RADAMASE CABRERA and his wife, Denise, a reporter for The Associated Press, moved to Prince George's County in 1987, settling in a formerly all-white working-class neighborhood where blacks were becoming the majority. "It was about 50-50 then, and I knew it was only a matter of time before the white folks would leave and you'd have yourself a nice suburban African-American community."

For Cabrera, life in Prince George's County has become part of a mission. Though he works in Washington, he has become an outspoken activist in his community—consumed with its demographic, political and economic statistics. "Prince George's County will be, if it is not already, the most educated and affluent African-American community on the planet, and it has the opportunity to be a model of how black folks can control their political, economic and social institutions," Cabrera says. "This place is unique because usually black folks inherit things like a Newark or a Gary when it's depressed and all the wealth is gone and it has no potential."

Prince George's now has more than 8,000 black-owned businesses. Financing for the smaller businesses—beauty parlors and home-based companies—often comes from a black-owned bank and a black-controlled savings and loan in Washington. Some of the county's larger black-owned companies—high-tech firms and a million-dollar-a-year trash-hauling business—have received financing for expansion by established banks in the county.

Although commercial development in the county has grown, many retailers have declined the county's invitations to open stores there while entering counties with a lower median income but a larger white population. Nordstrom and Macy's have opened stores in Baltimore County, which had a median household income of $38,837, compared with $43,127 in Prince George's County in 1989. But Baltimore County is 85 percent white. Many Prince George's shoppers, like Linda Williams-Brown, often ride two counties away to shop, pouring tax dollars into other communities. "For me to go to a nice mall with a Saks and a Macy's, I have to go all the way to Virginia," Williams-Brown says. "When they put new stores in the shopping centers here, they put in a T.J. Maxx, in a place like Mitchellville, across the street from $200,000 and $300,000 homes that black people own. Why?"

Daniel Russell, who spent 20 years as a private developer based in the Washington area and who now runs a development-training institute and consulting firm, has spent the past five years meeting with retailers, trying to bring them into the county. "In meetings, they say they don't know how to merchandise to a market like this or how to do promotion for this market or other excuses, like the people won't buy the merchandise, when what you have is people going to other counties to buy the merchandise."

An editorial in *The Prince George's County Journal* last year implied retailers like Saks Fifth Avenue and Bloomingdale's were snubbing the county. Spokesmen for both stores deny race is a factor. Some white county officials say the county's image still carries the baggage of its blue-collar days. "We've just now become a white-collar community with a large expendable income," says Prince George's county executive, Parris N. Glendening, who is expected to enter the 1994 Maryland race for governor. "The market hasn't caught up to us. But it will."

However, Douglas Massey, a professor of sociology at the University of Chicago, would not be surprised if it did not. "I think that a group that raises residential segregation to be an ideal is going to cut itself off from many of the benefits of society," he says. "You make it easier for the larger white population to eventually decapitalize it, and it basically becomes an easy target for racist attitudes. It becomes isolated politically.

"It's not a matter of liking whites. You don't have to want to live near whites or like whites. If you talk to Mexicans, who are more integrated than blacks residentially, they may not like Anglos and may prefer to live in Mexican neighborhoods, but they realize services are better in integrated neighborhoods than in Mexican neighborhoods."

Economics aside, the rapid racial change has created a sense of political uncertainty for many white politicians. Alvin Thornton led a citizens' group that lobbied to carve a new Congressional district. Two black candidates won the primaries in March, thereby guaranteeing that Prince George's will have its first black Congressman this November. Thornton's group also lobbied for the redrawing of the county council lines that will give five out of nine districts a black majority in the 1994 election. Currently only two of the nine council members are black.

Some black activists in the community have complained that the council makes zoning decisions to benefit developers who don't live in the county. "We need to look at this zoning process and get the council members, who allocate the county's financial resources, to distribute that wealth with the business people who live here and care about the county's future," Thornton says. "Otherwise Prince George's will become like cities where banking and commercial corridors are owned and controlled by people who don't live there. All we'll own are our nice houses."

However, some black Prince Georgians don't live in nice houses, but in rundown apartments. These pockets of poverty, inside the Beltway, closer to the Washington border, seem far away from the well-kept lawns of Enterprise Estates. "This is now one of the wealthiest black Congressional districts in the country," says Thornton. "If the county wants to maintain that image, it's going to have to redevelop many of the inner-Beltway communities. If it doesn't, you are going to have the same separate cores of poverty and affluence that you find in many inner cities."

The distance between the two worlds of the county leaves many in the middle class with a false sense of comfort, according to State Representative Michael E. Arrington, 36, who grew up in Prince George's.

"What's missing is a sense of activism," Arrington says. "Part of the problem is that you have a lot of people here doing well, and they don't see the problems in other communities firsthand."

Some black middle-class Prince Georgians say inner Beltway problems are thrust upon them, no matter how many miles separate the two communities. One week after Jack B. Johnson, a Prince George's County prosecutor, spent hours discussing the Rodney King verdict with his three children, his 13-year-old son came to him with another incident. One of his classmates, Joseph, a straight-A student from an inner Beltway neighborhood, was gunned down, caught in the crossfire between two drug dealers.

Johnson, an active member of the Coalition of 100 Black Men and the graduate chapter of his fraternity, often spends hours in mentoring programs for low-income males. "There are so many programs here to help teenagers," he says. "There are a substantial number of black middle-class people who are out in the poorer community."

O THER BLACK MIDDLE-CLASS PARENTS say they must first keep *their* children free of the racism and peer pressure that leads to social alienation, crime and teen-age pregnancy. Those parents are reaching back to the days of segregation to extract the elements of black culture that nurtured self-esteem and a commitment to family and community.

Both Frank and Kathryn Weaver grew up in segregated black communities. Frank Weaver, who holds a B.S. from Howard and an M.B.A. from the

University of North Carolina at Chapel Hill, says his academic and professional successes are rooted in the intellectual grooming, pride and discipline instilled in him by his parents, his church, his segregated neighborhood and his high school in Raleigh, N.C., from which he graduated in 1968. "I was always taught I could compete with the best," says Weaver. "Out of the top 10 of my class, two became Harvard lawyers, one a Duke medical doctor. All of us went on to college and graduate school. I find today many of us are searching to rediscover what some of us took for granted while growing up in a segregated society."

Frank and Kathryn Weaver say they don't want to re-create a segregated society for their daughter, but they do want their daughter to grow up with an appreciation of her heritage and culture as they did. They fear she will not be able to compete with others as equals if she is conditioned to see herself as a subordinate American. "Although we mix and mingle in the mainstream culture, we are proud of our African past," says Frank Weaver. "Our daughter does not have to shade everything black or wear a dashiki or kente cloth, but I want her to develop a sense of pride in her identity as a black person."

Could sheltering black middle-class children from racism and the inner city produce black adults with a vision of the world as narrow as that of many upper- and middle-income whites? The Alexanders have struggled with that question. They say they don't worry about their children's ability to interact with whites, since their daughters attend private, predominantly white schools. They did send their youngest daughter, Starsha, 11, to dance classes in the heart of Washington so that inner-city culture wouldn't seem alien to her. While accompanying Starsha to class one day, her mother and older sister, Shelique, 14, passed a group of winos sitting on the street outside the school. Shelique turned her nose up at the winos. Her parents were stunned. "That's when it hit me," Patricia Alexander says. "She said she had never seen anything like that."

Harold Alexander adds: "We both grew up in single-parent working-class situations. We are sensitive to problems in the inner city, and we want our children to have that same sensitivity."

Parents say their children do need protection from racism, poverty and the negative images of blacks that flood the media. "Two doors down from us is a black cardiologist," says Barron Harvey. "There's a dentist on the block, a couple of lawyers, an airline pilot, a college professor, an entrepreneur. My daughter needs to be exposed to that."

Ball adds, "If my son grows up to be a knucklehead, it won't be because I didn't expose him to other possibilities."

In some ways, the need for black role models embodies the powerful impact of racism in defining achievement in America, according to Bart Landry, a sociologist and the author of "The New Black Middle Class." Landry says the sight of a white achiever doesn't offer strong signs of encouragement to many black children. "In this country, where we are polarized along racial lines, seeing a white cardiologist doesn't reaffirm their abilities. That's those people achieving. That's not us achieving. What their parents want them to see is us achieving."

The decision to live in a black community should not be equated with a desire to live in a one-race world. While many black Prince Georgians say integration shouldn't be a priority, they also say they wouldn't move away if more whites moved into the county.

"If they want to come and enjoy, help build the county and take advantage of the economic benefits of living here, that's great," says Fred Sims, who owns a management and secretarial company that grosses $5 million a year. "But we are not begging them to come."

Most residents of the black neighborhoods in Prince George's County work or function in other ways in the integrated American culture. "One of things black folks never really have to worry about in America is being outside the realm of integration," says Harvey. "We will always have to interface with the other culture."

The rise of affluent black neighborhoods could enhance the relationship between the races, Landry says. "I think to the extent that it strengthens feelings of self-worth, it's good for integration, because you have to believe you are O.K. first before you can mingle with others."

Even Radamase Cabrera can see a slight ray of hope for the cause of integration in a strong black community. "Creating black wealth, black power and black stability will enable my children to go hand in hand in society with little white children. My children can integrate society from their own cultural taste, their own historical base, and meet on a level playing field. Right now, there is no level playing field. How are you going to successfully integrate something that is historically disparate?"

For the Harveys, the move to Prince George's may not be a step away from the Rev. Dr. Martin Luther King Jr.'s dream, but a step toward the realization of that dream. "We are advancing," says Barron Harvey. "We were fighting for the right to go where we want to go, to make the choice to live where we want to live. We have the freedom of choice, which we have exercised."

Discussion Questions

Content

1. According to Dent, what are the reasons many African Americans have for wanting to live in predominantly black suburbs? What do the people he interviews from Prince George's County in particular say that they want from their suburban communities?

2. According to Dent, the rise of black suburbs follows the successes of the Civil Rights movement and the emergence of a large African American middle-class population in the 1970s. Keeping in mind what the people in Dent's article say, how are the Civil Rights movement of the 1960s and the rise of black suburbs in the 1980s related? In what ways do the black suburbanites continue the Civil Rights movement? In what ways do they not continue it?

3. What does the rise of black suburbs suggest to you about the current state of race relations in this country? Are the black suburbs a step closer to African American empowerment and equal race relations? Or do they represent a step backward toward deeper racial divisions?

Form

1. In his essay, Dent quotes from interviews with quite a few residents of Prince George's County. None of the people quoted seems to share the same view on any topic. How does this diversity of opinions and voices contribute to the essay? In what ways do you think it adds to, or even takes away from, the narrative?

2. Most of the representations of suburbia in this part portray it as a place almost devoid of values. Citing specific passages in Dent's essay, describe the values promoted in the black suburbs. Where do these values come from? How and why are they different from the values of white suburbs?

3. Dent's style seems distinctly objective. He seems to be reporting what he finds as opposed to arguing for one position over another. Still, he must be writing about black suburbs for a reason; and his reasons for writing about this topic would determine to some extent the ways in which he writes about it. What seems to you to be Dent's interest in black suburbs? What can you say about his attitude toward black suburbs from the way he has written about the topic? Just what is it that he is trying to get us to think or feel about black suburbs?

Writing Prompts

1. Write a dialogue between three people about what segregation in the suburbs means. All three people should have different racial identities. Each person should talk at least three times, each bit of dialogue should consist of at least three lines, and no one person's point of view should prevail in the end.

2. Write a position paper on the issue of self-segregation. Explain why you think groups that are discriminated against respond to discrimination by either actively integrating with the majority or actively isolating themselves from the majority. Argue your position with reference to a particular group.

*Robert B. Reich is the former secretary of labor in the Clinton administra-
tion. Prior to his cabinet appointment, Reich taught political economics at
Harvard University. He is the author or editor of numerous books on
American social and political issues, including* Tales of a New America
(1987), The Power of Public Ideas *(1988), and* The Work of Nations
(1991). "Secession of the Successful" first appeared in the New York Times
Magazine *in January 1991. In this essay, Reich explains how the unequal
distribution of wealth among communities has led to unequal access to
basic public institutions such as schools. Reich uses the proliferation of suburbs and the privatization of communities in the United States as evidence
to demonstrate that Americans are losing their sense of community. As you
read "Secession of the Successful," pay attention to how Reich uses the
words* we *and* they. *Try to be aware of the ways in which these terms, and
others like them, encourage you to identify yourself with one group and not
another.*

Secession of the Successful

Robert B. Reich

THE IDEA OF "COMMUNITY" has always held a special attraction for
Americans. In a 1984 speech, President Ronald Reagan celebrated America's
"bedrock"—"its communities where neighbors help one another, where
families bring up kids together, where American values are born." Governor
Mario M. Cuomo of New York, with a very different political leaning, has been
almost as lyrical. "Community . . . is the reality on which our national life has
been founded," he said in 1987.

There is only one problem with this picture. Most Americans no longer
live in traditional communities. They live in suburban subdivisions bordered
by highways and sprinkled with shopping malls, or in tony condominiums
and residential clusters, or in ramshackle apartment buildings and housing
projects. Most of them commute to work and socialize on some basis other

than geographic proximity. And most people pick up and move to a different neighborhood every five years or so.

But Americans generally have one thing in common with their neighbors: They have similar incomes. And that simple fact lies at the heart of the new community. This means that their educational backgrounds are likely to be similar, that they pay roughly the same in taxes, and that they indulge in the same consumer impulses. Tell me someone's ZIP code," the founder of a direct-mail company once bragged, "and I can predict what they eat, drink, drive—even think."

Americans who own their homes usually share one political cause with their neighbors: a near obsessive concern with maintaining or upgrading property values. And this common interest is responsible for much of what has brought neighbors together in recent years. Complete strangers, although they may live on the same street or in the same condominium complex, suddenly feel intense solidarity when it is rumored that low-income housing will be constructed in their midst or that a poorer school district will be consolidated with their own.

The renewed emphasis on "community" in American life has justified and legitimized these economic enclaves. If generosity and solidarity end at the border of similarly valued properties, then the most fortunate can be virtuous citizens at little cost. Since most people in one neighborhood or town are equally well off, there is no cause for a guilty conscience. If inhabitants of another area are poorer, let them look to one another. Why should *we* pay for *their* schools?

So the argument goes, without acknowledging that the critical assumption has already been made: "We" and "they" belong to fundamentally different communities. Through such reasoning, it has become possible to maintain a self-image of generosity toward, and solidarity with, one's "community" without bearing any responsibility to "them"—the other "community."

America's high earners—the fortunate top fifth—thus feel increasingly justified in paying only what is necessary to insure that everyone in their community is sufficiently well educated and has access to the public services they need to succeed.

LAST YEAR, the top fifth of working Americans took home more money than the other four-fifths put together—the highest portion in postwar history. These high earners will relinquish somewhat more of their income to the Federal Government this year than in 1990 as a result of last fall's tax changes, although considerably less than in the late 1970s, when the tax code was more progressive. But the continuing debate over whether the wealthy are paying their fair share of taxes obscures a larger issue, with more profound implications for America: The fortunate fifth is quietly seceding from the rest of the nation.

This is occurring gradually, without much awareness by members of the top group—or, for that matter, by anyone else. And the government is speeding this process as Washington shifts responsibility for many public services to state and local governments.

The secession is taking several forms. In many cities and towns, the wealthy have in effect withdrawn their dollars from the support of public spaces and institutions shared by all and dedicated the savings to their own private services. As public parks and playgrounds deteriorate, there is a proliferation of private health clubs, golf clubs, tennis clubs, skating clubs, and every other type of recreational association in which costs are shared among members. Condominiums and the omnipresent residential communities dun their members to undertake work that financially strapped local governments can no longer afford to do well—maintaining roads, mending sidewalks, pruning trees, repairing street lights, cleaning swimming pools, paying for lifeguards, and, notably, hiring security guards to protect life and property. (The number of private security guards in the United States now exceeds the number of public police officers.)

Of course, wealthier Americans have been withdrawing into their own neighborhoods and clubs for generations. But the new secession is more dramatic because the highest earners now inhabit a different economy from other Americans. The new elite is linked by jet, modem, fax, satellite, and fiber-optic cable to the great commercial and recreational centers of the world, but it is not particularly connected to the rest of the nation.

That is because the work this group does is becoming less tied to the activities of other Americans. Most of their jobs consist of analyzing and manipulating symbols—words, numbers, or visual images. Among the most prominent of these "symbolic analysts" are management consultants, lawyers, software and design engineers, research scientists, corporate executives, financial advisers, strategic planners, advertising executives, television and movie producers, and other workers whose job titles include terms like "strategy," "planning," "consultant," "policy," "resources," or "engineer."

These workers typically spend long hours in meetings or on the telephone and even longer hours in planes or hotels—advising, making presentations, giving briefings, and making deals. Periodically, they issue reports, plans, designs, drafts, briefs, blueprints, analyses, memorandums, layouts, renderings, scripts, or projections. In contrast with people whose jobs tend to be tedious and repetitive, symbolic analysts find their work varied and intellectually challenging. In fact, the work is often enjoyable.

These symbolic analysts are in ever greater demand in a world market that places an increasing value on identifying and solving problems.

Requests for their software designs, financial advice, or engineering blue-prints come from all parts of the globe. This largely explains why most (but by no means all) symbolic analysts have become wealthier, even as the ever-growing worldwide supply of unskilled labor continues to depress the wages of other Americans.

SUCCESSFUL AMERICANS have not completely disengaged themselves from the lives of their less fortunate compatriots. Some devote substantial resources and energies to helping the rest of society, not through their tax payments, but through voluntary efforts. "Generosity is a reflection of what one does with his or her resources—and not what he or she advocates the government do with everyone's money," Ronald Reagan said in 1984.

The argument is fair enough. Government is not the only device for redistributing wealth. In his speech accepting the Presidential nomination at the Republican National Convention in 1988, George Bush said that the real magnanimity of America was to be found in a "brilliant diversity" of private charity "spread like stars, like a thousand points of light in a broad and peaceful sky."

No nation congratulates itself more enthusiastically on its charitable acts than America; none engages in a greater number of charity balls, bake sales, benefit auctions, and border-to-border hand holdings for good causes. Much of this is sincerely motivated and admirable.

But close examination reveals that many of these acts of benevolence do not help the needy. Particularly suspect is the private giving of those in the top income-tax bracket. Studies have revealed that their largess does not flow mainly to social services for the poor—to better schools, health clinics, or recreational centers. Instead, most voluntary contributions of wealthy Americans go to the places and institutions that entertain, inspire, cure, or educate wealthy Americans—art museums, opera houses, theaters, orchestras, ballet companies, private hospitals, and elite universities.

And even these charitable contributions are relatively skimpy. Last year, American households with incomes of less than $10,000 gave an average of 5.5 percent of their earnings to charity or to a religious organization; those making more than $100,000 a year gave only 2.9 percent. After the 1986 tax-code overhaul reduced the benefits of charitable giving, the very rich became even stingier. According to Internal Revenue Service data, taxpayers earning $500,000 or more slashed their average donations to $16,062 in 1988 from $47,432 in 1980.

Corporate philanthropy is following the same general pattern. In recent years, the largest American corporations have been sounding the alarm about the nation's fast deteriorating primary and secondary schools. Few are more eloquent and impassioned about the need for better schools than

American executives. "How well we educate all of our children will determine our competitiveness globally, and our economic health domestically, and our communities' character and vitality," said a report of the Business Roundtable, a New York–based association of top executives.

Accordingly, there are numerous "partnerships" between corporations and public schools: scholarships for poor children qualified to attend college, and programs in which businesses adopt individual schools by making conspicuous donations of computers, books, and, on occasion, even money. That such activities are loudly touted by corporate public relations staffs should not detract from the good they do.

Despite the hoopla, business donations to education and charitable causes actually tapered off markedly in the 1980s, even as the economy boomed. In the 1970s, corporate giving to education jumped an average of 15 percent a year. In 1990, however, giving was only 5 percent over that in 1989; In 1989 it was 3 percent over 1988. Moreover, most of this money goes to colleges and universities—in particular, to the alma maters of symbolic analysts, who expect their children and grandchildren to follow in their footsteps. Only 1.5 percent of corporate giving in the late 1980s was to public primary and secondary schools.

Notably, these contributions have been smaller than the amounts corporations are receiving from states and communities in the form of subsidies or tax breaks. Companies are quietly procuring such deals by threatening to move their operations—and jobs—to places around the world with a more congenial tax climate. The paradoxical result has been even less corporate revenue to spend on schools and other community services than before. The executives of General Motors, for example, who have been among the loudest to proclaim the need for better schools, have also been among the most relentless in pursuing local tax abatements and in challenging their tax assessments. G.M.'s successful efforts to reduce its taxes in North Tarrytown, N.Y., where the company has had a factory since 1914, cut local revenues by $1 million in 1990, part of a larger shortfall that forced the town to lay off scores of teachers.

THE SECESSION of the fortunate fifth has been most apparent in how and where they have chosen to work and live. In effect, most of America's large urban centers have splintered into two separate cities. One is composed of those whose symbolic and analytic services are linked to the world economy. The other consists of local service workers—custodians, security guards, taxi drivers, clerical aides, parking attendants, salespeople, restaurant employees—whose jobs are dependent on the symbolic analysts. Few blue-collar manufacturing workers remain in American cities. Between 1953 and

1984, for example, New York City lost about 600,000 factory jobs; in the same interval, it added about 700,000 jobs for symbolic analysts and service workers.

The separation of symbolic analysts from local service workers within cities has been reinforced in several ways. Most large cities now possess two school systems—a private one for the children of the top-earning group and a public one for the children of service workers, the remaining blue-collar workers, and the unemployed. Symbolic analysts spend considerable time and energy insuring that their children gain entrance to good private schools, and then small fortunes keeping them there—dollars that under a more progressive tax code might finance better public education.

People with high incomes live, shop, and work within areas of cities that, if not beautiful, are at least esthetically tolerable and reasonably safe; precincts not meeting these minimum standards of charm and security have been left to the less fortunate.

Here again, symbolic analysts have pooled their resources to the exclusive benefit of themselves. Public funds have been spent in earnest on downtown "revitalization" projects, entailing the construction of clusters of post-modern office buildings (complete with fiber-optic cables, private branch exchanges, satellite dishes, and other communications equipment linking them to the rest of the world), multilevel parking garages, hotels with glass-enclosed atriums, upscale shopping plazas and galleries, theaters, convention centers, and luxury condominiums.

Ideally, these complexes are entirely self-contained, with air-conditioned walkways linking residences, businesses, and recreational space. The lucky resident is able to shop, work, and attend the theater without risking direct contact with the outside world—that is, the other city.

When not living in urban enclaves, symbolic analysts are increasingly congregating in suburbs and exurbs where corporate headquarters have been relocated, research parks have been created, and where bucolic universities have spawned entrepreneurial ventures. Among the most desirable of such locations are Princeton, N.J.; northern Westchester and Putnam Counties in New York; Palo Alto, Calif.; Austin, Tex.; Bethesda, Md.; and Raleigh-Durham, N.C.

Engineers and strategists of American auto companies, for example, do not live in Flint or Saginaw, Mich., where the blue-collar workers reside; they cluster in their own towns of Troy, Warren, and Auburn Hills. Likewise, the vast majority of the financial specialists, lawyers, and executives working for the insurance companies of Hartford would never consider living there; after all, Hartford is the nation's fourth-poorest city. Instead, they flock to Windsor, Middlebury, West Hartford, and other towns that are among the wealthiest in the country.

This trend, too, has been growing for decades. But technology has accelerated it. Today's symbolic analysts linked directly to the rest of the globe can choose to live and work in the most pastoral of settings.

The secession has been encouraged by the Federal Government. For the last decade, Washington has in effect shifted responsibility for many public services to local governments. At their peak, Federal grants made up 25 percent of state and local spending in the late 1970s. Today, the Federal share has dwindled to 17 percent. Direct aid to local governments, in the form of programs introduced in the Johnson and Nixon Administrations, has been the hardest hit by budget cuts. In the 1980s, Federal dollars for clean water, job training and transfers, low-income housing, sewage treatment, and garbage disposal shrank by some $50 billion a year, and Washington's share of spending on local transit declined by 50 percent. (The Bush Administration has proposed that states and localities take on even more of the costs of building and maintaining roads, and wants to cut federal aid for mass transit.) In 1990, New York City received only 9.6 percent of all its revenue from the Federal Government, compared with 16 percent in 1981.

States have quickly transferred many of these new expenses to fiscally strapped cities and towns, with a result that by the start of the 1990s, localities were bearing more than half of the costs of water and sewage, roads, parks, welfare, and public schools. In New York State, the local communities' share has risen to about 75 percent of these costs.

Cities and towns with affluent inhabitants can bear these burdens relatively easily. Poorer ones, faced with the twin problems of lower incomes and greater demand for social services, have had far more difficulty. And as the gap between the richest and poorest communities has widened, the shift in responsibility for public services to cities and towns has functioned as another means of relieving wealthier Americans of the cost of aiding less fortunate citizens.

The result has been a growing inequality in basic social and community services. While the city tax rate in Philadelphia, for example, is about triple that of communities around it, the suburbs enjoy far better schools, hospitals, recreation, and police protection. Eighty-five percent of the richest families in the greater Philadelphia area live outside the city limits, and 80 percent of the region's poorest live inside. The quality of a city's infrastructure—roads, bridges, sewage, water treatment—is likewise related to the average income of its inhabitants.

The growing inequality in government services has been most apparent in the public schools. The Federal Government's share of the costs of primary and secondary education has dwindled to about 6 percent. The bulk of the cost is divided about equally between the states and local school districts. States with a higher concentration of wealthy residents can afford to spend more on their schools than other states. In 1989, the average public-school teacher in Arkansas, for example, received $21,700; in Connecticut, $37,300.

Even among adjoining suburban towns in the same state the differences can be quite large. Consider three Boston-area communities located within minutes of one another. All are predominantly white, and most residents within each town earn about the same as their neighbors. But the disparity of incomes between towns is substantial.

Belmont, northwest of Boston, is inhabited mainly by symbolic analysts and their families. In 1988, the average teacher in its public schools earned $36,100. Only 3 percent of Belmont's eighteen-year-olds dropped out of high school, and more than 80 percent of graduating seniors chose to go on to a four-year college.

JUST EAST OF BELMONT is Somerville, most of whose residents are low-wage service workers. In 1988, the average Somerville teacher earned $29,400. A third of the town's eighteen-year-olds did not finish high school, and fewer than a third planned to attend college.

Chelsea, across the Mystic River from Somerville, is the poorest of the three towns. Most of its inhabitants are unskilled, and many are unemployed or only employed part time. The average teacher in Chelsea, facing tougher educational challenges than his or her counterparts in Belmont, earned $26,200 in 1988, almost a third less than the average teacher in the more affluent town just a few miles away. More than half of Chelsea's eighteen-year-olds did not graduate from high school, and only 10 percent planned to attend college.

Similar disparities can be found all over the nation. Students at Highland Park High School in a wealthy suburb of Dallas, for example, enjoy a campus with a planetarium, indoor swimming pool, closed-circuit television studio and state-of-the-art science laboratory. Highland Park spends about $6,000 a year to educate each student. This is almost twice that spent per pupil by the towns of Wilmer and Hutchins in southern Dallas County. According to Texas education officials, the richest school district in the state spends $19,300 a year per pupil; its poorest, $2,100 a year.

The courts have become involved in trying to repair such imbalances, but the issues are not open to easy judicial remedy.

The four-fifths of Americans left in the wake of the secession of the fortunate fifth include many poor blacks, but racial exclusion is neither the primary motive for the separation nor a necessary consequence. Lower-income whites are similarly excluded, and high-income black symbolic analysts are often welcomed. The segregation is economic rather than racial, although economically motivated separation often results in de facto racial segregation. Where courts have found a pattern of racially motivated segregation, it usually has involved lower-income white communities bordering on lower-income black neighborhoods.

In states where courts have ordered equalized state spending in school districts, the vast differences in a town's property values—and thus local tax revenues—continue to result in substantial inequities. Where courts or state governments have tried to impose limits on what affluent communities can pay their teachers, not a few parents in upscale towns have simply removed their children from the public schools and applied the money they might otherwise have willingly paid in higher taxes to private school tuitions instead. And, of course, even if statewide expenditures were better equalized, poorer states would continue to be at a substantial disadvantage.

In all these ways, the gap between America's symbolic analysts and everyone else is widening into a chasm. Their secession from the rest of the population raises fundamental questions about the future of American society. In the new global economy—in which money, technologies, and corporations cross borders effortlessly—a citizen's standard of living depends more and more on skills and insights, and on the infrastructure needed to link these abilities to the rest of the world. But the most skilled and insightful Americans, who are already positioned to thrive in the world market, are now able to slip the bonds of national allegiance, and by so doing disengage themselves from their less-favored fellows. The stark political challenge in the decades ahead will be to reaffirm that, even though America is no longer a separate and distinct economy, it is still a society whose members have abiding obligations to one another.

Discussion Questions

Content

1. According to Reich, what has happened to the traditional community? What is a traditional community? How has it changed? Whom does he blame for this change?

2. What reasons does Reich give for viewing the secession of the successful as negative? Do you agree with the reasons he gives? In what ways do you think that the secession of the successful might be positive? Explain your answers in terms of what Reich writes about community and success.

3. What is your vision of the American dream? How does the secession of the successful described by Reich relate to that vision? Are your vision and Reich's description the same or different? In what ways are they the same or different? After reading Reich's essay, what do you think the relationship is between your vision and the lives of other people?

Form

1. How does Reich's language attempt to persuade you to agree with his main point? Is his language more objective? Or more subjective? Does it attempt to persuade you through appeal to your reason? Or through appeal to your emotions?

2. In his essay, Reich casts the lifestyle choices of the affluent in a negative light. How do Reich's negative assessments of the wealthy's lifestyle evoke what he feels would be a better world? What would this better world be like? Draw from several of Reich's examples to support your views. Then consider whether Reich's is an effective strategy. Are you persuaded by him? Who do you think he might not persuade? Why?

3. Reich's essay is divided into four sections. What does he do differently in each of these four sections? What do the sections add up to when taken together?

Writing Prompts

1. Write an essay defending your position on what a wealthy person's responsibility to his or her community should be. Consider such issues as our beliefs in private property and civic responsibility. Make the discussion as concrete as possible by including examples such as health care, social services, and aid to the poor. Weigh our responsibilities to ourselves against our responsibilities to each other.

2. Write a fictional account in which you imagine what your city would be like if people from all social and economic classes participated equally in the community. Would it be a place where everyone shared everything all the time? Would it be a place where everyone argued all the time about how to share everything? Or might it even be a place where everyone shared nothing?

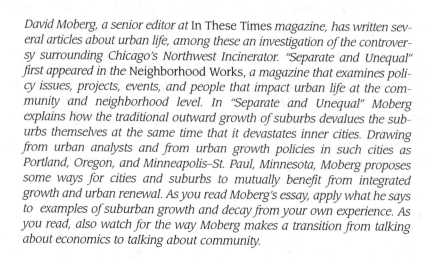

David Moberg, a senior editor at In These Times *magazine, has written several articles about urban life, among these an investigation of the controversy surrounding Chicago's Northwest Incinerator. "Separate and Unequal" first appeared in the* Neighborhood Works, *a magazine that examines policy issues, projects, events, and people that impact urban life at the community and neighborhood level. In "Separate and Unequal" Moberg explains how the traditional outward growth of suburbs devalues the suburbs themselves at the same time that it devastates inner cities. Drawing from urban analysts and from urban growth policies in such cities as Portland, Oregon, and Minneapolis–St. Paul, Minnesota, Moberg proposes some ways for cities and suburbs to mutually benefit from integrated growth and urban renewal. As you read Moberg's essay, apply what he says to examples of suburban growth and decay from your own experience. As you read, also watch for the way Moberg makes a transition from talking about economics to talking about community.*

Separate and Unequal

David Moberg

For YEARS, organizers and advocates have chipped away at the corrosive forces of urban decline. They market old factories, offer job training, rehab housing, preserve mass transit, reform local schools, and much more. Yet it's clear that saving the city requires something more.

Perverse government subsidies (especially for housing and transit) and uncoordinated, balkanized government encourage development that draws away from the urban core. National trends—such as economic globalization, mass computerization, the decline of labor unions and the conservative drive to deregulate business—are likely to increase metropolitan disparities and deprive central cities of crucial federal dollars.

But cities and suburbs form a metropolitan whole that rises and falls together. Many blue collar suburbs are losing factories; resegregated poor black suburbs are emerging; and old satellite cities don't share in the subur-

David Moberg. "Separate and Unequal." In *Neighborhood Works* (Aug./Sept. 1995): 9–11+. David Moberg is a senior editor at *In These Times* magazine.

ban boom around them. Recent research demonstrates that even wealthy suburbs' incomes and growth rates flow in tandem with those of the central city.

The central problem is uneven development, which is linked to the broader issue of inequality. Metropolitan areas are most likely to flourish if social and economic inequality between the central city (or poorer suburbs) and rich suburbs is reduced.

Consider the evidence of metropolitan economic health in relationship to that of the central city: A 1993 study by Cleveland State University professor Larry C. Ledebur and National League of Cities researcher William R. Barnes demonstrates clear income connections between city and suburban jobs. From 1979 to 1989, when central city incomes rose by $1, incomes in surrounding suburbs rose $1.12. Where suburban incomes declined, central city incomes dropped as well. They found these links grew stronger over the period they studied, even as the gap between suburban and central city poverty and unemployment grew. Indeed, the greater the region's gap in per capita income, the slower its job growth.

Conversely, the most economically integrated metro areas have the highest incomes, finds Hank Savitch and fellow researchers at the University of Louisville. Suburbanites in the healthiest one-fourth of the nation's metropolitan areas earn $2,000 more each year when compared with suburbanites in the lowest quartile, Savitch says. "Healthier cities make for healthier metropolitan regions."

Suburbanites prosper from a healthy central city in part because they claim a growing share of the city's best jobs and income. Savitch found that while real per capita income rose in the cities in the 1970s and 1980s, suburbanites took more of the city jobs. "A decade ago," Savitch wrote in 1993 in *Economic Development Quarterly*, "47 percent of suburban income could be attributed to the density and income of the core city. Today, that number has risen to 61 percent."

THESE LINKS AREN'T IMMEDIATELY APPARENT to those fleeing the city. Traditionally, the city itself redistributed income among varied neighborhoods, forcing the rich to share in providing services for the poor. But the rapid suburbanization and sprawl of the past 50 years have amounted to class conflict played out in suburban space. In flight from the city and its problems, suburbanites search for comparative advantage over others by banding together with people of similar income. They pay only for services, especially education, to serve a narrow slice of society.

This is in itself a perverse redistribution benefitting the suburbs. Poverty—and related crime, blight, high tax rates and low tax bases—pushes job-creating investments from the center, leaving cities with less revenue to deal with a disproportionate share of problems, notes Henry R. Richmond, chairman of the Washington, D.C.-based National Growth Management Leadership Project.

The opposite attractions pull investment to the suburbs: good schools, low crime, strong tax bases, cheap and clean industrial sites and high levels of new public investment, Richmond adds. This push and pull simply deepens existing inequality, making it harder for the city to pull itself up.

Current statistics show this trend is accelerating. The fringes of Chicago metro population growth move out at about five miles per decade, according to a recent study by Chicago's nonprofit Metropolitan Planning Council, which used statistics released by the Northeast Planning Commission. While population in the six-county Chicago region grew 4 percent from 1970 to 1990, the region used 46 percent more land for housing and 74 percent more for business.

Throughout the process, general tax revenue subsidizes sprawl. First, there's the home mortgage interest deduction and other supports for home ownership. In 1988, the federal government spent $35 billion on subsidies for families making $50,000 or more through the interest deduction, aid that primarily built more suburbs. During the same period it spent a total of $10 billion on all forms of government housing assistance for families making less than $10,000 a year—people now disproportionately living in the cities.

Similarly, infrastructure spending and transportation policy favor the affluent and the suburbs. For example, in the 1980s, 85 percent of the capacity of the more than $1 billion in new highways built in the Twin Cities served an affluent southwest quadrant of Minneapolis suburbs, according to Minnesota State Representative Myron Orfield. Central city residents paid $6 million a year in the early 1990s to build new sewers in those same wealthy suburbs.

Richmond notes that, to the extent that public subsidies pay for amenities in the suburbs, the houses are more valuable. This benefits the local suburban government, because it permits tax rates to stay low yet still provide adequate income. Thus public subsidies and metro area structures both reflect and reinforce a stark class contrast. "In Europe, for example, you don't see the kind of wasted urban landscape and extensive chunks of urban solid waste and ghettoes that we allow in cities because we subsidize growth at the fringe," he explains.

But, how does that inequality hurt the metropolitan *region*? First, there's the fiscal contradiction: The jurisdictions within a metro region (especially rich suburbs) with the greatest resources frequently have the fewest problems, and vice versa. And even growth areas have problems of equity. Research released in January 1995 by the Federal Reserve Bank of Chicago showed that suburban communities near centers of commercial and industrial growth often suffered from rapidly rising tax rates. The influx of people brought by nearby growth increased demands on government without the requisite revenue.

One of Chicago's outlying suburbs, Schaumburg, had strong commercial and industrial development in the 1980s and saw its taxes as a percent of income decline from 4.11 percent in 1981 to 3.05 percent in 1991. In nearby Roselle Village, which shared in the costs of population growth but not revenue development, the tax share as a percentage of income rose during the same period from 4.12 percent to 4.49 percent.

There is a second mechanism that is harder to measure but may be quite important, especially in education and perpetuation of social class inequality: Different communities provide members varied amounts of what sociologists refer to as "social capital," analogous to financial capital or human capital (knowledge and training). This includes role models, peer relations, "old boy" networks, community associations such as churches and clubs, and recreational and cultural amenities.

Much of the "new regionalist" research on urban inequality emphasizes education and such informal community influence as key mechanisms for perpetuating and deepening inequality. University of Wisconsin economist Steven N. Durlauf has found that the combination of differences in formal education and in community social capital, which is unequally distributed through residential segregation, results in "persistent income inequality."

"As income inequality gets worse," he observes, "society organizes itself to increase stratification, and that increases intergenerational inequality even more. You get these cycles, and the long-run outcomes are ugly."

NOW ALL THIS MIGHT SEEM to work to the advantage of the upper middle class or rich, and to some extent it does. But New York University economist Roland Benabou's recent research questions that conclusion. Benabou observes that minor differences in education and wealth lead to high stratification, which increases inefficiency in the region. In the short run, Benabou writes, mixing of income could lead to slower growth, but in the long run, mixing yields higher output and productivity growth, eventually raising everyone's income, even that of the affluent.

"As an individual, I always have an incentive to make myself better off and to go with the select group," Benabou says, but "the pursuit of rational private interest collectively may hurt everyone. It always hurts the ones left behind."

Research by Mark Dynarksi of Mathematica Policy Research, Inc., a Princeton firm, largely confirms Benabou's ideas. He concludes that when children of different backgrounds and abilities are mixed in a classroom, the highest achievers are not held back as much as the lowest achievers gain. "The net result is a higher average outcome," he says, noting that it is not even clear that the higher achievers lose anything. "Higher-income people have a vested interest that may not be obvious to them in the well-being of lower-income people," he says, "because if society frays at the lower end, it hurts everyone. On the part of individuals it may be rational [to move to homogeneous suburbs and their schools], but what's the social perspective? Maybe it's better for everyone to take an interest in eliminating inequality. It's the tension between private choice and public good."

There are other ways equality may help efficiency and productivity. Workers may be more motivated to work or to cooperate with management if they believe rewards are fair. Also, high wages encourage investment in productivity-enhancing equipment. Finally, greater equality leads to more spending on education and health, since everyone shares in the same education or health-care system and has a stake in its success.

WHAT CAN A METROPOLITAN AREA DO about inequality? First, it could move away from relying so heavily on property tax for local school financing—an American anomaly—and adopt income or other broad-based taxes covering the metropolitan area, or draw from state or federal funds. Yet, precisely because the informal social capital of neighborhoods (and families) is important, equalization of financing would still not be adequate. Dynarski concludes that the local differences "can only be offset by large variations in spending." The well-to-do have a compound advantage—more money for schools as well as informal educational privileges. Only extraordinary efforts on behalf of the poor or working class kids can begin to level the playing field.

Some cities—Tucson, Ariz., Albuquerque, N.M., Columbus, Ohio, and Madison, Wis., to name a few—were able to annex parts of their growing fringe and retain a more stable tax base. Other metropolitan strategies include urban growth boundaries.

For example, since 1979 Portland has enforced boundaries to limit growth of the metropolitan area, including provisions to encourage mass transit and affordable housing.

"Urban growth boundaries deflect growth inward to the region, though not necessarily to the core, but it does reduce the outward flow," Richmond says. "By having urban growth boundaries in Portland and affirming that development is desired in certain locations inside the boundary, all controversy about development is eliminated. When residential or industrial developers want to build, they just need a building permit," which they typically get within 60 days.

Two decades ago in Minnesota, the St. Paul and Minneapolis metro area began sharing a portion of the growth in local government tax bases and established a weak metropolitan council that was—and still is—dominated by developers. Orfield recently forged a coalition of the central cities, older suburbs and low-tax base suburbs to strengthen those metropolitan structures. Orfield proposed greater tax base sharing, strong metropolitan land use planning, fair housing, and a combination of urban reinvestment, job creation and welfare reform.

Through state legislation, the young Minneapolis politician has expanded responsibilities of the metropolitan council, enlarging its authority over sewer and transit systems and thereby expanding its budgetary responsibility from $35 million to $800 million per year. He also strengthened metropolitan land use planning: Now local communities have to submit comprehensive plans to the metropolitan council, which must review and approve how those plans fit into a metropolitan strategy. He also pushed through fair housing goals after several defeats. If metropolitan communities do not take steps toward the fair housing goals, such as reducing zoning barriers or accepting subsidies that are offered, the communities could lose sewer, road and other funding they want.

Since 1971 Twin Cities suburbs and central cities have shared in a fund generated by taxes on 40 percent of the growth in the business tax base. As a result, the metro region now shares in slightly less than one-fourth of property tax revenue. Though the Minnesota legislature approved Orfield's plan, which would have gradually boosted tax sharing to nearly half of all property tax revenue over 15 years, the Republican governor vetoed the legislation.

Orfield's welfare reforms, which link work requirements with New Deal-style central city public works projects, were undermined by Republican cuts that eliminated job creation programs. But he did win $30 million in funds to reinvest in the city for environmental cleanup and removing blight to prepare land for redevelopment. By uniting disadvantaged suburbs and the central cities, while relying on church support to temper opposition in the richer suburbs, Orfield has rallied a coalition that is successfully fighting the trend toward metropolitan inequality.

Inequality is both a symptom of unsustainable social patterns underlying the development of America's metropolitan areas and a cause of slow growth, educational shortcomings and a wide range of other urban social problems. Making cities work will involve reversing both inequality and its causes. That requires forging new, regional political alliances and strategies, but such local efforts are only the start of a task that ultimately is national in scope.

Discussion Questions

Content

1. According to Moberg, how are the economic and social fates of cities and their surrounding suburbs connected?

2. Do you think people from the suburbs would be convinced by Moberg's argument that it is in their own best interest economically and socially to develop cities? How do you think people from cities would respond to Moberg's argument? Would they be convinced that their interests are best served by cooperating with suburbs? Why or why not?

3. Moberg concludes his essay by explaining that it is only through local efforts, such as those in Minneapolis–St. Paul, that the global problems of urban decline and inequality can be addressed. Just what do you think the relationship is between local action and seemingly global problems? Is local action enough to solve global problems? What might be some other ways of addressing the problems of separation and inequality?

Form

1. After reading Moberg's article, what sense do you make of its title, "Separate and Unequal"? In what ways are cities and suburbs both separate and unequal? In what ways do you think cities and their suburbs can in fact never be separate? In what ways do you think its possible for cities and suburbs never to be really equal? How do these many senses of separate and unequal get developed throughout the essay?

2. Moberg uses economic evidence to support his argument that suburbs benefit even more when they sustain the economic growth of cities. At what point in the essay does he turn from economic evidence to social evidence and social consequences? How effective is this shift in terms? Do you think it makes for a stronger or a weaker argument? Explain why.

3. What evidence do you find most convincing in Moberg's essay? Is it the economic evidence, which suggests that cities and suburbs are inextricably linked? Or is it the evidence of policies and practices from Portland and Minneapolis–St. Paul, which suggests that cooperation among cities and suburbs is difficult to achieve? On what basis do you make your decision? What is it about the ways in which the evidence is presented that make you prefer one to the other? Explain your choices through references to the article.

Writing Prompts

1. Compare and contrast a city and its suburbs. Explain the ways in which they are and are not separate and unequal.

2. Write a dialogue between suburbanites and city residents in which they consider a proposal for cooperative development. You must be specific about what the development plan is. Have them hash out the particulars of the plan. Consider what each side might want to get, what each side might not want to give up, and what each side would be willing to do economically and socially to see the proposal through.

Robert Fishman is a historian at Rutgers University in Camden, New Jersey. He studies American cities and the impact of urban experience and suburbanization on American culture. Among his many books and articles are "Urbanity and Suburbanity: Rethinking the 'Burbs," which appeared in American Quarterly; Bourgeois Utopias: The Rise and Fall of Suburbia; *and* Urban Utopias in the Twentieth Century. *The essay reprinted here, "America's New City: Megalopolis Unbound," is excerpted from a longer version of the article that appeared in the* Wilson Quarterly. *In this excerpt, Fishman traces the development of a "new kind of city" out of the vast industrial and commercial expansion of the American suburbs. Fishman frames his discussion with references to the architect Frank Lloyd Wright, whom Fishman refers to as one of the "great prophets" of urban decentralization. Wright is famous for his prairie-style architecture, as well as for his architectural use of gardens, trees, and even waterfalls. As you read "America's New City: Megalopolis Unbound," consider how the opening and closing references to Frank Lloyd Wright help Fishman introduce, develop, and conclude his main point.*

America's New City: Megalopolis Unbound

Robert Fishman

"THE BIG CITY," Frank Lloyd Wright announced prophetically in 1923, "is no longer modern." Although his forecast of a new age of urban decentralization was ignored by his contemporaries, we can now see that Wright and a few other thinkers of his day understood the fragility of the great behemoth—the centralized industrial metropolis—which then seemed to embody and define the modernity of the 20th century.

These capital cities of America's industrial revolution, with New York and Chicago at their head, were built to last. Their very form, as captured during the 1920s in the famous diagrams by Robert E. Park and Ernest W. Burgess of the Chicago School of sociology, seemed to possess a logic that was perma-

Robert Fishman. "America's New City: Megalopolis Unbound." From the *Wilson Quarterly* (Winter 1990): 25–45. Copyright © 1990 by The Woodrow Wilson International Center for Scholars.

nent. At the core was the "central business district," with its skyscraper symbols of local wealth, power, and sophistication; surrounding the core was the factory zone, the dense region of reinforced concrete factories and crowded workers' housing; and finally, a small ring of affluent middle-class suburbs occupied the outskirts. These were the triumphant American cities, electric with opportunity and excitement, and as late as the 1920s they were steadily draining the countryside of its population.

But modernism is a process of constant upheaval and self-destruction. Just when the centralized metropolis was at its zenith, powerful social and economic forces were combining to create an irresistible movement toward decentralization, tearing asunder the logic that had sustained the big city and distributing its prized functions over whole regions. The urban history of the last half-century is a record of this process.

Superficially, the process might be called "the rise of the suburb." The term "suburb," however, inevitably suggests the affluent and restricted "bedroom communities" that first took shape around the turn of the century in New York's Scarsdale, the North Shore of Chicago, and other locales on the edge of the l9th-century metropolis. These genteel retreats from urban life established the model of the single-family house on its own landscaped grounds as the ideal middle-class residence, just as they established the roles of commuter and housewife as social models for upper-middle-class men and women. But Scarsdale and its kind were limited zones of privilege that strictly banned almost all industry and commerce and excluded not only the working class but even the majority of the less-affluent middle class. The traditional suburb therefore remained an elite enclave, completely dependent on the central city for jobs and essential services.

Since 1945, however, the relationship between the urban core and the suburban periphery has undergone a startling transformation—especially during the past two decades. Where suburbia was once an exclusive refuge for a small elite, U.S. Census figures show that 45 percent of the American population is now "suburban," up from only 23 percent in 1950. Allowing for anomalies in the Census Bureau's methods, it is almost certain that a majority of Americans live in the suburbs. About one third remain in the central cities. Even more dramatic has been the exodus of commerce and industry from the cities. By 1980, 38 percent of the nation's workers commuted to their jobs from suburb-to-suburb, while only half as many made the stereotypical suburb-to-city trek. . . .

Commerce has also joined the exodus. Where suburbanites once had little choice but to travel to downtown stores for most of their clothing and household goods, suburban shopping malls and stores now ring up the majority of the nation's retail sales.

During the last two decades, the urban peripheries have even outpaced the cores in that last bastion of downtown economic clout, office employment. More than 57 percent of the nation's office space is now located outside the central cities. And the landscaped office parks and research centers that dot the outlying highways and interstates have become the home of the most advanced high-technology laboratories and factories, the national centers of business creativity and growth.... These multi-functional late-20th century "suburbs" can no longer be comprehended in the terms of the old bedroom communities. They have become a new kind of city.

Familiar as we all are with the features of the new city, most of us do not recognize how radically it departs from the cities of old. The most obvious difference is scale. The basic unit of the new city is not the street measured in blocks but the "growth corridor" stretching 50 to 100 miles. Where the leading metropolises of the early 20th century—New York, London, or Berlin—covered perhaps 100 square miles, the new city routinely encompasses two to three *thousand* square miles. Within such "urban regions," each element is correspondingly enlarged. "Planned unit developments" of cluster-housing are as large as townships; office parks are set amid hundreds of acres of landscaped grounds; and malls dwarf some of the downtowns they have replaced.

The new city, furthermore, lacks what gave shape and meaning to every urban form of the past: a dominant single core and definable boundaries. At most, it contains a multitude of partial centers, or "edge cities," more-or-less unified clusters of malls, office developments, and entertainment complexes that rise where major highways cross or converge.

If no one can find the center of the new city, its borders are even more elusive.

Low-density development tends to gain an inevitable momentum, as each extension of a region's housing and economy into previously rural areas becomes the base for further expansion. When one successful area begins to fill up, land values and taxes rise explosively, mushing the less affluent even farther out. During the past two decades, as Manhattan's "back offices" moved 30 miles west into northern New Jersey along interstates 78 and 80, new subdivisions and town-house communities began sprouting 40 miles farther west long these growth corridors in the Pocono Mountains of eastern Pennsylvania.

Baltimore and Washington, D.C., once separated by mile after mile of farms and forests, are now joined by an agglomeration of office parks, shopping strips, and housing. Census Bureau officials have given up attempting to draw a statistical boundary between the two metropolitan areas and have proposed combining them into a single consolidated region for statistical purposes. Indeed, as the automobile gives rise to a complex pattern of multi-directional travel that largely by-passes the old central cities, the very concept of "center" and "periphery" becomes obsolete.

But are the sprawling regions *cities*? Judged by the standards of the centralized metropolis, the answer is no. As I have suggested, this "city" lacks any definable borders, a center or a periphery, or a clear distinction between residential, industrial, and commercial zones. Instead, shopping malls, research and production facilities, and corporate headquarters all seem scattered amid a chaos of subdivisions, apartment complexes, and condominiums. It is easy to understand why urban planners and social scientists trained in the clear functional logic of the centralized metropolis can see only disorder in these "nonplace urban fields," or why ordinary people use the word "sprawl" to describe their own neighborhoods.

Nevertheless, I believe that the new city has a characteristic structure—one that departs radically not only from the old metropolis but from all cities of the past.

Comparing the new city with the old metropolis, we can see that the new city has yet to evolve anything comparable to the balance of community and diversity that the metropolis achieved. The urban neighborhood at its best gave a sense of rooted identity that the dispersed new city lacks. The downtowns provided a counterpoint of diversity, a neon-lit world where high and low culture met, all just a streetcar ride away. By comparison, even the most elaborate mall pales.

Of course, many residents of the new city were attracted there precisely because they were uncomfortable with both the community and diversity of the old. They wanted to escape from the neighborhood to a "community of limited liability," and they found the cultural and social mix of downtown more threatening than exciting. The new city represents the sum of these choices.

Inevitably, the central city will continue to shelter the dominant institutions of high culture—museums, concert halls, and theaters—but in our electronic age these institutions no longer monopolize that culture.... In the age of the compact disc and the VCR, we have concert halls, opera houses, theaters, and movie palaces without walls. The new city is still a cultural satellite of the old, but the electronic decentralization of high culture and the growing vitality of the new city could soon give it an independent cultural base to rival past civilizations.

The most fervent self-criticism coming from the new city has not, however, focused on the lack of art galleries or symphony orchestras. It comes from those who fear that the very success of the new city is destroying the freedom of movement and access to nature that were its original attraction. As new malls and subdivisions eat up acre after acre of land, and as highways clog with traffic, the danger arises that ... the city may break down. Too often the new city seems to be an environment as out of control as the old metropolis. The machine of growth is yet again gaining the upper hand over any human purpose. The early residents of the new city worried little about regulating growth because there was still a seemingly endless supply of open land. Now that it is disappearing, the residents of the new city must finally face the consequences of get-and-grab development.

Once again we must turn for wisdom to the great prophets of decentralization, especially Frank Lloyd Wright. Wright believed that the guiding principle of the new city must be the harmonization of development with a respect for the land in the interest of creating a beautiful and civilized landscape. "Architecture and acreage will be seen together as landscape—as was the best antique architecture—and will become more essential to each other," he wrote.... His plans show the same juxtapositions of housing, shopping, and industry that exist in the new city today. But they depict a world in which these are integrated into open space through the preservation of farmland, the creation of parks, and the extensive use of landscaping around buildings.

For Wright, an "organic" landscape meant more than creating beautiful vistas. It was the social effort to integrate the potentially disruptive effects of the machine in the service of a higher purpose. Wright, however, gave little practical thought to how this might be achieved.

Discussion Questions

Content

1. Why does Fishman refer to suburbs as "a new kind of city"? According to Fishman, what is it about suburbs that makes them cities? What is it about suburbs that does not make them cities?

2. Does Fishman seem more hopeful or more cautious about urban decentralization? What reasons does he give for hope and what reasons does he give for caution? What other reasons might you add to Fishman's to support either hope or caution?

3. What do you think it would take to make into a reality the dream of harmonizing development with a respect for land? Do you think that the dream of harmonizing development with a respect for land can be made a reality? Do you think it will be made a reality? Do you think there is anyone who even wants it to be made a reality? Why or why not?

Form

1. The subtitle of Fishman's essay, "Megalopolis Unbound," refers to the decentralization of American cities. How does Fishman arrange his discussion of urban sprawl in order to make sense of the sprawl? Do you think his essay is decentralized? Just how fully do you think his essay expresses the decentralization of American cities?

2. What do you think the opening reference to the famous architect Frank Lloyd Wright contributes to Fishman's argument? What do you think the closing reference contributes? How do you think the two references work together as a frame for the ideas in the essay? Just what do the references add to the essay? Do you think they are worth it to you as a reader? Why or why not?

3. Fishman's tone throughout the essay is fairly objective and matter-of-fact. Is this because the "new cities" are only facts to be reported? If so, then you should be able to find examples of new cities around you in the world. If not, then maybe new cities are realities only if we know how and where to look for them. Either way, don't they exist? Come up with several examples of places that might qualify as new cities. Then, consider whether they are new cities because of some quality they all share or whether they are new cities because you have defined them that way.

Writing Prompts

1. Write a description of the area in which you live. Use ideas from Fishman's essay to characterize your area as having features of a new city, an old city, or both.

2. Compare and contrast the demands for freedom of movement and access to nature with the realities of suburban living. Can these often competing demands ever be reconciled with each other?

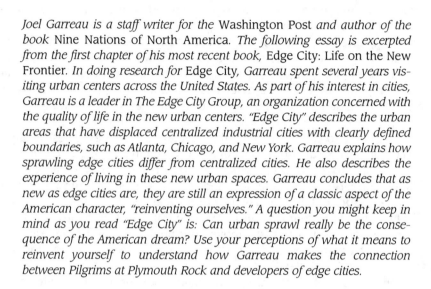

Joel Garreau is a staff writer for the Washington Post *and author of the book* Nine Nations of North America. *The following essay is excerpted from the first chapter of his most recent book,* Edge City: Life on the New Frontier. *In doing research for* Edge City, *Garreau spent several years visiting urban centers across the United States. As part of his interest in cities, Garreau is a leader in The Edge City Group, an organization concerned with the quality of life in the new urban centers. "Edge City" describes the urban areas that have displaced centralized industrial cities with clearly defined boundaries, such as Atlanta, Chicago, and New York. Garreau explains how sprawling edge cities differ from centralized cities. He also describes the experience of living in these new urban spaces. Garreau concludes that as new as edge cities are, they are still an expression of a classic aspect of the American character, "reinventing ourselves." A question you might keep in mind as you read "Edge City" is: Can urban sprawl really be the consequence of the American dream? Use your perceptions of what it means to reinvent yourself to understand how Garreau makes the connection between Pilgrims at Plymouth Rock and developers of edge cities.*

Edge City

Joel Garreau

AMERICANS ARE CREATING the biggest change in a hundred years in how we build cities. Every single American city that *is* growing, is growing in the fashion of Los Angeles, with multiple urban cores.

These new hearths of our civilization—in which the majority of metropolitan Americans now work and around which we live—look not at all like our old downtowns. Buildings rarely rise shoulder to shoulder, as in Chicago's Loop. Instead, their broad, low outlines dot the landscape like mushrooms, separated by greensward and parking lots. Their office towers, frequently guarded by trees, gaze at one another from respectful distances through bands of glass that mirror the sun in blue or silver or green or gold, like antique drawings of "the city of the future."

Our new city centers are tied together not by locomotives and subways, but by jetways, freeways, and rooftop satellite dishes thirty feet across. Their characteristic monument is not a horse-mounted hero, but the atria reaching for the sun and shielding trees perpetually in leaf at the cores of corporate headquarters, fitness centers, and shopping plazas. These new urban areas are marked not by the penthouses of the old urban rich or the tenements of the old urban poor. Instead, their landmark structure is the celebrated single-family detached dwelling, the suburban home with grass all around that made America the best-housed civilization the world has ever known.

I have come to call these new urban centers Edge Cities. Cities, because they contain all the functions a city ever has, albeit in a spread-out form that few have come to recognize for what it is. Edge, because they are a vigorous world of pioneers and immigrants, rising far from the old downtowns, where little save villages or farmland lay only thirty years before.

Edge Cities represent the third wave of our lives pushing into new frontiers in this half century. First, we moved our homes out past the traditional idea of what constituted a city. This was the suburbanization of America, especially after World War II.

Then we wearied of returning downtown for the necessities of life, so we moved our marketplaces out to where we lived. This was the malling of America, especially in the 1960s and 70s.

Today, we have moved our means of creating wealth, the essence of urbanism—our jobs—out to where most of us have lived and shopped for two generations. That has led to the rise of Edge City.

By any functional urban standard—tall buildings, bright lights, office space that represents white-collar jobs, shopping, entertainment, prestigious hotels, corporate headquarters, hospitals with CAT scans, even population—each Edge City is larger than downtown Portland, Oregon, or Portland, Maine, or Tampa, or Tucson. Already, two thirds of all American office facilities are in Edge Cities, and 80 percent of them have materialized in only the last two decades. By the mid-1980s, there was far more office space in Edge Cities around America's largest metropolis, New York, than there was at its heart—midtown Manhattan. Even before Wall Street faltered in the late 1980s there was less office space there, in New York's downtown, than there was in the Edge Cities of New Jersey alone.

Even the old-fashioned Ozzie and Harriet commute from a conventional suburb to downtown is now very much a minority pattern, U.S. Census figures show. Most of the trips metropolitan Americans take in a day completely skirt the old centers. Their journeys to work, especially, are to Edge Cities. So much of our shopping is done in Edge Cities that a casual glance at most Yellow Pages shows it increasingly difficult in an old downtown to buy such a commodity item as a television set.

Edge City is any place that:

- *Has five million square feet or more of leasable office space—the workplace of the Information Age.* Five million square feet is more than downtown Memphis. The Edge City called the Galleria area west of downtown Houston—crowned by the sixty-four-story Transco Tower, the tallest building in the world outside an old downtown—is bigger than downtown Minneapolis.
- *Has 600,000 square feet or more of leasable retail space.* That is the equivalent of a fair-sized mall. That mall, remember, probably has at least three nationally famous department stores, and eighty to a hundred shops and boutiques full of merchandise that used to be available only on the finest boulevards of Europe. Even in their heyday, there were not many downtowns with that boast.
- *Has more jobs than bedrooms.* When the workday starts, people head toward this place, not away from it. Like all urban places, the population increases at 9 A.M.
- *Is perceived by the population as one place.* It is a regional end destination for mixed use—not a starting point—that "has it all," from jobs, to shopping, to entertainment.
- *Was nothing like "city" as recently as thirty years ago.* Then, it was just bedrooms, if not cow pastures. This incarnation is brand new.

An example of the authentic, California-like experience of encountering such an Edge City is peeling off a high thruway, like the Pennsylvania Turnpike, onto an arterial, like 202 at King of Prussia, northwest of downtown Philadelphia. Descending into traffic that is bumper to bumper in *both* directions, one swirls through mosaics of lawn and parking, punctuated by office slabs whose designers have taken the curious vow of never placing windows in anything other than horizontal reflective strips. Detours mark the yellow dust of heavy construction that seems a permanent feature of the landscape.

Tasteful signs mark corporations apparently named after Klingon warriors. Who put Captain Kirk in charge of calling companies Imtrex, Avantor, and Synovus? Before that question can settle, you encounter the spoor of—the mother ship. On King of Prussia's Route 202, the mark of that mind-boggling enormity reads MALL NEXT FOUR LEFTS.

For the stranger who is a connoisseur of such places, this Dante-esque vision brings a physical shiver to the spine and a not entirely ironic murmur of recognition to the lips: "Ah! Home!" For that is precisely the significance of Edge Cities. They are the culmination of a generation of individual American value decisions about the best ways to live, work, and play—about how to create "home." That stuff "out there" is where America is being built. That "stuff" is the delicate balance between unlimited opportunity and rippling chaos that works for us so well. We build more of it every chance we get.

If Edge Cities are still a little ragged at the fringes, well, . . . Edge Cities, after all, are still works in progress.

They have already proven astoundingly efficient, though, by any urban standard that can be quantified. As places to make one's fame and fortune, their corporate offices generate unprecedentedly low unemployment. In fact, their emblem is the hand-lettered sign taped to plate glass begging people to come to work. As real estate markets, they have made an entire generation of homeowners and speculators rich. As bazaars, they are anchored by some of the most luxurious shopping in the world. Edge City acculturates immigrants, provides child care, and offers safety. It is, on average, an *improvement* in per capita fuel efficiency over the old suburbia-downtown arrangement, since it moves everything closer to the homes of the middle class.

That is why Edge City is the crucible of America's urban future. Having become the place in which the majority of Americans now live, learn, work, shop, play, pray, and die, Edge City will be the forge of the fabled American way of life well into the twenty-first century.

There are those who find this idea appalling.

I once spent a fair chunk of a Christmas season in Tysons Corner, Virginia, stopping people as they hurried about their holiday tasks, asking them what they thought of their brave new world. The words I recorded were searing. They described the area as plastic, a hodgepodge, Disneyland (used as a pejorative), and sterile. They said it lacked livability, civilization, community, neighborhood, and even a soul.

These responses are frightening, if Edge City is the laboratory of how civilized and livable urban American will be well into the next century. Right now, it is vertigo-inducing. It may have all the complexity, diversity, and size of a downtown. But it can cover dozens of square miles, and juxtapose schools and freeways and atria and shimmering parking lots with corporate lawns and Day-Glo-orange helicopter wind socks. Its logic takes a while to decode.

Will we ever be proud of this place? Will we ever drag our visiting relatives out to show off our Edge City, our shining city on the hill? Will we ever feel—for this generation and the ones that follow—that it's a good place to be young? To be old? To fall in love? To have a Fourth of July parade? Will it ever be the place we want to call home?

If Edge City still gives some people the creeps, it is partially because it confounds expectations. Traditional-downtown urbanites recoil because a place blown out to automobile scale is not what they think of as "city." They find the swirl of functions intimidating, confusing, maddening. Why are these tall office buildings so far apart? Why are they juxtaposed, apparently higgledy-piggledy, among the malls and strip shopping centers and fast-food joints and self-service gas stations? Both literally and metaphorically, these urbanites always get lost.

At the same time, Edge City often does not meet the expectations of traditional suburbanites, either. Few who bought into the idea of quarter-acre tranquillity ever expected to take a winding turn and suddenly be confronted with a 150-foot colossus looming over the trees, red aircraft-warning beacons flashing, its towering glass reflecting not the moon, but the sodium vapor of the parking lot's lights.

The question is whether this disorienting expectation gap is permanent or simply a phase, a function of how fast we've transformed our world.

The forces of change whose emblem is the bulldozer, and the forces of preservation whose totem is the tree, are everywhere at war in this country. The raging debate over what we have lost and what we have gained, as we flee the old urban patterns of the nineteenth century for the new ones of the twenty-first, is constant. Are we satisfying our deepest yearnings for the good life with Edge City? Or are we poisoning everything across which we sprawl?

Getting to the bottom of those questions leads directly to issues of national character, of what we value. They come down to who we are, how we got that way, and where we're headed. It is why, when the reeling feeling caused by Edge City finally subsides, I think it is possible to examine the place as the expression of some fundamental values. Nowhere in the American national character, as it turns out, is there as deep a divide as that between our reverence for "unspoiled" nature and our enduring devotion to "progress."

It comes to this. One vision of the American natural landscape was that it had inherent value and should be treasured for what it already was and had always been. The other saw in the land nothing but satanic wastes; there could be placed on it no value until it was bent to man's will—until civilization was forced into bloom.

The history of America is an endless repetition of this battle. We are fighting it to this day, nowhere more so than in our current frontier, Edge City. In the unsettled, unsettling environment of Edge City, great wealth may be acquired, but without a sense that the place has community, or even a center, much less a soul. And the resolution of these issues goes far beyond architecture and landscape. It goes to the philosophical ground on which we are building our Information Age society. It's possible that Edge City is the most purposeful attempt Americans have made since the days of the Founding Fathers to try to create something like a new Eden.

Edge City may be the result of Americans striving once again for a new, restorative synthesis. Perhaps Edge City represents Americans taking the functions of the city (the machine) and bringing them out to the physical edge of the landscape (the frontier). There, we try once again to merge the two in a new-found union of nature and art (the garden), albeit one in which the treeline is punctuated incongruously by office towers.

This goes to the ultimate significance of Edge City. The battles we fight today over our futures do not have echoes only back to 1956, when Dwight D. Eisenhower changed America forever with the creation of the interstate highway program. Nor does it go back only to the New Deal of the 1930s, during which Franklin Delano Roosevelt shaped America into a society of homeowners. It goes to the core of what makes America America, right back to the beginning, with the Pilgrims in 1620 and the Virginia Cavaliers of 1607.

It addresses profound questions, the answers to which will reverberate forever. It addresses the search for Utopia at the center of the American Dream. It reflects our perpetually unfinished American business of reinventing ourselves, redefining ourselves, restoring ourselves, announcing that our centuries-old perpetual revolution—our search for the future inside ourselves—still beats strong.

It suggests that the world of the immigrants and pioneers is not dead in America; it has just moved out to Edge City, where gambles are being lost and won for high stakes. It adds another level of history to places already filled with ghosts. That is why one day Edge City, too, may be seen as historic. It is the creation of a new world, being shaped by the free in a constantly reinvented land.

Discussion Questions

Content

1. According to Garreau, what is an "Edge City"?

2. What two competing values of the American character does Garreau see captured in Edge Cities? How does he think Edge Cities bring these values together? Think of an example of an Edge City you are familiar with that brings these values together.

3. According to Garreau, people in Tysons Corner, Virginia, describe their community as "plastic, a hodgepodge, Disneyland (used as a pejorative), and sterile" and say that it lacked "livability, civilization, community, neighborhood, and even a soul." What specific conditions would make people describe their community this way? And if they describe their community in this way, why do you think they would continue to live there? Would you use some of these same terms to describe your area? What words would you use to describe your area?

Form

1. After describing the disorienting newness of Edge Cities, Garreau concludes that their creation only repeats the old-fashioned American urge to reinvent ourselves. At what point in his essay does Garreau make the transition from describing the newness of Edge Cities to explaining that the newness of those cities expresses a traditional American value? Just how successful is this transition? Why are you or are you not persuaded by his claim?

2. Garreau writes that the significance of edge cities goes to the "core of what makes America America" and even goes back to the Pilgrims. What descriptions of Edge Cities does Garreau provide to convince his readers of this? What unwritten assumptions does Garreau rely on for the persuasiveness of his view? Do you share his assumptions? How important do you think it is to the persuasiveness of Garreau's argument that his readers share his assumptions? Explain why.

3. In what ways does Garreau position himself as an objective observer through the form of his essay? Indicate specific passages in the essay that make you think he is objective. What parts of his essay seem like subjective opinions to you? Indicate the passages that seem subjective. What sense do you make of Garreau's mixing of objective observation and subjective opinion? Can an essay have both and still be successful? Why or why not?

Writing Prompts

1. Write an essay that defines your character through descriptions of your area. Take into account not only the places where you like to hang out but also the places that you avoid. What part of your character is expressed in those places you avoid? In addition, how do you make sense of your individual character in the context of places that are everywhere, such as fast food restaurants and malls.

2. Think up your own term for suburban sprawl (just as Garreau thought up "Edge City"). It can be either a negative term, a positive term, or a fairly neutral or paradoxical term. Explain in a brief essay just what the term means, why you chose it, and how it captures the essence of rapid suburbanization.

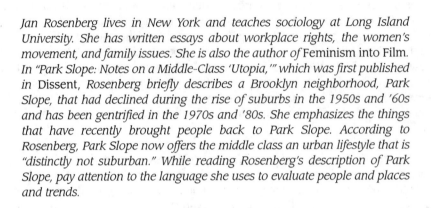

Jan Rosenberg lives in New York and teaches sociology at Long Island University. She has written essays about workplace rights, the women's movement, and family issues. She is also the author of Feminism into Film. *In "Park Slope: Notes on a Middle-Class 'Utopia,'" which was first published in* Dissent, *Rosenberg briefly describes a Brooklyn neighborhood, Park Slope, that had declined during the rise of suburbs in the 1950s and '60s and has been gentrified in the 1970s and '80s. She emphasizes the things that have recently brought people back to Park Slope. According to Rosenberg, Park Slope now offers the middle class an urban lifestyle that is "distinctly not suburban." While reading Rosenberg's description of Park Slope, pay attention to the language she uses to evaluate people and places and trends.*

Park Slope:
Notes on a Middle-Class "Utopia"

Jan Rosenberg

A FAMILIAR STORY, playing itself out in city after city: skyrocketing housing costs send upscale urban dwellers looking for new areas to "pioneer" (some would say invade) and to reshape to their taste. In Manhattan, it has transformed areas once filled with machine shops and printing plants into the luxury lofts and art spaces of Soho, Noho, and TriBeCa. And across the East River, similar changes march through Boerum Hill, Carroll Gardens, Cobble Hill, and particularly Park Slope—the "brownstone" neighborhoods ringing downtown Brooklyn.

Stroll through Park Slope on a warm Saturday night, past young middle-class crowds patronizing a cornucopia of chic new restaurants offering the latest in trendy cuisine: sushi, Tex-Mex, "continental," five types of Chinese, Thai, and various gourmet take-out shops. A lone shoemaker hangs on, but for a dime store or bodega where you can still get an ice cream sandwich for

Jan Rosenberg. "Park Slope: Notes on a Middle-Class 'Utopia.'" *Dissent* (Fall 1987): 565–67. Reprinted with the permission of the author.

under a dollar, you have to literally go down the Slope, an avenue or two away. Interspersed among the restaurants are numerous real estate offices and nearly as many "new wave" florists (there's almost a florist a block in the heart of the Slope's Seventh Avenue). New craft shops display expensive, elegant *objets*. Completing the ambience are those emblems of yuppiedom, Benetton's, a nearly-completed D'Agostino's, and a recently arrived "closet designer." (Those from Wall Street who specialize in restructuring corporations can now hire someone to restructure their closets, though some spouses have been known to view this as a hostile takeover.) These Saturday-night sidewalks are filled with well-dressed, well-coiffed people in their twenties, thirties, and forties (hardly any are beyond their forties). A tennis pro from Sheepshead Bay, accountants and teachers from Bensonhurst, are drawn to the shops, the people, the élan of Park Slope, where they encounter the full range of young professionals priced out of the Village and the Upper West Side, searching for an affordable "outer borough" alternative. The atmosphere is thick with style and expectation; this is a place to be, and to be seen. This is *New York Magazine*'s Park Slope.

BUT THERE ARE OTHER PARK SLOPES flourishing, in ways less familiar, less commercial. One is the Park Slope of neighborhood day-care centers and nursery schools, of after-school programs and Little League, of PS 321 and JHS 51, of religious institutions, nearly moribund only a few years ago, revitalized by the in-migration of families since the early 1970s. This child-centered, family-oriented Park Slope, anchored in its oun institutions, has its own landmarks and symbols: the area around "the monument" at Ninth Street and Prospect Park West on Saturday spring mornings is one of these. Awash in a maroon and yellow sea of St. Saviour's and St. Francis's baseball uniforms, elementary school kids (mostly boys, despite some organizers' best efforts) embody the neighborhood's vitality and—since many if not most are not Catholic—its ecumenical spirit. The kids, drawn from public, private, and parochial schools, wait at the monument for their teams to assemble and games to begin.

A six-year-old boy worries about his orthodox Jewish neighbors seeing him in his St. Saviour's uniforrn, and dons a yarmulke to offset his St. Saviour's shirt before visiting them on the Sabbath after his game. The priests ask the non-Catholic parents and children in the league to participate in and respect their preseason service, now nearly purged of specifically Catholic references. Congregation Beth Elohim (the Garfield Temple) also typifies the neighborhood. Faced with dwindling membership and bleak prospects in 1970, its former grandeur faded, temple members had the good sense and good luck to create one of the early neighborhood nursery schools. Its early-childhood programs helped revitalize the temple, drawing Jewish families into (or back into) Jewish institutional life. The churches and synagogues have made themselves centers of many family-oriented activities, from sports to preschool and after-school programs, potluck dinners and weekend retreats, that knit together some of the baby boomers with children.

PARKING IS NEARLY IMPOSSIBLE ("double Park Slope," my older son calls it) as I zoom up on a Saturday morning to drop off my child for his nine o'clock game. I pull away quickly to park and get back before the first inning, thinking of my friend, Fred I., the envy of the "silent majority": while most of us quietly grumble that our weeks are dominated by Little League (in our own case, practices on Wednesday, Thursday, and Friday afternoons and "official games" all day Saturday), Fred courageously manages to sneak off to his country house with his brood in tow every weekend.

It's a cold, drizzly Saturday in April and the parade to officially open the neighborhood baseball season is about to begin. Hundreds of kids and their parents huddle together by team, waiting to march up Union Street and over to "the monument." Mayor Koch is going to inaugurate the newly renovated playing fields near Prospect Park's new concert area and playground at Ninth Street, only a stone's throw from the beautifully restored Picnic House and Tennis House—all of which border the Park Slope side of Prospect Park. The southern and eastern sides of the park, bordered by predominantly black neighborhoods, seem a distant land. The park serves as more of a barrier than a meeting ground between white upper-middle-class and black and Hispanic Brooklyn. Connections between private neighborhood gentrification and the careful restoration of once-treasured, then-deteriorated public space suggest themselves to even the most casual visitor. But for even the most apolitical of Slopers, there is nagging doubt that their good fortune can endure in a Brooklyn increasingly overwhelmed by an underclass as cut off from prosperity as they are connected.

THE 1950s AND 1960s brought hard times to urban neighborhoods all over the country; Park Slope was no exception. This middle-class family neighborhood was losing out to newer, more promising suburban areas. Clashes between rival Hispanic and Italian gangs made the area inhospitable to the middle class. The park block residents of Third Street, always one of the Slope's most beautiful and desirable blocks (and Sidney Hook's home through the 1940s and 1950s) organized the Park Slope Betterment Committee to promote the neighborhood's revival. They pressured the banks to give mortgages and held meetings to advise prospective neighbors on buying and remodeling homes.

A trickle of newcomers, led by artists seeking affordable housing and studio space, flowed into the Slope. One early "pioneer," a writer-editor who moved to Park Slope with her artist husband in 1968, left Manhattan for the Slope's beautiful, ample space, and affordable homes. A *New York Times* article had trumpeted the neighborhood's virtues: its distinguished architecture and undervalued homes, its beautiful park, and the nearby presence of other artists. The couple bought a prime park block house, though it was occupied by numerous tenants and the neighborhood was still redlined by the banks, and converted it from a rooming house to a triplex for themselves and a floor-through rental. The single-room occupants they displaced have long since been forgotten by the current owners and their neighbors. Built in the 1890s as a one-family house with ample room for servants, the brownstone adapted quite readily to the changed circumstances of middle-class families in the 1970s.

Like artists, 1960s radicals were another important trickle in the early 1970s migration stream. They, too, were drawn by the affordable space, the park, and the presence of others like themselves. Veterans of the antiwar, civil rights, and feminist movements quickly found each other in, and drew each other to, this budding urban community.

MANY CAME IN COUPLES, expecting to settle in and eventually to have and raise their children here. Not surprisingly, these 1960s veterans remain central to community politics in Park Slope. Over the years, personal, community, and political interests have converged around issues of housing and education.

Early antiredlining campaigns were organized by people experienced with bankers' power to make and break neighborhoods. Ready but unable to buy houses in Park Slope, a neighborhood the banks did not yet believe in, activists successfully challenged the then-standard diversion of neighborhood resources to finance suburban and Sunbelt development. Ironically (but predictably) the end of redlining sped up the gentrification, which was soon to work against middle-class housing/investment opportunities. By the mid-1980s, despite considerable expansion of gentrified Park Slope's boundaries, only highly paid professionals, bankers and the like (and those lucky enough to have queued up on time), could afford to own a home in Park Slope.

School politics reflect the neighborhood's concentration of leftists and liberals. Several leading elementary schools have adopted the "Peace Curriculum"; the Community School Board has committed its resources to establishing an "alternative school" similar to the ones in Manhattan's District 4 founded by Deborah Meier.

To the middle class among a generation wary of suburbia's soured promise, places like Park Slope came to be seen as a contemporary alternative, the chance to build a family-centered urban life that is distinctly not suburban. The mix of people in public institutions, the subway rides to and from "the City," the architecture, the shared public grandeur of a partially restored Prospect Park—these eddies against the tide of privatization are reminders that one has embraced a post-suburban dream of a vital, complex, dynamic urban life.

Discussion Questions

Content

1. Rosenberg describes Park Slope from two different perspectives. What perspectives are these? What details of urban life does she describe from each perspective?

2. In what ways does Park Slope seem to you like a middle-class "utopia"? In what ways does it not seem like a utopia at all? How does its status as utopia for some relate to its status as dystopia for others? Do you think this compromises the utopian vision of Park Slope? What do you think would be a more realistic vision for Park Slope?

3. Rosenberg states that people have come to Park Slope in search of a lifestyle that is distinctly "not suburban." Does the community she describes seem to you "not suburban"? What elements of suburban life seem to have been brought to Park Slope? What elements of city life do you find in Rosenberg's description? Do you think that a distinctly "not suburban" lifestyle is even possible anymore? Just what kinds of lifestyles can we choose from? And how freely can we choose?

Form

1. How does Rosenberg's personal description of Little League baseball in Park Slope compare and contrast with her other descriptions of Park Slope's people and places? Does she use her description of her life in the neighborhood to distance herself from or identify herself with the other people and places of Park Slope? From these descriptions, what conclusions do you draw about the sense of community shared among residents in Park Slope?

2. Rosenberg places the resurgence of Park Slope in the context of forty years of urban development. How does her discussion of suburbanization and gentrification provide a wider context for her description of Park Slope? Do you think Park Slope can be seen as representative of larger trends in American urban culture? If not, why not? If so, just what do you think these trends might be?

3. How is Rosenberg's essay structured to encourage or discourage future projects like Park Slope? Does she tell a story of success or does she tell a story of failure? Do you think she has presented Park Slope in a way that makes its story relevant to everyone? Why or why not?

Writing Prompts

1. Describe a "stroll" through an area in your town. Give details about the people you would meet and the places you would pass in order to give your reader a sense of the urban, suburban, or postsuburban quality of the area.

2. Compare and contrast the advantages and disadvantages you would associate with a suburban and an urban lifestyle. In the end, which one might you be tempted to choose? On what basis would you make your choice?

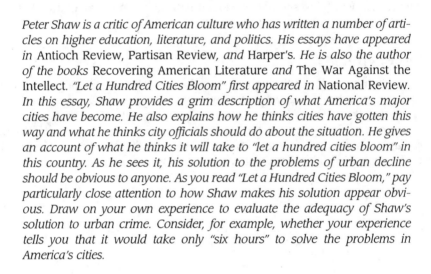

Peter Shaw is a critic of American culture who has written a number of articles on higher education, literature, and politics. His essays have appeared in Antioch Review, Partisan Review, *and* Harper's. *He is also the author of the books* Recovering American Literature *and* The War Against the Intellect. *"Let a Hundred Cities Bloom" first appeared in* National Review. *In this essay, Shaw provides a grim description of what America's major cities have become. He also explains how he thinks cities have gotten this way and what he thinks city officials should do about the situation. He gives an account of what he thinks it will take to "let a hundred cities bloom" in this country. As he sees it, his solution to the problems of urban decline should be obvious to anyone. As you read "Let a Hundred Cities Bloom," pay particularly close attention to how Shaw makes his solution appear obvious. Draw on your own experience to evaluate the adequacy of Shaw's solution to urban crime. Consider, for example, whether your experience tells you that it would take only "six hours" to solve the problems in America's cities.*

Let a Hundred Cities Bloom

Peter Shaw

A DOWNTOWN of deserted, mausoleum-like buildings, surrounded by black slums: this is the definition of most former cities of the United States. To contemplate what might be done about these forlorn places, it is necessary to understand who benefits from their present condition. Two groups stand out for their reluctance to see any changes. The first is those remaining in the inner city. They have accepted deteriorating living conditions in exchange for the lures of welfare. The law-abiding among them are obliged to live cheek by jowl with mentally disturbed and criminal elements once confined to asylums and jails. But all alike benefit from the welfare system and continue to live in its vicinity.

The second group is the suburbanites driven out of the city by the same conditions. The suburbanites regard the city as a convenient catchment area for the people they moved away from. This is why, despite their economic conservatism, they support the welfare system. They hope that, together with free medical services and subsidized housing, welfare will keep the underclass away from them.

Suburbanites no longer miss the cultural features of a genuine city: the bustle of diverse businesses generated by the haphazard crowding of a true downtown; enhanced educational opportunities like the teaching of obscure languages in high-school districts with enough students and teachers to offer specialized courses; professional sports teams; enough people to support a genuine French restaurant. Instead, the downtown and suburban populations alike send their children to segregated schools where the cultural diversity that is no more is assiduously celebrated.

The compelling advantages of present arrangements ensure that nothing will change. This leaves us free to offer solutions in confidence that they will be entirely ignored. Not to say that the following solutions are offered in a spirit of frivolity. They rest on the proposition that downtown redevelopment and the concentration of dependency populations are the cities' twin blights. Dealing with them must come first, followed by initiatives encouraging the return of population and investment.

First, then, must come the elimination of bureaucratic practices that perpetuate the location of dependency populations in the city core. Therefore, foolish and destructive as they are, allow the continuance of welfare payments, housing subsidies, drug-abuse treatment, food stamps. But provide these somewhere truly convenient for the state—that is, somewhere chosen not because it keeps undesirable people away from suburbanites, but because it keeps them away from the law-abiding.

The result would be to reduce the destructive and discouraging effects exerted by the cities' pathological populations. These effects removed, those left behind would come to resemble the viable poor populations of the past. Social pathology there always was in the slums, as well as crime and drugs. But none of these was on the scale made possible since the 1960s by government subsidy. Viable slums above all meant orderly behavior as the norm. If such behavior could have been maintained, American small and medium-sized cities need not have suffered their extinctions.

It is true that life can go on in an atmosphere of fear. But our society has also demonstrated that smaller cities do not survive in such an atmosphere. Clearly they stand no chance of being repopulated until fear has been banished. Yet to so much as refer to restored public safety is to run up against the syndrome in which our elites, racked with class and racial guilt, bereft of any conviction of legitimacy, deal with crime and violence by surrendering civic order.

How to Restore Order

How might law and order be restored? Easily. Yet it is a further comment on the ethos of the elites that the question, "How do we suppress crime?" needs to be asked. Time was that a decision to deal with crime would have been equivalent to a decision to clear the accumulated trash from along a city's curbs. One would not, after taking the decision, have gone on to detail how a street is swept. Today, one is obliged to explain how safety along the same street can be established.

Safe streets, then, are secured by trained agents of the state—policemen. These agents operate in a number of ways. Some display their uniformed presence in public places as a deterrent to crime and uncivil behavior. Others investigate crimes for the purpose of apprehending the perpetrators thereof. The latter activity tends to reduce crime in the short run and to deter it in the long run. After arrest, criminals come in contact with a functioning criminal-justice system as well as restraint and punishment centers called prisons. The key is maintaining each of the elements in working order. Police must deter and arrest, court systems try and sentence, prisons keep wrongdoers incarcerated.

In short, a decision has to be taken to enforce the law. At present, this is not even regarded as an option. Law enforcement has never been so much as suggested, for example, as a solution to the crime problem within a few square blocks in New York City's very center. After suffering decades of growing physical ugliness and violent crime, the city's authorities met to determine how Times Square might be restored to its former status as proud crossroads of the world.

The area is the size of the downtown in a medium-sized city. Beggars, bands of undisciplined youths, pornographic theaters and bookstores, and an atmosphere of menace rule. Only those respectable citizens unlucky enough to have jobs in the neighborhood, along with tourists, enter during the day. At night theatergoers are forced to run its gauntlet of beggars, three-card-monte dealers, and ever-wandering youths.

Accordingly, the Times Square master plan was arrived at through ratiocination of the highest order. The area would be transformed by architecture. Office buildings and hotels would replace the so-called seedy old buildings that, in urban-planning parlance, were "breeding" crime. The planners and civic-minded businessmen who approved this scheme, in other words, proposed to spend hundreds of millions of dollars over more than a decade on a problem that could be solved in under six hours.

The six-hour solution was the only one that could not be mentioned in the undoubtedly edifying meetings that led to the architectural initiative. No one in attendance can have been unrespectable enough to say: "Let us send police into the area to close down pornography operations, set derelicts on their feet, arrest anyone harassing fellow citizens, and stand in uniform along thoroughfares as a warning against uncivil behavior." Such an operation, if begun at 3 P.M. on a given day, could be completed by 9 P.M., after which a reduced number of policemen would have to remain in sight to maintain the newly restored order.

Instead of this unthinkable approach, the Times Square renewal committee, armed with expensive studies and subsidies, began its alternative. Viable office buildings were emptied; a few cold fortresses were erected to stand empty until at least the second millennium of the birth of Christ. The plan remained on the books, but with the recession it died a natural death, bequeathing to the city not only empty new buildings but also emptied old ones and an accelerated decline of both Times Square and the American theater.

Smaller American cities have gone the same route. But what if they were to address public safety directly? How much policing would they need? At what cost? Let us just say that they would require enough policing to restore safety, and at a cost undoubtedly less than the sum of costs from crime, property destruction, and irrelevant social services. There was a time when one foot patrolman every ten blocks or so could keep public order. In the suburbs, where those who used to be looked after by that patrolman have fled, several miles are adequately patroled by a single radio car. At first, though, there might have to be a patrolman on every block and numerous radio cars cruising the downtown.

To the tortured question, "How can we send police into minority neighborhoods without appearing racist?" the answer is simple. Send the police where there is crime and danger, and give them but one directive: "Enforce the law." Residents will be delighted: surveys show that blacks and other minorities enthusiastically support heavy police presence and strict enforcement of the law. Only advanced thinkers will react negatively.

Next Step

Making the city safe would not be enough. To make the safe city attractive, something else would have to be done.

First, kill all the city planners. That is, to make the safe city an attractive investment, shopping, and recreation center, halt all city planning and remove building and zoning restrictions. Much would ensue. The first changes might well involve building over the city planners' beloved plazas. These cold regions amount to unused wastelands offering little reward for the long, dreary walk required to cross them. The same distance, when dense with buildings, is easily, comfortably covered on foot as one goes from store window to store window, pausing occasionally, crossing streets, and being entertained by the rest of humanity.

Thrown open to development, the plazas—those desert places of the planners—would likely be filled with stores, and with apartments above them. The lonely white-elephant buildings at the center of the present plazas would be given a lifeline to the world, a chance to prosper as the city moves back toward its natural look of filled street spaces.

In the meantime, something might be done about the planners' free-standing, multi-story parking garages—those forbidding structures erected where once the sweet cash registers sang. Some of the uses to which these structures might be put would particularly distress city planners. The new investors might slaughter chickens in them, or set up semi-open-air markets, or tennis courts. The result will seem chaotic. But the city would be moving another step back toward its natural condition of mixed use and of mixed odors and mixed sounds as well.

The only foreseeable problem is that progressive thinkers, having initially disapproved the vulgar commercialization of the parking garages, will, as these are about to be sold at a profit by imaginative risk takers, make demands that their ethnic identity not be destroyed by greedy developers.

In residential sections let investors snap up undervalued homes and do whatever is necessary to make them competitive with the larger square footages and grounds in the suburbs. The investors can pair houses, adapting them for single-family living. Or let families combine three houses, renting out part of the space as apartments, subject only to health-code compliance.

Where planning was, there let innovation thrive; where fear was, there let safety reign.

On second thought, don't kill all the city planners. Make them into committees to review renovation and building plans. Whatever they disapprove, rush to support. Whatever they approve, scrutinize closely. Also set up a crime-control board made up of neighborhood activists, sociology professors, enlightened politicians, and representatives of the ACLU. Whatever this group disapproves, instantly establish as policy. Whatever it recommends, table until the city has revived . . . and it is time to begin the next cycle of decline.

Discussion Questions

Content

1. What suggestions does Shaw have for improving cities? How do his suggestions reflect a suburban bias and viewpoint?

2. According to Shaw, how has welfare destroyed American cities? Do you agree or disagree with his view? Find specific passages in the reading that could be used to support your position.

3. Referring specifically to the urban renewal of Times Square in New York City, Shaw argues that the renewal project was a waste of time and money. In his view, the problems of Times Square could have been solved in "six hours" by sending a large number of police to the area. Are more police the answer to urban problems? If so, why would "advanced thinkers . . . react negatively" to his answer? Are people simply uninterested in solving urban problems? Or is Shaw trying to make another point? What do you think that point is?

Form

1. Is Shaw serious when he writes, "kill all the city planners"? Find passages in the reading in which Shaw's language is exaggerated. What effect does his exaggerated language have on you as a reader? Why do you think he uses such exaggerated language? Do you think he wants you to react to his language as you do?

2. The title of Shaw's essay, "Let a Hundred Cities Bloom," invokes the image of cities blooming like flowers. In what ways do ideas about flowers and gardening (ideas such as "blooming," "growing," "weeding," "cultivation") inform Shaw's point of view? In what ways does the organic language of gardening seem inconsistent with Shaw's point of view?

3. Do you think Shaw's essay would persuade the city planners whom he is in disagreement with? If so, how? If not, why not? Is it possible that Shaw has another purpose in mind? Making references to the essay, explore other purposes for the essay.

Writing Prompts

1. Write a response to Shaw's essay using images of gardening to discuss ways of solving urban problems. Explain why you do or do not think his ideas will "Let a Hundred Cities Bloom."

2. Write a description of a major problem in your area. It could be anything from crime to economic decline to political corruption. Explain at least five different causes for the problem. Offer solutions in the spirit of Shaw, solutions that are thought provoking because they are so unrealistic.

PART 5 DISCUSSION QUESTIONS

1. Taking into account the views of Boulton, Garreau, Fishman, and the other writers in this part, what do you think suburbs are? Are they America's "new cities"? Are they stressful places? What do they say about America's future? What do they say about our past?

2. Compare Reich's idea of "community" to one of the other writers' ideas of community. In what ways is community an "urban" idea? In what ways is it a "suburban" idea? Which idea of community do you find more appealing, a suburban or an urban one?

3. The writers in this part largely agree that suburban living is characterized by a particular kind of lifestyle. What is the suburban lifestyle? What seems to you to be its promises? Its perils? What do you think citizens, city planners, and politicians should do in response to the promises and perils of a suburban lifestyle?

4. How would you characterize the lifestyle choices available in your area? Urban? Suburban? Postsuburban? Whose lifestyle is urban? Suburban? Postsuburban? What choices do these people have about how they live? What choices have been made for them? Explain how these options are part of the larger urban culture of the United States.

5. The writers in this part have all discussed the urban sprawl that has overtaken the American landscape over the last forty years. How accurately do you think they have represented suburbanization? Would you agree with their discussions of the consequences? What do you have to say to these writers about suburbanization?

PART 5 WRITING ASSIGNMENTS

1. Write an essay describing the area in which you live as either urban or suburban. Do so by explaining what you would do on a typical day in your area. Explain where you would go, what you would do, who you would do it with. Be sure to describe how you feel about the things you are describing. Specifically, try to account for whether you feel "decentered," "stressed out," fearful of crime, or any of the other emotions the writers in this part have invoked.

2. One of the consequences of the suburbanization of the United States is that the urban landscape has become "decentered." As a result, no matter where a person goes in this country, he or she can count on finding the same malls, fast food franchises, and entertainment options. Write an essay in which you evaluate this trend. Consider the implications of suburbanization for regionalism. Should we work to preserve the regional flavor of places such as the Southwest, the Pacific Northwest, the eastern seaboard, and the Great Plains? Or should we further encourage the decentering and homogenization of the American urban landscape?

3. Interview an older person in your area. Ask that person how his or her relationships with neighbors have changed over the course of his or her life. Using ideas and terms drawn from the essays in this part, evaluate the changes the person you interviewed has described. Explain how these changes may or may not reflect larger changes in American urban and suburban culture.

What Happened in L.A.?

IN THE CLASSROOMS of America in recent weeks, I heard no term more often than "multiculturalism." (You are not I.) We celebrate "our friends" the Guatemalans. In fact, our friends the Guatemalans are converting to the Mormon faith. And our friends the Guatemalans are working as nannies in Beverly Hills and teaching the children of 90210 how to ask and say thank you in Spanish. In fact, people influence one another, lives change, cultures mix....

Every mother tells men—her husband, her sons—what men cannot quite believe: Birth is traumatic. It is messy. It is slimy. It is painful beyond pain. There is blood. Birth begins with a scream.

I tell you, Los Angeles is being born. A city is forming within the terror and suspicion and fear that people have of one another. As an outsider, I can sense the city forming. People in Los Angeles are preoccupied with one another, can no longer forget one another.

You have lost your suburban innocence. It is better this way, I think. Better not to like one another than not to know the stranger exists.

—*Richard Rodriguez*

COVERT ACTION: What happened in Los Angeles? Was it a riot, an uprising, a rebellion, an insurrection, and why would you term it one or the other?

Mike Davis: I think the majority of the participants, particularly the youths who started it, see the events that began on April 29th as a rebellion.

When I was at a meeting of the Crips and Bloods in Inglewood in mid-May, it was referred to as a slave rebellion. Although the term "riot" doesn't have negative connotations for me as a labor historian, I think the wishes of the people who were the motive force should be honored.

In any case, you can't reduce the events to a single essence—one major characteristic or identity. L.A. was a hybrid social revolt with three major dimensions. It was a revolutionary democratic protest characteristic of African-American history when demands for equal rights have been thwarted by the major institutions. It was also a major postmodern bread riot—an uprising of not just poor people but particularly of those strata of poor in southern California who've been most savagely affected by the recession. Thirdly, it was an interethnic conflict—particularly the systematic destroying and uprooting of Korean stores in the Black community.

So it was all of those things at once and issues of rage, class, and race cannot be separated out. Sometimes they coalesced, sometimes they were parallel in time and space.

—Mike Davis

WHEN HE SPOKE TO THE PRESS during the Los Angeles uprising, Rodney King, in his own way, alluded implicitly to the limitations of the news format. "We're all stuck here for awhile," King said, in the course of his call for peace. Although he did not elaborate on his conception of what it is to be stuck, the generality of King's remark, with its unspecified "we" and its unspecified "here," suggested that being stuck is so basic and universal a condition as to be part of the essence of the uneventful. We are all stuck, but only for awhile, because we all eventually die. But before we die and wherever we are, we are prey to the world, routinely and relentlessly bound to circumstances and situations that lack the charisma essential to the news event.

Less well remembered than his T-shirt-commodified and much more newsy query, "Can we all get along?" Rodney King's reference to being stuck identified a condition that is at once ontological and social. Being stuck is an ontological condition (a condition constitutive of human existence), because each of us is, as existentialists insist, forever finding him- or herself saddled with a world that is not wholly a product of his or her creation. But being stuck is also a social condition, since the world and worlds which impinge on us are always and everywhere the products of social histories and ongoing social practices. Being stuck, then, is a matter of being inexorably caught up in a network of political, economic, and cultural legacies that escape the aura of the extraordinary. Neither news nor old news, these legacies constitute the uneventful conditions of social existence which useful analyses of the Rodney King incidents cannot possibly ignore. By calling our attention to the facticity of being stuck, Rodney King's own words provide an appropriate point of departure for such analyses.

—*Robert Gooding-Williams*

INTRODUCTION

I just want to say . . . can we all get along? Can we get along? Can we stop making it horrible for the older people and the kids? We've got enough smog here in Los Angeles, let alone to deal with the setting of fires and things. It's just not right. It's not right, and it's not going to change anything.

We'll get our justice. They won the battle but they haven't won the war. We will have our day in court and that's all we want. . . . I'm neutral. I love everybody. I love people of color. I'm not like they're . . . making me out to be.

We've got to quit. We've got to quit. You know. . . I can understand the first upset in the first two hours after the verdict, but to keep going on like this, and to see a security guard shot on the ground, it's just not right. It's just not right because those people will never go home to their families again. And I mean, please, we can get along here. We all can get along. We've just got to, just got to. We're all stuck here for a while. . . . Let's try to work it out. Let's try to work it out.

—*Rodney King, in a public statement given on May 1, 1992*

For three days, from April 29 through May 1, 1992, Los Angeles burned. Rage, frustration, and fear fueled the largest, most deadly, and most destructive urban uprising in recent United States history. By the end, fifty-eight people were dead, 2,383 people were injured, more than 17,000 had been arrested, and $785 million worth of property had been destroyed or stolen. Why? For a time, and at a price, questions of urban life, questions of justice, and questions of history rang out powerfully across the country. Perhaps you remember this time because of your concern for loved ones in areas engulfed in the violence. Or perhaps you recollect your feelings when the Simi Valley jury acquitted the four white police officers who had seemed so openly and excessively to beat Rodney King before the nation's eyes.

As Robert Gooding-Williams has noted, it is most important for us as citizens, to "explore the multiple connections between the Rodney King incidents and the quotidian exercise of political, economic, and cultural power throughout the United States." As we remember the uniqueness of those monumental days in Los Angeles, we must seek to understand how these three days are still part of the daily lives we lead. Although interpretations vary, some facts do exist: Rodney King was chased by police and, when caught, severely beaten. Rodney King is an African American. The officers who beat him are white. The officers were acquitted by a predominantly white jury in a predominantly white city. Parts of Los Angeles erupted in violence. The police lost control of the situation.

Eventually official order was restored. Keeping these facts in mind, you will be asked to read various interpretations people have had of the events. You will also be asked to write about and make connections between Los Angeles in 1992 and what gives the uprising meaning in your life—and in American life.

As you read this part, you will be asked to reflect upon issues raised by the civil disturbance in Los Angeles, including economic, social, political, and legal causes for the frustration in American cities. You will also be asked to comment critically on how various authors write about these issues and represent the reality of unrest in urban communities. As you begin, your writings will address your recollections of the unrest in Los Angeles. As you proceed, your writings will join the wider discussions of issues of race, ethnicity, class, opportunity, and justice in the United States.

Given the nature of mass communications, the uprising in Los Angeles has largely disappeared from our field of vision. Many of the writings in this part, however, implicitly claim that the events in Los Angeles in 1992 resonate powerfully with all of American history and suggest our possible future lives together. Thus, the opening essay in this part, William Broyles's "Letter from L.A.," examines the uprising in the context of many of the issues that figure prominently in our current discussions of urban life. Employing interviews with gang members, residents of damaged neighborhoods, and police, Broyles indicates that values such as respect, religion, safety, and equality played an important role in the urban relationships that broke down in Los Angeles. Broyles's essay, which narrates his own experiences with people involved in the uprising, begins to represent the diversity of perspectives that inform many of the later pieces.

Lewis Lapham's essay, "City Lights," suggests that the ways in which we understand cities influence both how we understand violence and what we learn from the Los Angeles incident. Lapham looks to American history in order to question what cities have meant to this culture since the early days of modernization. He uses both literature and popular culture to suggest that people in the United States fail to appreciate the forms of freedom that cities could offer citizens.

George Bush's speech to the nation, "Civil Disorder in Los Angeles," delivered on May 1, 1992—while much of Los Angeles was still in flames, begins by reassuring the nation that official order is being reestablished in Los Angeles. Bush's speech makes for an interesting study because of its need to appeal simultaneously to multiple audiences. Additionally, Bush's explanations of the causes for the violence and reasons for hope can be compared to other perspectives in this part, including those of Senator Bill Bradley, Cornel West, Elaine Kim, and members of two rival youth gangs who joined forces to produce a plan for the revitalization of Los Angeles. In "Bloods/Crips Proposal for LA's Face-Lift," the members of the rival gangs, the Bloods and the Crips, offer a set of plans for rebuilding the city that explain causes for violence and reasons for hope. It can be compared to the perspectives of official members of government and more authoritative voices in public debates.

In "The Real Lesson of L.A.," Senator Bill Bradley addresses the American public, arguing for what he calls a "conversion" in American policies concerning cities. In "Learning to Talk of Race," Cornel West also calls for a kind of conversion, but in contrast to Bradley, he sees the uprising itself in multiracial and multi-social-class terms; West says the uprising expresses a loss of real meaning in all of our lives.

In "Heat Wave," Joyce Ann Joyce explores the ways that the violence in Los Angeles can be understood as part of the racial dynamics of United States culture. She suggests that the meanings of difference must be reinterpreted in order for our society to realize its possibilities of a better future.

Elaine Kim contributes to the discussion of racial tension in "Home Is Where the Han Is," by reflecting, from a Korean American perspective, on the ways in which the upheaval in Los Angeles was represented and explained by the media and the wider public. She focuses on developing a more sophisticated understanding of the roles that Korean Americans played in the representations and explanations of the upheavals, in order to understand more fully the roles that Asian Americans play in United States culture. Finally, Holly Sklar and Peter Medoff's "Pathfinders," a description of an urban revitalization project in Boston, offers a way to think practically about the difficulties and potential rewards of struggling to improve urban communities.

Overall, these essays raise important questions for you to consider: How do the Rodney King beating, the jury decision, and the Los Angeles uprising connect to everyday life in the United States? What should we learn from the multifaceted tragedy in Los Angeles? How can individuals contribute to building a culture that has less economic, racial, and ethnic frustration? Reflecting on your own answers to these questions, the answers of your classmates, and the answers of the authors collected in this part will mean reflecting on fundamental questions about what cities mean in American life. You will also consider the ways in which language, debate, and reporting shape our perceptions of urban violence. You will be challenged to think critically about how others perceive important cultural events and how your own and others' potential solutions reflect personal experiences of day-to-day life.

PREREADING ASSIGNMENTS

1. Freewrite for ten minutes about your memories of the Rodney King beating and the Los Angeles uprising. Push yourself to remember details about what your family and friends said or did. Explain how you felt at this time and try to write down details that capture your feelings.

2. Spend ten minutes defining key words that are used in discussions of urban violence. Explore various connotations of words such as *riot, revolt, event, tragedy, aid, welfare,* and *underclass.*

3. Suggest a number of potential explanations of why urban uprisings seem an inevitable part of contemporary city life. Outline some possible solutions to the problems that you think make violent uprisings recurrent.

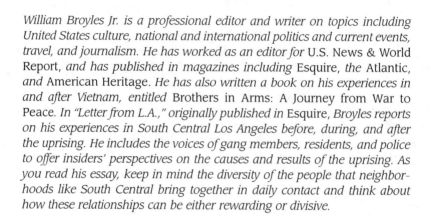

William Broyles Jr. is a professional editor and writer on topics including United States culture, national and international politics and current events, travel, and journalism. He has worked as an editor for U.S. News & World Report, *and has published in magazines including* Esquire, *the* Atlantic, *and* American Heritage. *He has also written a book on his experiences in and after Vietnam, entitled* Brothers in Arms: A Journey from War to Peace. *In "Letter from L.A.," originally published in* Esquire, *Broyles reports on his experiences in South Central Los Angeles before, during, and after the uprising. He includes the voices of gang members, residents, and police to offer insiders' perspectives on the causes and results of the uprising. As you read his essay, keep in mind the diversity of the people that neighborhoods like South Central bring together in daily contact and think about how these relationships can be either rewarding or divisive.*

Letter from L.A.

William Broyles Jr.

THE IMAGES ON TELEVISION sear into some fright-response region of the brain: fires, looting, anarchy. At the corner of Florence and Normandie, in the heart of South-Central, a white truck driver is beaten almost to death. The city panics. Fistfights break out as fleeing BMWs clog the Pacific Coast Highway. Car phones overload. Spago closes. Surfers abandon a perfect south swell.

"This isn't L.A., this isn't L.A.," a doctor friend from Malibu says over and over. Oh, but it is. I know one of the gang members I see screaming on TV. The last time I visited his house, his mother came home from work, told her children to do their schoolwork, then sat on her front porch to relax—with a .38 police special in her lap. While we sipped iced tea, gunfire rang out down the street. What horrifies us on television she lives with every day. For a time, at least, L.A. *is* South-Central, a city of ordinary people caught in a war zone.

For more than twenty years, this war has raged between gangs like rival local militias, with their own hierarchies, uniforms, and culture. So far it has been less about race than about power, respect, and revenge. One of the deadliest gang rivalries began over a perceived insult to a girl whose name no one remembers anymore. It's not just Bloods against Crips now. There aren't enough Bloods to go around, so Crips go to war with other Crips; neighbors become enemies. A gangbanger's manner, speech, dress, and actions—even his car—are all part of an elaborate set of rituals that convey status and respect, and respect is worth dying for. The riots that followed the Rodney King verdict brought these gang wars to an uneasy truce; for now, at least, the police are the common enemy.

But in South-Central, the police are just another militia. Though their codes and uniforms set them apart, their daily battles against gangbangers have the same goal: respect. Even before the verdict, King's case had crippled the police's traditional, righteous methods: "All we get now are citizen complaints," Sergeant David Nunez of the 77th Division told me as he patrolled near Florence and Normandie a few months ago. "You look at someone funny, you get a 181. And there goes that promotion. So maybe you pull back the next time, maybe you don't get quite as aggressive. And they know it."

Another cop expressed it even more graphically: "There were, what, eight hundred gang killings last year? Almost three people a day wasted by these assholes. We're at war down here. You go out and think today might be the day you don't get home. Then a few cops beat up one guy on videotape and the whole world goes crazy. Like we're the problem. You ask me, those priorities are fucked up."

The cops in the 77th talk about having a "stout" attitude toward the gangs they police. They keep themselves fit, they project confidence. But then they're out there late at night, alone, and they remember those stories about the stolen crossbows that penetrate their vests, about the missing truckload of AK-47's, about the hand grenades and machine guns. Everywhere they look, they see hatred looking back. And so they aren't surprised when it all finally blows on Florence and Normandie and someone starts to yell, "Let's go, let's go! It's not worth it!" And then the first cop breaks for his car, and then another.

At that moment, the thin shell of civilization cracks.

"We had them on the run," said Tee,* my friend from the Eight Trey (for Eighty-third Street) Gangster Crips who was there. "I couldn't believe it. They just left. It was like we won, we finally won." And then all the anger came out, and then came the beatings of motorists, and then the breaking into Tom's Liquor, and then the crowds started looting—not because they were angry but because they could, because no one was stopping them.

*Not his real gang name.

Anything goes. The gangbangers themselves were overwhelmed as the city seemed to go mad.

"We didn't think this was going to spread," Tee said. "It was just another day in the hood. Then it went crazy. There were families out there, Mexicans, whites, Orientals. I mean, this shit went worldwide. I just took a bottle of Olde English and went home and watched it on television."

By the weekend, the gangbangers were sobered. "We embarrassed the cops," Monster Kody told me on the phone from prison. Monster is an Eight Trey O.G. (original gangster), now retired, who's writing a book about his life on the streets. "They lost respect in front of the whole world. They've got to get their respect back. They're going to be coming down on us with everything they got. That's what I would do."

But the war to come could be even worse. "We've got a lot more weapons now. We've got vests. We've got grenades," Monster Kody said. "And now we've got fire—who would have known how effective fire was? Who would have known how easy L.A. was to burn?"

ON FRIDAY, the day after the worst riots, the fires are still burning. Smoke lies low in the sky, blotting out the sun. Cinders burn my shirt. My eyes water. I am with Bone, an O.G. from the Athens Park Bloods. Bone is twenty-six, tall, muscular, and clean-cut. Last year he was shot by a rival Crip. The bullet is still in his back.

We drive around for hours. Every gas station for miles has been hit, every supermarket, every bank every liquor store, every athletic-shoe store. Almost all the fast-food places are gone, as are health clinics, post offices, job-training centers. Whole strip centers look as if they've been hit by F-16's. Hastily scribbled signs that say BLACK OWNED have protected some buildings; elsewhere those signs flutter, charred, over piles of rubble.

Many Korean-owned businesses and all their "swap meets" have been torched. Others, like Johnny's Seafood, have not. "Everybody likes the Koreans there," Bone says. They treat you with respect." Bone takes me to 121st and Main. For more than forty years the grocery store here was run by an Asian named Al, who knew everyone in the neighborhood. Bone had gone there all his life. When the riots started, Al passed out shopping bags to help people carry their loot. He just asked that they not burn his store; he was too old to start again.

Al's is a bombed-out shell.

"The homeys were so angry," Bone says, "that when they found the Mexican guy who did it, they beat him up and turned him in. You see? You got homeys turning in a Mexican to the cops—who they hate—for burning a Jap store. So it's not as simple as they say."

In South-Central, almost nothing is.

On Manchester and Western, the Boys' Market looks as if it's been bombed. Around the corner, at Florence and Normandie, the riots began. Down the street, at Manchester and Vermont, we hear popping sounds. Some Eight Treys are shooting it out with the police.

"Hear that?" Bone says. "That's AKs. Problem is, the cops are so much better shots than we are. They shoot twice, we're dead. We shoot fifteen times, we're lucky to hit their car. That's why we got all those AKs. We go in equal, we don't have a chance."

Hundreds of people are inside the Boys' Market, but they aren't looting, even though there are no police in sight. I talk to Norma and Darryl Jackson. "We left because our five-year-old has asthma and the smoke was bothering him. Then we said, *This is our neighborhood,* so we came back to take care of it. We gave our kids brooms and put them to work. Maybe they'll learn something. Maybe they'll do better."

As she pushes her broom through the filthy water, Inez Johnson starts to sing, her voice deep and plaintive. "Wade in the water, wade in the water . . ."

From throughout the store, others join in the chorus: "God's gonna trouble the water."

The song vibrates out of the store, raspy, defiant, hypnotic, the only accompaniment the sound of swishing brooms and scraping shovels. And then a few men come in and start to take some cans off the shelves. The store convulses in outrage; a platoon of people with brooms advances on the intruders.

"Get out! Get out!" The chants rock the store. The looters drop their booty and run.

I had seen the determination to do good in the face of all obstacles in South-Central before. I had seen it at Sweet Alice Harris's cottage in Watts, jammed with volunteers, gang members, and Salvadoran mothers. I had seen it at Connie Wynn's parenting classes on Slauson. I had seen it in the programs to salvage gangbangers that Bobby Lavender runs at Manual Arts High School.

And then Bone takes me back to Athens Park where I see that spirit again, in the most unexpected way. A short young man with a slightly lopsided face is talking to a group of older kids in the middle of the street.

"That's Eric Gibson, Doctor Gibs. We used to run together, then he got shot in the face. He's banging for Christ now."

Eric and Bone greet each other in the usual way: "Zup, Blood?" (The Crips say "What's up, Cuz?" or "What's up, Loc?" which the Bloods refuse to say because the words contain the hated Crip letter *C*.)

"I've just been talking to 'em, trying to get 'em to see the Lord's way," Eric says with a beatific smile.

"They listen," Bone says. "They know you be real. You talk to any hard-heads in the next block?"

"Sure. They gonna come around, and we gonna have a peace rally in the park. Figure out what we can do. Reaganomics tore us down. We gonna build us back right, the way the Lord would."

"Maybe we see you there," Bone says.

"Okay, I love you."

"I love you too, man."

As we drive away, Bone talks about why all this happened. "These kids, they see Boesky and that guy Keating—look at how many people he hurt, but did you see President Bush give a news conference about him? And that Milken guy, how much did he steal in a year—$500 million? Those kids walk-ing out of Fedco with a VCR, I guarantee they'd be in some office stealing like respectable folks if they could."

As Monster Kody said, "These kids need a new message."

When Doctor Gibs starts banging for Christ, he's taking his reputation, which is all a gangbanger has, and putting it on the line out on the street. That's a lot more than all the politicians and preachers accomplish from their podiums and pulpits. Doctor Gibs's message is simple: "Hey, it's up to us. Can't blame those bad white people, nobody here but us. We gotta make our own bed."

He's out on the mean streets, talking to the hardheads about right and wrong and hope, smiling gently out of a face knocked off-center by a bullet.

Discussion Questions

Content

1. Broyles describes several positions on the uprisings and the public responses to them. Which position does he seem to favor and how does he communicate his preference?

2. Broyles quotes Bone as saying, "It's not as simple as they say." Who are "they," and what is more complicated than they believe? From your perspective, why do "they" misunderstand or misrepresent the situation?

3. Broyles suggests that police, gangs, and residents are all struggling for "respect." What do you think each group means by the term *respect*? How do the differences in the ways people understand the term *respect* influence the interac-tions between them?

Form

1. Broyles structures his piece as a narration of his encounters with various people affected by the uprising. How does this form enable his essay to make a unique contribution to the discussion of urban violence? What is the nature of that contribution?

2. Broyles creates many powerful descriptive images of individual lives in Los Angeles. Which of those images seems most important or memorable to you, and why?

3. How does the form that Broyles chooses for this essay relate to the idea of "respect"?

Writing Prompts

1. Narrate an event in your own city using at least three different types of characters, each of whom sees the event in a different way. Have the characters engage in a discussion of the event in which each character speaks about the causes of the event and no perspective wins.

2. In class, identify an important urban event in your area. Using your own individual knowledge, narrate the beginning of that event. Compare your story with those of other class members. Attempt to explain the differences and similarities.

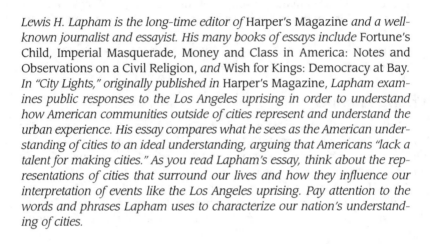

Lewis H. Lapham is the long-time editor of Harper's Magazine *and a well-known journalist and essayist. His many books of essays include* Fortune's Child, Imperial Masquerade, Money and Class in America: Notes and Observations on a Civil Religion, *and* Wish for Kings: Democracy at Bay. *In "City Lights," originally published in* Harper's Magazine, *Lapham examines public responses to the Los Angeles uprising in order to understand how American communities outside of cities represent and understand the urban experience. His essay compares what he sees as the American understanding of cities to an ideal understanding, arguing that Americans "lack a talent for making cities." As you read Lapham's essay, think about the representations of cities that surround our lives and how they influence our interpretation of events like the Los Angeles uprising. Pay attention to the words and phrases Lapham uses to characterize our nation's understanding of cities.*

City Lights

Lewis H. Lapham

Each person, withdrawn into himself, behaves as though he is a stranger to the destiny of all the others. His children and his good friends constitute for him the whole of the human species. As for his transactions with his fellow citizens, he may mix among them, but he sees them not; he touches them, but does not feel them, he exists only in himself and for himself alone. And if on these terms there remains in his mind a sense of family, there no longer remains a sense of society.

—*Alexis de Tocqueville*

DURING THE FIRST TWO WEEKS of May, I listened to a great many politicians worry about the scenes of urban apocalypse in South-Central Los Angeles, but the more often they mentioned "the crisis of the cities" or "the need for meaningful reform," the less convincing I found their expressions of concern. Most American politicians neither like nor trust the temperament of large cities, and their habitual animosity showed through the veneer of the speeches. They said what they were supposed to say—"healing the wounds of racial injustice," "a tragedy for us all," "human suffering," "rebuilding America's destiny"—and although many of them even went to the point of promising money—"enterprise zones," "relief funds," "bank loans"—it was clear that they would rather have been talking about something else. President George Bush appeared briefly in Los Angeles on May 7 and 8, a week after rioting and fire had laid waste to roughly fifty square miles of the landscape, and his palpable uneasiness defined the tenor of the response from the leading manufacturers of the country's conscience and opinion. What he said wasn't much different from what everybody else said (c.f., the anguish in *Time* and *Newsweek*, Governor Bill Clinton's campaign statements, the anguish on *Nightline* and *Meet the Press*, Governor Pete Wilson's press conferences, the anguish of Dan Rather), but Mr. Bush has a talent for embodying a falsity of feeling that lends itself to almost any solemn occasion, and his performance in Los Angeles admirably represented the attitudes of a social and political class that regards the city as its enemy. He arrived among the ruins of Vermont and Western avenues at dawn on Thursday, riding in a heavily armed limousine under the protective escort of the Secret Service, the L.A.P.D., and the National Guard. His advisers allowed him to remain in the neighborhood for no longer than three hours in the early morning, before too many people were abroad in the streets, and his entourage had gone before most of the local residents knew that it had come. Walking through streets still sour with the smell of smoke, the President was obviously disturbed by what he saw of the wreckage, and his unscheduled remarks veered off in the direction of unfamiliar emotion. Speaking to a small congregation in a Baptist church, he said, "We are embarrassed by interracial violence and prejudice. We are ashamed. We should take nothing but sorrow out of all of that and do our level best to see that it's eliminated from the American dream."

Clearly the President was chastened by the sorrow and resentment of the people to whom he spoke, but his words were somehow tentative and contingent, as if they could be withdrawn on a month's notice. C-Span's television cameras followed him on his pilgrim's progress through the ashes of an urban slum, and as I watched him keep to his schedule of condolence I understood that it was a small, drawing-room story about George Bush (his education, conduct, and deportment), not a large and tragic story about a society that could inflict upon itself the despairing ruin of South-Central Los Angeles.

By Friday morning the President had recovered his optimism and his sense of political proportion. He announced a gift of $19 million (for clinics and schools and the harrying of drug dealers) and he went to a hospital to visit a fireman severely wounded by gunfire on the first night of the rioting. Partially paralyzed and unable to speak, the fireman lay on his bed watching Bush sign autographs and hand out tie pins. The President was cheerful but nervous, and in a moment of awkward silence he said to the fireman's wife, "This is fantastic. We're glad to be here. Absolutely."

To the wife of another fireman injured in the riots, the President, still trying to make polite conversation and meaning to show that he, too, was acquainted with grief, spoke of the heavy seas that had come last October to Kennebunkport: "I'm sorry Barbara's not here. She's out repairing what's left of our house. Damn storm knocked down four or five walls. She says it's coming along."

The American ruling and explaining classes tend to live in the suburbs, or in cities as indistinguishable from suburbs as West Los Angeles and the government preserves of Washington, D.C., and their fear and suspicion of the urban landscape (as well as the urban turn of mind) would have been well understood by the gentlemen who founded the republic in Philadelphia in 1787. The idea of a great city never has occupied a comfortable place in the American imagination. Much of the country's political and literary history suggests that the city stands as a metaphor for depravity—the port of entry for things foreign and obnoxious, likely to pollute the pure streams of American innocence. Virtue proverbially resides in villages and small towns, and for at least two hundred years the rhetoric of urban reform has borrowed its images from the Bible and the visionary poets. Under the open sky (or a reasonable facsimile thereof) the faithful gather by the firelight to denounce the metropolitan spheres of crime and vice, and every now and then a knight errant—Jimmy Carter, Ralph Nader, Gary Hart, Ross Perot, et al.—rides off toward the dark horizon under the banners of redemption.

A similar bias informs the romantic spirit of American literature and provides the plots for popular melodrama. With remarkably few exceptions, the writers of genius decry the foul and pestilent air of the city, and instead of staying in town to paint the portraits of society they wander off into the wilderness in search of spiritual salvation. Thoreau beside his pond, Melville in the vastness of the southern ocean, Hemingway off the coast of Cuba—all of them glad of their escape from the stench of commerce in Boston and New York.

The conventional hero of the western or detective story (sometimes known as John Wayne or Humphrey Bogart, at other times taking the alias of Gary Cooper, Clint Eastwood, or Harrison Ford) rides into the dusty, wooden town and discovers evil in even the most rudimentary attempts at civilization. The hero appears as if he were a god come to punish the sin of pride and scourge the wicked with a terrible vengeance. After the requisite number of killings, the hero departs, leaving to mortal men and women (i.e., wretched citizens) the tedious business of burial, marriage, and settlement.

The movies and television series delight in showing the city as a killing ground. Predators of every known species (pimps, real estate speculators, drug addicts, prostitutes, dissolute prosecuting attorneys, and venal police captains) roam the streets as if they were beasts drifting across the Serengeti plain. The successful protagonists learn to rely on their animal instincts. If they make the mistake of remaining human (trusting to the civilized virtues of tolerance and compassion), they die a fool's death in the first reel.

Given the preferred image of the city as godforsaken heath, it's not surprising that so many American cities come to look the way that the audience wants and expects them to look. The proofs of worldly ruin give credence to the theorems of transcendental grace. If American cities have the feeling of makeshift camps, littered with debris and inhabited, temporarily, by people on the way to someplace else, it is because we conceive of them as sulfurous pits in which to earn the fortune to pay for the country rose garden and the house with the view of the sea. The pilgrims come to perform heroic feats of acquisition and then to depart with the spoils to the comforts of Florida or the safety of Simi Valley.

To the extent that we measure the distance between the city and the suburbs as the distance between virtue and vice, we confuse metaphysics with geography, and so imagine that blessedness is a property of the right address. During the Cuban Missile Crisis of 1962, in the early afternoon of the day on which the thermonuclear judgment was believed to be well on its way north from Havana, the city editor of the *New York Herald Tribune* sent me into Times Square to ask random citizens for opinions on their impending doom. Most of the respondents expressed a degree of anxiety appropriate to the circumstances, but I remember a woman from Lake Forest, Illinois, who told me that I had addressed my question to the wrong person, and who smiled as agreeably as President Bush handing out tie pins in the Los Angeles hospital room. "I wish I could help you," she said, "but I don't live here, you see. I'm just visiting from out of town."

The spirit of the age is feudal, and the fear of the cities allies itself not only with the fear of crime and disease and black people but also with the fear of freedom. The energy of the city derives from its hope for the future and the infinite forms of its possibility. The city offers its citizens a blank canvas on which to draw whatever portraits of themselves they have the wit and courage to imagine. Nobody asks them to constantly explain their purpose, and they remain free to join the minorities of their own choosing. Among people whom they regard as their equals, who share the same passions for seventeenth-century religious painting or Edwardian licentiousness, they can come and go in whatever direction their spirit beckons. The freedom of the city is the freedom of expression and the freedom of the mind.

So precious are these freedoms that the citizens judge the city's squalor as a fair price for its promise. What suburban opinion deplores as unmitigated abomination—bad air, poverty, noise, crowds, crime, traffic, heavy taxes, exorbitant rents, cynical government—the citizen accepts as the cost of liberty. It is in the nature of great cities to be dangerous, just as it is the nature of the future to be dangerous. The complexity of life in the city engenders in the inhabitants an equivalent complexity of thought and a tone of mind that can make a joke of paradox and contradiction.

The ideal of the city as an expression of man's humanity to man never has enjoyed much of a constituency in the United States. The stones of Paris and London and Rome speak to the citizens's high regard for the proofs of civilization. If it is possible to walk calmly through the streets of those cities late at night, it is not only because the government gladly spends money on public fountains but also because the other people in the streets take pride in their civility. Americans take pride in the building of roads and weapons systems as well as in their gifts for violence. We know how to mount expeditions—to the Persian Gulf or the California frontier or the moon—but we lack a talent for making cities.

The broad retreat to the suburbs over the last twenty or thirty years correlates to the fear of the future and the wish to make time stand still. The politics of the Nixon, Reagan, and Bush administrations made manifest a San Diego realtor's dream of Heaven and defined the great, good American place as an exclusive country club. Expressions of the same sentiment take forms as various as the judgments of the Rehnquist court, Senator Jesse Helms's suspicions of the National Endowment for the Arts, the ascendance of conservative and neoconservative socioeconomic theory, the sermons of George Will, the division of the county of Los Angeles into a series of residential enclaves (Bel-Air, Beverly Hills, Pasadena, etc.) as fiercely defended (by gates and electronic surveillance and regiments of liveried police) as the feudal manors of medieval Europe. As the larger business corporations come to employ as many people as lived in Renaissance Florence, they acquire the character of fiefs and dukedoms, and by shifting their headquarters into landscapes luxurious with English lawns and avenues of trees, they signify the splendor of their superiority—both moral and financial—to the urban mob.

Whenever I read in the papers that yet another corporation has quit New York City for a country estate in Virginia or Connecticut, I think of the United States receding that much farther into the past. The company of the elect becomes too quickly and too easily estranged from the democratic argument. Already protected from chance and uncertainty by the walls of bureaucratic protocol, the ladies and gentlemen of executive rank become ever more fearful of strangers—of Al Sharpton and Puerto Rican Day parades as well as of rats, pestilence, and crime—and their distrust of the city soon resembles the contempt so often and so smugly expressed by Vice President Quayle.

The fear is contagious, and as larger numbers of people come to perceive the city as a barren waste, the more profitable their disillusion becomes to dealers in guns and to the political factions that would destroy not only New York and Chicago but also the idea of the city. During the decade of the 1980s the federal government reduced by 60 percent the sum of money assigned to the nation's cities. Official Washington embraces the ethos of an expensive suburb, and the deductions embodied a cultural prejudice as well as a political doctrine. The same bias shows up in the seminars conducted by professors of urban science who blandly announce—invariably with many smiling references to the wonders of modern telecommunications—that the United States no longer has need for large cities. From the point of view of civil servants and Baptist ministers, the revelation might be construed as good news, but not from the point of view of anybody still interested in freedom.

The hatred of cities is the fear of freedom. Freedom implies change, which implies friction, which implies unhappiness, which disturbs the nervous complacency of the admissions committee at the country club. Because the city promises so many changes and transformations (a good many of them probably dangerous or unhealthy), the act of decision presents itself as a burden instead of an opportunity. Confronted with the dilemma of making moral and existential choices, the friends of Vice President Quayle and Chief Justice Rehnquist seek to escape their confusion by declaring freedom the enemy of the state. They prefer the orderliness of the feudal countryside, where few strangers ever come to trouble the villagers with news of Trebizond and Cathay.

In the whole of the editorial autopsy conducted by the news media in the days following the Los Angeles riots, I never heard anybody say anything about the popular hatred of the freedoms of a great city. I know that the topic is not one that the political and intellectual authorities like to discuss, but without at least mentioning it in passing, the familiar indices of poverty and crime make little sense. Until we learn to value the idea of the city, we can expect to see the streets paved with anger instead of gold.

The more well-intentioned the reforms announced by the politicians and the more theatrical the anguish of *Newsweek* or Barbara Walters, the more clearly I could hear the voice of suburban triumph. The guests assembled on a lawn in Arlington or Kennebunkport nod and frown and piously confuse New York or Los Angeles with the Inferno imagined by Dante or Mel

Gibson. A drift of smoke on the horizon confirms them in their best-loved suspicions and excuses their loathing for the multiplicity of both the human imagination and the human face.

Discussion Questions

Content

1. How does Lapham's essay differ from other responses to the Los Angeles uprising that you've encountered?

2. What does Lapham believe cities stand for? How does he explain the American fear of cities?

3. Lapham sees a connection between the ways U.S. cities are depicted in movies, television, advertisements, and music and the political responses to the Los Angeles uprising. What positive representations of cities can you think of from the media? Who is their intended audience? What does Lapham think makes cities attractive?

Form

1. Lapham argues that public responses to Los Angeles are connected to long-standing perceptions of cities in United States culture. How does he organize his essay to emphasize the historical nature of responses to the Los Angeles uprising?

2. Lapham writes his essay in the first person (using "I"). How does his use of the first person encourage the reader to agree with him?

3. How does the description of Bush's visit contribute to Lapham's idea that Americans fear freedom?

Writing Prompts

1. Using Lapham's essay as a model, write an essay describing a recent public event that you think demonstrates something fundamental about the American character. Justify your choice of event by explaining how and why that event typifies something "American."

2. Write an essay exploring the explicit and implicit messages about urban life contained in a popular representation (movie, television show, book, advertisement, song, etc.) of a city. Who is the intended audience? How are the explicit and implicit messages about urban life connected?

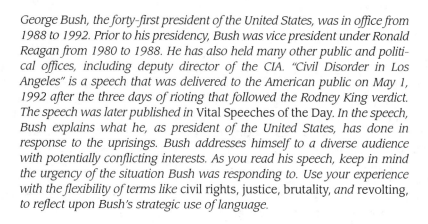

George Bush, the forty-first president of the United States, was in office from 1988 to 1992. Prior to his presidency, Bush was vice president under Ronald Reagan from 1980 to 1988. He has also held many other public and political offices, including deputy director of the CIA. "Civil Disorder in Los Angeles" is a speech that was delivered to the American public on May 1, 1992 after the three days of rioting that followed the Rodney King verdict. The speech was later published in Vital Speeches of the Day. In the speech, Bush explains what he, as president of the United States, has done in response to the uprisings. Bush addresses himself to a diverse audience with potentially conflicting interests. As you read his speech, keep in mind the urgency of the situation Bush was responding to. Use your experience with the flexibility of terms like civil rights, justice, brutality, and revolting, to reflect upon Bush's strategic use of language.

Civil Disorder in Los Angeles: Justice Will Be Served

George Bush
President of the United States of America

TONIGHT I WANT TO TALK TO YOU about violence in our cities and justice for our citizens, two big issues that have collided on the streets of Los Angeles. First, an update on where matters stand in Los Angeles.

Fifteen minutes ago I talked to California's Governor Pete Wilson and Los Angeles Mayor Tom Bradley. They told me that last night was better than the night before; today, calmer than yesterday. But there were still incidents of random terror and lawlessness this afternoon.

In the wake of the first night's violence I spoke directly to both Governor Wilson and Mayor Bradley to assess the situation and to offer assistance. There are two very different issues at hand: one is the urgent need to restore order. What followed Wednesday's jury verdict in the Rodney King case was

George Bush. "Civil Disorder in Los Angeles: Justice Will Be Served." From *Vital Speeches of the Day* (June 1, 1992): 482–83. Delivered to the Nation, Washington, D.C., May 1, 1992.

a tragic series of events for the city of Los Angeles. Nearly 4,000 fires, staggering property damage, hundreds of injuries; and the senseless deaths of over 30 people.

To restore order right now, there are 3,000 National Guardsmen on duty in the city of Los Angeles. Another 2,200 stand ready to provide immediate support. To supplement this effort I've taken several additional actions. First, this morning I've ordered the Justice Department to dispatch 1,000 federal riot-trained law enforcement officials to help restore order in Los Angeles beginning tonight. These officials include FBI swat teams, special riot control units of the U.S. Marshal's service, the border patrol and other federal law enforcement agencies. Second, another 1,000 federal law enforcement officials are on standby alert, should they be needed. Third, early today I directed 3,000 members of the 7th Infantry and 1,500 Marines to stand by at El Toro Air Station, California.

Tonight, at the request of the Governor and the Mayor, I have committed these troops to help restore order. I'm also federalizing the National Guard and I'm instructing General Colin Powell to place all those troops under a central command.

What we saw last night and the night before in Los Angeles is not about civil rights. It's not about the great cause of equality that all Americans must uphold. It's not a message of protest. It's been the brutality of a mob, pure and simple. And let me assure you: I will use whatever force is necessary to restore order.

What is going on in L.A. must—and will—stop. As your President I guarantee you this violence will end.

And now let's talk about the beating of Rodney King. Because beyond the urgent need to restore order is the second issue, the question of justice; whether Rodney King's federal civil rights were violated. What you saw and what I saw on the TV video was revolting. I felt anger. I felt pain. I thought: How can I explain this to my grandchildren?

Civil rights leaders just plain fearful of, and sometimes victimized by police brutality, were deeply hurt. And I know good and decent policemen who were equally appalled.

I spoke this morning to many leaders of the civil rights community. And they saw the video, as we all did. For 14 months they waited patiently, hopefully. They waited for the system to work. And when the verdict came in, they felt betrayed. Viewed from outside the trial, it was hard to understand how the verdict could possibly square with the video. Those civil rights leaders with whom I met were stunned. And so was I and so was Barbara and so were my kids.

But the verdict Wednesday was not the end of the process. The Department of Justice had started its own investigation immediately after the Rodney King incident and was monitoring the state investigation and trial. And so let me tell you what actions we are taking on the federal level to ensure that justice is served.

Within one hour of the verdict, I directed the Justice Department to move into high gear on its own independent criminal investigation into the case. And next, on Thursday, five federal prosecutors were on their way to Los Angeles. Our Justice Department has consistently demonstrated its ability to investigate fully a matter like this.

Since 1988, the Justice Department has successfully prosecuted over 100 law enforcement officials for excessive violence. I am confident that in this case, the Department of Justice will act as it should. Federal grand jury action is underway today in Los Angeles. Subpoenas are being issued. Evidence is being reviewed. The federal effort in this case will be expeditious and it will be fair. It will not be driven by mob violence, but by respect for due process and the rule of law.

We owe it to all Americans who put their faith in the law to see that justice is served. But as we move forward on this or any other case, we must remember the fundamental tenet of our legal system. Every American, whether accused or accuser, is entitled to protection of his or her rights.

In this highly controversial court case, a verdict was handed down by a California jury. To Americans of all races who were shocked by the verdict, let me say this: You must understand that our system of justice provides for the peaceful, orderly means of addressing this frustration. We must respect the process of law whether or not we agree with the outcome. There's a difference between frustration with the law and direct assaults upon our legal system.

In a civilized society, there can be no excuse—no excuse—for the murder, arson, theft and vandalism that have terrorized the law-abiding citizens of Los Angeles. Mayor Bradley, just a few minutes ago, mentioned to me his particular concern, among others, regarding the safety of the Korean community. My heart goes out to them and all others who have suffered losses.

The wanton destruction of life and property is not a legitimate expression of outrage with injustice—it is itself injustice. And no rationalization, no matter how heartfelt, no matter how eloquent, can make it otherwise.

Television has become a medium that often brings us together. But its vivid display of Rodney King's beating shocked us. And the America it has shown us on our screens these last 48 hours has appalled us. None of this is what we wish to think of as American. It's as if we were looking in a mirror that distorted our better selves and turned us ugly. We cannot let that happen. We cannot do that to ourselves.

We've seen images in the last 48 hours that we will never forget. Some were horrifying almost beyond belief. But there were other acts—small, but significant acts in all this ugliness that give us hope. I'm one who respects our police. They keep the peace. They face danger every day. They help kids. They don't make a lot of money—but they care about their communities and their country. Thousands of police officers and firefighters are risking their lives right now on the streets of L.A. and they deserve our support.

And then there are the people who have spent each night not in the streets, but in the churches of Los Angeles—praying that man's gentler instincts be revealed in the hearts of people driven by hate.

And finally, there were the citizens who showed great personal responsibility, who ignored the mob, who at great personal danger, helped the victims of violence—regardless of race.

Among the many stories I've seen and heard about these past few days, one sticks in my mind—the story of one savagely beaten white truck driver—alive tonight because four strangers, four black strangers, came to his aid. Two were men who had been watching television and saw the beating as it was happening, and came out into the street to help. Another was a woman on her way home from work—and the fourth, a young man whose name we may never know. The injured driver was able to get behind the wheel of his truck and tried to drive away. But his eyes were swollen shut. The woman asked him if he could see. He answered, no. She said, "Well, then I will be your eyes."

Together, those four people braved the mob and drove that truck driver to the hospital. He's alive today—only because they stepped in to help.

It is for every one of them that we must rebuild the community of Los Angeles—for these four people and the others like them who in the midst of this nightmare acted with simple human decency.

We must understand that no one in Los Angeles or any other city has rendered a verdict on America. If we are to remain the most vibrant and hopeful nation on Earth we must allow our diversity to bring us together, not drive us apart. This must be the rallying cry of good and decent people.

For their sake, for all our sakes, we must build a future where, in every city across this country, empty rage gives way to hope—where poverty and despair give way to opportunity. After peace is restored to Los Angeles, we must then turn again to the underlying causes of such tragic events. We must keep on working to create a climate of understanding and tolerance—a climate that refuses to accept racism, bigotry, anti-Semitism, and hate of any kind, anytime, anywhere.

Tonight, I ask all Americans to lend their hearts, their voices, and their prayers to the healing of hatred. As President, I took an oath to preserve, protect, and defend the Constitution—an oath that requires every President to establish justice and ensure domestic tranquility. That duty is foremost in my mind tonight.

Let me say to the people saddened by the spectacle of the past few days—to the good people of Los Angeles, caught at the center of this senseless suffering: The violence will end. Justice will be served. Hope will return. Thank you, and may God bless the United States of America.

Discussion Questions

Content

1. What important issues does this speech touch on? How would you describe and explain the tone of the speech?

2. Identify the most important word or phrase in this speech. How does it relate to Bush's main idea?

3. Could the Rodney King verdict have been the cause of the Los Angeles events as George Bush suggests? What other factors may have been involved and what options did the citizens have for dealing with them?

Form

1. In this speech, George Bush first discusses the need to restore order in Los Angeles, and then turns to the issue of civil rights. What do you see as the purpose of organizing his speech in this way?

2. What stylistic or organizational features identify this piece as a political speech? How would it be different if it were converted into an essay?

3. What conflicting demands are made on this speech by its audience, the American people? Which specific parts of the speech relate to different groups of people within America?

Writing Prompts

1. Imagine yourself as an important public figure in your community, and write a speech in which you respond to a significant public event. Make sure that your speech addresses the conflicting viewpoints of a diverse audience.

2. Write a response to George Bush's speech, explaining why you believe that a riot could or could not happen in your area.

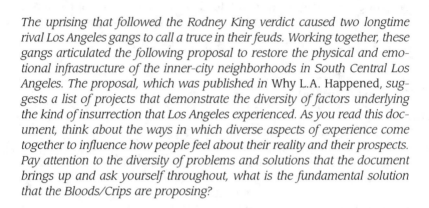

The uprising that followed the Rodney King verdict caused two longtime rival Los Angeles gangs to call a truce in their feuds. Working together, these gangs articulated the following proposal to restore the physical and emotional infrastructure of the inner-city neighborhoods in South Central Los Angeles. The proposal, which was published in Why L.A. Happened, *suggests a list of projects that demonstrate the diversity of factors underlying the kind of insurrection that Los Angeles experienced. As you read this document, think about the ways in which diverse aspects of experience come together to influence how people feel about their reality and their prospects. Pay attention to the diversity of problems and solutions that the document brings up and ask yourself throughout, what is the fundamental solution that the Bloods/Crips are proposing?*

Bloods/Crips Proposal
for LA's Face-Lift

Bloods and Crips

Burned and Abandoned Structures

Every burned and abandoned structure shall be gutted. The city will purchase the property if not already owned by the city, and build a community center. If the structure is on a corner lot or is a vacant lot, the city will build a career counseling center or a recreation area, respectively.

Repavement

All pavements/sidewalks in Los Angeles are in dire need of resurfacing. The Department of Transportation shall pay special attention to the pedestrian walkways and surface streets located in predominantly poor and minority areas. Our organization will assist the city in the identification of all areas of concern.

Bloods and Crips. "Bloods/Crips Proposal for LA's Face-Lift." In *Why L.A. Happened,* edited by Haki R. Madhubuti (1993). Reprinted with permission of Third World Press.

Lighting
All lighting will be increased in all neighborhoods. Additionally, lighting of city streets, neighborhood blocks and alleyways will be amended. We want a well-lit neighborhood. All alleys shall be painted white or yellow by the building owners and alley lights will be installed at the cost of the owner.

Landscaping
All trees will be properly trimmed and maintained. We want all weeded/shrubbed areas to be cleaned up and properly nurtured. New trees will be planted to increase the beauty of our neighborhoods.

Sanitation
A special task force shall be assigned to focus on the clean-up of all vacant lots and trashed areas throughout the deprived areas. Proper pest control methods shall be implemented by the city to reduce the chances of rodent scattering. The city will declare a neighborhood clean-up week wherein all residents will be responsible for their block—a block captain will be assigned to ensure cooperation. Residents will clean up the block in unisys.

$2 billion shall be appropriated for this effort over and above existing appropriations.

Bloods/Crips Economic Development Proposal

Loans shall be made available by the federal and state governments to provide interested minority entrepreneurs interested in doing business in these deprived areas. The loan requirements shall not be so stringent that it will make it impossible for a businessman to acquire these loans. These loans shall not exceed a 4% interest bearing charge per year. The businessman shall not be required to have security for the loan, however, the businessman must present at least two years of business operation and taxes, with a city license before funds will be allocated. The owner, must have either an established business desiring to expand or a sound business plan. Assistance for business plans shall be made available to these businessmen by the Small Business Administration. Additionally, the Small Business Administration will provide agents to help each business to develop a sound business plan from beginning to end. No one will be neglected in receiving adequate assistance. These business owners shall be required to hire 90% of their personnel from within their community and the monies shall not be distributed in a lump sum. Funds will be released in increments outlined by the business plan. Any businessman that doesn't conform to the hiring practices will have funding ceased until they conform.

$20 million shall be appropriated for this program over and above existing appropriations.

Please note all grants for these major reconstructions shall be granted to minority-owned businesses. While these minority-owned businesses are doing the work in our communities, they must hire at least 50% of their work force from within the community. <u>NO</u> front organizations will be tolerated!

Bloods/Crips Human Welfare Proposal

Hospitals and Health Care Centers

Federal government shall provide the deprived areas with three new hospitals and 40 additional health care centers. Dental clinics shall be made available within ten miles of each community. The services shall be free and supported by federal and state funds.

Welfare

We demand that welfare be completely removed from our community and these welfare programs be replaced by state work and product manufacturing plants that provide the city with certain supplies. State monies shall only be provided for individuals and the elderly. The State of California shall provide a child welfare building to serve as day care centers for single parents. We would like to encourage all manufacturing companies to vigorously hire these low income recipients and the state and federal governments shall commit to expand their institutions to provide work for these former welfare recipients.

Parks & Recreation

Los Angeles parks shall receive a complete face-lift, and develop activities and programs in the parks throughout the night. Stages, pools and courts shall be reconstructed and resurfaced, and the city shall provide highly visible security 24 hours a day for these parks and recreational centers. Programs at the park shall be in accordance with educational programs and social exchange programs developed by the city for adults and young adults.

$1 billion dollars shall be appropriated for this program over and above existing appropriations.

Bloods/Crips Educational Proposal

1. Maximizing education standards in the low income areas is essential to reduce the possibilities of repeated insurrection. The Bloods/Crips propose that:

a. $300 million will go into the reconstruction and refurbishment of the Los Angeles Unified School District (LAUSD) structures,

b. $200 million will be donated for computers, supplies and updated books (each student shall have the necessary books),

c. All teachers' salaries shall be no less than $30,000.00 a year to give them an incentive to educate in our districts, and

d. Re-election shall be held for all Los Angeles Board of Education members.

2. Reconstruction shall include repainting, sandblasting and reconstruction of all LAUSD schools: remodeling of classrooms, repainting of hallways and meeting areas; all schools shall have new landscaping and more plants and trees around the schools; completely upgrade the bathrooms, making them more modern: provide a bathroom monitor to each bathroom which will provide freshen-up toiletries at a minimum cost to the students (the selling of toiletries will support the salary of the bathroom monitor).

3. A provision for accelerated educational learning programs shall be implemented for the entire LAUSD to provide aggressive teaching methods and provide a curriculum similar to non-economically deprived areas. Tutoring for all subjects will be made available to all students after normal school hours. It will be mandatory for all students with sub-level grades to participate.

   In these after-school tutorial programs, those students whose grades are up to par will receive federally funded bonus bonds which will be applied to their continued education upon graduation from high school. They will also receive bonus bonds for extra scholastic work towards assisting their fellow students. All institutions shall maintain a second shift of substitute teachers in the schools to enforce educational excellence.

   Special financial bonuses shall be given to students who focus on education beyond the school's requirement in the areas of applied math and sciences. High achievers in these areas shall be granted a free trip to another country for educational exchange. Fifty students from each school will be granted this opportunity each year for an indefinite period.

4. The LAUSD will provide up-to-date books to the neglected areas and enough books to ensure that no student has to share a book with another. Supplies shall be made plentiful and school-sponsored financial programs shall be instituted in order to maintain equipment and supplies for the institution after the first donation.

5. LAUSD will remove all teachers not planning to further their education along with teachers who have not proven to have a passionate concern for the students in which they serve. All teachers shall be given a standard competency test to verify they are up-to-date with subjects and modern

teaching methods. Psychological testing will also be required for all teachers and educational administrators, including the Los Angeles School Board, every four years.

6. All curriculums shall focus on the basics in high school requirements and it shall be inundated with advanced sciences and additional applied math, English and writing skills.

7. Bussing shall become non-existent in our communities if all of the above demands are met.

$700 million shall be appropriated for these programs over and above existing appropriations.

Bloods/Crips Law Enforcement Program

The Los Angeles communities are demanding that they are policed and patrolled by individuals whom live in the community and the commanding officers be ten-year residents of the community in which they serve. Former gang members shall be given a chance to be patrol buddies in assisting in the protection of the neighborhood. These former gang members will be required to go through police training and must comply to all of the laws instituted by our established authorities. Uniforms will be issued to each and every member of the "buddy system," however, no weapons will be issued. All patrol units must have a buddy patrol notified and present in the event of a police matter. Each buddy patrol will be supplied with a video camera and will tape each event and the officers handling the police matter. The buddy patrol will not interfere with any police matter unless instructed by a commanding officer. Each buddy patrol will also be supplied with a vehicle.

$6 million shall be appropriated for this program over and above existing appropriations.

In Return for These Demands the Bloods/Crips Organization Will:

1. Request the drug lords of Los Angeles take their monies and invest them in business and property in Los Angeles.

2. Encourage these drug lords to stop the drug traffic and get them to use the money constructively. We will match the funds of the state government appropriations and build building-for-building.

3. Additionally, we will match funds for an AIDS research and awareness center in South Central and Long Beach that will only hire minority researchers and physicians to assist in the AIDS epidemic.

Conclusion

Meet these demands and the targeting of police officers will stop!!
You have 72 hours for a response and a commitment, in writing, to support these demands. Additionally, you have 30 days to begin implementation. And, finally, you have four years to complete the projects of construction of the major hospitals and restorations.
GIVE US THE HAMMER AND THE NAILS, WE WILL REBUILD THE CITY.

Budget Demands*

Proposal for LA's Face-Lift	$2,000,000,000
Educational Proposal	700,000,000
Law Enforcement Program	6,000,000
Economic Development Proposal	20,000,000
Human Welfare Proposal	<u>1,000,000,000</u>
TOTAL	$3,726,000,000

*To be appropriated over and above existing appropriations.

Discussion Questions

Content

1. What are the meanings of the words *proposal, program,* and *demand* in this text? How do the meanings change? How do you think each of these would affect an audience? Which term seems to you to be the most accurate as a description of the text's content?

2. Which of the changes that the Bloods/Crips propose or demand seem most important for people to consider? Why is that proposal important? What underlying values does it stress?

3. Public policy proposals are typically offered by elected officials and government figures. In what ways do you think that it is good for "civilians" to offer proposals like the Bloods/Crips's document? What values does this text express that are different from those found in other texts in this part like George Bush's speech or Senator Bradley's essay (which you'll read next)?

Form

1. The Bloods/Crips proposal first considers the physical environment, then the economy, human welfare, education, and law enforcement. How does this arrangement influence the way in which you understand the objectives and priorities of the text?

2. How would you characterize the tone of this piece? What specific words or phrases do the Bloods/Crips use to maintain a consistent tone throughout their proposal?

3. What does the Bloods/Crips proposal look like? In what ways do you think that the Bloods/Crips try to meet the expectations of their different audiences? What aspects of the proposal's form can you associate with specific possible audiences?

Writing Prompts

1. In a group or alone, choose one of the subheadings that the Bloods/Crips use and write an explanation of values that you think should underlie public policy in this area. Next, create a list of proposals that you think would enable governments and communities to better address or support these values.

2. Write a critical response to the Bloods/Crips proposal, explaining what you like about the proposal and how you would change it to develop those strengths.

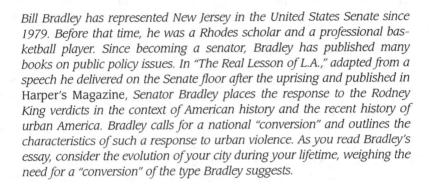

Bill Bradley has represented New Jersey in the United States Senate since 1979. Before that time, he was a Rhodes scholar and a professional basketball player. Since becoming a senator, Bradley has published many books on public policy issues. In "The Real Lesson of L.A.," adapted from a speech he delivered on the Senate floor after the uprising and published in Harper's Magazine, *Senator Bradley places the response to the Rodney King verdicts in the context of American history and the recent history of urban America. Bradley calls for a national "conversion" and outlines the characteristics of such a response to urban violence. As you read Bradley's essay, consider the evolution of your city during your lifetime, weighing the need for a "conversion" of the type Bradley suggests.*

The Real Lesson of L.A.

Bill Bradley

AMERICA HAS SEEN two tragedies this past spring: the horrible injustice of the Rodney King verdict and the deplorable violence that subsequently engulfed Los Angeles.

But we will all face a third tragedy if we don't learn the real lesson of this spring. Consider for example, a teenager who lived in Watts in the 1960s, who saw his neighborhood burned and his friends killed. Politicians came in and said they would restore opportunity, reform the criminal justice system, make the police evenhanded and disciplined, and change the conditions that created the context for the riots.

Now jump forward to 1992. The teenager is forty-five years old, and watches his neighborhood burn again and again sees his friends die. What will this man tell his teenage son about the police, the criminal justice system, the need for hard work, and the prospect of a job? What will he say about his personal safety in the neighborhood or the ability of the political system to help him take control of his life and build a better future?

The needs of our cities are obvious: more jobs, less violence, and stronger families, all in the context of a growing economy that takes everyone to a higher ground. The federal government must commit significant resources to meet the problems of urban America. It is ludicrous for anyone to pretend otherwise.

The fundamental changes, though, won't come from charismatic leaders or from federal bureaucracies. They will come from thousands of "leaders of awareness," in communities across the nation, men and women who will effect lasting change as they champion integrity and humility over self-promotion. But above all, the scapegoating and buck-passing must stop. A sense of urgency must inform our actions. The situation demands a new democratic movement—I call it a conversion, a willingness to convert the outrage of Los Angeles into positive efforts to rebuild our communities.

Conversion must start with the acknowledgment that slavery was America's original sin and race remains our unresolved dilemma. The future of American cities is inextricably bound to the issue of race and ethnicity. By the year 2000, only 57 percent of the people entering the work force in America will be native-born whites. That means that the economic future of the children of white Americans will increasingly depend on the talents of non-white Americans. If we allow this group to fail because of our penny-pinching or our timidity about straight talk, America will become a second-rate power. If this country's minorities succeed, America and all Americans will be enriched. If we don't move ahead and find common ground, we will all be diminished.

In national politics during the last twenty-five years, the issue of race and urban America has been shaped by distortion and silence. Both political parties have contributed to the problem. Republicans have played the race card in a divisive way in order to win votes—remember Willie Horton—and Democrats have suffocated discussion of the self-destructive behavior among parts of the minority population under a cloak of silence and denial. The result is that yet another generation of our children has been lost. We cannot afford to wait any longer. It is time for candor, time for truth, and time for action.

America's cities are poorer, sicker, less educated, and more violent than at any point in my lifetime. The physical problems are obvious: deteriorating schools; aging infrastructure; a diminished manufacturing base; a health care system, short of doctors, that fails to immunize against measles, much less educate about AIDS. The jobs have disappeared. The neighborhoods have been gutted. A genuine depression has hit the cities—unemployment, in some areas, matches the level of the 1930s.

What is less obvious, but equally important, in urban America is the crisis of meaning. Without meaning there can be no hope; without hope there can be no struggle; without struggle there can be no personal betterment. Absence of meaning, influenced by overt and subtle attacks from racist quarters over many years, as well as an increasing pessimism about the possibility of justice, fosters a context for chaos and irresponsibility. Meaning develops from birth. Yet, more than 40 percent of all births in the twenty largest cities of America are to women living alone; among black women, more than 65 percent.

For kids who have no family outside a gang, no connection to religion, no sense of place outside the territory, and no imagination beyond the violence of TV, our claims that government is on their side ring hollow. To them, government is at best incompetent and at worst corrupt. Instead of being rooted in values such as commitment and community service, their desires, like commodities, become rooted in the shallow ground of immediate gratification. TV bombards these kids with messages of conspicuous consumption. They want it now. They become trapped in the quicksands of American materialism, surfeited with images of sex, violence, and drugs.

THE PHYSICAL CONDITION of American cities and the absence of meaning in more and more lives come together at the barrel of a gun. If you were to select one thing that has changed most in cities since the 1960s, it would be fear. Fear covers the streets like a sheet of ice. The number of murders and violent crimes has doubled in the 20 largest cities since 1968. Ninety percent of all violence is committed by males, and they are its predominant victims. Indeed, murder is the leading cause of death for young black males.

For African-Americans in cities, violence isn't new. Mothers have sent their children to school through war zones for too many years. What *is* new is the fear among whites of random violence. No place in the city seems safe. Walking the streets seems to be a form of Russian roulette. At its core, this fear is a fear of young black men. Never mind that all black males have to answer for the actions of a few black males. Never mind that Asian-Americans fear both black and white Americans, or that in Miami and Los Angeles, some of the most feared gangs are Latinos and Chinese. Never mind that the ultimate racism was whites ignoring the violence when it wasn't in their neighborhoods, or that black Americans have always feared certain white neighborhoods.

Today many white Americans, whether fairly or unfairly, seem to be saying of some black males, "You litter the street and deface the subway, and no one, white or black, says stop. You cut school, threaten a teacher, 'dis' a social worker, and no one, white or black, says stop. You snatch a purse, you crash a concert, break a telephone booth, and no one, white or black, says stop. You rob a store, rape a jogger, shoot a tourist, and when they catch you—if they catch you—you cry racism. And nobody, white or black, says stop."

It makes no difference whether this white rap accurately reflects the reality of our cities. Millions of white Americans believe it's true. In a kind of ironic flip of fate, the fear of brutal white oppression experienced for decades in the black community and the seething anger it generated are now mirrored in the fear whites have of random attack from blacks and the growing anger that fear fuels. The white disdain grows when a frightened white politician convenes a commission to investigate charges of racism, and the anger swells when well-known black spokespersons fill the evening news with threats and bombast.

Most politicians don't want to confront the reality that causes the fear. But if politicians don't talk about the reality that everyone knows exists, they cannot lead us out of our current crisis. Because very few people of different races have real conversations with each other—when was the last time you had a conversation about race with a person of a different race?—the white vigilante groups and the black spokespersons who appear on television end up being the ones who educate the uneducated about race. The result is that the divide among races in our cities deepens and white Americans become less and less willing to spend the money to ameliorate the cities' condition or to understand that the absence of meaning in the lives of many urban children ultimately threatens the future of their own children.

Yet even in this atmosphere of disintegration, the power of the human spirit abides. Heroic families *do* overcome the odds, sometimes working four jobs to send their kids to college. Churches and mosques are peopled by the faithful who *do* practice the power of love. Neighborhood leaders have turned around local schools, organized health clinics, and rehabilitated blocks of housing. These islands of courage and dedication still offer the possibility of local renewal. And our system of government still offers the possibility of national rebirth.

THE FUTURE of urban America will take one of three paths: abandonment, encirclement, or conversion.

Abandonment will occur if people believe that the creation of suburban America, with its corporate parks and malls—along with the increasing availability of communications technology, which reduces the need for urban proximity—means that the city has outlived its usefulness. Like the small town whose industry leaves, the city will wither and disappear. Massive investment in urban America would be throwing money away, the argument would go, and trying to prevent the decline is futile.

Encirclement will occur if cities become enclaves of the rich surrounded by the poor. Racial and ethnic walls will rise higher. Class lines will be manned by ever-increasing security forces. Deeper divisions will replace communal life, and politics will be played by dividing up a shrinking economic pie into ever smaller ethnic, racial, and religious slices. It will be a kind of *Clockwork Orange* society in which the rich will pay for their security; the middle class, both black and white, will continue to flee as they confront violence; and the poor will be preyed upon at will or will join the army of violent predators. What will be lost by everyone will be freedom, civility, and the chance to build a common future.

Conversion can occur only by winning over all segments of urban life to a new politics of change, empowerment, and common effort. It is as different from the politics of dependency as it is from the politics of greed. Conversion requires listening to the disaffected as well as the powerful. Empowerment requires seizing the moment. It begins with the recognition that all of us advance together or each of us is diminished; that American diversity is not our weakness but our strength; that we will never be able to lead the world by example until we've come to terms with each other and overcome the blight of racial division on our history.

The first concrete step toward conversion is to bring an end to violence in the cities, intervene early in a child's life, reduce child abuse, establish some rule, remain unintimidated, and involve the community in its own salvation. That's what community policing, for example, is about.

The second step is to bolster families in urban America. That effort begins with the recognition that the most important year in a child's life is the first. Fifteen-month houses must be established for women seven months pregnant who want to live the first year of their lives as mothers in a residential program. We must also provide full funding for Head Start and WIC, more generous tax treatment of children, one-year parental leave, tough child support enforcement, and welfare reform that encourages marriage, work, and personal responsibility.

The third step is to create jobs for those who can work—through enterprise zones, the Job Corps, neighborhood reconstruction corps, and investment in the urban infrastructure. It is only through individual empowerment that we can guarantee long-term economic growth. Without economic growth, scapegoats will be sought and racial tensions will heighten. Without growth, hopes will languish.

Ultimately, the key to all this is the political process. It has failed to address our urban prospects because politicians feel accountable mainly to those who vote, and urban America has voted in declining numbers—so politicians have ignored them. Voter registration and active participation remain the critical link.

STEPHEN VINCENT BENÉT once said about American diversity: "All of these you are/and each is partly you/and none of them is false/and none is wholly true." For those citizens whose ancestors came generations ago there is a need to reaffirm principles—liberty, equality, democracy—even though these principles have always eluded complete fulfillment. The American city has always been the place where these ideas and cultures clashed—sometimes violently. But all people, even those brought here in chattel slavery, are not African or Italian or Polish or Irish or Japanese. They're American.

What we lose when racial or ethnic self-consciousness dominates are tolerance, curiosity, civility—precisely the qualities we need to allow us to live side by side in mutual respect. The fundamental challenge is to understand the suffering of others as well as to share in their joy. To sacrifice that sensitivity on the altar of racial chauvinism is to lose our future. And we *will* lose it unless we move quickly. The American city needs physical rejuvenation, economic opportunity, and moral direction, but above all what it needs is the same thing every small town needs: the willingness to treat a person of any race with the respect you show for a brother or sister, in the belief that together you'll build a better world than you would have ever done alone, a better world in which all Americans stand on common ground.

Discussion Questions

Content

1. What factors does Bradley suggest must be addressed in response to the Los Angeles uprising?

2. What does Bradley think is "new" about urban violence in America? How does he explain this new situation? In what ways would you agree with Bradley and in what ways do you see the situation differently?

3. Bradley states that as a result of fear and lack of communication, "the divide among races in our cities deepens and white Americans become less and less willing to spend the money to ameliorate the cities' condition." What are other results of the fear of cities? Of the lack of communication about them? Are these results more or less important than the lack of willingness to spend money? How can they be addressed?

Form

1. As a politician, Bradley uses this essay to communicate with voters. Which voters do you think Bradley has in mind, and how does the essay appeal to that audience?

2. Bradley's notion of "conversion" has three steps. What are the advantages of organizing and discussing ideas in terms of steps? What are some potential disadvantages?

3. What specific words and phrases does Bradley use to make the real lesson of L.A. apply to all Americans rather than simply urban Americans? Do you think he is successful?

Writing Prompts

1. Imagine that you were a U.S. senator at the time of the Rodney King verdict. Write a brief comment that you would have released to the public. Include a specific statement about who your constituents are and what they might expect from you.

2. Write an essay that reflects upon the three-step conversion process Bradley recommends. How would you adjust or change his priorities given your own experiences and beliefs?

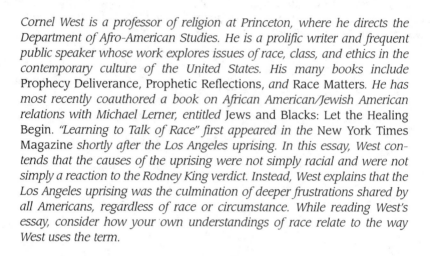

Cornel West is a professor of religion at Princeton, where he directs the Department of Afro-American Studies. He is a prolific writer and frequent public speaker whose work explores issues of race, class, and ethics in the contemporary culture of the United States. His many books include Prophecy Deliverance, Prophetic Reflections, *and* Race Matters. *He has most recently coauthored a book on African American/Jewish American relations with Michael Lerner, entitled* Jews *and* Blacks: Let the Healing Begin. *"Learning to Talk of Race" first appeared in the* New York Times Magazine *shortly after the Los Angeles uprising. In this essay, West contends that the causes of the uprising were not simply racial and were not simply a reaction to the Rodney King verdict. Instead, West explains that the Los Angeles uprising was the culmination of deeper frustrations shared by all Americans, regardless of race or circumstance. While reading West's essay, consider how your own understandings of race relate to the way West uses the term.*

Learning to Talk of Race

Cornel West

WHAT HAPPENED in Los Angeles this past April was neither a race riot nor a class rebellion. Rather, this monumental upheaval was a multiracial, trans-class, and largely male display of justified social rage. For all its ugly, xenophobic resentment, its air of adolescent carnival, and its downright barbaric behavior, it signified the sense of powerlessness in American society. Glib attempts to reduce its meaning to the pathologies of the black underclass, the criminal actions of hoodlums, or the political revolt of the oppressed urban masses miss the mark. Of those arrested, only 36 percent were black, more than a third had full-time jobs and most claimed to shun political affiliation. What we witnessed in Los Angeles was the consequence of a lethal linkage of economic decline, cultural decay, and political lethargy in American life. Race was the visible catalyst, not the underlying cause. The meaning of the earthshaking events in Los Angeles is difficult to grasp because most of us remain trapped in the narrow framework of the dominant liberal and conservative views of race in America, which with its worn-out vocabulary leaves us intellectually debilitated, morally disempowered, and personally depressed. The astonishing disappearance of the event from public dialogue is testimony to just how painful and distressing a serious engagement with race is. Our truncated public discussions of race suppress the best of who and what we are as a people because they fail to confront the complexity of the issue in a candid and critical manner. The predictable pitting of liberals against conservatives, Great Society Democrats against self-help Republicans, reinforces intellectual parochialism and political paralysis.

The liberal notion that more government programs can solve the problems is simplistic—precisely because it focuses *solely* on the economic dimension. And the conservative idea that what is needed is a change in the moral behavior of poor black urban dwellers (especially poor black men, who, they say, should stay married, support their children, and stop committing so many crimes) highlights immoral actions while ignoring public responsibility tor the immoral circumstances that haunt our fellow citizens.

The common denominator of these views of race is that each still sees black people as a "problem people," in the words of Dorothy I. Height, president of the National Council of Negro Women, rather than as fellow American citizens with problems. Her words echo the poignant "unasked question" of W. E. B. DuBois, who wrote:

> They approach me in a half-hesitant sort of way, eye me curiously or compassionately, and then instead of saying directly, How does it feel to be a problem? they say, I know an excellent colored man in my town.... Do not these Southern outrages make your blood boil? At these I smile, or am interested or reduce the boiling to a simmer, as the occasion may require. To the real question, How does it feel to be a problem? I answer seldom a word.

Nearly a century later, we confine discussions about race in America to the "problems" black people pose for whites rather than considering what this way of viewing black people reveals about us as a nation.

This paralyzing framework encourages liberals to relieve their guilty consciences by supporting public funds directed at "the problems"; but at the same time, reluctant to exercise principled criticism of black people, they deny them the freedom to err. Similarly, conservatives blame the "problems" on black people themselves and thereby render black social misery invisible or unworthy of public attention.

Hence, for liberals, black people are to be "included" and "integrated" into "our" society and culture, while for the conservatives they are to be "well behaved" and "worthy of acceptance" by "our" way of life. Both fail to see that the presence and predicaments of black people are neither additions to nor defections from American life, but rather *constitutive elements of that life.*

To ENGAGE IN A SERIOUS DISCUSSION of race in America, we must begin not with the problems of black people but with the flaws of American society—flaws rooted in historic inequalities and longstanding cultural stereotypes. How we set up the terms for discussing racial issues shapes our perception and response to these issues. As long as black people are viewed as a "them," the burden falls on blacks to do all the "cultural" and "moral" work necessary for healthy race relations. The implication is that only certain Americans can define what it means to be American—and the rest must simply "fit in."

The emergence of strong black-nationalist sentiments among blacks, especially young people, is a revolt against this sense of having to "fit in." The variety of black-nationalist ideologies, from the moderate views of Supreme Court Justice Clarence Thomas in his youth to those of Louis Farrakhan today, rest upon a fundamental truth: white America has been historically weak-willed in ensuring racial justice and has continued to resist accepting fully the humanity of blacks. As long as double standards and differential treatment abound—as long as the rap performer Ice-T is harshly condemned while former Los Angeles Police Chief Daryl F. Gates's antiblack comments are received in polite silence, as long as Dr. Leonard Jeffries's anti-Semitic statements are met with vitriolic outrage while presidential candidate Patrick J. Buchanan's are received with a genteel response—black nationalisms will thrive.

Afrocentrism, a contemporary species of black nationalism, is a gallant yet misguided attempt to define an African identity in a white society perceived to be hostile. It is gallant because it puts black doings and sufferings, not white anxieties and fears, at the center of discussion. It is misguided because—out of fear of cultural hybridization, silence on the issue of class, retrograde views on black women, homosexuals, and lesbians, and a reluctance to link race to the common good—it reinforces the narrow discussions about race.

To establish a new framework, we need to begin with a frank acknowledgment of the basic humanness and Americanness of each of us. And we must acknowledge that as a people—*E Pluribus Unum*—we are on a slippery slope toward economic strife, social turmoil, and cultural chaos. If we go down, we go down together. The Los Angeles upheaval forced us to see not only that we are not connected in ways we would like to be but also, in a more profound sense, that this failure to connect binds us even more tightly together. The paradox of race in America is that our common destiny is more pronounced and imperiled precisely when our divisions are deeper.

The Civil War and its legacy speak loudly here. Eighty-six percent of white suburban Americans live in neighborhoods that are less than one percent black, meaning that the prospects for the country depend largely on how its cities fare in the hands of a suburban electorate. There is no escape from our interracial interdependence, yet enforced racial hierarchy dooms us as a nation to collective paranoia and hysteria—the unmaking of any democratic order.

The verdict that sparked the incidents in Los Angeles was perceived to be wrong by the vast majority of Americans. But whites have often failed to acknowledge the widespread mistreatment of black people, especially black men, by law-enforcement agencies, which helped ignite the spark. The Rodney King verdict was merely the occasion for deep-seated rage to come to the surface. This rage is fed by the "silent" depression ravaging the country—in which real weekly wages of all American workers since 1973 have declined nearly twenty percent, while at the same time wealth has been upwardly distributed.

The exodus of stable industrial jobs from urban centers to cheaper labor markets here and abroad, housing policies that have created "chocolate cities and vanilla suburbs" (to use the popular musical artist George Clinton's memorable phrase), white fear of black crime, and the urban influx of poor Spanish-speaking and Asian immigrants—all have helped erode the tax base of American cities just as the federal government has cut its supports and programs. The result is unemployment, hunger, homelessness, and sickness for millions.

Driving that rage is a culture of hedonistic self-indulgence and narcissistic self-regard. This culture of consumption yields coldhearted and mean-spirited attitudes and actions that turn poor urban neighborhoods into military combat zones and existential wastelands.

And the pervasive spiritual impoverishment grows. The collapse of meaning in life—the eclipse of hope and absence of love of self and others, the breakdown of family and neighborhood bonds—leads to the social deracination and cultural denudement of urban dwellers, especially children. We have created rootless, dangling people with little link to the supportive networks—family, friends, school—that sustain some sense of purpose in life. We have witnessed the collapse of the spiritual communities that help us face despair, disease, and death and that transmit through the generations dignity and decency, excellence, and elegance.

The result is lives of what we might call "random nows," of fortuitous and fleeting moments preoccupied with "getting over"—with acquiring pleasure, property, and power by any means necessary. (This is not what Malcolm X meant by this famous phrase.) Postmodern culture is more and more a market culture dominated by gangster mentalities and self-destructive wantonness. This culture engulfs all of us—yet its impact on the disadvantaged is devastating, resulting in extreme violence in everyday life. Sexual violence against women and homicidal assaults by young black men on one another are only the most obvious signs of this empty quest for pleasure, property, and power.

Lastly, this rage is fueled by a political atmosphere in which images, not ideas, dominate, where politicians spend more time raising money than issues. The functions of parties have been displaced by public polls, and politicians behave less as thermostats that determine the climate of opinion than as thermometers registering the public mood. American politics has been rocked by an unleashing of greed among opportunistic public officials—following the lead of their counterparts in the private sphere, where, as of 1989, one percent of the population owned thirty-seven percent of the wealth—leading to a profound cynicism and pessimism among the citizenry.

And given the way in which the Republican party since 1968 has appealed to popular xenophobic images—playing the black, female, and homophobic cards and realigning the electorate along race, sex, and sexual-orientation lines—it is no surprise that the notion that we are all part of one garment of destiny is discredited. Appeals to special interests rather than public interests reinforce this polarization. The Los Angeles upheaval was an expression of utter fragmentation by a powerless citizenry that includes not just the poor but all of us.

WHAT IS TO BE DONE? How do we capture a new spirit and vision to meet the challenges of the postindustrial city, postmodern cultures and postparty politics? First, we must admit that the most valuable sources for help, hope, and power consist of ourselves and our common history. As in the ages of Lincoln, Roosevelt, and King, we must look to new frameworks and languages to understand our multilayered crisis and overcome our deep malaise.

Second, we must focus our attention on the public square—the common good that undergirds our national and global destinies. The vitality of any public square ultimately depends on how much we *care* about the quality of our lives together. The neglect of our public infrastructure, for example—our water and sewage systems, bridges, tunnels, highways, subways, and streets reflects not only our myopic economic policies, which impede productivity, but also the low priority we place on our common life.

The tragic plight of our children clearly reveals our deep disregard for public well-being. With about one out of five children living in poverty in this country and one out of two black children and two out of five Hispanic children doing so and with most of our children ill-equipped to live lives of spiritual and cultural quality, neglected by overburdened parents, and bombarded by the market values of profit-hungry corporations—how do we expect ever to constitute a vibrant society?

One essential step is some form of large-scale public intervention to ensure access to basic social goods—housing, food, health care, education, child care, and jobs. We must invigorate the common good with a mixture of government, business, and labor that does not follow any existing blueprint. After a period in which the private sphere has been sacralized and the public square gutted, the temptation is to make a fetish of the public square. We need to resist such dogmatic swings.

Last, the major challenge is the need to generate new leadership. The paucity of courageous leaders—so apparent in the response to the events in Los Angeles—requires that we look beyond the same elites and voices that recycle the older frameworks. We need leaders—neither saints nor sparkling television personalities—who can situate themselves within a larger historical narrative of this country and world, who can grasp the complex dynamics of our peoplehood and imagine a future grounded in the best of our past, yet attuned to the frightening obstacles that now perplex us. Our ideals of freedom, democracy, and equality must be invoked to invigorate all of us, especially the landless, propertyless, and luckless. Only a visionary leadership that can motivate "the better angels of our nature," as Lincoln said, and activate possibilities for a freer, more efficient, and stable America—only that leadership deserves cultivation and support.

This new leadership must be grounded in grass-roots organizing that highlights democratic accountability. Regardless of whether Bill Clinton's cautious neoliberal programs or George Bush's callous conservative policies prevail in November, the challenge to America will be determining whether a genuine multiracial democracy can be created and sustained in an era of global economies and a moment of xenophobic frenzy.

Let us hope and pray that the vast intelligence, imagination, humor, and courage in this country will not fail us. Either we learn a new language of empathy and compassion, or the fire this time will consume us all.

Discussion Questions

Content

1. What is West's vision of a revitalized public culture? What does he think is needed in order to achieve this?

2. What change in discussions of social issues in the United States does West call for? What does he believe such a change would achieve? What do you think?

3. What do you see as West's main criticism of American public discussion of social issues? Find at least one piece of writing in this part to which you think West's criticism applies and explain why.

Form

1. West uses the incident in Los Angeles to begin a discussion of a many-sided "crisis" in American culture. What terms from West's description of Los Angeles are important to his later discussion, and what is their effect on you as a reader?

2. How would you characterize West's writing style? Is it forceful? emotional? straightforward? What effect does his style have on how you respond to him? Is he authoritative? Upon reflection, are his suggestions practical enough for you? Are they reasonable?

3. What is West's primary concern in this essay? How is the essay organized to emphasize this concern?

Writing Prompts

1. Write an essay in which you describe the "new languages" that can help us "understand our multilayered crisis and overcome our deep malaise."

2. Choose the issue that strikes you as most important from West's analysis of our current situation. Write an essay that imagines what one person can do positively to change the situation.

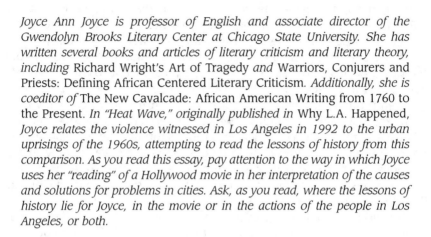

Joyce Ann Joyce is professor of English and associate director of the Gwendolyn Brooks Literary Center at Chicago State University. She has written several books and articles of literary criticism and literary theory, including Richard Wright's Art of Tragedy *and* Warriors, Conjurers and Priests: Defining African Centered Literary Criticism. *Additionally, she is coeditor of* The New Cavalcade: African American Writing from 1760 to the Present. *In "Heat Wave," originally published in* Why L.A. Happened, *Joyce relates the violence witnessed in Los Angeles in 1992 to the urban uprisings of the 1960s, attempting to read the lessons of history from this comparison. As you read this essay, pay attention to the way in which Joyce uses her "reading" of a Hollywood movie in her interpretation of the causes and solutions for problems in cities. Ask, as you read, where the lessons of history lie for Joyce, in the movie or in the actions of the people in Los Angeles, or both.*

Heat Wave

Joyce Ann Joyce

APPROXIMATELY TWO WEEKS after the fires began to cool in South Central Los Angeles, I wandered into a video store, looking for something to distract me from the disappointment and pain I was feeling because of the loss of real political leadership in this so-called greatest country on the planet. Because it was a Friday afternoon, all of the newly released tapes had been rented: *The Fisher King, Robin Hood, Frankie and Johnny, The Super* and all the *Lethal Weapons.* So I sauntered around the store and ended up in the drama section of old tapes. Black faces on one tape stood out. And because those faces included James Earl Jones and Cicely Tyson, I decided that they would keep me well enough entertained.

Once I got the tape home and put it in the VCR, I remembered that I already had seen this movie on television. I realized that if the Elders were correct (as they usually are), some good reason (that was not clear to me at the time) was responsible for my stumbling upon the movie *Heat Wave,*

Joyce Ann Joyce. "Heat Wave." In *Why L.A. Happened,* edited by Haki R. Madhubuti (1993). Reprinted with permission of Third World Press.

recorded by Turner Entertainment and based on the true story of Robert Richardson's account of the Watts riots in 1965. The movie (or Richardson's account) did not provide me with the solace that I was seeking when I entered the video store. Providing the answers to the many questions that I have heard posed since the Simi Valley jury returned its 'not guilty' verdict, *Heat Wave* demonstrates quite effectively and poignantly the causes of both the Watts riots in August 13, 1965 and of the most recent Los Angeles riot following the jury's decision.

Even though I myself find it quite a conundrum that I currently live in Nebraska, I have always wondered why and how so many Blacks ended up in California, a state quite a distance from those southern states which were the breeding places of millions of children of slaves. *Heat Wave* not only answers this question, but it also makes it quite clear that the white mentality in California was as hostile toward Blacks as it was in the South from which the Blacks had fled.

Thinking that California was the real land of opportunity, Clifford Turbin, his wife, son J. T and a cousin slightly older than their son, Richard Robertson, sing and clap their hands along the road as they discuss happily the good schools and the airplane and aluminum factories that will provide them with a livelihood quite different from that in Alabama. They tease each other and discuss with pride those Black movie stars, like Lena Horne and Dorothy Dandridge, whom they see as having crossed racial boundaries.

As they drive into the community where Clifford's mother-in-law (Ma Dear) lives, the wholesomeness of this Black California neighborhood contrasts sharply to the shanties and poverty of Black Alabama in the 1950s displayed at the very beginning of the movie. Of course, the street on which Ma Dear (Cicely Tyson) lives is in Watts. Thus, though her house is comfortable and nicely furnished, it soon becomes clear to Clifford and his family that Alabama's rural squalor and racism is even more vicious and debilitating in sunny California.

At dinner, Ma Dear cautions J.T. and Bobby (Richardson) against going on Alameda Street. Since the two young men think that California is nothing like Alabama, they pay no attention to the warning nor to where they are when they end up lost on Alameda Street searching for Hollywood. Suddenly, these two young men find themselves in a dilemma quite characteristic of their life in Alabama. A car full of young white ruffians (easily recognized as rednecks in Alabama) chase J.T. and Bobby for a short while in the car. When the car proves ineffective, they get out of the car and run after the two Black men until they escape across a railroad track just in front of a passing train. After the train passes and the Blacks are safe outside the forbidden territory, one of the young whites screams, "Niggers, stay out of Linwood."

This incident proves to be merely an introduction to what follows. The spirit with which Clifford Turbin and his family sang "If you traveling on the road tell him what you want" as they crossed the California state line slowly fades as they struggle to make a new life. While Clifford first experiences California's unwritten Jim Crow laws as he struggles for employment, his son J.T. faces what racism has done to the mentality of middle-class Blacks who have adopted the Booker T. Washington strategy. In suit, tie, suspenders and a cheerful smile, Clifford goes from one construction site to another for weeks looking for employment, only to be told that either the position has been filled or the company is looking for someone with more experience. This proud, capable Black man who had been a construction foreman with 45 men working under him in the South has to take a job as a janitor in order to provide, even to a small degree, for his family.

Facing similar obstacles, J.T. goes excitedly into the counselor's office at school to explain that he wants to be a pilot like his great uncle who was one of the Tuskegee pilots. The counselor discourages him by saying that a knowledge of navigation and hydraulics is required for which calculus and physics are prerequisites. J.T. explains that he made a B– in chemistry before coming West and that he even tutored some of the other students in his school. The counselor continues her attack of his spirit by saying that J.T.'s college board scores are quite low. The look on J.T.'s face acknowledges that he finally understands the kind of Black person he is talking to. After saying he is not stupid, he walks out of the room. When he meets Bobby (Richardson) who is waiting for him outside, J.T. says he told the woman he wanted to go into auto mechanics. When Bobby asks J.T. what the counselor said, J.T. responds, "Nothing I don't already know." What J.T. knows is the same thing that Richard Wright's Bigger Thomas knows: that being a pilot and being able to fulfill one's potential to its fullest is not an activity allowed a Black man in America. Even many Black people, such as the school counselor, believe that Black men should not aim too high. Thus, Clifford's and his son's dreams are destroyed, and they become victims of alcohol. Their spirits broken, they become aloof and full of self-hatred.

When Bobby returns from the army, he barely recognizes his cousins. Clifford boasts and talks incessantly in the neighborhood barber shop owned by Junius Jackson (James Earl Jones), and he is unable to keep a job as janitor because of his drinking. J.T. is bitter and hostile toward Bobby who is excited about his new job at the *Los Angeles Times*. Bobby, however, is not used as a reporter. He is a message "boy" in a suit. While he is struggling to gain his supervisor's recognition, he and the rest of Watts are constantly harassed by policemen. Clifford and his wife are pulled over; the police throw Clifford against the car and push his wife's purse in her stomach after searching it. Bobby and his girlfriend are stopped because they are walking down the street. When one of the policemen refers to Bobby's girlfriend as "Tricksy Trim," Bobby and she turn and walk away as this same policeman aims a gun at them and orders them to stop. If a new, more sensible and sensitive policeman had not caught up with Bobby and talked to him, the other policeman would have fired without any provocation whatsoever.

The incident from which the Black community was unable to recover began in the same way as the now historical Rodney King beating. On August 13, 1965, a policeman pulled over two young Black brothers and said that they were speeding. When the policeman detected alcohol on the driver's breath, he asked him to step out of the car. After a crowd gathered, including the driver's mother, he became outraged and said that he would rather die than go to jail. At this point, policemen flooded the Watts neighborhood. Outraged that one Black man was being manhandled by a throng of policemen, the community became angry. One policeman, mistakenly thinking that a pregnant woman spat on his neck, grabbed her and threw her up against the car and into it. By the time the police left with the two brothers and the pregnant woman in custody, the Watts community was uncontrollable. Centuries of racism, powerlessness and disappointment were unleashed in looting and rioting.

News media all over the country compared the pictures of Watts burning in 1965 with the recent fires in South Central L.A. These same media, particularly CNN and Dan Rather, have aired stories about the brave and talented children who live in South Central L.A. They have shown pictures of the young Black men arrested for beating the truck driver. They have even interviewed the mothers of some of these young men. But where are the stories behind what made these young men react as they did? Where are the stories that make it clear that J.T.'s children and Clifford's grandchildren have inherited their father's and grandfather's powerlessness, hopelessness, bitterness and self-hatred?

What happened to Rodney King and the jury's verdict clearly responds to those white liberals and Black accommodationists who have a need to believe that class threatens the Black man in this country more than racism. Neither the Black community nor the white one has profited from history. When the trial was changed from L.A. to Simi Valley, Black leaders all over the country should have been protesting and leading demonstrations. If we had learned anything from the Watts riots, the Black community would never have allowed the site of the trial to be changed to the Simi Valley police stronghold. The brick we had at the pit of our stomachs after the verdict should have been hurled at the criminal justice system long before the trial began.

The fact that police brutality provided the ember that ignited the frustrations, anger, bitterness and stifled violence in 1965 and 1992 symbolizes the life of a people whose lives are still governed by the whims of overseers and pattyrollers hired to keep the underclass from forgetting their limitations. Ma Dear expresses these feelings best when she talks to the wealthy white Beverly Hills lawyer for whom she works and who has just brought a gun to shoot the "beast" when they come into his neighborhood. She asks him how he would feel if everything he had ever dreamed had always been close enough to see but never close enough to touch.

None of us are wise enough to know why one sibling from an impoverished family survives the horrors and limitations of that environment and becomes a doctor, lawyer, professor or journalist while another from the same home ends up an alcoholic or in prison. What we do know is that like J.T., many alcoholics, who should be airline pilots and who deserve the right to fulfill their dreams, roam the streets. The Watts riots ironically provided Bobby Richardson the opportunity to fulfill his dream. Because whites are beaten up in Watts, Bobby's supervisor is desperate for someone to go into Watts to report the news back to the paper. Bobby aggressively explains that he had saved the lives of two white reporters and that he was the only one at the *L.A. Times* qualified to go into Watts. Though the paper had never used a Black reporter before, the supervisor very reluctantly gives Bobby a reporter's badge. The first story that he telephones in is so good that the paper runs it without any changes.

In the end, a police chief refers to the Black community as monkeys in a zoo; the news media is castigated for looking the other way, and the mayor, who attended a $100 a plate dinner an hour before troops arrived in Watts, is condemned.

Almost thirty years later, L.A. still has a police chief who sees Blacks as monkeys. The news media, federal government and their parent corporations continue to look away from urban development. Black mayors now give the orders to drop bombs on women and children.

In 1966, the *L.A. Times* was awarded the Pulitzer Prize for Robert Richardson's coverage of the riots. Even after such a prestigious award, after the forming of a commission to study the riots and after a movie starring some of our finest and most committed Black actors and actresses—and after 27 years of so-called Black progress—more of South Central L.A. is in shambles today than it was in 1965. The actions we take today as Black people must go beyond newspaper stories, beyond the forming of commissions to study problems with causes even our children understand and beyond movies that get lost in the stacks if we are to prevent J.T.'s grandchildren and Clifford's great grandchildren from leading gangs that will destroy their lives and those of many others in the year 2019, 27 years from now. We have all the information we need as well as the brilliant young Black minds and energy to run our own airline and construction companies. What is missing is the means by which we can use this information to become leaders rather than followers in the decades to come.

Discussion Questions

Content

1. Early in her essay, Joyce contends that *"Heat Wave* demonstrates quite effectively and poignantly the causes of both the Watts riots in August 13, 1965 and of the most recent Los Angeles riot following the jury's decision." What do you think are the causes that Joyce believes the film points toward? In what sense do you agree with her suggestion that both Watts and Los Angeles riots grew out of the same causes? In what senses do you disagree?

2. Joyce argues that the people of the United States have failed to learn from history. What does she seem to think that we should have learned and how would we benefit from that knowledge?

3. Reread the last paragraph of the essay. What does Joyce leave the reader to think about? What do you believe we need to think about as we try to create a society in which people feel that they have options other than rioting?

Form

1. Joyce's essay combines a plot summary of *Heat Wave,* interpretation of the film's messages, and discussion of the circumstances surrounding the riots of 1965 and 1992. How does the movie help Joyce to make her argument? Point to specific places in her essay to explain how the movie helps her. What effect does her use of the movie have on you as a reader?

2. How does Joyce's personal opening influence the way you read her essay? Given what comes later in the essay, why do you think she opens it as she does? How effective is her strategy?

3. Use Joyce's title, "Heat Wave," to explain the way she organizes her essay.

Writing Prompts

1. Write an essay explaining how a mass media text (movie, TV show, radio program) helped you to see a public issue in a different way.

2. Write an essay that begins by discussing a particular incident in your own life and then use that experience to explain your understanding of uprisings, such as the one in Los Angeles.

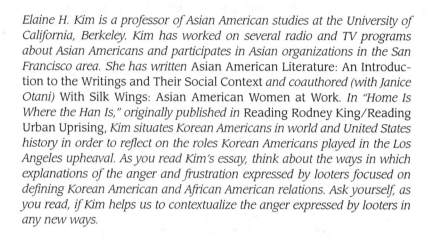

Elaine H. Kim is a professor of Asian American studies at the University of California, Berkeley. Kim has worked on several radio and TV programs about Asian Americans and participates in Asian organizations in the San Francisco area. She has written Asian American Literature: An Introduction to the Writings and Their Social Context *and coauthored (with Janice Otani)* With Silk Wings: Asian American Women at Work. *In "Home Is Where the Han Is," originally published in* Reading Rodney King/Reading Urban Uprising, *Kim situates Korean Americans in world and United States history in order to reflect on the roles Korean Americans played in the Los Angeles upheaval. As you read Kim's essay, think about the ways in which explanations of the anger and frustration expressed by looters focused on defining Korean American and African American relations. Ask yourself, as you read, if Kim helps us to contextualize the anger expressed by looters in any new ways.*

Home Is Where the *Han* Is: A Korean American Perspective on the Los Angeles Upheavals

Elaine H. Kim

ABOUT HALF of the estimated $850 million in estimated material losses incurred during the Los Angeles upheavals was sustained by a community no one seems to want to talk much about. Korean Americans in Los Angeles, suddenly at the front lines when violence came to the buffer zone they had been so precariously occupying, suffered profound damage to their means of livelihood. But my concern here is the psychic damage which, unlike material damage, is impossible to quantify.

I want to explore the questions of whether or not recovery is possible for Korean Americans, and what will become of our attempts to "become American" without dying of *han*. *Han* is a Korean word that means, loosely translated, the sorrow and anger that grow from the accumulated experiences of oppression. Although the word is frequently and commonly used by Koreans, the condition it describes is taken quite seriously. When people die of *han*, it is called dying of *hwabyong*, a disease of frustration and rage following misfortune.

Situated as we are on the border between those who have and those who have not, between predominantly Anglo and mostly African American and Latino communities, from our current interstitial position in the American discourse of race, many Korean Americans have trouble calling what happened in Los Angeles an "uprising." At the same time, we cannot quite say it was a "riot." So some of us have taken to calling it *sa-i-ku*, April 29, after the manner of naming other events in Korean history—3.1 (*sam-il*) for March 1, 1919, when massive protests against Japanese colonial rule began in Korea; 6.25 (*yook-i-o*), or June 25, 1950, when the Korean War began; and 4.19 (*sa-il-ku*), or April 19, 1960, when the first student movement in the world to overthrow a government began in South Korea. The ironic similarity between 4.19 and 4.29 does not escape most Korean Americans.

Los Angeles Koreatown has been important to me, even though I visit only a dozen times a year. Before Koreatown sprang up during the last decade and a half, I used to hang around the fringes of Chinatown, although I knew that this habit was pure pretense. For me, knowing that Los Angeles Koreatown existed made a difference; one of my closest friends worked with the Black-Korean Alliance there, and I liked to think of it as a kind of "home"—however idealized and hypostatized—for the soul, an anchor, a potential refuge, a place in America where I could belong without ever being asked, "Who are you and what are you doing here? Where did you come from and when are you going back?"

Many of us watched in horror the destruction of Koreatown and the systematic targeting of Korean shops in South Central Los Angeles after the Rodney King verdict. Seeing those buildings in flames and those anguished Korean faces, I had the terrible thought that there would be no belonging and that we were, just as I had always suspected, a people destined to carry our *han* around with us wherever we went in the world. The destiny (*p'aljja*) that had spelled centuries of extreme suffering from invasion, colonization, war, and national division had smuggled itself into the U.S. with our baggage.

African American and Korean American Conflict

As someone whose social consciousness was shaped by the African American-led civil rights movement of the 1960s, I felt that I was watching our collective dreams for a just society disintegrating, cast aside as naive and irrelevant in the bitter and embattled 1990s. It was the courageous African American women and men of the 1960s who had redefined the meaning of

"American," who had first suggested that a person like me could reject the false choice between being treated as a perpetual foreigner in my own birthplace, on the one hand, and relinquishing my identity for someone else's ill-fitting and impossible Anglo American one on the other. Thanks to them, I began to discern how institutional racism works and why Korea was never mentioned in my world-history textbooks. I was able to see how others besides Koreans had been swept aside by the dominant culture. My American education offered nothing about Chicanos or Latinos, and most of what I was taught about African and Native Americans was distorted to justify their oppression and vindicate their oppressors.

I could hardly believe my ears when, during the weeks immediately following *sa-i-ku,* I heard African American community leaders suggesting that Korean American merchants were foreign intruders deliberately trying to stifle African American economic development, when I knew that they had bought those liquor stores at five times gross receipts from African American owners, who had previously bought them at two times gross receipts from Jewish owners after Watts. I saw anti-Korean flyers that were being circulated by African American political candidates and read about South Central residents petitioning against the reestablishment of swap meets, groups of typically Korean immigrant-operated market stalls. I was disheartened with Latinos who related the pleasure they felt while looting Korean stores that they believed "had it coming" and who claimed that it was because of racism that more Latinos were arrested during *sa-i-ku* than Asian Americans. And I was filled with despair when I read about Chinese Americans wanting to dissociate themselves from us. According to one Chinese American reporter assigned to cover Asian American issues for a San Francisco daily, Chinese and Japanese American shopkeepers, unlike Koreans, always got along fine with African Americans in the past. "Suddenly," admitted another Chinese American, "I am scared to be Asian. More specifically, I am afraid to be mistaken for Korean." I was enraged when I overheard European Americans discussing the conflicts as if they were watching a dogfight or a boxing match. The situation reminded me of the Chinese film "Raise the Red Lantern," in which we never see the husband's face. We only hear his mellifluous voice as he benignly admonishes his four wives not to fight among themselves. He can afford to be kind and pleasant because the structure that pits his wives against each other is so firmly in place that he need never sully his hands or even raise his voice.

Battleground Legacy

Korean Americans are squeezed between black and white and also between U.S. and South Korean political agendas. Opportunistic American and South Korean presidential candidates toured the burnt ruins, posing for the television cameras but delivering nothing of substance to the victims. Like their

U.S. counterparts, South Korean news media seized upon *sa-i-ku,* featuring sensational stories that depicted the problem as that of savage African Americans attacking innocent Koreans for no reason. To give the appearance of authenticity, Seoul newspapers even published articles using the names of Korean Americans who did not in fact write them.

Those of us who chafe at being asked whether we are Chinese or Japanese as if there were no other possibilities or who were angered when the news media sought Chinese and Japanese but not Korean American views during *sa-i-ku* are sensitive to an invisibility that seems particular to us. To many Americans, Korea is but the gateway to or the bridge between China and Japan, or a crossroads of major Asian conflicts.

It can certainly be said that, although little known or cared about in the Western world, Korea has been a perennial battleground. Besides the Mongols and the Manchus, there were the *Yŏjin* (Jurched), the *Koran* (Khitan), and the *Waegu* (Wäkö) invaders. In relatively recent years, there was the war between China and Japan that ended in 1895 and the war between Japan and Russia in 1905, both of which were fought on Korean soil and resulted in extreme suffering for the Korean people. Japan's 36 years of brutal colonial rule ended with the U.S. and what was then the Soviet Union dividing the country in half at the 38th parallel. Thus, Korea was turned into a Cold War territory that ultimately became a battleground for world superpowers during the conflict of 1950–53.

Becoming American

One of the consequences of war, colonization, national division, and superpower economic and cultural domination has been the migration of Koreans to places like Los Angeles, where they believed their human rights would be protected by law. After all, they had received U.S.-influenced political educations. They started learning English in the seventh grade. They all knew the story of the poor boy from Illinois who became president. They all learned that the U.S. Constitution and Bill of Rights protected the common people from violence and injustice. But they who grew up in Korea watching "Gunsmoke," "Night Rider," and "McGyver" dubbed in Korean were not prepared for the black, brown, red, and yellow America they encountered when they disembarked at the Los Angeles International Airport. They hadn't heard that there is no equal justice in the U.S. They had to learn about American racial hierarchies. They did not realize that, as immigrants of color, they would never attain political voice or visibility but would instead be used to uphold the inequality and the racial hierarchy they had no part in creating.

Most of the newcomers had underestimated the communication barriers they would face. Like the Turkish workers in Germany described in John

Berger and Jean Mohr's *A Seventh Man,* their toil amounted to only a pile of gestures and the English they tried to speak changed and turned against them as they spoke it. Working 14 hours a day, six or seven days a week, they rarely came into sustained contact with English-speaking Americans and almost never had time to study English. Not feeling at ease with English, they did not engage in informal conversations easily with non-Koreans and were hated for being curt and rude. They did not attend churches or do business in banks or other enterprises where English was required. Typically, the immigrant, small-business owners utilized unpaid family labor instead of hiring people from local communities. Thanks to Eurocentric American cultural practices, they knew little or nothing good about African Americans or Latinos, who in turn and for similar reasons knew little or nothing good about them. At the same time, Korean shopowners in South Central and Koreatown were affluent compared with the impoverished residents, whom they often exploited as laborers or looked down upon as fools with an aversion to hard work. Most Korean immigrants did not even know that they were among the many direct beneficiaries of the African American–led civil rights movement, which helped pave the way for the 1965 immigration reforms that made their immigration possible.

Korean-immigrant views, shaped as they were by U.S. cultural influences and official, anticommunist, South Korean education, differed radically from those of many poor people in the communities Korean immigrants served: unaware of the shameful history of oppression of nonwhite immigrants and other people of color in the U.S., they regarded themselves as having arrived in a meritocratic "land of opportunity" where a person's chances for success are limited only by individual lack of ability or diligence. Having left a homeland where they foresaw their talents and hard work going unrecognized and unrewarded, they were desperate to believe that the "American dream" of social and economic mobility through hard work was within their reach.

Sa-i-ku

What they experienced on 29 and 30 April was a baptism into what it really means for a Korean to "become American" in the 1990s. In South Korea, there is no 911, and no one really expects a fire engine or police car if there is trouble. Instead, people make arrangements with friends and family for emergencies. At the same time, guns are not part of Korean daily life. No civilian in South Korea can own a gun. Guns are the exclusive accoutrement of the military and police who enforce order for those who rule the society. When the Korean Americans in South Central and Koreatown dialed 911, nothing happened. When their stores and homes were being looted and burned to the ground, they were left completely alone for three horrifying days. How betrayed they must have felt by what they had believed was a democratic system that protects its people from violence. Those who trusted the government to protect them lost everything; those who took up arms after waiting for help for two days were able to defend themselves. It was as simple as that. What they had to learn was that, as in South Korea, protection in the U.S. is by and large for the rich and powerful. If there were a choice between Westwood and Koreatown, it is clear that Koreatown would have to be sacrificed. The familiar concept of privilege for the rich and powerful would have been easy for the Korean immigrant to grasp if only those exhortations about democracy and equality had not obfuscated the picture. Perhaps they should have relied even more on whatever they brought with them from Korea instead of fretting over trying to understand what was going on around them here. That Koreatown became a battleground does seem like the further playing out of a tragic legacy that has followed them across oceans and continents. The difference is that this was a battle between the poor and disenfranchised and the invisible rich, who were being protected by a layer of clearly visible Korean American human shields in a battle on the buffer zone.

This difference is crucial. Perhaps the legacy is not one carried across oceans and continents but one assumed immediately upon arrival, not the curse of being Korean but the initiation into becoming American, which requires that Korean Americans take on this country's legacy of five centuries of racial violence and inequality, of divide and rule, of privilege for the rich and oppression of the poor. Within this legacy, they have been assigned a place on the front lines. Silenced by those who possess the power to characterize and represent, they are permitted to speak only to reiterate their acceptance of this role.

Silencing the Korean American Voice

Twelve years ago, in Kwanju, South Korea, hundreds of civilians demonstrating for constitutional reform and free elections were murdered by U.S.-supported and -equipped South Korean elite paratroopers. Because I recorded it and played it over and over again, searching for a sign or a clue, I remember clearly how what were to me heartrendingly tragic events were represented in the U.S. news media. For a few fleeting moments, images of unruly crowds of alien-looking Asians shouting unintelligible words and phrases and wearing white headbands inscribed with unintelligible characters flickered across the screen. The Koreans were made to seem like insane people from another planet. The voice in the background stated simply that there were massive demonstrations but did not explain what the protests were about. Nor was a single Korean ever given an opportunity to speak to the camera.

The next news story was about demonstrations for democracy in Poland. The camera settled on individuals' faces which one by one filled the screen as each man or woman was asked to explain how he or she felt. Each Polish person's words were translated in a voice-over or subtitle. Solidarity leader Lech Walesa, who was allowed to speak often, was characterized as a heroic human being with whom all Americans could surely identify personally. Polish Americans from New York and Chicago to San Francisco, asked in man-on-the-street interviews about their reactions, described the canned hams and blankets they were sending to Warsaw.

This was for me a lesson in media representation, race, and power politics. It is a given that Americans are encouraged by our ideological apparatuses to side with our allies (here, the Polish resisters and the anti-communist South Korean government) against our enemies (here, the communist Soviet Union and protesters against the South Korean government). But visual-media racism helps craft and reinforce our identification with Europeans and whites while distancing us from fearsome and alien Asiatic hordes.

In March of last year, when two delegates from North Korea visited the Bay Area to participate in community-sponsored talks on Korean reunification, about 800 people from the Korean American community attended. The meeting was consummately newsworthy, since it was the first time in history that anyone from North Korea had ever been in California for more than 24 hours just passing through. The event was discussed for months in the Korean-language media—television, radio, and newspapers. Almost every Korean-speaking person in California knew about it. Although we sent press releases to all the commercial and public radio and television stations and to all the Bay Area newspapers, not a single mainstream media outfit covered the event. However, whenever there was an African American boycott of a Korean store or whenever conflict surfaced between Korean and African Americans, community leaders found a dozen microphones from all the main news media shoved into their faces, as if they were the president's press secretary making an official public pronouncement. Fascination with interethnic conflicts is rooted in the desire to excuse or minimize white racism by buttressing the mistaken notion that all human beings are "naturally" racist, and when Korean and African Americans allow themselves to be distracted by these interests, their attention is deflected from the social hierarchies that give racism its destructive power.

Without a doubt, the U.S. news media played a major role in exacerbating the damage and ill will toward Korean Americans, first by spotlighting tensions between African Americans and Koreans above all efforts to work together and as opposed to many other newsworthy events in these two communities, and second by exploiting racist stereotypes of Koreans as unfathomable aliens, this time wielding guns on rooftops and allegedly firing wildly into crowds. In news programs and on talk shows, African and Korean American tensions were discussed by blacks and whites, who pointed to these tensions as the main cause of the uprising. I heard some European Americans railing against rude and exploitative Korean merchants for ruining peaceful race relations for everyone else. Thus, Korean Americans were used to deflect attention from the racism they inherited and the economic injustice and poverty that had been already well woven into the fabric of American life, as evidenced by a judicial system that could allow not only the Korean store owner who killed Latasha Harlins but also the white men who killed Vincent Chin and the white police who beat Rodney King to go free, while Leonard Peltier still languishes in prison.

As far as I know, neither the commercial nor the public news media has mentioned the many Korean and African American attempts to improve relations, such as joint church services, joint musical performances and poetry readings, Korean merchant donations to African American community and youth programs, African American volunteer teachers in classes for Korean immigrants studying for citizenship examinations, or Korean translations of African American history materials.

While Korean immigrants were preoccupied with the mantra of day-to-day survival, Korean Americans had no voice, no political presence whatsoever in American life. When they became the targets of violence in Los Angeles, their opinions and views were hardly solicited except as they could be used in the already-constructed mainstream discourse on race relations, which is a sorry combination of blaming the African American and Latino victims for their poverty and scapegoating the Korean Americans as robotic aliens who have no "real" right to be here in the first place and therefore deserve whatever happens to them.

The *Newsweek* Experience

In this situation, I felt compelled to respond when an editor from the "My Turn" section of *Newsweek* magazine asked for a 1000-word personal essay. Hesitant because I was given only a day and a half to write the piece, not enough time in light of the vastness of American ignorance about Koreans and Korean Americans, I decided to do it because I thought I could not be made into a sound bite or a quote contextualized for someone else's agenda.

I wrote an essay accusing the news media of using Korean Americans and tensions between African and Korean Americans to divert attention from the roots of racial violence in the U.S. I asserted that these lie not in the Korean-immigrant-owned corner store situated in a community ravaged by poverty and police violence, but reach far back into the corridors of corporate and government offices in Los Angeles, Sacramento, and Washington, D.C. I suggested that Koreans and African Americans were kept ignorant about each other by educational and media institutions that erase or distort their experiences and perspectives. I tried to explain how racism had kept my parents from ever really becoming Americans, but that having been born here, I considered myself American and wanted to believe in the possibility of an American dream.

The editor of "My Turn" did everything he could to frame my words with his own viewpoint. He faxed his own introductory and concluding paragraphs that equated Korean merchants with cowboys in the Wild West and alluded to Korean/African American hatred. When I objected, he told me that my writing style was not crisp enough and that as an experienced journalist, he could help me out. My confidence wavered, but ultimately I rejected his editing. Then he accused me of being overly sensitive, confiding that I had no need to be defensive—because his wife was a Chinese American. Only after I had decided to withdraw the piece did he agree to accept it as I wrote it.

Before I could finish congratulating myself on being able to resist silencing and the kind of decontextualization I was trying to describe in the piece, I started receiving hate mail. Some of it was addressed directly to me, since I had been identified as a University of California faculty member, but most of it arrived in bundles, forwarded by *Newsweek*. Hundreds of letters came from all over the country, from Florida to Washington state and from Massachusetts to Arizona. I was unprepared for the hostility expressed in most of the letters. Some people sent the article, torn from the magazine and covered with angry, red-inked obscenities scratched across my picture. "You should see a good doctor," wrote someone from Southern California, "you have severe problems in thinking, reasoning, and adjusting to your environment."

A significant proportion of the writers, especially those who identified themselves as descendants of immigrants from Eastern Europe, wrote *Newsweek* that they were outraged, sickened, disgusted, appalled, annoyed, and angry at the magazine for providing an arena for the paranoid, absurd, hypocritical, racist, and childish views of a spoiled, ungrateful, whining, bitching, un-American bogus faculty member who should be fired or die when the next California earthquake dumps all of the "so-called people of color" into the Pacific Ocean.

I was shocked by the profound ignorance of many writers' assumptions about the experiences and perspectives of American people of color in general and Korean and other Asian Americans in particular. Even though my essay revealed that I was born in the U.S. and that my parents had lived in the U.S. for more than six decades, I was viewed as a foreigner without the right to say anything except words of gratitude and praise about America. The letters also provided some evidence of the dilemma Korean Americans are placed in by those who assume that we are aliens who should "go back" and at the same time berate us for not rejecting "Korean-American identity" for "American identity."

How many Americans migrate to Korea? If you are so disenchanted, Korea is still there. Why did you ever leave it? Sayonara.

Ms. Kim appears to have a personal axe to grind with this country that has given her so much freedom and opportunity. . . . I should suggest that she move to Korea, where her children will learn all they ever wanted about that country's history.

[Her] whining about the supposedly racist U.S. society is just a mask for her own acute inferiority complex. If she is so dissatisfied with the United States why doesn't she vote with her feet and leave? She can get the hell out and return to her beloved Korea—her tribal afinity [sic] where her true loyalty and consciousness lies [sic].

You refer to yourself as a Korean American and yet you have lived all your life in the United States . . . you write about racism in this country and yet you are the biggest racist by your own written words. If you cannot accept the fact that you are an American, maybe you should be living your life in Korea.

My stepfather and cousin risked their lives in the country where your father is buried to ensure the ideals of our country would remain. So don't expect to find a sympathetic ear for your pathetic whining.

Many of the letter writers assumed that my family had been the "scum" of Asia and that I was a college teacher only because of American justice and largesse. They were furious that I did not express gratitude for being saved from starvation in Asia and given the opportunity to flourish, no doubt beyond my wildest dreams, in America.

Where would she be if her parents had not migrated to the United States? For a professor at Berkeley University [sic] to say the American dream is only an empty promise is ludicrous. Shame, shame, shame on Elaine!

[Her father and his family] made enough money in the USA to ship his corpse home to Korea for burial. Ms. Kim herself no doubt has a guaranteed life income as a professor paid by California taxpayers. Wouldn't you think that she might say kind things about the USA instead of whining about racism?

At the same time some letters blamed me for expecting "freedom and opportunity":

It is wondrous that folks such as you find truth in your paranoia. No one ever promised anything to you or your parents.

Besides providing indications of how Korean Americans are regarded, the letters revealed a great deal about how American identity is thought of. One California woman explained that although her grandparents were Irish immigrants, she was not an Irish American, because "if you are not with us, you are against us." A Missouri woman did not seem to realize that she was conflating race and nationality and confusing "nonethnic" and "nonracial," by which she seems to have meant "white," with "American." And, although she insists that it is impossible to be both "black" and "American," she identifies herself at the outset as a "white American."

> I am a white American. I am proud to be an American. You cannot be black, white, Korean, Chinese, Mexican, German, French, or English or any other and still be an American. Of course the culture taught in schools is strictly American. That's where we are and if you choose to learn another [culture] you have the freedom to settle there. You cannot be a Korean American which assumes you are not ready to be an AMERICAN. Do you get my gist?

The suggestion that more should be taught in U.S. schools about America's many immigrant groups and people of color prompted many letters in defense of Western civilization against non-Western barbarism:

> You are dissatisfied with current school curricula that excludes Korea. Could it possibly be because Korea and Asia for that matter has [*sic*] not had . . . a noticeable impact on the shaping of Western culture, and Korea has had unfortunately little culture of its own?

> Who cares about Korea, Ms. Kim? . . . And what enduring contributions has the Black culture, both here in the US and on the continent contributed to the world, and mankind? I'm from a culture, Ms. Kim, who put a man on the moon 23 years ago, who established medical schools to train doctors to perform open heart surgery, and . . . who created a language of music so that musicians, from Beethoven to the Beatles, could easily touch the world with their brilliance forever and ever and ever. Perhaps the dominant culture, whites obviously, "swept aside Chicanos . . . Latinos . . . African-Americans . . . Koreans," because they haven't contributed anything that made—be mindful of the cliche—a world of difference?

> Koreans' favorite means of execution is decapitation . . . Ms. Kim, and others like her, came here to escape such injustice. Then they whine at riots to which they have contributed by their own fanning of flames of discontent. . . . Yes! Let us all study more about Oriental culture! Let us put matters into proper perspective.

> Fanatical multiculturalists like you expect a country whose dominant culture has been formed and influenced by Europe . . . , nearly 80% of her population consisting of persons whose ancestry is European, to include the history of every ethnic group who has ever lived here. I truly feel sorry for you. You and your bunch need to realize that white Americans are not racists. . . . We would love to get along, but not at the expense of our own culture and heritage.

> Kim's axe-to-grind confirms the utter futility of race-relations—the races were never meant to live together. We don't get along and never will. . . . Whats [*sic*] needed is to divide the United States up along racial lines so that life here can finally become livable.

What seemed to anger some people the most was their idea that, although they worked hard, people of color were seeking handouts and privileges because of their race, and the thought of an ungrateful Asian

American siding with African Americans, presumably against whites, was infuriating. How dare I "bite the hand that feeds" me by siding with the champion "whiners who cry 'racism'" because to do so is the last refuge of the "terminally incompetent"?

> The racial health in this country won't improve until minorities stop erecting "me first" barriers and strive to be Americans, not African-Americans or Asian-Americans expecting privileges.

> Ms. Kim wants preferential treatment that immigrants from Greece-to-Sweden have not enjoyed.... Even the Chinese ... have not created any special problems for themselves or other Americans. Soon those folk are going to express their own resentments to the insatiable demands of the Blacks and other colored peoples, including the wetbacks from Mexico who sneak into this country then pilfer it for all they can.

> The Afroderived citizens of Los Angeles and the Asiatic derivatives were not suffering a common imposition.... The Asiatics are trying to build their success. The Africans are sucking at the teats of entitlement.

As is usual with racists, most of the writers of these hate letters saw only themselves in their notions about Korea, America, Korean Americans, African Americans. They felt that their own sense of American identity was being threatened and that they were being blamed as individuals for U.S. racism. One man, adept at manipulating various fonts on his word processor, imposed his preconceptions on my words:

> Let me read between the lines of your little hate message:
>
> ..."The roots ... stretch far back into the corridors of corporate and government offices in Los Angeles, Sacramento, and Washington, D.C."
>
> All white America and all American institutions are to blame for racism.
>
> ..."I still want to believe the promise is real."
>
> I have the savvy to know that the American ideals of freedom and justice are a joke but if you want to give me what I want I'm willing to make concessions.
>
> Ms. Kim, ... if you want to embody the ignorant, the insecure, and the emotionally immature, that's your right! Just stop preaching hate and please, please, quit whining.
>
> > Sincerely, A proud White-American teaching
> > my children not to be prejudicial

Especially since my essay had been subdued and intensely personal, I had not anticipated the fury it would provoke. I never thought that readers would write over my words with their own. The very fact that I used words, and English words at that, particularly incensed some: one letter writer complained about my use of words and phrases like "manifestation" and "zero-sum game," and "suzerain relationship," which is the only way to describe Korea's relationship with China during the T'ang Dynasty. "Not more than ten people in the USA know what [these words] mean," he wrote. "You are on an ego trip." I wondered if it made him particularly angry that an Asian American had used those English words, or if he would make such a comment to George Will or Jane Bryant Quinn.

Clearly I have encountered part of America's legacy, the legacy that insists on silencing certain voices and erasing certain presences, even if it means deportation, internment, and outright murder. I should not have been surprised by what happened in Koreatown or by the ignorance and hatred expressed in the letters to *Newsweek,* any more than African Americans should have been surprised by the Rodney King verdict. Perhaps the news media, which constituted *sa-i-ku* as news, as an extraordinary event in no way continuous with our everyday lives, made us forget for a moment that as people of color many of us simultaneously inhabit two Americas: the America of our dreams and the America of our experience.

Who among us does not cling stubbornly to the America of our dreams, the promise of a multicultural democracy where our cultures and our differences might be affirmed instead of distorted in an effort to destroy us?

After *sa-i-ku,* I was able to catch glimpses of this America of my dreams because I received other letters that expressed another American legacy. Some people identified themselves as Norwegian or Irish Americans interested in combating racism. Significantly, while most of the angry mail had been sent not to me but to *Newsweek,* almost all of the sympathetic mail, particularly the letters from African Americans, came directly to me. Many came from Korean Americans who were glad that one of their number had found a vehicle for self-expression. Others were from Chinese and Japanese Americans who wrote that they had had similar experiences and feelings. Several were written in shaky longhand by women fervently wishing for peace and understanding among people of all races. A Native American from Nashville wrote a long description of cases of racism against African, Asian, and Native Americans in the U.S. criminal-justice system. A large number of letters came from African Americans, all of them supportive and sympathetic—from judges and professors who wanted better understanding between Africans and Koreans to poets and laborers who scribbled their notes in pencil while on breaks at work. One man identified himself as a Los Angeles African American whose uncle had married a Korean woman. He stated that as a black man in America, he knew what other people feel when they face injustice. He ended his letter apologizing for his spelling and grammar mistakes and asking for materials to read on Asian Americans. The most touching letter I received was written by a prison inmate who had served twelve years of a 35-to-70-year sentence for armed robbery during which no physical injuries occurred. He wrote:

I've been locked in these prisons going on 12 years now ... and since being here I have studied fully the struggles of not just blacks, but all people of color. I am a true believer of helping "your" people "first," but also the helping of all people no matter where there at or the color of there skin. But I must be truthful, my struggle and assistance is truly on the side of people of color like ourselves. But just a few years ago I didn't think like this.

I thought that if you wasn't black, then you was the enemy, but ... many years of this prison madness and much study and research changed all of this.... [I]t's not with each other, blacks against Koreans or Koreans against blacks. No, this is not what it's about. Our struggle(s) are truly one in the same. What happened in L.A. during the riot really hurt me, because it was no way that blacks was suppose to do the things to your people, my people (Koreans) that they did. You're my sister, our people are my people. Even though our culture may be somewhat different, and even though we may worship our God(s) different ... white-Amerikkka [doesn't] separate us. They look at us all the same. Either you're white, or you're wrong.... I'm just writing you to let you know that, you're my sister, your people's struggle are my people's struggle.

This is the ground I need to claim now for Korean American resistance and recovery, so that we can become American without dying of *han*.

Although the sentiments expressed in these letters seemed to break down roughly along racial lines—that is, all writers who were identifiably people of color wrote in support—and one might become alarmed at the depth of the divisions they imply, I like to think that I have experienced the desire of many Americans, especially Americans of color, to do as Rodney King pleaded on the second day of *sa-i-ku:* "We're all stuck here for awhile... . Let's try to work it out."

In my view, it's important for us to think about *all* of what Rodney King said and not just the words "we all can get along," which have been depoliticized and transformed into a Disneyesque catchphrase for Pat Boone songs and roadside billboards in Los Angeles. It seems to me the emphasis is on the being "stuck here for awhile" together as we await "our day in court."

Like the African American man who wrote from prison, the African American man who had been brutally beaten by white police might have felt the desire to "love everybody," but he had to amend—or rectify—that wish. He had to speak last about loving "people of color." The impulse to "love everybody" was there, but the conditions were not right. For now, the most practical and progressive agenda may be people of color trying to "work it out."

Finding Community through National Consciousness

The place where Korean and American legacies converge for Korean Americans is the exhortation to "go home to where you belong."

One of the letters I received was from a Korean American living in Chicago. He had read a translation of my essay in a Korean language newspaper. "Although you were born in the U.S.A.," he wrote, noticing what none of the white men who ordered me to go back to "my" country had, "your ethnical background and your complexion belong to Korea. It is time to give up your U.S. citizenship and go to Korea."

Some ruined merchants are claiming that they will pull up stakes and return to Korea, but I know that this is not possible for most of them. Even if their stores had not been destroyed, even if they were able to sell their businesses and take the proceeds to Korea, most of them would not have enough to buy a home or business there, since both require total cash up front. Neither would they be able to find work in the society they left behind because it is plagued by recession, repression, and fierce economic competition.

Going back to Korea. The dream of going back to Korea fed the spirit of my father, who came to Chicago in 1926 and lived in the United States for 63 years, during which time he never became a U.S. citizen, at first because the law did not allow it and later because he did not want to. He kept himself going by believing that he would return to Korea in triumph one day. Instead, he died in Oakland at 88. Only his remains returned to Korea, where we buried him in accordance with his wishes.

Hasn't the dream of going back home to where you belong sustained most of America's unwanted at one time or another, giving meaning to lives of toil and making it possible to endure other people's hatred and rejection? Isn't the attempt to find community through national consciousness natural for people refused an American identity because racism does not give them that choice?

Korean national consciousness, the resolve to resist and fight back when threatened with extermination, was all that could be called upon when the Korean Americans in Los Angeles found themselves abandoned. They joined together to guard each other's means of livelihood with guns, relying on Korean-language radio and newspapers to communicate with and help each other. On the third day after the outbreak of violence, more than 30,000 Korean Americans gathered for a peace march in downtown L.A. in what was perhaps the largest and most quickly organized mass mobilization in Asian American history. Musicians in white, the color of mourning, beat traditional Korean drums in sorrow, anger, and celebration of community, a call to arms like a collective heartbeat. I believe that the mother of Edward Song Lee, the Los Angeles–born college student mistaken for a looter and shot to death in the streets, has been able to persevere in great part because of the massive outpouring of sympathy expressed by the Korean-American community that shared and understood her *han*.

I have been critical lately of cultural nationalism as detrimental to Korean Americans, especially Korean American women, because it operates on exclusions and fosters intolerance and uniformity of thought while stifling self-criticism and encouraging sacrifice, even to the point of suicide. But *sa-i-ku* makes me think again: what remains for those who are left to stand alone? If Korean Americans refuse to be victims or political pawns in the U.S. while rejecting the exhortation that we go back to Korea where we belong, what will be our weapons of choice?

In the darkest days of Japanese colonial rule, even after being stripped of land and of all economic means of survival, Koreans were threatened with total erasure when the colonizers rewrote Korean history, outlawed the Korean language, forced the subjugated people to worship the Japanese emperor, and demanded that they adopt Japanese names. One of the results of these cultural-annihilation policies was Koreans' fierce insistence on the sanctity of Korean national identity that persists to this day. In this context, it is not difficult to understand why nationalism has been the main refuge of Koreans and Korean Americans.

While recognizing the potential dangers of nationalism as a weapon, I for one am not ready to respond to the antiessentialists' call to relinquish my Korean American identity. It is easy enough for the French and Germans to call for a common European identity and an end to nationalisms, but what of the peoples suppressed and submerged while France and Germany exercised their national prerogatives? I am mindful of the argument that the resurgence of nationalism in Europe is rooted in historical and contemporary political and economic inequality among the nations of Europe. Likewise, I have noticed that many white Americans do not like to think of themselves as belonging to a race, even while thinking of people of color almost exclusively in terms of race. In the same way, many men think of themselves as "human beings" and of women as the ones having a gender. Thus crime, small businesses, and all Korean-African American interactions are seen and interpreted through the lens of race in the same dominant culture that angrily rejects the use of the racial lens for viewing yellow/white or black/white interactions and insists suddenly that we are all "American" whenever we attempt to assert our identity as people of color. It is far easier for Anglo Americans to call for an end to cultural nationalisms than for Korean Americans to give up national consciousness, which makes it possible to survive the vicious racism that would deny our existence as either Korean Americans or Americans.

Is there anything of use to us in Korean nationalism? During one thousand years of Chinese suzerainty, the Korean ruling elite developed a philosophy called *sadaejui,* or reliance of the weak on the strong. In direct opposition to this way of thought is what is called *jaju* or *juche sasang,* or self-determination. Both *sadaejui* and *juche susang* are ways of dealing with unequal power relationships and resisting the transformation of one's homeland into a battlefield for others, but *sadaejui* has never worked any better for Koreans than it has for any minority group in America. *Juche sasang,* on the other hand, has the kind of oppositional potential needed in the struggle against silence and invisibility. From Korean national consciousness, we can recover this fierce refusal to accept subjugation, which is the first step in the effort to build community, so that we can work with others to challenge the forces that would have us annihilate each other instead of our mutual oppression.

What is clear is that we cannot "become American" without dying of *han* unless we think about community in new ways. Self-determination does not mean living alone. At least for now, that may mean mining the rich and haunted lode of Korean national consciousness while we struggle to understand how our fate is entwined with the fate of others lying prostrate before the triumphal procession of the winners of History. During the past fifteen years or so, many young Korean nationalists have been studying the legacies of colonialism and imperialism that they share with peoples in many Asian, African, and Latin American nations. At the same time that we take note of this work, we can also try to understand how nationalism and feminism can be worked together to demystify the limitations and reductiveness of each as a weapon of empowerment. If Korean national consciousness is ever to be such a weapon for us, we must use it to create a new kind of nationalism-in-internationalism to help us call forth a culture of survival and recovery, so that our *han* might be released and we might be freed to dream fiercely of different possibilities.

Discussion Questions

Content
1. What position does Kim suggest Korean Americans occupy in the American hierarchies of race and power?

2. What specific images or representations of Asian Americans can you think of from mainstream American media? How are those images related to the stereotypes of Asian people Kim describes?

3. Kim uses the letters she received to represent many different responses to her *Newsweek* article. Which of these responses is most powerfully important to understanding contemporary America, and why?

Form
1. What changes in tone and style accompany the shift from the first part of Kim's essay to the discussion of the *Newsweek* article and the letters written in response to it?

2. In the latter part of this essay, Kim quotes extensively from letters she received after publication of her *Newsweek* article. To what degree does her essay become a conversation of many voices in this section and to what degree does Kim's voice frame or control the other voices? Does her tone or style change in this section in order to frame more powerfully the other voices?

3. Kim's essay discusses the L.A. incident from at least three perspectives: that of the "rioters," that of the Korean immigrants, and that of the "audience" who witnessed parts of the incident through the media. What particular words or phrases bring these perspectives into her essay? What do those words or phrases show about Kim's perspective?

Writing Prompts

1. Write an essay that uses some of the quotations from Kim's essay to discuss how people make arguments in debates over public policies.

2. Think about the term *han*. Invent and define a term that could somehow capture an important feeling that is particularly applicable to your "people."

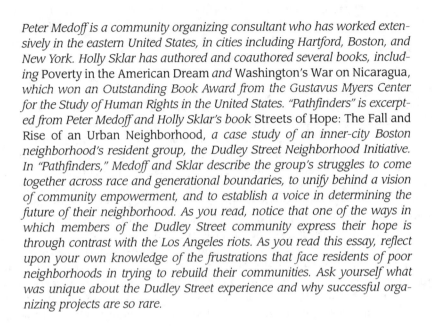

Peter Medoff is a community organizing consultant who has worked exten-
sively in the eastern United States, in cities including Hartford, Boston, and
New York. Holly Sklar has authored and coauthored several books, including Poverty in the American Dream *and* Washington's War on Nicaragua,
which won an Outstanding Book Award from the Gustavus Myers Center
for the Study of Human Rights in the United States. "Pathfinders" is excerpt-
ed from Peter Medoff and Holly Sklar's book Streets of Hope: The Fall and
Rise of an Urban Neighborhood, *a case study of an inner-city Boston*
neighborhood's resident group, the Dudley Street Neighborhood Initiative.
In "Pathfinders," Medoff and Sklar describe the group's struggles to come
together across race and generational boundaries, to unify behind a vision
of community empowerment, and to establish a voice in determining the
future of their neighborhood. As you read, notice that one of the ways in
which members of the Dudley Street community express their hope is
through contrast with the Los Angeles riots. As you read this essay, reflect
upon your own knowledge of the frustrations that face residents of poor
neighborhoods in trying to rebuild their communities. Ask yourself what
was unique about the Dudley Street experience and why successful orga-
nizing projects are so rare.

Pathfinders

Peter Medoff and Holly Sklar

IN APRIL 1992, dispossessed Los Angeles burned in rage. Embers of anger
and despair flared up the coast in San Francisco, Oakland and Seattle and
across the country in Las Vegas and Atlanta. A few weeks earlier, the Dudley
community had come together in celebration. L.A. exploded with the
crushed dreams of inner city America. Dudley surged with the power and
pride of dreams unfolding. As DSNI [Dudley Street Neighborhood Initiative]
President Ché Madyun put it in the 1992 DSNI annual report, "Hope is the
great ally of organizing."

Peter Medoff and Holly Sklar. "Pathfinders." In *Streets of Hope: The Fall and Rise of an Urban Neighborhood,* pp. 245–87, by Peter Medoff and Holly Sklar. Used with the permission of South End Press. South End Press is a nonprofit, collectively run book publisher committed to the politics of radical change.

The riots were a multiracial explosion of rage against past injustice and "a perception of a future already looted." South Central L.A. Congresswoman Maxine Waters told a Senate committee, "The verdict in the Rodney King case ... was only the most recent injustice piled upon many other injustices ... I have seen our community continually and systematically ravaged—ravaged by banks who would not lend to us, ravaged by governments which abandoned us or punished us for our poverty, and ravaged by big business who exported our jobs."

Waters quoted Robert Kennedy's words from 1968: "There is another kind of violence in America, slower but just as deadly, destructive as the shot or bomb in the night ... This is the violence of institutions; indifference and inaction and slow decay. This is the violence that afflicts the poor, that poisons relations between men and women because their skin is different colors. This is the slow destruction of a child by hunger, and schools without books and homes without heat in the winter." Waters added, "What a tragedy it is that America has still ... not learned such an important lesson."

As in South Central Los Angeles, the residents of Dudley have suffered exploitation and exclusion. Their community has been used as a dumping ground for the waste of wealthier neighborhoods and starved of jobs and government services. They saw downtown Boston undergo an economic boom while Dudley continued to go bust. They have borne the burden of redlining while their tax dollars are used to bail out Savings and Loan spendthrifts. They have endured cops with a colonial mentality.

"Riots are the voices of the unheard," said Martin Luther King. Dudley's pathfinders found a way to be heard. The city found a way to listen.

DSNI board member Stephen Hanley remarks, "The people in this community know even when there were good times [in Boston], they were shafted. So while things are bad right now, at least they're on the right track."

On April 3, 1992, over 800 people filled the historic Strand Theatre in Uphams Corner to celebrate DSNI's accomplishments and thank the outgoing executive director, Gus Newport. Youth leader John Barros drew the portrait of Newport that graced the program booklet. Newport's old friend, actor Danny Glover, was the master of ceremonies. Hundreds of Dudley residents were joined by community activists from other neighborhoods, funders, politicians, the mayor and various city officials, businesspeople and others of many different backgrounds committed to seeing Dudley's rebirth.

There was a short video history of Dudley and DSNI—part of a longer film in progress by Leah Mahan and Mark Lipman. The video clip of Gus Newport rapping with kids from Dudley's Young Architects and Planners— Heavy G and the Young APs—brought the house down. Everyone shared a multiethnic meal prepared by Dudley residents and enjoyed performances by local dancers, actors, singers and musicians—among them Ché Madyun, who performed an original solo dance, and DSNI Director Paul Yelder in his persona of blues singer Luap Redley. Newell Flather presented Newport with a framed piece of the Riley Foundation's rug, which Newport had frequently trod. It was a symbolic bridge between Dudley's past—the disinvestment represented by the old worn rug at La Alianza Hispana—and the more constructive, contemporary relationship between Dudley and downtown.

When Boston city official Lisa Chapnick was asked if she had thought of DSNI at the time of the L.A. riots, she responded quickly, "I certainly did. I said, 'If there were more DSNIs, L.A. wouldn't have happened.'" Chapnick continues, "I think DSNI is the future of our country. I think the challenge is, how do you replicate it? . . . How do you find residents who have hope and heart when they should be bitter?" The riot, she says, "was a wake-up call that's long overdue. Of course, it looks like nothing is going to happen with it."

The embers of disrespect, discrimination and disinvestment still smolder in cities around the country. Rebuild L.A., launched after the riots with much fanfare and promises of inclusion and "greenlining," has not delivered in process or product. Rebuild L.A.'s first director, Peter Ueberroth—impresario of the commercialized 1984 Olympics and chairman of the California Council on Competitiveness, which advocated rolling back environmental and land use regulations—represented "corporatism dressed up in the language of cooperation," says Eric Mann, director of the Labor/Community Strategy Center in Los Angeles. Power on the Rebuild L.A. (R.L.A.) board "is firmly in the hands of representatives of Arco, I.B.M., Warner Brothers, Southern California Edison, U.S.C., Disney and the Chamber of Commerce."

In July 1992, says Mann, Ueberroth cheered when General Motors announced that it would channel $15 million in contracts from its Hughes Aircraft subsidiary to inner-city suppliers. The move, which would generate a few hundred jobs at most, was hyped by R.L.A. as corporate benevolence in action. One month later G.M. shut down the Van Nuys automobile assembly plant, its last in L.A., eliminating 3,000 workers, about two-thirds of whom are Latino and black." At a job training conference sponsored by Toyota and the Urban League in fall 1992, "Ueberroth hailed *minimum*-wage jobs as bringing 'dignity to those who labor in them.' Workers from Justice for Janitors, a campaign of the Service Employees International Union, marched on R.L.A. shortly after to tell him that for hundreds of thousands of Angelenos who already have full-time jobs, the minimum wage means living below the federal poverty line, usually without health insurance or job security."

"'Nothing, nothing at all has been learned from the riots,' says María Elena Durazo, leader of the mostly Latino Hotel and Restaurant Employees Local 11. . . . Since the riots the business community has been pushing the city and the state to roll back environmental, tax, and workers' compensation regulations. What it means is that they want to squeeze even more out of a vulnerable work force.' Durazo adds, 'Don't they see they are creating more of the very same conditions that led to the riots?'"

In the words of author Mike Davis, California "Governor Wilson and the state legislature in Sacramento figuratively burned down the city a second time with billions of dollars of school and public-sector cutbacks." Legislators ignored "a report on the state's children that showed youth unemployment and homicide rates soaring in tandem."

In January 1994, on the day the nation celebrates Martin Luther King's birthday, Los Angeles shook and burned from the force of a catastrophic earthquake. Angelenos must now rebuild from riots sparked by repression and economic depression, nature's earthquake and the fires in between. Pacific News Service editor Rubén Martínez contemplated how, in the Latino immigrant *barrios*, the solidarity Angelenos showed each other in responding to the earthquake "is the survival mechanism of daily life." Martínez looked beyond one of the poignant events shown widely on television: the rescue of Salvador Peña, an immigrant from El Salvador, from "the pancaked parking lot of the Northridge Fashion Mall" where he was driving a street sweeper. "An army of hundreds of thousands of Salvador Peñas toils from dusk to dawn in L.A., cleaning office buildings, preparing meals for the white collars. They do so because without work there is no future, and without a future there is no hope."

"Yes, this rescue assured us, good will can guide us through tragedy," Martínez observes. But the economic, racial and ethnic fault lines that divide Angelenos remain. Looking to the future, the question is, will Los Angeles rebuild together—or apart and volatile? That's a question many others around the country can ask of their communities and their nation.

"Together, We'll Find the Way"

While he was directing Rebuild L.A., Peter Ueberroth said that many businesses gutted in the riot were "not of any great, huge value." He said that local activists demanding a faster flow of money should "get out of the way."

In Dudley, residents successfully got "in the way" of both a city redevelopment plan that threatened to displace them and an agency/funder-driven coalition to rebuild the neighborhood. Dudley residents got in the way—and created a new way forward. As DSNI board member Paul Bothwell affirms, "Together, we'll find the way."

Bothwell offers three lessons he finds true to Dudley as it rebuilds. . . . First, "the heart is far more important than the head. Lots of efforts are head efforts. Lots of things have money and expertise, they have this and that and everything else, but they don't have any heart. Anybody on the street can read that. If there isn't a heart to it then the head doesn't even matter."

Second, says Bothwell, "being is really more important than doing. What something *is* is more important even than what it can do. What you are or what I am—what's going on in the nature of heart, spirit, personhood and all that—that, in the end, is all we have. In the end . . . if we're crippled and broken by accident or anything else, what does that mean? That you're not worth something anymore? There's nothing here anymore? Of course not. Being is far more important than doing." Bothwell adds, "People don't trust DSNI just because it can do something. That's a big factor—because nobody else has been able to do anything. [But] I think people trust DSNI . . . because of what it is . . . People see themselves reflected here."

Third, says Bothwell, "doing together, living together is far more important than doing alone. I think that reflects that proverb I gave earlier: 'Together, we'll find the way.' You try to do that alone—we're all so broken, we're all so crippled, we're all so fragile, we're all so partial, and I'm talking about organizations as well as people and communities. You try to do it alone, it's not going to go anywhere."

Bothwell's lessons speak directly to DSNI's essence. The heart is more important than the head: DSNI's efforts are not guided by professional "experts" or leaders with swelled heads. Rather, DSNI is guided by those at the heart of the neighborhood—the residents—who are, in turn, guided by their hearts, hopes, dreams, knowledge and experiences. Being is more important than doing: DSNI emphasizes process before product, knowing that in the long run the products will be more and better if the process is empowering. DSNI's way of being is rooted in diversity and unity, self-esteem and community pride. Doing together is more important than doing alone: Dudley residents have shown that together they are powerful visionaries and together they can make their vision and plans for the neighborhood more real every day. . . .

Building on Neighborhood Assets

Community development must begin by recognizing and reinforcing the resources *within* the community. DSNI assumes and demonstrates that people in low-income neighborhoods—like people in all neighborhoods—have solutions as well as problems. Like people of every income level, they have individual and community assets—a mix of skills, talents, knowledge, experience and resources—that are vital elements of the redevelopment process.

As John McKnight, director of the Center for Urban Affairs and Policy Research at Northwestern University, puts it, "No community is built with a focus on deficiencies and needs. Every community, forever in the past and forever in the future, will be built on the capacities and gifts of the people who live there."

Andrea Nagel, who first served DSNI as an organizer and later as Human Development director, underscores the capacity-building approach. DSNI, she says, is continually "exposing, strengthening and building upon the gifts that this neighborhood has—its people, its vacant land, its businesses . . . The glass is half full to us, you know. We make an effort to look through the positive lens—understanding, not denying the reality, not minimizing or understating what hardships and difficult realities that people face in this neighborhood. But never, ever losing sight of what is often written off and completely overlooked, and that is its people and resources."

Low-income neighborhoods are often viewed as dependent receivers of services and dollars—ignoring the vast resources they export in the form of taxes; underpaid labor; bank savings invested in communities that have not been redlined; exorbitant interest and insurance payments; work and purchases at businesses located outside the neighborhood; volunteering in and donating to nonprofit, religious and civic organizations; and so on.

Government, private foundations and human service agencies often demean low-income residents, viewing them as incapable, culpable, "at risk," dependent clients—clients they treat as second-class citizens or worse. Many policymakers, funders and human service "providers" have fostered atomized communities that no longer recognize their own assets, their own vision, their own power. They are, in McKnight's words, "dominated by systems that have institutionalized degraded visions for devalued people."

Many human service agencies felt threatened by DSNI's resident-controlled agenda. McKnight predicts that this conflict will always arise: "Service systems act on the premise that the professional has the expertise and the client has the problem. The problem solving power of the people in the neighborhoods is unimportant. That professional idea is exactly the opposite of what community organizing attempts to do. The organizer tells the people that they have problem solving abilities and they can change their communities."

DSNI has worked hard to build an Agency Collaborative to strengthen agency accountability to residents, minimize competition, maximize cooperation and improve human development resources and policies. Funders, as emphasized later, can play an important role by encouraging collaboration and respecting the priorities of a resident-driven collaborative process—priorities which may well differ from funders' preconceived ideas.

The community of residents as a whole brings invaluable assets to the redevelopment process. Residents have experienced the history of the neighborhood. They have been the ones to stay and struggle as the neighborhood was being disinvested in, or made a new stake where others would not. Only residents working together can create a self-determined vision of the neighborhood's future. Only residents can foster the political will necessary to make the vision a reality. After years of being disrespected, dismissed and discriminated against, residents may not always realize they have these capacities. Through organizing together, they reveal and reinforce their individual and collective assets.

In the words of DSNI activist Najwa Abdul-Tawwab, what's "key about DSNI is the word 'initiative.' It works to help people initiate."

Creating Vision and Political Will

Reflecting on the period before DSNI's formation, Paul Bothwell says, "What continued to break my heart, as well as mobilize this terrific fire inside me personally and others," was that neighborhood decline "is not something that happens in communities by itself . . . it's not something that's just sheer chance. It's not because people here are stupid . . . This is the result of city policy, of other kinds of large-scale things that systematically cripple or dismember a community. Nobody who can do anything about it really cares. Everybody who is here, who really to a great degree can't do anything about it, cares." DSNI's challenge was to translate caring into control.

Creating a vision begins by building up expectations and stoking a constructive "fire inside." As Bill Slotnik puts it, "First, the people have to care about the neighborhood in which they live, and I think that exists in most neighborhoods. Second, they've got to have a feeling that things aren't going to get better unless we get involved. Third, there has to be a sense of confidence that something can come together that will make a difference."

Most bureaucrats, whether in public or private agencies, will advise keeping expectations low. If expectations aren't fulfilled, they claim, people will become disappointed and lose interest in staying involved. This approach fosters dependency and passivity. Higher expectations enable a community to Think Big—the kind of thinking not only needed to create a comprehensive vision, but needed to make it real. By thinking big and acting powerful, a neighborhood can create the political will and attract the attention and resources it needs to translate vision into reality.

"If you want to separate yourself from the traditional, you have to do something nontraditional," city official Lisa Chapnick observes. "If you want to create that flash point, that special moment, that special relationship, you've got to have a component that's unique and big and risky." A bureaucracy doesn't respond well to risky ventures, but good leaders do. And that is why DSNI held to the motto of "going to the top." Time and again, DSNI members learned that when bureaucracy ground to a halt, political leadership could quickly get it moving again. All that was necessary was for the leader to possess the political will. And that political will is created back in the neighborhood.

A unified, visionary community can create political will where there was none before and make government a partner rather than an obstacle or adversary. Comprehensive redevelopment requires significant resources from outside the neighborhood as well as inside it—resources people rightfully deserve, but which are often distributed unfairly.

Government policymakers often point to resource limitations to rationalize why they cannot meet citizen demands. Nonprofit service agencies too often conform, however unhappily, to government's top-down limitations on what is possible. Yet, lack of resources does not limit the most costly policies seen as necessary by those in power—such as the Gulf War and the Savings and Loan bailout. The problem is *not,* as often stated, "having more will than wallet." Rather, lack of political will limits what is possible. Communities must build enough power to make government truly representative and hold politicians and officials accountable.

In a community-controlled planning process neighborhood residents are organized to provide the vision, define the priorities and plans, and participate in the implementation. As Andrea Nagel emphasizes, residents also have the best understanding of what has *not* worked in their neighborhood.

Professional staff and consultants must see themselves as working for the residents. The notion that creating a successful plan relies more on organizing capacity than on technical skills flies directly against traditional, elitist views of planning. DSNI's choice of a firm like DAC, committed to DSNI's view of comprehensive community revitalization and a resident-driven process, was crucial. DAC differentiated itself from traditional planners in its original proposal: "The principles of planning for lower-income people and their communities are the same as those on behalf of the rich. Technicians are to be hired to serve the goals and objectives set by their employers ... When it comes to low-income residents, however, the rules tend to be reversed. 'The experts' seem intent on confusing their community clients with complex terms and coded jargon with the principal message of 'let the professionals handle it, because only they understand the process.'"

Organizing produces the political will necessary for the vision's adoption and successful implementation. While the content of the plan that DSNI created with DAC was technically sound, many technically solid plans are not implemented because they lack the necessary support inside and outside the neighborhood. DSNI successfully built a consensus around development that no politician or government official wanted to challenge. When Mayor Flynn announced his support for the plan, few people believed he had ever read the document. What led politicians and others to support the plan was not so much the details of its contents, but rather, its political power derived from an organizing process that assured inclusion of all segments of the Dudley community.

Comprehensive Community Revitalization

The Dudley Street Neighborhood Initiative has fostered an alternative, holistic approach to community development. While recognizing the importance of affordable housing and other physical development, DSNI sees that development as part of a much larger, dynamic process of community renewal led by neighborhood residents. In DSNI's view, a revitalized community is neighborly at heart, healthy in body and spirit, and socially, economically and culturally vibrant.

DSNI's successful methodology was to begin with organizing, create the long-term vision for the community and then assure the vision's implementation. Over the years, DSNI's capacity for comprehensive human, economic, physical and environmental development has grown stronger. It has had different priorities at different times—variously combining planning, organizing and implementation and variously addressing immediate and long-term goals. After its formation in 1984, DSNI was restructured in 1985 to reflect resident control and elected its first board. DSNI hired its first staff in early 1986. The 1986 priority was organizing—developing and expanding the membership base and strengthening board leadership; undertaking the "Don't Dump On Us" campaign; strengthening new and existing neighborhood associations; putting on the first multicultural festival; and restoring the commuter rail stop. In 1987, while organizing continued in full force—including the successful campaign to close down the trash transfer stations—DSNI's priorities expanded to include creating the comprehensive master plan for development and having the city adopt it. In 1988, the priorities expanded further to include implementation of the plan—gaining land control through eminent domain and winning a grant for the town common. DSNI also closed two largely vacant streets where dumping was still a terrible problem.

In 1989–90, DSNI emphasized "We Build Houses and People Too," pursuing major human development and organizing efforts such as Dudley's Young Architects and Planners; focus groups; the Agency Collaborative; tenant organizing; developing the Community Land Trust; completing and financing the build-out plan for the Dudley Triangle; choosing housing developers; and cofounding the antiredlining Community Investment Coalition. DSNI's 1991 priorities were reclaiming the local park through Community Summerfest, with its extensive youth programs; forming a Youth Committee; and launching the Dudley PRIDE campaign, stressing community esteem and initiative, public health and safety, and neighborhood greening; as well as strengthening child care and starting the Dudley Housing List.

In 1992, Dudley PRIDE was a continuing priority as DSNI began homebuyer classes to ensure access to the new housing and stepped up planning around economic development—the area that had lagged. The 1993 priorities were the groundbreaking and construction of DSNI's first new homes; economic development, as highlighted by the first economic summit; completing a Human Development Framework and Declaration of Community Rights; community design of the town common; organizing in broad coalition against a hazardous asphalt plant; pursuing joint planning with other agencies around existing and future community facilities; and continuing Dudley PRIDE.

At this writing, DSNI's 1994 priorities are completing an economic development plan and pursuing short- and long-term economic development projects; completing phase one construction in the Triangle and welcoming the new homeowners as members of the Community Land Trust; completing design and starting construction of the town common; finalizing plans and financing DSNI's community center while maximizing use of existing area facilities; carrying forward Dudley PRIDE; launching a major focus on education, from preschool to adult education; and organizing a major event celebrating DSNI's tenth anniversary.

In addition to everything above, the annual meeting, periodic community-wide meetings, neighborhood cleanups and multicultural festivals are major regular events. DSNI staff also respond to immediate resident concerns, whether by connecting residents to the proper public or private agencies (and following up as needed) or becoming directly involved in resolving problems such as specific incidents of illegal dumping, the unwarranted arrest of neighborhood youth or dangerous conditions (e.g., lack of winter heat) in apartments owned by unscrupulous landlords.

As this brief review highlights, DSNI has strengthened its commitment to comprehensive community revitalization.

Community

We're learning how to be a better community together," says DSNI's Sue Beaton. "But whether we look perfect at the end is really not, to me, the issue. It's how many people have participated along the way, who gets the benefits of whatever we can accomplish together, and how do we hang together and not get co-opted in the process of doing whatever we're doing." She adds, "I would like us to be a community of integrity."

Clayton Turnbull observes, "This community, along with Black people in America [generally, have long felt] like they rent their community. They don't feel like they own it even when they own a house ... Subconsciously or consciously, they don't feel like they own it." Turnbull points to the L.A. riots: "People say, 'Why do all these people burn down their own communities?' It wasn't their community! They didn't own the stores! They didn't work in them! They didn't own the houses! ... So, why do you call it 'your community'? Because you geographically, residentially live there? That's not what 'your community' means."

"DSNI has changed that attitude with the process, with the Community Land Trust and so on," says Turnbull. "People now say ... 'I own it' [and 'We own it.'] ... That's why I say to people, 'Urban America has to now set policies for politicians to come in and follow.'" That's what DSNI did, says Turnbull. "We set the policies."

The Dudley community has spent almost a decade renewing their dreams, their lives and their neighborhood. They found a way to forge a united vision of the future and institutionalize resident control. They have had many victories over the years. Yet, they have much more work ahead. Ultimately, what distinguishes the residents of Dudley is not their ability to stop dumping or create a comprehensive redevelopment plan for the neighborhood or get eminent domain or attract millions of dollars in resources into the neighborhood. What distinguishes Dudley residents from many other communities is this: They found a way to dream together and not allow their dreams—to borrow from Langston Hughes—to be deferred, to dry up like a raisin in the sun, or explode. Together, they found a way.

As stated in the preamble to DSNI's Declaration of Community Rights: "We—the youth, adults, seniors of African, Latin American, Caribbean, Native American, Asian and European ancestry—are the Dudley community. Nine years ago, we were Boston's dumping ground and forgotten neighborhood. Today, we are on the rise! We are reclaiming our dignity, rebuilding housing and reknitting the fabric of our communities. Tomorrow, we realize our vision of a vibrant, culturally diverse neighborhood, where everyone is valued for their talents and contributions to the larger community."

Dudley residents have a long way to go, but they have come a long way, and the journey itself has been rewarding. They have learned from others' experiences, and they hope others can learn from theirs. For ultimately, we as a nation must find a way to progress together—with diversity, not divisiveness—lest our children inherit a world even more impoverished and dangerous than today's. A world of chaos, not community. DSNI's local alternative of multiracial, mutual progress and holistic community development is no less relevant nationally. It is an alternative vision in which no one is disposable. Together, we must find a way.

Discussion Questions

Content

1. According to the authors, what similarities do the Dudley Street neighborhood and South Central Los Angeles share? How do the authors explain the most important difference between these two neighborhoods?

2. What is involved in comprehensive community development? Why do you think it is so difficult to achieve?

3. What role can you see yourself playing in a project like DSNI?

Form

1. Who "speaks" in this essay? Are any voices left out? What contributions could those voices have made to the essay?

2. How do the authors attempt to persuade readers that DSNI was and is successful? Are you convinced? Why or why not?

3. How does the beginning of the essay, an extended comparison of Dudley Street and South Central Los Angeles, prepare us to interpret the potential role of DSNI-type projects in United States cities?

Writing Prompts

1. Write an essay describing an experience with community involvement that you've had (organizing effort, block party, responding to a neighborhood crisis such as a car accident or a house fire). How did the experience make you feel about the power of community? How do you feel now?

2. The authors discuss the role of hope in efforts to improve the quality of our lives. Write an essay in which you discuss what you believe this hope is for.

PART 6 DISCUSSION QUESTIONS

1. Each of the authors in this part has ideas about what we can do in the wake of the Los Angeles violence to prevent violent uprisings in the future. What do these authors' ideas have in common? What are their differences? Do you think that the ideas they have in common address the fundamental issues? Why or why not?

2. The various authors in this part call the response to the Rodney King verdict an "uprising," a "riot," "looting," an "upheaval," and a "class rebellion." How well do you think each of the terms describes what happened? Why do the different authors use such different terms to characterize the same event? Which word would you use to characterize the events in Los Angeles? Why would you choose that particular word?

3. Several of the authors in this part describe the incident in Los Angeles as evidence of inner-city "misbehavior." Others describe the Los Angeles incident as the consequence of long-standing policies concerning inner cities and inner-city residents. Drawing from your own experiences, which of these positions do you support? Can you find ways to support the other position?

4. Medoff and Sklar use the Los Angeles uprising as an example of what can happen when cities are neglected. Is the Los Angeles uprising symbolic and representative of all that is wrong with urban America today? How might a city's character or its geography influence events in that particular city? In what ways is or is not the uprising representative of the problems that face your city? Why do you think this is so?

5. What do you think qualifies the authors in this part to discuss the Los Angeles uprising and to offer solutions? Who do you think has the right to discuss important political and social events and their possible solutions? Who has the responsibility to do so? What happens when people from different geographical locations and different backgrounds attempt to solve others' problems?

PART 6 WRITING ASSIGNMENTS

1. Write a personal essay describing in detail how your family reacted to the Los Angeles uprising. Include some especially memorable statements that members of your family made. Discuss what aspects of the uprising your family agreed upon and what it disagreed about.

2. Write an essay that attempts to persuade a specific group of people to reconsider their beliefs about urban violence.

3. Use an essay from another part of this book to explain what you think is the fundamental issue raised by the Los Angeles uprising.

4. Write an essay that tries to understand why people of different races, social classes, and occupations can all consider themselves to be good, kind, and honest people and yet still have very different ideas about who is to blame for urban violence.

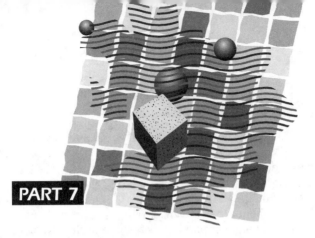

Urban Styles

OUT OF THE SOCIAL PAINS of industrialization, its spiritual and material deprivations, a consumer culture was born. In its imagery and ideology were powerful appeals from hitherto denied realms of leisure, beauty, and pleasure. Mail-order catalogs and department stores were prime examples in an array of institutions that provided vehicles for this new way of seeing. In exchange for adopting a consumerized understanding of survival, people could hope to enjoy aesthetic pleasures traditionally the province of the very rich or even unimaginable in times past. This enrichment was not proffered as a quantitative change, however. In order for people to enjoy the pleasures of the new order they had to abandon many old expectations. Simon Patten, one of the most important and outspoken apostles of industrial consumerism, argued in 1892 that the leap from "scarcity" to "abundance" demanded a break with the past. The universe of nature would be transcended by one of artifice; the old, familiar world would recede; a new one would take its place: "It is the reduction of old pleasures that forces the consumer to resort to new pleasures to make up for the loss of old ones.". . .

The politics of consumption must be understood as something more than what to buy, or even what to boycott. Consumption is a social relationship, the dominant relationship in our society—one that makes it harder and harder for people to hold together, to create community. At a time when for many of us the possibility of meaningful change seems to elude our grasp, it is a question of immense social and political proportions. To establish popular initiative, consumerism must be transcended—a difficult but central task facing all people who still seek a better way of life.

—*Stuart Ewen*

ON THE DAY before Memorial Day, 1983, a poet called me to describe a city he had just visited. He said that one section included mosques, built by the Islamic people who dwelled there. Attending his reading, he said, were large numbers of Hispanic people, forty thousand of whom lived in the same city. He was not talking about a fabled city located in some mysterious region of the world. The city he'd visited was Detroit.

A few months before, as I was leaving Houston, Texas, I heard it announced on the radio that Texas's largest minority was Mexican-American, and though a foundation recently issued a report critical of bilingual education, the taped voice used to guide the passengers on the air trams connecting terminals in Dallas Airport is in both Spanish and English. If the trend continues, a day will come when it will be difficult to travel through some sections of the country without hearing commands in both English and Spanish; after all, for some western states, Spanish was the first written language and the Spanish style lives on in the western way of life.

Shortly after my Texas trip, I sat in an auditorium located on the campus of the University of Wisconsin at Milwaukee as a Yale professor—whose original work on the influence of African cultures upon those of the Americas has led to his ostracism from some monocultural intellectual circles—walked up and down the aisle, like an old-time southern evangelist, dancing and drumming the top of the lectern, illustrating his points before some serious Afro-American intellectuals and artists who cheered and applauded his performance and his mastery of information. The professor was "white." After his lecture, he joined a group of Milwaukeeans in a conversation. All of the participants spoke Yoruban, though only the professor had ever traveled to Africa.

One of the artists told me that his paintings, which included African and Afro-American mythological symbols and imagery were hanging in the local McDonald's restaurant. The next day I went to McDonald's and snapped pictures of smiling youngsters eating hamburgers below paintings that could grace the walls of any of the country's leading museums. The manager of the local McDonald's said, "I don't know what you boys are doing, but I like it," as he commissioned the local painters to exhibit in his restaurant.

Such blurring of cultural styles occurs in everyday life in the United States to a greater extent than anyone can imagine and is probably more prevalent than the sensational conflict between people of different backgrounds that is played up and often encouraged by the media.

—*Ishmael Reed*

THE LOGO serves largely to position the audience within a combination of realism and amusement. Public truths revealed in Benetton's images, regardless of how horrifying or threatening, are offered, according to Dick Hebdige, "as a kind of joke in which the reader is invited to participate (the 'joke' is how low can we go?), but its potential dangers are also pretty clear: today aliens from Mars kidnap joggers, yesterday Auschwitz didn't happen, tomorrow who cares what happens?" Of course, the "joke" here is that anything is for sale and social commitment is just another gimmick for selling goods. In this type of representational politics, critical engagement is rendered ineffective by turning the photo and its political referent into an advertisement. If the possibility of social criticism is suggested by the ad, it is quickly dispelled by the insertion of the logo, which suggests that any complicity between the viewer and the event it depicts is merely ironic. The image ultimately references nothing more than a safe space where the logic of the commodity and the marketplace mobilize consumers' desires rather than struggle over social injustices and conflicts. In the case of the AIDS ad, the use of the Benetton logo juxtaposes human suffering and promotional culture so as to invite the viewer to position him- or herself between the playfulness of commodification and an image of apocalypse rendering social change either ironic or unimaginable. This serves less to situate a critical viewer who can mediate social reality and its attendant problems than to subordinate the viewer to the demands and aesthetic of commerce. One consequence of such a position has been captured by Stuart Ewen: "By reducing all social issues to matters of perception, it is on the perceptual level that social issues are addressed. Instead of social change, there is image change. Brief shows of flexibility at the surface mask intransigence at the core."

The politics at work in the Benetton photographs is also strikingly revealed in the use of photojournalistic images that are decontextualized from any meaningful historical and social setting and then recontextualized through the addition of the United Colors of Benetton logo. In the latter movement, the logo produces a representational "zone of comfort" confirming a playfulness which allows the viewer to displace any ethical or political understanding of the images contained in the Benetton ads.

—Henry Giroux

INTRODUCTION

We all use the term *style* and we all have a sense of what it means. But what is style? Although style may be seen in how people act, how they talk, and how they treat other people, it is most often thought of as external, a characteristic of how people or things look. Thus, individual people communicate through everything we see: through their clothes, jewelry, vehicle, choice of music, and choice of places in which to live or frequently spend their time. People use these styles to communicate information about themselves to other people around them. The styles that we use to identify ourselves can create an aura of individuality about us. They can also demonstrate that we are part of an ethnic or cultural group that shares that style—whether that group be Orthodox Jews, Latinos, bikers, or hip-hop music followers.

For many reasons, the majority of American styles are urban, or at least urban in origin. Cities and their suburbs are now home to the vast majority of Americans; urban areas are the economic, technological, and mass media centers of our nation. Information about how we should look and live, and about the latest products and trends, originates in these urban centers and is communicated throughout the culture more quickly and broadly than ever before. Also, the very conditions of city living, with people of various ethnic, subcultural, and socioeconomic backgrounds living in close proximity and daily crossing one another's paths, lend themselves to ways of identifying others through visual cues, such as their clothing, their cars, and the places they go frequently.

The essays in this part examine the relationships between cities and style and between individualism and group identity. They do this from a variety of perspectives and through the discussion of assorted styles. In Stuart Ewen's essay "First Impressions," he explains the history behind Americans' expression of individuality through clothing. He says that immigrants to U.S. cities in the late nineteenth and early twentieth centuries sought to lose their ethnic identities and gain instead the identities of individuality and "Americanness." They did this, in part, through careful attention to the messages given off by their choice of clothing.

E. Jean Carroll takes up the issues of race, group identity, and urban origins of style in a somewhat different manner. In her essay "The Return of the White Negro," she examines the issues involved in "racial incidents" at a nearly all-white high school in rural Indiana. At this high school, a small group of teens dress in the hip-hop fashions created by and associated with urban African American youth. Her article, through the use of sarcasm, conveys the issues at play in these incidents: whether some styles can be said to belong to certain groups, what it means to be rural, whether rural people can create styles to call their own, and whether style is really something important.

In "Punks in LA: It's Kiss or Kill," which originally appeared in *Journal of Popular Culture,* Jon Lewis offers a descriptive look at the various forms of expression that punk used to define itself during its brief existence as a youth subculture in Los Angeles. Charles Gandee, in "Off the Street . . . and Into the Future," looks at the relationship between cities and high fashions in the 1990s. Gandee demonstrates that many high fashions are derived from clothing that is worn on urban streets by youth of different races and various subcultures. Gandee's article suggests that the wealthy and the mainstream are now attempting to wear the styles of the streets, in comparison to the minorities and subculture members of one hundred years ago, who, according to Ewen, tried their hardest to look like the mainstream and the wealthy. Katherine Betts, in her arti-cle "Body Language," looks at what happens when mainstream urban people wear fashions—in this case body piercing and tattooing—created by and associ-ated with subcultures. Betts discusses how body piercing has moved beyond New York and San Fran-cisco gay culture and tattooing has moved out of biker culture, and how both have become popular with the mainstream as expressions of individuality and rebelliousness.

Two of the articles deal with expressions of style through vehicles. "Deep Clean," by Edward Zuckerman, examines the car wash industry in Los Angeles, a city in which people spend large amounts of time in their cars. Car washes in Los Angeles have developed into a high art called "detailing," which is high-priced, extremely thorough car washing. Los Angeles residents across the socio-economic spectrum, indulge in detailing and overall are very concerned with their cars' appearance. Zuckerman suggests that detailing confers stylishness not only on the cars, but on the car owners themselves, who are seen not only as having very clean cars, but as having the kind of prestigious style that comes with having spent a lot of money on something—and having people know they did. Similarly, in "Low Riders, High Stylers," Scott Martin discusses the low-rider bicycles favored by urban Latino and other youth in Los Angeles, Chicago, and elsewhere. Martin draws comparisons between the low-rider bicycles and simi-lar bicycles popular in the 1960s and 1970s and the low-riding cars that have been popular among Latinos since the late 1940s. He suggests the sense of both individual and cultural pride the youths feel when they are seen with their bicy-cles, which they spend many hours customizing.

Americans can also gain style from the places they frequent. In "Jiving with Java," Michel Marriott describes the current popularity of coffeehouses. He theo-rizes that coffeehouses have become popular partly because they offer an alternative to the alcohol, cigarettes, and sex of the bar scene. However, coffee-houses also offer an urban spot in which we can socialize, work or read alone in public, see others, and be seen by others. Marriott says that we are living in an era in which people have retreated into their homes to spend hours with cable television and the Internet, and thus they crave the atmosphere and style of the city. Also, because coffeehouses are associated with the young and trendy, they offer stylishness to those who frequent them. Marriott shows how coffeehouses reveal the importance of being seen by others in stylish places doing stylish things.

Although these essays may seem at first to have little in common, they do share some fundamental similarities. The essays describe different manifesta-tions of style—including clothing, cars, and places—but they all concern them-selves with the issues of style as individuality, style as group identification, and style as urban in origin. While reading these essays, you should consider the pur-pose, meaning, place, and origin of style. Let these authors help you to think about what people are trying to communicate through the style of their clothing and their presentation of their body. What are they trying to communicate through the car they drive or the bicycle or motorcycle they ride? And what about the places in which they hang out? Does a person's choice of where to go add to that person's style or the style he or she is associated with? When you think of people whom you consider to have style, do you assume that they live in cities? Why are rural people less associated with style? Does it have to do with the diversity of urban areas? If so, does a person's style demonstrate his or her individuality? Or does it mark that person's membership in a particular group that shares a similar ethnic or racial background, or musical or artistic tastes? Think about your answers to these questions, and as you read through the essays in this part, consider the impact style has on our feelings about ourselves and on our relationships with one another.

PREREADING ASSIGNMENTS

1. Take a few minutes to describe your own style. Describe the aspects of your appearance that you consider most important to who you are. Make sure to consider not only your clothes, but also the vehicle you ride in or drive, the music you listen to, and the places you hang out. What do all these things say about you?

2. Spend ten minutes freewriting about the possible connections between style and cities. Take into consideration the differences between cities, suburbs, and rural areas. What is it about densely populated areas like cities that lends to their being "style centers"?

3. List all the different styles that are available in your city for people to associate themselves with. Then, briefly, try to describe each style. What markers or features, what clothes or food, what music are specific to each style? What kinds of people have that style? How are things like age, race, sex, and income level related to that style?

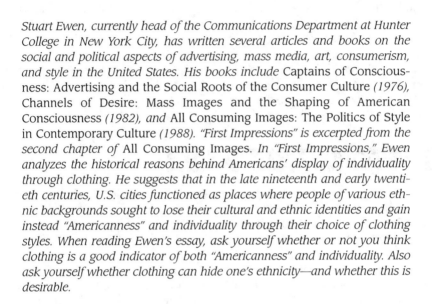

Stuart Ewen, currently head of the Communications Department at Hunter College in New York City, has written several articles and books on the social and political aspects of advertising, mass media, art, consumerism, and style in the United States. His books include Captains of Consciousness: Advertising and the Social Roots of the Consumer Culture *(1976),* Channels of Desire: Mass Images and the Shaping of American Consciousness *(1982), and* All Consuming Images: The Politics of Style in Contemporary Culture *(1988). "First Impressions" is excerpted from the second chapter of* All Consuming Images. *In "First Impressions," Ewen analyzes the historical reasons behind Americans' display of individuality through clothing. He suggests that in the late nineteenth and early twentieth centuries, U.S. cities functioned as places where people of various ethnic backgrounds sought to lose their cultural and ethnic identities and gain instead "Americanness" and individuality through their choice of clothing styles. When reading Ewen's essay, ask yourself whether or not you think clothing is a good indicator of both "Americanness" and individuality. Also ask yourself whether clothing can hide one's ethnicity—and whether this is desirable.*

First Impressions

Stuart Ewen

THE DEVELOPMENT of consumer capitalism in the United States was fueled by a series of massive migrations—from within and without—which supplied a cheap, continually replaceable work force. Over time, these migrations also created a population whose hopes for a better life became the building blocks out of which a responsive, mass market of consumers would be constructed. With an immigration of millions between the late nineteenth century and 1920, the meaning and power of style underwent prodigious changes.

Immigrants from foreign lands came, during these years, primarily from Eastern Europe and the southern tier of Italy. In addition to these Europeans, there were also millions of migrants—black and white—who came from rural poverty to burgeoning industrial cities, seeking employment and improved conditions.

In these cities—New York City, particularly—the iconography of style was touched and molded by a new multiplicity of influences. If the meaning of style had previously emanated from the consumption patterns of European elites, new, more democratic influences now began to assert themselves. With its infusion of different nationalities and cultures, and as a center of global commerce, the metropolis became a battleground, a vibrant cacophony of contending and cross-fertilizing cultural meanings. This heterogeneity and swarming energy, along with the relative tolerance of metropolitan life, turned the city into an always-moving repository of images, a perpetually expanding, and changing, inventory of "looks" and expressions. The jagged and vital quality of urban life has given shape to the definition of style ever since. Nearly anything that bubbles to the surface of the city can find its way into the style market.

Yet the city was more than a stylistic resource. It was also an environment that made style into an essential tool for everyday life. For people coming from agrarian or small-town artisanal roots, the move to urban industrialism posed a shock of world historic proportions. Uprooted from familiar patterns of work, kinship, and community, and also from customary ways of comprehending the world, they now entered a terrain that included countless strangers. Social life itself was being transformed from something known, set and transmitted by custom, into something increasingly anonymous; custom was inadequate to provide measures and lessons for survival.

In the shadow of this dislocation, people's customary conception of *self* was challenged. First, life became an experience of repeated and regular encounters with the unknown. As one navigated this vast new world of strangers, one quickly learned that to the eyes of countless others one becomes a "stranger" oneself. Anonymity was not only the characteristic of others; it was also becoming a component of subjectivity, part of the way one came to understand oneself. Part of surviving this strange new world was the ability to make quick judgments based, largely, on immediate visual evidence. The city was a place where surfaces took on a new power of expression. The very terms of everyday experience required, as part of the rules of survival and exchange, a sense of *self as alien,* as an object of scrutiny and judgment. From this vantage point, immigrants learned that matters of dress and personal appearance were essential for success in the public world. Writing in 1902, Jane Addams described the imperative of dress among urban working girls:

> The working girl, whose family lives in a tenement, or moves from one small apartment to another, who has little social standing and has to make her own place, knows full well how much habit and style of dress has to do with her

position. Her income goes into her clothing, out of all proportion to the amount which she spends upon other things. But, if social advancement is her aim, it is the most sensible thing she can do. She is judged largely by her clothes. Her house furnishing, with its pitiful little decorations, her scanty supply of books, are never seen by the people whose social opinions she most values. Her clothes are her background, and from them she is largely judged.

In an environment where being labeled a "greenhorn" left one open to swindles and mockery, assuming the look of an "American" was a device of survival. Leonard Covello, who immigrated as a boy from Italy, described his acquisition of acceptable American attire before anything else. "My long European trousers had been replaced by the short knickers of the time, and I wore black ribbed stockings and new, American shoes. To all outward appearances I was an American," he confided ironically, "except that I did not speak a word of English." The visual vernacular of style was the lingua franca of the city.

With the guidance of various Americanizing forces and institutions, young people began to learn that when one applied or interviewed for a job, or sought acceptance in school, it was important to make a good impression. This reality gave rise to a divided self. "Family obligations" and traditional codes of behavior were often enforced in the home, but outside the home these young people were seduced by the American social environment. If Ira Steward's "middle class" was torn between the longing for status and the struggle for the legal tender, these new Americans experienced a similar dissonance in their lives, this one marked by a toe-to-toe struggle between cultures.

For example, Pauline Young, a social worker writing in *Survey* magazine (15 March 1928), spoke of a sixteen-year-old son in a family of Jewish immigrants from Poland: "Jim is in almost daily contact with two divergent cultures: the older Jewish culture symbolized by the home, and the newer American culture symbolized by the school, industry and the larger community." Within the context of the home, she related, "family obligations . . . are still set in the foreground, and individual members are expected to conform to family tradition." Alongside this, however, was the opposing pull of the new world he inhabited:

> In the larger community . . . Jim tends to become an "American Citizen." The English language and the associations at school open up to him a new world of social practices, customs, attitudes, and social values. This newer culture fosters, moreover, traits of independence, personal resourcefulness, individuality, and cultivates desires for personal distinction.

This example repeated itself again and again. The old world of the parents was rooted in a continuity, an ongoing connection among closely tied people over generations. Familiar cultural resources were drawn upon, to navigate and envision the possibilities and limits of everyday life. The new world, on the other hand, demanded a sense of self that was malleable, sensitive to the power of increasingly volatile surfaces. Addressing the historical transformation of individual identity, historian Warren Susman described it as a shift from the importance of "character" (intrinsic self) to the importance of "personality" (a moldable, extrinsic self). In this transition, the problem was invariably who one *was*. Who one could *become* was the solution. In the finding of solutions, the emerging consumer culture would gladly oblige.

Patterns of courtship were also affected by this transformation. The customary cultures of these immigrants and migrants were—for the most part—shaped by patterns of traditional patriarchal authority. Courtship, marriage, and sexuality were often arranged by parents, as agreements and exchanges between families from the same village or locale. Now, relations of love, sexuality, and matrimony were drawn from the new world of strangers. Young people, as they left the radius of the family, had unprecedented opportunities to develop relationships beyond the gaze of parents and matchmakers.

This mobility left a painful dent in the surface of the old culture. One Jewish matchmaker, interviewed by the New York *Tribune* in 1898, complained that the new American styles of courtship were leaving his business in ruin:

> Once I lived off the fat of the land, and most marriageable men and women in the quarter depended on me to make them happy. Now they believe in love and all that rot. They are making their own marriages.... They learned how to start their own love affairs from the Americans, and it is one of the worst things they have picked up.

This independence from habitual constraints required new tools of negotiation. Greenhorns were confronted in the streets with new patterns of adornment which signaled and beckoned toward a more independent mode of existence. A collision of cultures can be seen in one social worker's description of an encounter between a recent immigrant girl and her American counterparts:

> Each morning and evening as she covers her head with an old crocheted shawl and walks to and from the factory, she passes the daughters of her Irish and American neighbors in their smart hats, their cheap waists in the latest and smartest style, their tinsel ornaments and their gay hair bows. A part of the pay envelopes goes into the personal expenses of those girls. Nor do they hurry through the streets to their homes after working hours, but linger with a boy companion "making dates" for a movie or an affair.

"Inevitably," wrote the social worker, "the influence of the new life in which she spends nine hours a day begins to tell on her."

Here we see a second change in the definition of *self*. As people became what Raymond Williams calls "mobile individuals" they experienced a break from old patterns of hierarchy and authority, rooted for many in the history of feudalism and the conventional structures a localized, agrarian existence. This break was both disorienting and promising. It cast people adrift from known and internalized strategies of survival, but it also posed the seductive possibility of greater autonomy and freedom, of democracy.

The industrial society that these people confronted was simultaneously oppressive and liberating. The machine, and its relentless rhythms, supplied the modern context for misery and exploitation, but it also contained an ability to reproduce—on a mass scale—pregnant images and symbols of luxury, abundance, and distinction, powerful suggestions of privilege and franchise. Styled objects, once the province of an upper class, now became reproducible, if only as surface images.

To some extent this development was triggered by the mass production of chromolithographs, as objects of desire and alluring tools of commerce. Extended access to style was also effected by the great public expositions of the late nineteenth century, where urban dwellers could come to witness the wonders of industrialism on display. Exposition halls—their plaster and horsehair surfaces molded to imitate the grandeur of Renaissance palaces— offered the public entry into environments traditionally inhabited by elites. The democratic privilege suggested by such spectacles can be heard in a promotional claim made for the Columbian Exposition: "We are all princes, for the time being, in this little realm."

Perhaps the most significant area in which stylized goods became common possessions of working-class people was that of fashionable, mass-produced clothing. From the 1880s onward, men's and women's gar- ment industries began to mass produce inexpensive fashions, cut to imitate the ornamental elegance of upper-class styles. Coming from societies where the prerogatives of dress were intimately connected to one's elevated class position, European immigrants, in particular, perceived the availability of mass-produced fashions as a mark of social mobility, of materially improved circumstances. People who had previously been denied access to images of magnificence now found them in reach, for a price.

Beginning in the nineteenth century, and catapulting in the twentieth, a wide-ranging consumer market in style was reaching deeply into nearly all aspects of life. Style was in the process of being transformed from a prerog- ative of the few to an amusement of the millions. Though the implication of exclusivity and privilege would remain, the expressive and connotative arena of style was becoming an essential part of the modern vernacular. With this alluring access to fashion, old world notions of quality and durabil- ity gave way to new world priorities of consumption and frequent changes in style. This transformation of values between mothers and daughters was described by a social worker, Sophinisba Breckenridge, in her 1929 book, *New Homes for Old:*

> In her [daughter's] main contention that if she is to keep up with the fashions
> she need not buy clothing that will last more than one season, she is probably

right. It is also natural that this method of buying should be distressing to her mother, who has been accustomed to clothes of unchanging fashions which were judged entirely by their quality.

In such a broad milieu of strangers, style was a dramatic necessity. One was repeatedly made aware of *self as other,* of one's commodity status within a vast social marketplace, and style provided its user with a powerful medium of encounter and exchange. Whereas contacts between people had once been familiar, the city was unfamiliar, and daily life, at times, seemed threatening.

In the face of this apparently "hostile" environment, style allowed one to put up a front, to protect one's inner self. As a kind of armor for city life, style taught people that they could gain comfort from self-estrangement, from erecting a visible line of defense for a subjectivity that often experienced a sense of jeopardy. As a basic lesson in *modernization,* immigrant and migrant workers learned to be "presentable," to rely on the tools of presentation while navigating the treacherous waters of everyday life. True moderns, they were learning to internalize the dictum of Bishop Berkeley, that "to be is to be perceived."

In its mimicry of upper-class elegance, as well as in its piracy of emerging forms of popular expression, the marketplace of consumer goods, from the early twentieth century onward, provided instruments for the construction of a self—a surrogate self, perhaps—to be seen, to be judged, to simultaneously scale and maintain the wall of anonymity. In worlds of work and love, status and aspiration, the assembly of "self" was becoming compulsory for ventures into the society at large. The appeal of "style" was not a matter of aesthetics alone; it was also a functional acquisition of metropolitan life.

This can be seen in the story of one woman, a Russian immigrant, who described her own relationship with style. In Russia she wore the customary clothes of the poor, made crudely out of scraps of cloth. "It was not a question of style," she explained, "but of how to cover one's body in those days." When she came to America in the 1920s, one of the first articles of clothing she bought was an item she had admired from afar while still in Russia: a leather jacket, a "symbol of both the Revolution and elegance." Yet when she wore this prized acquisition while looking for work, she discovered that employers would not hire her; they, too, understood the political connotations of the jacket. They were afraid its wearer might cause problems, as a unionist or agitator. Employers were looking for signs of docility, adaptability, and conformity in their prospective employees. Finally, the woman was forced to make a concession to the codes of the job market:

> I dressed myself in the latest fashion with lipstick in addition, although it was so hard to get used to at first that I blushed, felt foolish and thought myself vulgar. But I got the job.

Style provided an extension of personality on a physical plane, leaving its mark on the sundry accessories of life: personal apparel, the home, even the foods one ate. In a world where scrutiny by unknown others had become the norm, style provided people with an *attractive otherness,* a "phantom objectivity" (to borrow a phrase from Georg Lukacs), to publicly define oneself, to be weighed in the eye's mind.

A central appeal of style was its ability to create an illusory transcendence of class or background. While hierarchy and inequities of wealth and power were—in many ways—increasing, the free and open market in style offered a symbolic ability to name oneself; to become a "lady" or a "gentleman," a "Sir" or a "Madam." Mass-produced, often shoddy, nevertheless style seemed to subvert ancient monopolies over the image that had predominated in the cultures out of which many of these "greenhorns" were drawn. If style was essentially a matter of surface and mystification, it was—and continues to be—a surface that offered a democratic charm.

Discussion Questions

Content

1. What, according to Ewen, is the relationship between urban life and the emergence of contemporary styles? Do you agree with Ewen that style is an essentially urban creation? Do rural areas create style? Why or why not?

2. Ewen claims that style has meaning and power. What does he mean by this? What is the meaning of style? What is its power? Use examples from your own experience to either support or contest Ewen's ideas about the meaning and power of style. In your own experience, when has style had meaning and/or power? When has it not? In what ways do your experiences support and/or contest Ewen's views? At the same time, how does Ewen help you make better sense of your experiences of the meaning and power of style?

3. Do you agree that people—at least people today—sometimes use clothing styles to hide their ethnic and socioeconomic origins? Do people ever use clothing styles to do the opposite, to proudly display their origins? Provide some examples to support your answer. Whatever your answer, to what degree do you think a purchased product can authentically represent one's roots? After all, if it can be bought, can't just anyone buy it? And what does it mean to you to be able to purchase an authentic identity?

Form

1. Ewen's article is argumentative and persuasive. How does he put together his essay so that we are convinced that immigrants at the turn of the century used clothing styles to hide their ethnicity and become more American? Just how convinced are you by his essay? Why? Refer to the article itself to explain what is most and what is least persuasive for you.

2. Ewen uses primarily discussion of the late nineteenth and early twentieth centuries to illustrate his point about immigration, cities, and style. In what ways would his article be different if he instead used the 1990s to make his point? What examples of style and fashion do you think he would have to use? In what ways do you think the article would still be quite similar? To what extent are the fashions and styles of the 1990s used to do the same things as the fashions and styles of the late 1800s to the early 1900s?

3. What is Ewen's tone? Does he seem to you to have a positive, negative, or mixed attitude toward the fact that immigrants Americanized themselves through clothing? Find examples of his words and phrases that support your opinion about Ewen's attitude toward his topic.

Writing Prompts

1. Write a short essay in which you make a connection between some person or some group's style and the meaning of that style. Describe how this person's or group's style reflects who they are and who they want to be. Take into consideration issues of power, race, ethnicity, social class, urban living versus rural living, etc.

2. Write an essay based upon an interview with an elderly person who either is foreign-born or had foreign-born parents and who has lived in an urban area. Ask this person about how he or she perceived the pressures to use clothing to hide ethnicity and promote "Americanness." Also ask this person whether he or she sought to hide or promote his or her ethnicity and how the person feels about that idea now.

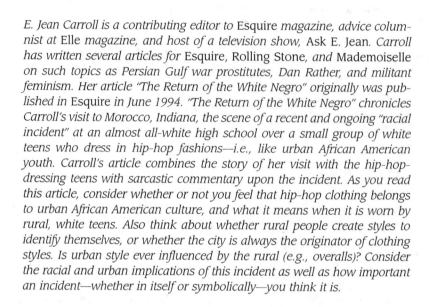

E. Jean Carroll is a contributing editor to Esquire magazine, advice colum-
nist at Elle magazine, and host of a television show, Ask E. Jean. Carroll
has written several articles for Esquire, Rolling Stone, and Mademoiselle
on such topics as Persian Gulf war prostitutes, Dan Rather, and militant
feminism. Her article "The Return of the White Negro" originally was published in Esquire in June 1994. "The Return of the White Negro" chronicles
Carroll's visit to Morocco, Indiana, the scene of a recent and ongoing "racial
incident" at an almost all-white high school over a small group of white
teens who dress in hip-hop fashions—i.e., like urban African American
youth. Carroll's article combines the story of her visit with the hip-hop-
dressing teens with sarcastic commentary upon the incident. As you read
this article, consider whether or not you feel that hip-hop clothing belongs
to urban African American culture, and what it means when it is worn by
rural, white teens. Also think about whether rural people create styles to
identify themselves, or whether the city is always the originator of clothing
styles. Is urban style ever influenced by the rural (e.g., overalls)? Consider
the racial and urban implications of this incident as well as how important
an incident—whether in itself or symbolically—you think it is.

The Return of the White Negro

E. Jean Carroll

FIFTY MILES SOUTH OF GARY and a hundred miles west of Fort Wayne, running down Highway 41 at about 23 miles an hour through one of your thick
north-Indiana fogs—thank God it obliterates the view—is a rented Tracer
bearing me into ... nowhere. The middle of nowhere. Oh, not the middle of
nowhere like the rest of Indiana, but a nowhere so flat and ugly you want to
lie down in a ditch and never get up again. A shriveled, worn-out, beat-up
cornstalk nowhere, the kind of place where the cream of society is the owner
of the IGA grocery mart. The sort of spot where a girl is said to have "made it
big" when she ascends to the position of lap-counter for Mario Andretti.
Where the men strive in the Hammond steel mills or strain in the barley
fields in which they were born to die. This is the sticks, honey.

It's the dung-colored area on the map halfway between the birthplaces of David Letterman (Indianapolis) and Michael Jackson (Gary). It's the "bread-basket," the "crossroads of America," the "heart of the heart of the nation"— the point where the farm belt, the Bible belt, and the rust belt intersect and the women are so homely that even the big-legged coeds of Purdue, famed nationwide for their ugliness and surliness, look like prom queens in comparison.

North Newton Junior-Senior High, however, is a large, good-looking building and stands in the middle of a cornfield some eight miles north of the town of Morocco—a melancholy hamlet of lawyers' offices, abandoned buildings, closed cafés, and a boarded-up pool hall. And that, really, is all. Not much else to include about a place gripped by the fear in every street, every house, every farm, barn, and coop that the Nigger Hoards are coming....

"**S**O WHAT DO YOU DO around here?"

"We ride around town."

"There *is* no town."

"We ride around anyway," says Mikey, a strapping son of Morocco.

"And then what?"

"Set there."

"Where?"

"In the bank parking lot."

He's a sharp youngster. Eighteen. A senior at North Newton Junior-Senior High. In fact, one look at his apricot goatee and flaming pumpkin flattop with the neck fringe hanging down like a big piece of peat moss and I hire Michael Blakeney to be my driver.

"What else do kids do around here?" I ask.

"Shoot their guns," says Mikey. He's so excited about getting fifty dollars a day just to drive somebody around in a rented Tracer, his whole upper body has turned the color of tomato aspic.

"They hunt?" I ask.

"Every night," says Mikey. Last year he sat up in a tree for three or four days. "I seen a doe," he says, "but, you know, I don't shoot women deer."

He is wearing a baby-blue-and-white hooded sweatshirt, rolled jeans, basketball shoes, a gold thing hanging around his neck ("my senior *key!*"— humping his shoulders proudly), a big silver ID bracelet ("my dad's name's on it; he doesn't live with us anymore, he lives in Kankakee"), a gold earring, a leather bracelet, and a class ring ("my girlfriend's; she graduated three years ago"). It's plain I'm talking to a sophisticated young dog here. And, indeed, Mikey has been on Channel 7 speaking about the "disturbance at the school" with such eloquence you might think you were listening to a young Dan Quayle.

His first job is to drive me over to Roselawn and introduce me to the Van Winkle girls, who are causing the "race riots." On the way, he slows down to 73 miles an hour and shows me where the flowers "grow wild all over the place" and explains how the combines leave the fields all "stubbly lookin'."

When he finally gets around to explaining how the controversy began, he says, "The school's so boring they had to bring all this stuff up 'cause the school's so boring." He pauses a second to ruminate.

"We only have one race at our school!" he say, shaking his head. "How can there be a racial disturbance?"

In Mikey's opinion, the Van Winkle girls dress a little "dumb," but they're "all right," and he thinks that when the kids at school started calling them wiggers, "it bothered them, and then the more of a fit they threw the more of a fit everybody else threw," and it ended up with Principal Bell having to empty the school last week because of a bomb threat.

"What does *wiggers* mean, exactly?" I ask.

"White nigger," says Mikey. "*Wiggers*. Like that."

NORTH NEWTON COUNTY has been alive with rumors of "carfuls" of black men speeding through the hamlets of Morocco, Lake Village, Roselawn, De Motte, and Thayer (communities so moribund that James Dean's grave over in Marion looks like a Hoosier hoedown in comparison). But it turns out that the "carfuls" are nothing but Spanky Gee Highbaugh and DuShaun Goings, ages eighteen and nineteen, respectively, two young African-Americans from Lafayette who read about the Van Winkle girls in the paper and have driven up to lend moral support "to the struggle."

When Mikey and I arrive, Spanky Gee and DuShaun are sitting in the Van Winkles' attractive little Cape Cod house (in a subdivision in the middle of a cornfield), watching MTV with the Van Winkle sisters, Andrea and Kerry, and a third little girl in fiery-red lipstick, Alizabeth Grzych.

"Some guys started saying that we're trying to dress black and everything," says Kerry, flipping violently through the pages of a fashion magazine. "And they started calling us wiggers, and at first they were just writing stuff on desks like 'Wiggers' and 'White Power' and 'KKK' and a bunch of stuff. So we went to the office and told the principal, Mr. Bell, and all he did was make two of the boys wash off the desks. And then they started shoving us and they started spitting on us. . . . And then this one teacher, Miss Tillman, she came up to me and told me that I was going to have to remove my headband, and I said, 'No. I don't have to.' I didn't cuss at all. I said I wasn't going to remove it, and she said, 'Well, you're going to have to go to the office.'"

I ask to see the "black clothes" that Kerry was wearing when she, Andrea, Alizabeth, and seven other girls were suspended from school. Kerry, a riper, rounder, brainier version of Christina Applegate on *Married . . . with Children*, with a saucy little build and long blond hair, finds the outfit in the dryer and a couple of minutes later appears in a turquoise headband, her dad's blue-plaid flannel shirt, and a pair of semibaggy purple skater shorts.

Jane Austen's ball gown was more hip-hop.

"That's *it*?" I cry.

Yes, Kerry nods, this is one of the outfits that caused a bomb threat at school, the phoning of four death threats into the Van Winkles' home, the installation of a police wiretap on the family's telephone, the expulsion of several students from school, an ongoing FBI investigation, protests by the National Organization for Women, denunciations from the NAACP, a *Montel Williams* show, a *Jerry Springer* show, a *Ricki Lake* show, a profile in *People*, the filing of a lawsuit by the Van Winkles and eight other families against the North Newton Schools Corporation, and a filthy little race war in a school where all the students except two little eighth graders are white.

(Actually, there is only one black eighth grader now. The other, Jacob Campbell, a quiet, shy, light-skinned, green-eyed thirteen-year-old, declined to return to school after getting "hit" and "shoved." "I was punched," Jacob told me later. "And shoved into my locker. I'd walk down the hall and they'd punch me. I don't like it there.")

The North Newton County sheriff's office has repeatedly declined to comment on the troubles, and poor Gene Bell, principal of North Newton, is under orders from Larry Hanna, superintendent of the North Newton Schools Corporation, not to speak to the press. (I whisked Principal Bell, a fifty-year-old man who plays the trumpet, away to romantic Merchant's Bar and Restaurant out on Highway 41. He did not, in fact, have much to say. He remarked calmly that he was "surprised" by all the "excitement" the "incident" was causing. He did not condone such "unladylike" behavior. He wondered if he would keep his job. And he thought the "trouble" would "blow over" if the press "stayed away.")

Ivan Bodensteiner, a Hoosier attorney well known for winning civil-rights cases, was hired to defend the freedoms of the Van Winkles, Alizabeth Grzych, and the seven other schoolgirls. He says, "Students have filed suit against the North Newton Schools Corporation and several school officials, claiming compensatory damages for the emotional and mental distress suffered by the students and their parents, plus punitive damages to punish and deter the school officials for what they have done. The message the school is sending is that the girls who are expressing the idea of racial equality in their way of dress are in the wrong and that the boys who are harassing them represent the norm."

So there it is.

"So WHAT'S YOUR LIFE LIKE now?" I ask Alizabeth Grzych. "Who're you dating?"

"Nobody," says Alizabeth.

She shrugs. She is wearing a FREE TO BE ME note safety-pinned to her big orange Cross Colors shirt.

"Any guys calling?"

She shakes her head. "No."

"Has this hurt your social life or helped it?"

"Well," says Alizabeth, glumly, "I can't go to school and say, you know, hi to anybody because, you know, they *hate* me now."

ONLY A SQUAD OF LIPIZZANS could equal the beauty and form of the North Newton cheerleaders at Friday night's basketball game, but the idea of watching hoops in the middle of a cornfield with no black people where every member of the visiting team is shorter than I am is too much to deal with. So for the fourth quarter Mikey and I go and sit in the car in the school parking lot and talk to a couple of North Newton boys and their young mother.

Naturally, the boys deny everything and say the girls are the ones going around shouting, "Fuck you, you cornbread-eating country hicks."

"Yeah, and I mean if they want to be black so bad," says the first boy, "why don't they go get some Indian paint or something to dump all over them and move up into the slums of Chicago?"

"Would you ever date a black girl?" I say.

He socks himself in the head.

"No!"

He's a simple-looking boy, wearing an aquamarine San Jose Sharks cap and an aquamarine Hornets sweatshirt.

"Are you sure?" I say.

His mother, who sports a long Tonya Harding hairdo and a headband that matches her slacks, nods violently the whole time he speaks.

"Yes," he says. "I'm sure."

"What if you meet a really nice black girl," I say, "who's really intelligent, very beautiful, and very rich. Would you date her?"

He can scarce contain himself at the idea.

"No!"

I have many conversations with North Newton boys during the next few days, including the so-called ringleaders of the attacks, and every single one of the silly little buggers answers the same way.

THOUGH MIKEY'S GIRLFRIEND in Kankakee says she hopes the fifty dollars a day I'm giving him to drive me around will pay for his funeral when the KKK kills him, his girlfriend in Roselawn just flops on her bed and cries when he stops by her house after the basketball game to tell her that we're going on to the dance at the fire station in Thayer to meet Kerry, Andrea, and Alizabeth.

And Mother of Creeping Grain Silos! The deejay at the Thayer dance is playing Dr. Dre when we arrive, and sixty or seventy teen rubes from North Newton High are standing in a circle, watching Spanky Gee in his Dickie suit spin on his head on the floor. Marco Polo's appearance in China was nothing to it. The Morocco kids are stunned! A black boy! On his head! *Twirling*! Meanwhile, our girls, Andrea, Kerry, and Alizabeth, the only significant group of rebels in the whole state of Indiana, are bumping against DuShaun, front, back, and side, like En Vogue in a malarial fever.

The difference between the girls' clothes and those of the rest of the kids is so slight that an outsider would have trouble picking out the "wiggers" in the crowd. (The truth is that our girls don't have the money to buy the real hip-hop fashion—the big-jeaned, big-logoed, big-booted look that's broadcast across the nation—and they're too countrified to dress straight out of the trash can like the street-savvy homegirls.) But one glance at their faces—at Andrea's expression, for instance, which says *I'm so fly*!—and there is no confusion.

Norman Mailer wrote in his supremely cool 1957 essay, "The White Negro": "So there was a new breed of adventurers … who drifted out at night looking for action with a black man's code to fit their facts. The hipster had absorbed the existentialist synapses of the Negro, and for practical purposes could be considered a white Negro." Our girls, of course, don't care diddly-squat about the existentialist synapses of the Negro, white or black. They've been brought up among the sons and daughters of the most perniciously boring clan of Caucasians ever to roll over the surface of the earth on a John Deere, and by cracky, they want *fun*. And since the biggest, nastiest fun to be found on this godforsaken landscape is a watered-down, distorted, MTV-brand, black fun, well, then … *cool*. They've gotta have it.

Rotten little "incidents" like this happen all the time in Indiana, birthplace of the Ku Klux Klan. Where else would a little girl wearing big pants represent the imminent obliteration of the white race? What other locale North or South would look upon a turquoise headband as synonymous with "coon riots"? Frankly, it just makes you dull to be in Indiana. All except of course, for young Mikey, who shows up Saturday morning attired in what he majestically calls his Malcolm X outfit—a teal-green-and-royal-purple shirt and matching green-and-purple pants with a big fringed knee patch that says FIGHT THE POWER.

He is wearing this getup specifically because we are going with the Mr. Robert Van Winkles and Spanky Gee and the girls as guests of DuShaun Goings to an African-American Kwanza Celebration at the Purdue Student Union in West Lafayette.

AFTER A PERFORMANCE of old Negro spirituals, Spanky Gee, DuShaun, and their Mexican friend, Sal, a young man of high fashion who works at a West Lafayette venetian-blind factory, take Mikey and the girls to an all-black fraternity party at the Purdue Armory.

If one male model thirty feet distant on a runway is enough to set the girls' hearts bouncing like basketballs, the reader won't be surprised to discover the shocking effect of a *hundred and thirteen black men* on our gals. In short, Miss Andrea, Miss Kerry, and Miss Alizabeth crash through the coliseum doors of the Armory like wild beasts getting their first smell of the Christians.

Then they stop dead in their tracks.

Kerry, for instance, after a quick intake of air, ceases breathing completely; Andrea moves only her eyeballs, and after a full minute, during which Alizabeth keeps drawling in a loud, excited voice, "I've got jungle *feeeeeever*, I've got jungle *feeeeeeever*," they spring to life again and flutter forward like butterflies, jerking their wings, snapping their long tongues, and settle at last in the midst of the darkest, heaviest flowers.

Mikey, meanwhile, has put on the multicolored African hat he purchased at the Kwanza and is happy just swaggering around the perimeter of the fraternity party in his fabulous Malcolm X outfit.

The evening ends with Spanky Gee, DuShaun, and Mexican Sal producing huge bottles of neon-colored beverages, which are ripped from their hands and immediately knocked down the gullets of the three shapely rustics.

AFTER SUNDAY BREAKFAST at Denny's we drop by the Word of Life Fellowship Church to see Spanky Gee's parents. Spanky Gee's father is a well-known disc jockey. He leans his head in the car and looks at the three white girls in the backseat, then pulls his head out and looks at Spanky Gee, then leans his head in again and looks at the girls and says, "Have you taken Jesus for your savior?"

"Yes, sir!" they all sing like little canaries.

"Okay," says Mr. Highbaugh. And he pats Spanky Gee on the back. "I don't have anything to worry about."

Ten minutes later they're all necking up in Spanky Gee's room while Mikey straddles a stool, clutching a Japanese kimono around his neck, waiting for Spanky Gee to give him a haircut.

"You can do anything you want," says Mikey. "Just don't touch the back where I've got my *length*. I need that for my girlfriend," he says, rolling his shoulders and looking over at the girls.

Spanky Gee's room is paneled in fake birch wood.

He puts Naughty By Nature in the tape deck, changes into his Orlando Magic shirt, strolls through the clothes on the floor, looking for his implements and his attachment, which he locates in various plastic bags, and then plugs in his clippers.

"It's going to be *real* short," says Spanky Gee, shaking his cutting arm and loosening up like Mikhail Baryshnikov. "But you're not going to be bald."

"*Oh, shit!*" says Mikey.

Spanky Gee inclines into Mikey's sides and rims Mikey's ears as if they're whitewall tires.

"Now, what's this called?" I say.

"This is a fade," says Spanky Gee.

Spanky Gee's pants are hanging almost down to his knees.

"Why's it called a fade?" I ask.

The girls are lying over on the bed while Mexican Sal cuts lines into Alizabeth's eyebrows.

"'Cause it fades into the skin," says Spanky Gee.

Three minutes later:

"What's this called?" I ask.

I point to a big *J* carved into the top of Mikey's scalp.

"That's called a part," says Spanky Gee.

Three minutes later:

"And what's this called?"

I indicate the whole upper region of hair, which rises off Mikey's red forehead like an orange crate.

"That's a box," says Spanky Gee.

Meantime, DuShaun, wearing his beautiful Montel Williams cap, is standing behind Mikey with a felt-tipped marker writing "Sweat Pee" into what's left of the hair on the back of Mikey's head. But Spanky Gee tells him to get the hell away, rubs it off with a washcloth, and buzzes in "Sweet P" with an elegant flourish of the clippers, after which he cuts in three or four waves from the front of Mikey's skull to the back, and then the girls unroll Mikey's Malcolm X pants and braid his fringe hanging on his neck. By the time they've put the sunglasses on him, Mikey's head has turned the shade of a cherry blossom.

Indeed, the whole fierce look is completely destroyed by the expression on his face of almost intolerable bliss.

AND NOW IT'S TIME to bid adieu to Spanky Gee, DuShaun, and Mexican Sal and head back to Morocco. We've been to the movies and ordered fifty dollars' worth of junk to eat and now we're cruising back up Interstate 65, staring out the windows at the soybean fields and the farmhouses all lit up, and we're swaying our heads, listening to Too Short rap about "fat dicks," when suddenly young Mikey turns around to the girls in the backseat and says:

"We got our shit *hooked!*"

The girls screech happily.

"I want to go to school tomorrow," says Mikey, "and I want to tell these guys who make fun of you all exactly what they missed. And how much fun you can have with people if you just get to know them. No matter what color they are or what race."

"Go, Mike, go!" cries Andrea.

"Goddamn right!" says Mikey, straightening his multicolored African hat. "A lot of teachers told me to keep my mouth shut."

"And now," cries Andrea, "it's like, 'Well, I partied with about three hundred black guys!'"

And if these young girls, by their rude rebellion, have managed to turn one Morocco yokel into what looks like a cross between President Mobutu and L. L. Cool J, they are pretty wise women indeed. In fact, we all feel wonderful even though we're heading toward unbearable Morocco, because . . . well, because there is hope.

"No shit, man!" shouts Mikey, thumping on the steering wheel. "Three hundred? *Shit!* There was about five or seven hundred of them there!"

Discussion Questions

Content

1. The author says that the clothes worn by the girls in Indiana are not authentic hip-hop and that the girls really don't understand African American culture at all. What do you think of this? Do white youths have to wear hip-hop clothes in a certain way in order for their hip-hop style to be valid? Do they have to wear the style the same way that African American youths do?

2. The author makes fun of the girls and their community because they are naive about black culture yet want to be part of it in a "watered-down, distorted, MTV" way—in other words, they want the urban style, but not the substance of real urban experience. Just what might the difference be between urban style and urban substance? What does each term mean? Do you agree with the author that the girls' attitudes toward urban African American culture are deplorable? Why or why not?

3. In this article, white, rural teens are wearing clothing styles originally worn by urban African Americans. Do you believe that fashions should be worn by people who are not part of the group that originated a particular style of clothing? Why or why not?

Form

1. What is the tone of the article? Identify words and phrases that you think most strongly state the author's attitude toward the white teens. What attitude do you have toward the topic as a result of the author's language? How might the author change her tone to achieve a different effect?

2. Carroll's article is told in the form of a narrative describing her activities in Indiana. How does this form influence how you read her article and the kinds of information you learn about the town and these teens? Are you more drawn in by it? Does it put you off? Why? How would your response to the article be different if, instead of a narrative, it was a straightforward report on the events in Morocco, Indiana?

3. Why does the author include so much about Mikey in the article? What is the effect of Mickey's presence in the article? Consider what his attitude is toward the incidents, and try to explain how his attitude might influence the way Carroll writes.

Writing Prompts

1. Write a straightforward, argumentative essay in which you take a position on the style worn by the teens in "The Return of the White Negro." Try not to use the narrative elements or the sarcastic humor that Carroll uses.

2. Write an essay that presents your opinion on the desirability of subcultural styles being worn and becoming popular among people outside those subcultures. Should hip-hop fashion be accessible to everyone? What happens to it as a fashion statement when it can be mass-marketed? Discuss both the negative and the positive aspects of people wearing clothing usually associated with specific groups.

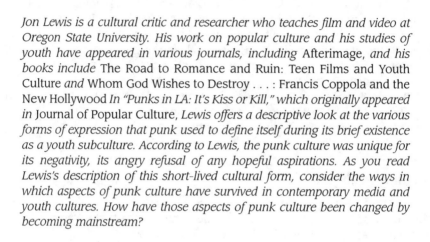

Jon Lewis is a cultural critic and researcher who teaches film and video at Oregon State University. His work on popular culture and his studies of youth have appeared in various journals, including Afterimage, *and his books include* The Road to Romance and Ruin: Teen Films and Youth Culture *and* Whom God Wishes to Destroy . . . : Francis Coppola and the New Hollywood *In "Punks in LA: It's Kiss or Kill," which originally appeared in* Journal of Popular Culture, *Lewis offers a descriptive look at the various forms of expression that punk used to define itself during its brief existence as a youth subculture. According to Lewis, the punk culture was unique for its negativity, its angry refusal of any hopeful aspirations. As you read Lewis's description of this short-lived cultural form, consider the ways in which aspects of punk culture have survived in contemporary media and youth cultures. How have those aspects of punk culture been changed by becoming mainstream?*

Punks in LA:
It's Kiss or Kill

Jon Lewis

Punk SURFACED IN LOS ANGELES in the late seventies as a curious blend of anarchy and anomie—as one last desperate attempt for white, urban, lower middle class youths to dramatically express their distaste for a society that had long since expressed its disinterest in them. What follows is a selective description of the movement; an analysis of its ideology and its symbiotic relationship to mainstream rock and roll and an attempt to contextualize punk as a unique moment in the history of American youth culture.

The LA punk movement began around 1977 and ended in the first few years of the 1980s. For the duration of its brief hold on the disenfranchised youth of urban LA, punk unapologetically paraded a variety of misanthropic and misogynist tendencies: Nazism, fascism, racism and self-hate. No youth movement before or since has hinged so tenuously on bizarre and frighten-

Jon Lewis. "Punks in LA: It's Kiss or Kill." From *Journal of Popular Culture* (Fall 1988): 87–97. Reprinted by permission of Popular Press.

ing ceremonies of attraction and repulsion and public displays of absolute anti-social behaviour. No youth movement before or since has laid so bare the desperation residing at the heart of the now failed urban American dream.

Like the New York or London based punk movements, the LA variation gained definition as an urban performance art form. The chaos and penchant for public obscenity which were punk's stock in trade found a milieu in the Masque, Madame Wong's and the Hong Kong Cafe—punk clubs in the heart of LA's very worst neighborhoods. Imminent danger characterized every venture to a punk club and the media attention to the savagery and very real violence integral to every punk performance and experience made it virtually impossible for anyone to "be there" completely by mistake.

From the start punk's droll, black comic and only marginally ironic celebration of urban squalor and senseless violence generated a kind of outsider mystique. Punk performance—here a very broad term indeed—generally manifested itself in ritual terms; shared acts or activities displaying a ceremonial and privileged significance. Punk attire and behaviour was opposed to convention; which was consistent with the movement's tendency towards celebrating its members' alienation from the mainstream of bourgeois city life. As a rejection of the late seventies/early eighties gearing up of the yuppie lifestyle, the LA punk movement paraded a glib and steadfast embrace of the frustrations inherent to their outsider status, maintaining an essential insider sub-culture; one which was simply too extreme to court the likes of the urban bourgeoisie as anything more than dumbfounded spectators.

As with so many urban sub-cultures, punk generated its own peculiar performance art scene, headed up by the redoubtable Sergio Premoli. In his most famous performance to date, Premoli, stationed in front of Gucci's status-packed Italian boutique on Beverly Hills' famed Rodeo Drive, hefted a 120-pound wooden American flag up on his back. "To carry something this heavy, it takes a lot of faith to do it," Premoli told spectators, "That's why Christ was so special." Viewing Premoli bearing his cross down the ritziest commercial LA street, the proprietor of ("the intelligent and tasteful mens' store") Madonna Man suggested that Premoli (clad topless, with loose fitting sweatpants over his bottom half) should have worn something more elegant, like a black raincoat by Benedetto (the Blessed One) of New York. Premoli, citing the true gravity of his task was hardly thinking of fashion, even on so auspicious an avenue. When asked how he felt once he secured the flag on his shoulders, Premoli replied, "Eeets a fucking heavy."

Premoli's art is provocation and it is meant to be offensive. By mixing his metaphors to God and country, Premoli complicates matters with his choice of locale (commercial America; the one street on earth most completely associated with conspicuous consumption). That there is an element of social commentary here is not all that unusual for punk. And that the commentary is obscene (in the Henry Miller sense of the word: as not pornographic or titillating, but ugly and revelatory), and to a great extent confusing and confused, is quite consistent with the peculiar artistic oeuvre of the LA punk scene.

The punk predilection for obscenity is similarly exposed in the LA punk literature: godfathered by the now legendary Charles Bukowski, featured in the unique punk fanzines like *Wet, Slash, Contagion, No Mag* and *The Lowest Common Denominator* and publically exhibited on bathroom walls and decaying building edifices in the often misanthropic/misogynist, existential or absurdist punk graffiti.

Bukowski, like his more famous counterpart William Burroughs in New York, has been credited as the movement's literary avatar, its truly gifted muse. But like Burroughs, whose reputation and income soared due to an identification with the movement, Bukowski's relationship to the punks themselves is peripheral at most. His readership is comprised primarily of those who viewed punk with fascination (but at arms' length). Bukowski's alcohol-soaked prose and anti-heroic, macho, barbrawling heroes coincide and resonate with punk anti-social behaviour and lifestyle, but aside from his alleged influence on the punk band X, Bukowski and the punks literally live at opposite ends of town; he in Venice by the sea, the punks far east of La Brea in the heat and smog of downtown.

For those on the inside, graffiti was the "pure punk" form, as it is public, obscene, often misspelled and ungrammatical, generally reductive and emblematic (rather than symbolic or allusive) and illegal. A familiar mix of crude drawing and aphoristic outrage, punk graffiti effaced already crumbling property, calling attention to (but never asking anyone to change) the dreadful landscape of decaying urban America.

The graffiti look and literary style is clearly evident in the unique and irreverent punk fanzines. These fan magazines, staffed, funded and distributed from within the punk subculture, provided information on the punk bands and featured pseudo-gonzo New Journalism (apeing Hunter Thompson and Terry Southern) replete with anti-social and often paradoxical and paranoid nihilist rants (for example Richard Meltzer's bizarre punk treatise on communism, "Go for the hammer/go for the sickle/you'll be glad you did....Hitler was just a fairy who dug blue-eyed South Bay surfer boys.").

The fanzines all featured a graffiti layout style, literalizing the effect of cutting and pasting. Unlike *Rolling Stone* and the other popular music magazines, the punk fanzines de-emphasized the stardom of the bands. While *Rolling Stone* et al institutionalized the glamour of the industry, the fanzines wallowed in the glamourlessness of punk.

The punk sense of humour exhibited in the fanzines was characteristically irreverent. For example, when Ronald Reagan's Commission on the Eighties found that for the first time in US history more than one-half of the

American population lived west of the Mississippi, *Wet* responded to the rising political influence of the conservative southwest with a black-comical mock advertisement for a solar powered electric chair, touting "Organic Executions for the Sunbelt." The ad credits the chair to New York designer James Hong and guarantees that the device "provides effectiveness even on a partly cloudy day." The chair, as advertised, is "slow rotisserie effective," with "capabilities for torture most of us haven't dreamed about since the days of the Protestant Reformation." And with a typical bit of (not really tongue in cheek) punk social theory, the ad concludes: "Just the thing to stamp out those food stamp cheating single mothers."

Two films, both by UCLA film school graduates who were in LA in the late seventies, articulate (for audiences outside LA) the essence of the LA punks: Penelope Spheeris' *The Decline of Western Civilization* and Alex Cox's cult-hit *Repo Man,* a film that juxtaposes the punk hallmark anti-commercialism to the crude narratives and visual styles of truly bad B-films.

The attraction of punk culture to graduate students, to upper middle class, white, well educated men and women (despite the fact that they were often the target of punk tirades), was a curious phenomenon in the late seventies' LA. For those in search of a youth movement in postVietnam America, punk positioned itself in diametric opposition to the optimistic and idealistic flower children of the previous decade. In fact, the punks often railed against the hippies. One punk (sporting a swasticka medallion on his chest) wryly quips (in an interview with Penelope Spheeris in *The Decline of Western Civilization*): "Like I'm not going to go out and kill some Jew. C'mon—Maybe a hippie." Such blank, emotionless threats of violence abound in Spheeris' film. One punk argues that fighting is the only thing that makes him feel good. Claude Bessy, AKA Kickboy Face, *Slash* editor and lead singer of the punk band Catholic Discipline puts it all in the peculiar punk perspective: "We're not grooving on the same vibes anymore. We're grooving on different vibes . . . ugly vibes."

Eugene, a skinhead who opens *The Decline of Western Civilization* with a treatise on how punk has "no stars—no bullshit," expresses his rationale for rebellion via vague references to buses and poseurs. For him, as for so many other punks, the city is both subject and object, at once sacred and profane, a kind of indecipherable, repugnant yet seductive fact of life.

The most obvious performative outlet for this familiar urban frustration was the phenomenon of pogo. A dance, done to music executed at 250 beats a minute (disco for example is performed at half that speed), pogo (and its offspring, the even less structured slam dance) was pure and simple the performance of violence. Whereas mainstream rock and roll sugarcoats an essential misanthropy and misogyny as teenage romance and rebellion, the punks accepted the "teenage wasteland" for what it is. Punk was the celebration of resignation. It was anomie as artistic impulse. And in a cult of aggressive egalitarianism (everyone is worthless/everyone is the same) everyone involved in the punk performance was part of the performance.

To Spheeris' credit (and coincident with her decision to document rather than comment on the LA punk scene), the concert material in *The Decline of Western Civilization* is almost exclusively shot from the point of view of the audience. There the camera is obscured, jostled, harassed, threatened, knocked over, kicked and cursed and abused by the maniacal pogo dancing punks. "Actually there is no difference between dancing and fighting," a bouncer muses as he grabs a security guard by the throat. Shaking his co-worker like a rag doll he adds, "This, for example, is dancing."

Alex Cox's cult-fiction film *Repo Man* purposefully attends to the significance of the city to LA punk culture. The film's focus on the unglamorous East LA city-scape as opposed to the fun, sun and surf allure of Santa Monica, Malibu or Venice (where the majority of mainstream TV and cinema are shot) depicts the city as just one large bad neighborhood.

From the opening credit sequence to the closing scene hovering above the night-lit city in a radioactive automobile, *Repo Man* leaps and lunges from one thing to the next, never effacing (in fact celebrating) the anti-aesthetics of the low budget B movie. Much of the film is comical and ridiculous, banking on postmodern pastiche, kitsch and camp. The film features aliens, a radioactive car and an obscure plot involving repo men battle g-men. The film's truth-teller, Miller, who waxes philosophical while burning garbage under the striking LA smog sunset, talks of the cosmic relevance of "plates of shrimp" and argues that (in of all places LA) "the more you drive the less intelligent you are." His revelations are characteristically off-center which explains why he has such authority in the film.

Repo Man rather blankly wades through hackneyed dialogue reminiscent of the strained seriousness of 50's B movie teenage melodramas, as evident in the following scene: Duke (dying from a gunshot wound suffered while robbing a 7-11): "I know a life of crime has led me to this sorry fate. And yet I blame society—Society made me what I am." Otto (the punk cum repo man hero of the film played by Emilio Estevez): "That's bullshit. You're a white suburban punk just like me." Duke: "But it still hurts," (and he dies).

The helter skelter pace of the film not only punctuates the searing punk music score, but allows filmic material to simply appear and disappear without much coherence or apparent authorial organization, as if any pretense to order would betray the punk sensibility of the film. But despite its B-movie cliches and scatterbrained narrative, *Repo Man* successfully posits a realistic and depressing view of the city and its youth. When Kevin, Otto's straight friend, mindlessly stacks and prices cans of generic cling peaches in a small city supermarket he sings the 7-Up jingle ("Feeling' 7-Up/I'm feelin' 7-Up"). Later on in the film, Kevin peruses the want ads, "There's room to move as a fry cook," he says, "in two years I'll be assistant manager. It's key." That Otto rejects such acquiescence helps to define his separation and heroism.

There is a progressive argument to be made about *Repo Man*—a critical position seldom staked with regard to punk art and lifestyle. Fred Pfeil argues that *Repo Man* "reproduces the relation between the bonenumbing vacuity and circularity of daily life ..." noting that the film's "sudden jolts of idiotic violence" offer a profound if parodic (Pfeil would argue postmodern) critique of "the nowhere city." Pfeil then comments on "the simultaneous desire and dread of some ultimate, externally imposed moment of truth" in *Repo Man;* a moment that "once and for all would put an end to the endless, senseless repetitions of which our lives seem to be made."

Repo Man, though deliberately narratologically incoherent, does evince a coherent tract on the effect of the city on its disenfranchised youth. And though the film has been championed by its primarily postpunk, white urban and suburban youth audience—and I suppose in effect misunderstood by them as a camp teen film comedy, a *Beach Party* with 80's nudity, bad language and technology—*Repo Man* should not be disparaged because of its popularity. It is just unfortunate that punk, as with all other youth movements, has been annexed into mainstream popular culture, and, as is so often the case, it has re-surfaced as far less threatening and far less politically important to those too young or too rich or too suburban to really understand what the movement meant less than a decade past.

CERTAINLY MAINSTREAM ROCK AND ROLL has had a significant effect on the American teenage population. And apropos to Tipper Gore, the music and the multi-billion dollar consumer culture that accompanies it stupidly celebrates sex and drugs and anti-social behaviour.

Punk on the other hand offered no escapist merchandising scheme. The self-effacing, self-mutilating, self-abusive tendencies of punk—shared by its performers and fans to the point of establishing the movement's most significant bond—were dramatically "performed" in ceremonies of complete sexual and physical surrender. Punk slam and pogo dancing guaranteed physical injury. The indiscriminate abuse of drugs and alcohol common among the punks involved none of the glamour and pretense to being cool commonly associated with mainstream rock and roll. Rather, substance abuse among the punks was purposeful. It was a ritual of self-destruction; subsuming the self, not to the commodity (as in conventional rock and roll), but to a senseless, stupid culture revealed in a decaying urban environment where glamour, romance and petty teenage angst are comical and unacceptable.

A sense of desperation is captured in the music. And despite the speed and volume of the songs, the lyrics are audible and (because they are simplistic and repeated several times) comprehensible. In the baiting, the heckling, the fistfights between band members and the crowd, a kind of bizarre kinship is maintained. Club owner Brenden Mullen called punk the folk music of the 1980's; and in the purest sense of the term "folk," he is right. For the appropriately initiated, the ritual nature of punk was far more significant than it has ever been or ever will be for mainstream rock and roll.

The cultural importance of popular music since the advent of rock and roll some thirty years ago is the subject of a rather divergent debate. Some culture critics, here most notably the proponents of the Frankfurt School, cite the almost immediate commodification of rock and roll by "the culture industry." Just as "youth culture" surfaced as a critical term, the same 9–14 and 15–24 year olds became the principal media and consumer target groups. Other critics, many of them rock and roll historians like Robert Christgau, Greil Marcus and Dick Hebdige maintain arguments regarding rock and roll's unifying, even emancipatory function. Bernard Gendron summarizes this idealistic approach as follows: ". . . rock and roll's appearance at a particular juncture of class, generational and cultural struggle has given it a preeminent role among mass cultural artifacts as an instrument of opposition and liberation."

In "On Popular Music" (first published in 1941) Theodor Adorno juxtaposes mass market, assembly line commodity production with the "Tin Pan Alley culture industry" that "standardizes" popular music. By connecting popular music to factory production Adorno vents his rage against a popular culture industry that stupefies its audience. In punk, Adorno's fears regarding the repetitive and reductive tendencies of popular music are dramatically played out, but to a significantly different ideological effect.

Punk music is fast, loud and for the most part simplistic. The songs seldom last more than a scant two minutes and are often indistinguishable from one another. LA punk bands like Black Flag and the Circle Jerks actually highlight the indistinguishability of their songs, allowing one number to run into (or over) another. This standardization, so abhorred by Adorno and so much a part of his critique of the culture industry, is in punk music part of a unifying ceremonial performance. For punk, musical and lyrical repetition bears a dramatic political and collective ritual import.

Punk music is simple enough and standard enough to consistently incite violence and riot. In the purest sense punk, however politically confused on the surface, realizes the ever so elusive emancipatory popular culture so optimistically envisioned by Walter Benjamin and so skeptically lamented by Adorno, fellow Frankfurt School theorists Max Horkheimer and Herbert Marcuse, C. Wright Mills and Robert Warshow, who argues the following in his landmark study, *The Immediate Experience:* ". . . the chief function of mass culture is to relieve one of the necessity of experiencing one's life directly."

However we view the function and significance of popular culture in America today, the issue of the specific ideological agenda of punk remains a difficult issue. The songs performed by X, Black Flag, the Circle Jerks, the Germs, Catholic Discipline and Fear often feature overtly political lyrics, but given the setting and performance the precise point is often obscure or paradoxical. Black Flag, for example, a band fronted by an Hispanic lead singer who lives in a gutted church, perform "White Minority," a fascist, racist rant made altogether paradoxical by the lead singer's ethnicity. Another of their songs, "Depression," heralds a conventional rock and roll sentiment, teenage angst, but with a clearly more angry and desperate subtext: "Got no friends/No girls want to touch me/I don't need your fucking sympathy."

X, the one LA punk band to achieve commercial success (by necessarily abandoning the movement), match high speed rhythms essential for pogo and slam dancing with ironic, black comic lyrics. Their best known song "Nausea," about vomiting blood after drinking too much is a classic rock and roll bar song with a shifted focus (to the morning after) and "Johnny Hit and Run Pauline," which uncritically tells of a violent rape fantasy, takes the mainstream rock and roll penchant for misogyny and sexual violence to graphic extremes. X, who were discovered by former Doors' member Ray Manzarek, also display a more self-conscious and ironic side with songs about Jacqueline Susann, "sex and dying in high society," and landlord tenant relations (in the classic, "We're Desperate," lyrics as follows: We're desperate/Get used to it/We're desperate/It's kiss or kill.).

Exene, the lead singer of X who met fellow X member John Doe at a poetry workshop in Venice, argues that "the only performance that 'makes it' is the one that achieves total madness." Curiously, Exene's remark is a direct quote from the British New Wave film *Performance*, written and directed by Nick Roeg in 1970. In *Performance*, Rolling Stones' lead singer Mick Jagger plays a down and out rock and roll performer who finally decides that suicide is (on so many levels) the ultimate public act.

The LA punk bands all seem to share Exene's fixation with madness. In the late seventies the most interesting bands made their reputation by getting barred from one club or another for inciting riots. Black Flag for example, introduce one of their numbers in *The Decline of Western Civilization* with the following: "This song is for the *L.A.P.D.* We got arrested the other night ... for playing punk rock music ... they called it a public nuisance. This song is for them and it's called 'Revenge'."

Since musicianship and professionalism are the trappings of commercial rock and roll, many of the LA punk bands made a spectacle out of their own lack of musical talent. (In this too there are the seeds of a true egalitarian, proletarian art, supported by standardization and simplicity.) Here the Germs provide a most telling example. Germs' performances were never organized around songs but "gained meaning" from the bizarre ramblings and completely drug-altered behaviour of their lead singer Darby Crash. As it may not have been evident at the time, Crash's on stage performance was a thinly veiled public suicide ritual. What had its perversely funny moments (Crash's habit for forgetting to sing into the microphone, for example) also had its darker side. Every Germs performance ended with Crash hurling himself limp-limbed into the audience. When he'd emerge he'd be effaced with magic marker drawings all over his face and chest, or worse, cut by a knife or piece of glass in the melee on the floor. When Crash died of a drug overdose at the height of his "fame," he became the movement's unlikely martyr, its rebel, its James Dean.

Though terms like "star" and "fame" were anathema to the punks, Crash was the movement's best known figure—a kind of scene-maker who precisely because of his lack of true star qualities (charisma, attractiveness, wit, etc.) became a punk legend. His death, a familiar fate to so many punks who similarly abused drugs, seemed appropriate, like Dean's death (which so symbolized living fast and dying young to his teenage fans).

The Circle Jerks, whose "hits" include "Red Tape," "Beverly Hills" (beginning with the lyrics: "Beverly Hills/Century City/everything/looks so pretty/all the people/look the same/don't they know they're fucking lame"), "I Just Want Some Skank" and "Back Against the Wall" (featuring the chorus: "You can curse/spit/throw bottles . . . but it all ends with a swift kick in the ass") efface musicality and professional performance by standardizing their songs to lengths under sixty seconds. Every Circle Jerks' song reveals an identical chord pattern. One song simply begins as another ends. There are no refrains, no codas, no hooks and no payoff endings.

Catholic Discipline, a band founded by a charismatic, misplaced Paris aesthete Claude Bessy, takes its name from graffiti found on the men's room wall in the Masque. Bessy's performance features a caustic harangue at the audience, which is typical of punk. "I just want (the audience) to hate me," Bessy says, "It makes me feel good." Bessy, like performance artist Sergio Premoli, fashions himself an artiste and his songs bear out an irreverent penchant for the mixed metaphor. Catholic Discipline's best know compositions are "Barbie Doll Love," chronicling Bessy's habit of fondling the famous doll in his pocket and "Underground Babylon," featuring references to the Bible, DW Griffith's *Intolerance* and Kenneth Anger's *Hollywood Babylon*.

Of all the bands, Fear was the most provocative and charismatic. Once featured on "Saturday Night Live," their performance was so savage and anarchic and their pogo dancing entourage so out of control that NBC executives forced the show's producer, Lorne Michaels, to cut to commercial long before the set was complete. Their front man, Lee Ving (now something of a film star after his role as a sleazy club owner in *Flashdance*), like Bessy, purposefully provoked the audience between numbers. His remarks were characteristically obscene and bitter and his disdain for public propriety was the kind of punk performance that "made it"—that achieved the madness of public outrage and riot.

In response to a heckler in *The Decline of Western Civilization*, Ving shouts: "Next time don't bite so hard when I come." Preceding their final number in the film, Ving attacks the record industry: "If there are any A and R people out there, go die!" Ving is unapologetic and he is not ironic or parodic. When he mocks homosexuals ("We're from Frisco," he says hanging his wrist limply, "We think you're a bunch of queers . . ."), there is no liberal critical distance. When he says "You know why chicks have their holes so close together? . . . so you can carry them around like sixpacks," his disdain for public propriety is the point of his performance; it is the only real rationale for performance.

Fear's live set includes: "Beef Bologna" (revealing Ving's girlfriend's taste with regard to cuts of meat), "Let's Have a War/So You Can Go Die" (Fear's answer to the population explosion), "I Don't Care About You/Fuck You," and the punk anthem "I Love Livin' in the City" (lyrics as follows: "My house smells just like a zoo/It's chock full of shit and puke/cockroaches on my walls/crabs are crawlin' on my balls/oh I'm so clean cut/I just want to fuck some slut/I love livin' in the city . . . suburban scumbags/they don't care/they just get fat/and dye their hair/I love livin' in the city."). Their performance in *The Decline of Western Civilization* closes with a satire of the national anthem: "O'er the land of the free/and the homos and Jews."

As a cultural artifact—as a cultural phenomenon—the LA punks dramatically raise certain central questions regarding the relative autonomy of youth culture and the liberating potential of popular culture in general and rock and roll in specific. Bernard Gendron, deferring to the Birmingham School of Culture Theory, paraphrases Dick Hebdige when he writes: "One cannot understand the meaning of a rock and roll record without situating it within the youth cultures which typically consume it. In effect . . . the punks rewrite the recorded text . . . by recontextualizing it within their practices and rituals."

Citing such a point of view in conjunction with Roland Barthes' concept of a "readerly text," Gendron posits the following (familiar) ideological conclusion: "If either the artist or the consuming public is the primary creator of . . . meaning, then rock and roll does have the liberatory power so often claimed for it."

David E. James characterizes punk "as the final modernist capitulation to decadence, irrationality and despair," and posits his argument, finally, in ideological (mass cultural), terms: "(Punk is) a recalcitrant stance against the bland conformity of mass society." James goes on to cite punk as "avant garde and populist," though here is "progressive ideological" approach and desire to affix a method to the madness that so dominated downtown LA in the late seventies gets the better of him. Certainly punk has many of the qualities of an avant garde practice akin to the Dadaists and Surrealists, though it is stretching things to view the LA of the late seventies as a rebirth of the Paris of the 1920's. More obvious and telling are the unsettling parallels to Berlin circa 1925–1933.

By 1981 punk had all but vanished from the LA club scene. X appeared on "American Bandstand" with Dick Clark and accepted a major label record contract. The clubs that had made their reputations on the riots incited by Fear, Black Flag and the other punk bands began showcasing "safer" acts.

Punk's brief hold on a very unhappy segment of the urban LA population testifies to a mass cultural conclusion made by Dana Polan in "Brief Encounters': Mass Culture and the Evacuation of Sense": ". . . the new mass culture may operate by offering no models whatsoever, preferring instead a situation in which there are no stable values, in which there are no effective roles that one can follow from beginning to end." In such a scenario, all popular culture becomes part of an intertextual spectacle in which punk was (at the very least) a very significant and disturbing scene.

Discussion Questions

Content

1. Early in his essay, Lewis calls the punk movement "a unique moment in the history of American youth culture." What does he think made the punk movement unique? Are you inclined to agree with him? If punk was unique, what do you think it can tell us about youth movements in urban culture in general?

2. Throughout his essay, Lewis refers to the relationship between punk and the city. For example, Lewis reports that punk clubs were located in the worst neighborhoods of the city and contends that punk culture appropriated graffiti to "[call] attention to (but never asking anyone to change) the dreadful landscape of decaying urban America." Do you think that, as an urban youth movement, punk has any relationship to current urban cultural forms? Do the ways that the city is seen, either from inside or outside, seem to you to have been influenced at all by the punk ethic of accepting the decay of cities and the social relationships within them?

3. Lewis's article reveals that punk culture expanded beyond music and clothing into dance, literature, magazines, performance art, and other cultural forms. Do you see any consistency in the ways that punk culture used these forms? What do you understand to be the central ethic of this movement?

Form

1. At various points in his essay, Lewis discusses the ways that other critics have interpreted punk's meanings and values. After listing these interpretations in the order that Lewis offers them in his text, discuss how you think his organization of these explanations influences readers to interpret punk's meanings.

2. Lewis writes his essay as an objective account of the punk scene. In what ways does his objectivity shape the form of his final product? How does his essay seek to avoid being personal? How does it seek to avoid being opinionated? Do you think that it successfully achieves objectivity?

3. Does the form of this essay seem appropriate to you given its stated purposes and topic? What aspects of the punk aesthetic does it seem to you to demonstrate through its form? What parts of the punk aesthetic do you think the essay ignores or challenges through the way that Lewis writes? How can you imagine that the essay would have a different form if it had been written by a member of the punk scene rather than by an observer?

Writing Prompts

1. Lewis writes that punk expressed "the desperation residing at the heart of the now failed urban American dream." Write an essay that describes what you think the urban American dream is or was. In what senses do you think that the American dream is still an urban dream?

2. Write an essay that tries to recognize and describe the ways in which a particular youth culture leaks out of its primary medium and into other cultural forms. As a model, look at Lewis's description of the ways that punk music informed more mainstream writing, performance art, film making, etc.

Charles Gandee is a staff writer for Vogue *who has written dozens of articles on beauty and fashion for the magazine since the early 1990s. Previously, Gandee wrote for many years on architectural and interior design topics for* Architectural Record *and* House & Garden, *and at* House & Garden *he wrote a column entitled "Gandee at Large" from 1988 to 1992. Gandee's article "Off the Street . . . and Into the Future" first appeared in* Vogue *in April 1994. In the article, Gandee demonstrates that many fashions being shown on runways are obviously inspired by clothing worn on the streets of American cities by members of subcultures and young people of various races. Gandee sees the direct influence on high fashion of the hip-hop, grunge, biker, and punk revival subcultures, as well as of the general sloppiness, thrift-shop fashions, body piercing, and tattooing favored by many young people. While reading Gandee's article, think about his idea that various street fashions have influenced high fashion—which will presumably be sold at high prices and worn by people other than those who originally created and wore the style. Does this change the meaning of the clothing style—for instance, if someone who is not a member of the hip-hop or punk revival subculture wears the clothing styles associated with that subculture? Is it even possible for the clothing fashions of the wealthy to originate on city streets?*

Off the Street . . . and Into the Future

Charles Gandee

OVER THE LAST FEW YEARS, strident elitism and let-'em-eat-cake exclusivity have taken a well-documented plunge in the polls. The new image of choice is populist rather than elitist, inclusive rather than exclusive. Its provenance is South Beach, not Southampton; the East Village, not the Upper East Side; Melrose Avenue, not Rodeo Drive; raves, not Regine's. One of the consequences of this revised agenda has been the erosion of the time-honored notion that fashion originates on the runway, then trickles down to the street. Today, it seems, it's the inverse notion—that fashion originates on the street, then percolates up to the runway—that's holding sway.

As the staples of the street become the staples of the runway, it becomes increasingly difficult to identify who the contemporary arbiters of style and taste really are. Whom, for example, do we thank for T-shirts, hooded sweatshirts, baseball caps, bibbed overalls, and denim jeans? Whom do we thank for high-top basketball sneakers, rubber flip-flops, and combat boots? And whom do we thank for creating the fashion for tattoos and body piercing, for flapping shirttails, for beyond-baggy pants, for underwear worn as outerwear, for *le style Goodwill*?

That designers should attempt to get in step with the changing times by looking for inspiration not to the heavens but to the earth is understandable. But while few would argue that the runway should not reflect the reality of the street, the closer that reflection comes to mirror accurate, the more in jeopardy becomes the definition of the word *designer*—as someone who actually designs, rather than refines.

Perhaps the most surreal example, at least to date, of the rerouting of influence occurred last October in Paris when Karl Lagerfeld sent model Stephanie Roberts sailing down the Chanel runway in beige Rollerblades adorned with black interlocking C's. Though Roberts moved so fast that it was hard to get a good look at what she was wearing, Claudia Schiffer and Cindy Crawford were close on her (w)heels, which gave the rapt audience a chance to check out the familiar uniform of the boyz 'n the 'hood that Lagerfeld had appropriated for Chanel's spring/summer '94 collection. While there's nothing remotely populist about $970 Rollerblades, $140 elastic suspenders, and $620 oversize jeans with $55 cotton bandannas poking out of the back pocket, clearly the guaranteed-to-get-a-collection-noticed idea was to show that the door to the House of Chanel is open wide to the street. That a hip-hop homeboy happened to walk in is surprising only to those who have forgotten that three seasons back it was the Hell's Angels who roared up to 31 rue Cambon inspiring Lagerfeld to sew the Chanel label onto black leather motorcycle boots, black leather motorcycle caps, and black leather motorcycle jackets.

THAT HOMEBOYS, Hell's Angels, bicycle messengers, and awkward teenagers dressed in two-sizes-too-small T-shirts and three-sizes-too-large jeans are now regarded as muses is a phenomenon that Christian Lacroix views with some ambivalence. "I think that we are tired of 'salon' fashion, of 'ivory tower' fashion," opines the couturier who gave us the pouf. "Even for the couture we need the impact of real life, because if you keep couture in the windows and in the museums, you will kill it. You need to have the impulse and the energy of the street." On the other hand, cautions Lacroix, "we have to be very, very, very careful and not do expensive fashion based on the problems of other people—even if, and it's terrible to say, very often the most exciting outfits are from the poorest people." The subject is on the designer's mind because he's just seen the January Comme des Garçons show, which he "loved" but found unsettling. "They looked exactly like the homeless. It's exactly the same: The poor guy sleeping in a cardboard box on the street and the guy on the runway this weekend were clad exactly the same. That's very disturbing. At some point you must wonder, is that interesting for a customer? And is that, I don't say 'politically correct' because I'm not interested in being politically correct, but is that humanly correct?" . . .

Gianni Versace . . . claims that "the most important thing is to represent through fashion the present time." To stay in tune with the present time, Versace keeps one eye on MTV—"I am an addict"—and the other on the street. "The influence of the street is enormous—the attitude of the young, the elegance of the elderly. The past, present, and future are always in the street. It is up to the designer to translate the street fashion onto the runway, then to the people, and, finally, to bring it back to the street."

Among the street fashions that Versace has chosen to "translate" most recently is punk, which is currently enjoying a revival in London, New York, and L.A., and which provided the foundation for Versace's spring/summer '94 ready-to-wear collection—especially memorable because the dresses were literally held together by that most iconic of punk symbols, the safety pin. Three months later, for his spring/summer '94 couture collection, it was bibbed overalls that caught Versace's ever-roving eye.

Safety pins and bibbed overalls may seem peculiar points of departure, but they are certainly no more peculiar than the "street leather" that inspired the designer and his sister, Donatella, two years ago to come up with what was sometimes referred to as the bondage collection, sometimes referred to as the dominatrix collection. "I believe that fashion can start from the most unexpected places," reports Versace, whose edgy rendition of fetish wear brought to mind bondage clubs named the Vault, the Dungeon and Hell, and specialty boutiques named the Pink Pussycat, the Pleasure Chest, and the Marquis de Suede.

In addition to raising the somewhat provocative question of which street Gianni Versace is spending time on, the designer's basically black-leather collection—like his punk and bibbed overalls collections—vividly illustrates the point that the street is a place of dramatic extremes. Particularly those streets where the young and the hip and the cool and the trendy promenade.

Unlike on the runway, where there tends to be an organizing principle, a stylistic theme, on the street there is visual chaos, aesthetic anarchy. Along Melrose Avenue in West Hollywood, for example, the visual cacophony is cranked up to a near deafening decibel. There are longhaired "grungies" in Birkenstocks, flannel shirts, and knit ski caps, and no-hair skinheads in storm-trooper boots and black T-shirts with what can only be described as antisocial messages written on them. There are boys in skirts and girls with pierced noses, pierced tongues, pierced eyebrows . . . pierced whatevers. There are teenagers driving new Porsches but dressed in old blue-collar work shirts with VERNON written on the pocket, right below TEXACO. There are the more than vaguely vampirish "gothic kids"—devotees of the bands Christian Death and Ministry—who wear lots of black velvet and even more white makeup, which make them look like *Addams Family* extras.

There are homeboys wearing overalls and biker boys wearing chains. There are androgynous girls in pajama-like scrub suits and girly girls in heels, hot pants, and halters.

"You can see 50 years of fashion walking up and down this street," boasts Tracy Morse, who works at Aaardvark's, a secondhand clothing store on Melrose where you can deck yourself out in your decade of choice—from forties furs to fifties poodle skirts to sixties bellbottoms to seventies double knits to eighties shoulder pads. "The seventies thing is very big," reports Morse, who adds that *The Partridge Family* is a strong influence. "But the newest trend is the eighties thing—the Michael Jackson zipper look, the punk-rock ripped-fishnet-stocking look, the sexpot look." As it happens, Christian Lacroix anticipates the return of the style of the early eighties for the late nineties, a time, he predicts, when fashion will fall under the spell of the vintage early eighties work of Guy Bourdin, Helmut Newton, and Francesco Scavullo. "It's very interesting to rediscover these images of very kinky glamour" notes Lacroix.

GIVEN THE BLINDING RANGE of options available on the streets and in the clubs, precisely what a designer chooses to take as "inspiration" is as revealing as what that designer makes of it.

Asked what he has picked up from the street recently, Todd Oldham quips, "I had colors dyed to match spilled antifreeze on the street, and I've picked up pieces of twigs and broken glass from the street that we've cast into buttons. But as far as mopping street style, I don't have to, I have enough ideas. It seems absurd to me to mop ideas from eighteen-year-olds on the street. Why do we need to see things on the runway that we see on the street? It's truly proof that the designer as dictator is dead. Very dead." Which is something Oldham doesn't mourn. "If influence is coming from what people are already wearing, then surely people are not that interested in what we're doing. Which is good because it means that people are thinking for themselves, that they're not all frothy about what length or silhouette we're pushing. It's an interesting time in fashion; there's a lot of confusion, which is good."

Even though Oldham is skeptical of the penchant for appropriation, he acknowledges that certain street fashions have had a positive—and powerful—impact. "Rap style is probably the most important influence on clothes we've had in years. It shook loose boundaries beyond belief. It changed everybody's concept of size, of fit, of proportion, of color. It doesn't influence my design, because I have a specific sensibility in what I do. But the freedom of it is inspiring."

A designer with a well-deserved reputation for being in touch with the young and the hip, Marc Jacobs reports that "the influence of the street goes without saying. When people ask, 'What's your inspiration?' you don't even want to utter the word *street,* because you take it for granted." Of the allure the street holds, 30-year-old Jacobs says, "The reason kids look so cool is that they do it with such abandon. There's none of that sort of preciousness. In the end, the attitude gives it a contemporary edge."

Commercial attempts to re-create that contemporary edge by dressing millionaire models up like downtown hipsters is a doomed endeavor, according to Norma Kamali: "The reality is it looks better when it's on the street." So although the designer responsible for taking cotton fleece out of the locker room in the early eighties still keeps her eye on the street, what inspires Kamali now is the mood on the sidewalk, the message implicit in the clothes people wear every day. Which is? "I see active clothes, athletic clothes. I see real, easy fabrics—cotton, fleece, denim. I see T-shirts. I see shorts, shorts, shorts. I see jackets, jackets, jackets in everything from nylon to twill. I see clothes under $100. To me, that's what's really happening—active clothes, sports clothes, and clothes that cost under $100 ... well, under $200."

ECHOING KAMALI, downtown designer Patricia Field—whose basement boutique on Manhattan's hipsters-on-parade Eighth Street has been a bell-wether of style since 1973—regards activewear and sportswear as "the big fashion statement" of the last decade. Of the current popularity of the three stripes that signal Adidas, Field says, "That's just this year's model." How Adidas stripes came to be this year's model—came to sweep the New York runways last October—might have something to do with the fact that Queen Latifah and her rapper brothers have been onto Adidas stripes for some time now, which is to say well before either Madonna or Donna.

The elevation of sportswear to fashion, according to Field, reflects the trend toward populism: "In the second half of the eighties, everything sort of melted down to the same thing. Whether you bought it at Giorgio Armani or the Gap, the message was the same—it was sort of a Depression look."

And now, looking ahead to the second half of the nineties? According to Field: "When the higher levels are looking to the lower levels, when fashion is going from the street up, it's usually at a point when the higher levels are losing the energy and the momentum. The street is much younger, let's say, than the houses of haute couture. Kids have a different energy. Youth has a different perspective, a different motivation, a different budget."

So what will influence the runway tomorrow? "The streets tell me technology," says Field, sounding a bit like a fortune teller looking into her crystal ball. "Everything is sort of coming together with this consciousness of technology. Technology is the main thing that is leading the way. The fashion is aligned with the music, which is techno-music, which is basically music coming out of computers. It's sort of a pop-techno-commercialism, where kids take well-known brand names that they see on TV or in the supermarket, like Tide or Bold, and twist them around—like that T-shirt with a marijuana leaf superimposed on the word *Adidas*. I think that's connected with this whole techno influence. These kids have been brought up in a techno age—their references are television and computers, as opposed to books."

Discussion Questions

Content

1. According to the article, what are designers looking for when they look at the streets of our cities? What is it that they see in urban clothing styles that they want to capture?

2. Gandee quotes designers who say that street fashion has "energy" and "anarchy." Are these the qualities that you see in urban fashions? What makes energy and anarchy important parts of city life? Are these qualities maintained when the fashions are turned into expensive designer clothing? What do you think it even means for energy and anarchy to be qualities of a particular style?

3. Can street fashions really be turned into designer fashions, considering the changes in cost, materials, and the people who will be purchasing and wearing them? Even if the look is successfully copied, do the changes in cost and in who's wearing it make it no longer a street fashion? What is lost and what is gained in the evolution from street style to high fashion?

Form

1. Who does this article seem to be written for? Designers? People on the street? People who wear designer clothing? What clues from the article itself suggest to you one audience as opposed to another? In what ways do you think his article would be different if it were aimed at a different audience?

2. What kinds of examples does Gandee provide in his article? Are they all of the same type? Do they provide different perspectives on the issue of designers mimicking street fashions, or do they all demonstrate the same perspective? What for you is the cumulative effect of Gandee's examples? Are they persuasive enough? Why or why not?

3. Gandee starts his essay by saying that the new fashions are "populist rather than elitist" and "inclusive rather than exclusive." What does this opening cause you as a reader to expect? How does the remainder of his essay develop from this statement in the way you expected? In what ways does Gandee not develop the statement as you expected him to? How might you develop the article differently?

Writing Prompts

1. Write a short essay that discusses one of your favorite fashions. Compare and contrast the meaning of the style for you now with the meaning of the same style when worn by people who seem to you to identify themselves differently. Consider, for example, whether baggy pants means the same thing for you as it does for someone who is older or poorer, or who has a different ethnic background.

2. Gandee discusses the moral issues inherent in the idea of high, expensive fashions copying the styles of poorer people living in urban areas. Write an essay in which you argue whether it is morally acceptable for high fashion to copy street fashion.

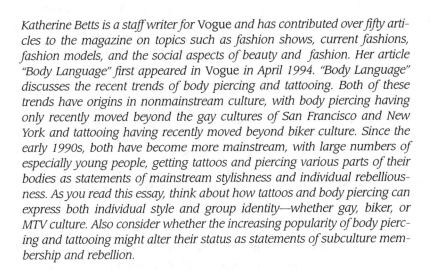

Katherine Betts is a staff writer for Vogue *and has contributed over fifty articles to the magazine on topics such as fashion shows, current fashions, fashion models, and the social aspects of beauty and fashion. Her article "Body Language" first appeared in* Vogue *in April 1994. "Body Language" discusses the recent trends of body piercing and tattooing. Both of these trends have origins in nonmainstream culture, with body piercing having only recently moved beyond the gay cultures of San Francisco and New York and tattooing having recently moved beyond biker culture. Since the early 1990s, both have become more mainstream, with large numbers of especially young people, getting tattoos and piercing various parts of their bodies as statements of mainstream stylishness and individual rebelliousness. As you read this essay, think about how tattoos and body piercing can express both individual style and group identity—whether gay, biker, or MTV culture. Also consider whether the increasing popularity of body piercing and tattooing might alter their status as statements of subculture membership and rebellion.*

Body Language

Katherine Betts

THE TWO ENGLISH GIRLS poring over the neat rows of barbell- and hoop-shaped jewelry in the black-velvet-lined display cases at Manhattan's Gauntlet piercing parlor look worried. Maybe they're not worried, just nervous. I definitely am worried, and my name's not even listed in the Gauntlet's appointment calendar to get one of those increasingly popular $35 navel piercings. I'm just here to interview the manager.

"Just sit down and we're gonna show you the after-care video we've put together to teach you how to care for your navel while it's healing," says a superpolite piercer called Bobby who will be doing the damage (literally) on these two relatively prissy-looking girls. I sit down to watch the video with them, but when a close-up of some guy's nipple ring flashes on the screen, I'm already averting my eyes. Unfortunately, there's little else to look at in this preeminent parlor without cringing, from the raunchy photos of pierced models lining the walls to the heavily pierced employees behind the jewelry counter to the clients themselves—a peculiar mix of long-haired heavy-metal types, Generation-Xers with major grunge hangovers, a few daffy New Agers from Silicon Valley, and a handful of very well groomed European tourists. This is not the East Village, by the way; this is Fifth Avenue, one block down from Emporio Armani.

"We get all types in here," says manager Mark Seitchik, the senior piercer with several of his own badges of courage placed strategically around his face—nose, ear, lip (he had his tongue pierced too but felt there was too much metal going on around his mouth, so he took it out)."From 18-year-old street punks to 80-year-old retired judges. I wouldn't say piercing's gone mainstream, but it's definitely attracting a pretty diverse crowd lately." Likewise, Leo Zulueta, a co-owner of the Black Wave tattoo parlor on Los Angeles's La Brea, says he has tattooed every type—from dental instructors to federal prosecutors, and even a Catholic priest.

Indeed, five years ago body piercing was to the downtown gay and punk-rock scenes of big cities like New York and San Francisco what tattooing was to the Harley-Davidson biker crowd. Back then the act of tattooing or piercing had its own kind of clan or tribal identification, which was resolutely underground and usually, in the case of piercing, sexual. But if the streets of New York and San Francisco or the runways of Paris and Milan are any indication, body piercings have replaced tattoos—and even hairstyles—as the latest expression of individuality. And it's a different kind of clanning—now one ascribed to the hip and very diverse tribes of MTV, rap music, fashion, sports, and megamalls.

Like hairstyles, tattoos have been around forever. As far back as the Crusades, men were tattooed with crucifixes to ensure a Christian burial should they die on foreign soil. And for centuries the Maori of New Zealand, Tahitians, Japanese, and Native Americans tattooed for religious, tribal, social, or superstitious reasons. Although tattooing has always had deviant connotations (think circus acts, sailors, bikers, gangs, and prison inmates), some surprisingly staid historical figures have been "inked," including Winston Churchill's mother, Lady Randolph Churchill, who had herself tattooed to commemorate Edward VII's coronation. Other European crowned heads, including Edward VII and George V, had royal emblems etched discreetly on their arms. And even former secretary of state George Schultz had a tiger tattooed on his posterior while a student at Princeton.

Of course those small tattoos, tucked away underneath clothing, were meant for intimate admirers' eyes only. It wasn't until the eighties, when supermodels like Stephanie Seymour and Carré Otis and Hollywood actresses like Julia Roberts and Drew Barrymore began flaunting very public "pieces" on their shoulders, ankles, and lower backs, that tattooing took a decidedly glamorous turn. (Call me conservative, but I still do a double take when I see tattooed limbs on the likes of squeaky-clean teenagers like Niki Taylor.)

In the nineties tattooing has become so routine that jaded fashion watchers barely flinch when more elaborately tattooed models like one-time car mechanic Jenny Shimizu (who has a bawdy tattoo of a near-naked woman riding a wrench on her upper arm) or the buzz-cut model Eve Salvail (who has a large tattoo of a serpent across one side of her head) strut down the Chanel, Versace, and Calvin Klein runways of Paris, Milan, and New York. Although many tattoo artists still discourage visible pieces that can jeopardize employment, it's now common to see tattoos prominently displayed in television commercials, on lawyers in courtrooms, or even peeking out of waiters' sleeves at renowned New York City restaurants.

Tattoo "studios" have responded by upgrading their image and treating their service as an art. Places like the Inkspot II in Linden, New Jersey, cater to an elite clientele, which co-owner Steve Ferguson defines as "business-class people." "We also get our share of housewives," he adds. "They feel comfortable here, they bring the kids. It's not a freaky atmosphere like you might find on the Lower East Side. There's none of that piercing going on here; that stuffs just for shock value. Tattooing for me is an art."

In a society that rewards shock value with dollars, it makes sense that tattooing would make way for piercing. And, thanks to media vehicles like MTV and high-profile personalities like football players, piercing is everywhere, not just on the Lower East Side. At a recent Buffalo Bills game, fans and players alike flaunted multiple earrings. Models like Stella Tennant stare out from Versace couture ads with conspicuous nose rings; kids roam through malls across the country sporting hoops all over their ears and studs on their lips; and Howard Stern has invited volunteers to pierce their tongues live on television. With the blessing of fashion, piercing—like makeup, tanning, plastic surgery, and tattooing—is shedding its sexual connotations and moving from the underground to the mainstream. Let's not forget that applying makeup, now an everyday ritual for most women, was initially done to inspire erotic arousal. And tans, once a mark of lower-class status or south-of-the-border eroticism, became the height of chic when Coco Chanel and company began taking sun on the French Riviera in the 1920s (only to go out of fashion again in the 1980s because of the threat of bodily harm).

Nobody seems to be able to pinpoint the exact moment that piercing went from wrong to right—and, yes, the jury's still out—but two milestones at the European collections last October provide clues: (1) Jean Paul Gaultier's Paris runway show and (2) the morning Christy Turlington called a professional piercer to her London hotel room to pierce her navel. Gaultier, French fashion's veritable outlaw, is one thing. But Christy Turlington? The clean-cut Audrey Hepburn of supermodels piercing her navel? "I just wanted to try it," she told me sheepishly backstage at a London show hours after the deed was done. "Why not?"

Why not indeed. That's what I said to my mom when I was fifteen and desperate to get my ears pierced, and she pleaded, "Why do you want to destroy your body that way? Why do you want to put holes through your skin?" I had no real answer, it was just the thing to do. And besides, deep down I felt that urge to decorate myself. Let's face it, at fifteen the idea of wearing earrings is enchanting.

After seasons of drab black minimalism, after women quietly tucked their jewelry away so they wouldn't stand out as beacons for burglars, Gaultier's body-art show of real tattoo and piercing "collectors," followed by supermodels wearing clip-on face jewelry and sheer T-shirts decorated to look like tattoos, was enchanting too. If nothing else, he succeeded in reigniting an interest in ornamentation at a time in fashion when the slightest trace of decoration has been scorned. Then Christy took the plunge, and before you knew it couturiers like Christian Lacroix were turning out couture suits cut to expose the navel. Despite the deviant connotations, body piercing has, indirectly, helped reinstate a certain degree of femininity and sexiness in fashion—whether that means simple decoration with jewelry or more exposure of skin.

Ever since Gaultier's show and Christy's daring move, places like the Gauntlet in New York, San Francisco, and L.A. have seen a steady stream of young women between the ages of 18 and 30 signing up for navel-piercing appointments (you have to be at least 18). Nonetheless, Seitchik and his staff caution people about getting pierced just because it's trendy. "It's not a haircut, it's not a piece of clothing. You can't just throw it away," insists Seitchik. "Piercing and tattooing are things you have to be passionate about," agrees 22-year-old Shimizu, who has four substantial tattoos and a pierced navel. "You can't just do it to be trendy or you will definitely regret it. These are two things you have to live with for the rest of your life."

True. Tattoos don't come out without expensive and very painful laser surgery. And although piercings seem less complicated because they're easier to undo, the holes require cleaning at least twice a day while they heal—which can take up to nine months—and, if mistreated or neglected, can lead to infection. Gaultier's show was beautiful, but it was a show. Christy is a model; perhaps for that reason she can get away with a navel ring. But beyond those two examples, what makes a woman pierce her nose, her tongue, or her navel? Not to mention that face and body jewelry is not like your standard earring for pierced ears—the posts are much, much thicker, which means the hole is much, much bigger. Strangely, vanity is the most common answer to that nagging question.

"You can play with your body in ways other than plastic surgery," says Gaultier, who has several piercings on his ears. "It's a kind of art, it's not only sexual or sensual. People do it for beauty." Although I personally still can't see the beauty in it, I can see Gaultier's point. Piercing has been around for a long time and has meant different things to different cultures. In ancient Egypt, a navel ring indicated royalty, while in India a nose ring still signifies Hindu and Muslim devotion. Even in proper Victorian England women pierced their nipples so they could wear jewels in them.

"It's just like buying a beautiful dress," explains Maria Tashjian, an owner of Venus Modern Body Arts, a piercing studio in Manhattan's East Village. "Why do you buy a beautiful dress? Because it makes you feel beautiful, it enhances your natural features; and that's what piercing does." This comes from someone who has enhanced her natural features a lot: Tashjian has long, wild Tallulah Bankhead hair with green stripes through it and major piercings along her earlobes, in her nose, and on her lower lip. "When I first started getting into piercing, my mother asked, 'Why do you want to mutilate yourself?' But I think it's a natural human tendency to decorate."

"I pierced my tongue because I think it looks beautiful," echoes nineteen-year-old Anouche Wise, a waiflike freshman at New York University who was also contemplating getting the skin on her collarbone pierced. "It's not *that* permanent; it's just not that big a deal," she says, even though she admits that she couldn't eat for three days afterward and that the jewelry ripped up the bottom of her mouth. Why go through that kind of pain? "For vanity. So many things women do for beauty are painful. It's the same thing as getting your legs waxed or having a facelift. You just have to really want to do it."

"When you look back over history, every period is connected to some sort of body modification," Seitchik agrees. "Whether it's the plastic surgery and breast implants of the eighties or the corsets of Victorian times. This idea of falsely enhancing your beauty is human. Some parents won't let their kid get their nose pierced, but they'll pay a lot of money for them to get a nose job."

There is an important, if superficial, difference between nose jobs and piercings: The former satisfies social standards while the latter intentionally flouts them. Similarly, most body modifications in the past were practiced in order to fit in, not stand out. Piercing may be increasingly popular, but it's still a statement. Tennant, for one, says she pierced her nose as an in-your-face gesture. "Piercing has become a lot like wearing a leather jacket," says Valerie Steele, a professor at the Fashion Institute of Technology who is currently working on a book about fashion and fetishism. "For a lot of people, piercing symbolizes being a sex radical: it's a very antibourgeois gesture, and fashion is more and more about that. It's part of an ongoing fascination with the look of deviance in our society. More and more people are drawing on sadomasochistic themes in fashion without being involved with them or conscious of them."

What keeps piercing exotic is the pain factor. Unlike plastic surgeons, piercers cannot offer any kind of anesthetic, because they're not licensed, and, essentially, a shot of Novocain would probably be as painful as a piercing. "In a way, that's what makes it more attractive to some," says Harold Koda, associate curator of the Metropolitan Museum of Art's Costume Institute. "Pain is implicit, so there's always that forbidden zone, that danger." Although the idea of putting a piece of metal through some part of the body as decoration may sound exotic, consider the fact that no one thinks twice about pierced earlobes anymore.

Decoration and vanity aside, some aficionados see piercing and tattooing as a modern rite of passage or a form of outlaw bonding for an alienated generation. "For me, getting pierced was not about taking part in a fashion trend," explains Shimizu. "It was about going from a delinquent to a mature person." In a mass-market culture so immune to nudity or vulgarity, it makes sense that kids—even adults—would alter their physical appearance so blatantly in order to express and enhance their individuality. Soon nobody will think twice about visible piercings, either.

"Piercing is not really mutilation anymore, it's decorating an object," says Barbara Ilardi, a professor of psychology at the University of Rochester, who explains piercing as the result of society's objectification of the body. "In advertising and in the movies, body parts have been taken out of context as if they don't belong to the person. In doing this, we've created a culture of persons whose bodies don't belong to them." Body manipulation is now a means of gaining social acceptance, which makes it an accessory of sorts, argues Ilardi. "The message is: If you don't like the body you were given, get another one."

Discussion Questions

Content

1. As Betts explains, body piercing and tattooing have become socially acceptable and mainstream. She also states that one reason that people have them done is to make a rebellious statement. How can body piercing and tattooing be both mainstream and rebellious at the same time?

2. What reasons does the author give to explain why so many people are having their bodies pierced and/or tattooed? What do you think the stylistic meanings of tattooing and body piercing are? Why do you think they are so popular? And what does their popularity say about who we are?

3. How are body piercing and tattooing urban styles? Are only their origins urban? Or are they still predominantly stylistic statements of people who live in cities and identify themselves with having a type of urban experience?

Just what statement might someone be making by having his or her body pierced or tattooed?

Form

1. What is the author's attitude toward body piercing and tattooing? What writing devices does she use to convey her attitude? Does she persuade you to her opinion through her writing? If so, why? If not, why not?

2. How does Betts relate the popularity of body piercing and tattooing to larger current fashion trends? Does her argument seem to you to work? Try to come up with other explanations that relate body piercing and tattooing to larger trends in fashion.

3. How does Betts ask you to feel about the topic? Is there a difference between how she wants you to feel about the topic and how you do feel about it? If there is a difference, is it because of prior experiences you have had and thinking you have done on the topic? Or are there other reasons?

Writing Prompts

1. Write an essay in which you attempt to define the style of body piercing and tattooing. Are they a statement of individuality? A statement of being part of a youthful, rebellious group? A statement of being part of the subcultures that created them? Or are they possibly more than one of these?

2. Write an essay in which you compare the movement of body piercing and tattooing into the mainstream to the movement of other urban or subcultural "street" styles into the mainstream, as discussed by Charles Gandee in "Off the Street . . . and Into the Future."

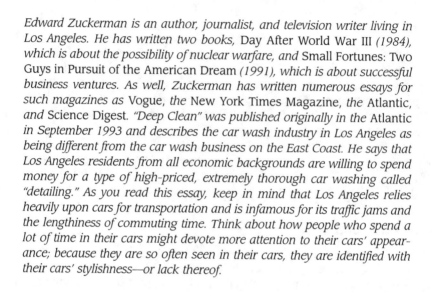

Edward Zuckerman is an author, journalist, and television writer living in Los Angeles. He has written two books, Day After World War III *(1984), which is about the possibility of nuclear warfare, and* Small Fortunes: Two Guys in Pursuit of the American Dream *(1991), which is about successful business ventures. As well, Zuckerman has written numerous essays for such magazines as* Vogue, *the* New York Times Magazine, *the* Atlantic, *and* Science Digest. *"Deep Clean" was published originally in the* Atlantic *in September 1993 and describes the car wash industry in Los Angeles as being different from the car wash business on the East Coast. He says that Los Angeles residents from all economic backgrounds are willing to spend money for a type of high-priced, extremely thorough car washing called "detailing." As you read this essay, keep in mind that Los Angeles relies heavily upon cars for transportation and is infamous for its traffic jams and the lengthiness of commuting time. Think about how people who spend a lot of time in their cars might devote more attention to their cars' appearance; because they are so often seen in their cars, they are identified with their cars' stylishness—or lack thereof.*

Deep Clean

Edward Zuckerman

SHORTLY AFTER MOVING from New York to Los Angeles, I went to get my car washed. The price was $7.50, which seemed a little steep until I realized that the car wash was different from the car washes I had known in New York City. At this car wash, they washed the car.

In New York, my car had been dragged down a mechanical track and sloshed with soap and water. Then a handful of unmotivated employees had swiped at it with wet rags. I would drive off toward the Queensboro Bridge in a dripping, smudged car that was cleaner that it used to be, but not by much.

In Los Angeles, my car was set upon by what appeared to be an entire village of Central Americans. They vacuumed the interior, attacked the hubcaps with hoses and brushes, ran the car through a mechanical wash—and then washed it again by hand.

Edward Zuckerman. "Deep Clean." From *Harper's Magazine* (Sept. 1993): 74–77. Reprinted by permission.

While this went on, I passed the time browsing in the car-wash shop, inspecting the air fresheners and cassette-tape compilations of Elvis's greatest love songs, as well as earthquake survival kits, metallized packets of emergency water rations, and several books in the Tell-a-Maid series, which contain tear-out bilingual instruction sheets to be checked off and handed to Spanish-speaking household workers (e.g., "Please clean the baby from the waist down"). Then I joined my fellow customers on the car-wash veranda, where I relaxed with a shoe shine and an enchilada while I watched a man meticulously dry my 1984 Nissan Sentra. I tipped him a dollar and drove away feeling clean.

I had no idea how mistaken I was....

[I had moved] to Los Angeles to try my fortune as a television writer.

Not long after arriving, I had an appointment at Steven Spielberg's production company, which is housed in its own hacienda on the Universal lot. I drove up in my Sentra, and the discreetly suited security guard assumed I was a messenger. I realized that this kind of thing could be a problem in Los Angeles. I couldn't afford to buy a new car, but I thought maybe I could get this one to look better. And so I eventually discovered "detailing."

People in New York City do not know what car detailing is. If they have any ideas at all, they tend to think it involves the painting of fine decorative lines on the hood and fenders, an art that I believe is known as pinstriping.

Detailing is the cleaning of a car beyond all reason. It typically costs $100 or more, and it is routinely indulged in by all kinds of people in Los Angeles. Rich executives have people come to their houses to do it once a week. Secretaries (known, in Los Angeles, as assistants) have it done a couple of times a year. The Yellow Pages are filled with ads for detailers promising to employ toothbrushes and Q-Tips in cleaning your car. There are several specialists in the detailing of black cars (which have a stubborn tendency to highlight tiny imperfections in the finish) and many in the removal of "overspray," which is a problem you probably did not know you have. (Overspray is what the wind may carry onto your car in infinitesimal quantities if someone is spraypainting something a few blocks away.)

The parking lots at the movie studios are studded with mobile detailers erecting canopies over cars they are about to work on (no decent detailer will work in direct sunlight; it makes the car too hot to hold a proper wax job). One of my first neighbors in Los Angeles was a sloppy, disorganized woman whose BMW lost its rear window in a crash. Months went by, and she never got around to getting the window replaced. But once a month she had the car detailed.

I TOOK MY CAR to Bill Larzelere, a car detailer of such excellent reputation that until recently his business had an unlisted phone number. He got more customers than he could handle through personal referral.

The recession put a dent in his prosperity—the waiting time to get your car cleaned by Larzelere has dipped to as little as a couple of weeks—so he put his number in the book. But there's still no sign to mark his establishment, just a blank concrete wall on a commercial strip in Burbank.

Behind the wall, I found Larzelere working on a partially disassembled 1972 Ferrari Daytona, a show car whose owner had recently driven it for the first time in fourteen years. From the open road he had taken it directly to Larzelere.

Larzelere explained, "When a car's like this"—i.e., driven—"you've got to semi-disassemble it to get it clean. You take the bumpers off, take the grille off, the wheels off." He pointed to the car's gleaming red body. "It has chips from pebbles and bugs," he said. I couldn't see any. "That's the biggest problem you get with driving them. That, plus they get dirty."

Larzelere, with neat graying hair and mustache, has an unassuming manner. He wears work pants and a work shirt with "Bill" in an oval stitched on his chest. His dogs wander around the shop, and there is a ferret in a cage. Counters are littered with brushes, rags, spray bottles, and rubber gloves. But the work is not casual. The day I visited, a bulletin board held a list of things to be done to a BMW, including "Replace frayed cloth tape around brackets on underside of vehicle."

Larzelere spends ten to twenty hours (at $25 per) on what he calls a "regular cleanup and polish." Treating the body paint is an eight-step process, starting with sanding and ending with glazing. Larzelere applies three layers of wax from the Brazilian carnauba palm, rubbing it in with a soft fabric used in sanitary napkins (he finds diapers too harsh). He washes the engine and the engine compartment, and he removes everything from the trunk, including the carpeting, to clean thoroughly there. He waxes the seatbelt hardware. He massages preservative into leather upholstery with his fingertips. He lines up adjacent screw heads so they point the same way. He does a lot of other things as well, and he does these things not only to old cars that his clients have been so audacious as to drive but also to new cars they bring him directly from dealer showrooms.

Larzelere's customers tend to be even fussier than he is. The owner of a black Porsche was driving through Hollywood one night when, Larzelere recalled, somebody threw "something syrupy, like Coke" onto his car. So he drove straight to Larzelere, arriving at the garage at 1:30 A.M. Larzelere was there (he often works late and sleeps at the shop). He spent an hour and a half cleaning up the mystery substance. He has also made emergency house calls to clients who have driven through puddles.

I asked Larzelere to have a look at my Sentra, which had deteriorated rather alarmingly, cleanliness-wise, in the weeks since my $7.50 car wash, and hadn't really ever been much to look at. It was one of the cheapest cars sold in America when it was new. I'd bought it used for $1,700.

Larzelere walked toward it cheerfully. "Aha!" he said. "It's dirty. It's filthy. It's from New York." He peered at the paint on the roof. "It's oxidized." He rubbed a finger over the finish. "It's dirty, but it's not *just* dirty." He rubbed the dirt off his finger. "It's dull, chalky, flat."

He looked inside. "It's Japanese. Not top of the line. The fabrics, seats, are not good. There's a lot of plastic. The carpeting's not good. You haven't used mats." His tone wasn't *too* condemning.

He examined body nicks and dings and damage from the half-dozen break-ins the car had endured in New York. He was not happy to see bird shit on the roof. "Some cars," he reflected, "are used but not abused. This I have to categorize as abused." He said he could clean it up—or at least "get this in as good condition as you could get it"—for $700. That didn't include any repairs. If I wanted to cut corners, he'd do the exterior only for $450.

There was no hard sell. He didn't need the work.

I told him I'd think about it.

I DECIDED to find a less lofty detailer than Bill Larzelere to work on my Sentra. Consulting the Yellow Pages, I settled on Detail Wizard. "Q-Tips and Toothbrushes Used!" its ad promised. "The Mobile Service That Brings Its Own Water & Power."

Two young men, an animated Salvadoran and a stone-faced Guatemalan, arrived in a van equipped with a water tank and a gasoline-powered generator to give my Sentra a $139 car wash. They erected a framework of pipes to hold a canopy over the car and began by straightforwardly washing it. This eliminated the bird shit on the roof, but it also exposed some rust spots I hadn't seen before. "The paint," pronounced the Salvadoran, who was the leader of the team, "Is not good." He said they would do what they could.

While the Guatemalan scrubbed my tires, then vacuumed and shampooed the interior of the trunk, the Salvadoran polished, glazed, waxed, and buffed my oxidized paint job. When he was done with a fender, he invited me to compare it to the hood. To my amazement, it had luster. My car had never had luster.

Pleased by my reaction, the Salvadoran turned confidently to the interior and said, "We have something for the leather." He stopped short when he saw that there was no leather. I asked if he would polish the wood beads on the taxi-style seat pad I'd bought from a vendor at a stoplight in upper Manhattan.

The Guatemalan scrubbed the dashboard with a toothbrush and cleaned out the heater vents with a Q-Tip. Then he scoured the backseat with a stiff brush, removing a black stain that had come with the car. The Salvadoran polished the exterior keyholes. When they were finished, the car looked great. I climbed in to drive it and found a greasy (but clear) film on the steering wheel and dashboard. A little too much cleanser, I supposed. Then I glanced toward the window in the passenger door and was shocked to see it missing. Had the men from Detail Wizard smashed it and fled without copping? I looked again, carefully. The window was there. It was so clean it was invisible.

I TOOK MY NEWLY DETAILED CAR for an expert evaluation to Bill Larzelere, who does not conceal his contempt for most other detailers. ("Some of them can't even wash a car. You get butter swirls. You get polish in the cracks. That's not what it's all about.") I wanted to know what he thought of Detail Wizard's work, and I was curious to know what he would have done for $561 more.

He approached the Nissan with skepticism and a wooden barbecue skewer. "They got the tires to look good," he granted. (The Guatemalan had applied a treatment that turned them a solid matte black.) "They got the paint to do okay," he said. Then he peered closely at the windshield wipers and the vent intakes beside them. "There are splatters of polish here, here, here."

He picked at them with a fingernail. He opened the driver's door and found some glue residue from an old oil-change sticker. He shook his head. "This is the big thing," he said. "They didn't clean the rubber." He ran his finger along the rubber seal at the base of the windshield. It was streaked with gray. He dug his skewer into the crack between the rubber and the glass, and it found black gunk.

Inside the car, the news was better. "It's really pretty nice, considering how bad it was. You didn't have mats. How much did it cost?"

I told him $139 plus tax and tip, and he exhaled sharply, amazed. "You certainly got your money's worth! It's good for that!"

He opened the hood and examined the paint along the thin edge. "They didn't buff through," he observed. And added, "Whether it was by accident or not, we don't know," which struck me as a little ungenerous. But apparently those narrow edges are notorious trouble spots, where careless detailers buff through exterior coats. "That's one way to ruin a $50,000 paint job," Larzelere said.

Excuse me?

It seems the Ferrari I had first seen Larzelere working on had a $50,000 paint job from Junior's House of Color, which is another southern California car institution. And another story.

Discussion Questions

Content

1. Why do you think that people in Los Angeles put so much effort into washing their cars? From what the author says, what value does a "deep clean" have for the people of Los Angeles?

2. What kind of style does a very clean car evoke? Is the style just in the car's cleanliness, or does it mean more than that? What might that something more be? Does the style have something to do with the cost of a deep clean and prestige involved?

3. Is a very clean car an expression of individual style or part of identifying with the expectations of a group—in this case Los Angeles residents? In what ways do you think individual choices about style are determined by group expectations?

Form

1. Throughout the essay, the author refers to various people who wash his car. The people who wash his car at the $7.50 car wash he refers to as "the Guatemalans" and "the Salvadorans." He refers to the most expensive detailer by name, however. What effect does referring to these people in this way have on how you picture the people who do this work? Are these judgments fair?

2. How would you describe Zuckerman's attitude toward the detailing car washes? Does his attitude change during the course of the article? Support your answer with specific references to the article.

3. Zuckerman's essay unfolds as a narrative of his education in Los Angeles car washing. What sequence of events in "Deep Clean" functions as a narrative and what parts function as an essay? How do the two elements—narrative and essay—work together to inform the reader about the topic?

Writing Prompts

1. Tell the story of the things that happened as you learned about someone else's style. Try to relate learning about that style through the series of incidents in which you learned them—i.e., teach the reader about the style in the same piecemeal method by which you learned it. At the beginning of the story, communicate what you learned first as well as the feelings (such as confusion) evoked in you by what you were learning. As the narrative progresses, communicate your growing confidence and insight into the real meaning of that style.

2. Reflect on the other essays in this part to explain how a certain style or trend can be very popular in one city but not in others. Describe a style or trend in your city, or a city that you have visited, that is not practiced elsewhere. Try to account for the reasons why the trend is particular to your city.

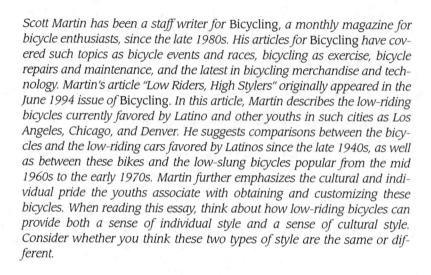

Scott Martin has been a staff writer for Bicycling, *a monthly magazine for bicycle enthusiasts, since the late 1980s. His articles for* Bicycling *have covered such topics as bicycle events and races, bicycling as exercise, bicycle repairs and maintenance, and the latest in bicycling merchandise and technology. Martin's article "Low Riders, High Stylers" originally appeared in the June 1994 issue of* Bicycling. *In this article, Martin describes the low-riding bicycles currently favored by Latino and other youths in such cities as Los Angeles, Chicago, and Denver. He suggests comparisons between the bicycles and the low-riding cars favored by Latinos since the late 1940s, as well as between these bikes and the low-slung bicycles popular from the mid 1960s to the early 1970s. Martin further emphasizes the cultural and individual pride the youths associate with obtaining and customizing these bicycles. When reading this essay, think about how low-riding bicycles can provide both a sense of individual style and a sense of cultural style. Consider whether you think these two types of style are the same or different.*

Low Riders, High Stylers

Scott Martin

YEP, THAT'S A BIKE you're looking at. A little different . . . OK, a lot different. But still a bike.

You remember lowrider cars—those rolling candy-colored showpieces that Chicanos chop and shape until you can barely squeeze a pack of cigarettes between the undercarriage and the pavement. This is the cycling version. And suddenly, it's cool.

In L.A. and other California cities you don't have to look hard to see kids on lowriders cruisin' the 'hood or hangin' at the mall. Word is that old Schwinn StingRay frames (the preferred mount) sell for upwards of $100. The demand for hardware is fed by mail-order businesses hawking reproduction parts and frames (such as Low Styler Bikes, 408/292-6546, CA). The bicycle divisions of lowrider car shows across the Southwest draw 50 or 60 entries, with the tricked-out winners valued at as much as $5,000. It's rumored that a new music video by top-selling rapper Snoop Doggy Dogg will feature lowrider bikes.

There's even a new magazine devoted to the trend. L.A.-based *Lowrider Bicycle* (909/598-9300) debuted last winter with 75,000 copies.

Nobody knows how big the craze is, just that it's spreading.

"It's growing by leaps," says *Lowrider Bicycle* publisher Alberto Lopez. "And it's not just Chicanos now. It's gone Anglo, black, Asian. Westside kids, surfers, skateboarders—they're all into it."

The phenomenon is rooted in Southern California but clubs are sprouting in northern California, Texas, Denver, and elsewhere. The bikes are popular in Hawaii and Puerto Rico, too.

"The trend has come from L.A., and it's spreading like wildfire," says Victor Flores, president of Chicago's Just Cruising Bicycle Club, a beach-cruiser group with a half-dozen ground-hugging members. "Lowriders are what's on the street right now."

LOW-SLUNG CARS have been part of Hispanic life in the U.S. since the post-World War II boom years of the late '40s and early '50s. Many Mexican-Americans who were able to afford automobiles for the first time began modifying and decorating them as a way to express pride and cultural identity.

Bikes copying the fashion appeared in the late '60s as boys too young to drive emulated their older brothers. (It's a mostly male domain.)

This was America's muscle-car era—dragsters, GTOs, Mustangs—and the youth-driven bicycle market reflected this. Every kid wanted a Schwinn Sting-Ray with a 16-inch front wheel and drum brake, springer fork, 5-speed stick shift, banana seat, mag-wheel chainring, "ape-hanger" high-rise handlebar, "sissy bar" rear strut, slick rear tire, and—if you were lucky—electric turn indicators and checkerboard rearview mirror.

The fad peaked when Schwinn began producing the Krate series of colorful Sting-Rays: the Orange Krate, Apple Krate, Pea Picker, Lemon Peeler, Cotton Picker, and Grey Ghost. The company made 17 million StingRay-style bikes from '63–'73, according to bicycle historian Jim Hurd.

"Chicanos went berserk with 'em," says Bill Blake, *Lowrider Bicycle's* technical editor and owner of Dennison Schwinn Cyclery, an L.A. shop that's served the Chicano market for generations.

Just as their older brothers removed body sections to bring the cars closer to the ground, kids cut top tubes and installed longer forks until their chainrings practically kissed the street. These machines were barely ridable, but the main idea was to be seen, not to get somewhere.

Then in the mid-'70s, BMX became popular. The new bikes were fast and light. Awkward, heavy lowriders were hip no more.

"Lowrider bikes died out," says Blake. "They took a siesta."

THE STYLE BEGAN SHOWING UP on the street again in the early '90s and then at lowrider car shows as novelties. In '91, publisher Lopez started featuring photos of bikes in his lowrider car magazine. The craze was refueled.

One reason could be nostalgia. Boys who created lowriders 20 years ago are now dads. They want to share with their sons the joy and satisfaction of crafting a personalized piece of art.

It's also a way for kids in the barrio to learn mechanical skills and stay away from gangs and drugs. The early lowrider scene—fairly or not—carried gangster connotations. Nowadays, proponents say it's a positive influence in a culture with its share of negative ones.

"I don't want to see kids roaming the streets, 'cause I got brothers who got killed on the streets," says Paul Tula. "I grew up a drug addict. I never had nothing. I didn't want kids to see me like that. I want to teach kids how to do a lot of stuff."

The Tulas are involved in the Old Style Club, a lowrider-bike group in L.A.'s San Gabriel Valley. They work on their machines, sell candy to raise money, hold barbecues and display their work at local shows.

"It's a community," says Paul Tula. "And we've got rules. These kids are not gangbangers. They don't dress in all that gangster stuff or do drugs."

WHAT THESE KIDS DO to their bikes makes traditional bicycle collectors weep all over their pristine Schwinn Black Phantoms. But even the staunchest purists must be amazed by the ingenuity, creativity, and sweat involved. The kids haunt swap meets looking for parts. They spend months perfecting their creations, whether they're humble street machines or gleaming show bikes that never touch asphalt. They don't scrimp, either.

"Kids come to me and drop $500–$600 for pinstriping," says car detailer Danny Galvez of L.A. "These kids are working odd jobs to pay for stuff. It's pretty cool."

Today's lowriders are in a different league from their crude ancestors. Besides cutting the frames and installing longer forks, builders often add bondo or fiberglass to the frame to create a smooth, sculpted look. Also big are gold-chromed parts, chainlink steering wheels, rearview mirrors and lights, upholstered seats, spare wheels mounted on rear fenders, and elaborate paint-jobs and murals. Some bikes sport cellular phones.

Lately, things have gotten even wilder as lowriders race to outdo their buddies, impress their girlfriends, or win show awards. A new development is trailers, often holding a boom box. One kid put a complete couch on wheels. Someone has even put together a 5-wheeler. And in Japan, the newest lowrider-bike hotbed, the rage is hydraulics and built-in aquariums.

Silly? Sure. In some ways. But not in others. Especially for kids who don't have much to begin with, these bikes say. "I did this. This bike is me. I'm somebody."

Lopez agrees. "Pride plays a big part in the whole lowrider movement. These bikes are their masterpieces."

Take a closer look. We think you'll agree.

Discussion Questions

Content

1. According to the author, why are low-rider bicycles so popular? What kind of style do the bicycles provide for the youths who decorate and ride them?

2. In what ways do you think that low-rider bicycles are a specifically urban experience? Why couldn't this style have evolved anyplace else? What is it about these bicycles that makes them urban?

3. How do the bicycles serve as sources of Latino cultural pride? Of individual style?

Form

1. What does the author most emphasize in his description of low-rider bicycle culture? What does he seem most interested in? As a result, is there anything he misrepresents or doesn't discuss about low-rider bicycle culture?

2. Martin indicates that low-rider bicycles mimic both low-rider cars,which have been popular since the late 1940s, and the low-riding bicycles that were popular in the 1960s and 1970s. How does this historical information serve his purpose of discussing low-rider bicycles as a current trend among Latino and other youths? Is the historical information necessary? Is there enough historical information here to make clear why low-riding cars and bicycles have been popular at certain times and with certain groups of people? What other information would be needed to make the history of these vehicles clearer?

3. What about Martin's writing demonstrates that he is writing for people who read *Bicycling* and not for the general American public? Can you point to examples of his wording that illustrate this? What might he do differently to appeal to a wider audience?

Writing Prompts

1. Take an example of a customized car, bicycle, motorcycle, or other vehicle that you've seen in your city. Describe the ways in which that vehicle has been customized and explain why you think the owner has customized the vehicle in that way. Explain how the vehicle's customized appearance identifies the owner's individual style or the style of his or her group. Explain also just what that particular style is.

2. Write a short essay in which you compare and contrast the style of low-rider bicycles and the style of deeply clean cars discussed in Zuckerman's essay "Deep Clean."

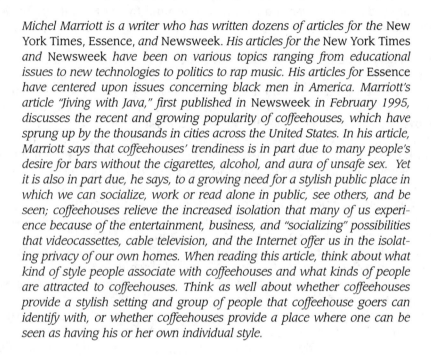

Michel Marriott is a writer who has written dozens of articles for the New York Times, Essence, *and* Newsweek. *His articles for the* New York Times *and* Newsweek *have been on various topics ranging from educational issues to new technologies to politics to rap music. His articles for* Essence *have centered upon issues concerning black men in America. Marriott's article "Jiving with Java," first published in* Newsweek *in February 1995, discusses the recent and growing popularity of coffeehouses, which have sprung up by the thousands in cities across the United States. In his article, Marriott says that coffeehouses' trendiness is in part due to many people's desire for bars without the cigarettes, alcohol, and aura of unsafe sex. Yet it is also in part due, he says, to a growing need for a stylish public place in which we can socialize, work or read alone in public, see others, and be seen; coffeehouses relieve the increased isolation that many of us experience because of the entertainment, business, and "socializing" possibilities that videocassettes, cable television, and the Internet offer us in the isolating privacy of our own homes. When reading this article, think about what kind of style people associate with coffeehouses and what kinds of people are attracted to coffeehouses. Think as well about whether coffeehouses provide a stylish setting and group of people that coffeehouse goers can identify with, or whether coffeehouses provide a place where one can be seen as having his or her own individual style.*

Jiving with Java

Michel Marriott

GREG CRACOLICE flies his coffee in from Milan every week. He even imports the sugar from France. But as good as the joe is at Soho, one of Washington, D.C.'s, newest coffeehouses, the customers clearly don't come for the taste alone. On their way to work, congressional drones fill the funky, mismatched chairs and stare at this month's art exhibit. At night the place belongs to twentysomethings, listening to live music or, laptops in hand, plugged into the gobs of outlets that stud Soho's gold, salmon and mint walls. And between dawn and dusk, Soho houses sippers of all stripes—slackers, secretaries, even the occasional socialite. "We had someone come in the other day who asked if one of us could stand by her Rolls-Royce while she came in and drank her coffee," says Cracolice, happy to oblige. "We have everyone."

That may be an exaggeration, but not by much. There are now at least 4,500 coffeehouses nationwide, and the Specialty Coffee Association of America predicts that that number will double in five years. (Even Mormons, who are forbidden to consume caffeine, have found a few coffeehouses in Provo, Utah, that slyly serve them cappuccinos in opaque 7Up cups.) The marketing of specialty coffees—bringing lattes, espressos and their haute-sounding cousins to the Maxwell House set—certainly helped establish the coffeehouse culture. But from Washington's Soho to the Starbucks that have claimed a corner in every city nationwide, what's goosed coffee's popularity as much as anything is the cross-generational appeal of the java joint. "People will sit in the coffeehouse and read and someone will make a comment, and pretty soon you've got a conversation," says Thomas Wyrner, who teaches English at Bowling Green University. "It's not so pretentious anymore. The coffeehouse has turned into 'Cheers' without booze."

Of course, the coffeehouse as social unit is not new. Italians probably started the first one in the 17th century, followed by the Viennese (who still flock to their rigidly stratified establishments) and the French (who are abandoning theirs in favor of their TV remote controls). Americans still want their MTV, too, but after a decade of cocooning and a silent night of cruising the Internet, they've begun to crave real conversation. "Fifty years ago you didn't have the social situation to merit this," says Marshall Fishwick, a humanities and communications professor at Virginia Polytechnic Institute. "The coffeehouse has always been a sort of refuge for people who are in need of companionship." That describes Joseph Zuaiter perfectly. Zuaiter, a workaholic computer programmer in his late 20s, hits the nearest coffeehouse several times a day. "Sometimes I'll finish a movie at 11:30 p.m. and go find a cup," he says. "You don't need coffee at midnight, but we still go. There's no rush to go home. There's nothing to do at home."

The coffeehouse's easygoing culture also makes public solitude feel comfortable. Most houses permit customers to sit alone for hours, forming a subtle etiquette that allows people to be with people without feeling obligated to interact with them, says Doug Peters, a 30-year-old waiter from St. Paul, Minn. Coffeehouses do have more than their share of patrons who plant their faces behind books, newspapers and laptops. But the low-stress vibe also makes a perfect spot for first dates, says Michael Fiorito, 20. "If it works you can go someplace else." Coffeehouses are ideal, say businessmen, if you're looking for a quiet, cozy place to have a meeting or make a contact.

"Coffeehouses are still a wired thing," says Mark Frauenfelder, associate editor of Wired, the San Francisco-based monthly cyber-hip magazine that regularly lists what's in (wired) and what's out (tired). "You go in coffeehouses around here and it's hard not to find a couple of people working on laptops. They could be doing it at home or in their office, but there they are."

That's not to say that there's a one-stop cure for what Grant McCracken, a contemporary-culture anthropologist and the curator of Toronto's Royal Ontario Museum, calls "*fin de siècle* fatigue." As successful as coffeehouses have been in luring a cross-section of society, they're getting competition from niche shops tailored to specific audiences. Brain Wash in San Francisco offers live music, laundry machines and coin-operated computers to lure the young, unwashed masses. In Portland, Ore., there's a mad rush to buy old Fotomats and convert them into drive-up cappuccino vendors. And sometimes there just isn't enough caffeine anywhere to bridge the gap between the ages or classes. Jitters, in downtown Minneapolis, draws both Gen-Xers and boomers, though rarely at the same time. And people in their 50s hear the Monday night accordion player or look at the walls—no two painted the same color—and "laugh and walk away," says co-owner Dan Lessard, 38. "We made it a little fun and eclectic, and for some people that's not real familiar."

It's more than just funky décor that has built the growing coffeehouse culture. Now that all the old vices—smoking, sex, drinking before driving—have been deemed unsafe, coffeehouses provide one of the last unregulated drugs in America and the only one regularly taken with a wink and a muffin—caffeine. Ron Nordheimer, who operates Ferrara, one of many coffee shops and espresso stands in a 10-block radius of the White House, says he does a feverish trade with office workers. "A lot of people love the jolt," he says. "It gives them a feeling that they can work a couple more hours and not get drained." The sight of so many professionals bellying up to Washington espresso bars moved a local public-relations executive to remark that "coffeehouses are middle-class crackhouses." On campuses, some students are skipping the brewing and chewing the beans—coated in chocolate. "We started eating them to stay awake in lectures, and it worked," says Lori Czyscon, a University of Minnesota horticulture major.

Is that safe? Science hasn't even established the health impact of daily doses of mega mocha—and its megadose of caffeine—let alone chewing the beans straight. In Portland, Ore., some ex-coffee addicts have formed Caffeine Anonymous, a 12-step program for bean heads. Others, tired of the influence of coffee connoisseurs on the marketplace, grumble that they are sick of these high-calorie confections. An exasperated customer in Minneapolis recently cried out, "Does anyone know where I can get a damn cup of coffee?" Says Mark Vergilii, a 24-year-old insurance salesman standing at a coffee bar in Minneapolis: "It's sad. Why aren't all these people sitting at home drinking their coffee?" And miss out on the accordion player, the Internet hookup, the washing machines, the art exhibit and an unlimited supply of Swiss almond mochaccino? Forget it. Oh, and pass the cream, please.

Discussion Questions

Content

1. Are coffeehouses places for everyone, as the author says? If not, who are they for?

2. In what ways do coffeehouses seem to be urban environments? What examples of this are provided in Marriott's article? How do his statements about the relief from VCRs and the Internet that coffeehouses provide relate to the idea of an urban environment?

3. What places other than coffeehouses serve as similar types of gathering places in your city? Are coffeehouses unique in the type of atmosphere they offer? In what ways are they just like every place else?

Form

1. The article sets out to describe the culture and style of coffeehouses. Is it successful in doing so? Why do you think so? Is there enough detail? Is there anything the article excludes?

2. "Jiving with Java" was originally published in *Newsweek,* a weekly news-magazine whose purpose is to report facts. Does Marriott's article just report the facts about coffeehouses? Or does it also show some of his opinion toward them? Can you point to words and phrases he uses to indicate either his opinion or his lack of opinion?

3. Marriott mentions several people's names in his article. Why do you think he does this? How does this change the article?

Writing Prompts

1. Investigate a coffeehouse in your city. Describe its atmosphere, what kinds of people are there, and what kind of style overall it seems to have. Is your coffeehouse similar in style to those described in Marriott's article? Discuss the degree to which your coffeehouse provides or does not provide an urban gathering place where people can socialize, work or read alone, or meet for dates.

2. Write an essay that compares the type of style we associate with frequenting a coffeehouse with the style we associate with frequenting a different kind of place, such as a library, bar, bowling alley, etc.

PART 7 DISCUSSION QUESTIONS

1. The authors in this part all talk about style as having originated in and as being associated with cities. What are the different ways in which the authors see the relationship of cities and styles? What is similar about all of the authors' views of the city–style relationship? Do you agree that styles are intricately connected with cities? Why or why not? Just where do you locate styles?

2. Several of the articles on style deal with displays of style on people's bodies—through clothing, jewelry, hair styles, body piercing, tattooing, etc. Are people's bodies the primary site of style in the United States? Why or why not? What might some other sites of style be? When you think of your own style, for example, do you mostly think about your choice of clothing, hair style, etc. and not about other things?

3. Stuart Ewen says that one hundred years ago, minorities and members of other subcultures tried to look more mainstream by wearing the mainstream's clothing. Charles Gandee and Katherine Betts say that the mainstream is now wearing the clothing of minorities and subcultures. What does this change say about how American culture has changed in the past one hundred years? Does it mean that there has been a fundamental change in how we view being mainstream and how we view subcultures? Or is it simply a change in clothing styles? How do the other authors in this part comment upon this issue?

4. The authors all comment upon style as a way to demonstrate one's individuality. What do they see as the most common ways in which Americans show their individuality? What do they see as the purpose of communicating individuality in our society? Just how collective is this purpose? Why do you think this purpose is particularly necessary in cities?

5. One of the main purposes of style is to communicate identification with a subculture or group of some kind. Styles identify people's gender, ethnicity, age, musical taste, and sexual preference, as well as whether or not they are bikers, Hare Krishnas, etc. Why do we want to communicate our membership in groups? What does this say about American culture today? Does it indicate that individuality is in part an expression of group identity? Are the two types of identity separate?

PART 7 WRITING ASSIGNMENTS

1. Write a personal essay in which you describe your own style. Take into consideration not only your clothing, hair, makeup, jewelry, and tattoos, but also the vehicle you drive or ride and the places in which you hang out. What kind of style do you have? Is there a name for it? How is your style individual? How does it mark you as being part of one or more groups or subcultures? Which groups? What does membership in these groups signify? How does style signify it?

2. The essays discuss three main ways in which we can define our style: through our body and clothing, through our choice of vehicle, and through the places in which we choose to hang out. Can you think of any other ways in which we show our style? Drawing from the essays in this part, describe what you consider the most stylish bodies, clothes, vehicles, and places. Explain what makes these things so stylish and so attractive to you. Consider as well why you think people consider them important and what those bodies, clothes, vehicles, and places might say about who we are.

3. Write a persuasive essay that answers the question: Is it acceptable for people to use and wear styles associated with a group that they are not part of? Consider the opinions on this issue in the essays by E. Jean Carroll, Stuart Ewen, and Charles Gandee. Is it a problem that we potentially misrepresent ourselves and the style itself when we wear another group's style? Does it cause miscommunication about who we are? Is it somehow morally wrong? Or does it represent an "anything goes," "you can wear whatever you want" trend in our culture? If so, is this trend harmless?

4. Issues of individuality, communication in urban spaces, group identity, and the way things appear are evident both in this part and in other parts in this book. Take one essay in this part and one essay from another part, and compare and contrast how one of these issues is discussed in two essays.